Microprocessors and Introduction to Microcontroller

(8085, 8086, 8051 - Architecture, Interfacing and Programming)

[Conceptual Approach]

Atul P. Godse

M.S. Software Systems (BITS Pilani)
B.E. Industrial Electronics
Formerly Lecturer in Department of Electronics Engg.
Vishwakarma Institute of Technology
Pune

Dr. Deepali A. Godse

M.E., Ph.D. (Computer Engg.)
Head of Information Technology Department,
Bharati Vidyapeeth's College of Engineering for Women,
Pune

TABLE OF CONTENTS

Chapter - 17 8051 Microcontroller (17 - 1) to (17 - 36)

Chapter - 19 8051 I/O Ports, Timer, Serial Port & Interrupts (19 - 1) to (19 - 48)

Chapter - 20 Microcontroller Applications (20 - 1) to (20 - 32)

LAB EXPERIMENTS

8085A is an 8-bit microprocessor suitable for a wide range of applications. It is a single-chip, NMOS device implemented with approximately 6200 transistors on a 164 × 222 mil chip contained in a 40-pin dual-in-line package.

In this chapter we will see features, architecture, pin diagram and bus organization of 8085 microprocessor.

1.1 Features

April/May-04

The features of 8085 include :

1. It is an 8-bit microprocessor i.e. it can accept, process, or provide 8-bit data simultaneously.
2. It operates on a single +5 V power supply connected at V_{CC}; power supply ground is connected to V_{ss}.
3. It operates on clock cycle with 50 % duty cycle.
4. It has on chip clock generator. This internal clock generator requires tuned circuit like LC, RC or crystal. The internal clock generator divides oscillator frequency by 2 and generates clock signal, which can be used for synchronizing external devices.
5. It can operate with a 3 MHz clock frequency. The 8085A-2 version can operate at the maximum frequency of 5 MHz.
6. It has 16 address lines, hence it can access (2^{16}) 64 kbytes of memory.
7. It provides 8-bit I/O addresses to access (2^8) 256 I/O ports.
8. In 8085, the lower 8-bit address bus (A_0 - A_7) and data bus (D_0 - D_7) are multiplexed to reduce number of external pins. But due to this, external hardware (latch) is required to separate address lines and data lines.
9. It supports 74 instructions with the following addressing modes :

   a) Immediate b) Register c) Direct d) Indirect e) Implied.
10. The Arithmetic Logic Unit (ALU) of 8085 performs :

    a) 8-bit binary addition with or without carry.

    b) 16-bit binary addition. c) 2 digit BCD addition.

    d) 8-bit binary subtraction with or without borrow.

    e) 8-bit logical AND, OR, EX-OR, complement (NOT), and bit shift operations.
11. It has 8-bit accumulator, flag register, instruction register, six 8-bit general purpose registers (B, C, D, E, H and L) and two 16-bit registers (SP and PC). Getting the operand from the general purpose registers is more faster than from memory. Hence skilled programmers always prefer general purpose registers to store program variables than memory.

12. It provides five hardware interrupts : TRAP, RST 7.5, RST 6.5, RST 5.5 and INTR.
13. It has serial I/O control which allows serial communication.
14. It provides control signals ($IO/\overline{M}$, $\overline{RD}$, $\overline{WR}$) to control the bus cycles and hence external bus controller is not required.
15. The external hardware (another microprocessor or equivalent master) can detect which machine cycle microprocessor is executing using status signals ($IO/\overline{M}$, S_0, S_1). This feature is very useful when more than one processors are using common system resources (memory and I/O devices).
16. It has a mechanism by which it is possible to increase its interrupt handling capacity.
17. The 8085 has an ability to share system bus with Direct Memory Access controller. This feature allows to transfer large amount of data from I/O device to memory or from memory to I/O device with high speeds.
18. It can be used to implement three chip microcomputer with supporting I/O devices like IC 8155 and IC 8355.

1.2 Architecture of 8085

April/May-04, Nov./Dec.-04, Dec.-07, 08, 09, 10, June-06, May-10, 11

Fig. 1.1 (See Fig. 1.1 on next page) shows the architecture of 8085.

It consists of various functional blocks as listed below :

- Registers
- Arithmetic and Logic Unit
- Instruction decoder and machine cycle encoder
- Address buffer
- Address/Data buffer
- Incrementer/Decrementer address latch
- Interrupt control
- Serial I/O control
- Timing and control circuitry.

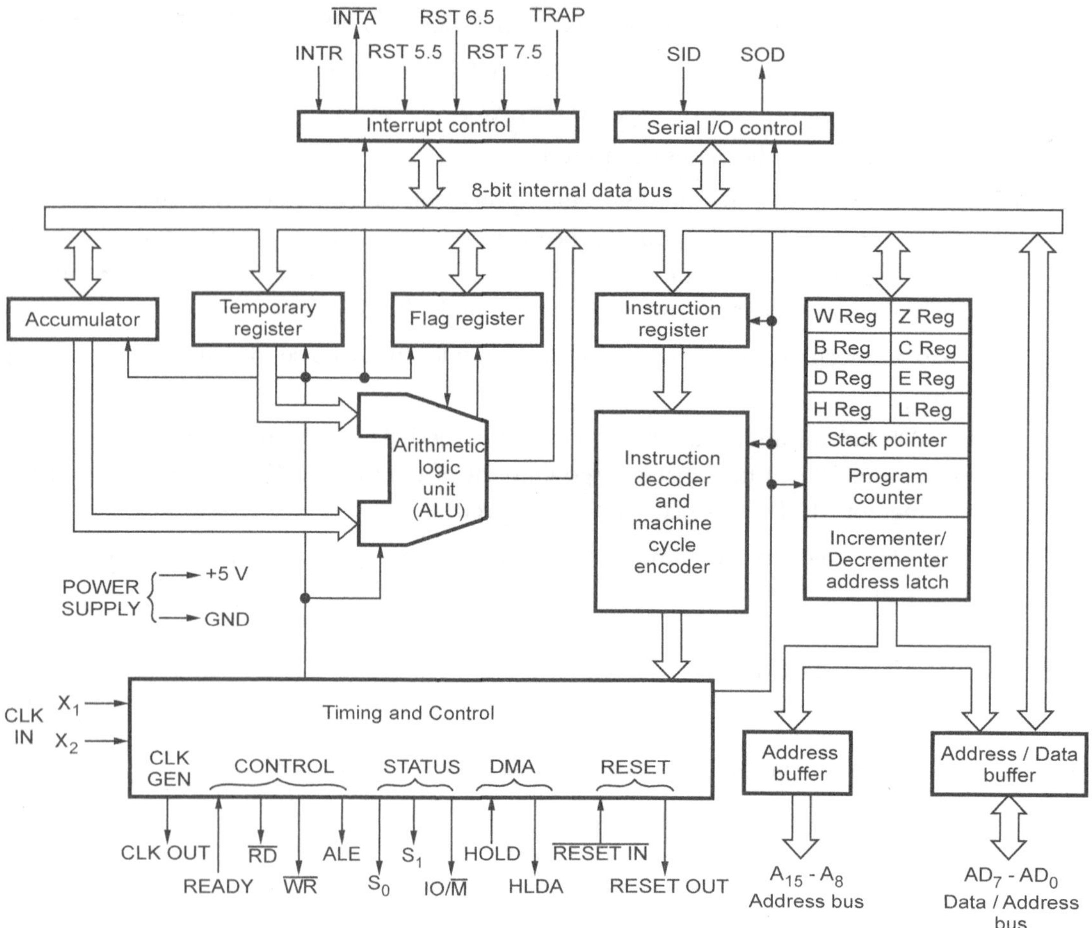

Fig. 1.1 Architecture of 8085

1.2.1 Register Structure

Temporary register	
W Reg	Z Reg
A Reg	Flag Reg
B Reg	C Reg
D Reg	E Reg
H Reg	L Reg
Stack Pointer (SP)	
Program Counter (PC)	

Fig. 1.2 Register structure of 8085

The Fig. 1.2 shows the register structure of 8085. The shaded portion of this register model is called **programmer's model** of 8085. It includes six 8-bit registers- (B, C, D, E, H and L) one accumulator, one flag register and two 16-bit registers (SP and PC). All these registers are accessible to programmer and hence they are included in the programmer's model. The remaining registers - temporary, W and Z are not accessible to the programmers; they are used by microprocessor for internal, intermediate operations.

The 8085 registers are classified as :

1. **General Purpose Registers**

2. **Temporary Registers**

   a) Temporary data register b) W and Z registers.

3. **Special Purpose Registers**

   a) Accumulator b) Flag registers c) Instruction register.

4. **Sixteen bit Registers**

   a) Program Counter (PC) b) Stack Pointer (SP).

1. General Purpose Registers :

B, C, D, E, H and L are 8-bit general purpose registers can be used as a separate 8-bit registers or as 16-bit register pairs, BC, DE and HL. When used in register pair mode, the high order byte resides in the first register (i.e. in B when BC is used as a register pair) and the low order byte in the second (i.e. in C when BC is used as a register pair).

HL pair also functions as a data pointer or memory pointer. These are also called **scratchpad registers,** as user can store data in them. To store and read data from these registers bus access is not required, it is an internal operation. Thus it provides an efficient way to store intermediate results and use them when required. The efficient programmer prefers to use these registers to store intermediate results than the memory locations which require bus access and hence more time to perform the operation.

2. Temporary Registers :

a) Temporary Data Register : The ALU has two inputs. One input is supplied by the accumulator and other from temporary data register. The programmer cannot access this temporary data register. However, it is internally used for execution of most of the arithmetic and logical instructions.

For example : ADD B is the instruction in the arithmetic group of instructions which adds the contents of register A and register B and stores result in register A. The addition operation is performed by ALU. The ALU takes inputs from register A and temporary data register. The contents of register B are transferred to temporary data register for applying second input to the ALU.

b) W and Z registers : W and Z registers are temporary registers. These registers are used to hold 8-bit data during execution of some instructions. These registers are not available for programmer, since 8085 uses them internally.

Use of W and Z registers :

The CALL instruction is used to transfer program control to a subprogram or subroutine. This instruction pushes the current PC contents onto the stack and loads the given address into the PC. The given address is temporarily stored in the W and Z registers and placed on the bus for the fetch cycle. Thus the program control is transferred to the address given in the instruction. XCHG instruction exchanges the contents of H with D and L with E. At the time of exchange W and Z registers are used for temporary storage of data.

3. Special Purpose Registers :

a) Register A (Accumulator) : It is a tri-state eight bit register. It is extensively used in arithmetic, logic, load and store operations, as well as in, input/output (I/O) operations. Most of the times the result of arithmetic and logical operations is stored in the register A. Hence it is also identified as **accumulator**.

b) Flag Register : It is an 8-bit register, in which five of the bits carry significant information in the form of flags : S (Sign flag), Z (Zero flag), AC (Auxiliary carry flag), P (Parity flag), and CY (carry flag), as shown in Fig. 1.3.

D_7	D_6	D_5	D_4	D_3	D_2	D_1	D_0
S	Z	X	AC	X	P	X	CY

Fig. 1.3 Flag register

S-Sign flag : After the execution of arithmetic or logical operations, if bit D_7 of the result is 1, the sign flag is set. In a given byte if D_7 is 1, the number will be viewed as negative number. If D_7 is 0, the number will be considered as positive number.

Z-Zero flag : The zero flag sets if the result of operation in ALU is zero and flag resets if result is non zero. The zero flag is also set if a certain register content becomes zero following an increment or decrement operation of that register.

AC-Auxiliary Carry flag : This flag is set if there is an overflow out of bit 3 i.e. , carry from lower nibble to higher nibble (D_3 bit to D_4 bit). This flag is used for BCD operations and it is not available for the programmer.

P-Parity flag : Parity is defined by the number of ones present in the accumulator. After an arithmetic or logical operation if the result has an even number of ones, i.e. even parity, the flag is set. If the parity is odd, flag is reset.

CY-Carry flag : This flag is set if there is an overflow out of bit 7. The carry flag also serves as a borrow flag for subtraction. In both the examples shown below, the carry flag is set.

ADDITION

	Hex	Binary
	9B H	1001 1011
+	75 H	+ 0111 0101
Carry	[1] 10 H	[1] 0001 0000

SUBTRACTION

	Hex	Binary
	89 H	1000 1001
−	AB H	− 1010 1011
Borrow	[1] DE H	[1] 1101 1110

c) Instruction Register : In a typical processor operation, the processor first fetches the opcode of instruction from memory (i.e. it places an address on the address bus and memory responds by placing the data stored at the specified address on the data bus). The CPU stores this opcode in a register called the instruction register. This opcode is further sent to the instruction decoder to select one of the 256 alternatives.

4. Sixteen Bit Registers :

a) Program Counter (PC) : Program is a sequence of instructions. As mentioned earlier, microprocessor fetches these instructions from the memory and executes them sequentially. The program counter is a special purpose register which, at a given time, stores the address of the next instruction to be fetched. Program Counter acts as a pointer to the **next** instruction. How processor increments program counter depends on the nature of the instruction; for one byte instruction it increments program counter by one, for two byte instruction it increments program counter by two and for three byte instruction it increments program counter by three such that program counter always points to the address of the next instruction.

In case of JUMP and CALL instructions, address followed by JUMP and CALL instructions is placed in the program counter. The processor then fetches the next instruction from the new address specified by JUMP or CALL instruction. In conditional JUMP and conditional CALL instructions, if the condition is not satisfied, the processor increments program counter by three so that it points the instruction followed by conditional JUMP or CALL instruction; otherwise processor fetches the next instruction from the new address specified by JUMP or CALL instruction.

b) Stack Pointer (SP) : The stack is a reserved area of the memory in the RAM where temporary information may be stored. A 16-bit stack pointer is used to hold the address of the most recent stack entry.

1.2.2 Arithmetic Logic Unit (ALU)

The 8085's ALU performs arithmetic and logical functions on eight bit variables. The arithmetic unit performs bitwise fundamental arithmetic operations such as addition and subtraction. The logic unit performs logical operations such as complement, AND, OR and EX-OR, as well as rotate and clear. The ALU also looks after the branching decisions.

1.2.3 Instruction Decoder

As mentioned earlier, the processor first fetches the opcode of instruction from memory and stores this opcode in the instruction register. It is then sent to the instruction decoder. The instruction decoder decodes it and accordingly gives the timing and control signals which control the register, the data buffers, ALU and external peripheral signals (explained in later sections) depending on the nature of the instruction.

The 8085 executes seven different types of machine cycles. It gives the information about which machine cycle is currently executing in the encoded form on the S_0, S_1 and $IO/\overline{M}$ lines. This task is done by machine cycle encoder.

1.2.4 Address Buffer

This is an 8-bit unidirectional buffer. It is used to drive external high order address bus (A_{15}-A_8). It is also used to tri-state the high order address bus under certain conditions such as reset, hold, halt, and when address lines are not in use.

1.2.5 Address/Data Buffer

This is an 8-bit bi-directional buffer. It is used to drive multiplexed address/data bus, i.e. low order address bus (A_7-A_0) and data bus (D_7-D_0). It is also used to tri-state the multiplexed address/data bus under certain conditions such as reset, hold, halt and when the bus is not in use.

The address and data buffers are used to drive external address and data buses respectively. Due to these buffers the address and data buses can be tri-stated when they are not in use.

1.2.6 Incrementer/Decrementer Address Latch

This 16-bit register is used to increment or decrement the contents of program counter or stack pointer as a part of execution of instructions related to them.

1.2.7 Interrupt Control

The processor fetches, decodes and executes instructions in a sequence. Sometimes it is necessary to have processor the automatically execute one of a collection of special routines whenever special condition exists within a program or the microcomputer system. The most important thing is that, after execution of the special routine, the program control must be transferred to the program which processor was executing before the occurrence of the special condition. The occurrence of this special condition is referred as interrupt. The interrupt control block has five interrupt inputs RST 5.5, RST 6.5, RST 7.5, TRAP and INTR and one acknowledge signal $\overline{INTA}$.

1.2.8 Serial I/O Control

In situations like, data transmission over long distance and communication with cassette tapes or a CRT terminal, it is necessary to transmit data bit by bit to reduce the cost of cabling. In serial communication one bit is transferred at a time over a single line. The 8085's serial I/O control provides two lines, SOD and SID for serial communication. The serial output data (SOD) line is used to send data serially and serial input data (SID) line is used to receive data serially.

1.2.9 Timing and Control Circuitry

The control circuitry in the processor 8085 is responsible for all the operations. The control circuitry and hence the operations in 8085 are synchronized with the help of clock signal. Along with the control of fetching and decoding operations and generating appropriate signals for instruction execution, control circuitry also generates signals required to interface external devices to the processor, 8085.

1.3 Pin Definitions of 8085

May/June-09, Nov./Dec.-09, April/May-10

Fig. 1.4 (a) and (b) show 8085 pin configuration and functional pin diagram of 8085 respectively. The signals of 8085 can be classified into seven groups according to their functions.

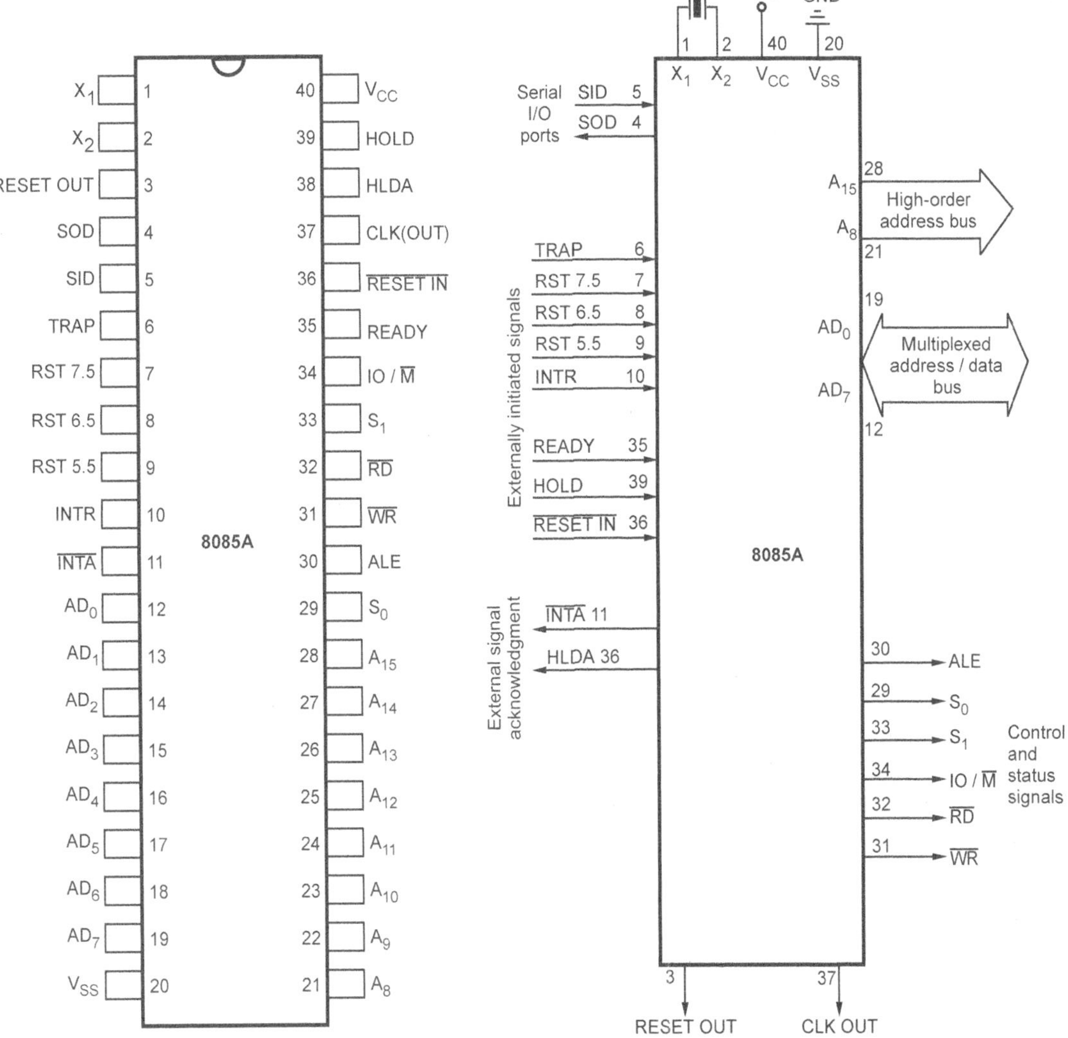

Fig. 1.4 (a) Pin configuration

Fig. 1.4 (b) Functional pin diagram

a) Power supply and frequency signals.

b) Data bus and address bus

c) Control bus

d) Interrupt signals

e) Serial I/O signals

f) DMA signals

g) Reset signals

1.3.1 Power Supply and Frequency Signals

i) V_{CC} : It requires a single +5 V power supply.

ii) V_{SS} : Ground reference.

iii) X_1 and X_2 : A tuned circuit like LC, RC or crystal is connected at these two pins. The internal clock generator divides oscillator frequency by 2, therefore, to operate a system at 3 MHz, the crystal of tuned circuit must have a frequency of 6 MHz.

iv) CLK OUT : This signal is used as a system clock for other devices. Its frequency is half the oscillator frequency.

1.3.2 Data Bus and Address Bus

A) AD_0 to AD_7 : The 8-bit data bus (D_0 - D_7) is multiplexed with the lower half (A_0 - A_7) of the 16-bit address bus. During first part of the machine cycle (T_1), lower 8 bits of memory address or I/O address appear on the bus. During remaining part of the machine cycle (T_2 and T_3) these lines are used as a bi-directional data bus.

B) A_8 to A_{15} : The upper half of the 16-bit address appears on the address lines A_8 to A_{15}. These lines are exclusively used for the most significant 8 bits of the 16-bit address lines.

1.3.3 Control and Status Signals

Nov./Dec.-06, 08

A) ALE (Address Latch Enable) : We know that AD_0 to AD_7 lines are multiplexed and the lower half of address (A_0 - A_7) is available only during T_1 of the machine cycle. This lower half of address is also necessary during T_2 and T_3 of machine cycle to access specific location in memory or I/O port. This means that the lower half of an address must be latched in T_1 of the machine cycle, so that it is available throughout the machine cycle. The latching of lower half of an address bus is done by using external latch and ALE signal from 8085.

B) $\overline{RD}$ and $\overline{WR}$: These signals are basically used to control the direction of the data flow between processor and memory or I/O device/port. A low on $\overline{RD}$ indicates that the data must be read from the selected memory location or I/O port via data bus. A low on $\overline{WR}$ indicates that the data must be written into the selected memory location or I/O port via data bus.

C) IO/$\overline{M}$, S_0 and S_1 : IO/$\overline{M}$ indicates whether I/O operation or memory operation is being carried out. S_1 and S_0 indicate the type of machine cycle in progress.

D) READY : It is used by the microprocessor to sense whether a peripheral is ready or not for data transfer. If not, the processor waits. It is thus used to synchronize slower peripherals to the microprocessor.

1.3.4 Interrupt Signals

April/May-10

The 8085 has five hardware interrupt signals : RST 5.5, RST 6.5, RST 7.5, TRAP and INTR. The microprocessor recognizes interrupt requests on these lines at the end of the current instruction execution.

The $\overline{INTA}$ (Interrupt Acknowledge) signal is used to indicate that the processor has acknowledged an INTR interrupt.

1.3.5 Serial I/O Signals

A) SID (Serial I/P Data) : This input signal is used to accept serial data bit by bit from the external device.

B) SOD (Serial O/P Data) : This is an output signal which enables the transmission of serial data bit by bit to the external device.

1.3.6 DMA Signal

A) HOLD : This signal indicates that another master is requesting for the use of address bus, data bus and control bus.

B) HLDA : This active high signal is used to acknowledge HOLD request.

1.3.7 Reset Signals

A) $\overline{\text{RESET IN}}$: A low on this pin

1) Sets the program counter to zero (0000H).
2) Resets the interrupt enable and HLDA flip-flops.
3) Tri-states the data bus, address bus and control bus.
   (Note : Only during RESET is active).
4) Affects the contents of processor's internal registers randomly.

On reset, the PC sets to 0000H which causes the 8085 to execute the first instruction from address 0000H. For proper reset operation reset signal must be held low for at least 3 clock cycles. The power-on reset circuit can be used to ensure execution of first instruction from address 0000H.

B) RESET OUT : This active high signal indicates that processor is being reset. This signal is synchronized to the processor clock and it can be used to reset other devices connected in the system.

1.4 Bus Organization

In this section we are going to see how we can use various buses of 8085, how to demultiplex address and data bus, how to generate control signals, how to provide clock and reset signals to 8085 and so on.

1.4.1 Clock Circuits

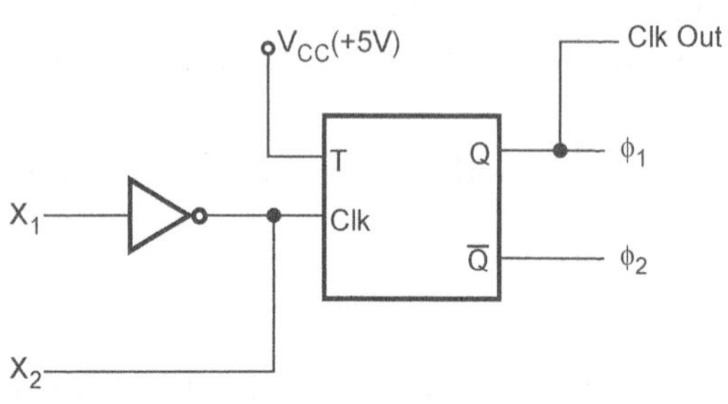

Fig. 1.5 Block diagram of built-in clock generator

The 8085 has on chip clock generator. Fig. 1.5 shows the internal block diagram of the on chip clock generator. The internal clock generator requires tuned circuit like LC, RC or crystal, or external clock source as an input to generate the clock. The internal T-flip flop divides the frequency by 2. Hence the operating frequency of the 8085 is always half of the oscillator frequency.

LC Tuned Circuit :

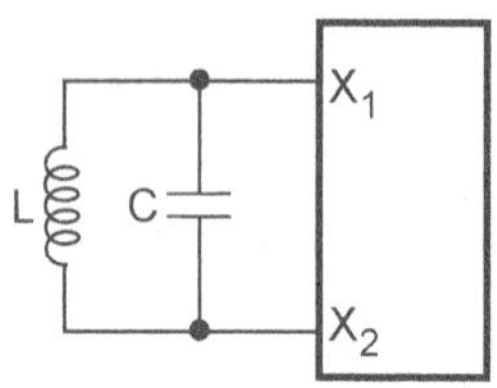

Fig. 1.6 LC circuit

It is a LC resonant tank circuit. The resonant frequency for this circuit is given by

$$f_r = \frac{1}{2\pi\sqrt{L(C_{ext} + C_{int})}}$$

Where C_{int} is the internal capacitance and it is normally 15 pF. The output frequency of this circuit has 10 % variations. To minimize the variations in the output frequency, it is recommended to have C_{ext} at least twice that of C_{int} i.e. 30 pF.

RC Tuned Circuit : Fig. 1.7 shows the RC tuned circuit. The output frequency of this circuit is also not exactly stable. But this circuit has an advantage that its component cost is less.

Crystal Oscillator Circuit : Fig. 1.8 shows the crystal oscillator circuit. It is the most stable circuit. The 20 pF capacitor in the circuit is connected to assure oscillator start-up at the correct frequency.

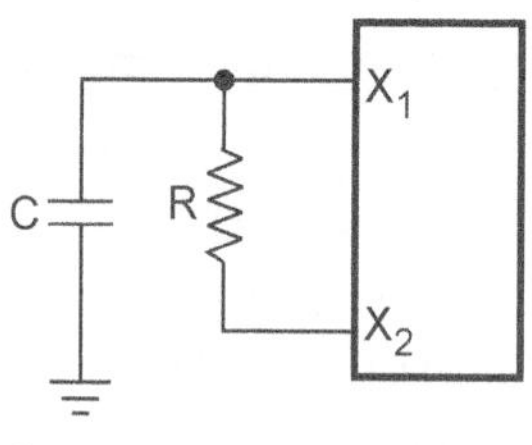

Fig. 1.7 RC Circuit

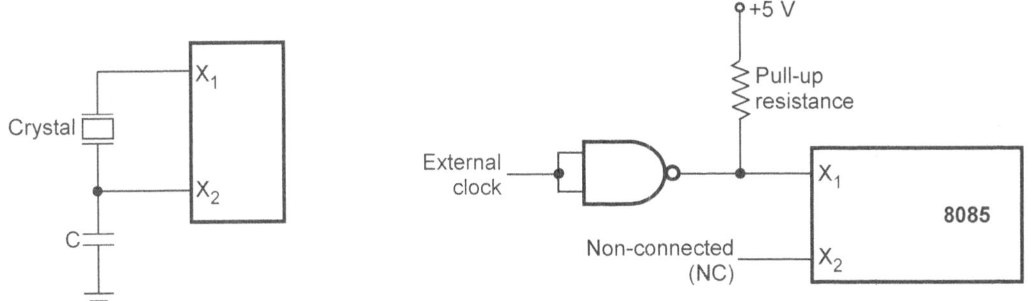

Fig. 1.8 Crystal clock circuit

Fig. 1.9 External frequency source

External Clock :

Fig. 1.9 shows how to drive clock input of 8085 with external frequency source. Here external clock is applied at X_1 input and X_2 input is kept open.

1.4.2 Demultiplexing AD_7-AD_0

Nov./Dec.-04

We know that AD_0 to AD_7 lines are multiplexed and the lower half of address (A_0 - A_7) is available only during T_1 of the machine cycle. This lower half of address is also necessary during T_2 and T_3 of machine cycle to access specific location in memory or I/O port. This means that the lower half of an address bus must be latched in T_1 of the machine cycle, so that it is available throughout the machine cycle. The latching of lower half of an address is done by using external latch and ALE signal from 8085. The Fig. 1.10 shows the hardware connection for latching the lower half of an address. The IC 74LS373 is an 8-bit latch, having 8 D flip-flops. The input is transferred to the output only when clock is high. This clock signal is driven by ALE signal from 8085. The ALE signal is activated only during T_1, so input is transferred to the output only during T_1 i.e. address (A_0 - A_7) on the AD_0 to AD_7 multiplexed bus. In the remaining part of the machine cycle, ALE signal is disabled so output of the latch (A_0 - A_7) remains unchanged. To latch lower half of an address, in each machine cycle, the 8085 gives ALE signal high during T_1 of every machine cycle.

1.4.3 Reset Circuit

On reset, the PC sets to 0000H which causes the 8085 to execute the first instruction from address 0000H. For proper reset operation reset signal must be held low for at least 3 clock cycles. The power-on reset circuit can be used to ensure execution of first instruction from address 0000H. Fig. 1.11 shows the power-on reset circuit with typical R, C values. (Note : R, C values may vary due to power supply ramp up time).

Upon power-up, $\overline{\text{RESET IN}}$ must remain low for at least 10 ms after minimum Vcc has been reached, in the circuit shown in Fig. 1.11. Upon power up or key press, the $\overline{\text{RESET IN}}$ goes low and slowly rises to +5 V, providing sufficient time for the processor to reset the system. The diode is connected to discharge the capacitor immediately when power supply is switched OFF.

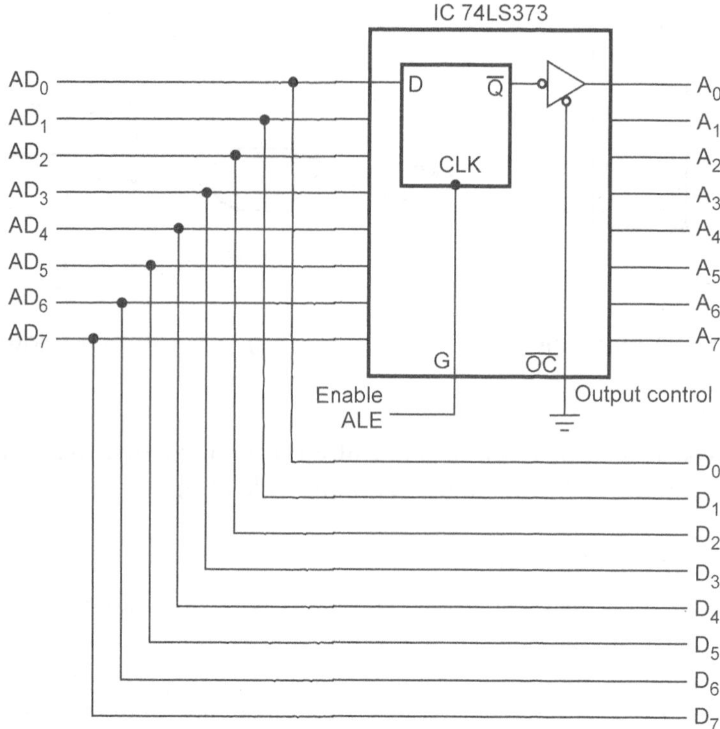

Fig. 1.10 Latching circuit

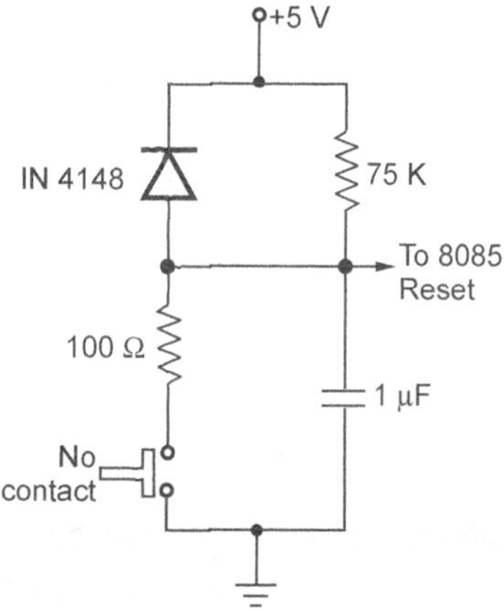

Fig. 1.11 Power on reset

After RESET, 8085 loads 0000H in PC register and clears the INTE flag. Before going to execute interrupt service routine, it is necessary to setup certain parameters, required to execute interrupt service routine. To avoid interrupt to occur before completion of these initial requirements, after power on or reset, INTE flip-flop is cleared to disable interrupts. It can be enabled by EI instruction after initial settings.

As we know that, after power up or reset 8085 fetches its first instruction from 0000H address, and it has to be the first instruction from monitor program. Therefore EPROM consisting of monitor program must be located from address 0000H in any 8085 microprocessor system.

1.4.4 Generation of Control Signals

The 8085 microprocessor provides $\overline{RD}$ and $\overline{WR}$ signals to initiate read or write cycle. Because these signals are used both for reading/writing memory and for reading/writing an input device, it is necessary to generate separate read and write signals for memory and I/O devices.

The 8085 provides IO/$\overline{M}$ signal to indicate whether the initiated cycle is for I/O device or for memory device. Using IO/$\overline{M}$ signal along with $\overline{RD}$ and $\overline{WR}$, it is possible to generate separate four control signals :

$\overline{MEMR}$	**(Memory Read)**	: To read data from memory.
$\overline{MEMW}$	**(Memory Write)**	: To write data in memory.
$\overline{IOR}$	**(I/O Read)**	: To read data from I/O device.
$\overline{IOW}$	**(I/O Write)**	: To write data in I/O device.

Fig. 1.12 shows the circuit which generates $\overline{MEMR}$, $\overline{MEMW}$, $\overline{IOR}$ and $\overline{IOW}$ signals.

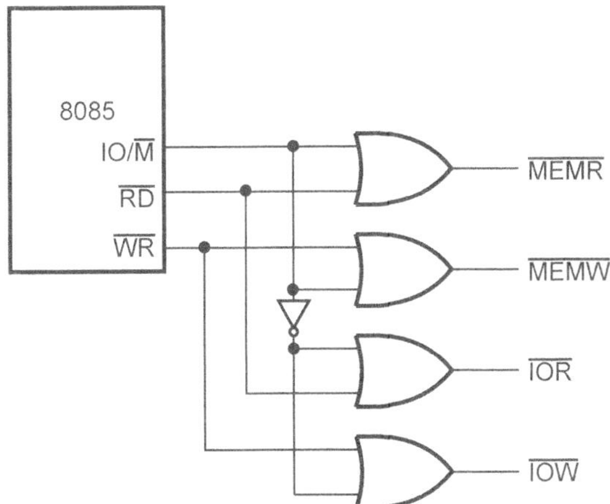

Fig. 1.12 Generation of $\overline{MEMR}$, $\overline{MEMW}$, $\overline{IOR}$ and $\overline{IOW}$ signals

We know that for OR gate, when both the inputs are low then only output is low. Table 1.1 shows the truth table used to generate $\overline{MEMR}$, $\overline{MEMW}$, $\overline{IOR}$ and $\overline{IOW}$ signals. The signal IO/$\overline{M}$ goes low for memory operation. This signal is logically ORed with $\overline{RD}$ and $\overline{WR}$ to get $\overline{MEMR}$ and $\overline{MEMW}$ signals. When both $\overline{RD}$ and IO/$\overline{M}$ signals go low, $\overline{MEMR}$ signal goes low. Similarly, when both $\overline{WR}$ and IO/$\overline{M}$ signals go low, $\overline{MEMW}$ signal goes low. To generate $\overline{IOR}$ and $\overline{IOW}$ signals for I/O operation, IO/$\overline{M}$ signal is first inverted and then logically ORed with $\overline{RD}$ and $\overline{WR}$ signals.

1.4.6 Typical Configuration

Fig. 1.16 shows schematic of the 8085 microprocessor demultiplexed address bus and control signals.

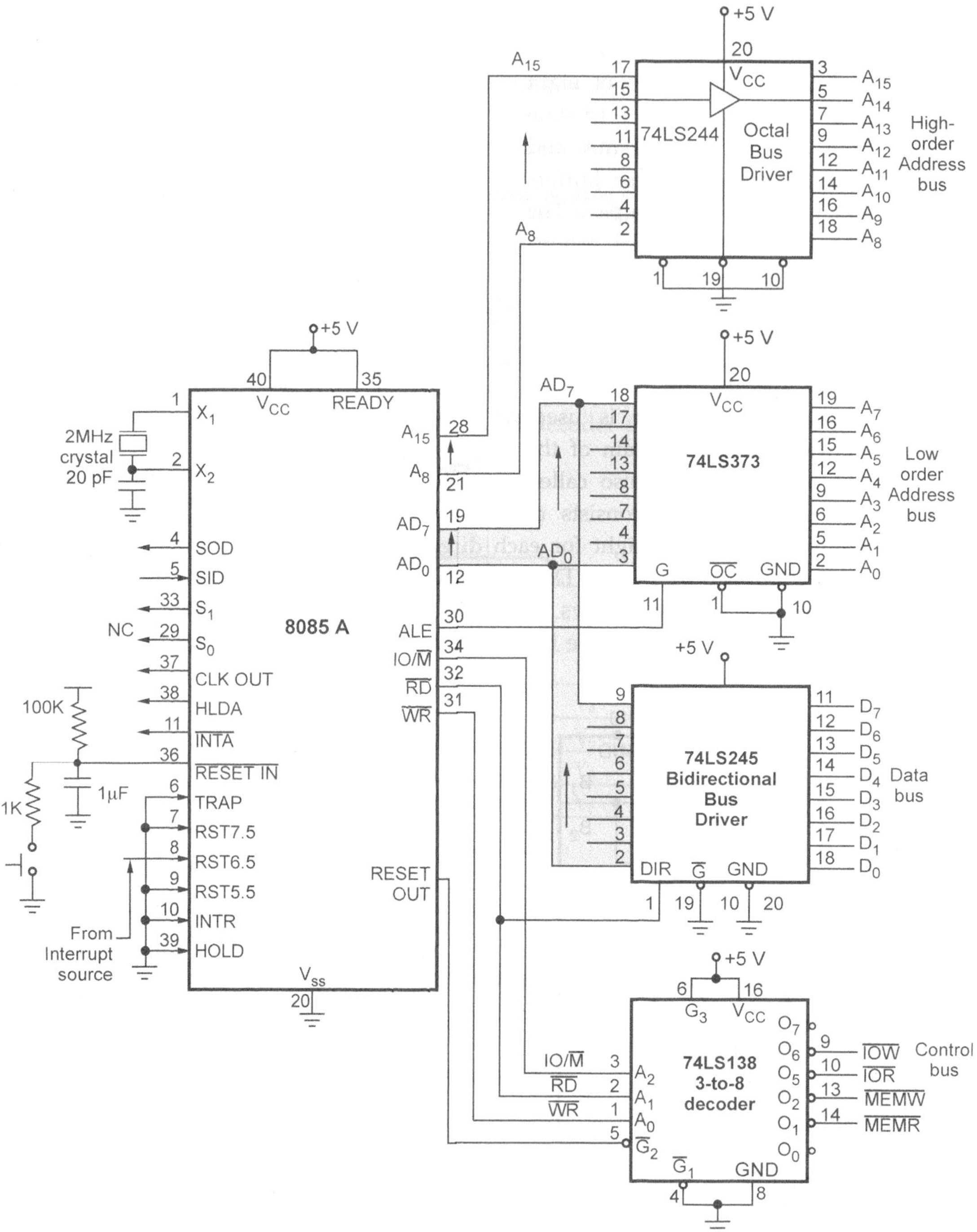

Fig. 1.16 Typical 8085 configuration

It also shows clock and reset circuits. Interrupt lines which are not in use are grounded. This is necessary because floating interrupt line may cause false triggering of interrupt. Similarly, since the DMA controller is not used, HOLD line is also grounded. As we know READY signal is used to synchronize slow peripherals with the microprocessor. When it is low, microprocessor enters in the wait state and when it is high, it indicates that the memory or peripheral is ready to send or receive data. Here, the READY signal is tied high to prevent the microprocessor from entering the wait state. ALE signal is connected to the clock input of the latch, to latch the low order address in T_1 of the machine cycle. To control the direction of the bi-directional buffer 74LS245, $\overline{RD}$ signal from 8085 is connected to DIR input of the bi-directional buffer. Thus, when $\overline{RD}$ signal is low, DIR is low and data flows from memory or I/O device to the microprocessor, performing read operation. When $\overline{RD}$ signal is high, DIR is high and data flows from microprocessor to memory or I/O device performing write operation.

Review Questions

Section 1.1

Q.1 *Explain architectural features of 8085.* **May-04, Marks 4**

Section 1.2

Q.1 *With neat functional block diagram, explain the architecture of 8085 microprocessor.* **June-06, Dec.-07, Dec.-04,08,09,10, May-04,10,11,12, Marks 16**

Q.2 *Explain the architecture, data flow and instruction execution of 8085 microprocessor.* **May-11, Marks 8**

Q.3 *Give the format of flag register in 8085. Explain each flag.*

Q.4 *Define the function of parity flag and zero flag in 8085.* **June-12, Marks 2**

Section 1.3

Q.1 *Write about the pin configuration of 8085 processor and explain them in detail.* **June-09, Marks 16**

Q.2 *Draw the pin diagram of 8085 microprocessor.* **June-12, Marks 4**

Q.3 *Explain different control signals used by 8085.*

Q.4 *What is the use of ALE signal ?*

Q.5 *What is the use of CLKOUT and RESET OUT signals of 8085 processor ?*

Q.6 *Describe the function of following pins in 8085.*
a. READY b. ALE c. IO/$\overline{M}$ d. HOLD e. RESET

Q.7 *Explain the signals used in DMA operation in 8085.*

Section 1.4

Q.1 *Draw the schematic of latching low-order address bus in 8085 microprocessor.*

Dec.-11, Marks 2

Q.2 *Why AD_0-AD_7 lines are multiplexed ?*

Q.3 *Draw and explain typical 8085 configuration.*

Q.4 *Write a note on bus drivers.*

Two Marks Questions with Answers

Q.1 ***What is Microprocessor? Give the power supply and clock frequency of 8085?***

Ans. : A microprocessor is a multipurpose, programmable logic device that reads binary instructions from a storage device called memory accepts binary data as input and processes data according to those instructions and provides result as output. The power supply of 8085 is +5 V and clock frequency in 3 MHz.

Q.2 ***What are the functions of an accumulator?***

Ans. : The accumulator is the register associated with the ALU operations and sometimes I/O operations. It is an integral part of ALU. It holds one of data to be processed by ALU. It also temporarily stores the result of the operation performed by the ALU.

Q.3 ***List the 16 - bit registers of 8085 microprocessor.***

Ans. : Stack pointer (SP) and Program counter (PC).

Q.4 ***List the allowed register pairs of 8085.***

Ans. :

B-C register pair

D-E register pair

H-L register pair

Q.5 ***Mention the purpose of SID and SOD lines.***

Ans. : SID (Serial input data line): It is an input line through which the microprocessor accepts serial data. SOD (Serial output data line): It is an output line through which the microprocessor sends output serial data.

Q.6 ***What is the function of $IO/\overline{M}$ signal in the 8085?***

Ans. : It is a status signal. It is used to differentiate between memory locations and I/O operations. When this signal is low ($IO/\overline{M} = 0$) it denotes the memory related operations. When this signal is high ($IO/\overline{M} = 1$) it denotes an I/O operation.

Q.7 ***What is the signal classification of 8085 ?***

Ans. : All the signals of 8085 can be classified into 6 groups

i) Address bus ii) Data bus

iii) Control and status signals iv) Power supply and frequency signals

v) Externally initiated signals vi) Serial I/O ports

Q.8 ***What is the use of bi-directional buffers?***

Ans. : It is used to increase the driving capacity of the data bus. The data bus of a microcomputer system is bi-directional, so it requires a bi-directional buffer that allows the data to flow in both directions.

Q.9 ***Explain the signals HOLD, READY and SID.***

Ans. : HOLD indicates that a peripheral such as DMA controller is requesting the use of address bus, data bus and control bus. READY is used to delay the microprocessor read or write cycles until a slow responding peripheral is ready to send or accept data. SID is used to accept serial data bit by bit.

Q.10 ***What is the need for ALE signal in 8085 microprocessor?*** **Dec.-04,09, May-10**

Ans. : The ALE signal is used to demultiplex (separate) AD_0 - AD_7 lines to A_0 - A_7 (address lines) and D_0 - D_7 (data lines). The separation of address lines and data lines is achieved by connecting a external latch to AD_0 - AD_7 lines and enabling the latch when ALE signal is active.

Q.11 ***How performance of a microprocessor is measured interms of MIPS ?*** **June-07**

Ans. : The performance of a microprocessor is measured interms of MIPS (Million Instructions per Second). It is given as,

$$\text{MIPS rate} = \frac{1}{\text{Average time required for the execution of instruction} \times 10^6}$$

Q.12 ***A microprocessor takes n μs is for executing an instruction. What design change will make the microprocessor to execute the same instruction in is n/2 μs ?*** **June-07**

Ans. : By replacing the crystal of double frequency than that of existing one we can execute the same instruction in half time.

Q.13 ***If a 5 MHz crystal is connected with 8085; what is the value of system clock frequency and one T-state ?*** **Dec.-07**

Ans. : $\text{System clock frequency} = \frac{\text{Crystal frequecny}}{2} = \frac{5\text{ MHz}}{2} = 2.5\text{ MHz},$

$\text{one T-state} = \frac{1}{2.5 \times 10^6} = 0.4\ \mu\text{sec}.$

Q.14 ***What are the important control signals in 8085 microprocessor ?*** **Dec.-08**

Ans. : The important control signals in 8085 microprocessor are : ALE, $IO/\overline{M}$, $\overline{RD}$ and $\overline{WR}$

Q.15 *What is tri-state logic ?* **June-09**

Ans. : Logic outputs have two normal states, LOW and HIGH, corresponding to logic values 0 and 1. However, some outputs have a third electrical state that is not logic state at all, called the high-impedance or floating state. In this state the output behaves as if it isn't even connected to the circuit, except for a small leakage current that may flow into or out of the output pin. The circuit having such three states is called tri-state logic.

Q.16 *What is the function of the Ready signal of 8085 ?*

Ans. : It is used by the microprocessor to sense whether a peripheral is ready or not for data transfer. If not, the processor waits. It is thus used to synchronize slower peripherals to the microprocessor.

Q.17 *List the five interrupt pins available in 8085.* **May-10**

Ans. : The five interrupt pins available in 8085 are : TRAP, RST 7.5, RST 6.5, RST 5.5, and INTR.

Q.18 *Specify the size of data, address, memory word and memory capacity of 8085 microprocessor.* **May-11**

Ans. : Size of data bus = 8-bits Size of address bus = 16-bits

Size of memory word = 8-bits Memory capacity = 64 kbytes

Q.19 *List the special purpose registers of 8085*

Ans. : The special purpose registers of 8085 are :

1. A (Accumulator) 2. Flag register

3. Instruction register 4. program counter 5. Stack pointer.

Q.20 *List the signals provided for DMA operation by 8085 and explain their use.*

Ans. : HOLD : This signal indicates that another master is requesting for the use of address bus, data bus and control bus.

HLDA : This active high signal is used to acknowledge HOLD request.

Q.21 *What are the content of PC and INTE flag after reset ?*

Ans. : After reset, PC is loaded with 0000H and INTE flag is cleared.

Q.22 *What is the need of bus drivers ?*

Ans. : Typically, the 8085 buses can source 400 μA and sink 2 mA of current, i.e. it can drive only **one** TTL load. Therefore, it is necessary to increase driving capacity of the 8085 buses. Bus drivers, buffers are used to increase the driving capacity of the buses.

Q.23 *What is the function of program counter ?*

Ans. : Program counter stores the address of the next instruction to be fetched. Thus it is used as pointer to the instruction.

Q.24 *What is stack and what is the function of stack pointer ?* **Dec.-07**

Ans. : The stack is a reserved area of the memory in the RAM where temporary information may be stored. A 16-bit stack pointer is used to hold the address of the most recent stack entry.

Q.25 *What are flags available in 8085 ?*

Ans. : Various flags in 8085 are : S (Sign flag), Z (Zero flag), AC (Auxiliary carry flag), P (Parity flag), and CY (Carry flag)

❑❑❑

2 8085 Instruction Set & ALP

Contents

In the previous chapter we have studied block diagram of microprocessor 8085. The block diagram shows microprocessor's functions for data processing and data handling. It also shows how each of these logic functions are connected together. Such microprocessor performs a particular task by executing proper sequence of instructions. Thus to perform a task in a particular microprocessor system, programmer has to know the instructions supported by microprocessor used in the microprocessor system.

This chapter explains the set of instructions supported by the 8085 microprocessor and explains how to write programs (set of instructions written in a proper sequence to perform a particular task) using them. This chapter also gives a large number of programs to perform different tasks.

2.1 Instruction Classification

The instructions provided by the 8085 can be categorized into five different groups based on the nature of function of the instructions.

- Data transfer operations
- Arithmetic operations
- Logical operations
- Branch operations and
- Stack, Input/Output and Machine control operations

2.1.1 Data Transfer Operations

The data transfer instructions load given data into register, copy data from register to register, copy data from register to memory location, and vice versa. In other words we can say that data transfer instructions copy data from source to destination. Source can be data or contents of register or contents of memory location whereas destination can be register or memory location. These instructions do not affect the flag register of the processor.

2.1.2 Arithmetic Operations

The arithmetic instructions provided by 8085 perform addition, subtraction, increment and decrement operations.

- **Addition :** Any 8-bit number, or the contents of a register, or the contents of a memory location can be added to the contents of the accumulator and the resulted sum is stored in the accumulator. The resulted carry bit is stored in the carry flag. In 8085, no two other registers can be added directly, i.e. the contents of B and C registers cannot be added directly. To add two 16-bit numbers the 8085 provides DAD instruction. It adds the data within the register pair to the contents of the HL register pair and resulted sum is stored in the HL register pair.

- **Subtraction :** Any 8-bit number, or the contents of a register, or the contents of a memory location can be subtracted from the contents of the accumulator and the result is stored in the accumulator. The resulted borrow bit is stored in the carry flag. In 8085, no two other registers can be added directly.
- **Increment/Decrement :** The 8085 has the increment and decrement instructions to increment and decrement the contents of any register, memory location or register pair by 1.

2.1.3 Logical Operations

The logical instructions provided by 8085 perform logical, rotate, compare and complement operations.

- **Logical :** Using logical instructions, any 8-bit number, or the contents of a register, or of a memory location can be logically ANDed, ORed, or Exclusive-ORed with the contents of the accumulator and the result is stored in the accumulator. The result also affects the flags according to definition of flags. For example, the zero result sets the zero flag.
- **Rotate :** These instructions allow shifting of each bit in the accumulator either left or right by 1 bit position.
- **Compare :** Any 8-bit number, or the contents of a register, or the contents of a memory location can be compared for equality, greater than, or less than, with the contents of the accumulator.
- **Complement :** The result of accumulator can be complemented with this instruction. It replaces all 0 s by 1s and all 1s by 0 s.

2.1.4 Branching Operations

These instructions allow the 8085 to change the sequence of the program, either unconditionally or under certain test conditions. These instructions include branch instructions, subroutine call and return instructions and restart instructions.

2.1.5 Stack, Input / Output and Machine Control Operations

These instructions control the stack operations, input/output operations and machine operations. The stack instructions allow the transfer of data from register pair to stack memory and from stack memory to the register pair. The input/output instruction allows the transfer of 8-bit data to input/output port. On the other hand machine instructions control the machine operations such as interrupt, halt, or do nothing.

2.2 Instruction Set of 8085

May/June-09; April/May-10

In this section, the instructions from all groups are explained with the help of examples. Before to discuss these instructions, let us get familiar with the notations used in the explanation of instructions. These are:

Notation	Meaning
M	Memory location pointed by HL register pair
r	8-bit register
rp	16-bit register pair
rs	Source register
rd	Destination register
addr	16-bit address / 8-bit address

2.2.1 Data Transfer Group

May/June-07, Nov./Dec.-07

1. **MVI r, data (8)** This instruction directly loads a specified register with an 8-bit data given within the instruction. The register r is an 8-bit general purpose register such as A, B, C, D, E, H and L.

Operation : r ← 8-bit data (byte)

Example :

MVI B, 60H ; This instruction will load 60H directly into the B register.

2. **MVI M, data (8)** This instruction directly loads an 8-bit data given within the instruction into a memory location. The memory location is specified by the contents of HL register pair.

Operation : M ← byte or (HL) ← byte

Example : H = 20H and L = 50H

MVI M, 40H ; This instruction will load 40H into memory whose address is 2050H.

Before Execution				After Execution	
204FH				204FH	
HL = 2050H		MVI M, 40H		HL = 2050H	40
2051H				2051H	

3. MOV rd, rs This instruction copies data from the source register into destination register. The rs and rd are general purpose registers such as A, B, C, D, E, H and L. The contents of the source register remain unchanged after execution of the instruction.

Operation : rd ← rs

Example : A = 20H

MOV B, A ; This instruction will copy the contents of register A (20H) into register B.

4. MOV M, rs This instruction copies data from the source register into memory location pointed by the HL register pair. The rs is an 8-bit general purpose register such as A, B, C, D, E, H and L.

Operation : (HL) ← rs

Example : If HL = 2050H, B = 30H.

MOV M, B ; This instruction will copy the contents of B register (30H) into the memory location whose address is specified by HL (2050H).

5. MOV rd, M This instruction copies data from memory location whose address is specified by HL register pair into destination register. The contents of the memory location remain unchanged. The rd is an 8-bit general purpose register such as A, B, C, D, E, H and L.

Operation : rd ← (HL)

Example : HL = 2050H, contents at 2050H memory location = 40H

MOV C, M ; This instruction will copy the contents of memory location pointed by HL register pair (40H) into the C register.

6. LXI rp, data (16) This instruction loads immediate 16 bit data specified within the instruction into register pair or stack pointer. The rp is 16-bit register pair such as BC, DE, HL or 16-bit stack pointer.

Operation : rp ← data (16)

Example :

LXI B,1020H ; This instruction will load 10H into B register and 20H into C register.

7. STA addr This instruction stores the contents of A register into the memory location whose address is directly specified within the instruction. The contents of A register remain unchanged.

Operation : (addr) ← A

Example : A = 50H

STA 2000H ; This instruction will store the contents of A register (50H) to memory location 2000H.

8. LDA addr This instruction copies the contents of the memory location whose address is given within the instruction into the accumulator. The contents of the memory location remain unchanged.

Operation : A ← (addr)

Example : (2000H) = 30H

LDA 2000H ; This instruction will copy the contents of memory location 2000H i.e. data 30H into the A register

9. SHLD addr This instruction stores the contents of L register in the memory location given within the instruction and contents of H register at address next to it. This instruction is used to store the contents of H and L registers directly into the memory. The contents of the H and L registers remain unchanged.

Operation : (addr) ← L and (addr + 1) ← H

Example : H = 30H, L = 60H

SHLD 2500H ; This instruction will copy the contents of L register at address 2500H and the contents of H register at address 2501H.

10. LHLD addr This instruction copies the contents of the memory location given within the instruction into the L register and the contents of the next memory location into the H register.

Operation : L ← (addr), H ← (addr + 1)

Example : (2500H) = 30H, (2501H) = 60H

LHLD 2500H ; This instruction will copy the contents of memory location 2500H i.e. data 30H into the L register and the contents at memory location 2501H i.e. data 60H into the H register.

11. STAX rp This instruction copies the contents of accumulator into the memory location whose address is specified by the specified register pair. The rp is BC or DE register pair. This register pair is used as a memory pointer. The contents of the accumulator remain unchanged.

Operation : (rp) $\leftarrow$ A

Example : BC = 1020H, A = 50H

STAX B ; This instruction will copy the contents of A register (50H) to the memory location specified by BC register pair (1020H).

12. LDAX rp This instruction copies the contents of memory location whose address is specified by the register pair into the accumulator. The rp is BC or DE register pair. The register pair is used as a memory pointer.

Operation : A $\leftarrow$ (rp)

Example : DE = 2030H, (2030H) = 80H

LDAX D This instruction will copy the contents of memory location specified by DE register pair (80H) into the accumulator.

13. XCHG This instruction exchanges the contents of the register H with that of D and of L with that of E.

Operation : H $\leftrightarrow$ D and L $\leftrightarrow$ E

Example : DE = 2040H, HL = 7080H

XCHG ; This instruction will load the data into registers as follows H = 20H, L = 40H, D = 70H and E = 80

2.2.2 Arithmetic Group

Nov./Dec.-07

1. ADD r This instruction adds the contents of the specified register to the contents of accumulator and stores result in the accumulator. The r is 8-bit general purpose register such as A, B, C, D, E, H and L.

Operation : $A \leftarrow A + r$

Example : A = 20H, C = 30H.

ADD C ; This instruction will add the contents of C register, i.e. data 30H to the contents of accumulator, i.e. data 20H and it will store the result 50H in the accumulator.

2. ADD M This instruction adds the contents of the memory location pointed by HL register pair to the contents of accumulator and stores result in the accumulator. The HL register pair is used as a memory pointer. This instruction affects all flags.

Operation : $A \leftarrow A + M$

Example : A = 20H, HL = 2050H, (2050H) = 10H

ADD M ; This instruction will add the contents of memory location pointed by HL register pair, 2050H i.e. data 10H to the contents of accumulator i.e. data 20H and it will store the result, 30H in the accumulator.

3. ADI data (8) This instruction adds the 8 bit data given within the instruction to the contents of accumulator and stores the result in the accumulator.

Operation : $A \leftarrow A + \text{data (8)}$

Example : A = 50H

ADI 70H ; This instruction will add 70H to the contents of the accumulator (50H) and it will store the result in the accumulator (C0H).

4. ADC r This instruction adds the contents of specified register to the contents of accumulator with carry. This means, if the carry flag is set by some previous operation, it adds 1 and the contents of the specified register to the contents of accumulator, else it adds the contents of the specified register only. The r is 8-bit general purpose register such as A, B, C, D, E, H and L.

Operation : A ← A + r + CY

Example : Carry flag = 1, A = 50H, C = 20H

ADC C ; This instruction will add the contents of C (20H) register to the contents of accumulator (50H) with carry (1) and it will store result, 71H (50H + 20H + 1 = 71H) in the accumulator

5. ADC M This instruction adds the contents of memory location pointed by HL register pair to the contents of accumulator with carry and stores the result in the accumulator. HL register pair is used as a memory pointer.

Operation : A ← A + M + CY

Example : Carry flag = 1, HL = 2050H, A = 20H, (2050H) = 30H.

ADC M ; This instruction will add the contents of memory location pointed by HL register pair, 2050H, i.e. data 30H to the contents of accumulator, i.e. data 20H with carry flag (1). It will store the result (30+20+1=51H) in the accumulator.

6. ACI data (8) This instruction adds 8 bit data given within the instruction to the contents of accumulator with carry and stores result in the accumulator.

Operation : A ← A + data (8) + CY

Example : A = 30H, Carry flag = 1

ACI 20H ; This instruction will add 20H to the contents of accumulator, i.e. data 30H with carry (1) and stores the result, 51H (30 + 20 + 1 = 51H) in the accumulator.

7. DAD rp This instruction adds the contents of the specified register pair to the contents of the HL register pair and stores the result in the HL register pair. The rp is 16-bit register pair such as BC, DE, HL or stack pointer. Only higher order register is to be specified for register pair within the instruction.

Operation : HL ← HL + rp

Example : DE = 1020H, HL = 2050H

DAD D ; This instruction will add the contents of DE register pair, 1020H to the contents of HL register pair, 2050H. It will store the result, 3070H in the HL register pair.

8. SUB r

This instruction subtracts the contents of the specified register from the contents of the accumulator and stores the result in the accumulator. The register r is 8-bit general purpose register such as A, B, C, D, E, H and L.

Operation : A ← A – r

Example : A = 50H, B = 30H.

SUB B ; This instruction will subtract the contents of B register (30H) from the contents of accumulator (50H) and stores the result (20H) in the accumulator.

9. SUB M

This instruction subtracts the contents of the memory location pointed by HL register pair from the contents of accumulator and stores the result in the accumulator. The HL register pair is used as a memory pointer.

Operation : A ← A – M

Example : HL = 1020H, A = 50H, (1020H) = 10H

SUB M ; This instruction will subtract the contents of memory location pointed by HL register pair, 1020H, i.e. data 10H from the contents accumulator, i.e. data 50H and stores the result (40H) in accumulator.

10. SUI data (8)

This instruction subtracts an 8 bit data given within the instruction from the contents of the accumulator and stores the result in the accumulator.

Operation : A ← A – data (8)

Example : A = 40H,

SUI 20H ; This instruction will subtract 20H from the contents of accumulator (40H). It will store the result (20H) in the accumulator.

11. SBB r

This instruction subtracts the specified register contents and borrow flag from the accumulator contents. This means, if the carry flag (borrow for subtraction) is set by some previous operation, it subtracts 1 and the contents of the specified register from the contents of accumulator, else it subtracts the contents of the specified register only. The register r is 8-bit register such as A, B, C, D, E, H and L.

Operation : $A \leftarrow A - r - CY$

Example : Carry flag = 1, C = 20H, A = 40H

SBB C ; This instruction will subtract the contents of C register (20H) and carry flag (1) from the contents of accumulator (40H). It will store the result (40H – 20H – 1 = 1FH) in the accumulator.

12. SBB M

This instruction subtracts the contents of memory location pointed by HL register pair from the contents of accumulator and borrow flag and stores the result in the accumulator.

Operation : $A \leftarrow A - M - CY$

Example : Carry flag = 1, HL = 2050H, A = 50H, (2050H) = 10H.

SBB M ; This instruction will subtract the contents of memory location; pointed by HL register pair, 2050H, i.e. data 10H and borrow (Carry flag=1) from the contents of accumulator (50H) and stores the result 3FH in the accumulator (50 – 10 – 1 = 3F).

13. SBI data (8)

This instruction subtracts 8 bit data given within the instruction and borrow flag from the contents of accumulator and stores the result in the accumulator.

Operation : $A \leftarrow A - \text{data}(8) - CY$

Example : Carry flag = 1, A = 50H

SBI 20H ; This instruction will subtract 20H and the carry flag (1) from the contents of the accumulator (50H). It will store the result (50H – 20H – 1 = 2FH) in the accumulator.

14. DAA

This instruction adjusts accumulator to packed BCD (Binary Coded Decimal) after adding two BCD numbers.

Instruction works as follows :

1. If the value of the low - order four bits (D_3-D_0) in the accumulator is greater than 9 or if auxiliary carry flag is set, the instruction adds 6 (06) to the low-order four bits.

2. If the value of the high-order four bits (D_7 - D_4) in the accumulator is greater than 9 or if carry flag is set, the instruction adds 6 (60) to the high-order four bits.

Example :

```
If,     A = 0011 1001 = 39 BCD
and       C = 0001 0010 = 12 BCD then
   ADD C        ; Gives A = 0100 1011 = 4BH
   DAA          ; adds 0110 because 1011>9,
                ; A=0101 0001 = 51 BCD
If      A = 1001 0110 = 96 BCD
and       D = 0000 0111 = 07 BCD  then
   ADD D        ; Gives A = 1001 1101 = 9DH
   DAA          ; adds 0110 because 1101 > 9,
                   A = 1010 0011 = A3H,
              1010 > 9 so adds 0110 0000,
                   A = 0000 0011 = 03 BCD, CF = 1.
```

15. INR r

This instruction increments the contents of specified register by 1. The result is stored in the same register. The register r is 8-bit general purpose register such as A, B, C, D, E, H and L.

Operation : $r \leftarrow r + 1$

Example : B = 10H

INR B ; This instruction will increment the contents of B register (10H) by one and stores the result (10+1 = 11H) in the same i.e. B register.

16. INR M

This instruction increments the contents of memory location pointed by HL register pair by 1. The result is stored at the same memory location. The HL register pair is used as a memory pointer.

Operation : $M \leftarrow M + 1$

Example : HL = 2050H, (2050H) = 30H

INR M ; This instruction will increment the contents of memory location pointed by HL register pair, 2050H, i.e. data 30H by one. It will store the result (30 + 1 = 31H) at the same place.

17. INX rp This instruction increments the contents of register pair by one. The result is stored in the same register pair. The rp is register pair such as BC, DE, HL or stack pointer (SP).

Operation : rp $\leftarrow$ rp + 1

Example : HL = 10FFH

INX H ; This instruction will increment the contents of HL register pair (10FFH) by one. It will store the result (10FF + 1 = 1100H) in the same i.e. HL register pair.

18. DCR r This instruction decrements the contents of the specified register by one. It stores the result in the same register. The register r is 8-bit general purpose register such as A, B, C, D, E, H and L.

Operation : r $\leftarrow$ r – 1

Example : E = 20H

DCR E ; This instruction will decrement the contents of E register (20H) by one. It will store the result (20 – 1 = 1FH) in the same, i.e. E register.

19. DCR M This instruction decrements the contents of memory location pointed by HL register pair by 1. The HL register pair is used as a memory pointer. The result is stored in the same memory location.

Operation : M $\leftarrow$ M – 1

Example : HL = 2050H, (2050H) = 21H

DCR M ; This instruction will decrement the contents of memory location pointed by HL register pair, 2050H, i.e. data 21H by one. It will store the result (21 – 1 = 20H) in the same memory location.

20. DCX rp This instruction decrements the contents of register pair by one. The result is stored in the same register pair. The rp is register pair such as BC, DE, HL or stack pointer (SP). Only higher order register is to be specified within the instruction.

Operation : rp ← rp – 1

Example : DE = 1020H

DCX D ; This instruction will decrement the contents of DE register pair (1020H) by one and store the result (1020 – 1 = 101FH) in the same, DE register pair.

2.2.3 Logic Group

1. ANA r

This instruction logically ANDs the contents of the specified register with the contents of accumulator and stores the result in the accumulator. Each bit in the accumulator is logically ANDed with the corresponding bit in register r, i.e. D_0 bit in A with D_0 bit in register r, D_1 in A with D_1 in r and so on upto D_7 bit. The register r is 8-bit general purpose register such as A, B, C, D, E, H and L.

Operation : A ← A ∧ r

Example : A = 10101010 (AAH), B = 00001111 (0FH)

ANA B ; This instruction will logically AND the contents of B register with the contents of accumulator. It will store the result (0AH) in the accumulator.

```
  1010 1010
  0000 1111
  ---------
  0000 1010 = 0AH
```

2. ANA M

This instruction logically ANDs the contents of memory location pointed by HL register pair with the contents of accumulator. The result is stored in the accumulator. The HL register pair is used as a memory pointer.

Operation : A ← A ∧ M

Example : A = 01010101 = (55H), HL = 2050H(2050H) → 10110011 = (B3H)

ANA M ; This instruction will logically AND the contents of memory location pointed by HL register pair (B3H) with the contents of accumulator (55H). It will store the result (11H) in the accumulator.

```
  0101 0101
  1011 0011
  ---------
  0001 0001 = 11H
```

3. ANI data This instruction logically ANDs the 8 bit data given in the instruction with the contents of the accumulator and stores the result in the accumulator.

Operation : $A \leftarrow A \wedge \text{data (8)}$

Example : A = 1011 0011 = (B3H)

ANI 3FH ; This instruction will logically AND the contents of accumulator (B3H) with 3FH. It will store the result (33H) in the accumulator.

```
1011  0011
0011  1111
----------
0011  0011 = 33H
```

The AND operation clears bits of a binary number. The task of clearing a bit in a binary number is called **masking.** The Fig. 2.1 shows the process of masking.

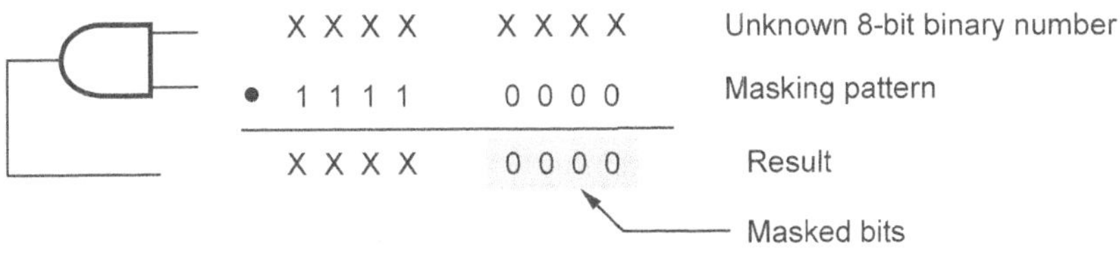

Fig. 2.1 Masking using AND operation

4. XRA r This instruction logically XORs the contents of the specified register with the contents of accumulator and stores the result in the accumulator. The register r is 8-bit general purpose register such as A, B, C, D, E, H and L.

Operation : $A \leftarrow A \oplus r$

Example : A = 1010 1010 (AAH), C = 0010 1101 (2DH)

XRA C ; This instruction will logically XOR the contents of C register with the contents of accumulator. It will store the result (87H) in the accumulator.

```
1010  1010
0010  1101
----------
1000  0111 = (87H)
```

5. XRA M This instruction logically XORs the contents of memory location pointed by HL register pair with the contents of accumulator. The HL register pair is used as a memory pointer.

Operation : $A \leftarrow A \oplus M$

Example : A = 0101 0101 = (55H), HL = 2050H (2050H) $\rightarrow$ 1011 0011 =(B3H)

XRA M ; This instruction will logically XOR the contents of memory location pointed by HL register pair (2050H) i.e. data B3H with the contents of accumulator (55H). It will store the result (E6H) in the accumulator.

```
0101  0101
1011  0011
----------
1110  0110 = E6H
```

6. XRI data

This instruction logically XORs the 8 bit data given in the instruction with the contents of the accumulator and stores the result in the accumulator.

Operation : A $\leftarrow$ A $\oplus$ data

Example : A = 10110011 = (B3H)

XRI 39H ; This instruction will logically XOR the contents of accumulator (B3H) with 39H. It will store the result (8AH) in the accumulator.

```
1011  0011
0011  1001
----------
1000  1010 = 8AH
```

The XOR instruction is used if some bits of a register or memory location must be inverted. This instruction allows part of a number to be inverted or complemented. This is illustrated in Fig. 2.2.

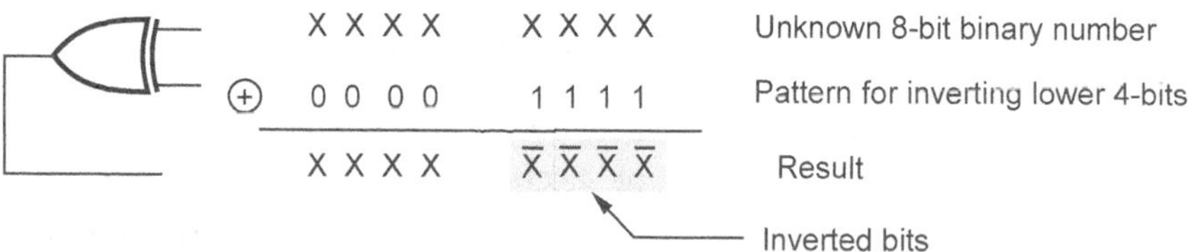

Fig. 2.2 Inversion of part of a number using XOR operation

7. ORA r

This instruction logically ORs the contents of specified register with the contents of accumulator and stores the result in the accumulator. Each bit in the accumulator is ORed with corresponding bit in register r. i.e. D_0 bit in accumulator is ORed with D_0 bit in register r, D_1 in A with D_1 in r and so on upto D_7 bit. The register r is 8-bit general purpose register such as A, B, C, D, E, H and L.

Operation : A $\leftarrow$ A $\vee$ r

Example : A = 1010 1010 (AAH), B = 0001 0010 (12H)

ORA B ; This instruction will logically OR the contents of B register with the contents of accumulator. It will store the result (BAH) in the accumulator.

```
1010  1010
0001  0010
----------
1011  1010 = BAH
```

8. ORA M This instruction logically ORs the contents of memory location pointed by HL register pair with the contents of accumulator. The result is stored in the accumulator. The HL register pair is used as a memory pointer.

Operation : A ← A ∨ M

Example : A = 0101 0101 = (55H) HL = 2050H

(2050H) → 1011 0011 = (B3H)

ORA M ; This instruction will logically OR the contents of memory location pointed by HL register pair (B3H) with the contents of accumulator (55H). It will store the result (F7H) in the accumulator.

```
0101  0101
1011  0011
----------
1111  0111 = F7H
```

9. ORI data This instruction logically ORs the 8 bit data given in the instruction with the contents of the accumulator and stores the result in the accumulator.

Operation : A ∨ data (8)

Example : A = 1011 0011 = (B3H)

ORI 08H ; This instruction will logically OR the contents of accumulator (B3H) with 08H. It will store the result (BBH) in the accumulator.

```
1011  0011
0000  1000
----------
1011  1011 = BBH
```

The OR instruction is used to set (make one) any bit in the binary number. This is illustrated in Fig. 2.3.

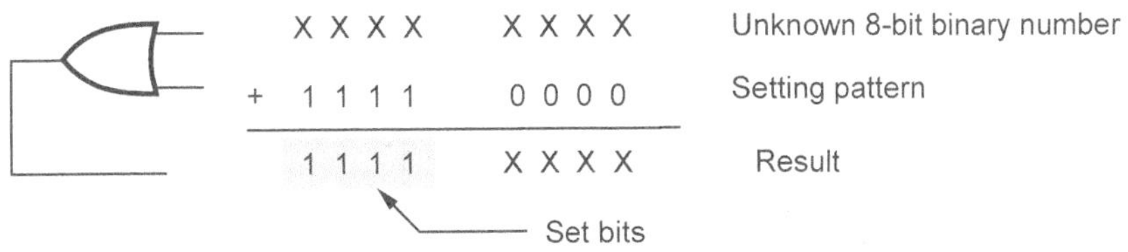

Fig. 2.3 Setting bit/s using OR operation

10. CMP r This instruction subtracts the contents of the specified register from contents of the accumulator and sets the condition flags as a result of the subtraction. It sets zero flag if A = r and sets carry flag if A < r. The register r is 8-bit general purpose register such as A, B, C, D, E, H and L.

Operation : A – r

Example : A = 1011 1000 (B8H) and D = 1011 1001 (B9H)

CMP D ; This instruction will compare the contents of D register with the contents of accumulator. Here A < D so carry flag will set after the execution of the instruction.

11. CMP M This instruction subtracts the contents of the memory location specified by HL register pair from the contents of the accumulator and sets the condition flags as a result of subtraction. It sets zero flag if A = M and sets carry flag if A < M. The HL register pair is used as a memory pointer.

Operation : A – M

Example : A = 1011 1000 (B8H), HL = 2050H and (2050H) = 1011 1000 (B8H)

CMP M ; This instruction will compare the contents of memory location (B8H) and the contents of accumulator. Here A = M so zero flag will set after the execution of the instruction.

12. CPI data This instruction subtracts the 8 bit data given in the instruction from the contents of the accumulator and sets the condition flags as a result of subtraction. It sets zero flag if A = data and sets carry flag if A < data.

Operation : A – data (8)

Example : A = 1011 1010 = (BAH)

CPI 30H ; This instruction will compare 30H with the contents of accumulator (BAH). Here A > data so zero and carry both flags will reset after the execution of the instruction.

13. STC This instruction sets carry flag = 1

Operation : CY ← 1

Example : Carry flag = 0

STC ; This instruction will set the carry flag = 1

14. CMC This instruction complements the carry flag.

Operation : $CY \leftarrow \overline{CY}$

Example : Carry flag = 1

CMC ; This instruction will complement the carry flag i.e. carry flag = 0

15. CMA This instruction complements each bit of the accumulator.

Operation : $A \leftarrow \overline{A}$

Example : A = 1000 1000 = 88H

CMA ; This instruction will complement each bit of accumulator A = 0111 0111 = 77H

2.2.4 Rotate Group

1. RLC This instruction rotates the contents of the accumulator left by one position. Bit B_7 is placed in B_0 as well as in CY.

Operation :

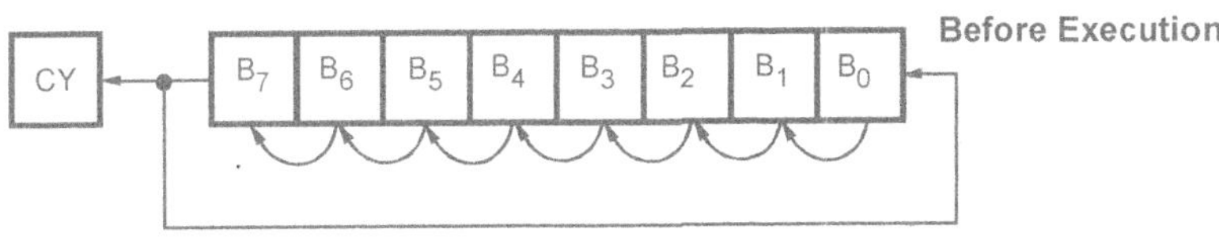

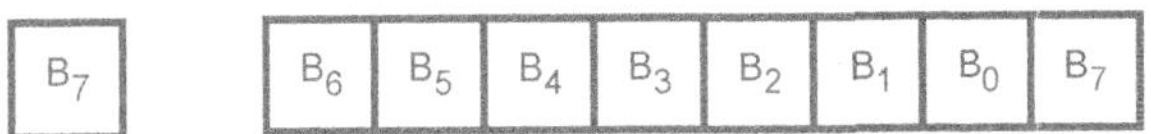

Example : A = 01010111 (57H) and CY = 1

RLC ; After execution of the instruction the accumulator contents will be (1010 1110) AEH and carry flag will reset.

2. RRC This instruction rotates the contents of the accumulator right by one position. Bit B_0 is placed in B_7 as well as in CY.

Operation :

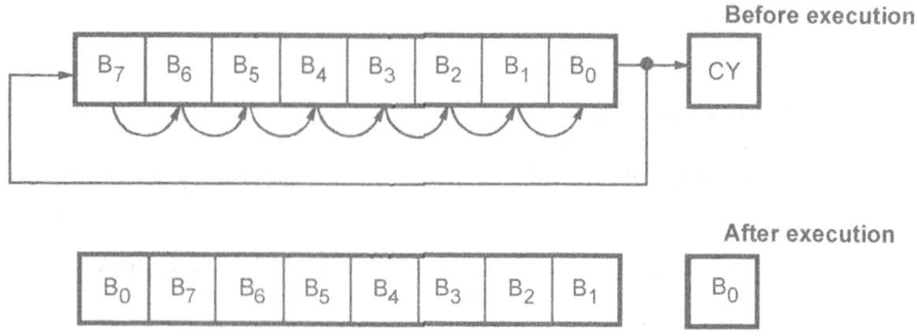

Example : A = 1001 1010 (9AH) and CY = 1

RRC ; After execution of the instruction the accumulator contents will be (0100 1101) 4DH and carry flag will reset.

3. **RAL** This instruction rotates the contents of the accumulator left by one position. Bit B_7 is placed in CY and CY is placed in B_0.

Operation :

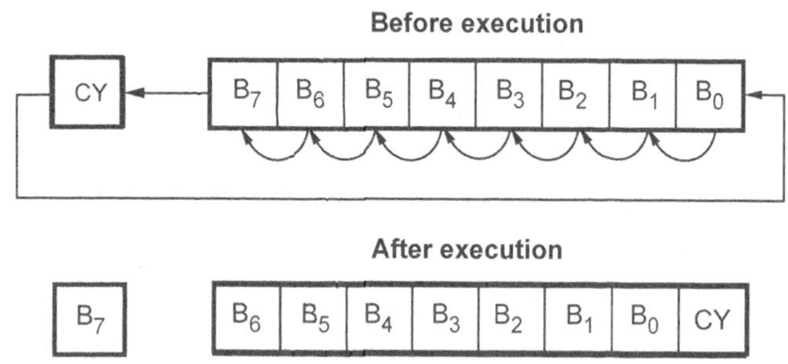

Example : A = 10101101 (ADH) and CY = 0

RAL ; After execution of the instruction accumulator contents will be (0101 1010) 5AH and carry flag will set.

4. **RAR** This instruction rotates the contents of the accumulator right by one position. Bit B_0 is placed in CY and CY is placed in B_7.

Operation :

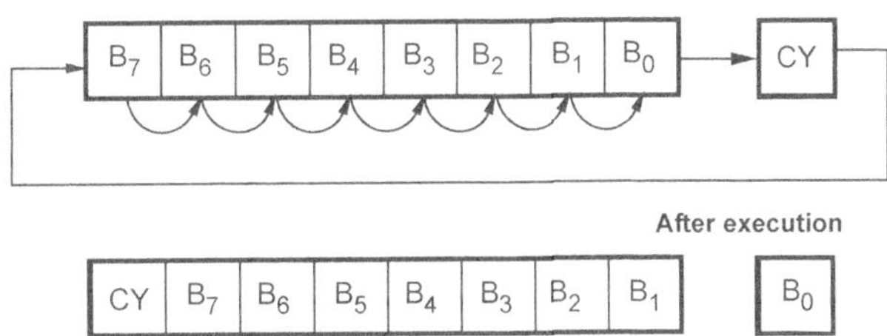

Example : A = 1010 0011 (A3H) and CY = 0

RAR ; After execution of the instruction accumulator contents will be (0101 0001) 51H and carry flag will set.

2.2.5 Stack Operations

April/May-04, 08; May/June-07, Nov./Dec.-07, 09

The stack is a portion of read/write memory set aside by the user for the purpose of storing information temporarily. When the information is written on the stack, the operation is called PUSH. When the information is read from stack, the operation is called POP.

The microprocessor stores the information, much like stacking plates. Using this analogy of stacking plates it is easy to illustrate the stack operation.

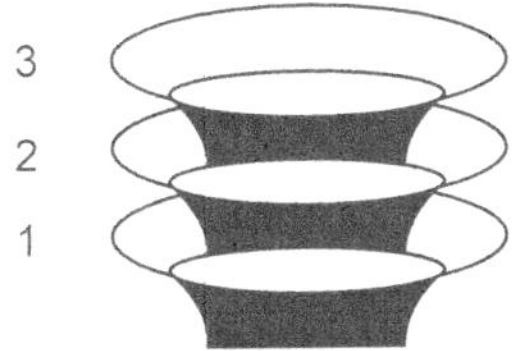

Fig. 2.4 Stacked plates

Fig. 2.4 shows the stacked plates. Here, we realize that if it is desired to take out the first stacked plate we will have to remove all plates above the first plate in the reverse order. This means that to remove first plate we will have to remove the third plate, then the second plate and finally the first plate. This means that, the first information pushed on to the stack is the last information popped off from the stack. This type of operation is known as a first in, last out (FILO). This stack is implemented with the help of special memory pointer register. The special pointer register is called the **stack pointer.** During PUSH and POP operation, stack pointer register gives the address of memory where the information is to be stored or to be read. The stack pointer's contents are automatically manipulated to point to stack top. The memory location currently pointed by stack pointer is called **top of stack**.

1. PUSH rp This instruction decrements stack pointer by one and copies the higher byte of the register pair into the memory location pointed by stack pointer. It then decrements the stack pointer again by one and copies the lower byte of the register pair into the memory location pointed by stack pointer. The rp is 16-bit register pair such as BC, DE, HL. Only higher order register is to be specified within the instruction.

(i.e. data 50H) into B register, and increment the stack pointer again by one.

Before Execution

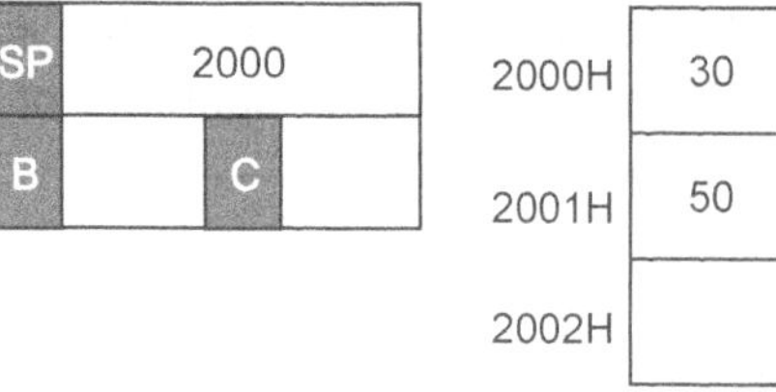

POP B

After Execution

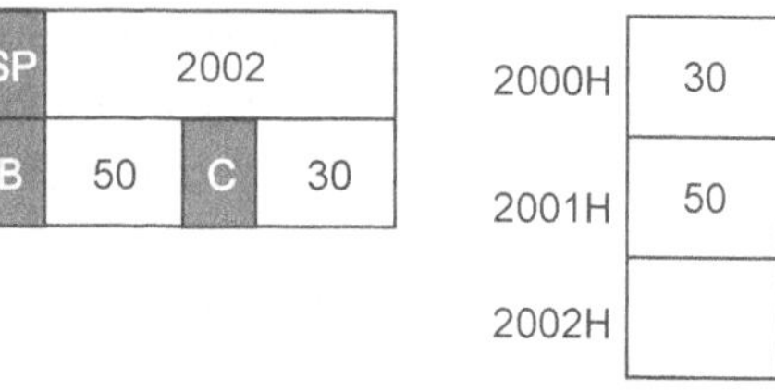

4. POP PSW

This instruction copies the contents of memory location pointed by the stack pointer into the flag register and increments the stack pointer by one. It then copies the contents of memory location pointed by stack pointer into the accumulator and increments the stack pointer again by one.

Operation : Flag register ← (SP)

SP ← SP + 1

A ← (SP)

SP ← SP + 1

Example : SP = 2000H, (2000H) = 30H, (2001H) = 50H

POP PSW ; This instruction will copy the contents of memory location pointed by the stack pointer, 2000H (i.e. data 30H) into the flag register. It will then increment the stack pointer by one, 2001H and will copy the contents of memory location pointed by stack pointer into the accumulator and increment the stack pointer again by one.

Before Execution **After Execution**

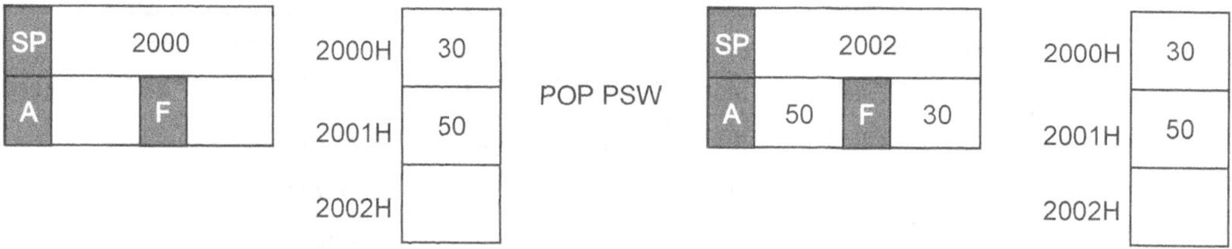

5. SPHL

This instruction copies the contents of HL register pair into the stack pointer. The contents of H register are copied to higher order byte of stack pointer and contents of L register are copied to the lower byte of stack pointer.

Operation : SP ← HL

Example : HL = 2500H

SPHL ; This instruction will copy 2500H into stack pointer. So after execution of instruction stack pointer contents will be 2500H.

6. XTHL This instruction exchanges the contents of memory location pointed by the stack pointer with the contents of L register and the contents of the next memory location with the contents of H register. This instruction does not modify stack pointer contents.

Operation : L ↔ (SP)

H ↔ (SP + 1)

Example : HL = 3040H and SP = 2700H, (2700H) = 50H, (2701H) = 60H

XTHL ; This instruction will exchange the contents of L register(40H) with the contents of memory location 2700H (i.e. 50H) and the contents of H register (30H) with the contents of memory location 2701H (i.e. 60H).

Before Execution

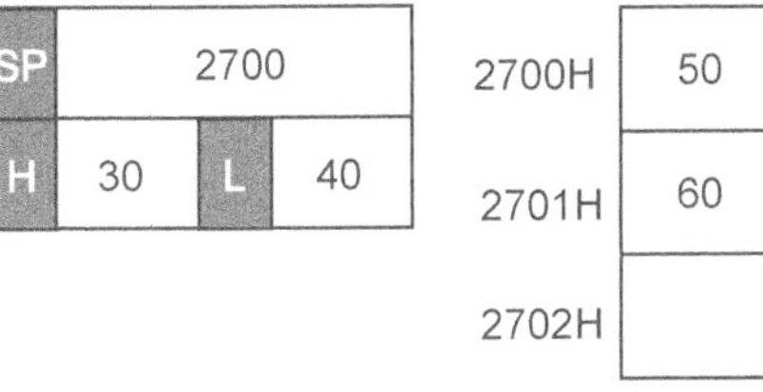

XTHL

After Execution

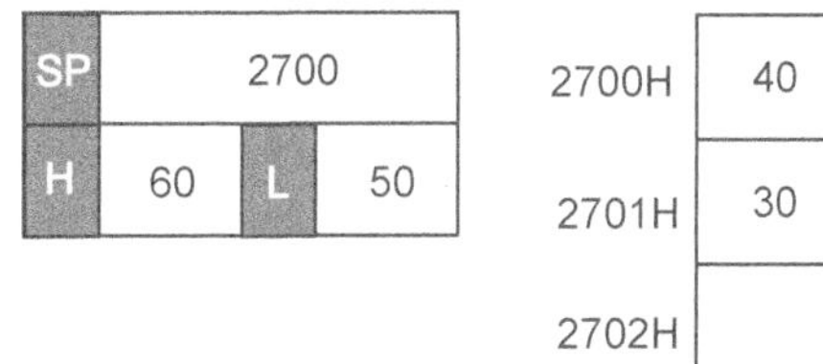

2.2.6 Branch Group

May/June-07, Nov./Dec.-07, 09, April/May-10

1. JMP addr This instruction loads the PC with the address given within the instruction and resumes the program execution from this location.

Operation : PC ← addr

Example :

JMP 2000H ; This instruction will load PC with 2000H and processor will fetch next instruction from this address.

2. Jcond addr This instruction causes a jump to an address given in the instruction if the desired condition occurs in the program before the execution of the instruction. The Table 2.1 shows the possible conditions for jumps.

Instruction code	Description	Condition for jump
JC	Jump on carry	CY = 1
JNC	Jump on not carry	CY = 0
JP	Jump on positive	S = 0
JM	Jump on minus	S = 1
JPE	Jump on parity even	P = 1
JPO	Jump on parity odd	P = 0
JZ	Jump on zero	Z = 1
JNZ	Jump on not zero	Z = 0

Table 2.1 Conditional jumps

Example : Carry flag = 1

JC 2000H ; This instruction will cause a jump to an address 2000H i.e. program counter will load with 2000H since CF =1.

3. CALL addr

A subroutine is a group of instructions, performs a particular subtask which is executed number of times. It is written separately. The microprocessor executes this subroutine by transferring program control to the subroutine program. After completion of subroutine program execution, the program control is returned back to the main program.

The CALL instruction is used to transfer program control to a subprogram or subroutine. This instruction pushes the current PC contents onto the stack and loads the given address into the PC. Thus the program control is transferred to the address given in the instruction. Stack pointer is decremented by two.

When the subroutine is called, the program control is transferred from calling program to the subroutine. After execution of subroutine it is necessary to transfer program control back to the calling program. To do this processor must remember the address of the instruction next to the CALL instruction. Processor saves this address on the stack when the CALL instruction is executed.

Note : The stack is a part of read/write memory set aside for storing intermediate results and addresses.

Operation : $(SP - 1) \leftarrow PC_H$

$(SP - 2) \leftarrow PC_L$

$SP \leftarrow SP - 2$

$PC \leftarrow addr$

Example : Stack pointer = 3000H.

6000H CALL 2000H ; This instruction will store the address of instruction next to CALL (i.e. 6003H) on the stack and load PC with 2000H.

6003H —-

4. C cond addr This instruction calls the subroutine at the given address if a specified condition is satisfied. Before call it stores the address of instruction next to the call on the stack and decrements stack pointer by two. The Table 2.2 shows the possible conditions for calls.

Instruction code	Description	Condition for CALL
CC	Call on carry	CY = 1
CNC	Call on not carry	CY = 0
CP	Call on positive	S = 0
CM	Call on minus	S = 1
CPE	Call on parity even	P = 1
CPO	Call on parity odd	P = 0
CZ	Call on zero	Z = 1
CNZ	Call on not zero	Z = 0

Table 2.2 Conditional calls

Operation : If condition true (SP – 1) ← PCH
(SP – 2) ← PCL
PC ← addr
else PC ← PC + 3

Example : Carry flag = 1, stack pointer = 4000H.

2000H CC 3000H ; This instruction will store the address of the next instruction i.e. 2003H on the stack and load the program counter with 3000H, since the carry flag is set.

5. RET This instruction pops the return addr (address of the instruction next to CALL in the main program) from the stack and loads program counter with this return address. Thus transfers program control to the instruction next to CALL in the main program.

Operation : $PC_L \leftarrow (SP)$
$PC_H \leftarrow (SP+1)$
$SP \leftarrow SP + 2$

Example : If SP = 27FDH and contents on the stack are as shown then

SP →	27FD	00
	27FE	62
	27FF	

RET ; This instruction will load PC with 6200H and it will transfer program control to the address 6200H. It will also increment the stack pointer by two.

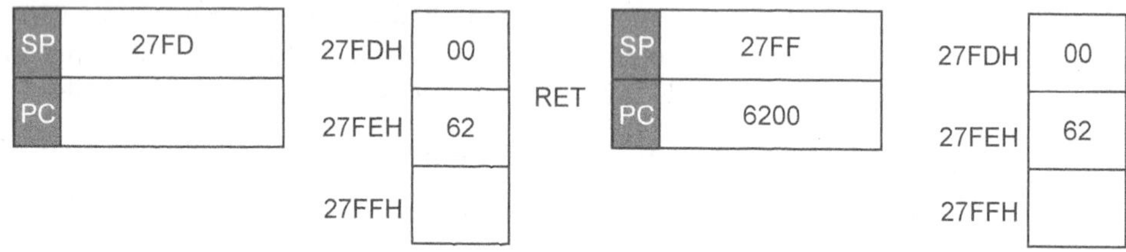

6. R condition This instruction returns the control to the main program if the specified condition is satisfied. Table 2.3 shows the possible conditions for return.

Instruction code	Description	Condition for RET
RC	Return on carry	CY = 1
RNC	Return on not carry	CY = 0
RP	Return on positive	S = 0
RM	Return on minus	S = 1
RPE	Return on parity even	P = 1
RPO	Return on parity odd	P = 0
RZ	Return on zero	Z = 1
RNZ	Return on not zero	Z = 0

Table 2.3 Conditions for return

7. PCHL This instruction loads the contents of HL register pair into the program counter. Thus the program control is transferred to the location whose address is in HL register pair.

Operation : $PC \leftarrow HL$

Example : HL = 6000H

PCHL ; This instruction will load 6000H into the program counter.

8. RST n This instruction transfers the program control to the specific memory address as shown in Table 2.4. This instruction is like a fixed address CALL instruction. These fixed addresses are also referred to as vector addresses. The processor multiplies the RST number by 8 to calculate these vector addresses. Before transferring the program control to the instruction following the vector address RST instruction saves the current program counter contents on the stack like CALL instruction

Instruction code	Vector Address
RST 0	0×8 = 0000H
RST 1	1×8 = 0008H
RST 2	2×8 = 0010H
RST 3	3×8 = 0018H
RST 4	4×8 = 0020H
RST 5	5×8 = 0028H
RST 6	6×8 = 0030H
RST 7	7×8 = 0038H

Table 2.4 Vector addresses for return instructions

Operation : $(SP - 1) \leftarrow PC_H$

$(SP - 2) \leftarrow PC_L$

$SP \leftarrow SP - 2$, $PC \leftarrow (n \times 8)$ in hex

Example : SP = 3000H

2000H RST 6 ; This instruction will save the current contents of the program counter (i.e. address of next instruction 2001H) on the stack and it will load the program counter with vector address $6 \times 8 = 48_{10} = 30H$) 0030H.

2.2.7 Input/Output

April/May-10

1. IN addr(8-bit) This instruction copies the data at the port whose address is specified in the instruction into the accumulator.

Operation : $A \leftarrow (addr)$

Example : Port address = 80H, data stored at port address 80H, (80H) = 10H

IN 80H ; This instruction will copy the data stored at address 80H, i.e. data 10H in the accumulator.

2. OUT addr(8-bit) This instruction sends the contents of accumulator to the output port whose address is specified within the instruction.

Operation : (addr) ← A

Example : A = 40H

OUT 50H ; This instruction will send the contents of accumulator(40H) to the output port whose address is 50H.

2.2.8 Machine Control Group

Nov./Dec.-08

1. EI This instruction sets the interrupt enable flip flop to enable interrupts. When the microprocessor is reset or after interrupt acknowledge, the interrupt enable flip-flop is reset. This instruction is used to reenable the interrupts.

Operation : IE (F/F) ← 1

2. DI This instruction resets the interrupt enable flip-flop to disable interrupts. This instruction disables all interrupts except TRAP since TRAP is non-maskable interrupt (cannot be disabled. It is always enabled).

Operation : IE (F/F) ← 0

3. NOP No operation is performed.

4. HLT This instruction halts the processor. It can be restarted by a valid interrupt or by applying a RESET signal.

5. SIM This instruction masks the interrupts as desired. It also sends out serial data through the SOD pin. For this instruction command byte must be loaded in the accumulator.

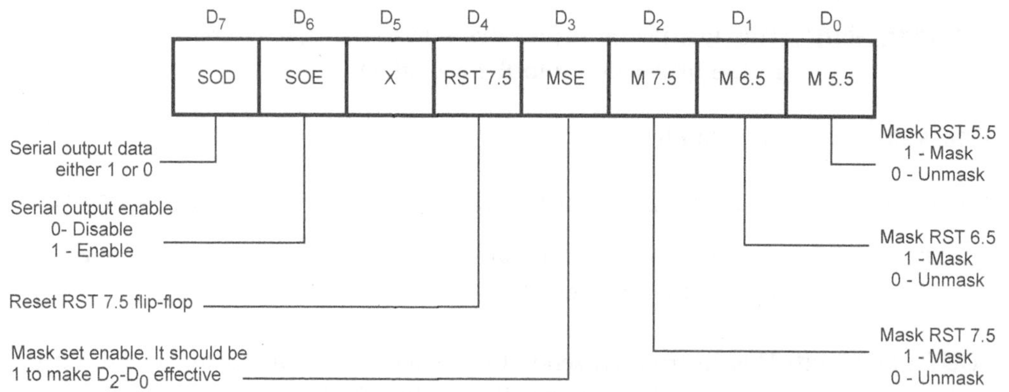

Example : i) A = 0EH

D_7	D_6	D_5	D_4	D_3	D_2	D_1	D_0		Register A
SOD	SOE	X	RST7.5	MSE	M7.5	M6.5	M5.5		
0	0	0	0	1	1	1	0	=	0EH

SIM ; This instruction will mask RST 7.5 and RST 6.5 interrupts where as RST 5.5 interrupt will be unmasked. It will also disable serial output.

6. RIM : This instruction copies the status of the interrupts into the accumulator. It also reads the serial data through the SID pin.

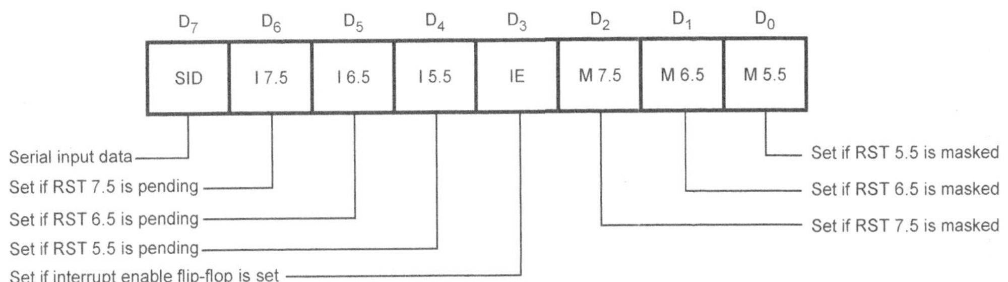

Example :

RIM ; After execution of RIM instruction if the contents of accumulator are 4BH then we get following information.

D_7	D_6	D_5	D_4	D_3	D_2	D_1	D_0		Register A
SID	I 7.5	I 6.5	I 5.5	IE	M7.5	M6.5	M5.5		
0	1	0	0	1	0	1	1	=	4BH

i.e. a) RST 7.5 is pending

b) RST 5.5 and RST 6.5 are masked

c) Interrupt Enable flip-flop is set

d) Serial i/p data is zero.

2.3 Addressing Modes

Part of the programming flexibility for each microprocessor is the number and different kind of ways the programmer can refer to data stored in the memory. The different ways that a microprocessor can access data are referred to as **addressing modes**. The 8085 has 5 addressing modes. These are :

1. Immediate
2. Register
3. Direct
4. Indirect
5. Implied

1. Immediate addressing mode :

In an immediate addressing mode, 8 or 16 bit data can be specified as a part of instruction. In 8085, the instructions having 'I' letter fall under this category. 'I' indicates immediate addressing mode.

Example :

```
MVI A, 20H      ; Moves 8 bit immediate data (20H) into accumulator
MVI M, 30H      ; Moves 8 bit immediate data (30H) into the
                ; memory location pointed by HL register pair.
LXI SP, 2700H   ; Moves 16 bit immediate data (2700H) into SP.
LXI D, 10FFH    ; Moves 16 bit immediate data (10FFH) into DE
                ; register pair ( D = 10H and E = FFH).
```

2. Register addressing mode :

The register addressing mode specifies the source operand, destination operand, or both to be contained in an 8085 registers. This results in faster execution, since it is not necessary to access memory locations for operands.

Example :

```
MOV A, B   ; Moves the contents of register B into the accumulator.
SPHL       ; Moves the contents of HL register pair into stack pointer.
ADD C      ; Adds the contents of register C into the contents of accumulator
           ; and stores result in the accumulator.
```

3. Direct addressing mode :

The direct addressing mode specifies the 16 bit address of the operand within the instruction itself. The second and third bytes of instruction contain this 16 bit address.

Example :

```
LDA 2000H    ; Loads the 8 bit contents of memory location
             ; 2000H into the accumulator.
SHLD 3000H   ; Stores the HL register pair into two consecutive memory
             ; locations. Lower byte i.e. the contents of L register into memory
             ; location 3000H and higher byte i.e. the contents of H register
             ; into memory location 3001H.
```

4. Indirect addressing mode :

In indirect addressing mode, the memory address where the operand located is specified by the contents of a register pair.

Example :

```
LDAX B      ; Loads the accumulator with the contents of
            ; memory location pointed by BC register pair.
MOV M, A    ; Stores the contents of accumulator into the
            ; memory location pointed by HL register pair.
```

5. Implied Addressing Mode :

In implied addressing mode, opcode specifies the address of the operands.

Example :

```
CMA         ; Complements contents of accumulator.
RAL         ; Rotates the contents of accumulator left through carry.
```

Note : Many of the advanced processors support addressing mode called **index addressing mode**. In this mode, the address of the operand within the memory is generated by adding the offset/displacement to the register specified in the instruction. The offset/displacement is also a part of the instruction. In 8085 such addressing mode is not available. However, we can implement such kind of program structure, by using memory pointer (HL register), any other register pair and a instruction sequence given below :

```
LXI H, Base_addr             ; Loads the base address
LXI B, Offset/Displacement   ; Loads the offset or displacement
DAD B                        ; Gives the addition of HL and BC in HL register pair.
MOV A, M                     ; Load the data from memory in the accumulator
```

By incrementing or decrementing contents of BC register or loading another contents, we can change the index/offset/displacement.

2.4 Instruction Set Summary

Data Transfer Group					
Sr. No.	**Instruction**	**Operation**	**Flags affected**	**No. of bytes**	**Addressing mode**
1.	MVI r, data (8)	r ← data(8)	No	2	Immediate
2.	MVI M, data (8)	(HL) ← data (8)	No	2	Immediate and Indirect
3.	MOV rd, rs	rd ← rs	No	1	Register
4.	MOV M, rs	(HL) ← rs	No	1	Indirect
5.	MOV rd, M	rd ← (HL)	No	1	Indirect
6.	LXI rp, data (16)	rp ← data (16)	No	3	Immediate
7.	STA addr	(addr) ← A	No	3	Direct

8.	LDA addr	A ← (addr)	No	3	Direct
9.	SHLD addr	(addr) ← L (addr + 1) ← H	No	3	Direct
10.	LHLD addr	L ← (addr) HL ← (addr+1)	No	3	Direct
11.	STAX rp	(rp) ← A	No	1	Indirect
12.	LDAX rp	A ← (rp)	No	1	Indirect
13	XCHG	H ↔ D, L ↔ E	No	1	Register

Arithmetic Group

Sr. No.	Instruction	Operation	Flags affected	No. of bytes	Addressing mode
1.	ADD r	A ← A + r	All	1	Register
2.	ADD M	A ← A + (HL)	All	1	Register Indirect
3.	ADI data(8)	A ← A + data (8)	All	2	Immediate
4.	ADC r	A ← A + r + CY	All	1	Register
5.	ADC M	A ← A + (HL) + CY	All	1	Register indirect
6.	ACI data (8)	A ← A + data(8) + CY	All	2	Immediate
7.	DAD rp	HL ← HL + rp	CY	1	Register
8.	Sub r	A ← A – r	All	1	Register
9.	Sub M	A ← A – (HL)	All	1	Register Indirect
10.	SUI data (8)	A ← A – data (8)	All	2	Immediate
11.	SBB r	A ← A – r – CY	All	1	Register
12.	SBB M	A ← A – (HL) – CY	All	1	Register Indirect
13.	SBI data	A ← A – data(8) – CY	All	2	Immediate
14.	DAA	A(BCD) ← A(Binary)	All	1	Implied
15.	INR r	r ← r + 1	S, Z, P, A, C	1	Register
16	INR M	(HL) ← (HL) + 1	S, Z, P, A, C	1	Register Indirect
17.	INX rp	rp ← rp + 1	No	1	Register
18.	DCR r	r ← r – 1	S, Z, P, A, C	1	Register
19.	DCR M	(HL) ← (HL) – 1	S, Z, P, A, C	1	Register Indirect
20.	DCX rp	rp ← rp – 1	No	1	Register

Logic Group					
1.	ANA r	A ← A ∧ r	All, CY = 0 AC = 1	1	Register
2.	ANA M	A ← A ∧ (HL)	All, CY = 0 AC = 1	1	Register Indirect
3.	ANI data(8)	A ← A ∧ data(8)	All, CY = 0 AC = 1	2	Immediate
4.	XRA r	A ← A ⊕ r	All, CY = 0 AC = 0	1	Register
5.	XRA M	A ← A ⊕ (HL)	All, CY = 0 AC = 0	1	Register Indirect
6.	XRI data (8)	A ← A ⊕ data (8)	All, CY = 0 AC = 0	2	Immediate
7.	ORA r	A ← A ∨ r	All, CY = 0 AC = 0	1	Register
8.	ORA M	A ← A ∨ (HL)	All, CY = 0 AC = 0	1	Register Indirect
9.	ORI data (8)	A ← A ∨ data (8)	All, CY = 0 AC = 0	2	Immediate
10.	CMP r	A – r	All	1	Register
11.	CMP M	A – (HL)	All	1	Register Indirect
12.	CPI data (8)	A – data (8)	All	2	Immediate
13.	STC	CY ← 1	CY	1	Implied
14.	CMC	$CY \leftarrow \overline{CY}$	CY	1	Implied
15.	CMA	$A \leftarrow \overline{A}$	No	1	Implied

Rotate Group

Sr. No.	Instruction	Operation	Flags affected	No. of bytes	Addressing mode
1.	RLC	$B_{i+1} \leftarrow B_i$, $B_0 \leftarrow B_7$ $CY \leftarrow B_7$	CY	1	Implied
2.	RRC	$B_{i-1} \leftarrow B_i$, $B_7 \leftarrow B_0$ $CY \leftarrow B_0$	CY	1	Implied
3.	RAL	$B_{i+1} \leftarrow B_i$, $B_0 \leftarrow CY$ $CY \leftarrow B_7$	CY	1	Implied
4.	RAR	$B_{i-1} \leftarrow B_i$, $B_7 \leftarrow CY$ $CY \leftarrow B_0$	CY	1	Implied

Branch Group

Sr. No.	Instruction	Operation	Flags affected	No. of bytes	Addressing mode
1.	JMP addr	PC ← addr	No	3	Immediate
2.	J cond addr	If condition true PC ← addr	No	3	Immediate
3.	PCHL	PC ← HL	No	1	Register

4.	CALL addr	$(SP-1) \leftarrow PC_H$ $(SP-2) \leftarrow PC_L$ $SP \leftarrow SP-2$ $PC \leftarrow addr$	No	3	Immediate
5.	CALL cond addr	If condition true $(SP-1) \leftarrow PC_H$ $(SP-2) \leftarrow PC_L$ $SP \leftarrow SP-2$ $PC \leftarrow addr$	No	3	Immediate
6.	RET	$PC_L \leftarrow (SP)$ $PC_H \leftarrow (SP+1)$ $SP \leftarrow SP+2$	No	1	Register Indirect
7.	RET cond	If condition true $PC_L \leftarrow (SP)$ $PC_H \leftarrow (SP+1)$ $SP \leftarrow SP+2$	No	1	Register Indirect
8.	RST n	$(SP-1) \leftarrow PC_H$ $(SP-2) \leftarrow PC_L$ $SP \leftarrow SP-2$ $PC \leftarrow (n \times 8)$ in hex	No	1	Register Indirect

Stack Group

Sr. No.	Instruction	Operation	Flags affected	No. of bytes	Addressing mode
1.	PUSH rp	$SP \leftarrow SP-1$ $(SP) \leftarrow rpH$ $SP \leftarrow SP-1$ $(SP) \leftarrow rpL$	No	1	Register Indirect
2.	PUSH PSW	$SP \leftarrow SP-1$ $(SP) \leftarrow A$ $SP \leftarrow SP-1$ (SP) flag register	No	1	Register Indirect
3.	POP rp	$rpL \leftarrow (SP)$ $SP \leftarrow SP+1$ $rPH \leftarrow (SP)$ $SP \leftarrow SP+1$	No	1	Register Indirect

4.	POP PSW	flag register ← (SP) SP ← SP + 1 A ← (SP) SP ← SP + 1	No	1	Register Indirect
5.	SPHL	SP ← HL	No	1	Register
6.	XTHL	L ↔ (SP) H ↔ (SP + 1)	No	1	Register Indirect

Input/Output Group

Sr. No.	Instruction	Operation	Flags affected	No. of bytes	Addressing mode
1.	IN addr (8)	A ← (addr)	No	2	Direct
2.	OUT addr (8)	(addr) ← A	No	2	Direct

Machine Control Group

Sr. No.	Instruction	Operation	Flags affected	No. of bytes	Addressing mode
1.	EI	IE(F/F) ← 1	No	1	–
2.	DI	IE(F/F) ← 0	No	1	–
3.	NOP	No operation	No	1	–
4.	HLT	Halts the processor	No	1	–
5.	SIM	Serial interrupt mask	No	1	–
6.	RIM	Read interrupt mask	No	1	–

2.5 Assembly Language Programming

A program is a set of instructions arranged in the specific sequence to do the specific task. It tells the microprocessor what it has to do. The process of writing the set of instructions which tells the microprocessor what to do is called "**Programming**". In other words, we can say that programming is the process of telling the processor exactly how to solve a problem. To do this, the programmer must "**speak**" to the processor in a language which processor can understand.

2.5.1 Steps Involved in Programming

- **Specifying the problem** : The first step in the programming is to find out which task is to be performed. This is called specifying the problem. If the programmer does not understand what is to be done, the programming process cannot begin.
- **Designing the problem-solution** : During this process, the exact step by step process that is to be followed (program logic) is developed and written down.
- **Coding** : Once the program is specified and designed, it can be implemented. Implementation begins with the process of coding the program. Coding the program means to tell the processor the exact step by step process in its language. Each processor has a set of instructions. Programmer has to choose appropriate instructions from the instruction set to build the program.
- **Debugging** : Once the program or a part of program is coded, the next step is debugging the code. Debugging is the process of testing the code to see if it does the given task. If program is not working properly, debugging process helps in finding and correcting errors.

To write a program, programmer should know :

- How to develop program logic?
- How to tell the program to the processor?
- How to code the program?
- How to test the program?

2.5.2 Flowchart

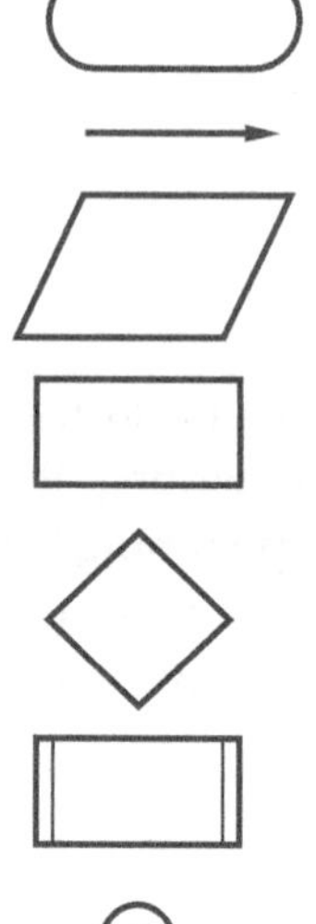

Fig. 2.7 Graphic symbols used in flowchart

To develop the programming logic programmer has to write down various actions which are to be performed in proper sequence. The flow chart is a graphical tool that allows programmer to represent various actions which are to be performed. The graphical representation is very useful for clear understanding of the programming logic.

The Fig. 2.7 shows the graphic symbols used in the flowchart.

Oval : It indicates start or stop operation.

Arrow : It indicates flow with direction.

Parallelogram : It indicates input/output operation.

Rectangle : It indicates process operation.

Diamond : It indicates decision making operation.

Double sided Rectangle : It indicates execution of pre-defined process (subroutine).

Circle with alphabet : It indicates continuation.

A : Any alphabet

The Fig. 2.8 shows sample flowchart.

2.5.3 Assembly Language Program

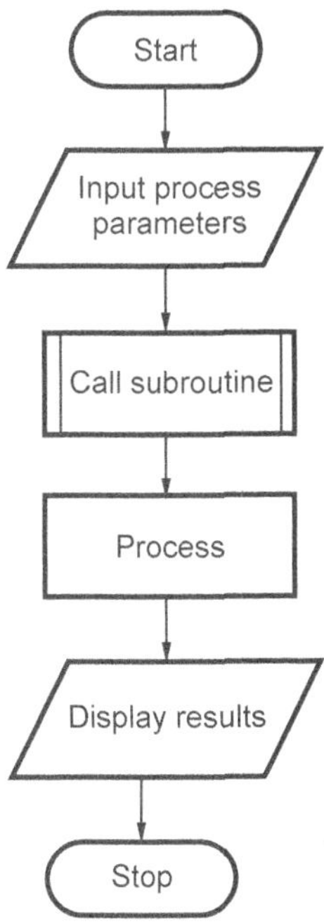

Fig. 2.8 Sample flowchart

Let us define a program statement as 'write an assembly language program to add two numbers'. The three tasks are involved in this program :

- Load two hex numbers
- Add numbers and
- Store the result in the memory

These tasks can be symbolically presented as flow chart, as shown in the Fig. 2.9. (See Fig. 2.9 on next page)

Next job is to find the suitable 8085 assembly language instruction/s for each task. These instructions are as follows :

Task 1 instructions :

```
MVI A, 20H    ; Load 20H as a first number in register A
MVI B, 40H    ; Load 40H as a second number in register B
```

Task 2 instruction :

```
ADD B         ; Add two numbers and save result in register A
```

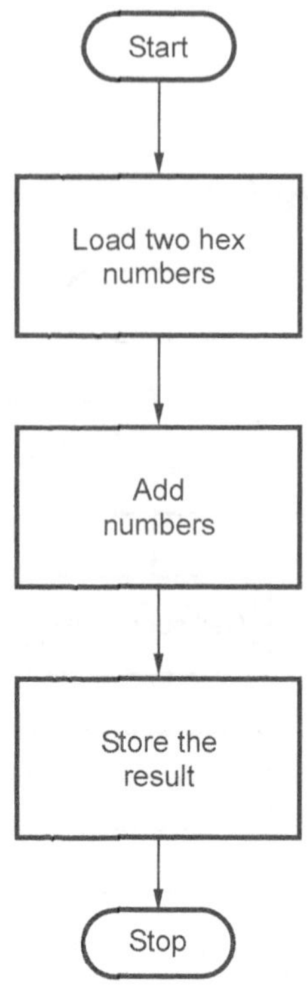

Fig. 2.9 Flowchart for addition of two numbers

Task 3 instruction :

STA 2200H ; Store the result in memory location 2000H

HLT ; Stop the program execution

We want to execute three tasks in a sequence, thus writing corresponding instructions in the same sequence constitutes an assembly language program.

2.5.4 Assembly Language Program to Machine Language Program

Once the assembly language program is ready, it is necessary to convert it in the machine language program. It is possible to do this by referring the proper hex code for each assembly instruction from the 8085 instruction set manual. This process is known as **hand assembly** and the resulted machine language program is also known as **hex code**. Let us see the hex code for our program.

Mnemonics	Hex code
MVI A, 20H	3EH ← Opcode
	20H ← Operand
MVI B, 40H	06H ← Opcode
	40H ← Operand

ADD B	80H ←	Opcode
STA 2200H	32H ←	Opcode
	00H ←	Operand (lower byte of address)
	22H ←	Operand (higher byte of address)
HLT	76H ←	Opcode

2.5.5 Storing Hex Code in the Memory

Once the hex code is ready, it has to be loaded in the memory of specially designed microprocessor system (Microprocessor training kit) for execution. To perform this task we should know the address range of read/write memory in the system. Let us assume that the read/write memory ranges from 2000H to 22FFH. The microprocessor training kit has keypad to enter the hex code in the memory. It provides a special routines (monitor program) to enter a hex code byte by byte and execute the program. Typical steps for storing hex code in the memory from address from address 2000H are as follows :

1. Reset the microprocessor system by pressing the RESET key.
2. Enter into store mode by pressing SET key.
3. Enter the address of the memory 2000H, where the first hex code (starting address of the program) is to be stored using hex keys.
4. Enter the hex code using hex keys.
5. Increment the memory address by 1 using INC key.
6. Repeat steps 4 and 5 until the last hex code.

2.5.6 Executing the Program

The microprocessor training kit provides a procedure to execute the program. To activate the procedure we have to enter the starting address of the program (2000H in our example). To enter this address we have to go into execute mode by pressing GO key and enter the starting address using hex keys. Once the starting address is entered, the program can be executed by pressing EXECUTE key. The EXECUTE key procedure loads the starting address of our program, 2000H into the program counter and program control is transferred from monitor program to our program.

After this microprocessor reads one hex code at a time, and when it fetches the complete instruction, it executes that instruction. Then it fetches the next instruction and this process continues until the last instruction in the program is executed.

2.6 Programming Examples

Lab Experiment 1 : Store 8-bit data in memory.

Statement : Store the data byte 52H into memory location 2000H.

Program 1 :

```
 A, 52H   ; Store 52H in the accumulator
STA 2000H   ; Copy accumulator contents at address 2000H
HLT         ; Terminate program execution
```

Program 2 :

```
LXI H, 2000H  ; Load HL with 2000H
MVI M, 52H    ; Store 52H in memory location pointed
              ; by HL register pair (2000H)
HLT           ; Terminate program execution
```

The result of both programs will be the same. In program 1 direct addressing instruction is used, whereas in program 2 indirect addressing instruction is used.

Lab Experiment 2 : Exchange the contents of memory locations.

Statement : Exchange the contents of memory locations 1000H and 2000H

Program 1 :

```
LDA 1000H ; Get the contents of memory location 1000H into accumulator
MOV B, A  ; save the contents in B register
LDA 2000H ; Get the contents of memory location 2000H into accumulator.
STA 1000H ; Store the contents of accumulator at address 1000H.
MOV A, B  ; Get the saved contents back into A register
STA 2000H ; Store the contents of accumulator at address 2000H
HLT       ; Terminate program execution
```

Program 2 :

```
LXI H, 1000H  ; Initialize HL register pair as a pointer
              ; to memory location 1000H
LXI D, 2000H  ; Initialize DE register pair as a pointer
              ; to memory location 2000H
MOV B, M      ; Get the contents of memory location 1000H into B register
LDAX  D       ; Get the contents of memory location 2000H into A register
MOV M, A      ; Store the contents of A register into memory location 1000H
MOV A, B      ; Copy the contents of B register into accumulator
STAX D        ; Store the contents of A register into memory location 2000H.
HLT           ; Terminate program execution
```

In Program 1 direct addressing instructions are used, whereas in Program 2 indirect addressing instructions are used.

Lab Experiment 3 : Add two 8-bit numbers.

Statement : Add the contents of memory locations 2000H and 2001H and place the result in memory location 2002H.

Flowchart

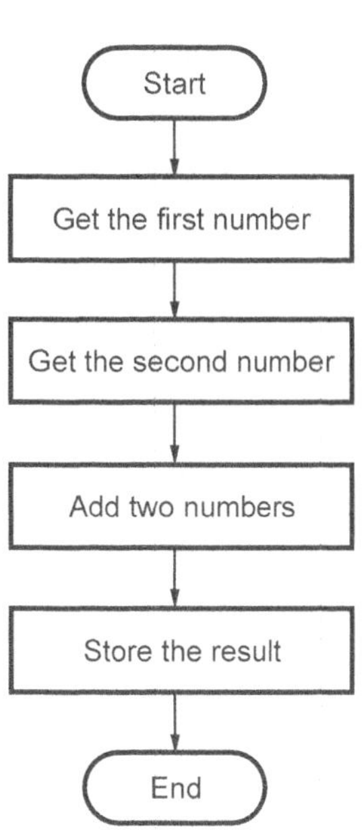

Sample problem

(2000H) = 14H

(2001H) = 89H

Result = 14H + 89H = 9DH

Source program

```
LXI H, 2000H   ; HL points 2000H
MOV A, M       ; Get first operand
INX H          ; HL points 2001H
ADD M          ; Add second operand
INX H          ; HL points 2002H
MOV M, A       ; Store result at 2002H
HLT            ; Terminate program execution
```

Lab Experiment 4 : Subtract two 8-bit numbers.

Statement : Subtract the contents of memory location 2001H from the memory location 2000H and place the result in memory location 2002H.

Flowchart

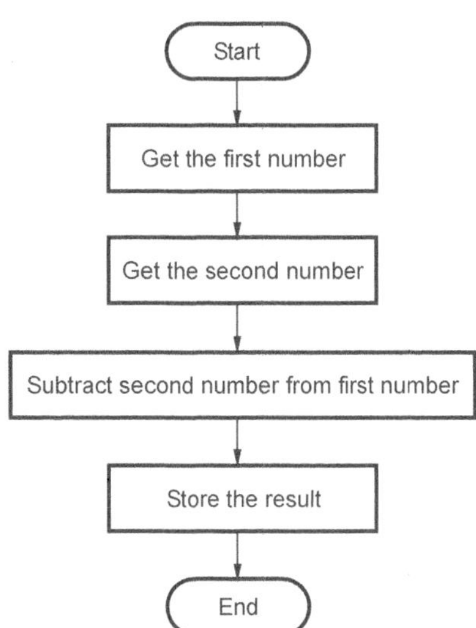

Sample problem

(2000H) = 51H

(2001H) = 19H

Result = 51H – 19H = 38H

Source program

```
LXI H, 2000H   ; HL points 2000H
MOV A, M       ; Get first operand
INX H          ; HL points 2001H
SUB M          ; Subtract second operand
INX H          ; HL points 2002H
MOV M, A       ; Store result at 2002H
HLT            ; Terminate program execution
```

Lab Experiment 5 : Add two 16-bit numbers.

Statement : Add the 16-bit number in memory locations 2000H and 2001H to the 16-bit number in memory locations 2002H and 2003H. The most significant eight bits of the two numbers to be added are in memory locations 2001H and 2003H. Store the result in memory locations 2004H and 2005H with the most significant byte in memory location 2005H.

Sample problem

(2000H) = 15H
(2001H) = 1CH
(2002H) = B7H
(2003H) = 5AH
Result = 1C15 + 5AB7H = 76CCH
(2004H) = CCH
(2005H) = 76H

Flowchart

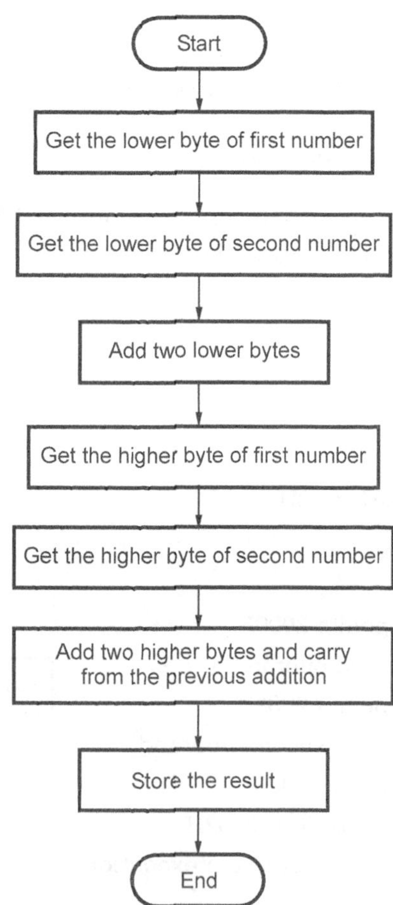

Source Program 1

```
LHLD 2000H   ; Get first 16-bit number in HL
XCHG         ; Save first 16-bit number in DE
LHLD 2002H   ; Get second 16-bit number in HL
MOV A, E     ; Get lower byte of the first number
ADD L        ; Add lower byte of the second number
MOV L, A     ; Store result in L register
MOV A, D     ; Get higher byte of the first number
ADC H        ; Add higher byte of the second number with carry
MOV H, A     ; Store result in H register
SHLD 2004H   ; Store 16-bit result in memory locations 2004H and 2005H.
HLT          ; Terminate program execution
```

Source program 2

```
LHLD 2000H   ; Get first 16-bit number
XCHG         ; Save first 16-bit number in DE
LHLD 2002H   ; Get second 16-bit number in HL
DAD D        ; Add DE and HL
SHLD 2004H   ; Store 16-bit result in memory locations 2004H and 2005H.
HLT          ; Terminate program execution
```

In program 1 eight bit addition instructions are used (ADD and ADC) and addition is performed in two steps. First lower byte addition using ADD instruction and then higher byte addition using ADC instruction. In program 2 16-bit addition instruction (DAD) is used.

Lab Experiment 6 : Subtract two 16-bit numbers.

Statement : Subtract the 16-bit number in memory locations 2002H and 2003H from the 16-bit number in memory locations 2000H and 2001H. The most significant eight bits of the two numbers are in memory locations 2001H and 2003H. Store the result in memory locations 2004H and 2005H with the most significant byte in memory location 2005H.

Sample problem

(2000H) = 19H

(2001H) = 6AH

(2002H) = 15H

(2003H) = 5CH

Result = 6A19H – 5C15H = 0E04H

(2004H) = 04H

(2005H) = 0EH

Source program

```
LHLD 2000H   ; Get first 16-bit number in HL
XCHG         ; Save first 16-bit number in DE
LHLD 2002H   ; Get second 16-bit number in HL
MOV A, E     ; Get lower byte of the first number
SUB L        ; Subtract lower byte of the second number
MOV L, A     ; Store the result in L register
MOV A, D     ; Get higher byte of the first number
SBB H        ; Subtract higher byte of second number with borrow
MOV H, A     ; Store 16-bit result in memory locations 2004H and 2005H.
SHLD 2004H   ; Store 16-bit result in memory locations 2004H and 2005H.
HLT          ; Terminate program execution.
```

Flowchart

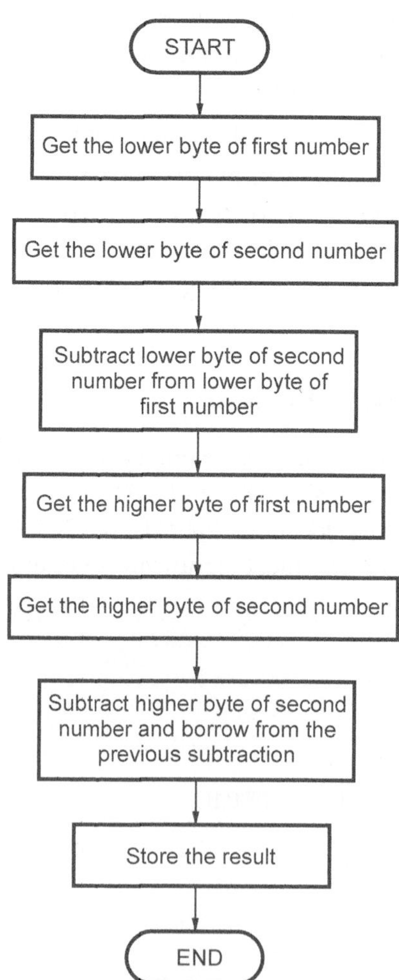

Lab Experiment 7 : Check results after execution of INR B, INR C and INX B instructions.

Statement : If the contents of B = FFH and C = FFH then after execution of following instructions give the contents of register B and register C.

Instructions :

1. INR B
2. INR C
3. INX B

1. INR B

   B → FFH
   + 01H
   00H → B

   ∴ B = 00H and C = FFH

2. INR C

   C → FFH
   + 01H
   00H → C

   ∴ B = FFH and C = 00H

3. INX B

   BC → FF FF H
   + 00 01 H
   00 00 H → B C

   ∴ B = 00H and C = 00H

Lab Experiment 8 : Check results after execution of DCR C, DCR B and DCX B instructions.

Statement : If the contents of B = 00H and C = 00H then after execution of following instructions give the contents of register B and register C.

Instructions :

1. DCR C
2. DCR B
3. DCX B

1. DCR C

   C → 00H
   – 01H
   FFH → C

   ∴ B = 00H and C = FFH

2. DCR B

```
B →  00H
   - 01H
     ---
     FFH  → B
```

∴ B = FFH and C = 00H

3. DCX B

```
BC →    0 0 0 0 H
      - 0 0 0 1 H
        ---------
        F F F F H  → BC
```

∴ B = FFH and C = FFH

Lab Experiment 9 : Find the 1's complement of a number.

Start

Get the number

Complement the number

Store the result

End

Statement : Find the 1's complement of the number stored at memory location 2200H and store the complemented number at memory location 2300H.

Sample problem

(2200H) = 55H

Result = (2300H) = AAH

Source program

```
LDA 2200H    ; Get the number
CMA          ; Complement number
STA 2300H    ; Store the result
HLT          ; Terminate program execution
```

Lab Experiment 10 : Find the 2's complement of a number.

Statement : Find the 2's complement of the number stored at memory location 2200H and store the complemented number at memory location 2300H.

Sample problem

(2200H) = 55H

Result = (2300H) = AAH + 1 = ABH

Source program

```
LDA 2200 H   ; Get the number
CMA          ; Complement the number
ADI, 01H     ; Add one in the number
STA 2300H    ; Store the result
HLT          ; Terminate program execution
```

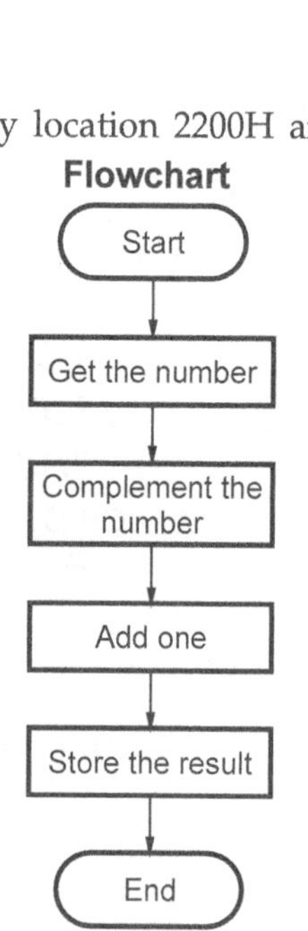

Lab Experiment 11 : Pack the two unpacked BCD numbers.

Statement : Pack the two unpacked BCD numbers stored in memory locations 2200H and 2201H and store result in memory location 2300H. Assume the least significant digit is stored at 2200H.

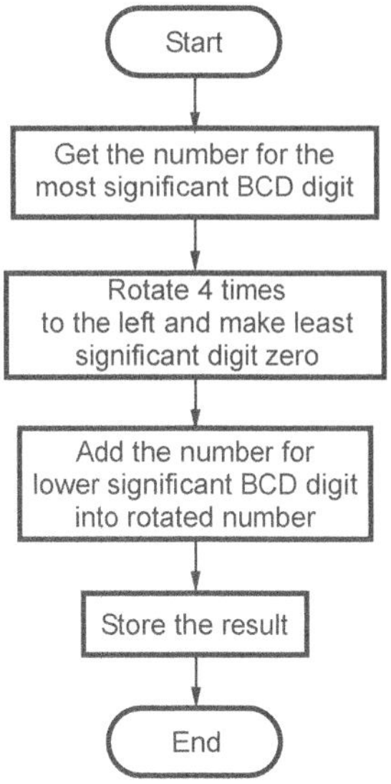

Sample problem

(2200H) = 04

(2201H) = 09

Result = (2300H) = 94

Source program

```
LDA 2201H  ; Get the Most significant BCD digit
RLC
RLC
RLC
RLC        ; Adjust the position
ANI F0H    ; Make least significant BCD digit zero
MOV C, A   ; store the partial result
LDA 2200H  ; Get the lower BCD digit
ADD C      ; Add lower BCD digit
STA 2300H  ; Store the result
HLT        ; Terminate program execution
```

Flowchart

Lab Experiment 12 : Unpack the BCD number.

Statement : Two digit BCD number is stored in memory location 2200H. Unpack the BCD number and store the two digits in memory locations 2300H and 2301H such that memory location 2300H will have lower BCD digit.

Sample problem

(2200H) = 58

Result = (2300H) = 08 and (2301H) = 05

Flowchart

(See flowchart on next page)

Source program

```
LDA 2200H  ; Get the packed BCD number
ANI F0H    ; Mask lower nibble
RRC
RRC
RRC
RRC        ; Adjust higher BCD digit as a lower digit
```

```
STA 2301H  ; Store the partial result
LDA 2200H  ; Get the original BCD number
ANI 0FH    ; Mask higher nibble
STA 2201H  ; Store the result
HLT        ; Terminate program execution
```

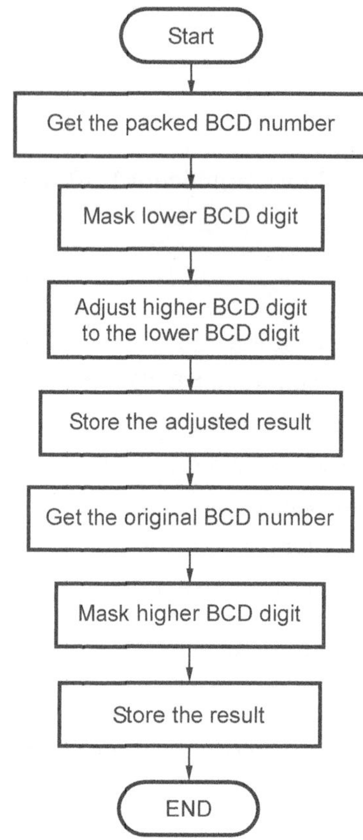

Lab Experiment 13 : Sample subroutine program.

Statement : Read the program given below and state the contents of all registers after the execution of each instruction in sequence.

Main program :

```
6000H    LXI SP, 27FFH
6003H    LXI H, 2000H
6006H    LXI B, 1020H
6009H    CALL SUB
600CH    HLT
```

Subroutine program :

```
6100H  SUB : PUSH B
6101H        PUSH H
6102H        LXI B, 4080H
6105H        LXI H, 4090H
6108H        DAD B
6109H        SHLD 2200H
610CH        POP H
610DH        POP B
610EH        RET
```

Solution : The Table 2.5 shows the instruction sequence and the contents of all registers and stack after execution of each instruction.

Sr. No.	Instructions	Registers contents in Hex									Memory locations (addresses are in Hex)
		A	B	C	D	E	H	L	SP	PC	
1	LXI SP,27FF	X	X	X	X	X	X	X	27FF	6003	
2	LXI H,2000	X	X	X	X	X	20	00	27FF	6006	
3	LXI B,1020	X	10	20	X	X	20	00	27FF	6009	
4	CALL SUB	X	10	20	X	X	20	00	27FD	6100	27FE ← 60, 27FD ← 0C
5	PUSH B	X	10	20	X	X	20	00	27FB	6101	27FC ← 10, 27FB ← 20
6	PUSH H	X	10	20	X	X	20	00	27F9	6102	27FA ← 20, 27F9 ← 00
7	LXI B,4080	X	40	80	X	X	20	00	27F9	6105	
8	LXI H,4090	X	40	80	X	X	40	90	27F9	6108	
9	DAD B	X	40	80	X	X	81	10	27F9	6109	
10	SHLD 2200	X	40	80	X	X	81	10	27F9	610C	2200 ← 10, 2201 ← 81
11	POP H	X	40	80	X	X	20	00	27FB	610D	
12	POP B	X	10	20	X	X	20	00	27FD	610E	
13	RET	X	10	20	X	X	20	00	27FF	600C	
14	HLT	X	10	20	X	X	20	00	27FF	600D	

Table 2.5

Lab Experiment 14 : Add contents of two memory locations.

Statement : Add the contents of memory locations 2000H and 2001H and place the result in the memory locations 2002H and 2003H.

Sample problem :

(2000H) = 7FH

(2001H) = 89H

Result = 7FH + 89H = 108H

(2002H) = 08H

(2003H) = 01H

Flowchart

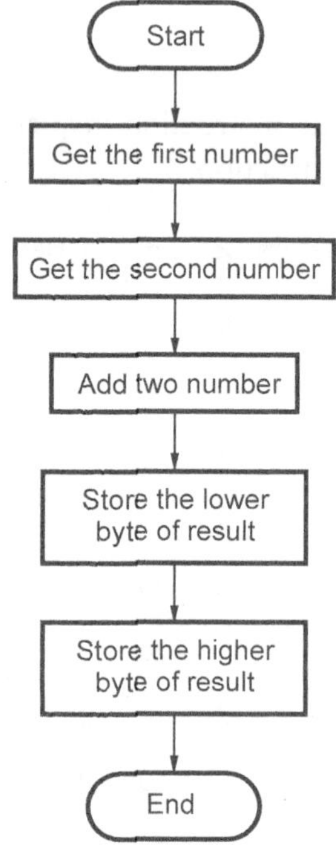

Source program :

```
LXI H, 2000H   ; HL Points 2000H
MOV A, M       ; Get first operand
INX H          ; HL Points 2001H
ADD M          ; Add second operand
INX H          ; HL Points 2002H
MOV M, A       ; Store the lower byte of result at 2002H
MVI A, 00      ; Initialize higher byte result with 00H
ADC A          ; Add carry in the high byte result
INX H          ; HL Points 2003H
MOV M, A       ; Store the higher byte of result at 2003H
HLT            ; Terminate program execution
```

Lab Experiment 15 : Right shift data within the 8-bit register.

Statement : Write a program to shift an eight bit data four bits right. Assume that data is in register C.

Source program :

```
MOV A, C
RAR
RAR
RAR
RAR
MOV C, A
HLT
```

Flowchart

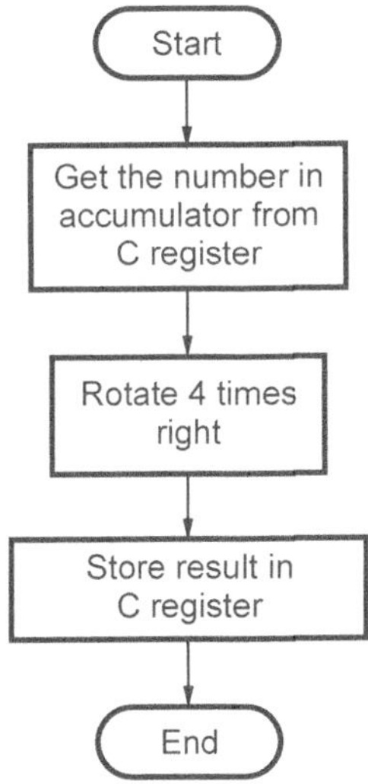

Lab Experiment 16 : Right shift data within 16-bit register.

Statement : Write a program to shift an 16-bit data 1 bit right. Assume data is in the BC register pair.

Flowchart

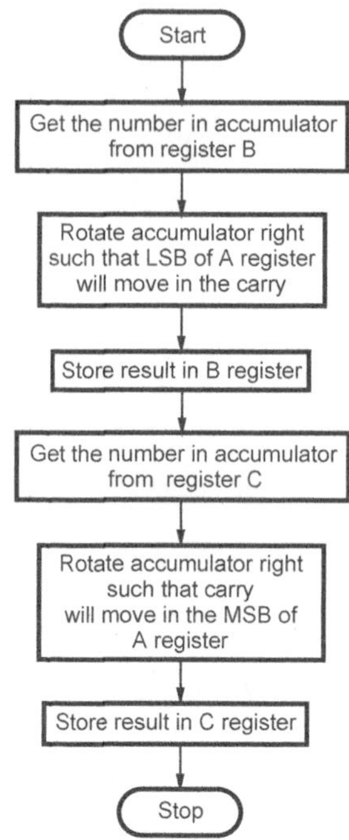

Source program :

```
MOV A, B
RAR
MOV B, A
MOV A, C
RAR
MOV C, A
HLT
```

Lab Experiment 17 : Left shift 16-bit data within 16-bit register.

Statement : Write a program to shift an 16-bit data 1 bit left. Assume data is in the HL register pair.

Flowchart

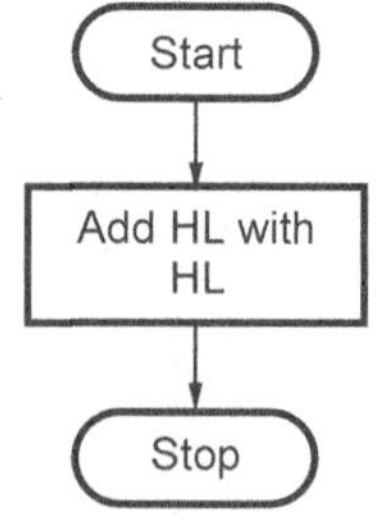

Sample problem :

```
HL = 1025   = 0001 0000 0010 0101
∴     HL    = 0001 0000 0010 0101
    + HL    = 0001 0000 0010 0101
    ---------------------------------------------
    Result  = 0010 0000 0100 1010
```

Source program :

```
DAD H
```

Lab Experiment 18 : Alter the contents of flag register.

Statement : Write a set of instructions to alter the contents of flag register in 8085.

Source Program :

```
PUSH PSW  ; Save flags on stack
POP H     ; Retrieve flags in 'L'
MOV A, L  ; Flags in accumulator
CMA       ; Complement accumulator
MOV L, A  ; Accumulator in 'L'
PUSH H    ; Save on stack
POP PSW   ; Back to flag register
HLT       ; Terminate program execution
```

Lab Experiment 19 : Find 2's complement of 16-bit number.

Let	$x = 2000$ H		$y = 4000$ H
∴	$x + 1 = 2001$ H	∴	$y + 1 = 4001$ H

Source Program :

```
LDA 2000H ; Load Accumulator with contents of 2000H location
CMA       ; complement the lower byte
ADD 01H   ; add 01 to the accumulator
STA 4000H ; Store the accumulator data to 4000H location
LDA 2001H ; Load accumulator with data from memory location 2001H
CMA       ; complement the higher byte
ADC 00H   ; add with carry to accumulator
HLT       ; Stop
```

Lab Experiment 20 : Simulation of CALL and RET instructions.

Statement : If CALL and RET instructions are not provided in the 8085, could it be possible to write subroutines for this microprocessor ? If so how will you call and return from the subroutine?

Solution : We know that,

1. CALL instruction transfers the program control to the subroutine program by loading the address of the subroutine program in the program counter, and before transferring program control it saves the address of the instruction after the CALL instruction on the stack.
2. RET instruction loads the program counter with return address from the stack and thus transfers the program control back to the instruction following the CALL.

Now our task is to implement the operation performed by these two instructions with the help of other instructions of 8085.

Let us implement RET instruction first. To implement this it is necessary to load program counter with return address. To load program counter with 16-bit address we have two instructions : JMP address and PCHL. But JMP address instruction cannot be used for our purpose because JMP address loads program counter with fix address and the return address is not fix, it depends on, from where the subroutine is 'CALLed' in the main program. The other instruction, PCHL loads 16-bit contents of HL register pair into PC. If we manage to load return address into HL register pair, every time subroutine is called, then it is possible to implement RET instruction with the help of PCHL instruction. We can load the HL register pair with return address before we make a CALL for subroutine program.

The task to implement CALL instruction is simplified because we are going to store return address into the HL register pair before we make a 'CALL' for subroutine program. Now it is only required to load program counter with the subroutine address. This can be implemented by executing JMP instruction. Here JMP instruction is suitable because subroutine starting address is a 'fix' address. The table shows how we can 'Call' and 'Return' from the subroutine without using CALL and RET instructions.

Main program	Main program without CALL instruction		
6000H LXI SP, 27FFH	6000H	LXI SP, 27FFH	; Initialize stack pointer
	: :		
6010H CALL 2200H	6010H	PUSH H	; Saves HL register contents in stack, since HL is used for implementation of CALL and RET. After subroutine program execution the original HL contents are retrieved by executing POP H instruction
6013H	6011H	LXI H, 6018H	; Loads HL with return address.

	6014H	PUSH H	; Stores return address in the stack
	6015H	JMP 2200H	; Loads program counter with 2200H
	6018H	POP H	; Loads HL with original contents of HL ; from the stack

Table 2.6

Subroutine program	Subroutine program without RET instruction		
2200 . . .	2200H	: :	
2200H RET	2220H	POP H	; Loads HL with return address
	2221H	PCHL	; Loads program counter with return ; address

Table 2.7

Lab Experiment 21 : Find the factorial of a number.

Statement : Write a program to calculate the factorial of a number between 0 to 8.

Solution : **Main Program :**

```
        LXI SP, 27FFH ; Initialize stack pointer
        LDA 2200H     ; Get the number
        CPI 02H       ; Check if number is greater than 1
        JC LAST
        MVI D, 00H    ; Load number as a result
        MOV E, A
        DCR A
        MOV C, A      ; Load counter one less than number
        CALL FACTO    ; Call subroutine facto
        XCHG          ; Get the result in HL
        SHLD 2201H    ; Store result in the memory
        JMP END
LAST :  LXI H,0001H   ; Store result = 01
        SHLD 2201H    ;
END:    HLT
```

Flowchart :

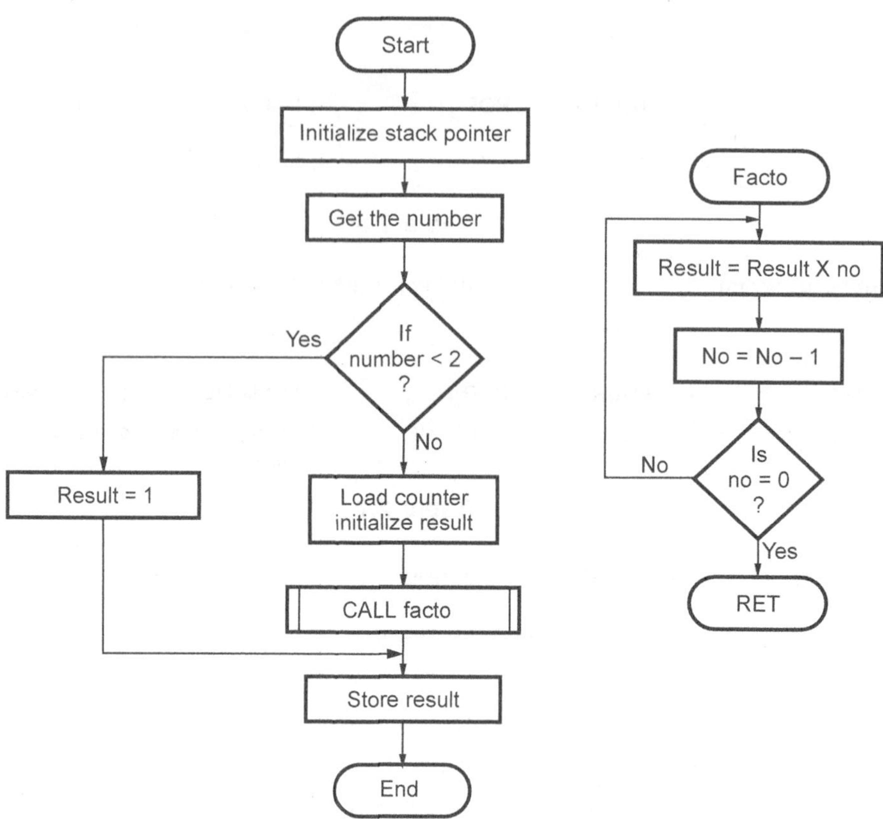

Subroutine Program :

```
FACTO : LXI H,0000H
        MOV B, C       ; Load counter
BACK :  DAD D          ;
        DCR B          ;
        JNZ BACK       ; Multiply by successive addition
        XCHG           ; Store result in DE
        DCR C          ; Decrement counter
        CNZ FACTO      ; Call subroutine FACTO
        RET            ; Return to main program
```

2.7 Instruction Comparisons

Example 2.1 : *Compare instructions SUB A and MVI A, 00H.*

Solution :

Parameter	SUB A	MVI A, 00H
Number of instruction bytes	One byte instruction	Two byte instruction
Opcode	97H	3EH
Operation	This instruction subtracts the contents of register A from itself and stores result (00H) in register A	This instruction loads 00H in register A.
Addressing mode	Register addressing mode	Immediate addressing mode
Flags	This instruction affects all flags.	This instruction does not affect flags
T-states required	4	7
Machine cycles required	1. Opcode fetch	1. Opcode fetch 2. Memory read

Example 2.2 : *Compare instructions SUB B and CMP B.*

Solution :

Parameter	SUB B	CMP B
Number of instruction bytes	One byte instruction	One byte instruction
Opcode	90H	B8H
Operation	This instruction subtracts the contents of register B from register A and stores result in register A and affects the flags according to contents of register A and B.	This instruction subtracts the contents of register B from register A and affects the flags according to contents of registers A and B.
Result	Result of A – B is stored in register A	Result of A – B is not stored in register A. The contents of register A are unchanged.
Addressing mode	Register	Register
Flags	This instruction affects all flags	This instruction affects all flags

T-states required	4	4
Machine cycles required	1. Opcode fetch	1. Opcode fetch

Example 2.3 : *Compare instructions LXI H, 2000H and LHLD 2000H.*

Solution :

Parameter	LXI H, 2000 H	LHLD 2000 H
Number of instruction bytes	Three byte instruction	Three byte instruction
Opcode	21H	2AH
Operand	2000H	2000H
Operation	This instruction loads 2000 H in the HL register pair	This instruction loads contents of 2000H memory location into L register and contents of 2001H memory location into H register
Addressing mode	Immediate	Direct
Flags	This instruction does not affect flags	This instruction does not affect flags
Required T-states	10	16
Required machine cycles	1. Opcode fetch 2. Memory read 3. Memory read	1. Opcode fetch 2. Memory read 3. Memory read 4. Memory read 5. Memory read

Example 2.4 : *Compare instruction JMP 2000 H and PCHL*

Solution :

Parameter	JMP 2000H	PCHL
Number of bytes	Three byte instruction	One byte instruction
Opcode	C3H	E9H

Operand	2000H	Contents of HL register
Operation	This instruction copies 2000H in PC so that processor fetches next instruction from address 2000H	This instruction copies the contents of HL register pair into PC so that processor fetches next instruction from address specified by HL register pair.
Addressing Mode	Direct	Indirect
Flags	This instruction does not affect flags	This instruction does not affect flags
Required T-states	10	6
Required Machine Cycles	1. Opcode fetch 2. Memory read 3. Memory read	1. Opcode fetch

Example 2.5 : *Compare instructions HLT and NOP*

Solution :

Parameter	HLT	NOP
Number of instruction byte	One byte instruction	One byte instruction
Opcode	76H	00H
Operation	This instruction halts the processor	No operation is performed
Flags	This instruction does not affect flags	This instruction does not affect flags
Required T-states	T-states required are undefined because this instruction halts the processor. The processor can be restarted by a valid interrupt or by applying a RESET signal	4-T states. After this instruction processor fetches the next instruction after NOP

Example 2.6 *List out differences and similarities between CALL - RET and PUSH-POP instructions.*

Solution : Differences :

Sr. No.	CALL-RET	PUSH-POP
1	These instructions are used for the execution of subroutine	These instructions are used to store register data temporarily in memory.
2	CALL instruction store the address of next instruction after it in the stack and loads PC with address given in the instruction.	PUSH instruction stores register contents in the stack.
3	RET instruction loads the address from stack into PC.	POP instruction gets the register contents from the stack.

Similarities :

1. They use stack memory.
2. CALL and PUSH instructions decrement stack pointer by 2.
3. RET and POP instructions increment stack pointer by 2
4. Instructions do not affect flags except POP PSW instruction.

2.8 Instruction Formats

The 8085A instruction set consists of one, two and three byte instructions. The first byte is always the opcode; in two-byte instructions the second byte is usually data; in three byte instructions the last two bytes present address or 16-bit data.

1. One byte instruction :

Format : | Opcode |
1 byte

For Example : MOV A, B whose opcode is 78H which is one byte. This instruction copies the contents of B register in A register.

2. Two byte instruction :

Format : | Opcode | Operand |
2 bytes

For Example : MVI B, 02H. The opcode for this instruction is 06H and is always followed by a byte data (02H in this case). This instruction is a two byte instruction which copies immediate data into B register.

3. Three byte instruction :

For Example : JMP 6200H. The opcode for this instruction is C3H and is always followed by 16-bit address (6200H in this case). This instruction is a three byte instruction which loads 16-bit address into program counter.

Review Questions

Section 2.1

Q.1 *Explain the classification of the instruction set of 8085 microprocessor with suitable examples.*

Section 2.2

Q.1 *Explain the operations carried out when 8085 executes the instructions.*
i) MOV A, M ii) XCHG
iii) DAD B iv) DAA **Dec.-07, Marks 16**

Q.2 *With suitable examples, Explain the function of various data transfer and data manipulation instructions of 8085.* **May-10,11, Marks 10**

Q.3 *How are the 8085 instructions classified according to the functional categories ?* **Dec.-11, Marks 2**

Q.4 *Describe with suitable examples the data transfer, loading and storing instructions.* **June-12, Marks 8**

Q.5 *What is stack ? And what is the function of stack pointer ?* **Dec.-07, Marks 2**

Q.6 *Explain the operations carried out when 8085 executes the instructions.*
POP PSW **Dec.-07, Marks 16**

Q.7 *Discuss the organizations of the 8085 stack and the various instructions that will operate on the stack.* **Dec-09, June-11, Marks 10**

Q.8 *Describe with a suitable example the operation of stack.* **June-12, Marks 8**

Q.9 *How is PUSH B instruction executed ? Find the status after the execution.* **May-11, Marks 2**

Q.10 *Explain the sequence of events in the execution of CALL and RET instructions.* **June-07, Marks 8**

Q.11 *What is the use of branching instructions ? Give Example.* **June-12, Marks 2**

Q.12 *State the function of given 8085 instructions : JP, JPE, JPO, JNZ* **May-11, Marks 2**

Q.13 *Give examples for machine control instructions.* **June-11, Marks 2**

Section 2.3

Q.1 *With example explain the different addressing modes of 8085 and the different types of instruction.* **Dec.-04, Marks 16**

Q.2 *Define and explain the addressing modes of 8085 with example.*
June-06,07,11, May-08,10,11,12 Dec.-09,10, Marks 16

Q.3 *Explain in detail about the indirect addressing mode in 8085.*
June-09, Marks 4

Section 2.4

Q.1 *Explain the instruction set of 8085 with examples.* **Dec.-08, Marks 16**

Section 2.5

Q.1 *What is program ?*

Q.2 *Give the steps involved in programming.*

Q.3 *What is flowchart ? Explain its use.*

Q.4 *Explain the process of writing assembly language program with the help of example.*

Q.5 *What do you mean by hand assembly ? Explain with the help of example.*

Q.6 *Explain the process of executing the program on the microprocessor training kit.*

Section 2.6

Q.1 *Write a program with a flowchart to multiply two 8-bit numbers.*
Dec.-11, Marks 8

Q.2 *Sixteen bytes are stored in memory locations at XX50h to XX5Fh.*
Transfer the entire block of data to new memory locations starting at XX70h.
Dec.-11, Marks 8

Q.3 *Write an assembly language program for arranging an array of 8-bit unsigned number in ascending order.* **June-12, Marks 8**

Section 2.7

Q.1 *Compare the similarities and differences of CALL and RET instructions with PUSH and POP instructions.* **Dec.-11, Marks 8**

Q.2 *Explain the operational difference between the following pairs of instructions.*
i) SPHL and XTHL *ii) CALL addr and JMP addr*
iii) LHLD and SHLD addr *iv) XRA A and MVI A, 00H*
v) INR A and ADI 01 H *vi) DAD RP and DAA.*

Section 2.8

Q.1 *Describe the instruction format of 8085 microprocessor.* **May-11, Marks 4**

Two Marks Questions with Answers

Q.1 *What is an operand ?*

Ans. : The data on which the operation is to be performed is called an operand.

Q.2 *How many operations are there in the instruction set of 8085 microprocessor ?*

Ans. : There are 74 operations in the 8085 microprocessor.

Q.3 *What is an opcode ?*

Ans. : The part of the instruction that specifies the operation to be performed is called the operation code or opcode.

Q.4 *List out the five categories of the 8085 instructions. Give examples of the instructions for each group.*

Ans. :

- Data transfer group - MOV, MVI, LXI.
- Arithmetic group - ADD, SUB, INR.
- Logical group -ANA, XRA, CMP.
- Branch group - JMP, JNZ, CALL.
- Stack I/O and Machine control group – PUSH, POP, HLT.

Q.5 *Explain the purpose of the I/O instructions IN and OUT.*

Ans. : The IN instruction is used to move data from an I/O port into the accumulator. The OUT instruction is used to move data from the accumulator to an I/O port. The IN and OUT instructions are used only on microprocessor, which use a separate address space for I/O interfacing.

Q.6 *What is the difference between the shift and rotate instructions?*

Ans. : A rotate instruction is a closed loop instruction. That is, the data moved out at one end is put back in at the other end. The shift instruction loses the data that is moved out of the last bit locations.

Q.7 *What are operations performed on data in 8085.*

Ans. : The various operations performed are :

- Store 8-bit data
- Perform arithmetic and logical operations
- Test for conditions
- Sequence the execution of instructions
- Store data temporarily during execution in the defined R/W memory locations called the stack

Q.8 ***What is an instruction?***

Ans. : An instruction is a binary pattern or code which is interpreted by the microprocessor to perform that specific function

Q.9 ***Explain the different instruction formats with examples.***

Ans. : The instruction set is grouped into the following formats.

- One byte instruction -MOV C,A
- Two byte instruction -MVI A,39H
- Three byte instruction -JMP 2345H

Q.10 ***What is the use of addressing modes, mention the different types.***

Ans. : The various formats of specifying the operands are called addressing modes, it is used to access the operands or data. The different types are as follows :

- Immediate addressing
- Register addressing
- Direct addressing
- Indirect addressing
- Implicit addressing

Q.11 ***What is the type of stack used in 8085?*** **May-04**

Ans. : Memory type stack is used in 8085

Q.12 ***What are the different addressing modes of 8085?*** **Dec.-04,09**

Ans. : The 8085 has 5 addressing modes. These are :

1. Immediate 2. Register
3. Direct 4. Indirect
5. Implied

Q.13 ***Define addressing modes.***

Ans. : The different ways that a microprocessor can access data are referred to as **addressing modes**

Q.14 ***What is the significance of 'XCHG' and 'SPHL' instructions ?*** **June-07**

Ans. : **XCHG :** This instruction exchanges the contents of the register H with that of D and of L with that of E.

SPHL : This instruction copies the contents of HL register pair into the stack pointer. The contents of H register are copied to higher order byte of stack pointer and contents of L register are copied to the lower byte of stack pointer. This allows indirect way of initializing stack pointer.

Q.15 ***Differentiate cascade stack and memory stack.*** June-07

Ans. : In a cascaded stack, CPU registers are used as a stack. In memory stack, the part of memory is used for stack.

Q.16 ***What is the function of SIM instruction in 8085 ?*** Dec.-07

Ans. : The sim instruction masks the interrupts as desired. It also sends out serial data through the SOD pin.

Q.17 ***Write the operation carried out when 8085 executes RST0 instruction.*** Dec.-07

Ans. : When 8085 executes RST0 instruction, the program control is transferred to memory address 0000H. Before transfer of program control RST0 instruction saves the current program counter contents on the stack and decrements stack pointer by 2.

Q.18 ***Write the difference between opcode and operand.*** May-08

Ans. : Opcode indicates the operation to be performed and operand is a data on which the operation is performed.

Q.19 ***Write the stack related instructions in 8085 microprocessor.*** May-08

Ans. : The stack related instructions in 8085 microprocessor are :

1. PUSH rp 2. PUSH PSW
3. POP rp 4. POP PSW
5. SPHL 6. XTHL

Q.20 ***Write the machine control instructions of 8085 microprocessor.*** Dec.-08

Ans. : Machine control instructions of 8085 microprocessor are :

1. EI 2. DI
3. NOP 4. HLT
5. SIM 6. RIM

Q.21 ***How the instruction sets are grouped ?*** June-09

Ans. : Refer section 2.2.

Q.22 ***What are the use of CALL and RET instructions of 8085?*** Dec-09

Ans. : Refer section 2.2.6.

Q.23 ***Mention the instructions used for data transfer with I/O ports.*** May-10

Ans. : The instructions used for data transfer with I/O ports are : 1. IN addr 2. OUT adder

Q.24 ***Differentiate CALL instruction from JUMP instruction.*** May-10

Ans. :

Sr. No.	CALL	JMP
1.	A CALL instruction leaves information on the stack so that the original program execution sequence can be resumed.	A JMP instruction permanently changes the program counter.
2.	It requires 5 machine cycles.	It requires three machine cycles.
3.	It requires 18 T-states time for execution.	It requires 10 T-states time for execution.
4.	After execution of CALL sp is sp - 2.	Stack pointer contents are unchanged after execution of JMP instruction.

Q.25 ***What do you understand by the term 'program status word' and state how it can be read ?*** Dec.-10

Ans. : Program status word is the flag register of microprocessor. In 8085 microprocessor the program status word can be read as follows :

PUSH PSW

POP r_P

Now contents of PSW are available in lower byte of specified register pair

Q.26 ***What is the value of register A after each of the following instructions ?***

MOV A, # 26H

RR A

RR A

RR A

RR A

SWAP A Dec.-10

Ans. : A = 26 H

❑❑❑

3 Looping, Counting, Time Delays and Code Conversion

Contents

In the last chapter we have seen the instruction set of 8085 and some simple assembly language programs using it. We know that, the program is an implementation of certain logic by executing group of instructions. To implement program logic we need to take help of some common programming techniques such as looping, counting, indexing and code conversion.

In this chapter, we are going to study how to implement these programming techniques using 8085 assembly language and some programming examples using them. This chapter also introduces the BCD arithmetic and programming techniques to implement BCD arithmetic using 8085 assembly language.

3.1 Looping, Counting and Indexing

Before going to implement these techniques, we get conversant with these techniques and understand the use of them.

Looping : In this technique, the program is instructed to execute certain set of instructions repeatedly to execute a particular task number of times. For example, to add ten numbers stored in the consecutive memory locations we have to perform addition ten times.

Counting : This technique allows programmer to count how many times the instruction/set of instructions are executed.

Indexing : This technique allows programmer to point or refer the data stored in sequential memory locations one by one. Let us see the program loop to understand looping, counting and indexing.

The program loop is the basic structure which forces the processor to repeat a sequence of instructions. Loops have four sections.

1. Initialization section.
2. Processing section.
3. Loop control section
4. Result section.

Flowchart : (See on next page)

1. The initialization section establishes the starting values of
   - loop counters for counting how many times loop is executed,
   - address registers for indexing which give pointers to memory locations and
   - other variables.

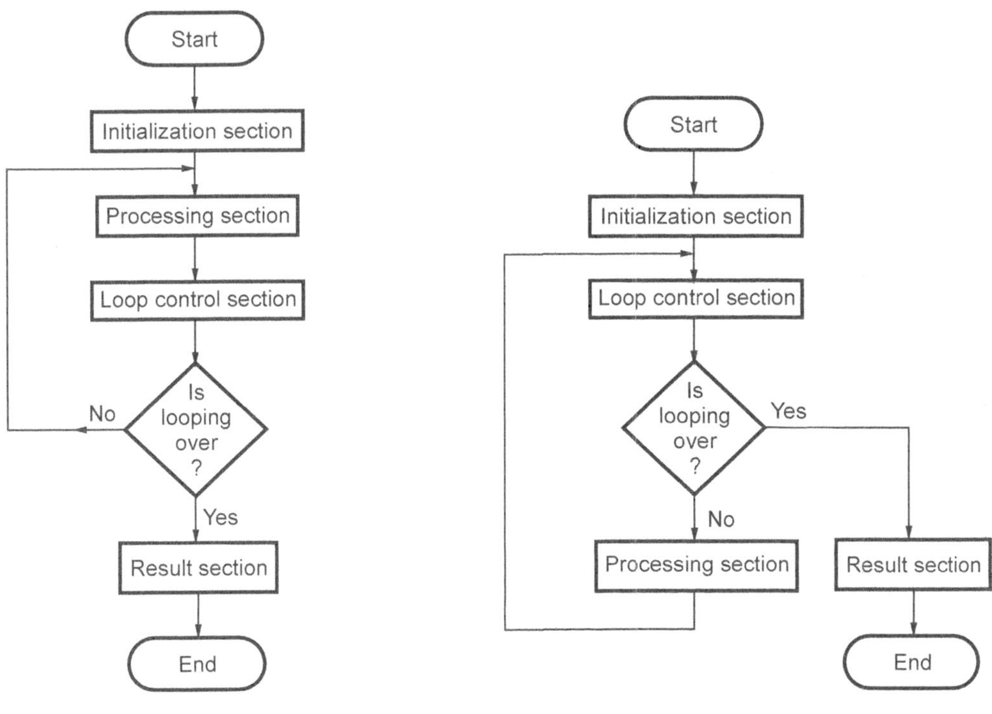

Flowchart 1 **Flowchart 2**

2. The actual data manipulation occurs in the processing section. This is the section which does the work.
3. The loop control section updates counters, indices (pointers) for the next iteration.
4. The result section analyzes and stores the results.

Note : The processor executes initialization section and result section only once, while it may execute processing section and loop control section many times. Thus, the execution time of the loop will be mainly dependent on the execution time of the processing section and loop control section. The flowchart 1 shows typical program loop. The processing section in this flowchart is always executed at least once. If you interchange the position of the processing and loop control section then it is possible that the processing section may not be executed at all, if necessary. Refer flowchart 2.

Program Examples

Lab Experiment 22 : Calculate the sum of series of numbers.

Statement : Calculate the sum of series of numbers. The length of the series is in memory location 2200H and the series itself begins from memory location 2201H.

a. Assume the sum to be 8 bit number so you can ignore carries. Store the sum at memory location 2300H.

b. Assume the sum to be 16 bit number. Store the sum at memory locations 2300H and 2301H.

a. Sample problem :

2200H = 04H

2201H = 20H

2202H = 15H

2203H = 13H

2204H = 22H

Result = 20 + 15 + 13 + 22 = 6AH

∴ 2300H = 6AH

Flowchart :

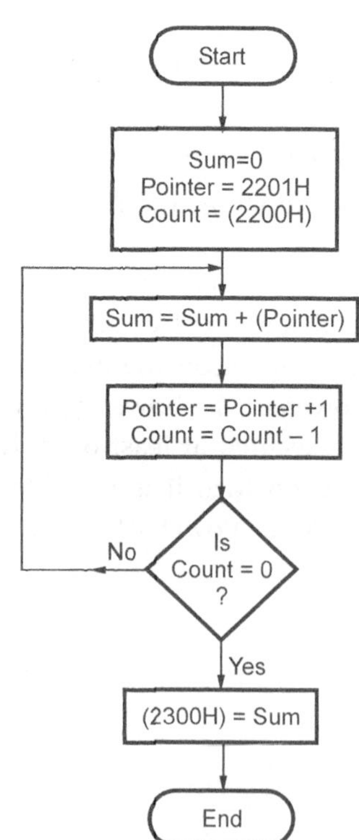

Source program :

```
        LDA 2200H
        MOV C, A        ; Initialize counter
        SUB A           ; sum = 0
        LXI H, 2201H    ; Initialize pointer
BACK :  ADD M           ; SUM = SUM + data
        INX H           ; Increment pointer
        DCR C           ; Decrement counter
        JNZ BACK        ; If counter ≠ 0 repeat
        STA 2300H       ; Store sum
        HLT             ; Terminate program execution
```

b. Sample problem :

2200H = 04H 2201H = 9AH

2202H = 52H 2203H = 89H 2204H = 3EH

Result = 9AH + 52H + 89H + 3EH = 1B3H

$\therefore$ 2300H = B3H Lower byte 2301H = 01H Higher byte

Flowchart :

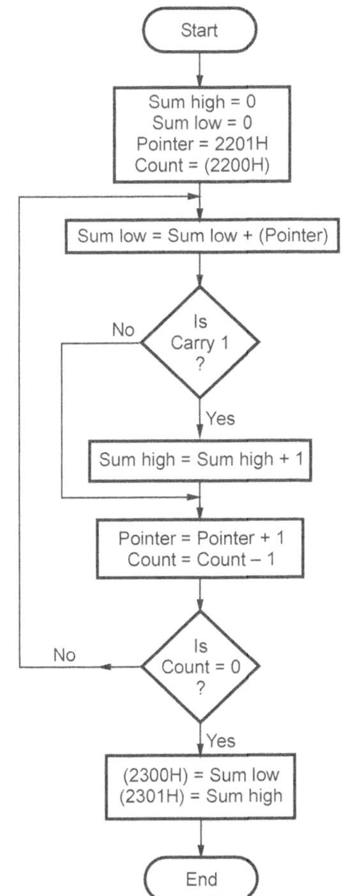

Source program :

```
        LDA 2200H
        MOV C, A        ; Initialize counter
        LXI H, 2201H    ; Initialize pointer
        SUB A           ; Sumlow = 0
        MOV B, A        ; Sumhigh = 0
BACK :  ADD M           ; Sum = sum + data
        JNC SKIP
        INR B           ; Add carry to MSB of SUM
SKIP :  INX H           ; Increment pointer
        DCR C           ; Decrement counter
        JNZ BACK        ; Check if counter ≠ 0 repeat
        STA 2300H       ; Store lower byte
        MOV A, B
        STA 2301H       ; Store higher byte
        HLT             ; Terminate program execution
```

Lab Experiment 23 : Data transfer from memory block B1 to memory block B2.

Statement : Transfer ten bytes of data from one memory to another memory block. Source memory block starts from memory location 2200H where as destination memory block starts from memory location 2300H.

Flowchart :

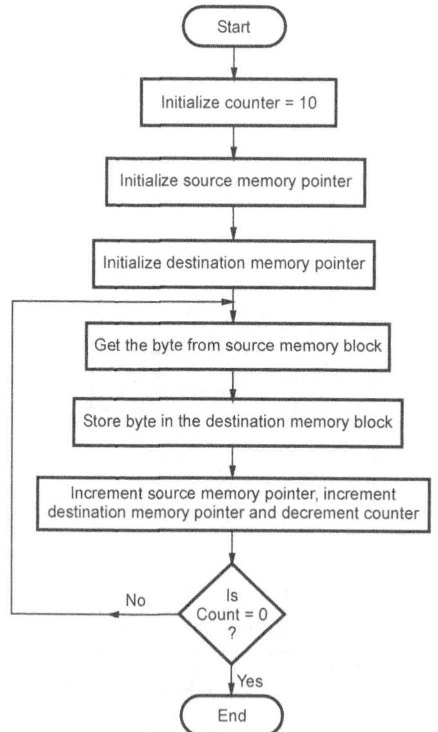

Source program :

```
        MVI C, 0AH     ; Initialize counter
        LXI H, 2200H   ; Initialize source memory pointer
        LXI D, 2300H   ; Initialize destination memory pointer
BACK :  MOV A, M       ; Get byte from source memory block
        STAX D         ; Store byte in the destination memory block
        INX H          ; Increment source memory pointer
        INX D          ; Increment destination memory pointer
        DCR C          ; Decrement counter
        JNZ BACK       ; If counter ≠ 0 repeat
        HLT            ; Terminate program execution
```

Lab Experiment 24 : Multiply two 8-bit numbers.

Statement : Multiply two 8-bit numbers stored in memory locations 2200H and 2201H. Store the result in memory locations 2300H and 2301H.

Sample problem :

(2200H) = 03H
(2201H) = B2H
Result = B2H + B2H + B2H
= 216H
(2300H) = 16H
(2301H) = 02H

Note : In 8085 multiplication can be done by repetitive addition.

Flowchart :

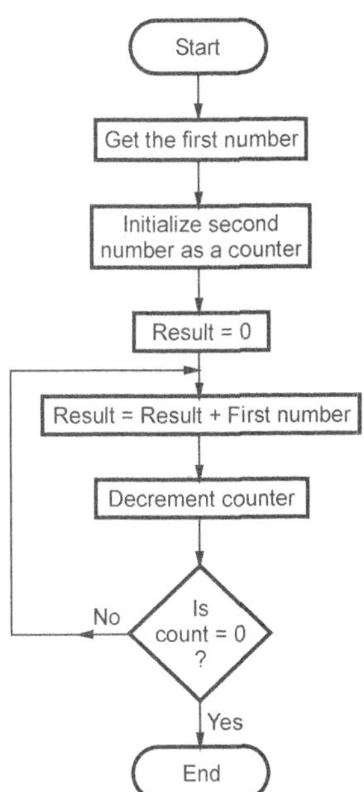

Source program :

```
        LDA 2200H
        MOV E, A
        MVI D, 00       ; Get the first number in DE register pair
        LDA 2201H
        MOV C, A        ; Initialize counter
        LXI H, 0000H    ; Result = 0
BACK :  DAD D           ; Result = result + first number
        DCR C           ; Decrement count
        JNZ BACK        ; If count ≠ 0 repeat
        SHLD 2300H      ; Store result
        HLT             ; Terminate program execution
```

Lab Experiment 25 : Divide 16-bit number by 8-bit number.

Statement : Divide 16 bit number stored in memory locations 2200H and 2201H by the 8 bit number stored at memory location 2202H. Store the quotient in memory locations 2300H and 2301H and remainder in memory locations 2302H and 2303H.

Flowchart :

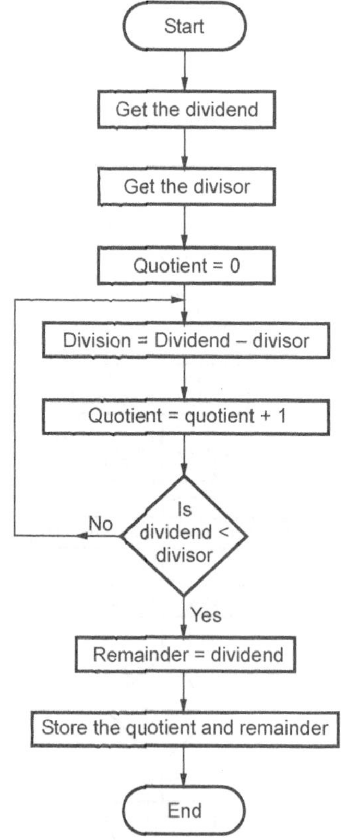

Sample problem :

(2200H) = 60H
(2201H) = A0H
(2202H) = 12H
Result = A060H/12H = 8E8H Quotient
and 10H remainder
(2300H) = E8H
(2301H) = 08H
(2302H) = 10H
(2303H) = 00H

Source program :

```
        LHLD 2200H    ; Get the dividend
        LDA 2202H
        MOV C, A      ; Get the divisor
        LXI D, 0000H  ; Quotient = 0
BACK :  MOV A, L
        SUB C         ; Subtract divisor
        MOV L, A      ; Save partial result
        JNC SKIP      ; If CY ≠ 1 jump
        DCR H         ; Subtract borrow of previous  subtraction
SKIP :  INX D         ; Increment quotient
        MOV A, H
        CPI, 00       ; Check if dividend < divisor
        JNZ BACK      ; If no repeat
        MOV A, L
        CMP C
        JNC BACK
        SHLD 2302H    ; Store the remainder
        XCHG
        SHLD 2300H    ; Store the quotient
        HLT           ; Terminate program execution
```

Lab Experiment 26 : Find the negative numbers in a block of data.

Statement : Find the number of negative elements (most significant bit 1) in a block of data. The length of the block is in memory location 2200H and the block itself begins in memory location 2201H. Store the number of negative elements in memory location 2300H.

Flowchart :

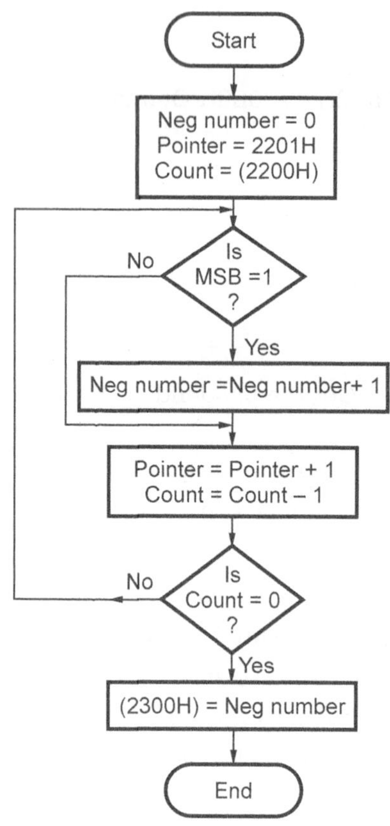

Sample problem :

(2200H) = 04H

(2201H) = 56H

(2202H) = A9H

(2203H) = 73H

(2204H) = 82H

Result = 02 since 2202H and 2204H contain numbers with a MSB of 1.

Source program :

```
        LDA 2200H
        MOV C, A        ; Initialize count
        MVI B, 00       ; Negative number = 0
        LXI H, 2201H    ; Initialize pointer
BACK :  MOV A, M        ; Get the number
        ANI 80H         ; Check for MSB
        JZ SKIP         ; If MSB = 1
```

```
        INR B       ; Increment negative number count
SKIP :  INX H       ; Increment pointer
        DCR C       ; Decrement count
        JNZ BACK    ; If count ≠ 0 repeat
        MOV A, B    ;
        STA 2300H   ; Store the result
        HLT         ; Terminate program execution
```

Lab Experiment 27 : Find the largest of given numbers.

Statement :

Find the largest number in a block of data. The length of the block is in memory location 2200H and the block itself start from memory location 2201H. Store the maximum number in memory location 2300H. Assume that the number in the block are all 8 bit unsigned binary numbers.

Flowchart :

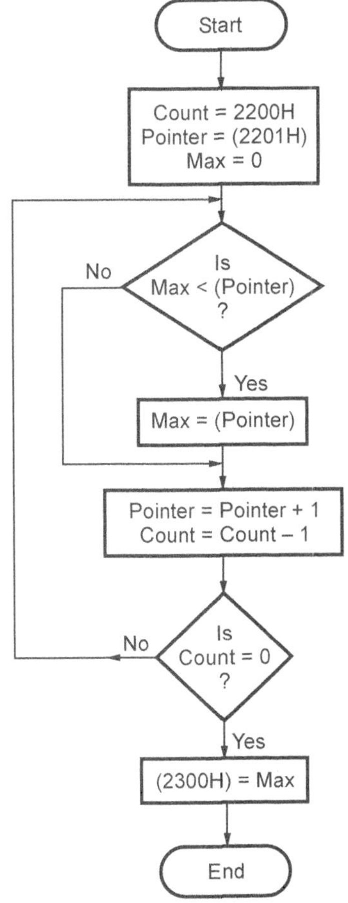

Sample problem :

(2200H) = 04
(2201H) = 34H
(2202H) = A9H
(2203H) = 78H
(2204H) = 56H
Result = (2202H) = A9H.

Source program :

```
        LDA 2200H
        MOV C, A        ; Initialize counter
        XRA A           ; Maximum = Minimum possible value = 0
        LXI H, 2201H    ; Initialize pointer
BACK  : CMP M           ; Is number > maximum
        JNC SKIP
        MOV A, M        ; Yes, replace maximum
SKIP  : INX H
        DCR C
        JNZ BACK
        STA 2300H       ; Store maximum number
        HLT             ; Terminate program execution
```

Lab Experiment 28 : Count number of one's in a number.

Statement : Write a program to count number of 1's in the contents of D register and store the count in the B register.

Source program :

```
        MVI B, 00H
        MVI C, 08H
        MOV A, D
BACK  : RAR
        JNC SKIP
        INR B
SKIP  : DCR C
        JNZ BACK
        HLT
```

Flowchart :

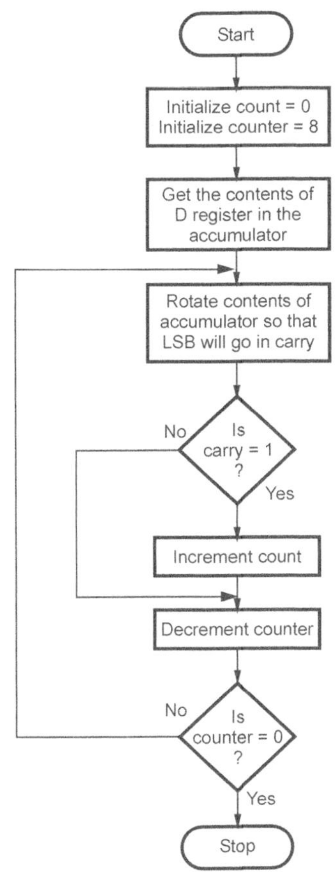

Lab Experiment 29 : Arrange numbers in the ascending order.

Statement : Write a program to sort given 10 numbers from memory location 2200H in the ascending order.

Source program :

```
         MVI B, 09      ; Initialize counter 1
START :  LXI H, 2200H   ; Initialize memory pointer
         MVI C, 09H     ; Initialize counter 2
BACK  :  MOV A, M       ; Get the number
         INX H          ; Increment memory pointer
         CMP M          ; Compare number with next number
         JC SKIP        ; If less, don't interchange
         JZ SKIP        ; If equal, don't interchange
         MOV D, M
         MOV M, A
         DCX H
```

```
        MOV M, D
        INX H           ; Interchange two numbers
SKIP :  DCR C           ; Decrement counter 2
        JNZ BACK        ; If not zero, repeat
        DCR B           ; Decrement counter 1
        JNZ START       ; If not zero, repeat
        HLT             ; Terminate program execution
```

Flowchart :

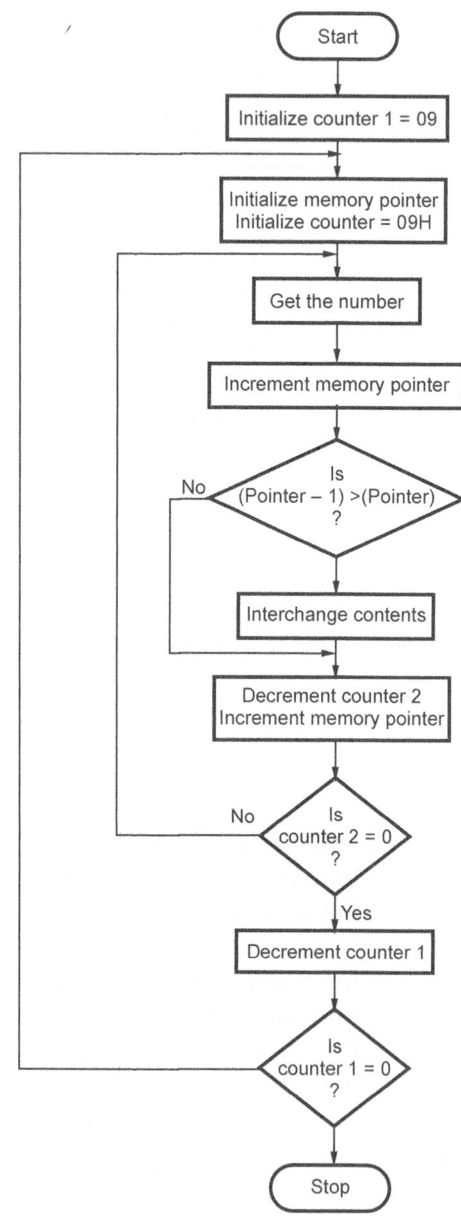

Lab Experiment 30 : Calculate the sum of series of even numbers.

Statement : Calculate the sum of series of even numbers from the list of numbers. The length of the list is in memory location 2200H and the series itself begins from memory location 2201H. Assume the sum to be 8 bit number so you can ignore carries and store the sum at memory location 2210H.

Sample problem :

2200H = 4H

2201H = 20H

2202H = 15H

2203H = 13H

2204H = 22H

Result = 20 + 22 = 42H

∴ 2210H = 42H

Flowchart :

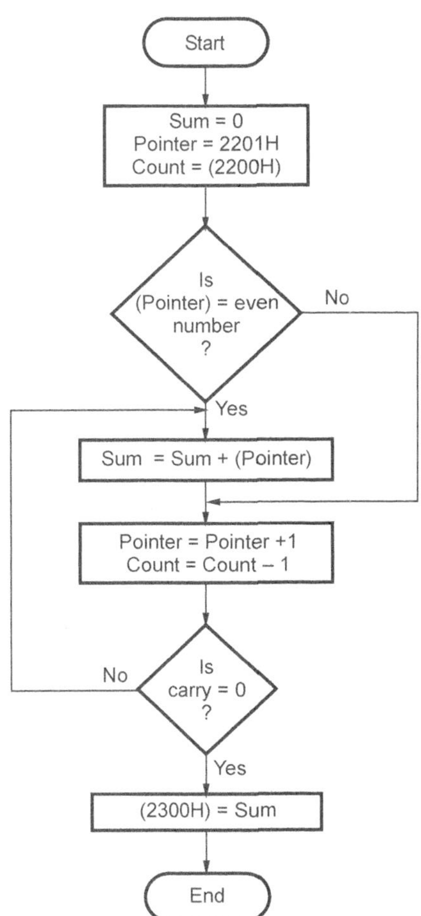

Source program :

```
        LDA 2200H
        MOV C, A       ; Initialize counter
        MVI B, 00H     ; sum = 0
        LXI H, 2201H   ; Initialize pointer
BACK :  MOV A, M       ; Get the number
        ANI 01H        ; Mask Bit1 to Bit7
        JNZ SKIP       ; Don't add if number is ODD
        MOV A, B       ; Get the sum
        ADD M          ; SUM = SUM + data
        MOV B, A       ; Store result in B register
SKIP :  INX H          ; Increment pointer
        DCR C          ; Decrement counter
        JNZ BACK       ; If counter 0 repeat
        STA 2210H      ; Store sum
        HLT            ; Terminate program execution
```

Lab Experiment 31 : Calculate the sum of series of odd numbers.

Statement : Calculate the sum of series of odd numbers from the list of numbers. The length of the list is in memory location 2200H and the series itself begins from memory location 2201H. Assume the sum to be 16-bit. Store the sum at memory locations 2300H and 2301H.

Sample program :

```
     2200H  = 4H
     2201H  = 9AH
     2202H  = 52H
     2203H  = 89H
     2204H  = 3FH
     Result = 89H + 3FH = C8H
∴    2300H  = 61H Lower byte
     2301H  = 01H Higher byte
```

Source program :

```
        LDA 2200H
        MOV C, A       ; Initialize counter
        LXI H, 2201H   ; Initialize pointer
        MVI E, 00      ; Sumlow = 0
        MOV D, E       ; Sumhigh = 0
BACK :  MOV A, M       ; Get the number
        ANI 01H        ; Mask Bit1 to Bit7
```

```
            JZ SKIP       ; Don't add if number is even
            MOV A, E      ; Get the lower byte of sum
            ADD M         ; Sum = sum + data
            MOV E, A      ; Store result in E register
            JNC SKIP
            INR D         ; Add carry to MSB of SUM
SKIP    :   INX H         ; Increment pointer
            DCR C         ; Decrement counter
            JNZ BACK      ; Check if counter ≠ 0 repeat
            MOV A, E
            STA 2300H     ; Store lower byte
            MOV A, D
            STA 2301H     ; Store higher byte
            HLT           ; Terminate program execution
```

Flowchart :

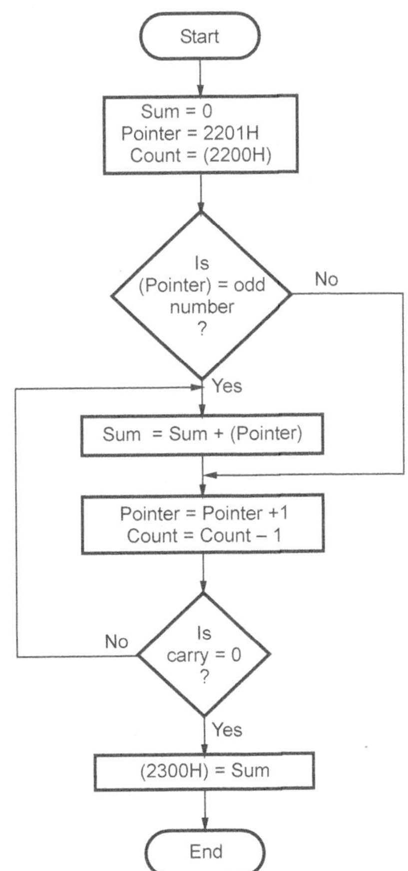

Lab Experiment 32 : Find the square of given number.

Statement : Find the square of the given numbers from memory location 6100H and store the result from memory location 7000H.

Source program :

```
        LXI H,6200H   ; Initialize lookup table pointer
        LXI D,6100H   ; Initialize source memory pointer
        LXI B,7000H   ; Initialize destination memory pointer
BACK :  LDAX D        ; Get the number
        MOV L, A      ; A point to the square
        MOV A, M      ; Get the square
        STAX B        ; Store the result at destination memory location
        INX D         ; Increment source memory pointer
        INX B         ; Increment destination memory pointer
        MOV A, C
        CPI 05H       ; Check for last number
        JNZ BACK      ; If not repeat
        HLT           ; End of program
```

Flowchart :

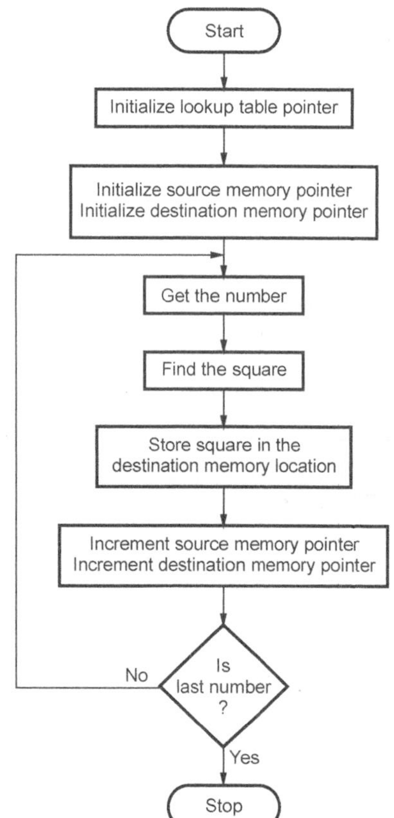

Lookup Table

Address	Digit	Square
6100H	0	0H
6101H	1	1H
6102H	2	4H
6103H	3	9H
6104H	4	10H
6105H	5	19H
6106H	6	24H
6107H	7	31H
6108H	8	40H
6109H	9	51H

Lab Experiment 33 : Search a byte in a given number.

Statement : Search the given byte in the list of 50 numbers stored in the consecutive memory locations and store the address of memory location in the memory locations 2200H and 2201H. Assume byte is in the C register and starting address of the list is 2000H. If byte is not found store 00 at 2200H and 2201H.

Source program :

```
        LXI H, 2000H    ; Initialize memory pointer
        MVI B, 52H      ; Initialize counter
BACK :  MOV A, M        ; Get the number
        CMP C           ; Compare with the given byte
        JZ LAST         ; Go last if match occurs
        INX H           ; Increment memory pointer
        DCR B           ; Decrement counter
        JNZ B           ; If not zero, repeat
        LXI H, 0000H
        SHLD 2200H
        JMP END         ; Store 00 at 2200H and 2201H
LAST :  SHLD 2200H      ; Store memory address
END  :  HLT             ; Stop
```

Flowchart :

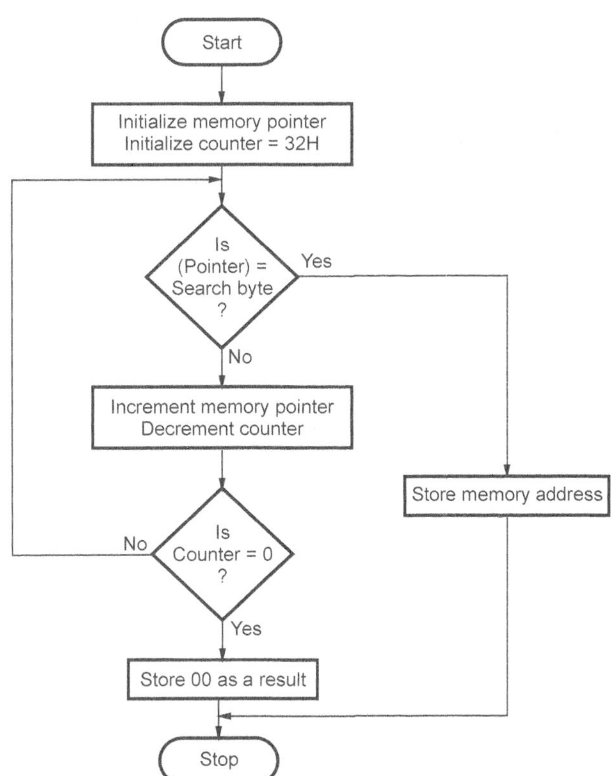

Lab Experiment 34 : Add two decimal numbers.

Statement : Two decimal numbers six digits each, are stored in BCD packed form. Each number occupies a sequence of byte in the memory. The starting address of first number is 6000H and second number is 6100H. Write an assembly language program that adds these two numbers and stores the sum in the same format starting from memory location 6200H.

Flowchart :

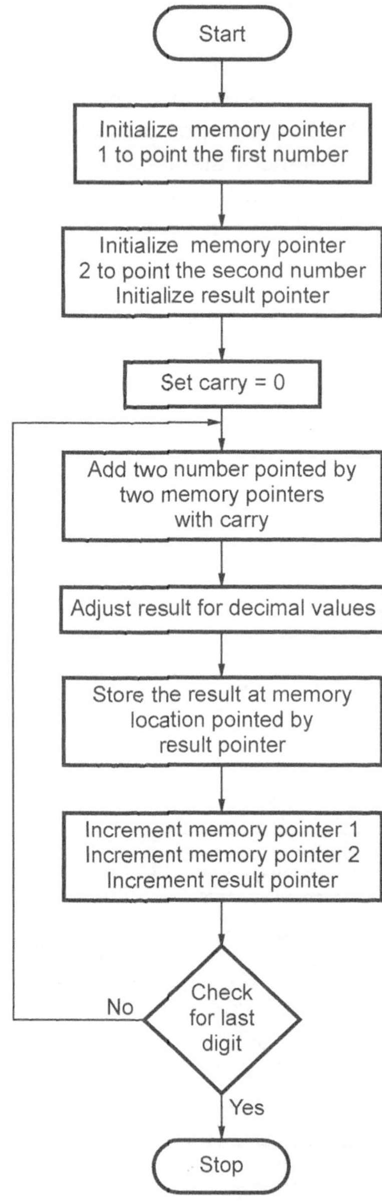

Source program :

```
        LXI H,6000H  ; Initialize pointer1 to first number
        LXI D,6100H  ; Initialize pointer2 to second number
        LXI B,6200H  ; Initialize pointer3 to result
        STC
        CMC          ; Carry = 0
BACK :  LDAX D       ; Get the digit
        ADD M        ; Add two digits
        DAA          ; Adjust for decimal
        STAX B       ; Store the result
        INX H        ; Increment pointer1
        INX D        ; Increment pointer2
        INX B        ; Increment result pointer
        MOV A, L
        CPI 06H      ; Check for last digit
        JNZ BACK     ; If not last digit repeat
        HLT          ; Terminate program execution
```

Lab Experiment 35 : Add each element of array with the elements of another array.

Statement : Add 2 arrays having ten 8-bit numbers each and generate a third array of result. It is necessary to add the first element of array1 with the first element of array-2 and so on. The starting addresses of array1, array2 and array3 are 2200H, 2300H and 2400H, respectively.

Flowchart : (See on next page)

Source program :

```
        LXI H, 2200H  ; Initialize memory pointer 1
        LXI B, 2300H  ; Initialize memory pointer 2
        LXI D, 2400H  ; Initialize result pointer
BACK :  LDAX B        ; Get the number from array 2
        ADD M         ; Add it with number in array 1
        STAX D        ; Store the addition in array 3
        INX H         ; Increment pointer1
        INX B         ; Increment pointer2
        INX D         ; Increment result pointer
        MOV A, L      ;
        CPI 0AH       ; Check pointer1 for last number
        JNZ BACK      ; If not, repeat
        HLT           ; Stop
```

Flowchart :

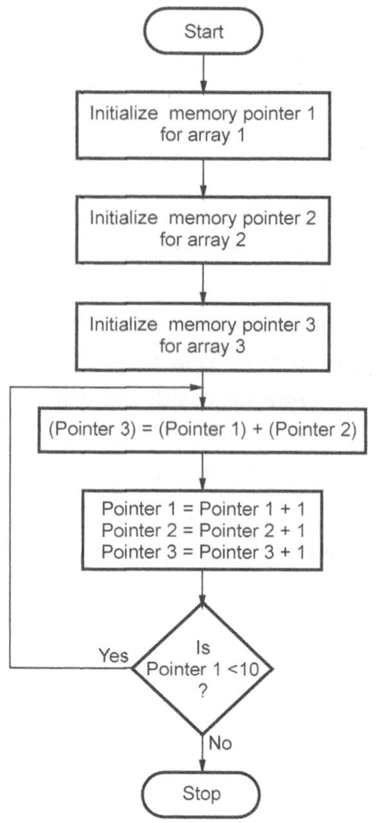

Lab Experiment 36 : Separate even numbers from given numbers.

Statement : Write an assembly language program to seperate even numbers from the given list of 50 numbers and store them in the another list starting from 2300H. Assume starting address of 50 number list is 2200H.

Flowchart : (See on next page)

Source program :

```
         LXI H, 2200H   ; Initialize memory pointer1
         LXI D, 2300H   ; Initialize memory pointer2
         MVI C, 32H     ; Initialize counter
BACK :   MOV A, M       ; Get the number
         ANI 01H        ; Check for even number
         JNZ SKIP       ; If ODD, don't store
         MOV A, M       ; Get the number
         STAX D         ; Store the number in result list
```

```
        INX D        ; Increment pointer 2
SKIP :  INX H        ; Increment pointer1
        DCR C        ; Decrement counter
        JNZ BACK     ; If not zero, repeat
        HLT          ; Stop
```

Flowchart : (For Lab Experiment 36)

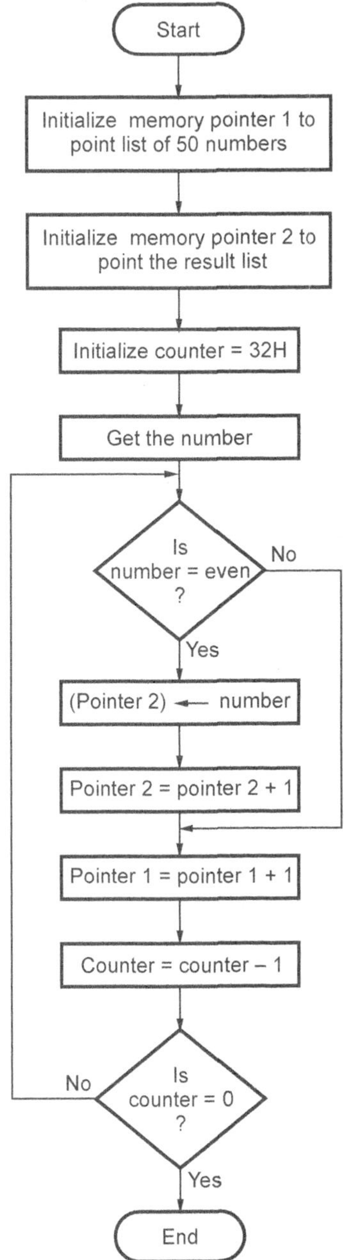

Lab Experiment 37 : Transfer contents to overlapping memory blocks.

Statement : Write assembly language program to with proper comments for the following : A block of data consisting of 256 bytes is stored in memory starting at 3000H. This block is to be shifted (relocated) in memory from 3050H onwards. Do not shift the block or part of the block anywhere else in the memory.

Source program :

Two blocks (3000 – 30FF and 3050 – 314F) are overlapping. Therefore it is necessary to transfer last byte first and first byte last.

```
        MVI C, FFH    ; Initialize counter
        LXI H, 30FFH  ; Initialize source memory pointer
        LXI D, 314FH  ; Initialize destination memory pointer
BACK :  MOV A, M      ; Get byte from source memory block
        STAX D        ; Store byte in the destination memory
                      ; block
        DCX H         ; Decrement source memory pointer
        DCX           ; Decrement destination memory pointer
        DCR C         ; Decrement counter
        JNZ BACK      ; If counter ≠ 0 repeat
        HLT           ; Stop execution
```

Lab Experiment 38 : Inserting string in a given array of characters.

Statement : Write an 8085 assembly language program to insert a string of four characters from the tenth location in the given array of 50 characters.

Solution :

Step 1 : Move bytes from location 10 till the end of array by four bytes downwards.

Step 2 : Insert four bytes at locations 10, 11, 12 and 13.

```
        LXI H, 2131H    ; Initialize pointer at the last location
                        ; of array.
        LXI D, 2135H    ; Initialize another pointer to point the
                        ; last location of array after insertion.
```

```
AGAIN : MOV A, M        ; Get the character
        STAX D          ; Store at the new location
        DCX D           ; Decrement destination pointer
        DCX H           ; Decrement source pointer
        MOV A, L        ; [ check whether desired bytes are
        CPI 08H         shifted or not]
        JNZ AGAIN       ; If not repeat the process
        INX H           ; Adjust the memory pointer
        LXI D, 2200H    ; Initialize the memory pointer to point
                        ; the string to be inserted
REPE  : LDAX D          ; Get the character
        MOV M, A        ; Store it in the array
        INX D           ; Increment source pointer
        INX H           ; Increment destination pointer
        MOV A, E        ; [ check whether the 4 bytes
        CPI 04          ;   are inserted]
        JNZ REPE        ;  If not repeat the process
        HLT             ; Stop
```

Lab Experiment 39 : Deleting string in a given array of characters.

Statement : Write an 8085 assembly language program to delete a string of 4 characters from the tenth location in the given array of 50 characters.

Solution : Shift bytes from location 14 till the end of array upwards by 4 characters i.e. from location 10 on words.

```
LXI H, 210DH  ; Initialize source memory pointer at the 14th
              ; location of the array.
LXI D, 2109H  ; Initialize destination memory pointer at the
              ; 10th location of the array.
MOV A, M      ; Get the character
STAX D        ; Store character at new location
INX D         ; Increment destination pointer
INX H         ; Increment source pointer
MOV A, L      ; [ check whether desired
CPI 32H       ;   bytes are shifted or not]
JNZ REPE      ; If not repeat the process.
HLT           ; Stop
```

Lab Experiment 40 : Add parity bit to 7-bit ASCII characters.

Statement : Add even parity to a string of 7-bit ASCII characters. The length of the string is in memory location 2040H and the string itself begins in memory location 2041H. Place even parity in the most significant bit of each character. Draw a flowchart and write an 8085 assembly language program with comment for each instruction.

Flowchart :

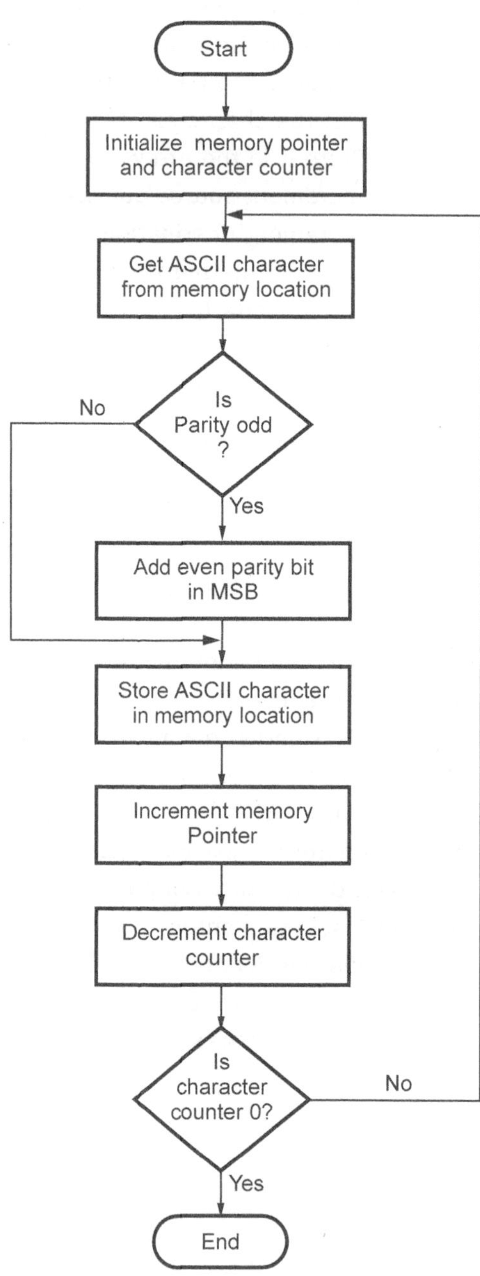

Source program :

```
          LXI H, 2040H
          MOV C, M       ; Counter for character
REPEAT  : INX H          ; Memory pointer to character
          MOV A, M       ; Character in accumulator
          ORA A          ; ORing with itself to check parity.
          JPO PEREVEN
          ORI 80H        ; If odd parity place even parity in
                         ; D7(80).
PEREVEN : MOV M, A       ; Store converted even parity character.
          DCR C          ; Decrement counter.
          JNZ REPEAT     ; If not zero go for next character.
          HLT            ; Terminate program execution
```

Lab Experiment 41 : Find the number of negative, zero and positive numbers.

Statement : A list of 50 numbers is stored in memory, starting at 6000H. Find number of negative, zero and positive numbers from this list and store these results in memory locations 7000H, 7001H, and 7002H respectively.

Source program :

```
          LXI H, 6000H   ; Initialize memory pointer
          MVI C, 00H     ; Initialize number counter
          MVI B, 00H     ; Initialize negative number counter
          MVI E, 00H     ; Initialize zero number counter
BEGIN   : MOV A, M       ; Get the number
          CPI 00H        ; If number = 0
          JZ ZERONUM     ; Goto zeronum
          ANI 80H        ; If MSB of number = 1 i.e. if
          JNZ NEGNUM     ; Number is negative goto NEGNUM
          INR D          ; Otherwise increment positive number Counter
          JMP LAST       ;
ZERONUM : INR E          ; Increment zero number counter
          JMP LAST
NEGNUM  : INR B          ; Increment negative number counter
LAST    : INX H          ; Increment memory pointer
          INR C          ; Increment number counter
          MOV A, C
          CPI 32H        ; If number counter = 50 (base 10) then
          JNZ BEGIN      ; Store otherwise check next number
```

```
LXI H, 7000    ; Initialize memory pointer.
MOV M, B       ; Store negative number.
INX H
MOV M, E       ; Store zero number.
INX H
MOV M, D       ; Store positive number.
HLT
```

Flowchart :

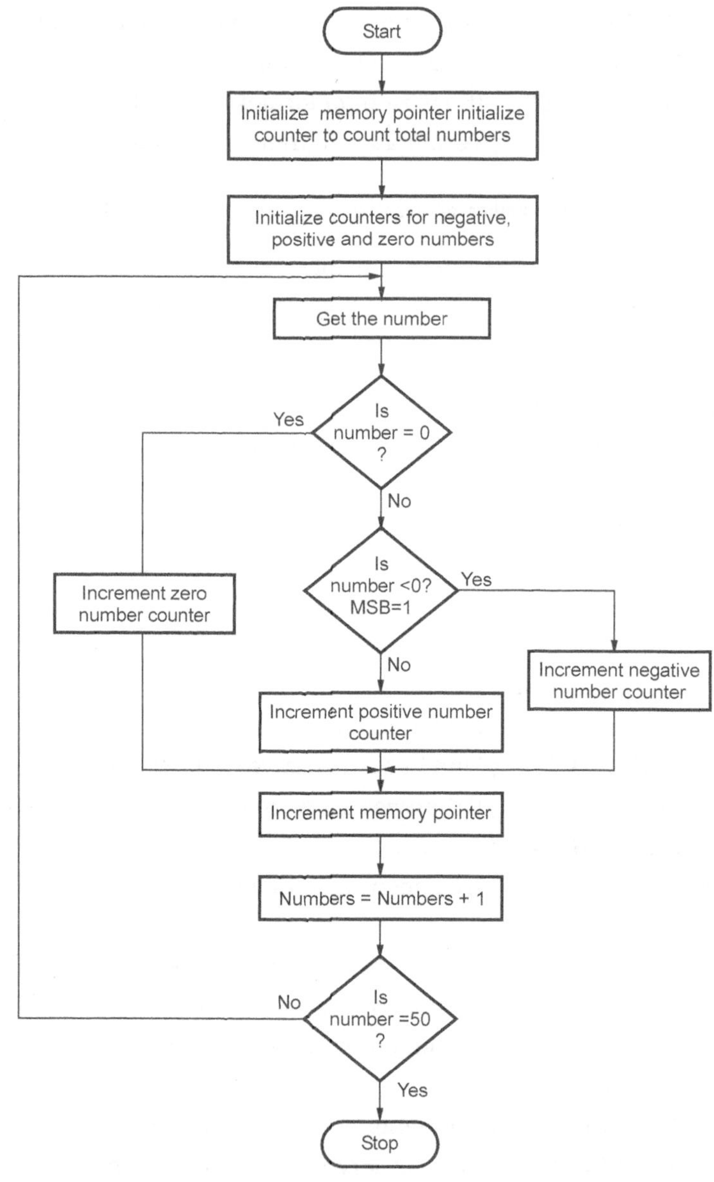

Lab Experiment 42 : Multiply two eight bit numbers with shift and add method.

Statement : Multiply the 8-bit unsigned number in memory location 2200H by the 8-bit unsigned number in memory location 2201H. Store the 8 least significant bits of the result in memory location 2300H and the 8 most significant bits in memory location 2301H.

Sample problems :

(2200) = 1100 (0CH)

(2201) = 0101 (05H)

Multiplicand	Multiplier	Result
1100 (12_{10})	0101 (5_{10})	$12 \times 5 = 60_{10}$

For simplicity, Multiplicand and Multiplier are taken 4-bit each.

Steps	Product								Multiplier					Comments
	B_7	B_6	B_5	B_4	B_3	B_2	B_1	B_0	CY	B_3	B_2	B_1	B_0	
	0	0	0	0	0	0	0	0	0	0	1	0	1	Initial stage
Step 1	0	0	0	0	0	0	0	0	0	1	0	1	0	Shift left by 1
	0	0	0	0	0	0	0	0	0	1	0	1	0	Don't Add since CY = 0
Step 2	0	0	0	0	0	0	0	0	1	0	1	0	0	Shift
	0	0	0	0	1	1	0	0	1	0	1	0	0	Add multiplicand Since CY = 1
Step 3	0	0	0	1	1	0	0	0	0	1	0	0	0	Shift left by 1
	0	0	0	1	1	0	0	0	0	1	0	0	0	Don't Add since CY=0
Step 4	0	0	1	1	0	0	0	0	1	0	0	0	0	Shift left by 1
	0	0	1	1	1	1	0	0	1	0	0	0	0	Add multiplicand Since CY = 1

Source program :

```
        LXI H, 2200H   ; Initialize the memory pointer
        MOV E, M       ; Get multiplicand
        MVI D, 00H     ; Extend to 16-bits
        INX H          ; Increment memory pointer
        MOV A, M       ; Get multiplier
        LXI H, 0000H   ; Product = 0
        MVI B, 08H     ; Initialize counter with count 8
MULT :  DAD H          ; Product = product × 2
        RAL
        JNC SKIP       ; Is carry from multiplier 1 ?
```

```
        DAD D          ; Yes, Product =Product + Multiplicand
SKIP :  DCR B          ; Is counter = zero
        JNZ MULT       ; no, repeat
        SHLD 2300H     ; Store the result
        HLT            ; End of program
```

Flowchart :

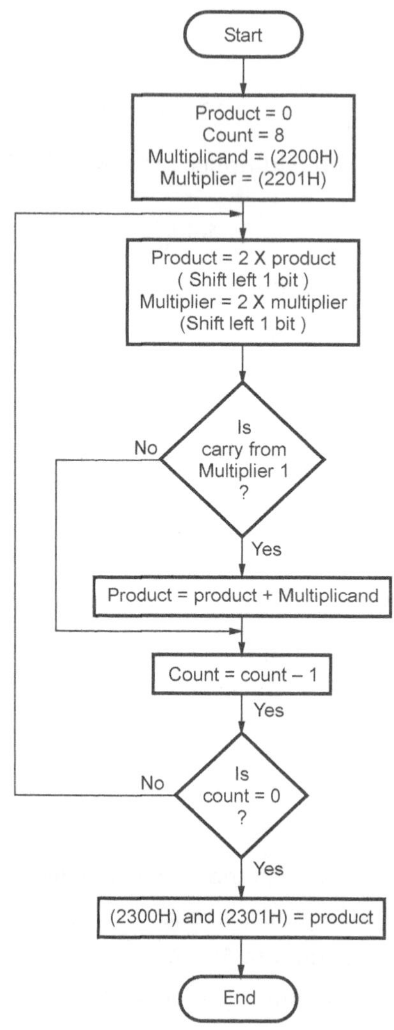

Lab Experiment 43 : Divide 16-bit number with 8-bit number using shifting technique.

Statement : Divide the 16-bit unsigned number in memory locations 2200H and 2201H (most significant bits in 2201H) by the 8-bit unsigned number in memory location 2300H store the quotient in memory location 2400H and remainder in 2401H.

Assumption : The most significant bits of both the divisor and dividend are zero.

Sample problem :

For simplicity, Dividend and divisor are taken 8-bit and 4-bit respectively

Dividend = 0110 0001 (61H) Divisor = 0111 (07H)

Steps	Dividend	Quotient	Comment
	B_7 B_6 B_5 B_4 B_3 B_2 B_1 B_0	B_3 B_2 B_1 B_0	
	0 1 1 0 0 0 0 1	0 0 0 0	Initial stage
Step 1	1 1 0 0 0 0 1 0	0 0 0 0	Shift left
	0 1 0 1 0 0 1 0	0 0 0 1	MSB of dividend = MSB dividend – divisor and Quotient = Quotient + 1 since MSB of dividend > divisor
Step 2	1 0 1 0 0 1 0 0	0 0 1 0	Shift left
	0 0 1 1 0 1 0 0	0 0 1 1	MSB of dividend = MSB dividend – divisor and Quotient = Quotient + 1 since MSB of dividend > divisor
Step 3	0 1 1 0 1 0 0 0	0 1 1 0	Shift left
	0 1 1 0 1 0 0 0	0 1 1 0	No change since MSB of dividend < divisor
Step 4	1 1 0 1 0 0 0 0	1 1 0 0	Shift left
	0 1 1 0 0 0 0 0	1 1 0 1	MSB of dividend = MSB dividend – divisor and Quotient = Quotient + 1 since MSB of dividend > divisor

Source program :

```
        MVI E, 00      ; Quotient = 0
        LHLD 2200H     ; Get dividend
        LDA 2300       ; Get divisor
        MOV B, A       ; Store divisor
        MVI C, 08      ; Count = 8
NEXT  : DAD H          ; Dividend = Dividend × 2
        MOV A, E
        RLC
        MOV E, A       ; Quotient = × 2
        MOV A, H       ;
        SUB B          ; Is most significant byte of Dividend
                       ; > divisor
        JC SKIP        ; No, go to Next step
        MOV H, A       ; Yes, subtract divisor
        INR E          ; and Quotient = Quotient + 1
```

```
SKIP : DCR C          ; Count = Count – 1
       JNZ NEXT       ; Is count = 0 repeat
       MOV A, E
       STA 2401H      ; Store Quotient
       MOV A, H
       STA 2401H      ; Store remainder
       HLT            ; End of program.
```

Flowchart :

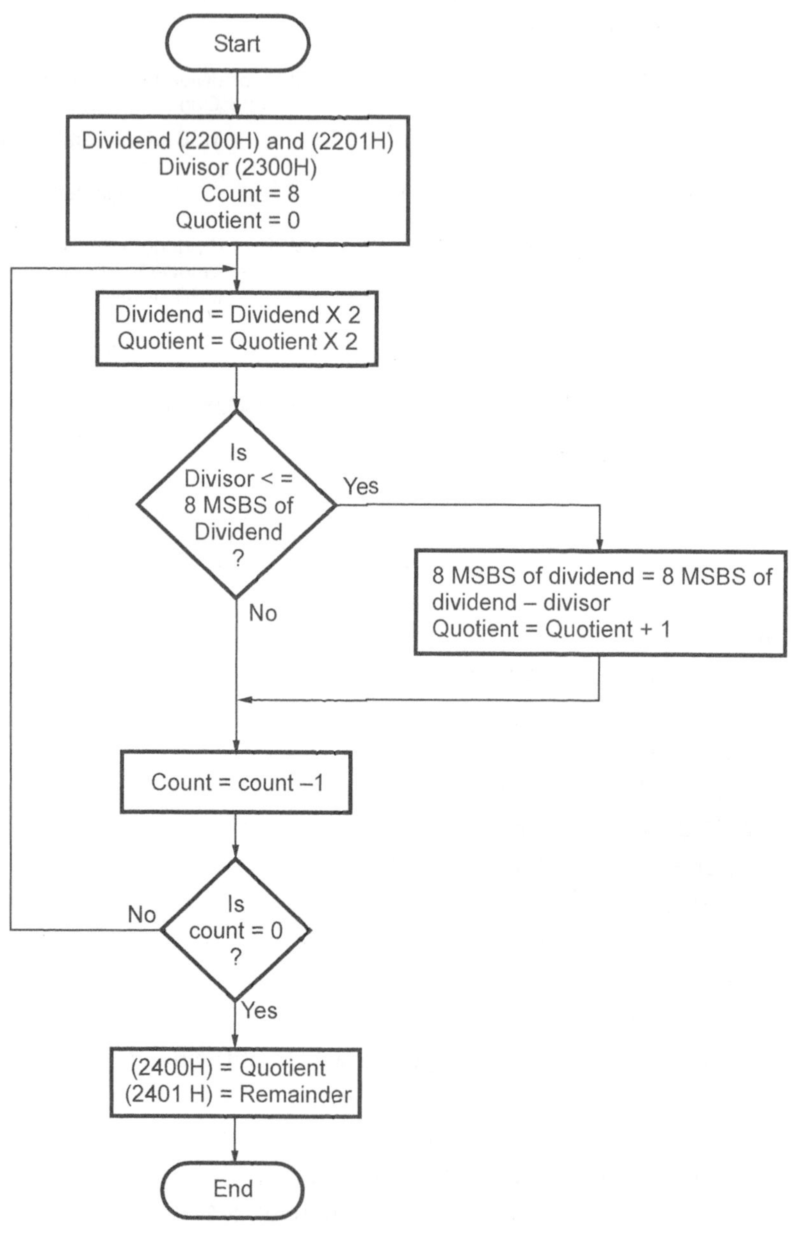

Lab Experiment 44 : Simulate DAA instruction.

Statement : Assume the DAA instruction is absent. Write a subroutine which will perform the same task as DAA instruction

Flowchart :

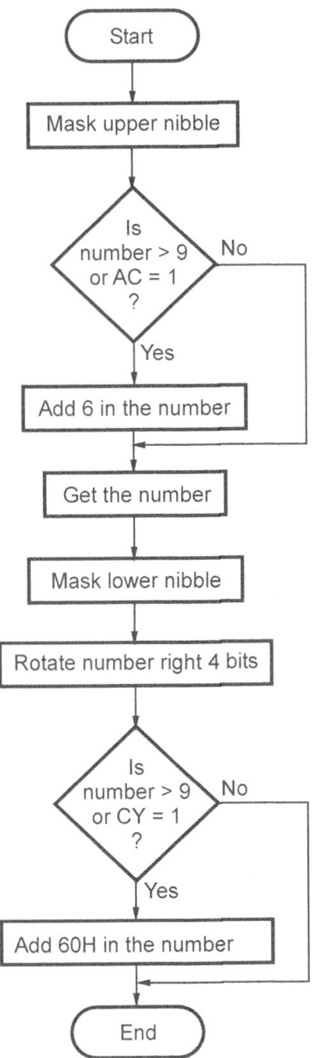

Sample Problem :

Let us see the execution of DAA instruction.

1. If the value of the low order four bits (D_3-D_0) in the accumulator is greater than 9 or if auxiliary carry flag is set, the instruction adds 6 (06) to the low-order four bits.

2. If the value of the high-order four bits (D_7-D_4) in the accumulator is greater than 9 or if carry flag is set, the instruction adds 6(06) to the high-order four bits.

Note : To check auxiliary carry flag it is necessary to get the flag register contents in one of the registers and then we can check the auxiliary carry flag by checking bit 4 of that register. To get the flag register contents in any general purpose register we require stack operation and therefore stack pointer is initialized at the beginning of the source program.

Source program :

```
          LXI SP, 27FFH    ; Initialize stack pointer
          MOV E, A         ; Store the contents of accumulator
          ANI 0FH          ; Mask upper nibble
          CPI 0AH          ; Check if number is greater than 9
          JC SKIP          ; If no go to skip
          MOV A, E         ; Get the number
          ADI 06H          ; Add 6 in the number
          JMP SECOND       ; Go for second check
SKIP :    PUSH PSW         ; Store accumulator and flag contents
                           ; in stack
          POP B            ; Get the contents of accumulator in B
                           ; register and
                           ; flag register contents in C register
          MOV A, C         ; Get flag register contents in
                           ; accumulator
          ANI 10H          ; Check for bit 4
          JZ SECOND        ; If zero, go for second check
          MOV A, E         ; Get the number
          ADI 06           ; Add 6 in the number
SECOND :  MOV E, A         ; Store the contents of accumulator
          ANI F0H          ; Mask lower nibble
          RRC
          RRC
          RRC
          RRC              ; Rotate number 4 bit right
          CPI 0AH          ; Check if number is greater than 9
          JC SKIP1         ; If no go to skip 1
          MOV A, E         ; Get the number
          ADI 60H          ; Add 60 H in the number
          JMP LAST         ; Go to last
```

```
SKIP1  : JNC LAST        ; If carry flag = 0 go to last
         MOV A, E        ; Get the number
         ADI 60 H        ; Add 60 H in the number
 LAST  : HLT
```

Lab Experiment 45 : Program to test RAM.

Statement : Write an assembly language program with proper comments to perform following operations :

To test RAM by writing '1' and reading it back and later writing '0' (zero) and reading it back. RAM addresses to be checked are 4000H to 40FFH. In case of any error, it is indicated by writing 01H at port 10H.

Source Program :

```
          LXI H, 4000H    ; Initialize memory pointer
 BACK  :  MVI M, FFH      ; Writing '1' into RAM
          MOV A, M        ; Reading data from RAM
          CPI FFH         ; Check for ERROR
          JNZ ERROR       ; If yes go to ERROR
          INX H           ; Increment memory pointer
          MOV A, H
          CPI 50H         ; Check for last check
          JNZ BACK        ; If not last repeat
          LXI H, 4000H    ; Initialize memory pointer
 BACK1 :  MVI M, 00H      ; Writing '0' into RAM
          MOV A, M        ; Reading data from RAM
          CPI 00H         ; Check for ERROR
          INX H           ; Increment memory pointer
          MOV A, H
          CPI 50H         ; Check for last check
          JNZ BACK1       ; If not last, repeat
          HLT             ; Stop execution
```

Lab Experiment 46 : Write an assembly language program to generate fibonacci number.

```
          MVI D, COUNT    ; Initialize counter
          MVI B, 00       ; Initialize variable to store previous
                          ; number
          MVI C, 01       ; Initialize variable to store current
                          ; number
 BACK :   MOV A, B        ; [Add two
```

```
        ADD C          ;   numbers ]
        MOV B, C       ; Current number is now previous number
        MOV C, A       ; Save result as a new current number
        DCR D          ; Decrement count
        JNZ BACK       ; If count ≠ 0 go to BACK
        HLT            ; Stop.
```

Lab Experiment 47 : Program to evaluate $a^2 + b^2$

Statement : Write 8085 assembly language program to perform the following, $a^2 + b^2$, where a and b are 8 - bit binary numbers. Explain with algorithm and flowchart.

Dec.-08, Marks 10

Algorithm

1. Read number a.
2. Find a^2 by performing $a \times a$ and store result 1.
3. Read number b.
4. Find b^2 by performing $b \times b$ and store result 2.
5. Result = Result 1 + Result 2

Flowchart

See flowchart on next page.

Refer Lab experiment 42 for the flowchart of multiplication routine.

Program

```
            MVI E, Number a ; Get the number a
            CALL MULTIPLY   ; Call multiply subroutine
            SHLD 2200H      ; Store result 1
            MVI E, Number b ; Get the number b
            CALL MULTIPLY   ; Call multiply subroutine
            XCHG            ; Store result 2 in DE
            LHLD 2200H      ; Get the result 1 in HL
            DAD D           ; HL ← HL + DE
            HLT             ; Stop
MULTIPLY :  MVI D, 00       ; Extend to 16-bit
            MOV A, E        ; Multiplier = multiplicand
            LXI H, 0000H    ; Product = 0
            MVI B, 08H      ; Initialize counter with count 8
MULT:       DAD H           ; Product = product × 2
```

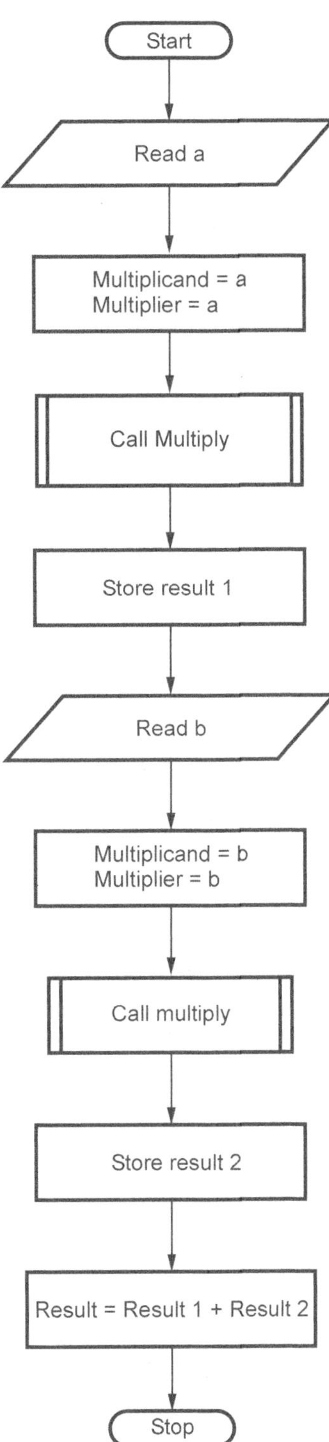
Start
Read a
Multiplicand = a
Multiplier = a
Call Multiply
Store result 1
Read b
Multiplicand = b
Multiplier = b
Call multiply
Store result 2
Result = Result 1 + Result 2
Stop

```
        RAL
        JNC SKIP        ; Is carry from multiplier 1 ?
        DAD D           ; Yes, Product =Product + Multiplicand
SKIP:   DCR B           ; Is counter = zero
        JNZ MULT        ; no, repeat
        RET             ; Return to main program
```

Lab Experiment 48 : Program to count given data in a set of numbers

Dec.-08, Marks 6

Statement : Write a program to count the number of times the data 02 is present in a set of 20 numbers.

It is assumed that set of 20 numbers are stored from memory location 2000H.

```
        LXI, 2000H      ; Initialize memory pointer
        MVI B, 14H      ; Initialize counter
        MVI C, 00H      ; Count = 0
BACK :  MOV A, M        ; Get the number
        CPI 02H         ; Compare with 02
        JNZ NEXT        ; If not zero skip next instruction
        INR C           ; Increment count
NEXT :  INX H           ; Increment memory pointer
        DCR B           ; Decrement counter
        JNZ BACK        ; If not zero, repeat
        HLT             ; Stop
```

Lab Experiment 49 : Program to multiply two 16-bit numbers

June-09, Marks 12

Statement : Write an assembly language program in 8085 to multiply two 16-bit numbers.

```
        LXI SP, 27FFH   ; Initialize stack pointer
        LXI H, 0000H    ; Result = 0 (Lower word)
        SHLD 2000H      ; Result = 0 (Higher word)
        LXI D, number 1 ; Multiplicand
        LXI B, number 2 ; Multiplier as a counter
BACK :  DAD D           ; Result (HL) = HL + DE
        JNC NEXT        ; If no carry goto NEXT
        PUSH H          ; Save HL register
        LHLD 2000H      ; Get the higher word
        INX H           ; Increment word by 1
        SHLD 2000H      ; Save higher word
        POP H           ; Get the lower word in HL
```

```
DCX B         ; Decrement counter
MOV A, B      ; Check whether
ORA C         ; BC is zero
JNZ BACK      ; if not zero, repeat
XCHG          ; Exchange DE and HL
LHLD 2000H    ; Get the higher word in HL
HLT           ; Stop
```

The 32-bit answer of multiplication is in HL and DE register. The lower word is in DE register and higher word is in HL register.

3.2 Timers

In the real time applications, such as traffic light control, digital clock, process control, serial communication, it is important to keep a track with time. For example in traffic light control application, it is necessary to give time delays between two transitions. These time delays are in few seconds and can be generated with the help of executing group of instructions number of times. This software timers are also called time delays or software delays. Let us see how to implement these time delays or software delays.

As you know microprocessor system consists of two basic components, Hardware and software. The software component controls and operates the hardware to get the desired output with the help of instructions. To execute these instructions, microprocessor takes fix time as per the instruction, since it is driven by constant frequency clock. This makes it possible to introduce delay for specific time between two events. In the following section we will see different delay implementation techniques.

3.2.1 Timer Delay using NOP Instruction

NOP instruction does nothing but takes 4T states of processor time to execute. So by executing NOP instruction in between two instructions we can get delay of 4 T-state

$$1 \text{ T state} = \frac{1}{\text{Operating frequency of 8085}}$$

3.2.2 Timer Delay using Counters

Counting can create time delays. Since the execution times of the instructions used in a counting routine are known, the initial value of the counter, required to get specific time delay can be determined.

Using 8-bit counter :

```
                                                 Number of T-states
        MVI C, count   ; Load count              7 T-states
BACK :  DCR C          ; Decrement count         4 T-states
        JNZ BACK       ; If count ≠ 0, repeat    10/7 T-states
```

In this program, the instructions DCR C and JNZ BACK execute number of times equal to count stored in the C register. The time taken by this program for execution can be calculated with the help of T-states. The column to the right of the comments indicates the number of T-states in the instruction cycle of each instruction. Two values are specified for the number of T-states for the JNZ instruction. The smaller value is applied when the condition is not met, and the larger value applied when it is met. The first instruction MVI C, count executed only once and it requires 7 T-states. There are count – 1 passes through the loop where the condition is met and control is transferred back to the first instruction in the loop (DCR C). The number of T-states that elapse while C is not zero are (count −1) × (4+10). On the last pass through the loop, the condition is not met and the loop is terminated. The number of T states that elapse in this pass are 4 + 7.

∴ Total T-states required to execute the given program

$$= \underset{\textbf{MVI C}}{7} + \underset{\textbf{Loops}}{(\text{count}-1) \times (4 + 10)} + \underset{\textbf{Last loop}}{(4 + 7)}$$

For count = 5

Number of T-state $= 7 + (5 - 1) \times (14) + (11)$

$= 7 + 56 + 11$

$= 74$

Assuming operating frequency of 8085A is 2 MHz,

Time required for 1 T-state $= \dfrac{1}{2\text{ MHz}}$

$= 0.5\ \mu\text{sec}$

Total time required to execute the given program $= 74 \times 0.5\ \mu\text{sec.}$

$= 37\ \mu\text{sec.}$

Maximum delay possible with 8-bit count.

The maximum count that can be loaded in the 8 bit register is FFH (255) so the maximum delay possible with 8 bit count, assuming operating frequency 2 MHz

$= (7 + (255 - 1) \times (14) + (11)) \times 0.5\ \mu\text{sec.}$

$= 1787\ \mu\text{sec.}$

With these calculations, it can be noticed that delay with 8 bit count suitable for small delays and not for large delays.

Using 16-bit counter :

```
                                                      Number of T-states
        LXI B, count   ; load 16 bit count            10 T-states
BACK :  DCX B          ; Decrement count              6  T-states
        MOV A, C       ;                              4  T-states
        ORA B          ; logically OR B and C         4  T-states
        JNZ BACK       ; If result is not 0, repeat   10 T-states
```

In this program, the instructions DCX B, MOV A, C, ORA B and JNZ BACK execute number of times equal to count stored in BC register pair. The instruction LXI B, count is executed only once. It requires 10 T-states. The number of T-states required for one loop = 6 + 4 + 4 + 10 = 24 T-states. The number of T-states required for last loop = 6 + 4 + 4 + 7 = 21 T-states. So total T-states required for execution of given program are

$$= \underset{\textbf{LXI B}}{10} + \underset{\textbf{Loops}}{(\text{count}-1)} \times \underset{\textbf{Last loop}}{24 + 21}$$

for count = 03FFH (1023_{10})

Number of T-states = 10 + (1022) × 24 + 21

= 24559

Assuming operating frequency of 8085A as 2 MHz, the time required for, T state = 0.5 μsec.

∴ Total time required to execute the given program

= 24559 × 0.5 μsec

= 12279.5 μsec

= 12.2795 msec

Maximum delay possible with 16-bit count

The maximum count that can be loaded in the 16 bit register pair is FFFFH (65535 H). So the maximum delay possible with 8 bit count, assuming operating frequency 2 MHz.

= 10(10 + (65535 – 1) × (24) + (21)) × 0.5 μsec

= 0.786425 sec

If the application requires the delays more than this, then the nested loop technique is used to implement the delays.

3.2.3 Timer Delay using Nested Loops

In this, there are more than one loops. The innermost loop is same as explained above. The outer loop sets the multiplying count to the delays provided by the innermost loop.

```
                                                              Number of T states
        MVI B, Multiplier count   ; Initialize multiplier           7  T-states
START : MVI C, Delay count        ; Initialize delay count          7  T-states
BACK  : DCR C                     ; Decrement delay count           4  T-states
        JNZ BACK                  ; If not 0, repeat             10/7  T-states
        DCR B                     ; Decrement multiplier count      4  T-states
        JNZ START                 ; If not 0, repeat             10/7  T-states
```

T-states required for execution of inner loop

$$T_{inner} = 7 + (\text{Delay count} - 1) \times 14 + 11$$

T-states required for execution of the given program

$$= (\text{Multiplier count} - 1) \times (T_{inner} + 14) + 11$$

For delay count = 65H (101) and multiplier count

= 51H (81)

T_{inner} = 7+(101–1) × 14 + 11

= 1418

Total time required to execute the given program is

(Operating frequency is 2 MHz) = [(81–1) × (1418 + 14) +11] × 0.5 μsec.

= 57.2855 msec.

Lab Experiment 50 : Generate a delay of 0.4 seconds.

Statement : Write a program to generate a delay of 0.4 sec if the crystal frequency is 5 MHz.

Solution : In 8085, the operating frequency is half of the crystal frequency,

$$\therefore \quad \text{Operating frequency} = 5/2 = 2.5 \text{ MHz}$$

$$\therefore \quad \text{Time for one T-state} = \frac{1}{2.5 \text{ MHz}} = 0.4\ \mu\text{sec}$$

$$\text{Number of T-states required} = \frac{\text{Required Time}}{\text{Time for 1 T-state}} = \frac{0.4 \text{ sec}}{0.4\ \mu\text{sec}}$$

$$= 1 \times 10^6$$

Delay Program :

```
        LXI B, count    ; 16-bit count
BACK :  DCX B           ; Decrement count
        MOV A, C
        ORA B           ; Logically OR B and C
        JNZ BACK        ; If result is not zero repeat
```

$$1 \times 10^6 = 10 + (\text{count} - 1) \times 24 + 21$$

$$\text{count} = \left(\frac{1 \times 10^6 - 31}{24} \right) + 1 \approx 41666_{10}$$

$$\text{count} = 41666_{10}$$

$$= \text{A2C2H}$$

Lab Experiment 51 : Generate and display binary up counter.

Statement : Write a program for displaying binary up counter. Counter should count numbers from 00 to FFH and it should increment after every 0.5 sec.

Assume operating frequency of 8085 equal to 2 MHz. Display routine is available.

Solution :

```
        LXI SP, 27FFH   ; Initialize stack pointer
        MVI C, 00H      ; Initialize counter
BACK :  CALL Display    ; Call display subroutine
        CALL Delay      ; Call delay subroutine
```

```
        INR C           ; Increment counter
        MOV A, C        ;
        CPI 00H         ; Check counter is > FFH
        JNZ BACK        ; If not, repeat
        HLT             ; Stop
```

Delay Subroutine :

```
Delay : LXI D, count    ; Initialize count
BACK :  DCX D           ; Decrement count
        MOV A, E        ;
        ORA D           ; Logically OR D and E
        JNZ BACK        ; If result is not 0 repeat
        RET             ; Return to main program
```

Flowchart :

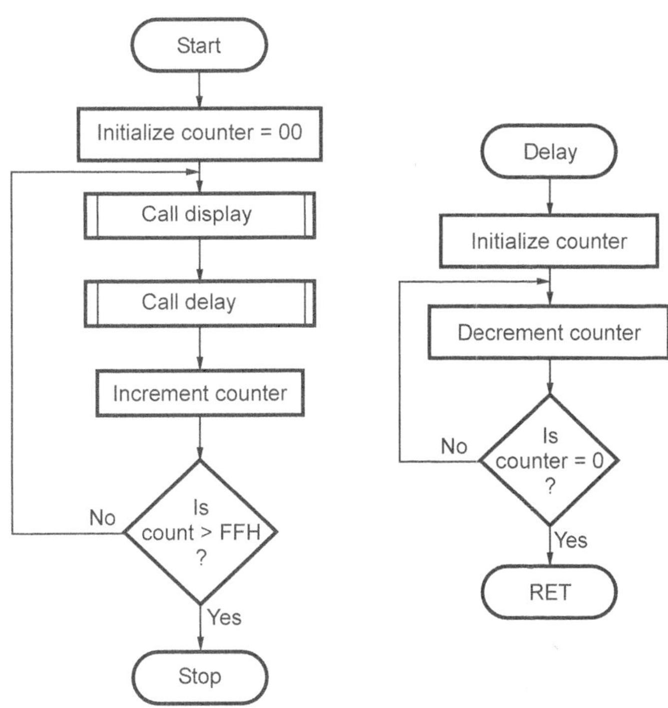

$$\text{Operating frequency} = 2 \text{ MHz}$$

$$\therefore \quad \text{Time for one T-state} = \frac{1}{2 \text{ MHz}} = 0.5 \, \mu\text{sec}$$

$$\text{Number of T-states required} = \frac{\text{Required Time}}{\text{Time for 1 T - state}} = \frac{0.5 \text{ sec}}{0.5 \, \mu\text{sec}} = 1 \times 10^6$$

$$1 \times 10^6 = 10 + (\text{count} - 1) \times 24 + 21$$

$$\text{count} = \left(\frac{1 \times 10^6 - 31}{24}\right) + 1 \approx 41666_{10}$$

$$\text{count} = 41666_{10} = \text{A2C2H}$$

Lab Experiment 52 : Generate and display BCD up counter with frequency 1 Hz.

Statement : Write a program for displaying BCD up counter. Counter should count numbers from 00 to 99H and it should increment after every 1 sec. Assume operating frequency of 8085 equal to 3 MHz. Display routine is available.

Solution :

```
        LXI SP, 27FFH     ; Initialize stack pointer
        MVI C, 00H        ; Initialize counter
BACK  : CALL Display      ; Call display subroutine
        CALL Delay        ; Call delay subroutine
        MOV A, C          ;
        ADI , 01          ; Increment counter
        DAA               ; Adjust it for decimal
        MOV C, A          ; Store count
        CPI ,00           ; Check count is > 99
        JNZ BACK          ; If not, repeat
        HLT               ; Stop
```

Delay Subroutine :

```
Delay  : MVI B, Multiplier-count ; Initialize multiplier count
BACK1:   LXI D, Initialize Count
BACK  :  DCX D            ; Decrement count
         MOV A, E         ;
         ORA D            ; Locally OR D and E
         JNZ BACK         ; If result is not 0, repeat
         DCR B            ; Decrement multiplier count
         JNZ BACK1        ; If not zero, repeat
         RET              ; Return to main program.
```

Operating frequency : 3 MHz

$\therefore$ Time for one T-state $= \frac{1}{3\text{ MHz}} = 0.333\ \mu\text{sec}$

Flowchart :

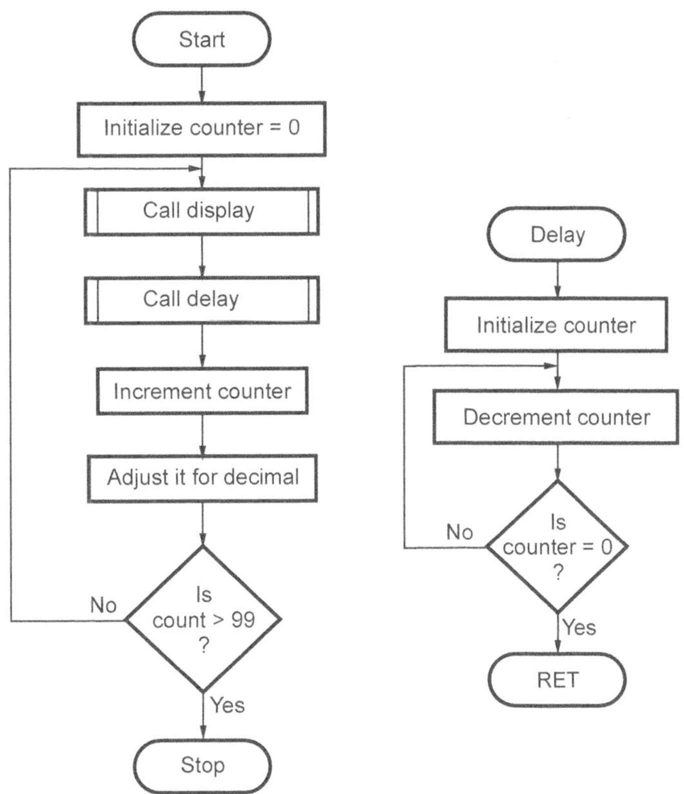

$\therefore$ Number of T-states required $= \dfrac{\text{Required Time}}{\text{Time for 1 - T state}} = 3 \times 10^6$

$= \dfrac{1 \text{ sec}}{0.333\ \mu\text{sec}}$

Let us take multiplier count = 3.

$\therefore$ Number of T-states required by inner loop $= \dfrac{3 \times 10^6}{3} = 1 \times 10^6$

$\therefore \quad 1 \times 10^6 = 10 + (\text{count} - 1) \times 24 + 21$

≈ 4166610

count = 4166610 = A2C2H

Lab Experiment 53 : Generate and display BCD down counter with frequency 1 Hz

Statement : Write a program for displaying BCD down counter. Counter should count numbers from 99 to 00 and it should decrement after every 1 sec. Assume display and delay routines are available.

Solution : Flowchart :

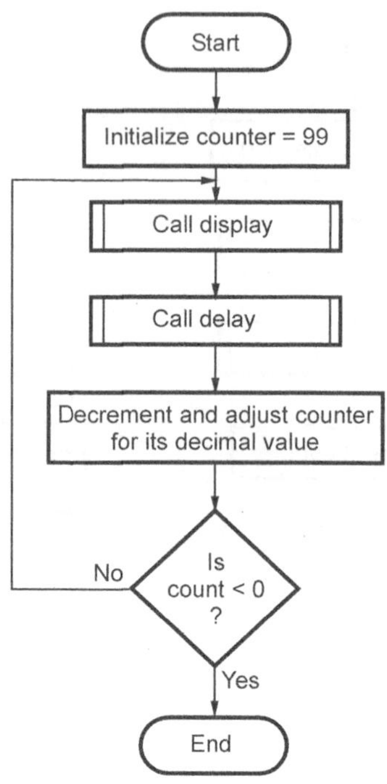

Source program with logic 1 :

```
        LXI SP, 27FFH   ; Initialize stack pointer
        MVI A, 99H      ; Initialize counter
BACK :  CALL Display    ; Call display subroutine
        CALL Delay      ; Call Delay subroutine
        ADI 99H         ; * (Explained later)
        DAA             ; Adjust for decimal
        CPI 99H         ; Compare with last count
        JNZ BACK        ; If no, repeat
        HLT
```

* **Addition** :

	1001	1001	99H
+	1001	1001	99H
	10011	0010	
DAA +	0110	0110	
	1001	1000	98H

Program with logic 2 :

```
        LXI SP, 27FFH   ; Initialize stack pointer
        MVI C, 99H      ; Initialize counter = 99
BACK :  Call Display    ; Call display subroutine
        Call Delay      ; Call delay subroutine
```

```
            MOV A, C        ; Get the count
            ANI 0FH         ; Check for lower nibble
            JNZ SKIP        ; If it is not 0FH go to skip
            MOV A, C        ; Else get the count
            SBI 06          ; and subtract 6
            MOV C, A        ; Store the count
SKIP      : DCR C           ; Decrement count
            MOV A, C        ; Get the count
            CPI 99H         ; Check it for last count
            JNZ BACK        ; If not, repeat
            HLT             ; Stop
```

Lab Experiment 54 : Generate and display the contents of decimal counter.

Statement : Write assembly language program to with proper comments for the following : To display decimal decrementing counter (99 to 00) at port 05 H with delay of half seconds between each count. Write as well the delay routine giving delay of half seconds. Operating frequency of microprocessor is 3.072 MHz. Neglect delay of the main program.

Source program :

```
            MVI C, 99H      ; Initialize counter
BACK :      MOV A, C        ;
            ANI 0F          ; Mask higher nibble
            CPI 0F
            JNZ SKIP
            MOV A, C
            SUI 06          ; Subtract 6 to adjust decimal count
            MOV D, A
SKIP :      MOV A, C
            OUT 05          ; send count on output port
            CALL Delay      ; Wait for 0.5 seconds
            DCR C           ; decrement count
            MOV A, C
            CPI FF
            JNZ BACK        ; If not zero, repeat
            HLT             ; Stop execution
```

Delay subroutine :

```
Delay  :    LXI D, Count
Back   :    DCX D           ; 6 T-states
            MOV A, D        ; 4 T-states
```

```
ORA E         ; 4 T-states
JNZ Back      ; 10 T-states
RET
```

$$1 \text{ T-state} = \frac{1}{\text{Operating frequency}} = \frac{1}{3.072 \times 10^6}$$

$$= 3.2552 \times 10^{-7}$$

$$\text{Number of T-states required} = \frac{0.5 \text{ sec}}{3.2552 \times 10^{-7}} = 1.536 \times 10^6$$

$$1.536 \times 10^6 = 10 + (\text{count} - 1) \times 24 + 21$$

$$\text{Count} = \frac{1.536 \times 10^6 - 31}{24} + 1 = 63999.708$$

$$= 64000$$

$$= \text{FA00H}$$

Lab Experiment 55 : Identify the error and correct the given delay routine.

Statement : The delay routine given below is in infinite loop, identify the error. Correct the program, give the machine cycles and T states of each instruction and also find the maximum delay generated. Assume 1 "T" state = 320 ns.

```
DELAY  :  LXI H, N
L1     :  DCX H
          JNZ L1
```

Solution : 1) The fault in the above program is at instruction JNZ L1. This condition always evaluates to be true hence loops keeps on executing and hence infinite loop.

2) Reason for infinite looping : - The instruction DCX H decrease the HL pair count one by one but it does not affect the zero flag. So when count reaches to 0000H in HL pair zero flag is not affected and JNZ L1 evaluates to be true and loop continues. Now HL again decrements below 0000H and HL becomes FFFFH and thus execution continues.

3) The modification in the program is as follows :

```
                                                 No. of T states
DELAY  :  LXI H, N    ; Load 16 bit count         → 10 T-states
   L1  :  DCX H       ; Decrement count           → 6  T-states
          MOV A, L    ;                           → 4  T-states
          ORA H       ; logically OR H and L      → 4  T-states
          JNZ L1      ; If result is not 0 repeat → 10 T-states
```

∴ Total number of T states required for program execution are

$$= 10 + (\text{count} - 1) \times 24 + 21$$

LXI H + Loops Last Loop

T-states for maximum delay = ?

Now maximum count that can be loaded in 16 bit register pair is FFFFH (65535H) so

$$[\text{T-states for max. delay} = 10 + (65535 - 1) \times 24 + 21]$$
$$= 1.57247 \times 10^6$$
$$\text{Time for 1 T state} = 320 \text{ ns}$$
$$\therefore \quad \text{Max. delay} = 1.575247 \times 10^6 \times 320 \text{ ns}$$
$$= 0.50407904 \text{ seconds}$$

3.3 Code Conversion

This technique allows programmer to translate a number represented using one coding system to another. For example, when we accept any number from the keyboard it is in ASCII code. But for processing, we have to convert this number in its hex equivalent. The code conversion involves some basic conversions such as

- BCD to binary conversion
- Binary to BCD conversion
- BCD to seven segment code conversion
- Binary to ASCII conversion and
- ASCII to binary conversion.

3.3.1 BCD to Binary Conversion

We are more familiar with the decimal number system. But the microprocessor understands the binary/hex number system. To convert BCD number into its binary equivalent we have to use the principle of positional weighting in a given number.

For example : $67 = 6 \times 0AH + 7$

$= 3CH + 7 = 43H$

To perform above operation it is necessary to separate an 8-bit packed BCD number into two 4-bit unpacked BCD digits : BCD_1 and BCD_2 and then convert each digit into its binary value according to its positions. Finally, add both binary numbers to obtain the binary equivalent of the BCD number. Let us see the program for 2-digit BCD to binary conversion.

Lab Experiment 56 : 2-Digit BCD to binary conversion.

Statement : Convert a 2-digit BCD number stored at memory address 2200H into its binary equivalent number and store the result in a memory location 2300H.

Sample Problem :

(2200H) = 67H

(2300H) = $6 \times 0AH + 7 = 3CH + 7 = 43H$

Source Program :

```
LDA 2200H    ; Get the BCD number
MOV B, A     ; Save it
ANI 0FH      ; Mask most significant four bits
MOV C, A     ; Save unpacked BCD1 in C register
MOV A, B     ; Get BCD again
ANI F0H      ; Mask least significant four bits
RRC          ; Convert most significant four
RRC          ; bits into unpacked BCD2
RRC          ;
RRC          ;
```

Flowchart :

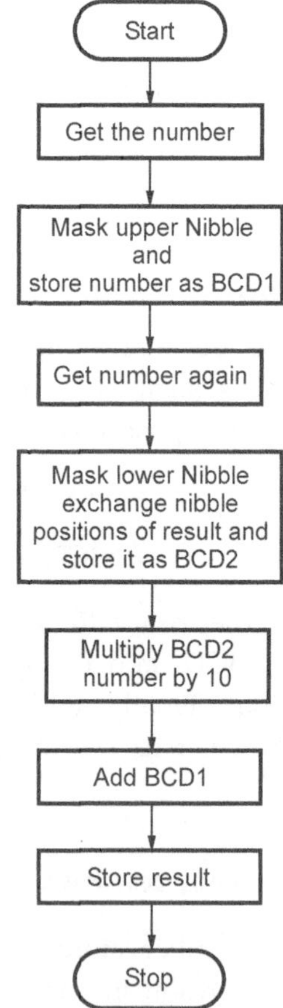

```
        MOV B, A      ; Save unpacked BCD2 in B register
        XRA A         ; Clear accumulator (sum = 0)
        MVI D, 0AH    ; Set D as a multiplier of 10
SUM :   ADD D         ; Add 10 until (B) = 0
        DCR B         ; Decrement BCD2 by one
        JNZ SUM       ; Is multiplication complete ?
                      ; if not, go back and add again
        ADD C         ; Add BCD1
        STA 2300H     ; Store the result
        HLT           ; Terminate program execution
```

3.3.2 Binary to BCD Conversion

We know that microprocessor processes data in the binary form. But when it is displayed, it is in the BCD form. In this case we need binary to BCD conversion of data. The conversion of binary to BCD is performed by dividing the number by the power of ten.

For example, assume the binary number as

0111 1011 (7BH) = 123_{10}

To represent the number in BCD requires twelve bits or three BCD digits as shown below

123_{10} = 0001 0010 0011

Digit_2 digit_1 digit_0

The conversion can be performed as follows

Step 1 : If the number is equal to or greater than 100, divide number by 100 (i.e. subtract 100 repeatedly until the remainder is less than 100). The quotient gives the most significant digit, digit 2 of the BCD number. If number is less than 100 go to step 2.

Step 2 : If the number i.e. remainder of first division is equal to or greater than 10 divide number by 10 repeatedly until the remainder is less than 10. The quotient gives the digit 1. If number is less than 10, go to step 3.

Step 3 : The remainder from step 2 gives the digit 3.

Let us see the program for binary to BCD conversion.

Lab Experiment 57 : Binary to BCD conversion.

Statement : Write a main program and a conversion subroutine to convert the binary number stored at 6000H into its equivalent BCD number. Store the result from memory location 6100H.

Sample Problem : (6000)H = 8AH

1. 8AH $\geq$ 64H (Decimal 100) $\therefore$ Divide by 64H (Decimal 100)
   8AH/64H $\rightarrow$ Quotient = 1 Remainder = 26H
   26H < 64H (Decimal 100) $\therefore$ goto step 2 and Digit 2 = 1
2. 26H $\geq$ 0AH (Decimal 10) $\therefore$ Divide by 0AH (Decimal 10)
   26H/0AH $\rightarrow$ Quotient = 3 Remainder = 08H
   08H < 0AH (Decimal 10) $\therefore$ goto step 3 and Digit 1 = 3
3. Digit 0 = 08H

Source Program :

```
LXI SP, 27FFH       ; Initialize stack pointer
LDA 6000H           ; Get the binary number in accumulator
CALL BIN TO BCD     ; Call subroutine BIN TO BCD
HLT                 ; Terminate program execution
```

Flowchart :

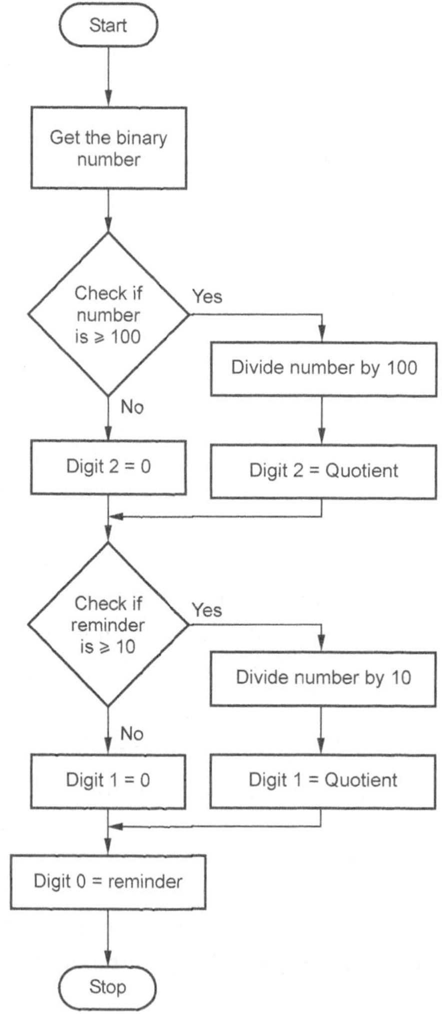

```
    Subroutine to convert binary number into its equivalent
    BCD number
   BIN TO BCD :
             PUSH B        ; Save BC register pair contents
             PUSH D        ; Save DE register pair contents
             MVI B, 64H    ; Load divisor decimal 100 in B register
             MVI C, 0AH    ; Load divisor decimal 10 in C register
             MVI D, 00H    ; Initialize Digit 1
             MVI E, 00H    ; Initialize Digit 2
   STEP1  :  CMP B         ; Check if number < Decimal 100
             JC STEP 2     ; If yes go to step 2
             SUB B         ; Subtract decimal 100
             INR E         ; Update quotient
             JMP STEP1     ; Go to step 1
   STEP2  :  CMP C         ; Check if number < Decimal 10
             JC STEP 3     ; If yes go to step 3
             SUB C         ; Subtract decimal 10
             INR D         ; Update quotient
             JMP STEP 2    ; Continue division by 10

   STEP3 :   STA 6100H     ; Store Digit 0
             MOV A, D      ; Get Digit 1
             STA 6101H     ; Store Digit 1
             MOV A, E      ; Get Digit 2
             STA 6102H     ; Store Digit 2
             POP D         ; Restore DE register pair contents
             POP B         ; Restore BC register pair contents
             RET           ; Return to main program
```

3.3.3 BCD to Seven Segment Conversion

Many times 7-segment LED display is used to display the results or parameters in the microprocessor system. In such cases we have to convert the result or parameter in 7-segment code. This conversion can be done using look-up technique. In the look-up table the codes of the digits (0-9) to be displayed are stored sequentially in the memory. The conversion program locates the code of a digit based on its BCD digit. Let us see the program for BCD to common cathode 7-segment code conversion.

Lab Experiment 58 : Find the 7-segment codes for given numbers.

Statement : Find the 7-segment codes for given 5 numbers from memory location 6000H and store the result from memory location 7000H.

Source Program :

```
             LXI H, 6200H    ; Initialize lookup table pointer
             LXI D, 6000H    ; Initialize source memory pointer
             LXI B, 7000H    ; Initialize destination memory pointer
```

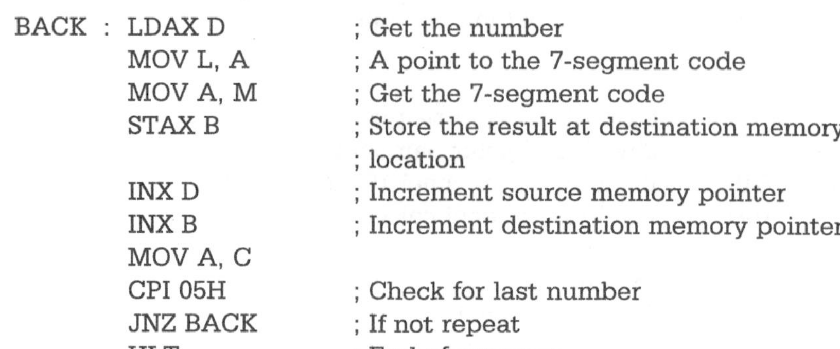

```
BACK : LDAX D       ; Get the number
       MOV L, A     ; A point to the 7-segment code
       MOV A, M     ; Get the 7-segment code
       STAX B       ; Store the result at destination memory
                    ; location
       INX D        ; Increment source memory pointer
       INX B        ; Increment destination memory pointer
       MOV A, C
       CPI 05H      ; Check for last number
       JNZ BACK     ; If not repeat
       HLT          ; End of program
```

Flowchart :

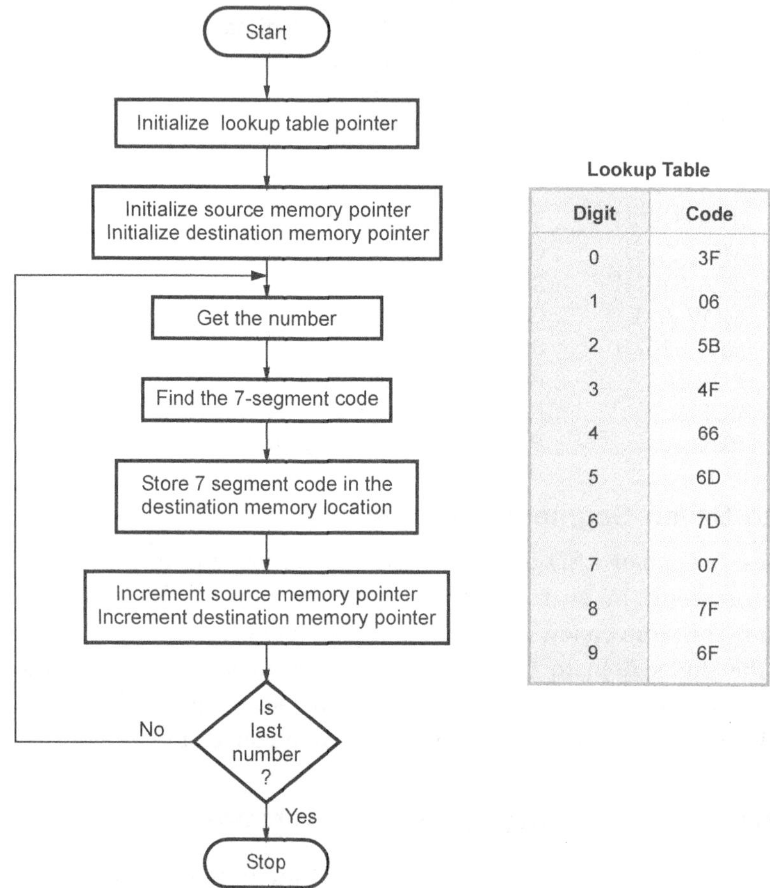

Lookup Table

Digit	Code
0	3F
1	06
2	5B
3	4F
4	66
5	6D
6	7D
7	07
8	7F
9	6F

3.3.4 Binary to ASCII Code Conversion

The ASCII Code (American Standard Code for Information Interchange) is commonly used for communication. In such cases we need to convert binary number to its ASCII equivalent. It is a seven bit code. In this code number 0 through 9 are represented as 30 through 39 respectively and letters A through Z are represented as 41H through 5AH.

Therefore, by adding 30H we can convert number into its ASCII equivalent and by adding 37H we can convert letter to its ASCII equivalent. Let us see the program for binary to ASCII code conversion.

Lab Experiment 59 : Find the ASCII character.

Statement : Write an assembly language program to convert the contents of the five memory locations starting from 2000H into an ASCII character. Place the result in another five memory locations starting from 2200H.

Flowchart :

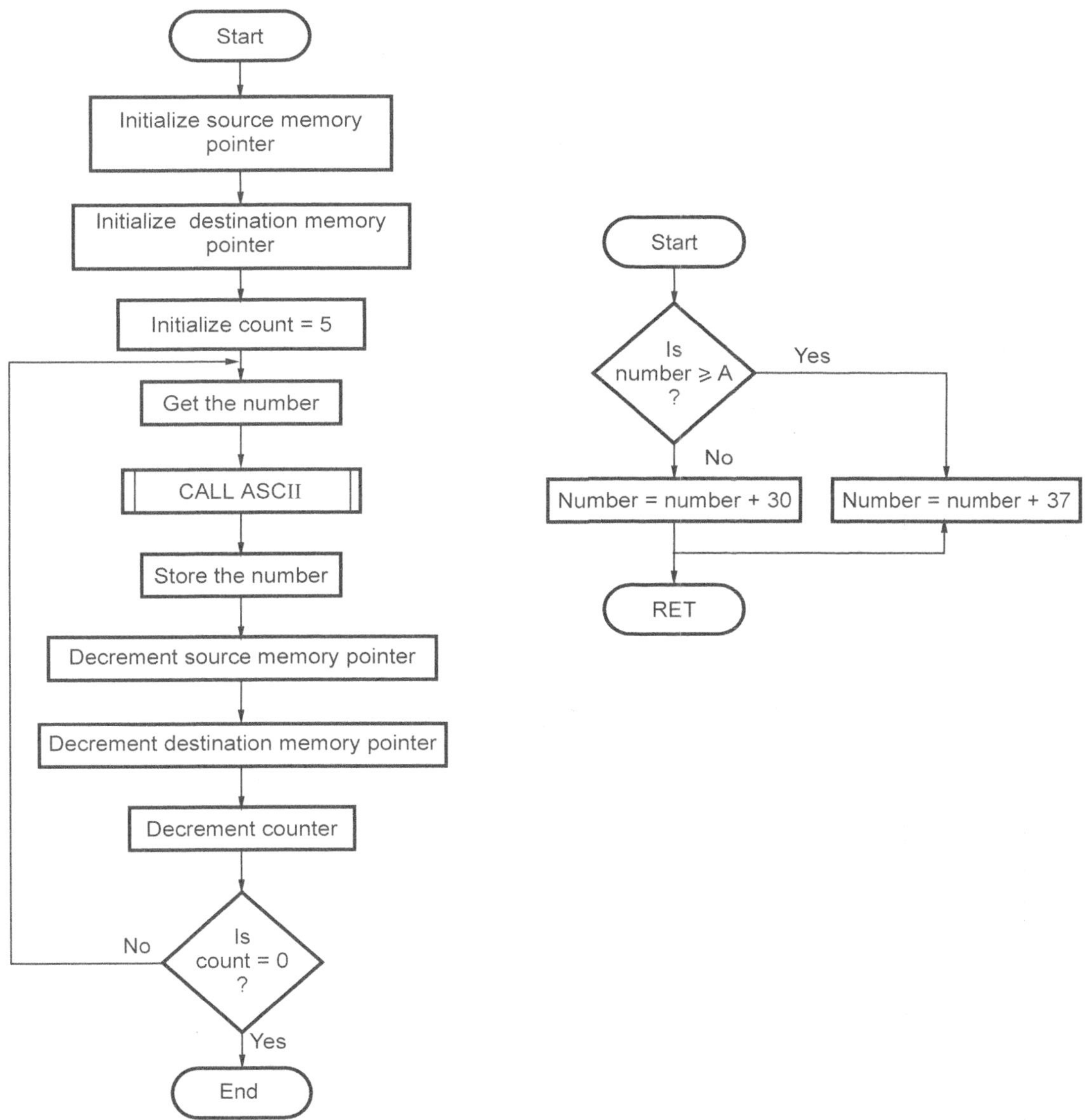

Sample Problem :

(2000H) = 1
(2001H) = 2
(2002H) = 9
(2003H) = A
(2004H) = B   Result (2200H) = 31
(2201H) = 32
(2202H) = 39
(2203H) = 41
(2204H) = 42

Subroutine Documentation :

Subroutine 'ASCII' converts a hexadecimal digit to ASCII.

Passing parameter	: The digit is passed using accumulator.
Return value	: In the accumulator.
Register used	: Accumulator.
Stack used	: From 27FEH to 27FDH

Source Program :

```
         LXI SP, 27FFH      ; Initialize stack pointer
         LXI H, 2000H       ; Source memory pointer
         LXI D, 2200H       ; Destination memory pointer
         MVI C, 05H         ; Initialize the counter
BACK  :  MOV A, M           ; Get the number
         CALL ASCII         ; Call subroutine ASCII
         STAX D             ; Store result
         INX H              ; Increment source memory pointer
         INX D              ; Increment destination memory pointer
         DCR C              ; Decrement count by 1
         JNZ BACK           ; if not zero, repeat
         HLT                ; Stop program execution subroutine ASCII
ASCII :  CPI, 0AH           ; Check if number is 0AH
         JNC NEXT           ; If yes goto next otherwise continue
         ADI 30H            ;
         JMP LAST
NEXT :   ADI 37H
LAST  :  RET                ; Return to main program
```

3.3.5 ASCII Code to Binary Conversion

It is exactly reverse process to binary to ASCII conversion. Here, if ASCII code is less than 3AH then 30H is subtracted to get the binary equivalent and if it is in between 41H and 5AH then 37H is subtracted to get the binary equivalent of letter (A-F).

3.4 BCD Arithmetic

3.4.1 BCD Addition

The addition of two BCD numbers can be best understood by considering the three cases that occur when two BCD digits are added.

Sum equals 9 or less with carry 0

Let us consider additions of 3 and 6 in BCD.

```
    6      0 1 1 0     ← BCD for 6
 +  3      0 0 1 1     ← BCD for 3
 -------   ---------
    9      1 0 0 1     ← BCD for 9
```

The addition is carried out as in normal binary addition and the sum is 1 0 0 1, which is BCD code for 9.

Sum greater than 9 with carry 0

Let us consider addition of 6 and 8 in BCD.

```
      6      0 1 1 0     ← BCD for 6
 +    8      1 0 0 0     ← BCD for 8
  --------   ----------
     14      1 1 1 0     ← Invalid BCD number     (1110) > 9
```

The sum 1 1 1 0 is an invalid BCD number. This has occurred because the sum of the two digits exceeds 9. Whenever this occurs the sum has to be corrected by the addition of six (0110) in the invalid BCD number, as shown below

```
      6      0 1 1 0     ← BCD for 6
 +    8      1 0 0 0     ← BCD for 8
  --------   ----------
     14      1 1 1 0     ← Invalid BCD number
 +           0 1 1 0     ← Add 6 for correction
-----------------------------
  0 0 0 1    0 1 0 0     ← BCD for 14
  \_____/    \_____/
     1          4
```

After addition of 6 carry is produced into the second decimal position.

Sum equals 9 or less with carry 1

Let us consider addition of 8 and 9 in BCD

```
    8             1 0 0 0      ← BCD for 8
 +  9             1 0 0 1      ← BCD for 9
 -------    -------------------
   17     0 0 0 1 0 0 0 1      ← Incorrect BCD result
```

In this, case, result (0001 0001) is valid BCD number, but it is incorrect. To get the correct BCD result correction factor of 6 has to be added to the least significant digit sum, as shown.

```
      8          1 0 0 0       ← BCD for 8
  +   9          1 0 0 1       ← BCD for 9
  -------    ----------------
     17    0 0 0 1 0 0 0 1     ← Incorrect BCD result
        +  0 0 0 0 0 1 1 0     ← Add 6 for correction
------------------------------
           0 0 0 1 0 1 1 1     ← BCD for 17
```

Going through these three cases of BCD addition we can summarize the BCD addition procedure as follows :

1. Add two BCD numbers using ordinary binary addition.
2. If four-bit sum is equal to or less than 9, no correction is needed. The sum is in proper BCD form.
3. If the four-bit sum is greater than 9 or if a carry is generated from the four-bit sum, the sum is invalid.
4. To correct the invalid sum, add 0110_2 to the four-bit sum. If a carry results from this addition, add it to the next higher-order BCD digit.

The 8085 supports DAA (Decimal Adjust Accumulator) instruction for adjusting the result of addition to the BCD number. (See chapter 2 for DAA instruction).

Lab Experiment 60 : Add two 2-digit BCD numbers.

Statement : Add two 2 digit BCD numbers in memory location 2200H and 2201H and store the result in memory location 2300H.

Sample problem :

(2200H) = 39
(2201H) = 45
Result = (2300H) = 39 + 45
= 7E + 6 = 84
(lower nibble is greater than 9 so add 6)

Source program :

```
LXI H, 2200H   ; Initialize pointer
MOV A, M       ; Get the first number
INX H          ; Increment the pointer
ADD M          ; Add two numbers
DAA            ; Convert HEX to valid BCD
```

Flowchart

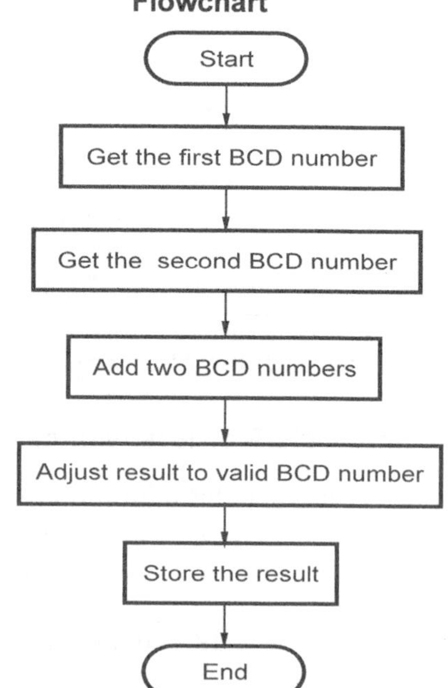

```
STA 2300H      ; Store the result
HLT            ; Terminate program execution
```

Lab Experiment 61 : Add two 4-digit BCD numbers.

Statement : Add two 4 digit BCD numbers in HL and DE register pairs and store result in memory locations, 2300H and 2301H. Ignore carry after 16 bit.

Sample problem :

(HL) = 3629

(DE) = 4738

Flowchart :

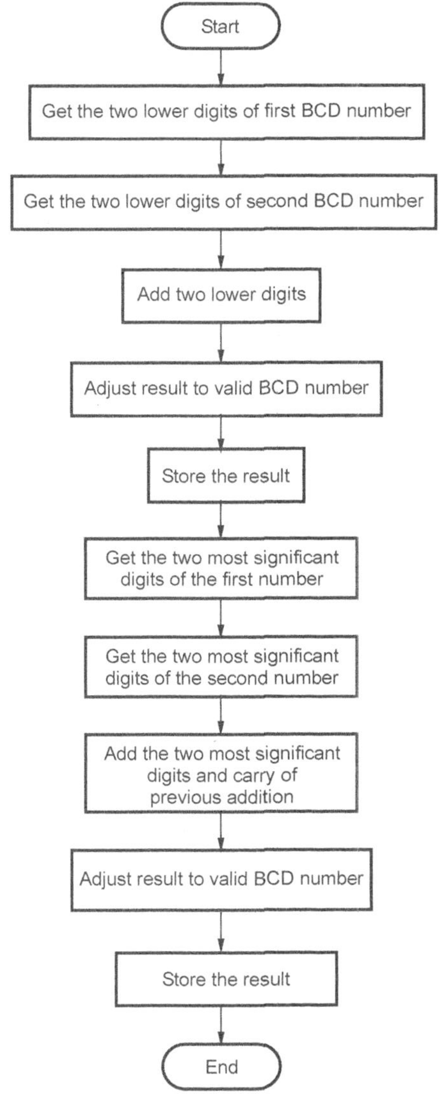

Step 1 : 29 + 38 = 61 and auxiliary carry flag = 1

∴ add 06

61 + 06 = 67

Step 2 : 36 + 47 + 0 (carry of LSB) = 7D

Lower nibble of addition is greater than 9

so add 6.

7D + 06 = 83

∴ Result = 8367

Source program :

```
MOV A, L      ; Get lower 2 digits of no. 1
ADD E         ; Add two lower digits
DAA           ; Adjust result to valid BCD
STA 2300H     ; Store partial result
MOV A, H      ; Get most significant 2 digits of no. 2
ADC D         ; Add two most significant digits
DAA           ; Adjust result to valid BCD
STA 2301H     ; Store partial result
HLT           ; Terminate program execution.
```

3.4.2 BCD Subtraction

When two BCD numbers are subtracted we can use DAA instruction for adjusting result to the BCD. Therefore, the subtraction of BCD number is carried out using 10's complement or 100's complement method.

The 10's complement of a decimal number is equal to the 9's complement plus 1 and the 100's complement of a decimal number is equal to the 99's complement plus 1. The 99's complement of a number can be found by subtracting the number from 99. The steps for 100's complement BCD subtraction are as follows :

- Find the 100's complement of subtrahend.
- Add two numbers using BCD addition.

Let us see the program for subtraction of two BCD numbers.

Lab Experiment 62 : Subtraction of two BCD numbers.

Statement : Subtract the BCD number stored in E register from the number stored in the D register.

Source Program :

```
MVI A,99H
SUB E         ; Find the 99's complement of subtrahend
INR A         ; Find 100's complement of subtrahend
```

```
      ADD D       ; Add minuend to 100's complement of subtrahend
      DAA         ; Adjust for BCD
      HLT         ; Terminate program execution
```

Lab Experiment 63 : Multiply two 2-digit BCD numbers

Statement : Write an assembly language program to multiply 2 BCD numbers

Source Program :

```
         MVI C, Multiplier    ; Load BCD multiplier
         MVI B, 00            ; Initialize counter
         LXI H, 0000H         ; Result = 0000
         MVI E, multiplicand  ; Load multiplicand
         MVI D, 00H           ; Extend to 16-bits
BACK :   DAD D                ; Result ← Result + Multiplicand
         MOV A, L             ; [ Get the lower
         ADI, 00H             ;   byte of the result
         DAA                  ;   Adjust it to BCD and
         MOV L, A             ;   store it]
         MOV A, H             ; [ Get the higher
         ACI, 00H             ;   byte of the result
         DAA                  ;   Adjust it to BCD and
         MOV H, A             ;   store it]
         MOV A, B             ; [ Increment
         ADI 01 H             ;   counter
         DAA                  ;   adjust it to BCD and
         MOV B, A             ;   store it]
         CMP C                ; Compare if count = multiplier
         JNZ BACK             ; if not equal repeat
         HLT                  ; Stop
```

Review Questions

Section 3.1

Q.1 *Explain the loop structure with counting and indexing in 8085 programming.* **May-10, Marks 8**

Q.2 *Write a program to arrange N numbers in ascending order.* **Dec.-05, Marks 8**

Q.3 *Write an assembly language program in 8085 to add N one byte binary numbers stored from location X + 1, where N is stored at location X, store the result in location Y and Y + 1. Display the result in address field.* **June-09, Marks 8**

Q.4 *Write an assembly language program in 8085 to find the maximum number from the given n numbers.* **June-09, Marks 8**

Q.5 *Write an 8085 program to count the number of even and odd numbers in a given set of numbers.* **Dec.-09, Marks 10**

Q.6 *Write an 8085 program to find the largest set of a n 8-bit numbers.* **Dec.-09, Marks 6**

Q.7 *Write an assembly language program for sorting 'n' elements in an array.* **May-10, Marks 8**

Q.8 *Write an assembly program to multiply a number by 8 program using the rotate instruction.* **June-09**

Q.9 *Write an ALP to add 5 data bytes stored in memory locations starting at 4500H and display the sum in next memory location.* **Dec.-10**

Section 3.2

Q.1 *Write a program to count from 0 to 9 with one second delay between each count. At the count of 9, the counter should reset itself to 0 and repeat the sequence continuously. Assume the clock frequency is 1 MHz.* **Dec.-11, Marks 8**

Q.2 *Explain the need of software timers.*

Q.3 *Explain how software delays can be implemented using counters.*

Section 3.3

Q.1 *Why do we need look-up table ?* **Dec.-11, Marks 2**

Q.2 *List the common code conversions required in the microprocessor systems.*

Q.3 *Explain BCD to Binary code conversion technique and write 8085 assembly language program for the same.*

Q.4 *Explain Binary to BCD code conversion technique and write 8085 assembly language program for the same.*

Q.5 *Explain BCD to Seven segment code conversion technique and write 8085 assembly language program for the same.*

Q.6 *Explain Binary to ASCII code conversion technique and write 8085 assembly language program for the same.*

Q.7 *Explain ASCII to Binary code conversion technique and write 8085 assembly language program for the same.*

Section 3.4

Q.1 *Explain the procedure for addition of two BCD numbers.*

Q.2 *Explain the procedure for subtraction of two BCD numbers.*

Two Marks Questions with Answers

Q.1 ***Write an 8085 assembly language program to subtract two 8-bit decimal numbers.*** **Dec-09**

Ans. : Refer Lab experiment 62.

Q.2 ***The last executable instruction in a procedure must be ....*** **Dec.-05**

Ans. : RET

❑❑❑

Notes

4 8085 Interrupts

Contents

Sometimes it is necessary to have microprocessor system which can automatically execute one of the collection of special routines whenever certain condition's exist within a program or in the microprocessor system. For example it is necessary that microprocessor system should give response to devices such as keyboard, sensor and other components when they request for service. When the microprocessor is asked to communicate with devices, we say that the microprocessor is servicing the devices. For example, each time when we type a character on a keyboard, a keyboard service routine is **called**. It transfers the character you typed from the keyboard I/O port into the processor and then to a data buffer in memory.

The interrupt driven I/O is one of the data transfer techniques used in the microprocessor systems. By using this technique, the external device or a peripheral can inform the processor that it is ready for communication. The request for communication informed by the peripheral is of asynchronous type, meaning that it can be initiated at any time without reference to the system clock. These type of requests are of two types : Maskable and Non-maskable. In case of maskable requests, the microprocessor has complete right to either service the requested communication or to deny it.

4.1 Necessity of Interrupts

May/June-06, 09

When you have one or more I/O devices connected to a microprocessor system, any one of them may demand service at any time. The microprocessor can service these devices in one of the two ways. One way is to use the polling routine. The other way is to use an interrupt. In the following section, we will see both ways.

In polling, the microprocessor's software simply checks each of the I/O devices every so often. During this check, the microprocessor tests to see if any device needs servicing. Fig. 4.1 shows the flowchart for polling subroutine.

This is a simple program which services I/O ports A, B, and C. The polling routine checks the status of I/O ports in proper sequence. It first transfers the status of I/O port A into the accumulator. Then the polling routine block checks the contents of accumulator to see if the service request bit is set. If it is, I/O port A service routine is called. After completion of service routine for I/O port A, the polling routine moves on to test port B and the process is repeated. This test and service procedure continues until all the I/O port status registers are tested and all the I/O ports requesting service are serviced. Once this is done, the microprocessor continues to execute the normal programs.

The polling routine assigns priorities to the different I/O devices. Once the polling routine is started, the service request bit at port A is always checked first. Once port A is checked, port B is checked, and then port C. However, the order can be changed by simply changing the polling routine and thus the priorities.

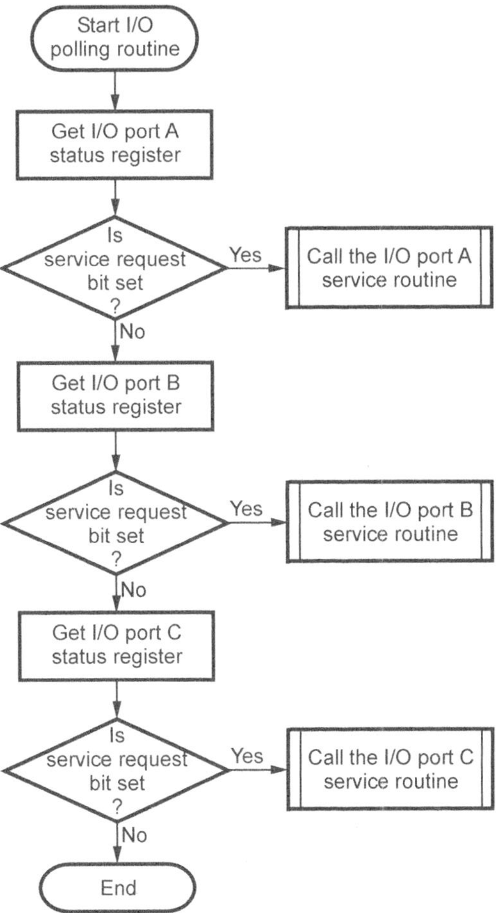

Fig. 4.1 Flowchart for polling routine

A more desirable method would be the one that allows the microprocessor to be executing its main program and only stop to service I/O devices when it is told to do so by the device itself. In effect, the method, would provide an external asynchronous input that would inform the processor that it should complete whatever instruction that is currently being executed and fetch a new routine that will service the requesting device. Once this servicing is completed, the processor would resume exactly where it left off. This method is called **interrupt method**. Before going in detail about the interrupt, we will see the analogy to the interrupt concept.

An analogy to the interrupt concept is the classroom, where the professor will serve as the CPU and the students as I/O ports. The classroom scenario for this interrupt analogy will be such that the professor is busy in writing on the blackboard and delivering his lecture. The student raises his hand when he wants to ask a question (student requesting for service). The professor then completes his sentence and acknowledges student's request by saying "Yes" (Professor acknowledges the interrupt request). After acknowledgement from the professor, student asks the question and professor gives answer to the question (professor services the interrupt) and resumes his respective work.

4.2 8085 Interrupt Structure and Operation

April/May-04, 05, 08, 10; May/June-07, 09; Nov./Dec.-09

4.2.1 Types of Interrupts

The 8085 has multilevel interrupt system. It supports two types of interrupts :

a. Hardware b. Software

Hardware : Some pins on the 8085 allow peripheral device to interrupt the main program for I/O operations. When an interrupt occurs, the 8085 completes the instruction it is currently executing and transfers the program control to a subroutine that services the peripheral device. Upon completion of the service routine, the MPU returns to the main program. These types of interrupts, where MPU pins are used to receive interrupt requests, are called **hardware interrupts**.

Software : In software interrupts, the cause of the interrupt is an execution of the instruction. These are special instructions supported by the microprocessor. After execution of these instructions microprocessor completes the execution of the instruction it is currently executing and transfers the program control to the subroutine program. Upon completion of the execution of the subroutine program, program control returns to the main program.

4.2.2 Overall Interrupt Structure

4.2.2.1 Hardware Interrupts in 8085

The 8085 has five hardware interrupts :

1. TRAP 2. RST 7.5 3. RST 6.5 4. RST 5.5 5. INTR

When any of these pins, except INTR, is active, the internal control circuit of the 8085 produces a CALL to a predetermined memory location. This memory location, where the subroutine starts is referred to as **vector location** and such interrupts are called **vectored interrupts**. The INTR is not a vectored interrupt. It receives the address of the subroutine from the external device.

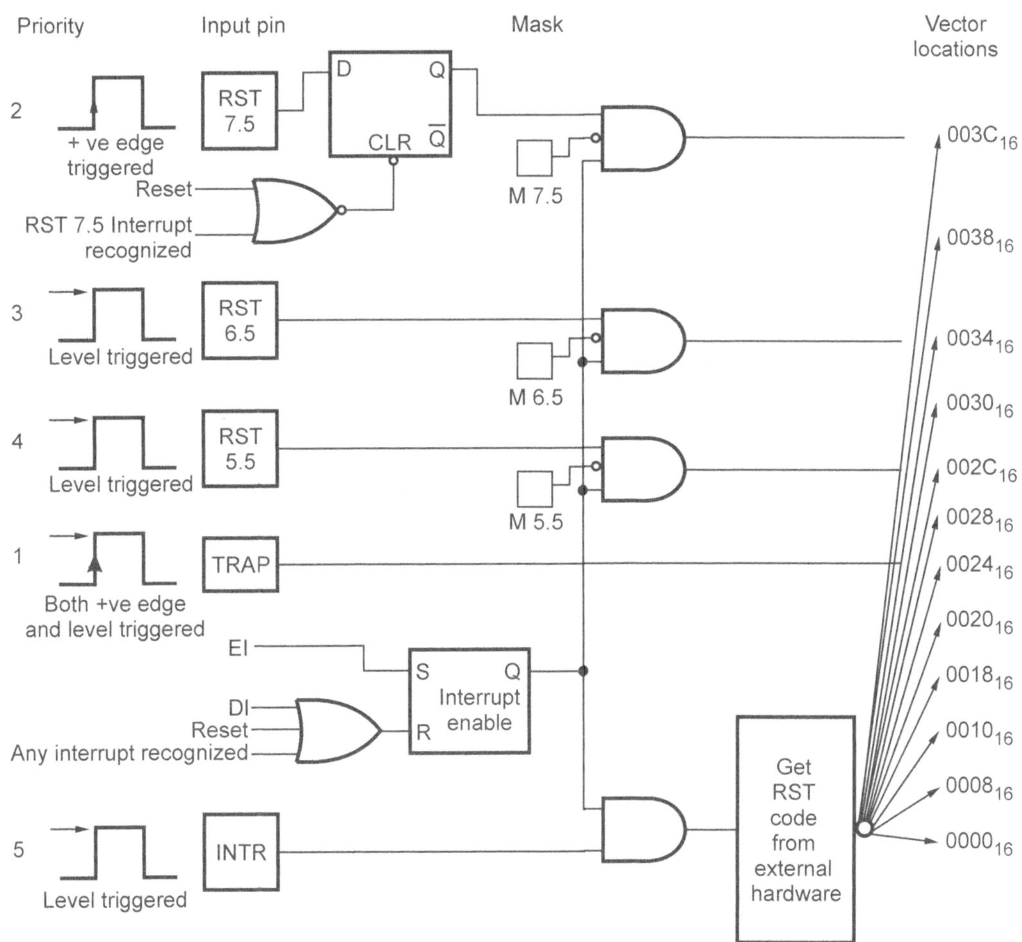

Fig. 4.2 Interrupt structure of 8085

In 8085, all interrupts except TRAP are maskable. When logic signal is applied to a maskable interrupt input, the 8085 is interrupted only if that particular input is enabled. These interrupts can be enabled or disabled under program control. If disabled, 8085 disables an interrupt request. The interrupt TRAP is non-maskable which means that it is not maskable by program control. The Fig. 4.2 shows the interrupt structure of 8085. The figure indicates that, the 8085 is designed to respond to edge triggering, level triggering or both.

TRAP : This interrupt is a non-maskable interrupt. It is unaffected by any mask or interrupt enable. TRAP has the highest priority. TRAP interrupt is edge and level triggered. This means that the TRAP must go high and remain high until it is acknowledged. This avoids false triggering caused by noise and transients.

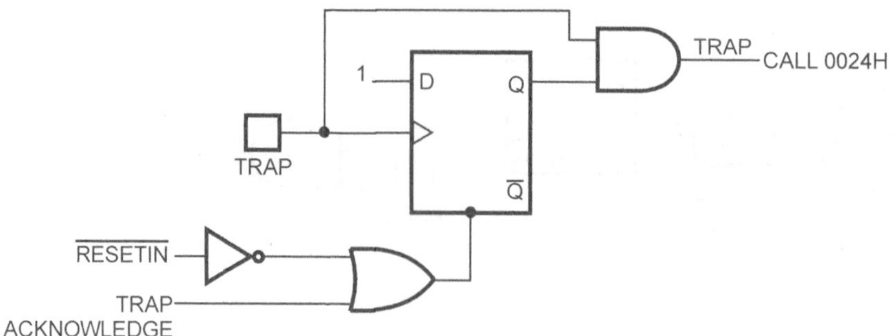

Fig. 4.3 Interrupt circuit for trap interrupt

As shown in the Fig. 4.3, the positive edge of TRAP signal sets the D flip-flop. However, due to the AND gate, it is necessary to sustain high level on the TRAP input. **There are two ways to clear TRAP interrupt :**

1. By resetting microprocessor i.e. giving a low signal on $\overline{\text{RESETIN}}$ pin (External signal).
2. By giving a high TRAP ACKNOWLEDGE (Internal signal).

After recognition of TRAP interrupt, 8085 internally generates a high TRAP ACKNOWLEDGE which clears the flip-flop. Once the TRAP is acknowledged, the 8085 completes its current instruction. It then pushes the address of the next instruction i.e. return address onto the stack and loads PC with the fixed vector address 0024H. Due to this, 8085 starts execution of instructions from address 0024H which is the starting address of an interrupt service routine for TRAP.

RST 7.5 : The RST 7.5 interrupt is a maskable interrupt. It has the second highest priority. As shown in Fig. 4.2, it is **positive edge triggered** and the positive edge trigger is stored internally by the D flip-flop until it is cleared by software reset using SIM instruction or by internally generated ACKNOWLEDGE signal.

The positive edge signal on the RST 7.5 pin sets the D flip-flop. If the mask bit M 7.5 is 0 i.e. RST 7.5 is unmasked then 8085 completes its current instruction. It then pushes the address of the next instruction onto the stack and loads PC with the fixed vector address 003CH. Due to this, 8085 starts execution of instructions from address 003CH which is the starting address of an interrupt service routine for RST 7.5.

RST 6.5 and RST 5.5 : The RST 6.5 and RST 5.5 both are **level triggered**. These interrupts can be masked using SIM instruction. The RST 6.5 has the third priority whereas RST 5.5 has the fourth priority. The vector addresses of RST 6.5 and RST 5.5 are 0034H and 002CH respectively. After recognition of RST 6.5 or RST 5.5 interrupt, 8085 completes its current instruction; pushes the address of next instruction onto the stack and loads PC with corresponding vector address.

INTR : INTR is a maskable interrupt, but not the vector interrupt. It has the lowest priority. The following sequence of events occur when INTR signal goes high.

1. The 8085 checks the status of INTR signal during execution of each instruction.
2. If INTR signal is high, then 8085 completes its current instruction and sends an active low interrupt acknowledge signal ($\overline{\text{INTA}}$) if the interrupt is enabled.

3. In response to the $\overline{INTA}$ signal, external logic places an instruction OPCODE on the data bus. In the case of multibyte instruction, additional interrupt acknowledge machine cycles are generated by the 8085 to transfer the additional bytes into the microprocessor.
4. On receiving the instruction, the 8085 saves the address of next instruction on stack and executes received instruction.

Note : Theoretically, the external logic can place any instruction code on the data bus in response to the $\overline{INTA}$. However, only CALL and RST codes save the contents of the PC on the stack and branch program control to the subroutine address.

Response for RST instruction : If the external device places an opcode for any one of the RST instruction (RST 0 - RST 7), then 8085 pushes the contents of PC onto the stack. It then branches the program control to the vector address of the corresponding RST instruction.

Response for CALL instruction : If the external device places an opcode for CALL instruction then 8085 generates two additional interrupt acknowledge cycles.

1. It sends an active low interrupt acknowledge signal second time.
2. In response to second $\overline{INTA}$ signal, external logic places the lower byte address for the CALL instruction.
3. After receiving lower byte address, 8085 sends the third interrupt acknowledge signal.
4. In response to third $\overline{INTA}$ signal, external logic places the higher byte address for the CALL instruction.
5. After receiving sixteen bit address for CALL, 8085 pushes the contents of the PC onto the stack and branches the program control to the subroutine whose address is received from the external logic.

Example : The Fig. 4.4 shows the diagram of external logic that gives the RST 7 instruction opcode on interrupt acknowledge.

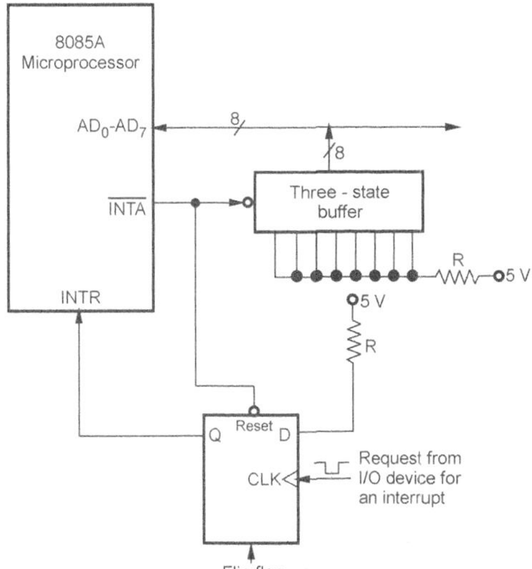

Fig. 4.4 External logic that gives the RST 7 instruction opcode

External logic controls a tri-state buffer with the $\overline{INTA}$ signal in order to place an opcode for RST 7 instruction. The $\overline{INTA}$ signal from the microprocessor is used as an Output Enable signal for the buffer as well as reset signal for D flip flop. The request from the I/O device is routed through the D flip-flop to the INTR. The D flip flop is used to hold the INTR signal high until 8085 gives interrupt acknowledge signal. The $\overline{INTA}$ signal that is generated enables the tri-state buffer whose data inputs are hardwired to the value equal to the opcode for RST 7 (FFH) instruction. The 8085 receives this opcode during interrupt acknowledge cycle. After receiving the opcode 8085 pushes the contents of program counter onto the stack, thus saving the return address. It then branches the program control to the address 0038H (Vector address of RST 7). Table 4.1 shows the summary of hardware interrupts in 8085.

Interrupt type	Trigger	Priority	Maskable	Vector address
TRAP	Edge and Level	1st (Highest)	No	0024H
RST 7.5	Edge	2nd	Yes	003CH
RST 6.5	Level	3rd	Yes	0034H
RST 5.5	Level	4th	Yes	002CH
INTR	Level	5th (Lowest)	Yes	-

Table 4.1

4.2.2.2 Software Interrupts in 8085

The 8085 has eight software interrupts from RST 0 to RST 7. The vector address for these interrupts can be calculated as follows :

Interrupt number $\times$ 8 = Vector address

For example :

$5 \times 8 = 40 = 28H$

$\therefore$ Vector address for interrupt RST 5 is 0028H.

The Table 4.2 shows the vector addresses of all interrupts.

Instruction	HEX code	Vector Address
RST 0	C7	0000H
RST 1	CF	0008H
RST 2	D7	0010H
RST 3	DF	0018H
RST 4	E7	0020H
RST 5	EF	0028H
RST 6	F7	0030H
RST 7	FF	0038H

Table 4.2 Vector addresses for software interrupts

4.2.3 Masking / Unmasking of Interrupts

As mentioned earlier, maskable interrupts are enabled and disabled under program control. In this section we will see how interrupts can be masked or unmasked using program control. There are four instructions used for control of interrupts :

1. EI
2. DI
3. RIM
4. SIM

EI : Enable Interrupt

The EI instruction sets the interrupt enable flip-flop, as shown in Fig. 4.2. Thus RST 7.5, RST 6.5, RST 5.5 and INTR are enabled using EI instruction.

It is important to note that when any interrupt is acknowledged, interrupt enable flip-flop resets and disables all interrupts. To enable interrupt in further process it is necessary to execute EI instruction within interrupt service routine.

DI : Disable Interrupt

The DI instruction resets the interrupt enable flip-flop, as shown in Fig. 4.2. Thus it disables RST 7.5, RST 6.5, RST 5.5 and INTR interrupts.

SIM : Set Interrupt Mask

This instruction is used to set interrupt mask and to send serial output. It transfers the contents of accumulator to interrupt control logic and serial I/O port. Thus it is necessary to load appropriate contents in the accumulator before execution of SIM instruction.

4.2.4 Pending Interrupts

The Read Interrupt Mask, RIM, instruction loads the status of the interrupt mask, the pending interrupts and the contents of the serial input data line, SID, into the accumulator. Thus, it is possible to monitor status of interrupt mask, pending interrupts and serial input. There are number of interrupts. When one interrupt is being serviced, other interrupt requests may occur. If the interrupt requests are of higher priority, 8085 branches program control to the requested interrupt service routines. But when the interrupt requests are of lower priority, 8085 stores the information about these interrupt requests. Such interrupts are called **pending interrupts**. The status of pending interrupts can be monitored using RIM instruction.

Example 1 : Write a program to display real time clock. Assume that a periodic signal is interrupting RST 7.5 signal after every 0.5 seconds.

Main program

```
        MVI C, 00H      ; Initialize counter
        LXI H, 0000H    ; Initialize seconds, and minutes
        MVI D, 00H      ; Initialize hours
        MVI A, 0BH      ;
        SIM             ;
        EI              ; Enable RST 7.5 interrupt
HERE  : JMP HERE        ; Wait for interrupt.
```

ISR - Interrupt Service Routine

```
        INR C           ; Increment counter
        MOV A, C
        CPI, 02H
        JNZ LAST        ; Check for 1 second
        MVI C, 00H      ; Reset counter
        MOV A, L        ; Get seconds counter
        ADI 01H         ; Increment seconds counter
        DAA             ; Adjust for BCD
        MOV L, A        ; Save seconds counter
        CPI 60H         ; check for 60 seconds
        JNZ LAST        ; if not 60, goto display
        MVI L, 00H      ; reset seconds counter
        MOV A, H        ; Get minutes counter
        ADI 01H         ; Increment minutes counter
        DAA             ; Adjust for BCD
        MOV H, A        ; save minutes counter
        CPI 60H         ; check for 60 minutes
        JNZ LAST        ; if not 60, goto display
        MVI H, 00H      ; reset minutes counter
        MOV A, D        ; Get hours counter
        ADI 01H         ; increment hours counter
        DAA             ; Adjust for BCD
        MOV D, A        ; save hours counter
        CPI 24 H        ; Check for 24 hours
        JNZ LAST        ; If not 24, goto display
        MVI D, 00H      ; Reset hours counter
LAST  : CALL DISPLAY    ; Call display subroutine
        EI              ; Enable Interrupt
        RET             ; Return to main program
```

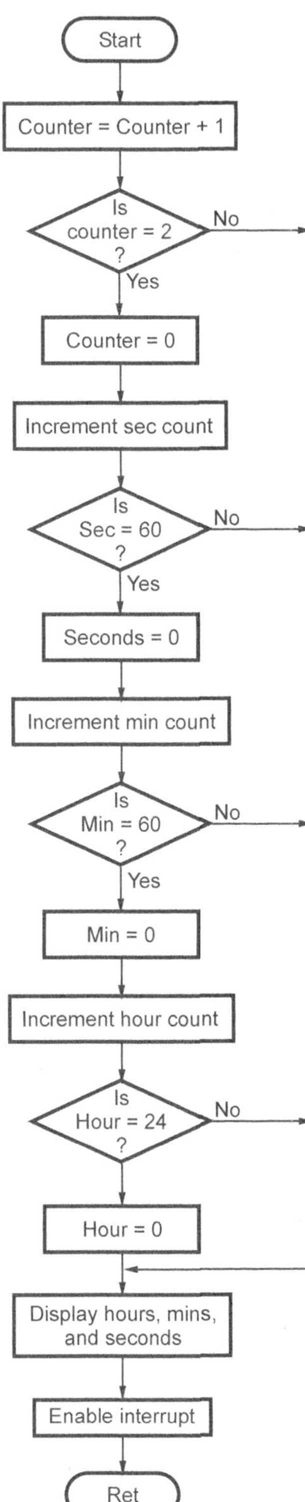

Fig. 4.5 Flowchart for interrupt subroutine

Review Questions

Section 4.1

Q.1 *What are interrupts ?* **June-09, Marks 2**

Q.2 *Explain the term polling with suitable example.*

Section 4.2

Q.1 *Explain the 8085 interrupts system in detail.* **May-04, Marks 10**

Q.2 *Write short notes on vectored interrupts of 8085.* **June-07, Marks 8**

Q.3 *With necessary diagrams, write short note on interrupt structure of 8085.* **May-08,10, Dec.-11, Marks 6**

Q.4 *Discuss the interrupts of 8085.* **Dec-09, May-12, Marks 10**

Q.5 *What is TRAP interrupt and its significance ?* **June-12, Marks 2**

Two Marks Questions with Answers

Q.1 ***What is meant by polling?***

Ans. : Polling or device polling is a process which identifies the device that has interrupted the microprocessor.

Q.2 ***What is interrupt ?*** **June-06**

Ans. : Interrupt is an external signal that causes a microprocessor to jump to a specific subroutine.

Q.3 ***Differentiate between software and hardware interrupts.*** **May-04, June-09**

Ans. : The type of interrupts where microprocessor pins are used to receive interrupt requests, are called **hardware interrupts**. In **software interrupts**, the cause of the interrupt is an execution of the instruction. These are special instructions supported by the microprocessor. After execution of these instructions microprocessor completes the execution of the instruction it is currently executing and transfers the program control to the subroutine program.

Q.4 ***Name the vectored and nonvectored interrupt of 8085 system.*** **May-05**

Ans. : Vectored interrupt of 8085 are : RST0 - RST7, TRAP, RS7.5, R6.5 and RST 5.5. The only nonvectored interrupt of 8085 system is INTR.

Q.5 ***What are all the hardware interrupts ?*** **June-09**

Ans. : Refer section 4.2.

❑❑❑

5 8085 Timing Diagrams

Contents

We have seen the instruction set of the 8085 microprocessor. For clear understanding of the each instruction, it is necessary to see how microprocessor executes these instructions, which signals are activated to execute a particular instruction and at what instant. All this information can be plotted graphically. The graphical representation of the instruction execution in steps with respect to the time (clock signal) is called **'timing diagram.'**

In this chapter, we will first see what do we mean by instruction cycle, machine cycles and T- states. After clear understanding of these things we will see the rules and standards used in the timing diagrams and then we will see the timing diagrams of all 8085 instructions.

5.1 Instruction Cycle, Machine Cycle and T-State April/May-08, Nov./Dec.-09

During normal operation, the microprocessor sequentially fetches, decodes and executes one instruction after another until a halt instruction () is executed. The fetching, decoding and execution of a single instruction constitutes an **instruction cycle**, which consists of one to five read or write operations between processor and memory or input/output devices. Each memory or I/O operation requires a particular time period, called **machine cycle**. In other words, to move byte of data in or out of the microprocessor, a machine cycle is required. Each machine cycle consists of 3 to 6 clock periods/cycles, referred to as **T-states**. Therefore we can say that, one instruction cycle consists of one to five machine cycles and one machine cycle consists of three to six T- states i.e. three to six clock periods, as shown in the Fig. 5.1.

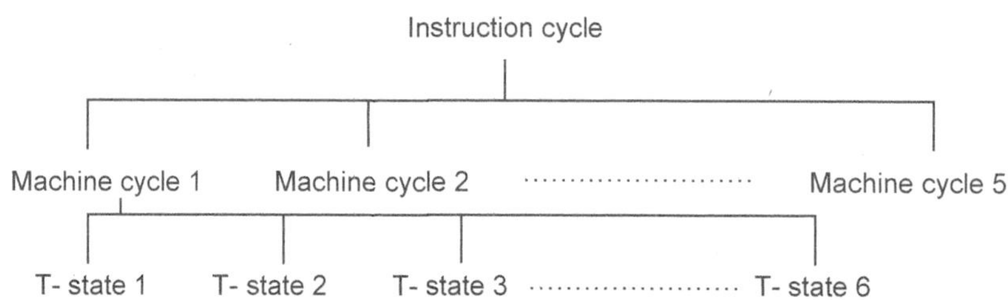

Fig. 5.1 Relation between instruction cycle, machine cycle and T-state

There are seven different types of machine cycles in the 8085A. Three status signals $IO/\overline{M}$, S_1 and S_0 identify each type as shown in Table 5.1. These signals are generated at the beginning of each machine cycle and remain valid for the duration of the cycle.

Machine cycle	Status			Control		
	$IO/\overline{M}$	S_1	S_0	$\overline{RD}$	$\overline{WR}$	INTA
Opcode Fetch	0	1	1	0	1	1
Memory Read	0	1	0	0	1	1
Memory Write	0	0	1	1	0	1
I/O Read	1	1	0	0	1	1
I/O Write	1	0	1	1	0	1
INTR Acknowledge	1	1	1	1	1	0
Bus Idle	0	0	0	1	1	1

Table 5.1 8085 machine cycles

5.2 Representation of Signals

Before going to see the timing diagram, we will see the signals and its representation used in the timing diagrams.

Clock Signal :

The 8085 divides the clock frequency provided at x_1 and x_2 inputs by 2, which is called **operating frequency**. All the operations within the 8085 are synchronized with this operating frequency. Therefore in the timing diagram operating frequency clock is shown on the top and then the signals are shown with reference to operating frequency clock. Ideally, the clock signal should be square wave with zero rise time and fall time, as shown in the Fig. 5.2. But in practice, we do not get zero rise time and fall time. Therefore the clock and other signals are always shown with finite rise and fall times. Fig. 5.2 shows the practical way of representing clock signal.

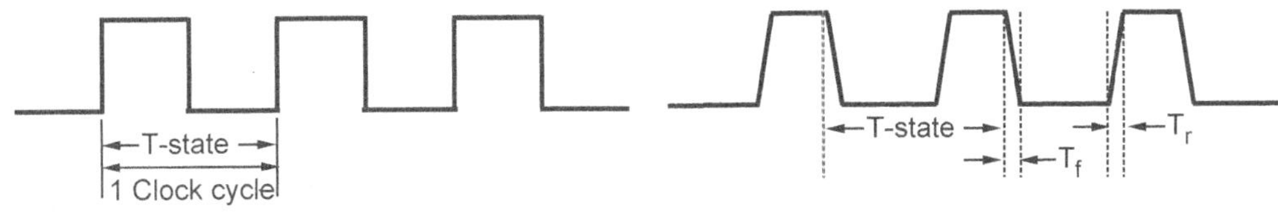

(a) Ideal **(b) Practical**

Fig. 5.2 Clock signal representation

Single Signal :

Single signal is represented by a line. It may have status either logic 0 or logic 1 or tri-state. The change in the state of the signal takes finite time and hence the state change of signal is represented with finite rise time and fall time, as shown in the Fig. 5.3.

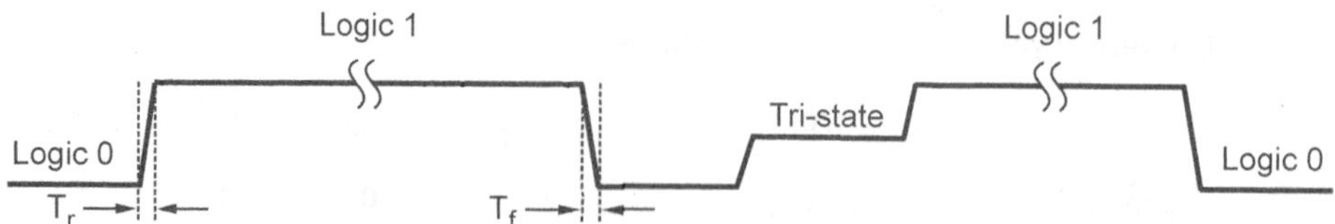

Fig. 5.3 Single signal representation

Group of Signals :

Group of signals is also called a bus e.g. address bus and data bus. To avoid complications in the timing diagram these signals are grouped and shown in the form of block as shown in Fig. 5.4.

Fig. 5.4 Group of signals representation

In the group representation individual state is not considered, but the group state is considered. Change in state of single signal changes the state of group. It is represented by the cross as shown the Fig. 5.4. The tri-state condition of the group signals is shown by dotted lines. Two straight lines represent valid state/stable state.

In microprocessor systems, activation of signal/signals depends on the state of other signal/signals. Such situations are shown in the timing diagrams with the help of specific symbols. There are four possibilities :

Activation of a signal with the change in state of other signal.

Activation of a signal with the change in state of other signals.

Activation of signals with the change in state of other signal.

Activation of signals with the change in state of other signals.

Fig. 5.5 shows the representation of dependence of the signal/signals, in the timing diagram.

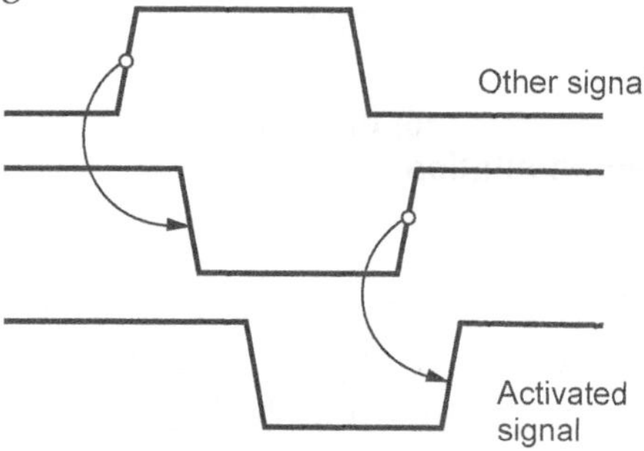

(a) Activation of a signal with the change in state of other signal

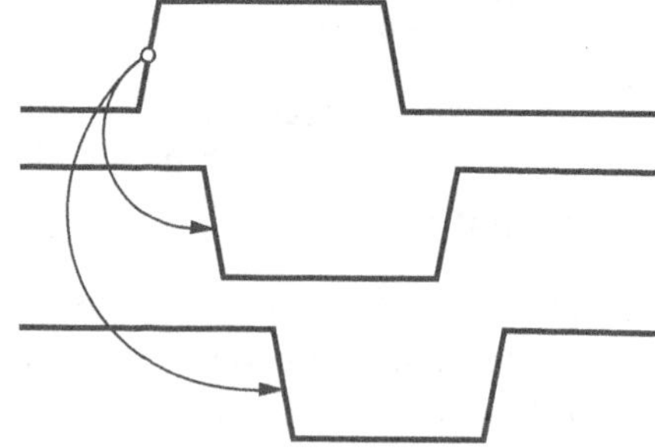

(b) Activation of signals with the change in state of other signal

Fig. 5.5

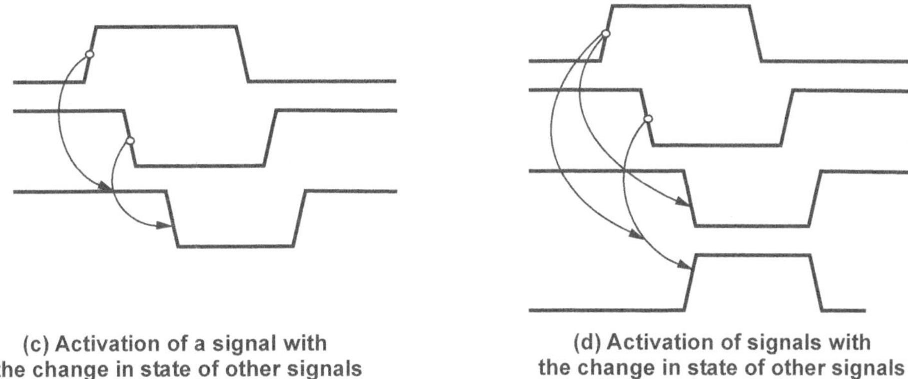

(c) Activation of a signal with the change in state of other signals

(d) Activation of signals with the change in state of other signals

Fig. 5.5

5.3 Signal Timings

In 8085 microprocessor, signals are activated at specific instant for specific time period. Once we understand this, it is very easy to draw timing diagrams. The following section explains when the signals are activated and for what period they remain in active state.

ALE (Address Latch Enable) :

This signal is active high signal. It is activated in the beginning of the T_1-state of each machine cycle, except bus idle machine cycle and it remains active in the T_1-state as shown in the Fig. 5.6.

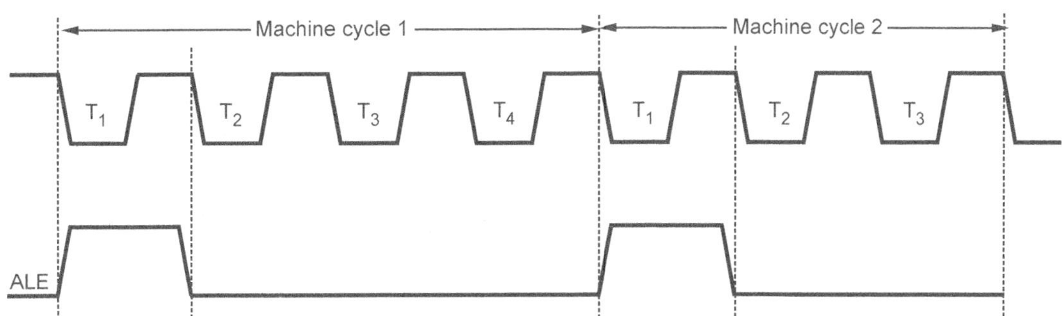

Fig. 5.6 ALE activation and its period

A_0 - A_7 (Lower byte address) :

The lower byte of address is available on the multiplexed address/data bus (AD_0-AD_7) during T_1-state of each machine cycle, except bus idle machine cycle, as shown in Fig. 5.7.

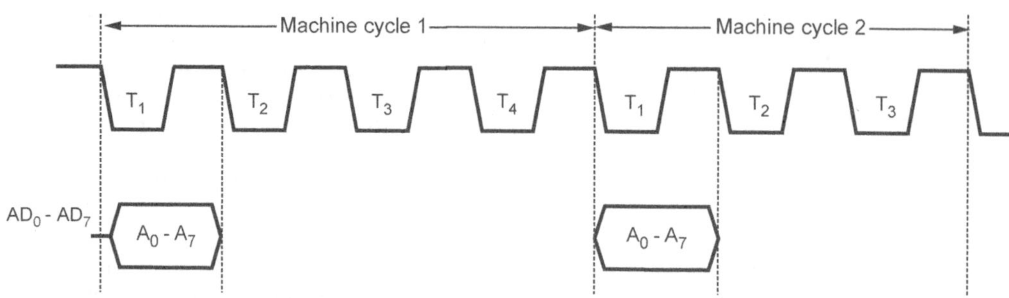

Fig. 5.7 Lower address on the multiplexed bus

D_0 - D_7 (Data bus) :

The data from memory or I/O device and from microprocessor to memory or I/O device is transferred during T_2 and T_3 - states. It is important to note that in read machine cycle, data will appear on the data bus during the later part of the T_2 - state, as shown in the Fig. 5.8, whereas in write cycle data will appear on the data bus at the beginning of the T_2 - state, as shown in the Fig. 5.8.

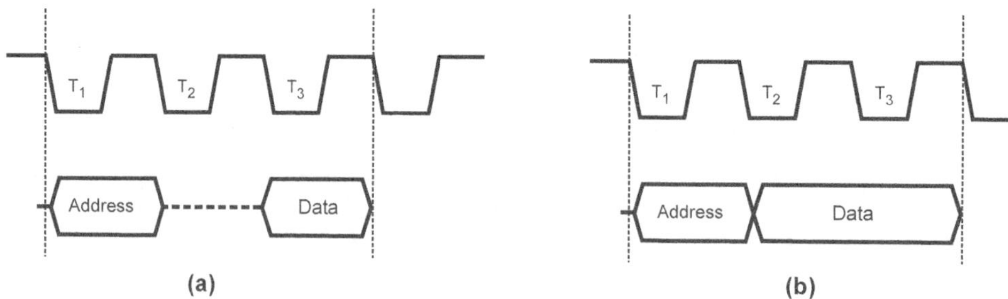

Fig. 5.8 Data bus

To read data from memory or I/O device it is necessary to select memory or I/O device. After selection, device will put the data from selected location on the data bus. This action needs finite time. This time is referred to as **'access time'**. In case of write cycle, data is available in the register set of the microprocessor and it can put that data on the data bus with zero access time.

A_8 - A_{15} (Higher byte address) :

The higher byte of address is available on the A_8 - A_{15} bus during T_1, T_2 and T_3 - state of each machine cycle, except bus idle machine cycle, as shown in Fig. 5.9.

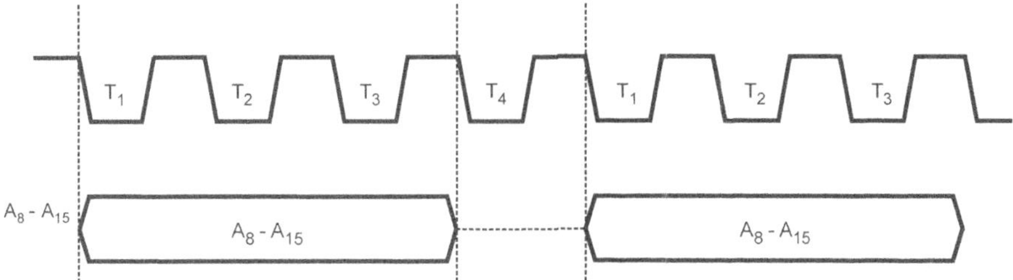

Fig. 5.9 Higher byte address on A_8 - A_{15}

IO/$\overline{M}$, S_0, S_1 :

These signals are called status signals. They decide the type of machine cycle to be executed. They are activated at the beginning of T_1 - state of each machine cycle and remain active till the end of the machine cycle.

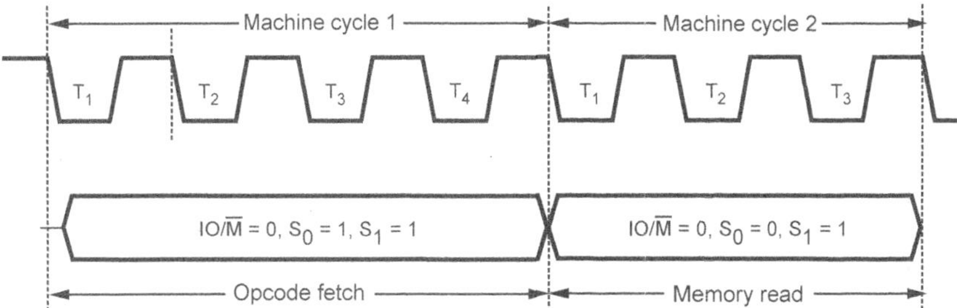

Fig. 5.10 Status signals

$\overline{RD}$ and $\overline{WR}$: These signals decide the direction of the data transfer. When $\overline{RD}$ signal is active, data is transmitted from memory or I/O device to the microprocessor and when $\overline{WR}$ signal is active, data is transmitted from microprocessor to the memory or I/O device. Both signals are never active at a time.

As we know data transfer in 8085 takes place during T_2 and T_3, these signals are activated during T_2 and T_3, as shown in the Fig. 5.11.

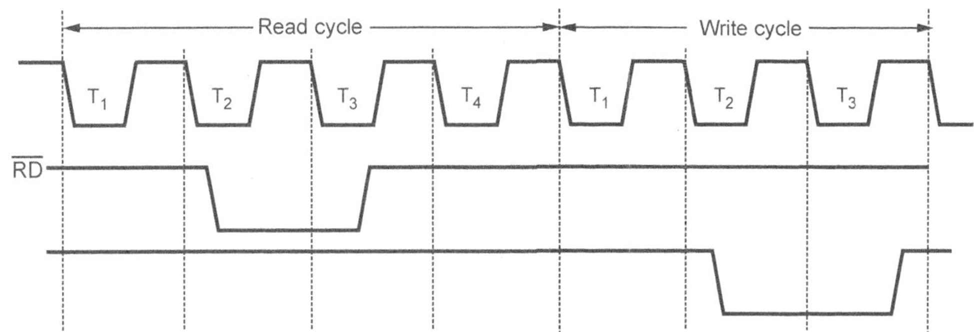

Fig. 5.11 $\overline{RD}$ and $\overline{WR}$ signals

5.4 8085 Machine Cycles and their Timings

April/May-04, Nov./Dec.-05

The 8085 has seven machine cycles. These are :

1. Opcode Fetch
2. Memory Read
3. Memory Write
4. I/O Read
5. I/O Write
6. Interrupt Acknowledge
7. Bus Idle.

1. Opcode fetch cycle

The first machine cycle of every instruction is opcode fetch cycle in which the 8085 finds the nature of the instruction to be executed. In this machine cycle, processor places the contents of the Program Counter on the address lines and through the read process, reads the opcode of the instruction. Fig. 5.12 (a) (See Fig. 5.12 (a) and (b) on next page) shows flow of data (opcode) from memory to the microprocessor and Fig. 5.12 (b) shows the timing diagram for opcode fetch machine cycle. The length of this cycle is not fixed. It varies from 4T-states to 6T-states as per the instruction. The following section describes the opcode fetch cycle in step by step manner.

Step 1 : (State T_1) In T_1-state, the 8085 places the contents of program counter on the address bus. The high-order byte of the PC is placed on the A_8-A_{15} lines. The low-order byte of the PC is placed on the AD_0 - AD_7 lines which stays on only during T_1. Thus microprocessor activates ALE (Address Latch Enable) which is used to latch the low-order byte of the address in external latch before it disappears.

In T_1, 8085 also sends status signals $IO/\overline{M}$, S_1 and S_0. $IO/\overline{M}$ specifies whether it is a memory or I/O operation, S_1 status specifies whether it is read/write operation; S_1 and S_0 together indicate read, write, opcode fetch, machine cycle operation or whether it is in HALT state. In opcode fetch machine cycle status signals are : $IO/\overline{M} = 0$, $S_1 = 1$, $S_0 = 1$.

Step 2 : (State T_2) In T_2, low-order address disappears from the AD_0 - AD_7 lines. (However A_0 - A_7 remain available as they were latched during T_1). In T_2, 8085 sends $\overline{RD}$ signal low to enable the addressed memory location. The memory device then places the contents of addressed memory location on the data bus (AD_0 - AD_7).

Step 3 : (State T_3) During T_3, 8085 loads the data from the data bus in its Instruction Register and raises $\overline{RD}$ to high which disables the memory device.

Step 4 : (State T_4) In T_4, microprocessor decodes the opcode and on the basis of the instruction received, it decides whether to enter state T_5 or to enter state T_1 of the next

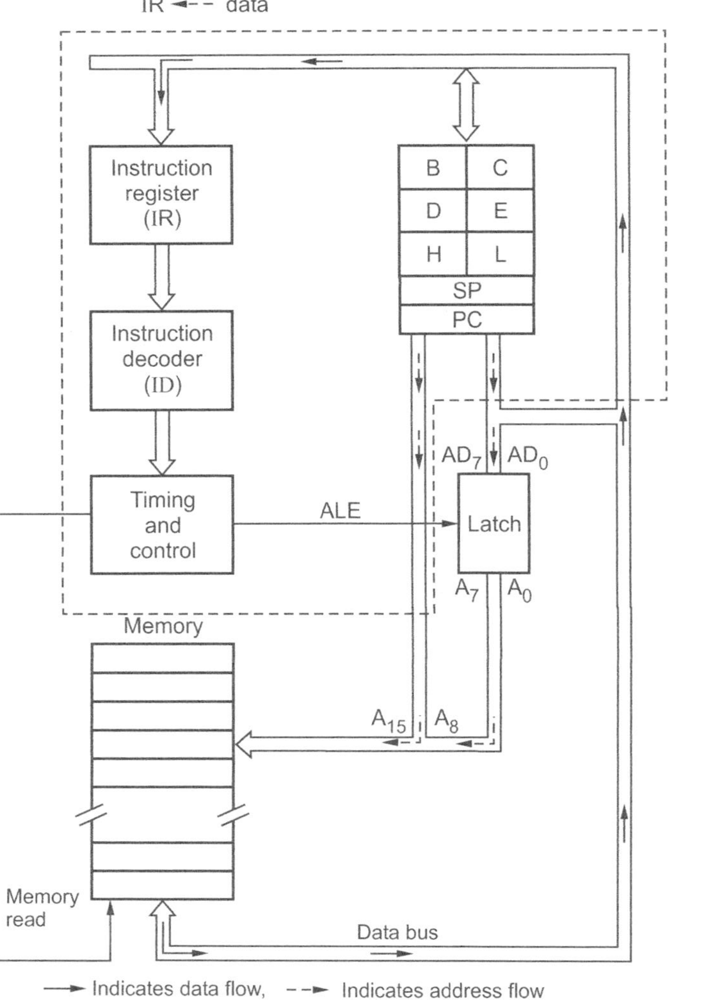

Fig. 5.12 (a) Data (opcode) flow from memory to micrprocessor

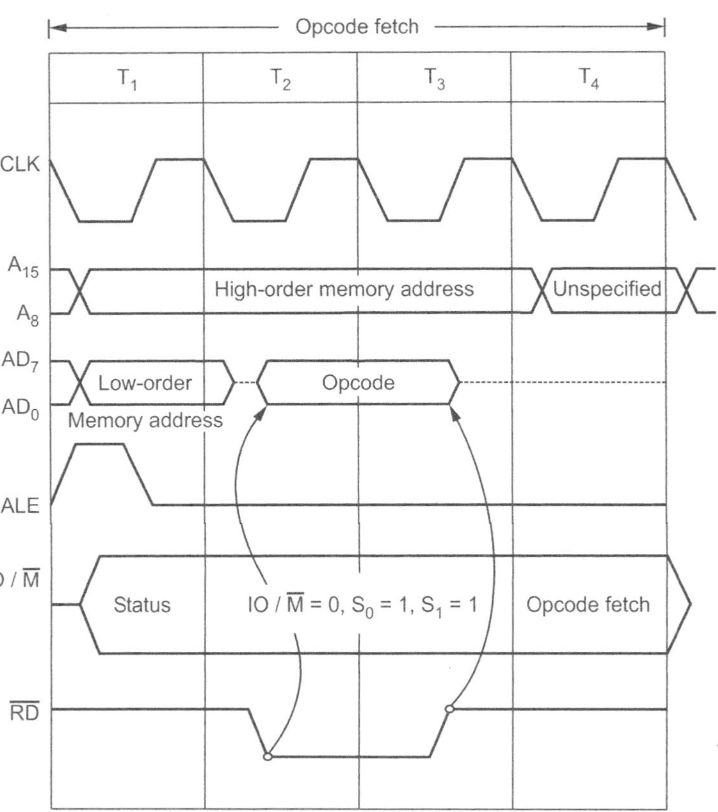

Fig. 5.12 (b) Opcode fetch machine cycle

machine cycle. One byte instructions those operate on eight bit data (8-bit operand) are executed in T_4.

For example : MOV A, B, ANA D, ADD B, INR L, DCR C, RAL and many more.

Note : For one byte instructions which operate on eight bit data, data is always available in the internal memory of 8085 i.e. registers.

Step 5 : (States T_5 and T_6) States T_5 and T_6, when entered, are used for internal microprocessor operations required by the instruction. During T_5 and T_6, 8085 performs stack write, internal 16-bit, and conditional return operations depending upon the type of instruction. One byte instructions those operate on sixteen bit data (16-bit operand) are executed in T_5 and T_6. For example : DCX H, PCHL, SPHL, INX H etc.

2. Memory read cycle

The 8085 executes the memory read cycle to read the contents of R/W memory or ROM. The length of this machine cycle is 3T-states (T_1 - T_3). In this machine cycle, processor places the address on the address lines from the stack pointer, general purpose register pair or program counter and through the read process, reads the data from the addressed memory location. Fig. 5.13 (a) (See Fig. 5.13 (a) and (b) on next page) shows flow of data from memory to the microprocessor and Fig. 5.13 (b) shows the timing diagram for memory read machine cycle. Memory read machine cycle is similar to the opcode fetch machine cycle. However, they use only states T_1 to T_3 and the status signal values ($IO/\overline{M}$ = 0, S_1 = 1, S_0 = 0) appropriate for memory read machine cycle are issued in T_1. The following section describes the memory read machine cycle in step by step manner.

Step 1 : (State T_1) In T_1-state, microprocessor places the address on the address lines from stack pointer, general purpose register pair or program counter and activates ALE signal in order to latch low-order byte of address.

During T_1, 8085 sends status signals : $IO/\overline{M}$ = 0, S_1 = 1 and S_0 = 0 for memory read machine cycle.

Step 2 : (State T_2) In T_2, 8085 sends $\overline{RD}$ signal low to enable the addressed memory location. The memory device then places the contents of addressed memory location on the data bus (AD_0 - AD_7).

Step 3 : (State T_3) During T_3, 8085 loads the data from the data bus into specified register (F, A, B, C, D, E, H and L) and raises $\overline{RD}$ to high which disables the memory device.

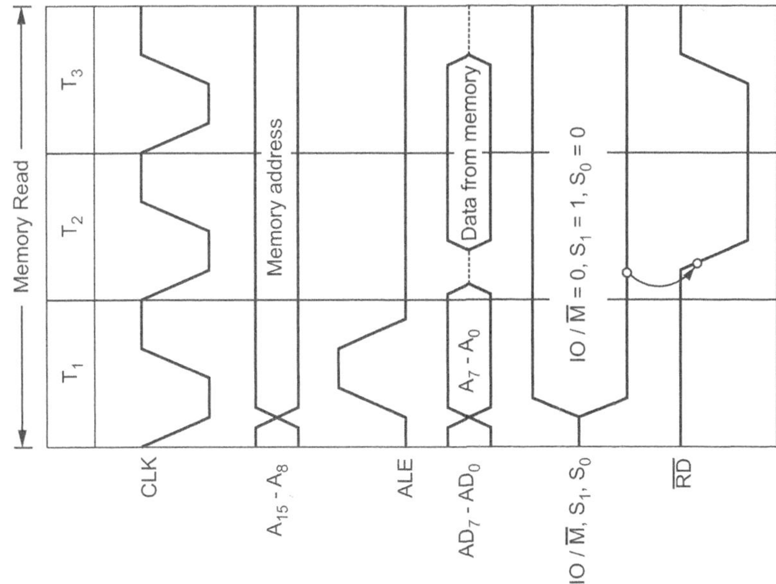

Fig. 5.13 (b) Memory read machine cycle

→ Indicates data flow, - -→ Indicates address flow

Fig. 5.13 (a) Data flow from memory to microprocessor

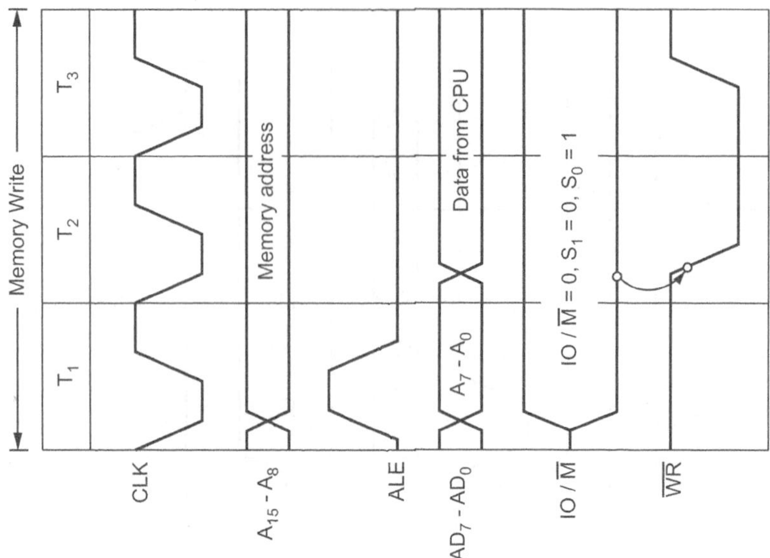

Fig. 5.14 (b) Memory write machine cycle

→ Indicates data flow, - - → Indicates address flow

Fig. 5.14 (a) Data flow microprocessor to memory

3. Memory write cycle

The 8085 executes the memory write cycle to store the data into data memory or stack memory. The length of this machine cycle is 3T-states (T_1 - T_3). In this machine cycle, processor places the address on the address lines from the stack pointer or general purpose register pair and through the write process, stores the data into the addressed memory location. Fig. 5.14 (See Fig. 5.14 on previous page) shows the timing diagram for memory write machine cycle. The memory write timing diagram is similar to the memory read timing diagram, except that instead of $\overline{RD}$, $\overline{WR}$ signal goes low during T_2 and T_3. The status signals for memory write cycle are : $IO/\overline{M} = 0$, $S_1 = 0$, $S_0 = 1$. The following section describes the memory write machine cycle in step by step manner.

Step 1 : (State T_1) In T_1-state, the 8085 places the address on the address lines from stack pointer or general purpose register pair and activates ALE signal in order to latch low-order byte of address. During T_1, 8085 sends status signals :

$IO/\overline{M} = 0$, $S_1 = 0$ and $S_0 = 1$ for memory write machine cycle.

Step 2 : (State T_2) In T_2, 8085 places data on the data bus and sends $\overline{WR}$ signal low for writing into the addressed memory location.

Step 3 : (State T_3) During T_3, $\overline{WR}$ signal goes high, which disables the memory device and terminates the write operation.

4, 5. I/O read and I/O write cycles

The I/O read and I/O write machine cycles are similar to the memory read and memory write machine cycles, respectively, except that the $IO/\overline{M}$ signal is high for I/O read and I/O write machine cycles. High $IO/\overline{M}$ signal indicates that it is an I/O operation. Fig. 5.15 (b) and Fig. 5.16 (b) shows the timing diagrams for I/O read and I/O write cycles, respectively.

6. Interrupt acknowledge cycle

In response to INTR signal, 8085 executes interrupt acknowledge machine cycle to read an instruction from the external device. Theoretically, the external device can place any instruction on the data bus in response to $\overline{INTA}$. However, only RST and CALL, save the PC contents (return address) before transferring control to the interrupt service routine. The next sections explain interrupt acknowledge cycles for RST and CALL instructions.

→ Indicates data flow, - - → Indicates address flow

Fig. 5.15 (a) Data flow from input device to microprocessor

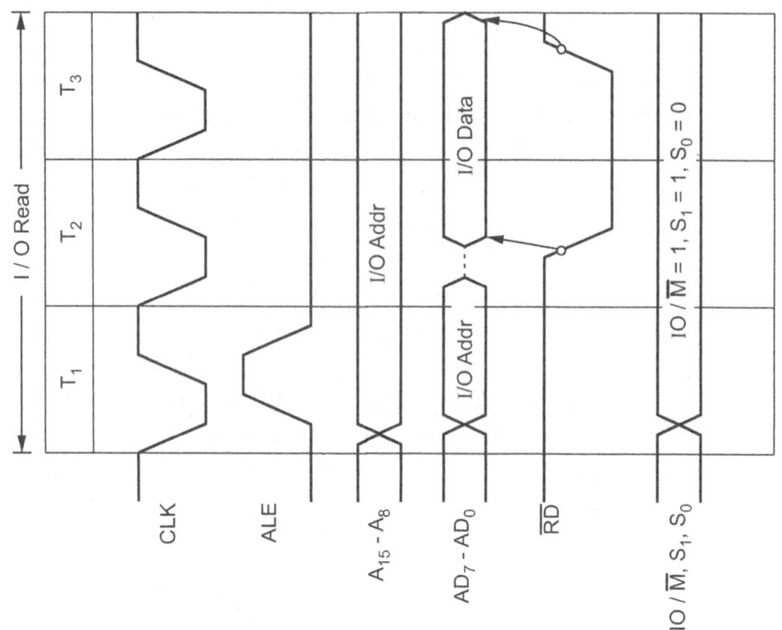

Fig. 5.15 (b) I/O read memory cycle

— Indicates data flow, - - → Indicates address flow

Fig. 5.16 (a) Data flow from microprocessor to output device

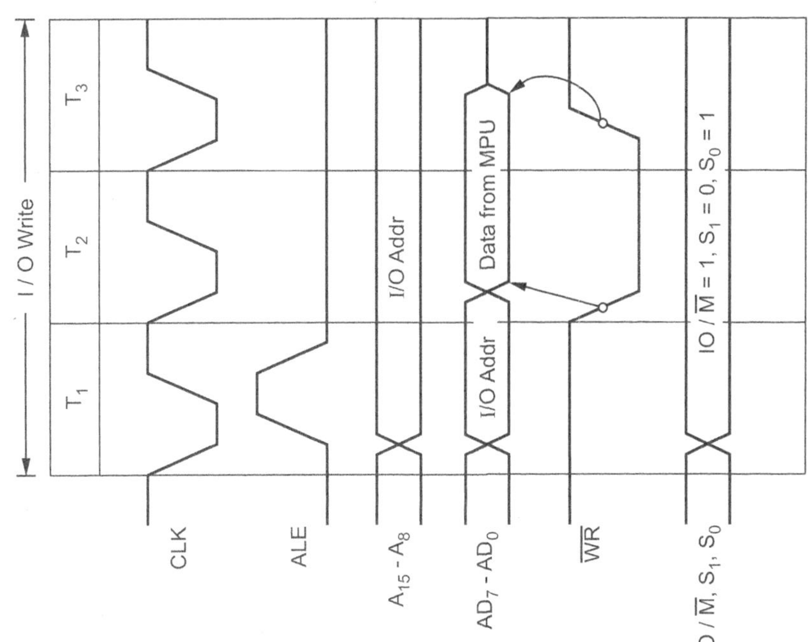

Fig. 5.16 (b) I/O write machine cycle

Interrupt acknowledge cycle for RST instruction

Fig. 5.17 shows the timing diagram of the interrupt acknowledge machine cycle and execution of RST instruction. The interrupt acknowledge cycle is similar to the opcode fetch cycle, with two exceptions.

1. The $\overline{INTA}$ signal is activated instead of the $\overline{RD}$ signal.

2. The status lines ($IO/\overline{M}$, S_0 and S_1) are 111 instead of 011.

During interrupt acknowledge machine cycle (M_1), the RST is decoded, which initiates 1 byte CALL instruction to the specific vector location. The machine cycles M_2 and M_3 are memory write cycles that store the contents of the program counter on the stack and then a new instruction cycle begins.

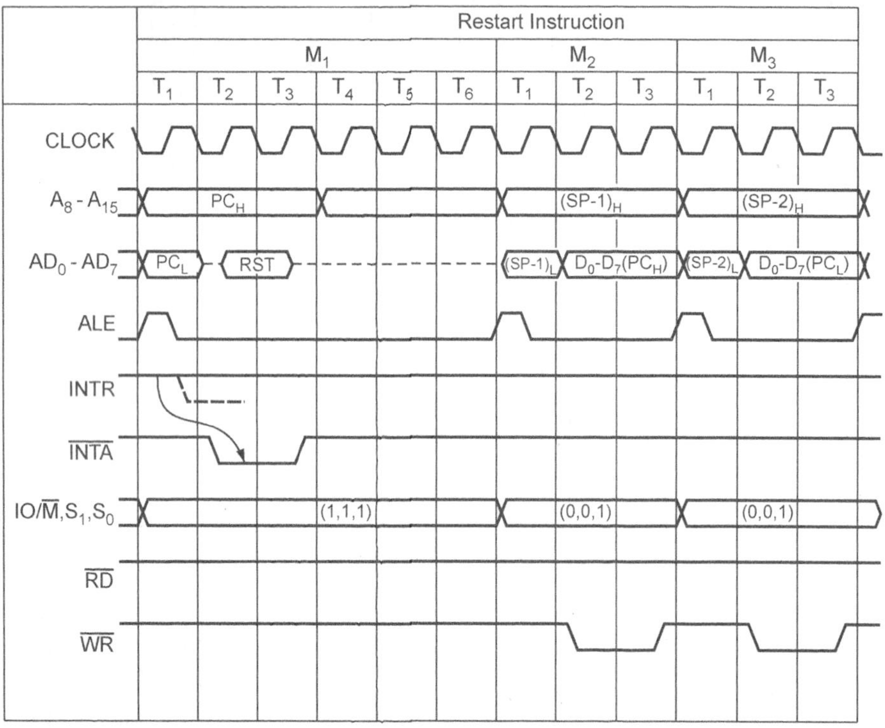

Fig. 5.17 Restart instruction

Interrupt acknowledge cycle for CALL instruction

Fig. 5.18 shows the timing diagram of the interrupt acknowledge machine cycle and execution of a CALL instruction. For CALL instruction, it is necessary to fetch the two bytes of the CALL address through two additional interrupt acknowledge machine cycles (M_2 and M_3 in the Fig. 5.18). The machine cycles M_4 and M_5 are memory write cycles that store the contents of the program counter on the stack and then a new instruction cycle begins.

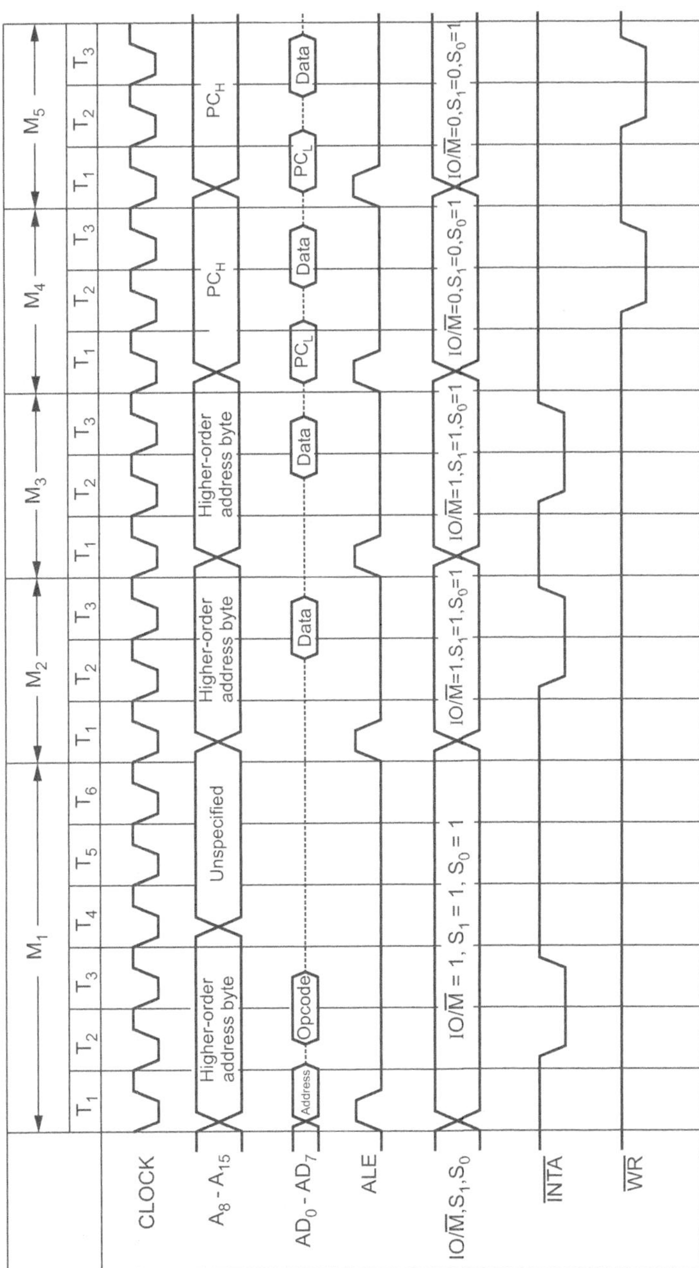

Fig. 5.18 Timing diagram of $\overline{INTA}$ machine cycle and execution of call instruction

7. Bus idle cycle

There are few situations where the machine cycles are neither Read nor Write. These situations are :

1. For execution of DAD instruction (this instruction adds the contents of a specified register pair to the contents of HL register pair) ten T-states are required. This means that

after execution of opcode fetch machine cycle, DAD instruction requires 6 extra T-states to add 16-bit contents of a specified register pair to the contents of HL register pair. These extra T-states which are divided into two machine cycles do not involve any memory or I/O operation. These machine cycles are called BUS IDLE machine cycles. Fig. 5.19 shows Bus Idle Machine Cycle for DAD instruction.

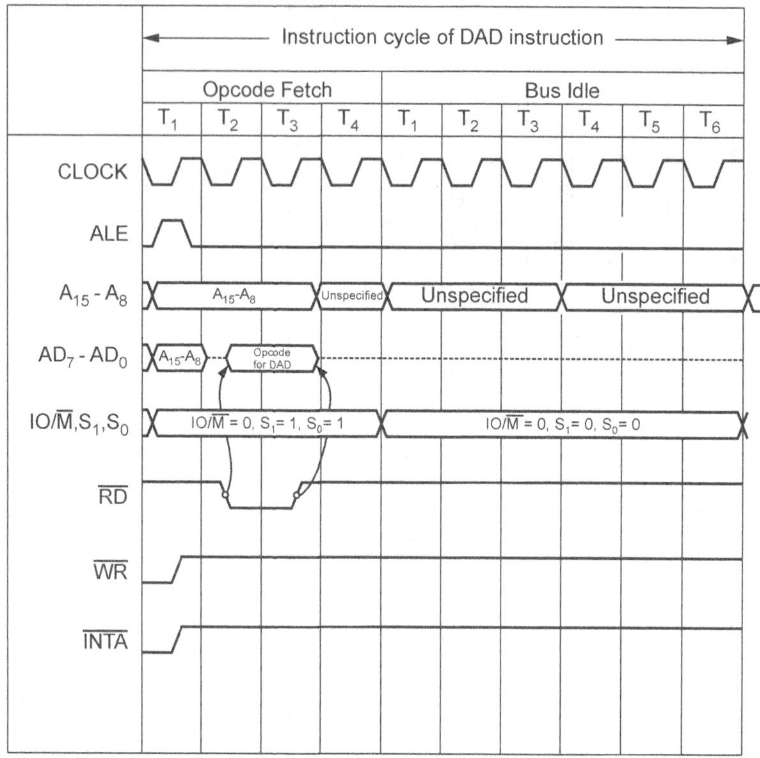

Fig. 5.19 Timing diagram for DAD instruction

In the case of DAD, these Bus Idle cycles are similar to memory read cycles, except $\overline{RD}$ and ALE signals are not activated.

2. During internal opcode generations, for TRAP and RST interrupts, 8085 executes Bus Idle Machine Cycles. Fig. 5.20 shows the Bus Idle Machine Cycle for TRAP. In response to TRAP interrupt, 8085 enters into a Bus Idle Machine Cycle during which it invokes restart instruction, stores the contents of PC onto the stack and places 0024H (Vector address of TRAP) onto the program counter.

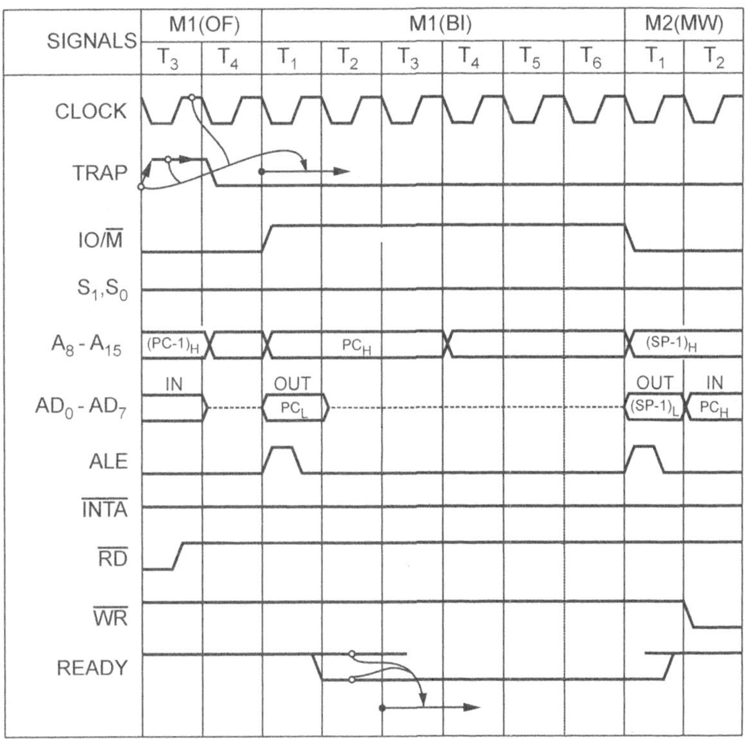

Fig. 5.20 Bus idle machine cycle for trap

The number of machine cycles required to fetch complete instruction depends on the instruction type :

1. One byte 2. Two byte or 3. Three byte.

One byte instruction does not require any additional machine cycle. Two byte instruction requires one additional memory read machine cycle, whereas three byte instruction requires two additional memory read machine cycles.

The number of machine cycles required to execute the instruction depends on the particular instruction. The total number of machine cycles required varies from one to five. It is possible that memory read and memory write machine cycles occur more than once in a single instruction cycle. The following examples illustrate the timing diagrams and machine cycles used for few 8085 instructions.

Example 5.1 : *Draw the timing diagram for instruction MVI A, 30H which is stored at address 2000H.*

2000H	*3E*
2001H	*30*

Solution : This instruction consists of two bytes; the first is the opcode for MVI A instruction and the second is the data byte. The 8085 needs to read these bytes first from memory and thus requires at least two machine cycles. The first machine cycle is opcode fetch and second is memory read. Fig. 5.21 shows the timing diagram for this instruction. This instruction cycle is described in the following paragraphs.

1. The first machine cycle is an opcode fetch machine cycle. In T_1, the microprocessor places the 16-bit memory address (2000H) from the program counter on the address bus, 20H on the A_{15}-A_8 and 00H on AD_7 - AD_0 and increments program counter to 2001H to point to the next memory location. It activates ALE signal (active high) to latch the low-order address 00H from the bus AD_7 - AD_0. It also gives the status signals (IO/$\overline{M}$, S_1 and S_0) 011 to indicate that it is an opcode fetch machine cycle. In T_2, the 8085 activates $\overline{RD}$ (active low) and reads the contents of memory location 2000H i.e. 3EH. Then 8085 places the opcode in the instruction register and disables the $\overline{RD}$ signal during T_3. During T_4, the 8085 decodes the opcode and recognizes that it needs memory read machine cycle to read second byte of the instruction. In T_4, the contents of the bus A_{15}-A_8 are unknown, and the data bus AD_7-AD_0 goes into high impedance state.

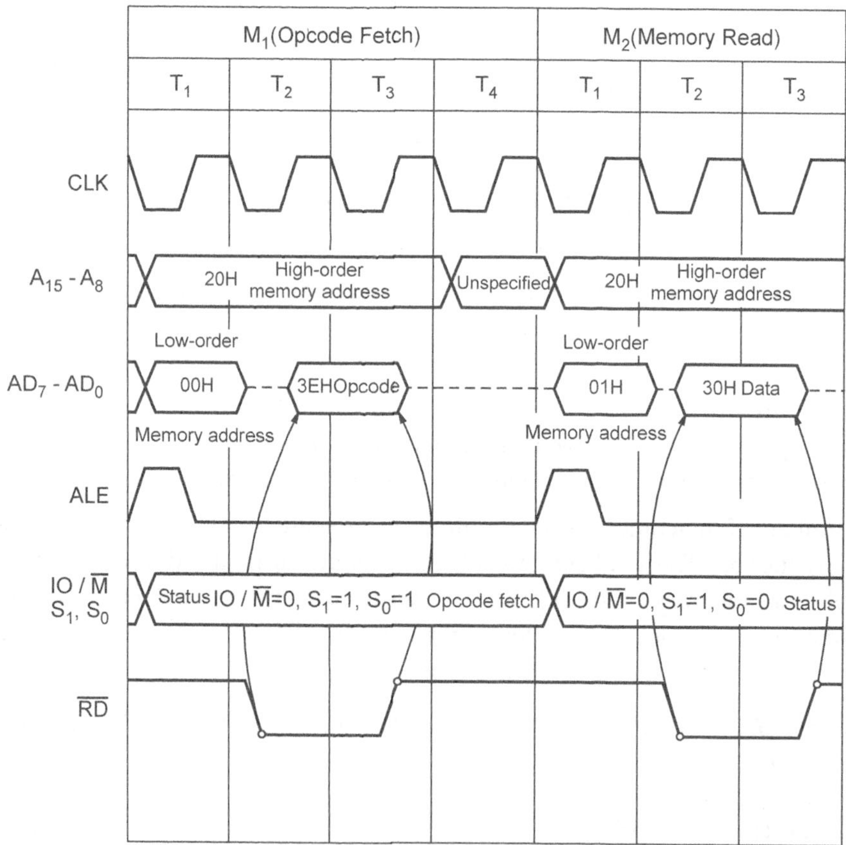

Fig. 5.21 Timing diagram for MVI A, 30H instruction

2. After opcode fetch machine cycle 8085 executes memory read machine cycle. In T_1 of memory read machine cycle, 8085 places the address 2001H on the address bus and increments the program counter to point the next memory location (2002H). 8085 then activates ALE signal and sends status signals ($IO/\overline{M}$, S_1 and S_0) 010 to indicate memory read machine cycle. During T_2 and T_3, 8085 activates $\overline{RD}$ signal and reads the 8-bit data from memory location 2001H (30H). The 8085 then stores this data into the accumulator.

Example 5.2 : *Indicate machine cycles and T-states required for execution of STA instruction.*

Solution : For instruction shown in Fig. 5.22, three machine cycles are required to fetch the instruction and one additional machine cycle is required to store the contents of accumulator into the memory. So following machine cycles are required for STA instruction.

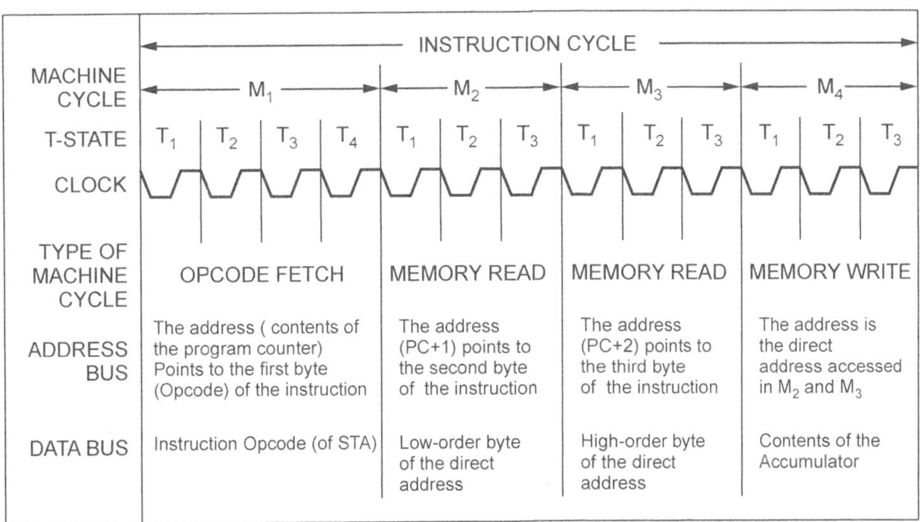

Fig. 5.22 Machine cycles for STA instruction

1. Opcode Fetch (4T- states).
2. Memory Read (3T- states).
3. Memory Read (3T- states).
4. Memory Write (3T- states).

Thus for STA instruction 13T-states are required.

Example 5.3 : *Indicate machine cycles and T-states required for execution of LXI instruction.*

Solution : For instruction shown in Fig. 5.23, three machine cycles are required to fetch the instruction. As it is an immediate instruction, operand i.e. immediate 16-bit data is given within the instruction, no further machine cycle is required.

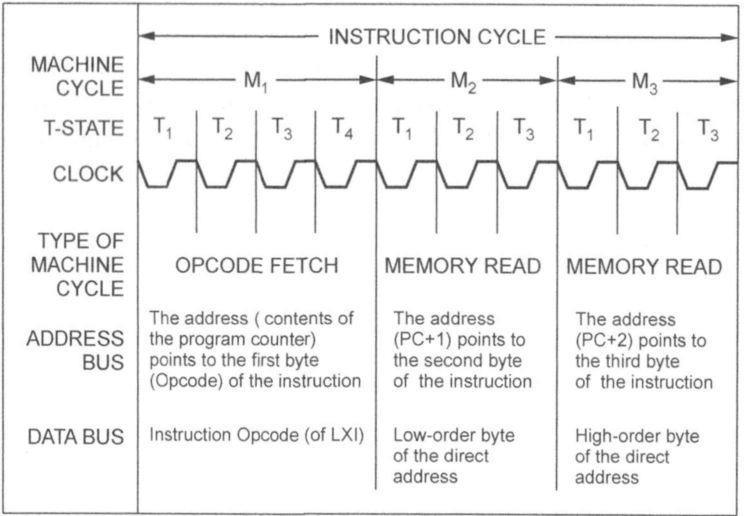

Fig. 5.23 Machine cycles required for LXI instruction(10)

Machine cycles required for LXI instruction.

1. Opcode Fetch (4T- states).
2. Memory Read (3T- states).
3. Memory Read (3T- states).

Thus for LXI instruction 10T-states are required.

Example 5.4 : *Indicate machine cycles and T-states required for execution of LHLD instruction.*

Solution : For instruction shown in Fig. 5.24, three machine cycles are required to fetch the instruction and two additional machine cycles are required to load 16-bit contents from two consecutive memory locations into HL register pair. So following machine cycles are required for LHLD instruction.

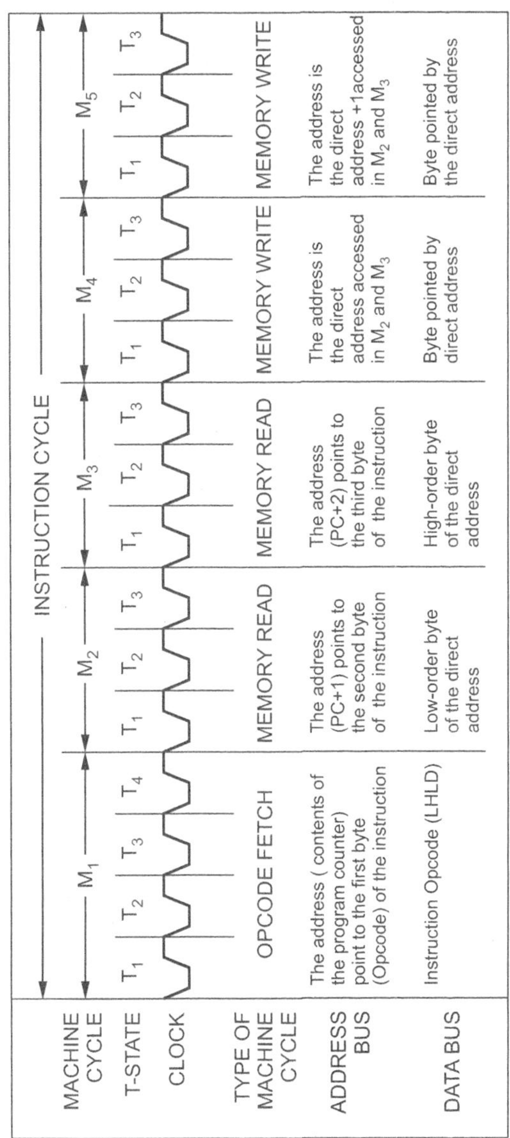

Fig. 5.24 Machine cycles and T-states required for execution of LHLD instruction

1. Opcode Fetch (4T-states).
2. Memory Read (3T-states).
3. Memory Read (3T-states).
4. Memory Write (3T-states).
5. Memory Write (3T-states).

Thus for LHLD instruction 16T-states are required.

5.5 Timing Diagrams for 8085 Instructions

In this section timing diagrams for all 8085 instructions are explained in detail. In 8085 many instructions require same machine cycles. Those instructions are grouped and represented with a single timing diagram with different opcodes shown in table along with timing diagram.

Timing diagram 1 :

MVI A, data ...... MVI L, data

These instructions directly load a specified register with a data byte specified within the instruction. They require the following machine cycles.

1. Opcode fetch : Program counter gives the memory address on low-order and high-order address bus. This machine cycle is required for reading the opcode into the microprocessor and decode it. Program counter is incremented by one.

2. Memory read : This machine cycle reads the data from addressed memory location into specified register of the microprocessor.

Fig. 5.25 shows the timings required for different signals. Table 5.2 gives the instructions for which the timing diagrams are same. Only difference is in opcode.

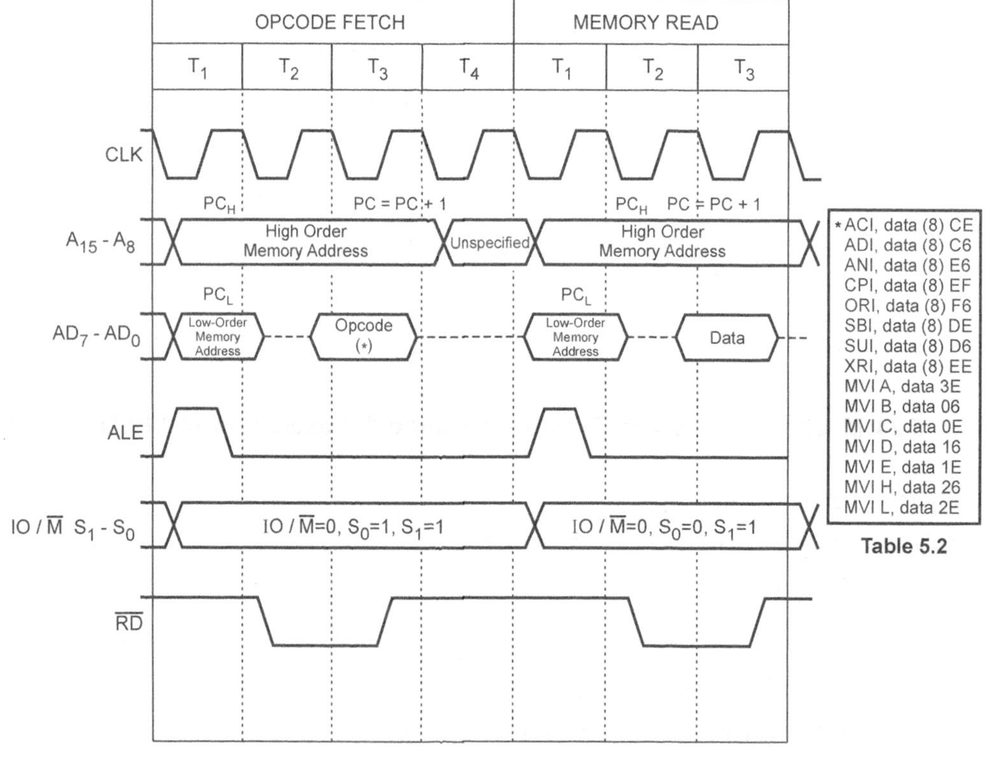

Instruction
*ACI, data (8) CE
ADI, data (8) C6
ANI, data (8) E6
CPI, data (8) EF
ORI, data (8) F6
SBI, data (8) DE
SUI, data (8) D6
XRI, data (8) EE
MVI A, data 3E
MVI B, data 06
MVI C, data 0E
MVI D, data 16
MVI E, data 1E
MVI H, data 26
MVI L, data 2E

Table 5.2

Fig. 5.25

ACI, data.. ADI, data.. ANI, data.. CPI, data.. ORI, data.. SBI, data.. SUI, data.. XRI, data..

These instructions perform logical operation specified in the instruction with the contents of accumulator and the data within the instruction. They require the following machine cycles.

1. Opcode fetch : Program counter gives the memory address on low-order and high-order address bus. This machine cycle is required for reading the opcode into the microprocessor and decode it. Program counter is incremented by one.

2. Memory read : This machine cycle reads the data from addressed memory location and after performing specified logical operation result is stored in the accumulator.

Timing diagram 2 :

LXI rp, data (16)

This instruction loads immediate 16-bit data specified within the instruction into register pair or stack pointer. It requires three machine cycles as explained below.

1. Opcode fetch : Program counter places address on low-order and high-order address bus. In this machine cycle, the opcode of LXI rp (e.g. 01 of LXI B) is read into the microprocessor and is decoded. Program counter is incremented by one.

2. Memory read : Program counter gives address on low-order and high-order address bus. The low-order byte of the data specified within the instruction is read into microprocessor (low-order register of rp) from this address. The program counter is incremented by one.

3. Memory read : Program counter keeps address on low-order and high-order address bus. The high-order byte of the data specified within the instruction is read into microprocessor (high-order register of rp) from this address. The program counter is incremented by one.

Fig. 5.26 shows the timing diagram of LXI rp, data (16) instruction.

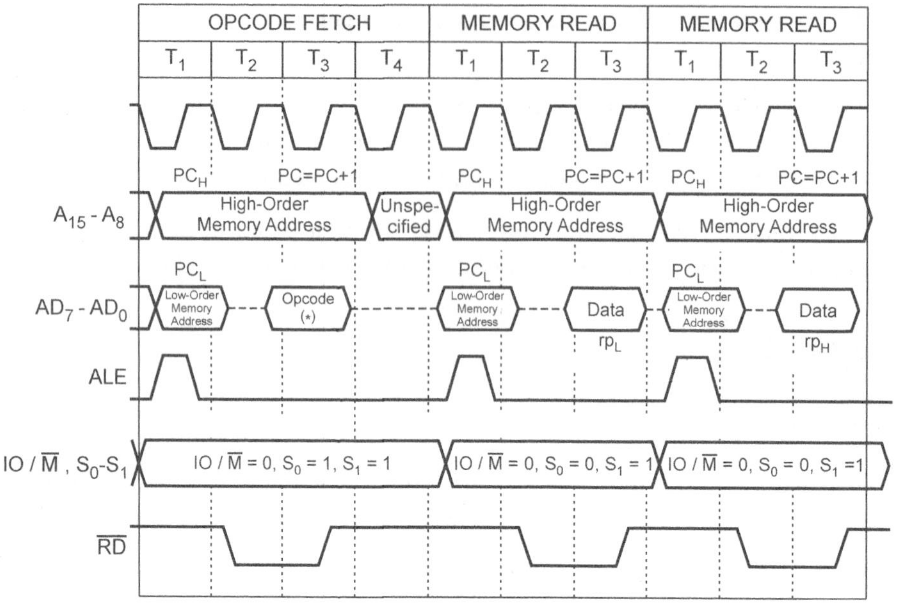

* LXI rp, data (16)	
LXI B	01
LXI D	11
LXI H	01
LXI SP	31

Table 5.3

Fig. 5.26

Timing diagram 3 :

MVI M, data (8)

This instruction loads the 8-bit data specified within the instruction into memory whose address is specified by HL register pair. It requires three machine cycles as explained below.

1. Opcode fetch : Program counter gives the address on low-order and high-order address bus. This machine cycle is required for reading the opcode (36H) into the microprocessor. Program counter is incremented by one.

2. Memory read : Program counter gives the address on low-order and high-order address bus. The data (given within the instruction) is read into the microprocessor in this machine cycle. Program counter is incremented by one.

3. Memory write : This machine cycle writes the data at the address given by HL register pair. The contents of H register are the higher-order byte of the address and the contents of L register are the lower-order byte of the address.

The timing diagram of MVI M, data (8) is shown in Fig. 5.27.

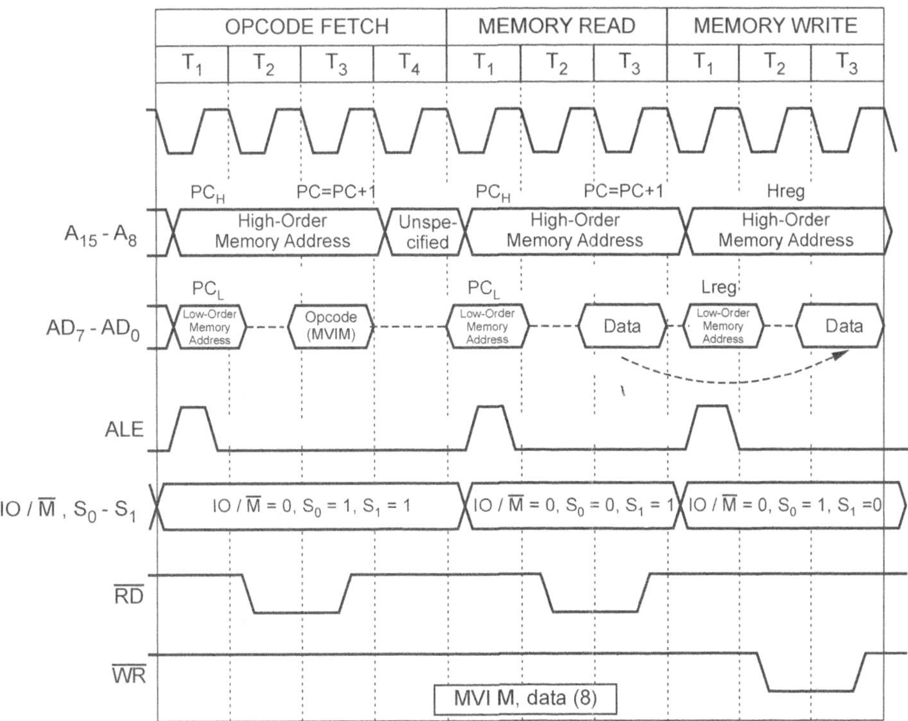

Fig. 5.27

Timing diagram 4 :

Fig. 5.28 gives the timing diagram for the instructions given in the Table 5.4. These instructions require only opcode fetch machine cycle. Program counter gives address on low-order and high-order address bus. The opcode of the instruction is read into the microprocessor from the addressed memory location and is decoded.

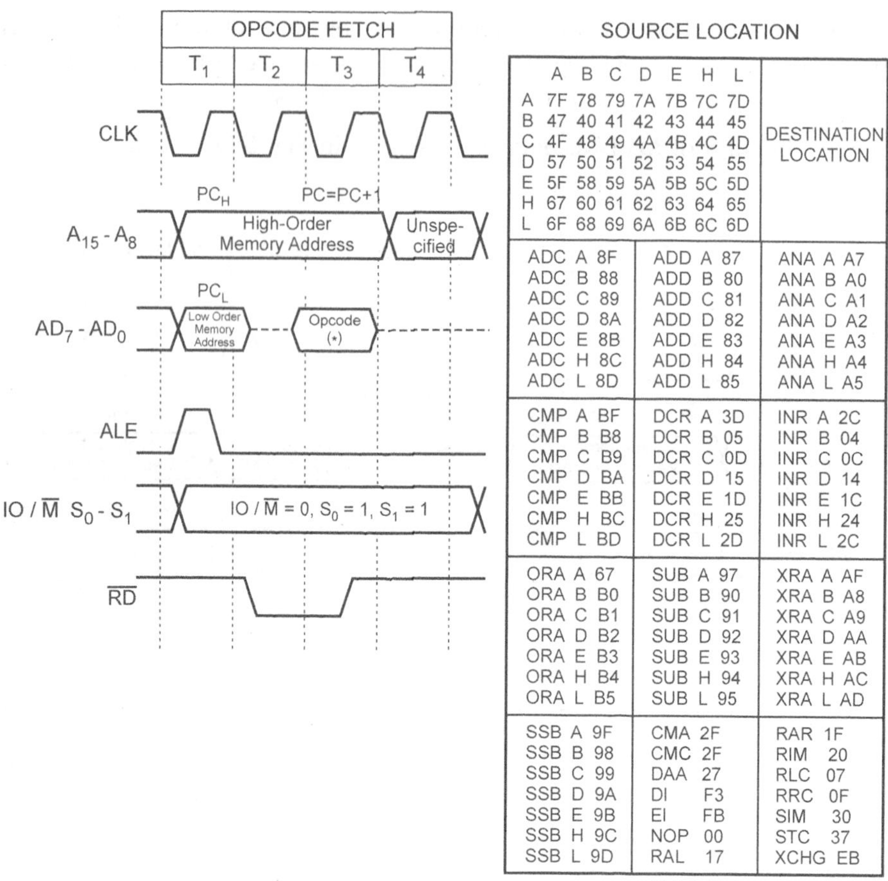

SOURCE LOCATION

	A	B	C	D	E	H	L	
A	7F	78	79	7A	7B	7C	7D	DESTINATION LOCATION
B	47	40	41	42	43	44	45	
C	4F	48	49	4A	4B	4C	4D	
D	57	50	51	52	53	54	55	
E	5F	58	59	5A	5B	5C	5D	
H	67	60	61	62	63	64	65	
L	6F	68	69	6A	6B	6C	6D	

ADC A 8F	ADD A 87	ANA A A7
ADC B 88	ADD B 80	ANA B A0
ADC C 89	ADD C 81	ANA C A1
ADC D 8A	ADD D 82	ANA D A2
ADC E 8B	ADD E 83	ANA E A3
ADC H 8C	ADD H 84	ANA H A4
ADC L 8D	ADD L 85	ANA L A5
CMP A BF	DCR A 3D	INR A 2C
CMP B B8	DCR B 05	INR B 04
CMP C B9	DCR C 0D	INR C 0C
CMP D BA	DCR D 15	INR D 14
CMP E BB	DCR E 1D	INR E 1C
CMP H BC	DCR H 25	INR H 24
CMP L BD	DCR L 2D	INR L 2C
ORA A 67	SUB A 97	XRA A AF
ORA B B0	SUB B 90	XRA B A8
ORA C B1	SUB C 91	XRA C A9
ORA D B2	SUB D 92	XRA D AA
ORA E B3	SUB E 93	XRA E AB
ORA H B4	SUB H 94	XRA H AC
ORA L B5	SUB L 95	XRA L AD
SSB A 9F	CMA 2F	RAR 1F
SSB B 98	CMC 2F	RIM 20
SSB C 99	DAA 27	RLC 07
SSB D 9A	DI F3	RRC 0F
SSB E 9B	EI FB	SIM 30
SSB H 9C	NOP 00	STC 37
SSB L 9D	RAL 17	XCHG EB

Table 5.4

Fig. 5.28

Timing diagram 5 :

These instructions performs logical operation between the contents of accumulator and the contents of memory location pointed by HL register pair. They require following machine cycles.

1. Opcode fetch : Program counter gives address on low-order and high-order address bus. The opcode of ADD (86H) is read into the microprocessor from the addressed memory location and is decoded. Program counter is incremented by one.

2. Memory read : The contents of H register give the high-order address and contents of L register give the low-order address. The data stored at this address is read into the microprocessor and after performing the specified logical operation result is stored in accumulator instruction (for example opcode for instruction ADD M is 86H). Fig. 5.29 gives the timing diagram for the instructions given in the Table 5.5.

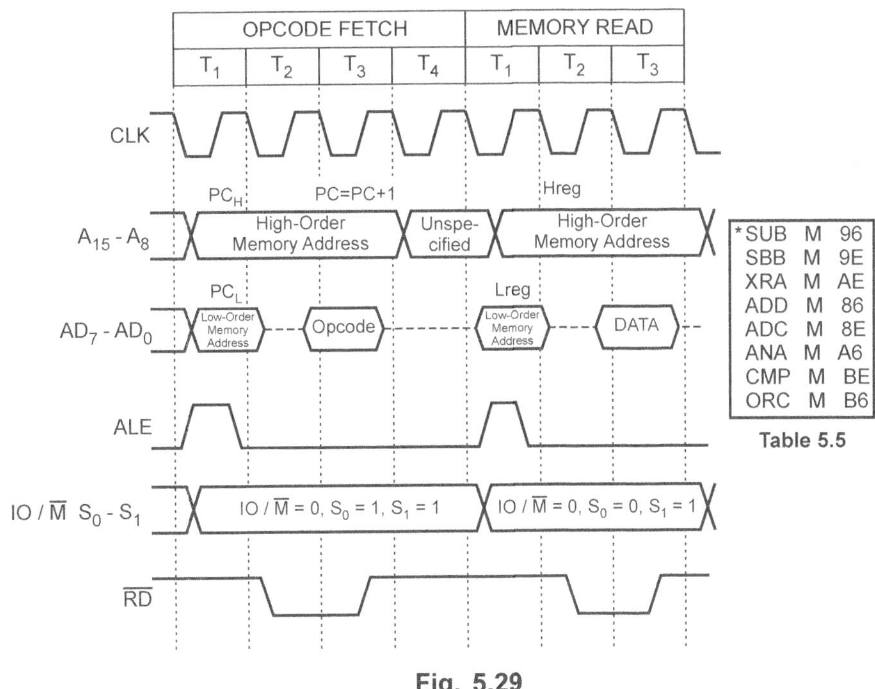

*SUB	M	96
SBB	M	9E
XRA	M	AE
ADD	M	86
ADC	M	8E
ANA	M	A6
CMP	M	BE
ORC	M	B6

Table 5.5

Fig. 5.29

Timing diagram 6 :

STA address :

This instruction stores the contents of A register at the address given within the instruction. It requires following machine cycles :

1. **Opcode fetch :** Program counter gives the memory address on high-order and low-order address bus. This machine cycle is required for reading the opcode (32H) into the microprocessor and to decode it. Program counter is incremented by one.

2. **Memory read :** Program counter gives the memory address on high-order and low-order address bus. In this machine cycle, the low-order byte of the address specified within the instruction is read into the microprocessor from the addressed memory location. Program counter is incremented by one.

3. **Memory read :** Program counter gives the memory address on high-order and low-order address bus. In this machine cycle the high-order byte of the address specified within the instruction is read into the microprocessor from addressed memory location. Program counter is incremented by one.

4. **Memory write :** This machine cycle is required for writing the data from the accumulator at the addressed memory location. This address is nothing but the data read into the microprocessor in previous two memory read cycles. Fig. 5.30 gives the timing diagram for STA address instruction.

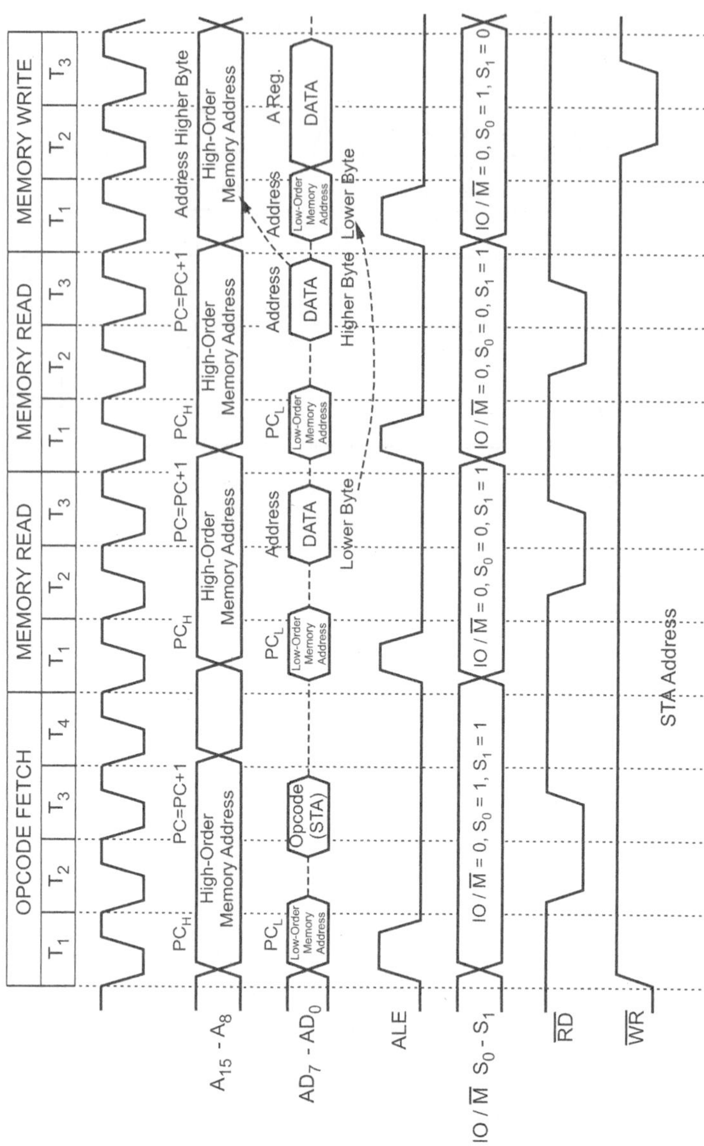

Fig. 5.30

Timing diagram 7 :

LDA address

This instruction loads the data into A register from the address given within the instruction. The machine cycles required for this instruction are explained below.

1. Opcode fetch : Program counter gives the memory address on high-order and low-order address bus. This machine cycle reads the opcode (3AH) into the microprocessor and decodes it. Program counter is incremented by one.

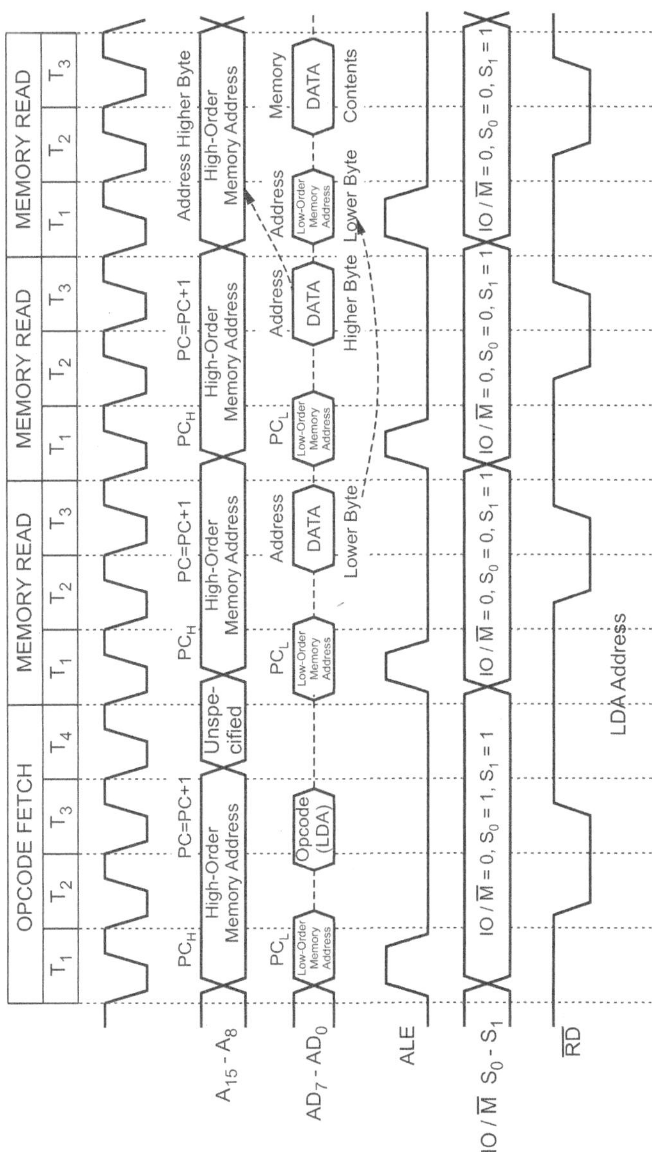

Fig. 5.31

2. Memory read : Program counter gives address on low-order and high-order address bus. In this machine cycle, the low order byte of the address specified within the instruction is read into the microprocessor from the addressed memory location. Program counter is incremented by one.

3. Memory read : Program counter gives the address on low-order and high-order address bus. In this machine cycle, the high-order byte of the address specified within the instruction is read into the microprocessor from the addressed memory location. Program counter is incremented by one.

4. Memory read : This machine cycle is required for reading the data into the A register from the addressed memory location. The address is nothing but data read into the microprocessor in previous two memory read cycles.

Timing diagram 8 :

STAX rp

This instruction stores the contents of A register in memory whose address is specified by register pair (BC or DE). It requires the following machine cycles :

1. Opcode fetch : Program counter places the memory address on low-order and high-order address bus. This machine cycle is required for reading the opcode of STAX rp (e.g. 02H for STAX B) into the microprocessor and decode it.

2. Memory write : Higher-order address is obtained from higher-order register and lower-address is obtained from lower-order register of the specified register pair. The contents of the accumulator are stored into the addressed memory location. Thus memory write machine cycle is required for writing the data from the microprocessor (A register) to the addressed memory location. Fig. 5.32 gives the timing diagram for STAX rp.

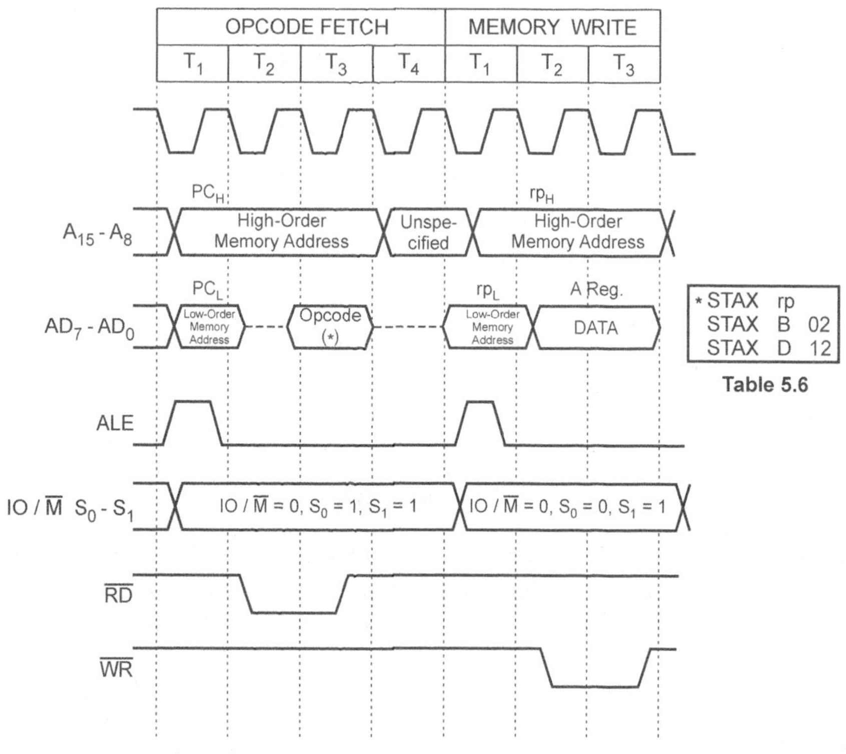

Fig. 5.32

* STAX	rp	
STAX	B	02
STAX	D	12

Table 5.6

Timing diagram 9 :

LDAX rp

This instruction loads A register with the contents of memory location whose address is specified by register pair (BC or DE). It requires the following machine cycles.

1. Opcode fetch : Program counter places the memory address on low-order and high-order address bus. This machine cycle is required for reading the opcode of LDAX rp (e.g. 0A for LDAX B) into the microprocessor and decode it.

2. Memory read : This machine cycle is required for reading the data into the accumulator. The address at which the data is stored is obtained from register pair specified within the instruction. In this machine cycle higher-order register contents are kept on higher-order address bus and lower-order register contents are kept on lower-order address bus. The data is read into the microprocessor (register A) from the addressed memory location. Fig. 5.33 gives the timing diagram.

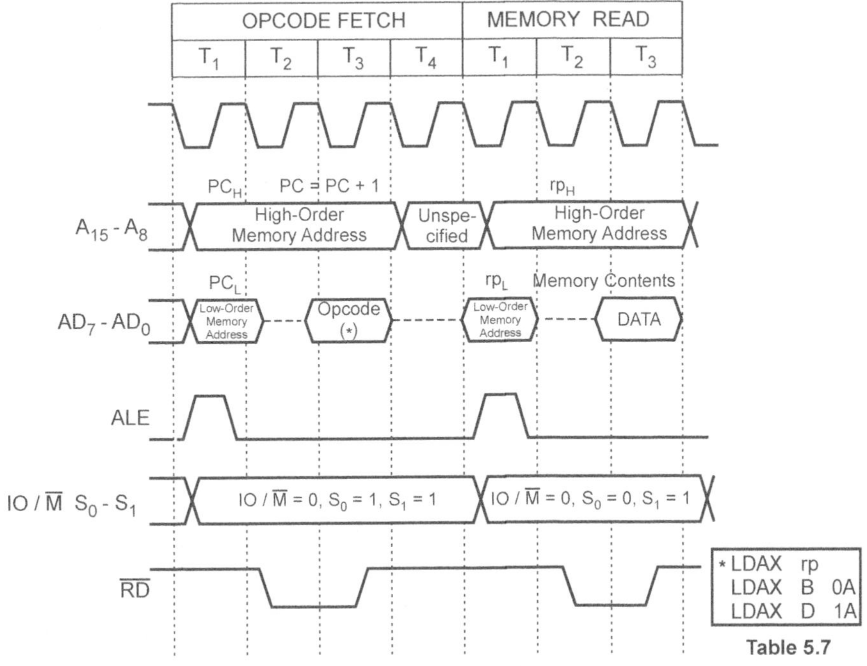

* LDAX	rp	
LDAX	B	0A
LDAX	D	1A

Table 5.7

Fig. 5.33

Timing diagram 10 :

DAD rp

This instruction adds 16-bit data from specified register pair or stack pointer in the contents of HL register pair and stores the result in the HL register pair. This instruction requires three machine cycles.

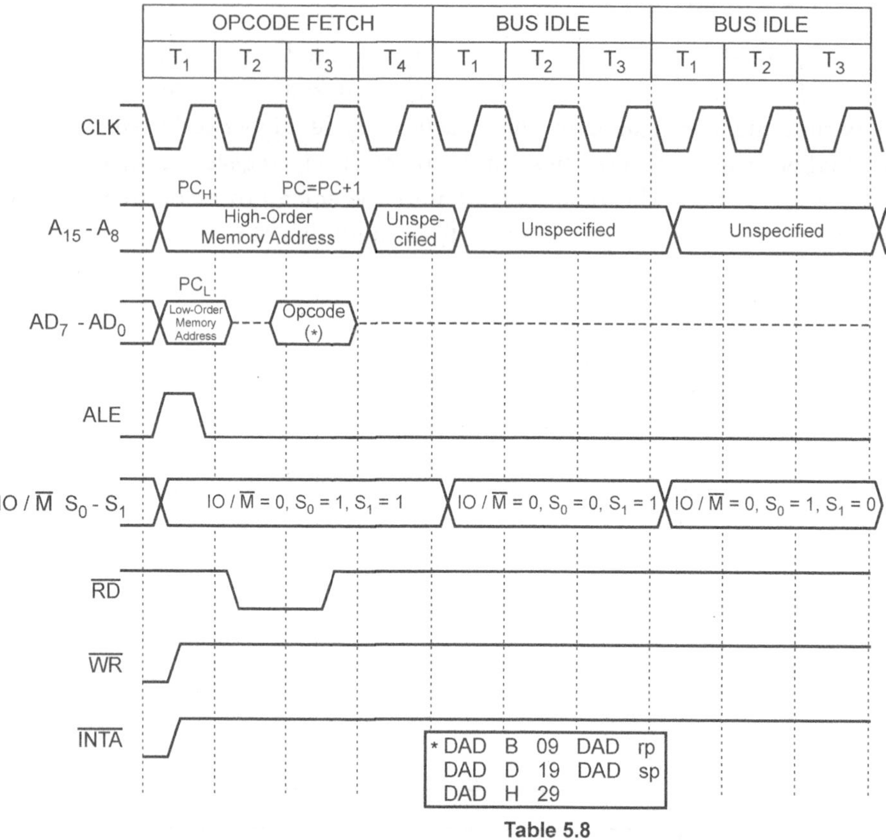

Fig. 5.34

1. Opcode fetch : Program counter places the memory address on low-order and high. order address bus. This machine cycle is required for reading the opcode of DAD (e.g. 09 for DAD B) into the microprocessor and decode it.

2. and 3. Bus idle

These machine cycles are required to do the internal operation i.e. to perform 16-bit addition. During these machine cycles buses are not in use.

Timing diagram 11 :

DCX rp and INX rp

These instructions decrement/increment the contents of register pair (rp) specified within the register by one and store result in the same register pair. It requires only opcode fetch machine cycle. In this cycle, program counter gives address on low-order and high-order address bus. The opcode of DCX rp (e.g. 0B of DCX B) is read into the microprocessor and it decodes it. This machine cycle requires 6 T-states. Fig. 5.35 gives the timing diagram of DCX rp. The instruction INX rp also has same timing diagram, the only difference is the opcode.

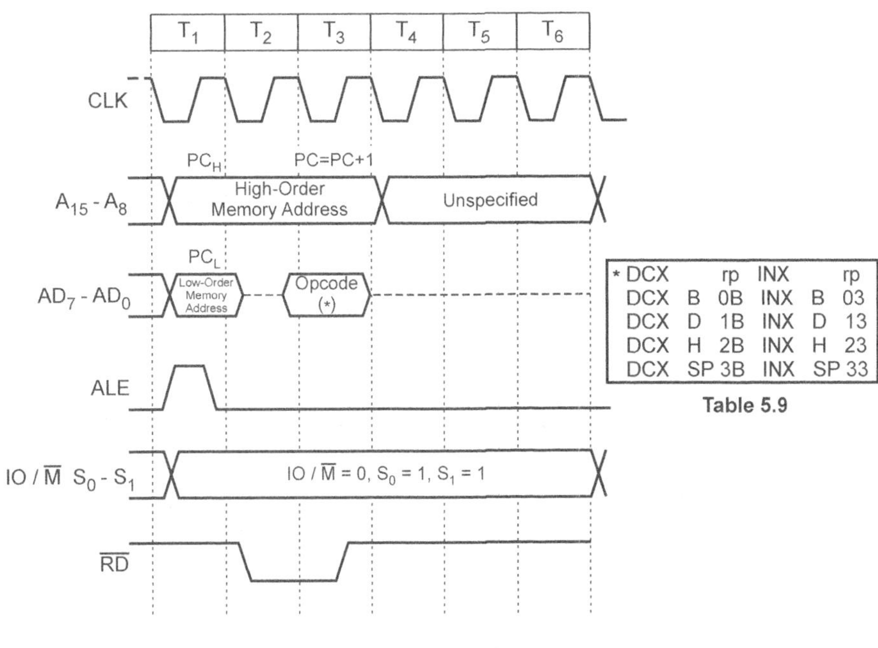

* DCX	rp	INX	rp
DCX B	0B	INX B	03
DCX D	1B	INX D	13
DCX H	2B	INX H	23
DCX SP	3B	INX SP	33

Table 5.9

Fig. 5.35

Timing diagram 12 :

INR M and DCR M

These instructions increment/decrement the contents of memory by one where memory address is specified by HL register pair. It requires three machine cycles as explained below.

1. Opcode fetch : Program counter gives the memory address on low-order and high-order address bus. This type of machine cycle is required for reading the opcode (e.g. 34H of INR M) into the microprocessor and to decode it.

2. Memory read : The contents of HL register pair give the address of memory where the data (which is to be incremented) is stored. In this machine cycle data is read into the microprocessor from this memory location.

3. Memory write : The microprocessor writes the incremented data at the memory location given by the contents of HL register pair.

Fig. 5.36 gives the number of T-states and timing required for each of the above operation. The DCR M instruction decrements the contents of memory by one where memory is specified by HL register pair. The timing diagram for DCR M is same as for INR M. Only difference is in opcode.

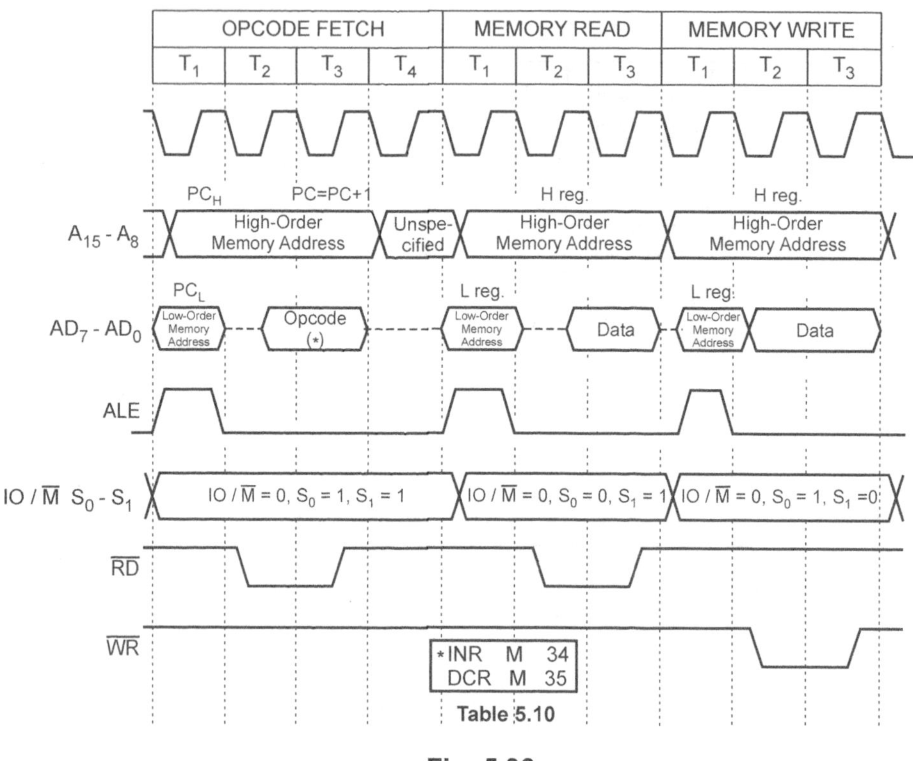

Fig. 5.36

Timing diagram 13 :

XTHL

This instruction exchanges the contents of memory location pointed by the stack pointer with the contents of L register and the contents of the next memory location with the contents of H register. This instruction requires five machine cycles as explained below.

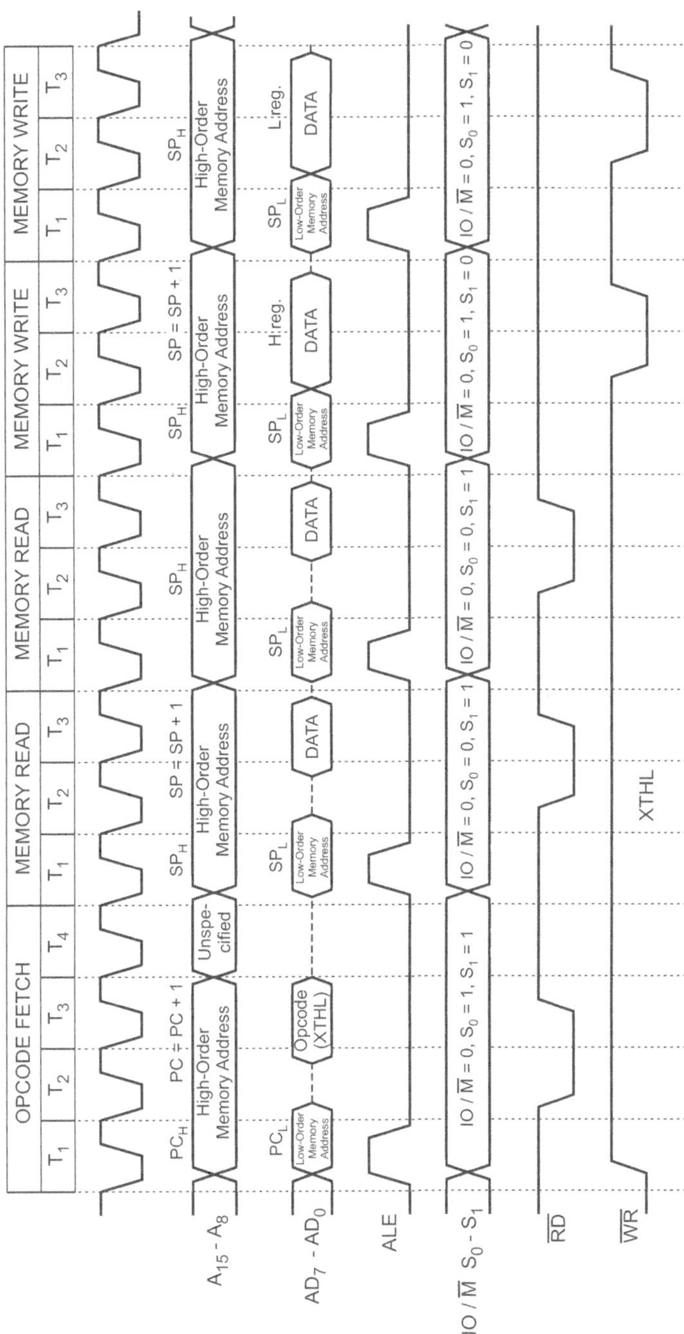

Fig. 5.37

1. Opcode fetch : Program counter places address on low-order and high-order address bus. The opcode of XTHL (E3H) is read from this address into the microprocessor and is decoded in this machine cycle. The program counter is incremented by one.

2. Memory read : Stack pointer gives address on low-order and high-order address bus. The data is read from this addressed memory location into the microprocessor. The stack pointer is incremented by one.

3. Memory read : Stack pointer gives address on low-order and high-order address bus. The data is read from this addressed memory location into the microprocessor.

4. Memory write : Stack pointer gives address on low-order and high-order address bus. This machine cycle is required for writing the data from H register of microprocessor into the addressed memory location. Stack pointer is again decremented by one.

5. Memory write : Stack pointer gives address on low-order and high-order address bus. This machine cycle is required for writing the data from L register of microprocessor into the addressed memory location.

Timing diagram 14 :

PCHL

This instruction loads the contents of HL register pair into the program counter. It requires only opcode fetch machine cycle. In this, the program counter gives address on low-order and high-order address bus. Microprocessor reads the opcode of PCHL (E9H) from this memory address and decodes it. This requires 6 T-states.

Fig. 5.38 gives the timing diagram of PCHL instruction.

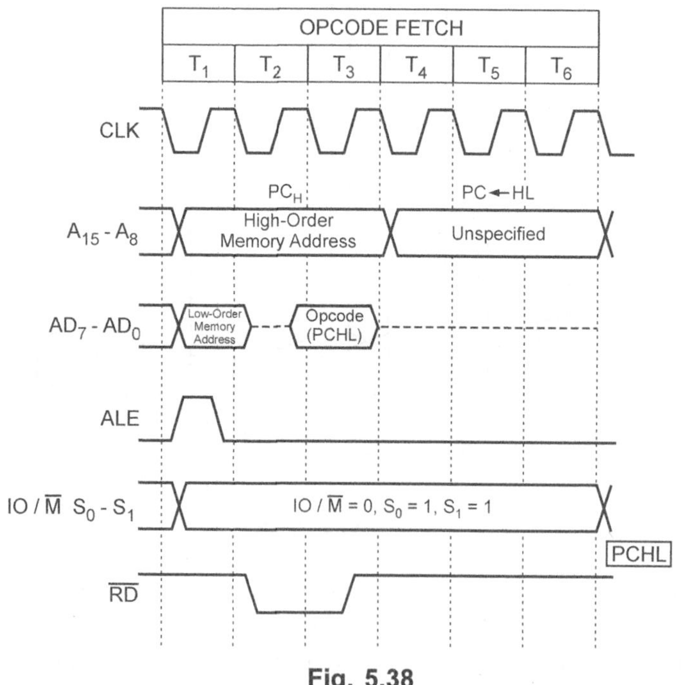

Fig. 5.38

Timing diagram 15 :

SPHL

This instruction copies the contents of HL register pair into the stack pointer. It requires only opcode fetch machine cycle. In this, program counter gives address on low-order and high-order address bus. Microprocessor reads the opcode of SPHL (F9H) from this addressed memory location and decodes it. Program counter is incremented by one. This machine cycle requires 6 T-states. Fig. 5.39 gives the timing diagram of SPHL.

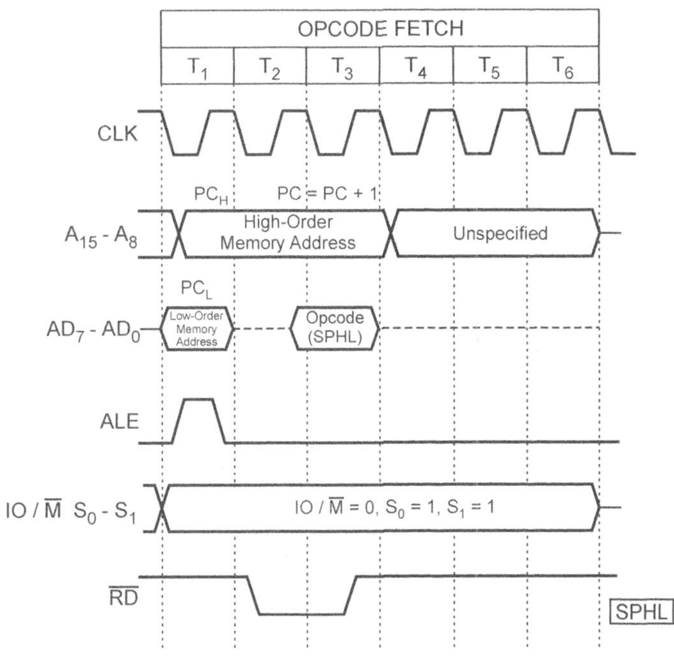

Fig. 5.39

Timing diagram 16 :

LHLD address

Fig. 5.40 gives the timing diagram of LHLD address instruction. This instruction loads L register with the contents of memory location given within the instruction and loads H register with the contents of memory location at address next to it. It requires the following five machine cycles.

1. Opcode fetch : Program counter places address on low-order and high-order address bus. Microprocessor reads the opcode of LHLD (2AH) from this memory location and decodes it. Program counter is incremented by one.

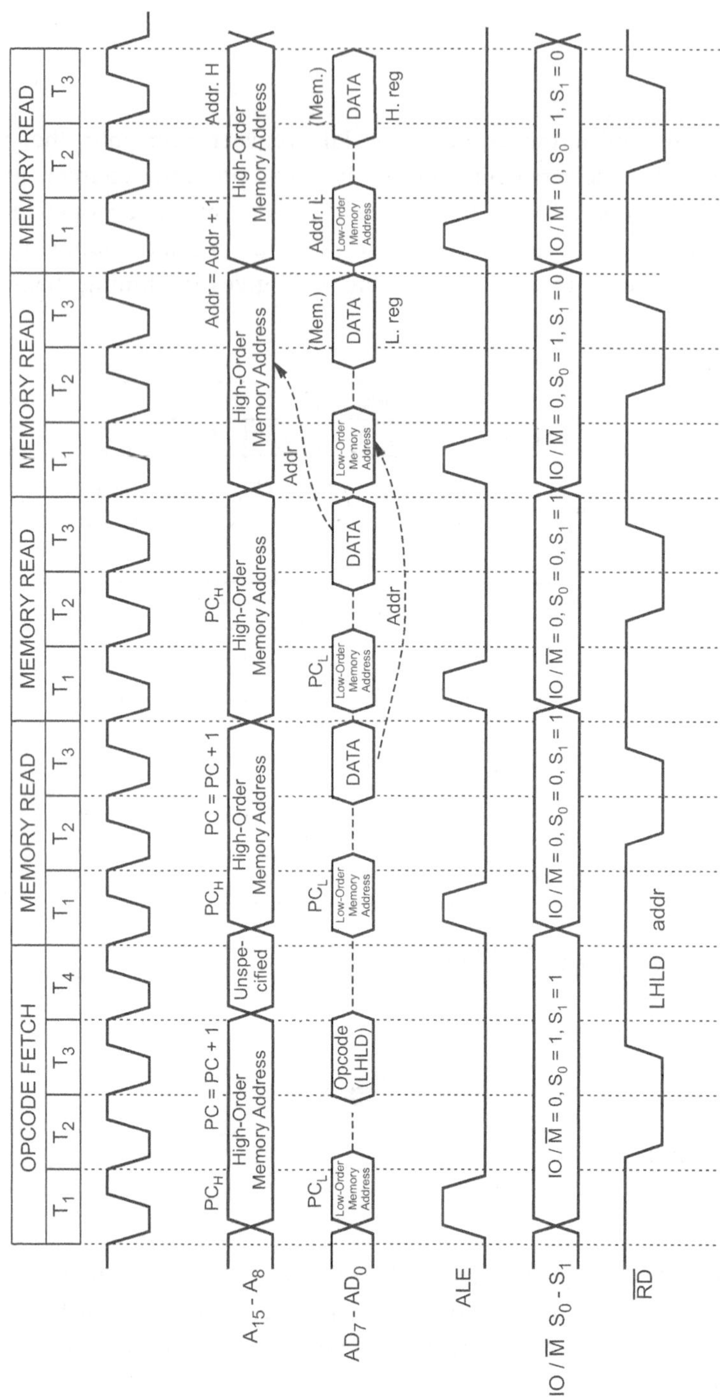

OPCODE FETCH
MEMORY READ
MEMORY READ
MEMORY READ
MEMORY READ
T_1 T_2 T_3 T_4
T_1 T_2 T_3
A_{15} - A_8
AD_7 - AD_0
ALE
IO / $\overline{M}$ S_0 - S_1
$\overline{RD}$
PC_H
PC_L
PC = PC + 1
High-Order Memory Address
Low-Order Memory Address
Opcode (LHLD)
Unspe-cified
DATA
Addr
Addr = Addr + 1
Addr. H
Addr. L
(Mem.)
L. reg
H. reg
IO / $\overline{M}$ = 0, S_0 = 1, S_1 = 1
IO / $\overline{M}$ = 0, S_0 = 0, S_1 = 1
IO / $\overline{M}$ = 0, S_0 = 1, S_1 = 0
LHLD addr

Fig. 5.40

2. Memory read : Program counter gives address on low-order and high-order address bus. Microprocessor reads data from the addressed memory location. This data is the low-order byte of the address specified within the instruction. Program counter is incremented by one.

3. Memory read : Program counter gives address on low-order and high-order address bus. Microprocessor reads data from the addressed memory location. This data is the high-order byte of the address specified within the instruction.

4. Memory read : The data read in the previous two memory read cycles is placed on the address bus. Microprocessor reads the contents of memory location and loads it in L register. This memory address is incremented by one.

5. Memory read : Now the incremented address is present on the address bus. Microprocessor reads the contents of memory location and loads it in H register.

Timing diagram 17 :

SHLD address

Fig. 5.41 gives the timing diagram of SHLD address instruction. This instruction stores the contents of L register in the memory location given within the instruction and contents of H register at address next to it. It requires the following five machine cycles.

1. Opcode fetch : Program counter places address on low-order and high-order address bus. Microprocessor reads the opcode of SHLD (22H) from this memory location and decodes it. Program counter is incremented by one.

2. Memory read : Program counter gives address on low-order and high-order address bus. Microprocessor reads data from the addressed memory location. This data is the low-order byte of the address specified within the instruction. Program counter is incremented by one.

3. Memory read : Program counter gives address on low-order and high-order address bus. Microprocessor reads data from the addressed memory location. This data is the high-order byte of the address specified within the instruction.

4. Memory write : The data read in the previous two memory read cycles is placed on the address bus. Microprocessor writes the contents of L register at this memory address. This memory address is incremented by one.

5. Memory write : Now the incremented address is present on the address bus. Microprocessor writes the contents of H register at this memory address.

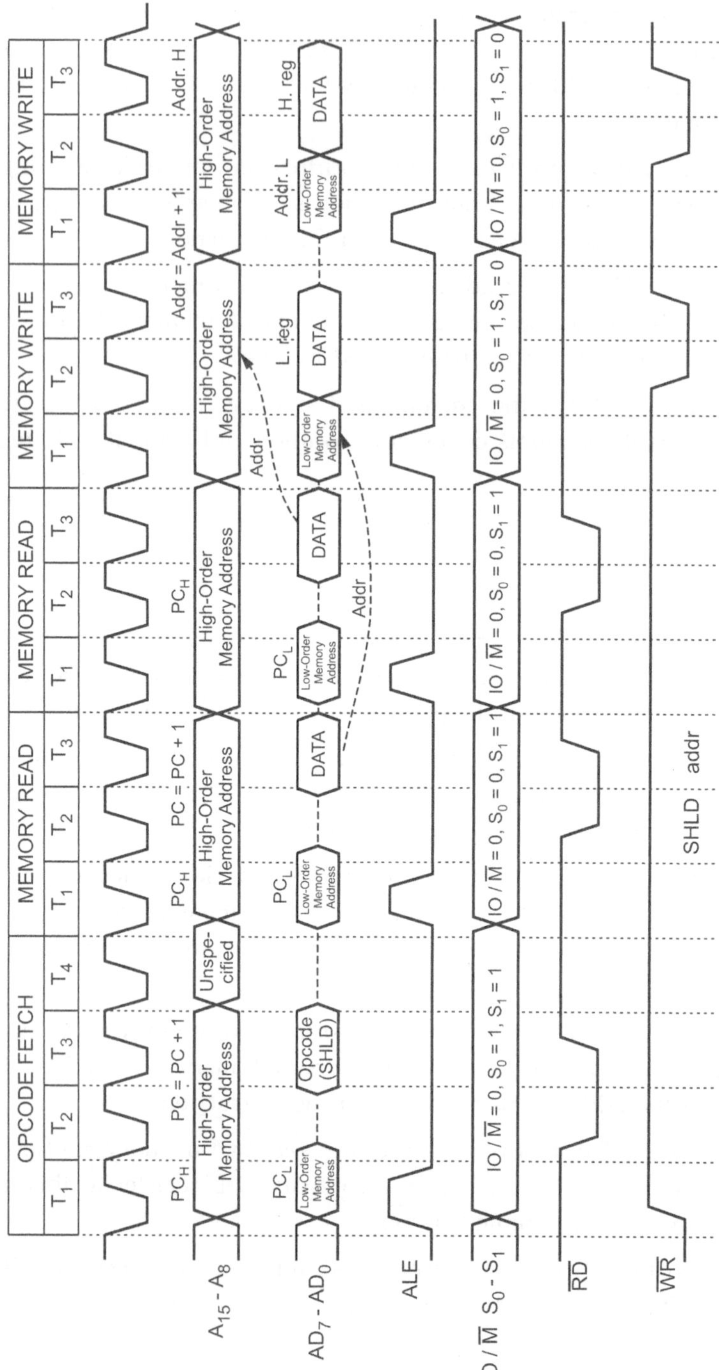
OPCODE FETCH
MEMORY READ
MEMORY READ
MEMORY WRITE
MEMORY WRITE
T1
T2
T3
T4
A_{15} - A_8
AD_7 - AD_0
ALE
IO / $\overline{M}$ S_0 - S_1
$\overline{RD}$
$\overline{WR}$
PC_H
PC = PC + 1
High-Order Memory Address
Unspe-cified
PC_L
Low-Order Memory Address
Opcode (SHLD)
DATA
Addr
Addr = Addr + 1
Addr. L
Addr. H
L. reg
H. reg
IO / $\overline{M}$ = 0, S_0 = 1, S_1 = 1
IO / $\overline{M}$ = 0, S_0 = 0, S_1 = 1
IO / $\overline{M}$ = 0, S_0 = 1, S_1 = 0
SHLD addr

Fig. 5.41

Timing diagram 18 :

JMP address

This instruction loads the program counter with the address given within the instruction and resumes the program execution from this location. It requires three machine cycles as explained below.

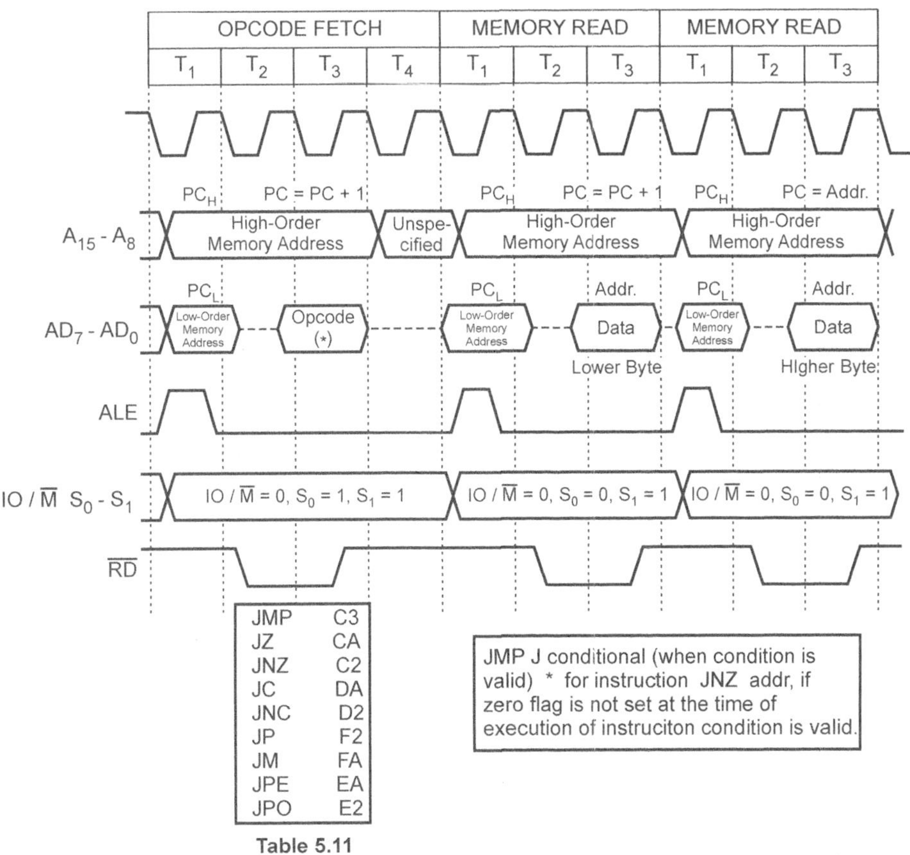

JMP	C3
JZ	CA
JNZ	C2
JC	DA
JNC	D2
JP	F2
JM	FA
JPE	EA
JPO	E2

Table 5.11

Fig. 5.42

1. Opcode fetch : Program counter places address on low-order and high-order address bus. The opcode of JMP (C3H) is read into the microprocessor from this address and is decoded. Program counter is incremented by one.

2. Memory read : Program counter gives address on low-order and high-order address bus. The data at this addressed memory location is read into the microprocessor. This data is nothing but the low-order byte of the address specified within the instruction. Program counter is incremented by one.

3. Memory read : Program counter gives address on low-order and high-order address bus. The data at this addressed memory location is read into the microprocessor. This data is nothing but the high-order byte of the address specified within the instruction. The data read into the microprocessor in these two memory read cycles is loaded into the program counter. So the program execution starts from the address specified within the instruction.

Fig. 5.42 gives the timing diagram of JMP address instruction. The timing diagram of J condition, when condition is valid is same as that of JMP address.

Timing diagram 19 :

J condition (When condition is not valid)

This instruction transfers program control to the next instruction written after this instruction. Due to fetch execution overlap flag are checked in the T-state of the next machine cycle. Hence it is not possible for 8085 to decide whether to jump or not at the given address after opcode fetch machine cycle. As a result, it executes memory read machine cycle. At T_1 of this machine cycle 8085 checks the necessary flag and goes to the next instruction if condition is not true.

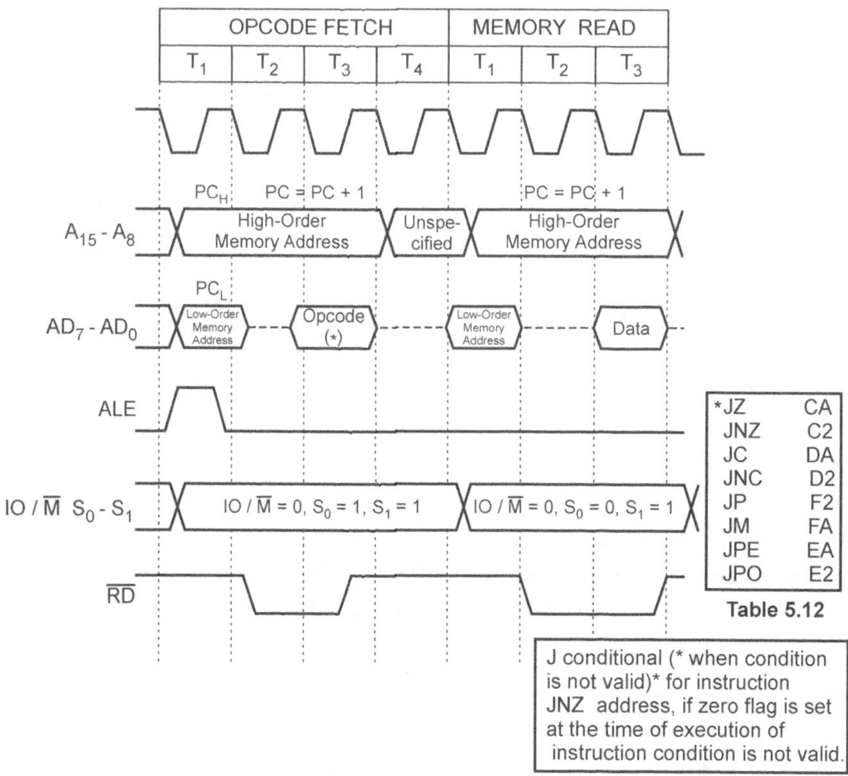

*JZ	CA
JNZ	C2
JC	DA
JNC	D2
JP	F2
JM	FA
JPE	EA
JPO	E2

Table 5.12

Fig. 5.43

Timing diagram 20 :

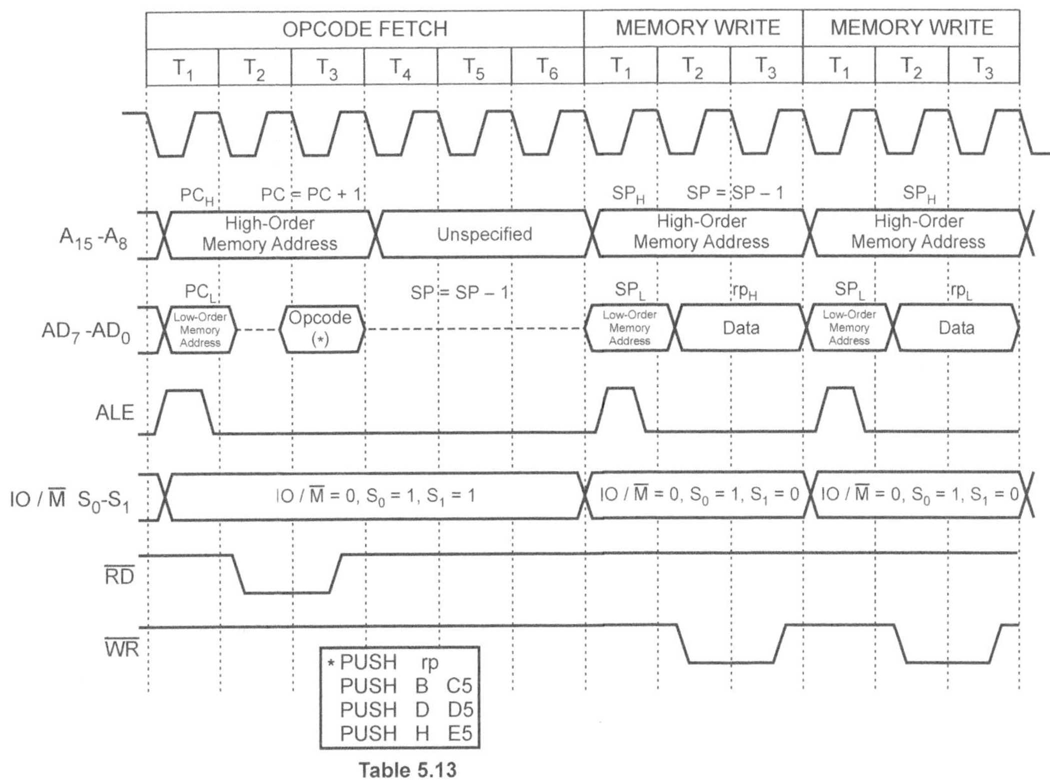

* PUSH	rp
PUSH B	C5
PUSH D	D5
PUSH H	E5

Table 5.13

Fig. 5.44

PUSH rp

The timing diagram of PUSH rp is shown in Fig. 5.44. This instruction decrements stack pointer by one and copies the higher byte of the register pair (rp) into the memory location pointed by stack pointer. It then decrements the stack pointer again by one and copies the lower byte of the register pair into the memory location pointed by stack pointer. The machine cycles required for this instruction are explained below.

1. Opcode fetch : Program counter places address on low-order and high-order address bus. The opcode of PUSH rp. (e.g. C5H of PUSH B) is read into the microprocessor. It decodes it. Program counter is incremented by one. Stack pointer is decremented by one.

2. Memory write : Stack pointer places address on low-order and high-order address bus. Microprocessor writes contents of high-order register (e.g. B in BC) at this address. Stack pointer is again decremented by one.

3. Memory write : Stack pointer gives address on low-order and high-order address bus.

Microprocessor writes contents of low-order register (e.g. C in BC) at this address.

Timing diagram 21 :

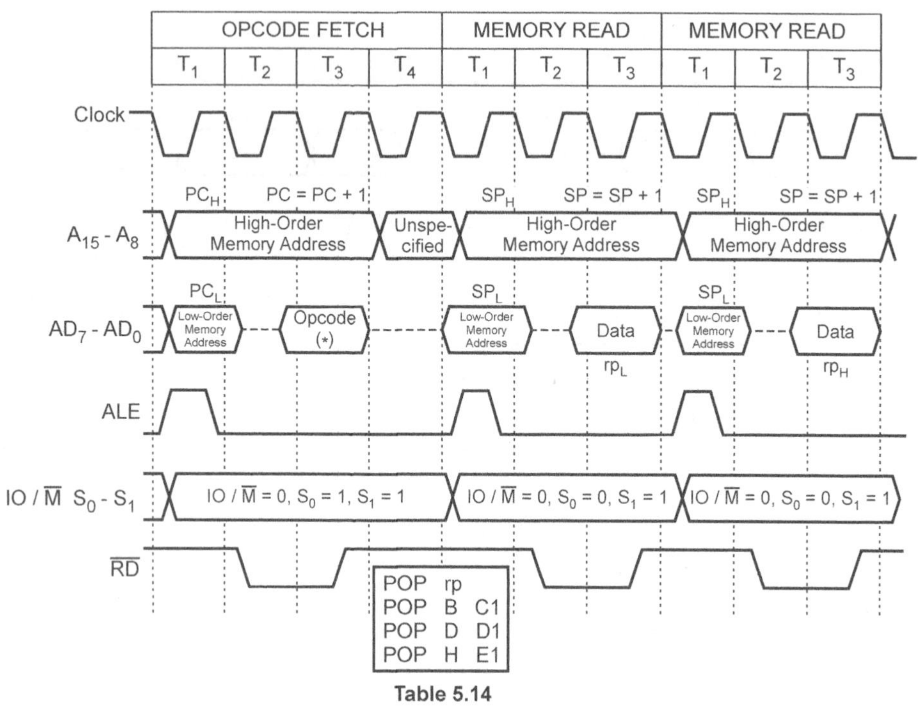

POP	rp	
POP	B	C1
POP	D	D1
POP	H	E1

Table 5.14

Fig. 5.45

POP rp

Fig. 5.45 shows the timing diagram of POP rp instruction. This instruction copies the contents of memory location pointed by the stack pointer into the lower byte of the specified register pair and increments the stack pointer by one. It then copies the contents of memory location pointed by stack pointer into the higher byte of the specified register pair and increments the stack pointer again by one.

This instruction requires the following machine cycles.

1. Opcode fetch : Program counter places address on low-order and high-order address bus. The opcode of POP rp (e.g. C1 of POP B) is read into the microprocessor and is decoded in this machine cycle. The program counter is incremented by one.

2. Memory read : The stack pointer gives address on low-order and high-order address bus. The data present at this address is loaded into the lower byte of the specified register pair (e.g. in C register for BC register pair). The stack pointer is incremented by one.

3. Memory read : The stack pointer gives address on low-order and high-order address bus. The data present at this address is loaded into high order byte of the specified register pair (e.g. in B register for BC register pair). The stack pointer is again incremented by one.

Timing diagram 22 :

PUSH PSW

This instruction decrements stack pointer by one and copies the accumulator contents into the memory location pointed by stack pointer. It then decrements the stack pointer again by one and copies the flag register into the memory location pointed by the stack pointer. The machine cycles required for this instruction are explained below.

1. Opcode fetch : Program counter places address on low-order and high-order address bus. The opcode of PUSH PSW (F5H) is read into the microprocessor. It decodes it. Program counter is incremented by one. Stack pointer is decremented by one.

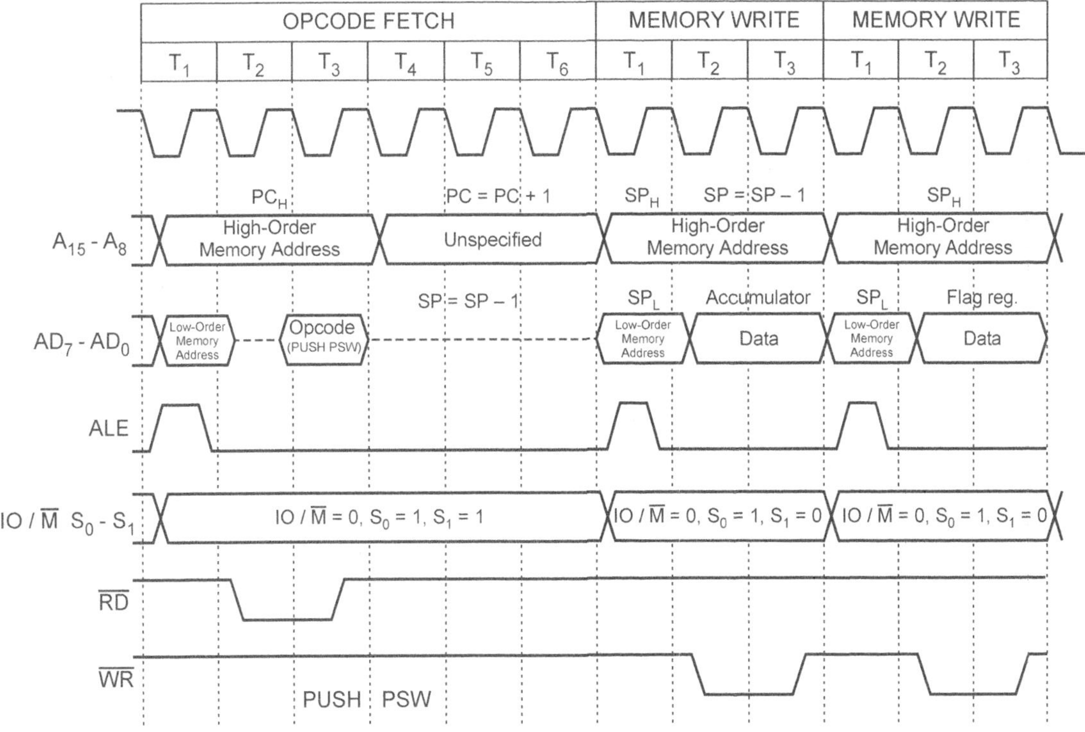

Fig. 5.46

2. Memory write : Stack pointer places address on low-order and high-order address bus. Microprocessor writes contents of accumulator at this address. Stack pointer is again decremented by one.

3. Memory write : Stack pointer gives address on low-order and high-order address bus. Microprocessor writes contents of flag register at this address. The timing diagram of PUSH PSW is shown in Fig. 5.46 (See Fig. 5.46 on previous page) .

Timing diagram 23 :

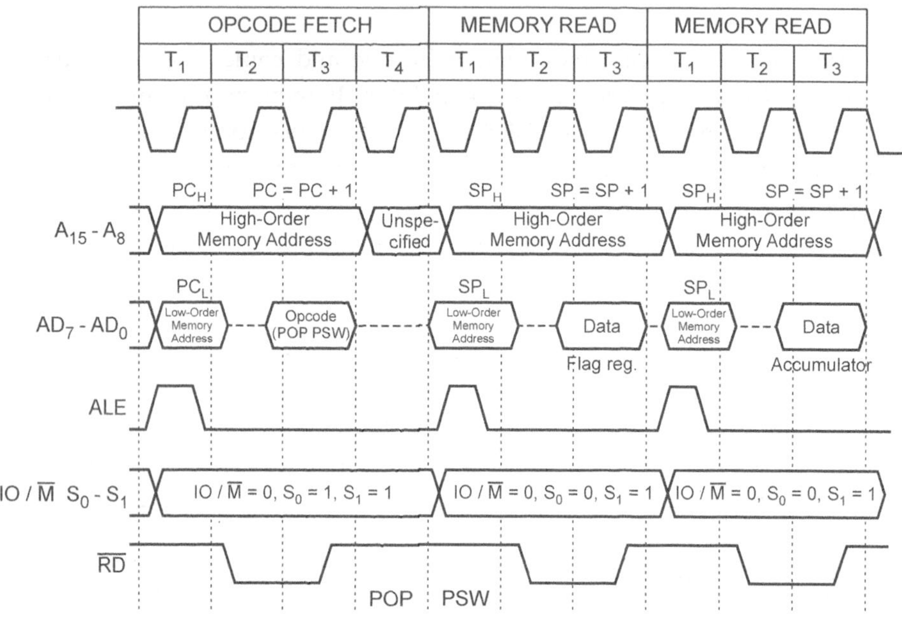

Fig. 5.47

POP PSW

Fig. 5.47 gives the timing diagram of POP PSW instruction. This instruction copies the contents of memory location pointed by the stack pointer into the flag register and increments the stack pointer by one. It then copies the contents of memory location pointed by stack pointer into the A register and increments the stack pointer again by one. This instruction requires the following machine cycles.

1. Opcode fetch : Program counter places address on low-order and high-order address bus. The opcode of POP PSW (C1H) is read into the microprocessor and is decoded in this machine cycle. The program counter is incremented by one.

2. Memory read : The stack pointer gives address on low-order and high-order address bus. The data present at this address is loaded (read) into the flag register of microprocessor. The stack pointer is incremented by one.

3. Memory read : The stack pointer gives address on low-order and high-order address bus. The data present at this address is loaded (read) into the A register of microprocessor. The stack pointer is again incremented by one.

Timing diagram 24 :

CALL address

Fig. 5.48 (See Fig. 5.48 on next page) gives the timing diagram of CALL address instruction. This instruction is used to transfer program control to a subprogram or subroutine. This instruction pushes the current program counter contents onto the stack and loads the given address into the program counter. It requires five machine cycles as explained below.

1. Opcode fetch : Program counter places address on low-order and high-order address bus. Microprocessor reads the opcode of CALL (CDH) from this memory address and decodes it. Program counter is incremented by one. This machine cycle requires 6 T-states.

2. Memory read : Program counter gives address on low-order and high-order address bus. Microprocessor reads the lower byte of address specified within the instruction from the addressed memory location. Program counter is incremented by one.

3. Memory read : Program counter gives address on low-order and high-order address bus. Microprocessor reads the higher byte of address specified within the instruction from the addressed memory location. Program counter is incremented by one. Stack pointer is decremented by one.

4. Memory write : Stack pointer places address on low-order and high-order address bus. Microprocessor writes the high-order byte of program counter at this addressed memory location. Stack pointer is again decremented by one.

5. Memory write : Stack pointer places address on low-order and high-order address bus. Microprocessor writes the low-order byte of program counter at this addressed memory location.

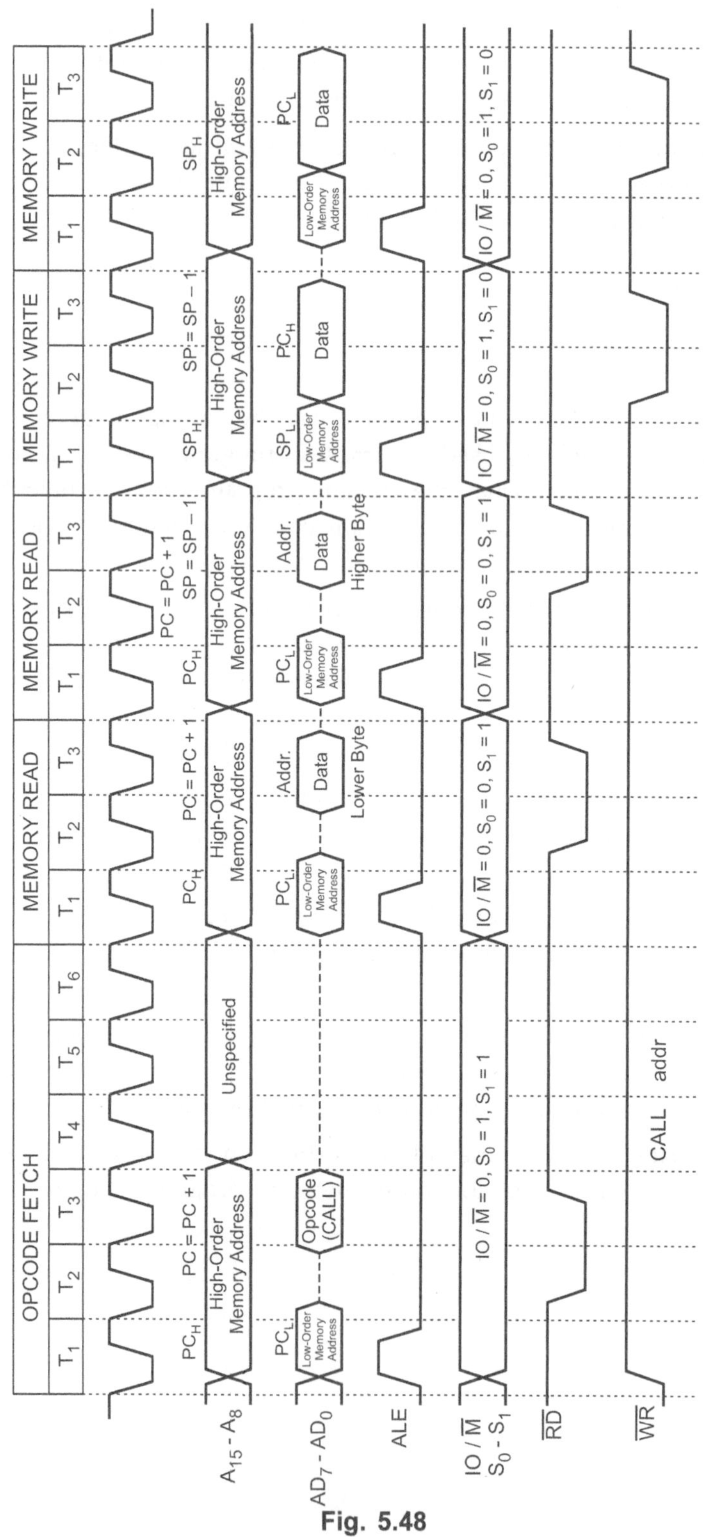

OPCODE FETCH
MEMORY READ
MEMORY READ
MEMORY WRITE
MEMORY WRITE
T1
T2
T3
T4
T5
T6
A15 - A8
AD7 - AD0
ALE
IO / M
S0 - S1
RD
WR
PCH
PC = PC + 1
High-Order Memory Address
Unspecified
PCL
Low-Order Memory Address
Opcode (CALL)
Addr.
Data
Lower Byte
Higher Byte
SP = SP – 1
SPH
SPL
PCH
PCL
IO / M = 0, S0 = 1, S1 = 1
IO / M = 0, S0 = 0, S1 = 1
IO / M = 0, S0 = 1, S1 = 0
CALL addr

Fig. 5.48

Timing diagram 25 :

C condition (When condition is not valid)

This instruction transfers program control to the next instruction written after this instruction. It is similar to J condition when condition is not valid.

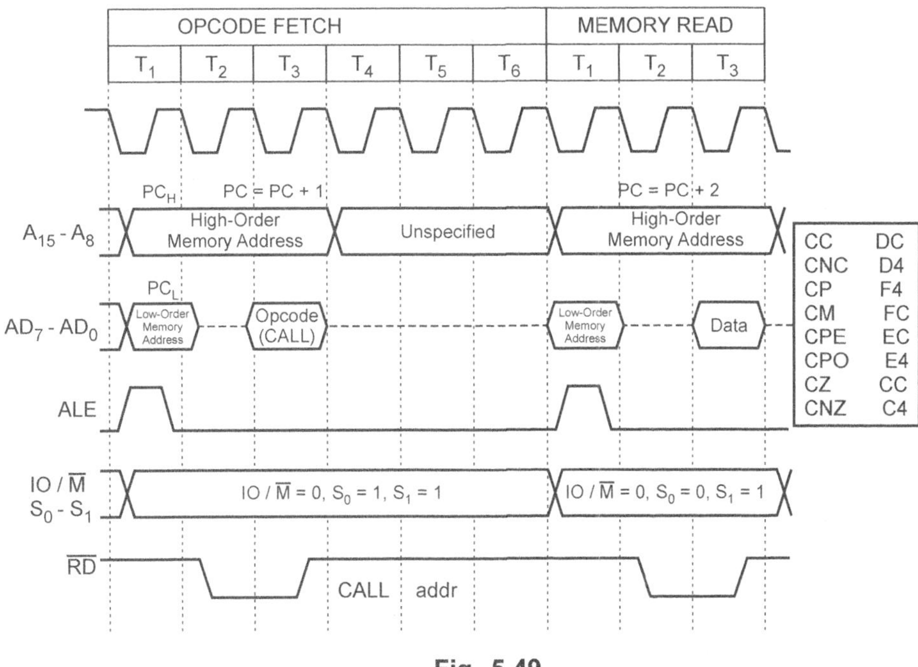

Fig. 5.49

Timing diagram 26 :

RET

This instruction POPs the return address (address of the instruction next to call in the main program) from the stack and loads program counter with this return address. Thus transfers program control to the instruction next to CALL in the main program. It requires three machine cycles as explained below.

1. Opcode fetch : Program counter places address on low-order and high-order address bus. From this address microprocessor reads the opcode of RET (C9H) and decodes it. Program counter is incremented by one.

2. Memory read : This machine cycle reads the "data" into the microprocessor from the memory whose address is the contents of stack pointer. This "data" is the low-order byte of the address to which the program control is to be transferred. Stack pointer is incremented by one.

3. Memory read : This machine cycle reads the "data" in the microprocessor from the memory whose address is the contents of stack pointer. This "data" is the high-order byte of the address to which the program control is to be transferred, Stack pointer is again incremented by one. Fig. 5.50 gives the timing diagram of RET instruction.

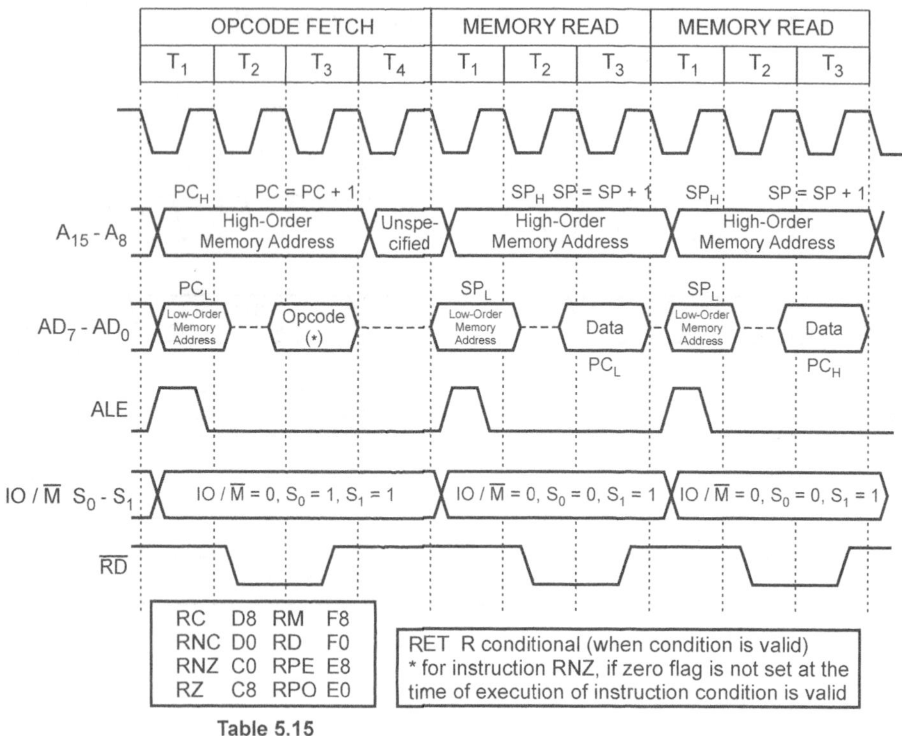

Table 5.15

Fig. 5.50

The timing diagram of $R_{condition}$, when condition is valid is same as that of RET instruction.

Timing diagram 27 :

R conditional (When condition is not valid)

This instruction requires opcode fetch machine cycle.

Fig. 5.51 gives the timing diagram of this instruction. 6 T-states are required for this opcode fetch machine cycle. This instruction transfers program control to next instruction written after this instruction. It requires opcode fetch machine cycle. In this cycle, program counter places address on low-order and high-order address bus. Opcode of Recondition (e.g. C0 of RNZ) is read into the microprocessor from the addressed memory location. Program counter is incremented by one.

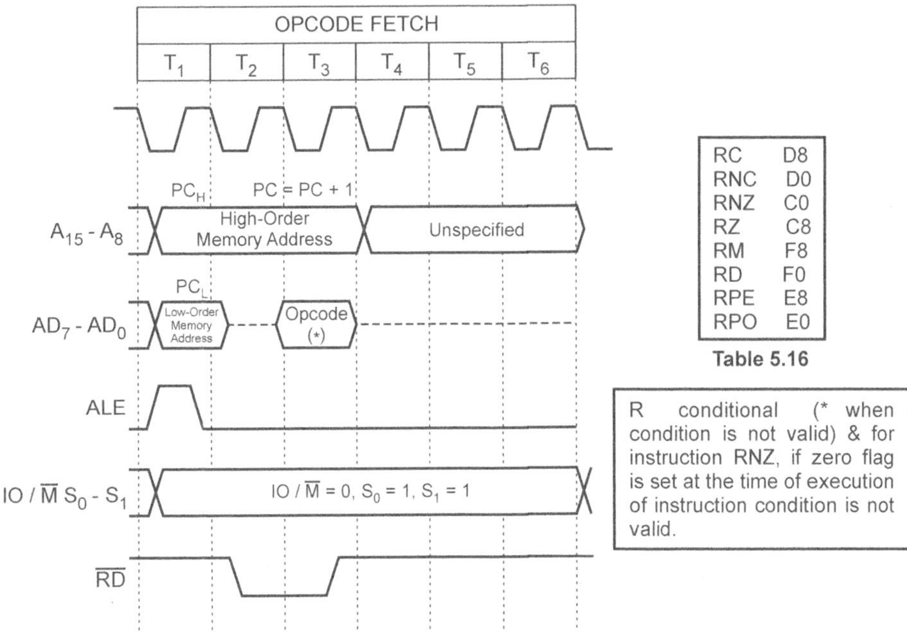

Fig. 5.51

Timing diagram 28 :

RST n

This instruction transfers the program control to the specific memory address, called as vector location. The processor multiplies the RST number (n) by 8 to calculate these vector addresses. Before transferring the program control to the instruction following the vector address, RST instruction saves the current program counter contents on the stack. This instruction requires the following machine cycles.

1. Opcode fetch : Program counter places address on low-order and high-order address bus. The opcode at this memory location (e.g. C7H of RST0) is read into the microprocessor and is decoded. 6 T-states are required for this machine cycle. The stack pointer is decremented by one. Program counter is incremented by one.

2. Memory write : Stack pointer gives address on low-order and high-order address bus. Microprocessor writes the high-order byte of the program counter at this addressed memory location. Stack pointer is again decremented by one.

3. Memory write : Stack pointer gives address on low-order and high-order address bus. Microprocessor writes the low-order byte of the program counter at this addressed memory location. The timing diagram of RST n is shown in Fig. 5.52.

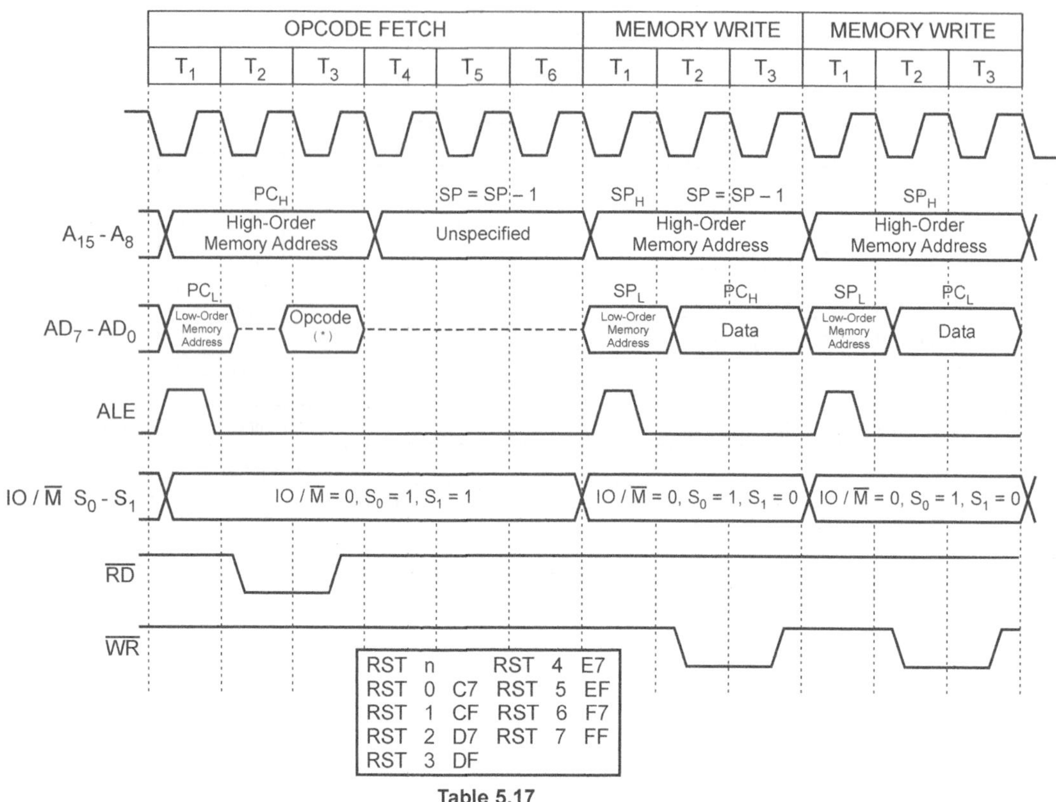

RST n		RST 4	E7
RST 0	C7	RST 5	EF
RST 1	CF	RST 6	F7
RST 2	D7	RST 7	FF
RST 3	DF		

Table 5.17

Fig. 5.52

Timing diagram 29 :

MOV r, M

Fig. 5.53 shows the timing diagram of MOV r, M instruction. This instruction copies the contents from memory location pointed by HL register pair into the register specified within the instruction. This instruction requires two machine cycles.

1. Opcode fetch : Program counter places address on low-order and high-order address bus. The opcode at this memory location (e.g. 7EH of MOV A, M) is read into the microprocessor and is decoded. 4 T-states are required for this machine cycle. Program counter is incremented by one.

2. Memory read : HL register pair gives address on low-order and high-order address bus. The data at this addressed memory location is read into the specified register of the microprocessor. Program counter is incremented by one.

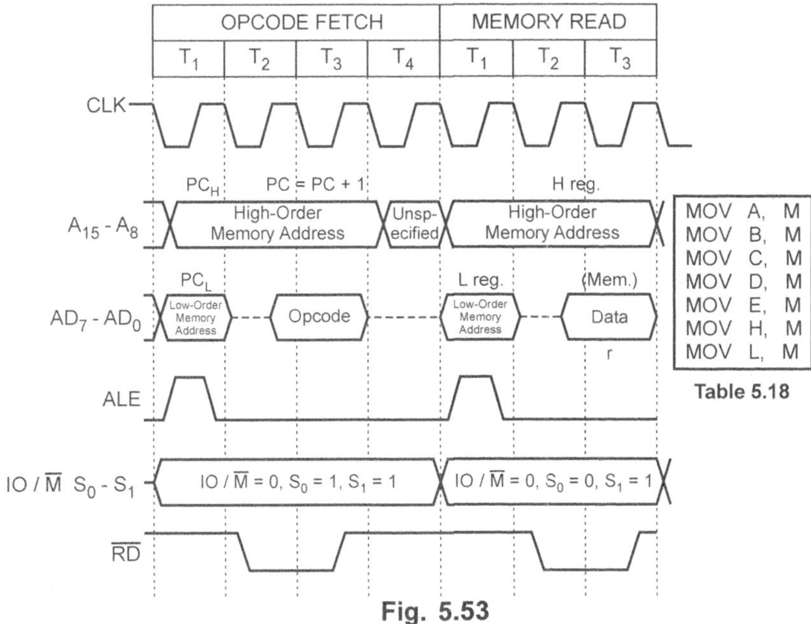

MOV	A,	M
MOV	B,	M
MOV	C,	M
MOV	D,	M
MOV	E,	M
MOV	H,	M
MOV	L,	M

Table 5.18

Fig. 5.53

Timing diagram 30 :

MOV M, r

Fig. 5.54 shows the timing diagram of MOV M, r instruction. This instruction copies the contents from the specified register into the memory location pointed by HL register pair. This instruction requires two machine cycles.

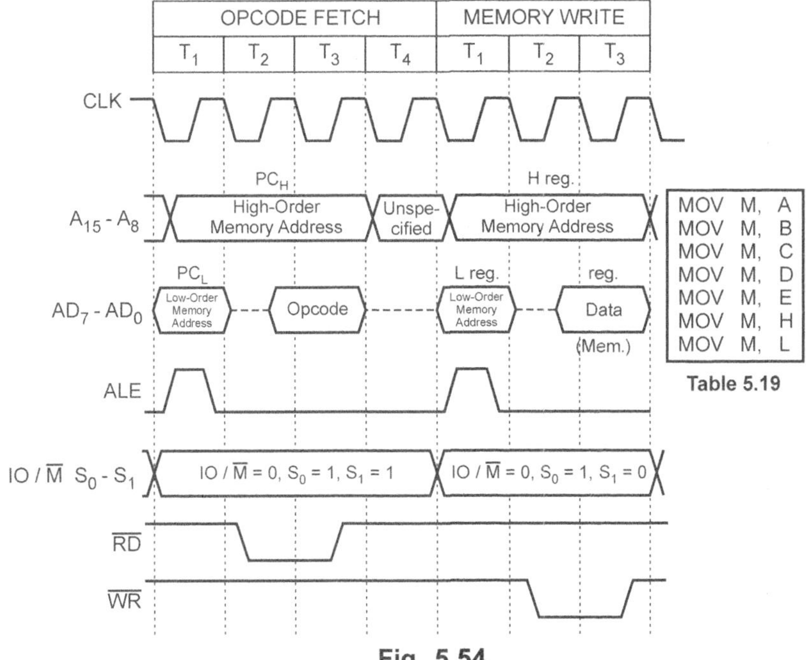

MOV	M,	A
MOV	M,	B
MOV	M,	C
MOV	M,	D
MOV	M,	E
MOV	M,	H
MOV	M,	L

Table 5.19

Fig. 5.54

1. Opcode fetch : Program counter places address on low-order and high-order address bus. The opcode at this memory location (e.g. 77H of MOV M, A) is read into the microprocessor and is decoded. 4 T-states are required for this machine cycle. Program counter is incremented by one.

2. Memory write : This machine cycle is required for writing the data from the specified register into the memory location specified by the HL register pair.

Timing diagram 31 :

IN addr

This instruction reads the data byte from the input port whose address is given within the instruction. This instruction requires two machine cycles.

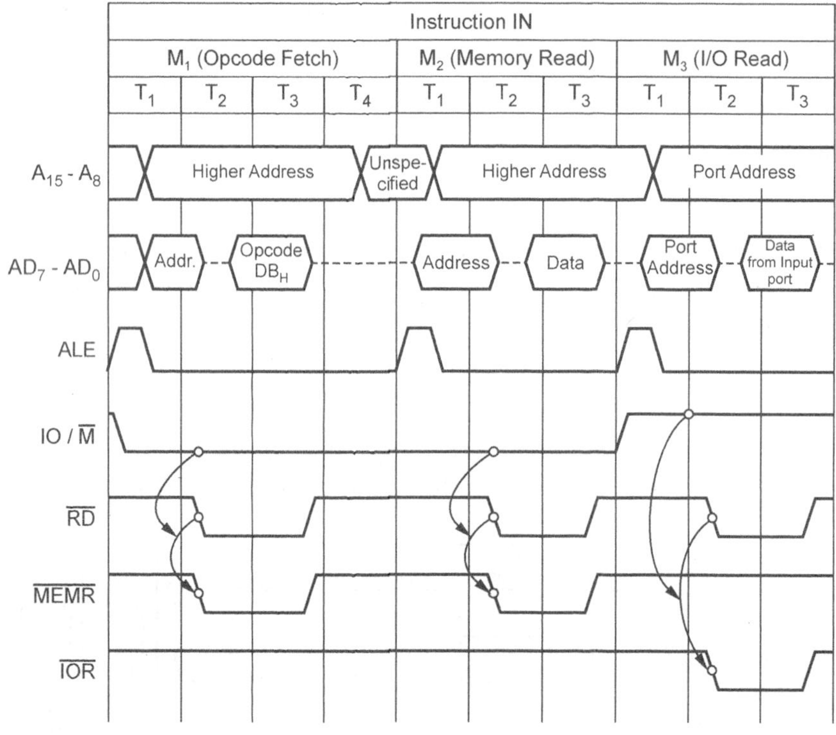

Fig. 5.55

1. Opcode fetch : Program counter places address on low-order and high-order address bus. The opcode at this memory location (e.g. DBH. of IN addr) is read into the microprocessor and is decoded. 4 T-states are required for this machine cycle. Program counter is incremented by one.

2. Memory read : Program counter gives 8-bit address on low-order as well as on high-order address bus. Microprocessor reads data byte from the addressed input port. The data byte is then stored in the accumulator. Program counter is incremented by one.

Timing diagram 32 :

OUT addr

This instruction writes the data byte from the accumulator into the output port whose address is given within the instruction. This instruction requires two machine cycles.

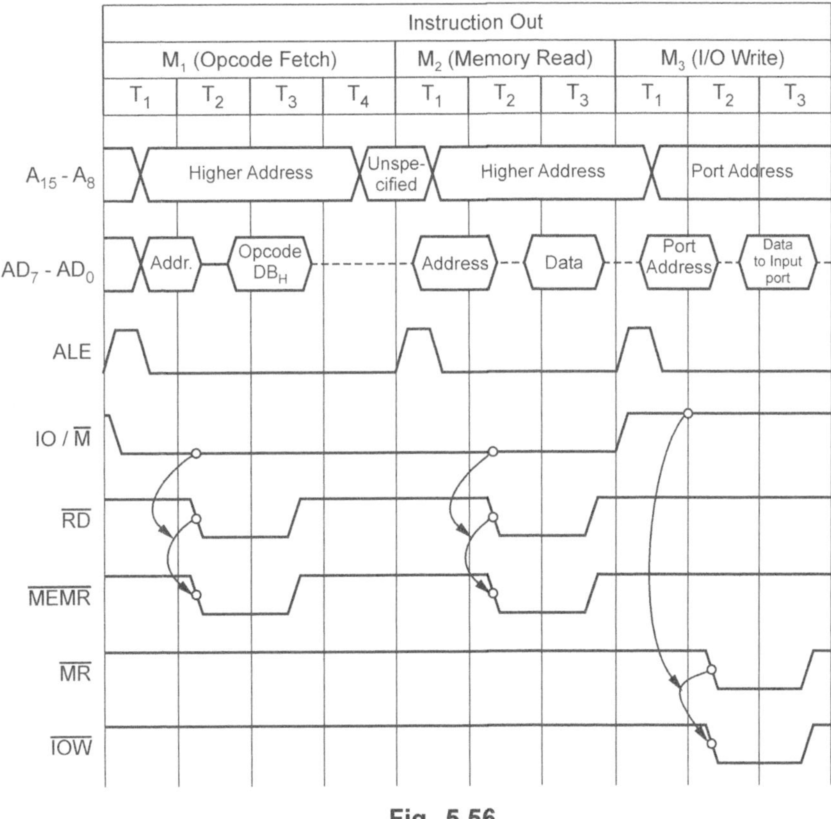

Fig. 5.56

1. Opcode fetch : Program counter places address on low-order and high-order address bus. The opcode at this memory location (e.g. D3H. of OUT addr) is read into the microprocessor and is decoded. 4 T-states are required for this machine cycle. Program counter is incremented by one.

2. Memory write : Program counter gives 8-bit address on low-order as well as on high order address bus. Microprocessor writes data byte from the accumulator into the addressed output port. Program counter is incremented by one.

Timing diagram 33 :

HLT

This instruction halts the processor. It requires only opcode fetch machine cycle. Program counter gives the memory address on low-order and high-order address bus. Opcode of HLT is read and decoded by the microprocessor. Program counter is incremented by one but all buses are tri-stated. The microprocessor can be restarted by a valid interrupt or by applying a RESET signal. Fig. 5.57 gives the timing diagram of HLT instruction

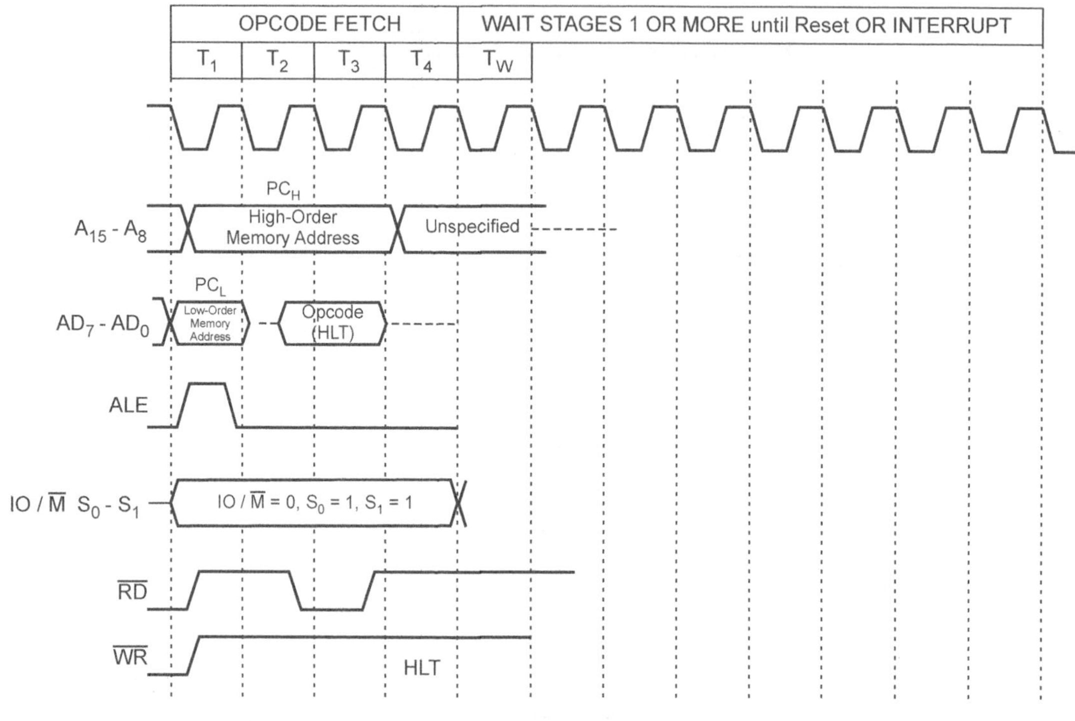

Fig. 5.57

Review Questions

Section 5.1

Q.1 *Distinguish between an instruction cycle, a machine cycle and a clock cycle with an example instruction.* **Dec-09, Marks 6**

Section 5.2

Q.1 *What is clock signal ?*

Q.2 *Show the representation of single signal.*

Q.3 *Show the representation of group of signals.*

Section 5.3

Q.1 *In which T-cycle the ALE signal is activated ?*

Q.2 *Explain how the multiplexed data/address bus is shared for data and address.*

Section 5.4

Q.1 *Draw the timing diagram for I/O read operation and explain.*
May-04, Marks 6

Q.2 *Draw and explain the timing diagram of opcode fetch machine cycle.*

Q.3 *Draw and explain the timing diagram of memory read machine cycle.*

Q.4 *Draw and explain the timing diagram of memory write machine cycle.*

Q.5 *Draw and explain the timing diagrams for I/O read and I/O write machine cycles.*

Q.6 *Explain the interrupt acknowledge cycle for RST instruction.*

Q.7 *Explain the interrupt acknowledge cycle for CALL instruction.*

Q.8 *Draw and explain the bus idle machine cycle.*

Q.9 *Indicate machine cycles and T-states required for execution of LDA instruction.*

Q.10 *Explain the use of Ready signal in 8085.*

Q.11 *Draw the timing diagram of opcode fetch machine cycle and I/O read cycle.*
June-12, Marks 8

Q.12 *With timing diagram, explain the memory read operation in 8085 microprocessor.*
May-11, Marks 2

Section 5.5

Q.1 *Illustrate the timing diagram for the execution of instruction MVI B, 08 in 8085.*
Dec.-10, Marks 10

Q.2 *Draw timing diagrams for the following instructions with appropriate control and status signals. Do not explain.*
i) INR M ii) RST.

Q.3 *Draw timing diagrams for the following instruction with appropriate control and status signal. Explain in brief CALL 2000.*

Q.4 *Draw timing diagram for the following instructions with appropriate control and status signals. Explain in brief :*
i) LXI H, 2000 H ii) DCR M.

Q.5 *Discuss with examples and their timing diagrams the following with respect to 8085 microprocessor.*

i) Instruction with one machine cycle

ii) Instruction with two machine cycles

iii) Instruction with three machine cycles

iv) Instruction with four machine cycles.

Q.6 *Draw and explain the timing diagram for the following instructions.*
i) LDA 2000 ii) INR M.

Q.7 *Draw and explain timing diagrams of the following instructions.*
i) IN ii) STA 4000.

Q.8 *Draw and explain timing diagrams of the following instructions.*
i) LDAX rp ii) DCX rp.

Two Marks Questions with Answers

Q.1 ***What is meant by wait state?***

Ans. : This state is used by slow peripheral devices. The microprocessor remains in wait state as long as READY line is low. During the wait state, the contents of the address, address/data and control buses are held constant.

Q.2 ***Give the steps involved in fetching a byte in 8085.***

Ans. :

- The PC places the 16-bit memory address on the address bus
- The control unit sends the control signal $\overline{RD}$ to enable the memory chip
- The byte from the memory location is placed on the data bus
- The byte is placed in the instruction decoder of the microprocessor and the task is carried out according to the instruction.

Q.3 ***Define instruction cycle, machine cycle and T-state.***

Ans. : Instruction cycle is defined, as the time required completing the execution of an instruction.
Machine cycle is defined as the time required completing one operation of accessing memory, I/O or acknowledging an external request.

T-cycle is defined as one subdivision of the operation performed in one clock period.

Q.4 ***How many machine cycles are needed to execute STA 1800 ?***

Dec.-05

Ans. : Four machine cycles are needed to execute STA 1800 instruction.

Q.5 ***What are the different machine cycles in 8085 microprocessor ?*** May-08

Ans. : The different machine cycles in 8085 microprocessor are :

1. Opcode fetch
2. Memory read
3. Memory write
4. I/O read
5. I/O write
6. Interrupt acknowledge
7. Bus idle

❑❑❑

Notes

6 8086 Processor

Contents

6.1 Introduction

In 1978, Intel came out with the 8086 processor. The Intel 8086 is a 16-bit microprocessor, implemented in N-channel, depletion load, silicon gate technology (HMOS) and packaged it in a 40 pin dual in line package. In this chapter, we study features, architecture, register organization, signal description, memory organization, bus operations, I/O addressing capability, minimum and maximum modes of 8086 processor. We also study the details of 8088 processor.

6.2 Features

Nov./Dec.-06

1. The 8086 is a 16-bit microprocessor. The term "16-bit" means that its arithmetic logic unit, internal registers and most of its instructions are designed to work with 16-bit binary words.
2. The 8086 has a 16-bit data bus, so it can read data from or write data to memory and ports either 16 bits or 8 bits at a time. The 8088, however, has an 8-bit data bus, so it can only read data from or write data to memory and ports 8 bits at a time.
3. The 8086 has a 20-bit address bus, so it can directly access 2^{20} or 10,48,576 (1 MB) memory locations. Each of the 10,48,576 memory locations is byte wide. Therefore, a sixteen-bit words are stored in two consecutive memory locations. The 8088 also has a 20-bit address bus, so it can also address 2^{20} or 10,48,576 memory locations.
4. The 8086 can generate 16-bit I/O address, hence it can access 2^{16} = 65536 I/O ports.
5. The 8086 provides fourteen 16-bit registers.
6. The 8086 has multiplexed address and data bus which reduces the number of pins needed, but does slow down the transfer of data (drawback).
7. The 8086 requires one phase clock with a 33 % duty cycle to provide internal timing.

Range of clock rates (Refer Fig. 6.1) are :-

5 MHz for 8086

8 MHz for 8086-2

10 MHz for 8086-1

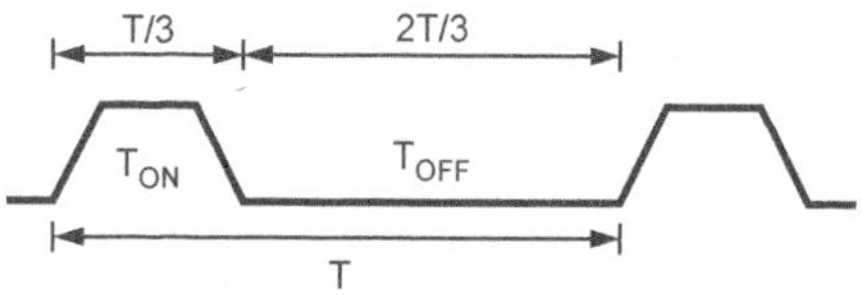

T/3 2T/3 T_{ON} T_{OFF} T

Fig. 6.1 Clock cycle

8. The 8086 is possible to perform bit, byte, word and block operations in 8086. It performs the arithmetic and logical operations on bit, byte, word and decimal numbers including multiply and divide.
9. The Intel 8086 is designed to operate in two modes, namely the minimum mode and the maximum mode. When only one 8086 CPU is to be used in a microcomputer system, the 8086 is used in the minimum mode of operation. In this mode the CPU issues the control signals required by memory and I/O devices. In multiprocessor (more than one processor in the system) system 8086 operates in

maximum mode. In maximum mode, control signals are generated with the help of external bus controller (8288).

10. The Intel 8086 supports multiprogramming. In multiprogramming, the code for two or more processes is in memory at the same time and is executed in a time-multiplexed fashion.
11. An interesting feature of the 8086 is that it fetches upto six instruction bytes (4 instruction bytes for 8088) from memory and queue stores them in order to speed up instruction execution. Later we will discuss this in detail.
12. The 8086 provides powerful instruction set with the following addressing modes : Register, immediate, direct, indirect through an index or base, indirect through the sum of a base and an index register, relative and implied.

6.3 Register Organization of 8086

The 8086 has a powerful set of registers. It includes general purpose registers, segment registers, pointers and index registers and flag register. The Fig. 6.2 shows the register organization of 8086. It is also known as programmer's model of 8086. The registers shown in programmer's model are accessible to programmer. As shown in the Fig. 6.2, all the registers of 8086 are 16-bit registers.

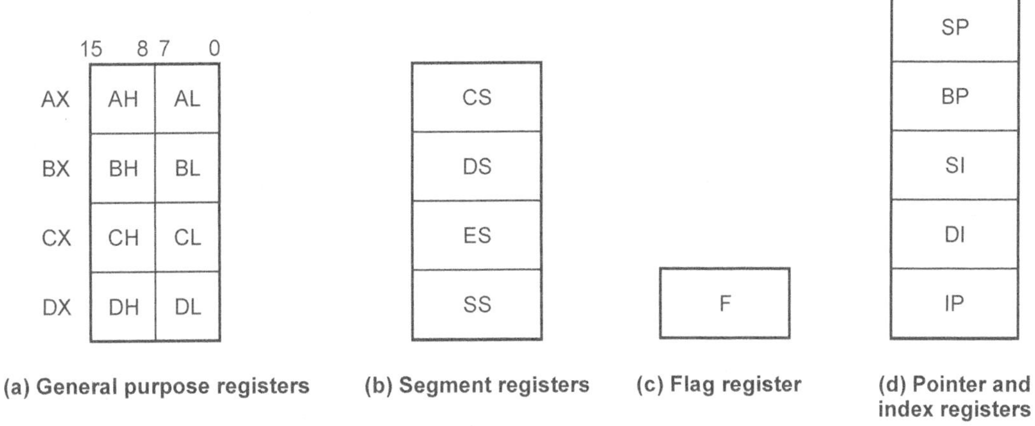

(a) General purpose registers (b) Segment registers (c) Flag register (d) Pointer and index registers

Fig. 6.2 Register organization of 8086

6.3.1 General Purpose Registers

The 8086 has four 16-bit general purpose registers labeled AX, BX, CX and DX. Each 16-bit general purpose register can be split into two 8-bit registers. The letters L and H specify the lower and higher bytes of a particular register. For example, BH means the higher byte (8-bits) of the BX register and BL means the lower byte (8-bits) of the BX register. The letter X is used to specify the complete 16-bit register.

The general purpose registers are either used for holding data, variables and intermediate results temporarily. They can also be used as a counters or used for storing offset address for some particular addressing modes. The register AX is used as 16-bit accumulator whereas register AL (lowerbyte of AX) is used as 8-bit accumulator. The register BX is also used as offset storage for generating physical addresses in case of certain addressing modes. On the other hand, the register CX is also used as a default counter in case of string and loop instructions.

6.3.2 Segment Registers

Nov./Dec.-06, 08

The physical address of the 8086 is 20-bits wide to access 1 Mbyte memory locations. However, its registers and memory locations which contain logical addresses are just 16-bits wide. Hence 8086 uses memory segmentation. It treats the 1 Mbyte of memory as divided into segments, with a maximum size of a segment as 64 kbytes. Thus any location within the segment can be accessed using 16 bits. The 8086 allows only four active segments at a time, as shown in the Fig. 6.3. For the selection of the four active segments the 16-bit segment registers are provided by the bus interface unit (BIU) of the 8086. These four registers are :

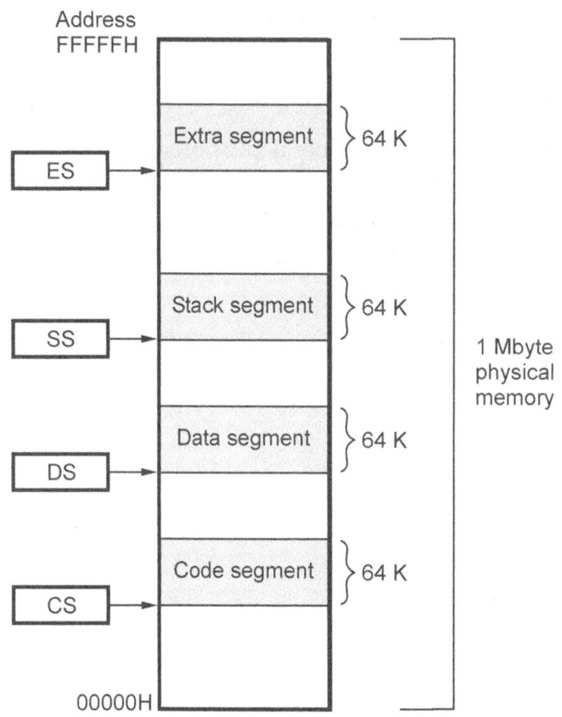

Fig. 6.3 Memory segmentation and segment registers

Code segment (CS) register, the data segment (DS) register, the stack segment (SS) register, and the extra segment (ES) register. These are used to hold the upper 16-bits of the starting addresses of the four memory segments, on which 8086 works at a particular time. For example, the value in CS identifies the starting address of 64 kbyte segment known as code segment. By "starting address", we mean the lowest addressed byte in the active code segment. The starting address is also known as **base address** or **segment base**.

The BIU always inserts zeros for the lower 4 bits (nibble) in the contents of segment register to generate 20-bit base address. For example, if the code segment register contains 348AH, then code segment will start at address 348A0H.

Functions of Segment Registers

1. The CS register holds the upper 16-bits of the starting address of the segment from which the is currently fetching the instruction code byte.
2. The SS register is used for the upper 16-bits of the starting address for the program stack (all stack related instructions will operate on stack)
3. ES register and DS register are used to hold the upper 16-bits of the starting address of the two memory segments which are used for data.

6.3.3 Pointers and Index Registers

All segment registers are 16-bit wide. But it is necessary to generate 20-bit address (physical address) on the address bus. To get 20-bit physical address one or more pointer or index registers are associated with each segment register. The pointer registers IP, BP and SP are associated with code, data and stack segments, respectively. They hold the offset within the code, data and stack segments, respectively. The index registers DI and SI are used as a general purpose registers as well as for offset storage in case of indexed, based indexed and relative based indexed addressing modes. The detail description of pointers and index register is given in section 6.4.3.4.

6.3.4 Flag Register

The contents of flag (F) register of 8086 indicate some conditions produced by the execution of an arithmetic or logical instruction. It also contains some flag bits to control the certain operations of the execution unit. The detail description of flag register is given in section 6.4.2.2.

6.4 Architecture of 8086

April/May-03, 05; Nov./Dec.-03, 04, 06; May/June-08

Fig. 6.4 shows a block diagram of the 8086 internal architecture. It is internally divided into two separate functional units. These are the Bus Interface Unit (BIU) and the Execution Unit (EU). These two functional units can work simultaneously to increase system speed and hence the throughput. Throughput is a measure of number of instructions executed per unit time.

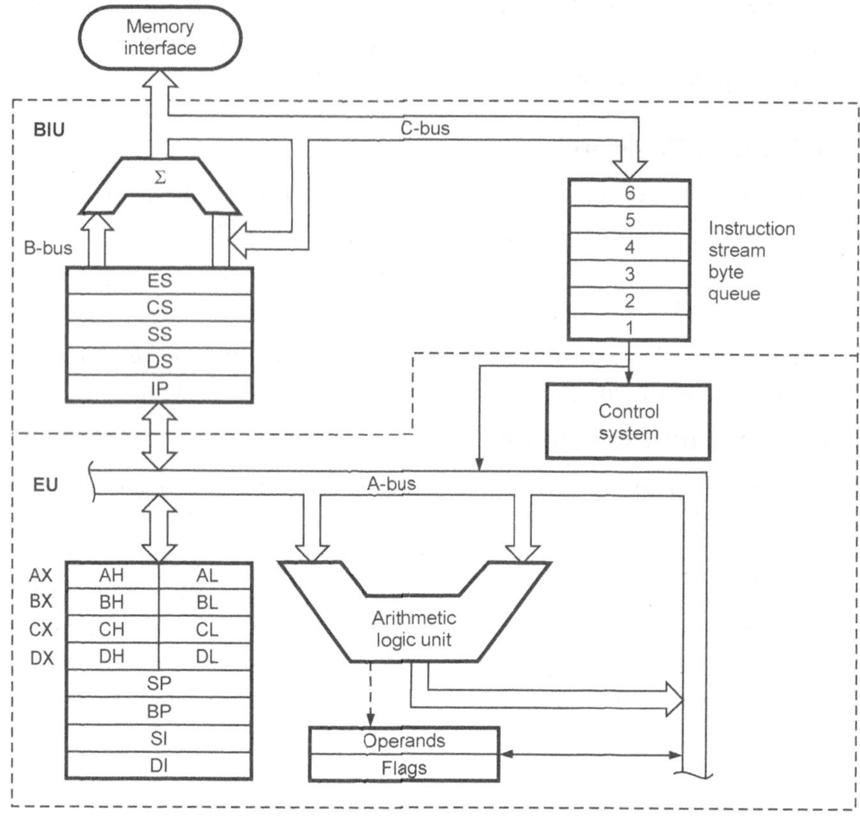

Fig. 6.4 8086 internal block diagram

6.4.1 Bus Interface Unit [BIU]

Nov./Dec.-06, 08, May/June-07

The bus interface unit is the 8086's interface to the outside world. It provides a full 16-bit bi-directional data bus and 20-bit address bus. The bus interface unit is responsible for performing all external bus operations, as listed below.

Functions of Bus Interface Unit

1. It sends address of the memory or I/O.
2. It fetches instruction from memory.
3. It reads data from port/memory.
4. It writes data into port/memory.
5. It supports instruction queuing.
6. It provides the address relocation facility.

To implement these functions the contains the instruction queue, segment registers instruction pointer, address summer and bus control logic.

Instruction Queue

To speed up program execution, the fetches **six instruction bytes** ahead of time from the memory. These prefetched instruction bytes are held for the execution unit in a group of six registers called **Queue**. With the help of queue it is possible to fetch next instruction when current instruction is in execution. For example, current instruction in execution is a multiplication instruction. In 8086, operands for multiplication operations are within registers. Still it requires 100 clock cycles to execute multiply instruction. Like multiplication there are number of other instructions in 8086 which need a quite a large number of clock cycles for execution. During this execution time the BIU fetches the next instruction or instructions from memory into the instruction queue instead of remaining idle. The BIU continues this process as long as the queue is not full. Due to this, execution unit gets the ready instruction in the queue and instruction fetch time is eliminated. This is illustrated in Fig. 6.5.

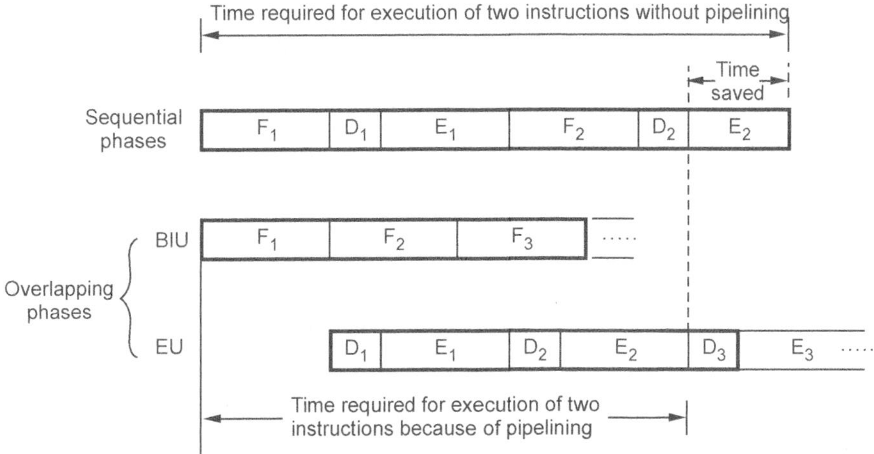

Fig. 6.5 Pipelining

The queue operates on the principle first in first out (FIFO). So that the execution unit gets the instructions for execution in the order they are fetched. In case of JUMP and CALL instructions, instruction already fetched in queue are of no use. Hence, in these cases queue is dumped and newly formed by loading instructions from new address specified by JUMP or CALL instruction. Feature of fetching the next instruction while the current instruction is executing is called **pipelining**.

6.4.2 Execution Unit [EU]

The execution unit of 8086 tells the BIU from where to fetch instructions or data, decodes instructions and executes instructions. It contains

- Control Circuitry
- Instruction Decoder
- Arithmetic Logic Unit (ALU)
- Flag Register
- General Purpose Registers
- Pointers and Index Registers

6.4.2.1 Control Circuitry, Instruction Decoder, ALU

The control circuitry in the EU directs the internal operations. A decoder in the EU translates the instructions fetched from memory into a series of actions which the EU performs. ALU is 16-bit. It can add, subtract, AND, OR, XOR, increment, decrements, complement and shift binary numbers.

6.4.2.2 Flag Register

Nov./Dec.-04, 06, 08; April/May-05, May/June-07

A flag is a flip-flop which indicates some condition produced by the execution of an instruction or controls certain operations of the EU. The flag register contains nine active flags as shown in the Fig. 6.6.

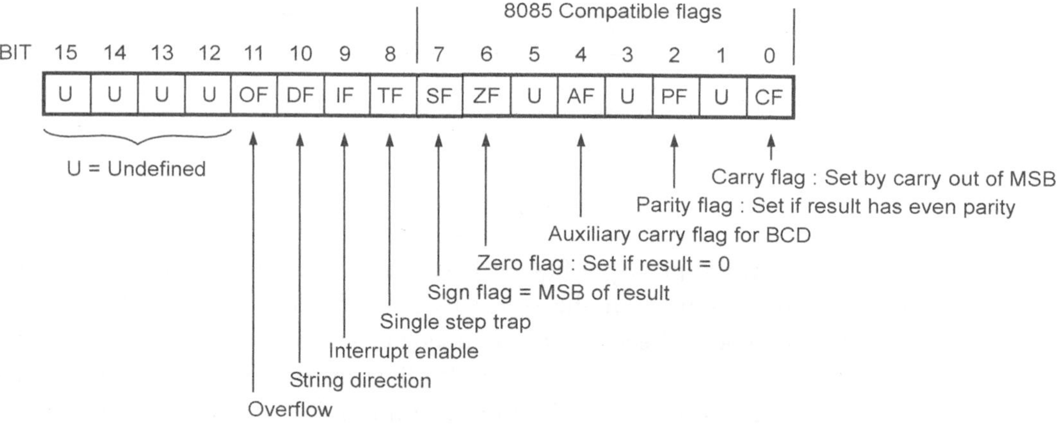

Fig. 6.6 8086 flag register bit pattern

Six of them are used to indicate some condition produced by instruction.

1. Carry Flag (CF) : In case of addition this flag is set if there is a carry out of the MSB. The carry flag also serves as a borrow flag for subtraction. In case of subtraction it is set when borrow is needed.

2. Parity Flag (PF) : It is set to 1 if result of byte operation or lower byte of the word operation contain an even number of ones; otherwise it is zero.

3. Auxiliary Flag (AF) : This flag is set if there is an overflow out of bit 3 i.e., carry from lower nibble to higher nibble (D_3 bit to D_4 bit). This flag is used for BCD operations and it is not available for the programmer.

4. Zero Flag (ZF) : The zero flag sets if the result of operation in ALU is zero and flag resets if the result is nonzero. The zero flag is also set if a certain register content becomes zero following an increment or decrement operation of that register.

5. Sign Flag (SF) : After the execution of arithmetic or logical operations, if the MSB of the result is 1, the sign bit is set. Sign bit 1 indicates the result is negative; otherwise it is positive.

6. Overflow Flag (OF) : This flag is set if result is out of range. For addition this flag is set when there is a carry into the MSB and no carry out of the MSB or vice-versa. For subtraction, it is set when the MSB needs a borrow and there is no borrow from the MSB, or vice-versa.

Example 6.1 : *Give the contents of the flag register after execution of following addition.*

```
  0110 0101 1101 0001
+ 0010 0011 0101 1001
---------------------
  1000 1001 0010 1010
```

Solution : SF = 1, ZF = 0, PF = 1, CF = 0, AF = 0 , OF = 1

Example 6.2 : *Give the contents of the flag register after execution of following subtraction*

```
  0110 0111 0010 1001
- 0011 0101 0100 1010
---------------------
  0011 0001 1101 1111
```

Solution : SF = 0, ZF = 0, PF = 1, CF = 0, AF = 1, OF = 0

The three remaining flags are used to control certain operations of the processor.

1. Trap Flag (TF) : One way to debug a program is to run the program one instruction at a time and see the contents of used registers and memory variables after execution of every instruction. This process is called '**single stepping**' through a program. Trap flag is used for single stepping through a program. If set, a trap is executed after execution of each instruction, i.e. interrupt service routine is executed which displays various registers and memory variable contents on the display after execution of each instruction. Thus programmer can easily trace and correct errors in the program.

2. Interrupt Flag (IF) : It is used to allow/prohibit the interruption of a program. If set, a certain type of interrupt (a maskable interrupt) can be recognized by the 8086; otherwise, these interrupts are ignored.

3. Direction Flag (DF) : It is used with string instructions. If DF = 0, the string is processed from its beginning with the first element having the lowest address. Otherwise, the string is processed from the high address towards the low address.

6.4.2.3 General Purpose Registers

The general purpose registers of 8086 is a part of execution unit. These are already explained in section 6.3.1.

6.4.3 Memory Segmentation / Real Mode Memory Addressing

Two types of memory organizations are commonly used. These are **linear addressing** and **segmented addressing**. In linear addressing the entire memory space is available to the processor in one linear array. In the segmented addressing, on the other hand, the available memory space is divided into "chunks" called segments. Such a memory is known as **segmented memory**. In 8086 system the available memory space is 1 Mbytes. This memory is divided into number of logical segments. Each segment is 64 kbytes in size and addressed by one of the segment registers. The 16-bit contents of the segment register gives the starting/base address of a particular segment, as shown in Fig. 6.7. To address a specific memory location within a segment we need an offset address. The offset address is also 16-bit wide and it is provided by one of the associated pointer or index register.

Note : The 80286 and above operate in either the real or protected mode. Only the 8086 and 8088 operate in the real mode. Real mode operation allows the microprocessor to address only the first 1 Mbyte of memory space.

6.4.3.1 Rules for Memory Segmentation

1. The four segments can overlap for small programs. In a minimum system all four segments can start at the address 00000H.
2. The segment can begin/start at any memory address which is divisible by 16.

6.4.3.2 Advantages of Memory Segmentation

Nov./Dec.-06, May/June-08

1. It allows the memory addressing capacity to be 1 Mbyte even though the address associated with individual instruction is only 16-bit.

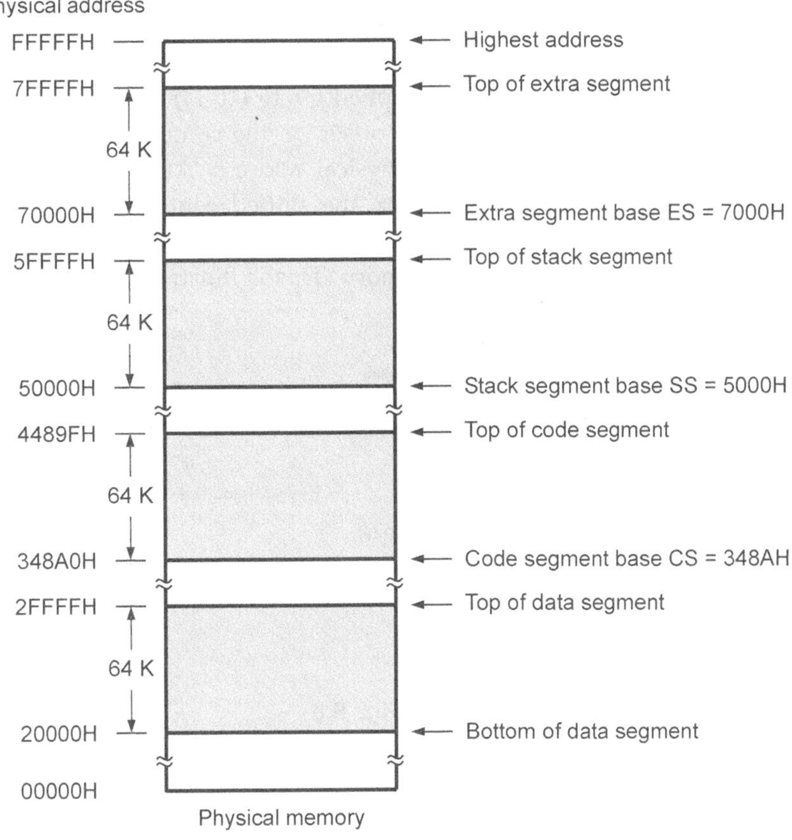

Fig. 6.7 Memory segmentation

2. It allows instruction code, data, stack, and portion of program to be more than 64 kB long by using more than one code, data, stack segment, and extra segment.
3. It facilitates use of separate memory areas for program, data and stack.
4. It permits a program or its data to be put in different areas of memory, each time the program is executed .e. program can be relocated which is very useful in multiprogramming.

6.4.3.3 Generation of 20-bit Address

Nov./Dec.-06, 07

To access a specific memory location from any segment we need 20-bit physical address. The 8086 generates this address using the contents of segment register and the offset register associated with it. Let us see how 8086 access code byte within the code segment.

We know that the CS register holds the base address of the code segment. The 8086 provides an instruction pointer (IP) which holds the 16-bit address of the next code byte within the code segment. The value contained in the IP is referred to as an **offset**. This value must be offset from (added to) the segment base address in CS to produce the required 20-bit physical address.

The contents of the CS register are multiplied by 16 (10 H) i.e. shifted by 4 positions to the left by inserting 4 zero bits and then the offset i.e. the contents of IP register are added to the shifted contents of CS to generate physical address. As shown in the Fig. 6.8, the contents of CS register are 348A H, therefore the shifted contents of CS register are 348A0 H. When the BIU adds the offset of 4214 H in the IP to this starting address, we get 38AB4 H as a 20-bit physical address of memory. This is illustrated in Fig. 6.8 (b).

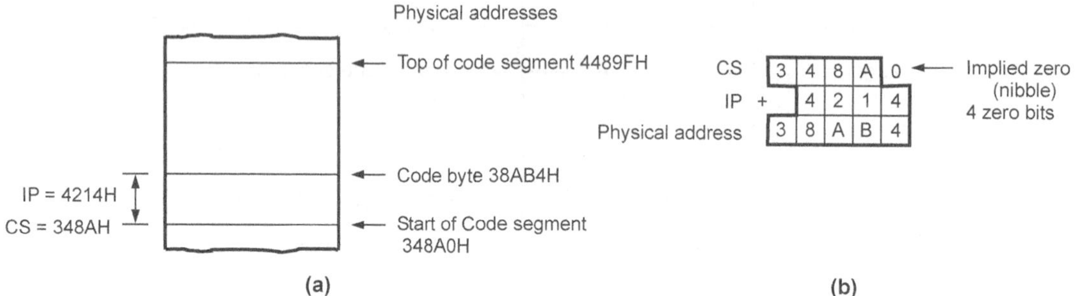

Fig. 6.8

We have seen that how 20-bit physical address is generated within the code segment. In the similar way the 20-bit physical address is generated in the other segments. However, it is important to note that each segment requires particular segment register and offset register to generate 20-bit physical address.

6.4.3.4 Pointers and Index Registers

All segment registers are 16-bit. But it is necessary to put 20-bit address (physical address) on the address bus. To get 20-bit physical address one more register is associated with each segment register the way IP is associated with CS.

These additional registers belong to the pointer and index group. The pointer and index group consists of Instruction Pointer (IP), Stack Pointer (SP), Base Pointer (BP), Source Index (SI) and Destination Index (DI) registers.

Stack Pointer (SP) : The stack pointer (SP) register contains the 16-bit offset from the start of the segment to the top of stack. For stack operation, physical address is produced by adding the contents of stack pointer register to the segment base address in SS. To do this the contents of the stack segment register are shifted four bits left and the contents of SP are added to the shifted result. If the contents of SP are 9F20H and SS are 4000H then the physical address is calculated as follows. (Refer Fig. 6.9).

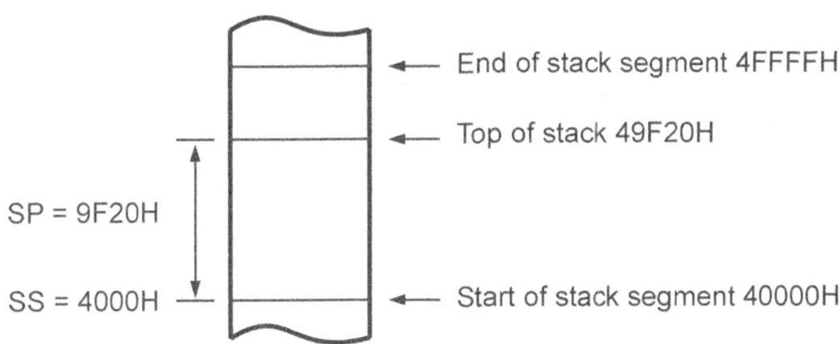

Fig. 6.9 Stack and stack pointer

SS = 4000H after shifting four bits left SS = 40000H

Now

SS	40000H
+ SP	9F20H
Physical address	49F20H

Base Pointer, Source Index and Destination Index (BP, SI and DI)

These three 16-bit registers can be used as general purpose registers. However, their main use is to hold the 16-bit offset of the data word in one of the segments.

Base pointer : We can use the BP register instead of SP for accessing the stack using the based addressing mode. In this case, the 20-bit physical stack address is calculated from BP and SS. Addressing modes are discussed in later section.

Source Index : Source index (SI) can be used to hold the offset of a data word in the data segment. In this case, the 20-bit physical data address is calculated from SI and DS.

Destination Index : The ES register points to the extra segment in which data is stored. String instructions always use ES and DI to determined the 20-bit physical address for the destination.

6.4.3.5 Default and Alternate Register Assignments

Table 6.1 shows that some memory references and their default and alternate segment definitions. For example, instruction codes can only be stored in the code segment with IP used as an offset. Similarly, for stack operations only SS and SP or BP registers can be used to give segment and offset addresses respectively. On the other hand, for accessing general data, string source, data pointed by BX and BP registers; it is possible to use alternate segments by using segment override prefix. See examples given after Table 6.1.

Type of memory reference	Default segment	Alternate segment	Offset (Logical address)
Instruction fetch	CS	None	IP
Stack operation	SS	None	SP, BP
General data	DS	CS, ES, SS	Effective address
String source	DS	CS, ES, SS	SI
String destination	ES	None	DI
BX used as pointer	DS	CS, ES, SS	Effective Address
BP used as pointer	SS	CS, ES, DS	Effective Address

Table 6.1 Default and alternate register assignments

For the following examples we have assumed

CS = 1000H, DS = 2000H, SS = 3000H, ES = 4000H, BP = 0010 H,

BX = 0020H, SP = 0030H, SI = 0040H, DI = 0050H

Example 1 :

1) MOV AL, [BP]

```
                   3000[0] H   SS
                 +  001 0  H   BP
Physical Address   3001 0  H
```

This instruction copies a byte from memory location to the AL register. The effective address for the memory location is contained in the BP register. By default, an effective address is added to the stack segment (SS) to produce the physical memory address (30010 H).

2) MOV CX, [BX]

```
                   2000[0] H   DS
                 +  002 0  H   BX
Physical Address   2002 0  H
```

This instruction copies a word from memory location to the CX register. The effective address is contained in the BX register. By default an effective address is added to the data segment (DS) to produce the physical memory address (20020 H).

3) MOV AL, [BP+SI]

```
                    001 0  H   BP
                 +  004 0  H   SI
Effective Address   005 0  H

                   3000[0] H   SS
                 +  005 0  H   EA
Physical Address   3005 0  H
```

This instruction copies a byte from memory location to the AL register. The effective address is the summation of the contents of the BP and SI register.

The effective address is added to the stack segment (SS) to get the physical address.

4) MOV CS : [BX], AL

```
                      1000[0] H   CS
                    +  002 0 H    BX
                    -----------
Physical Address      1002 0 H
```

This instruction copies a byte from the AL register to a memory location. The effective address for the memory location is contained in the BX register. By default an effective address in BX will be added to the data segment (DS) to produce the physical memory address. In this instruction, the CS: in front of [BX] indicates that we want BIU to add the effective address to the code segment (CS) to produce the physical address. The CS: is called **segment override prefix.**

6.4.3.6 Segment Override Prefix

Nov./Dec.-06

The segment override prefix allows the programmer to deviate from the default segment. The segment override prefix is an additional 8-bit code which is put in memory before the code for the rest of the instruction. This additional code selects the alternate segment register. The code byte for the segment override prefix as the format 001XX110. The XX represents a 2 bits which are as follows : ES = 00, CS = 01, SS = 10 and DS = 11. It is important to note that the segment override prefix may be added to almost any instruction in any memory addressing mode.

6.5 Addressing Modes

Dec.-07,08; June-07, 09; May/June-06; Nov./Dec.-06

We have seen how the 8086 fetches code bytes from memory by generating 20-bit physical address with the help of IP and CS. We have also seen how the 8086 accesses the stack using SS and SP. In this section we will see the different ways that an 8086 can access the data. The different ways that a processor can access data are referred to as **addressing modes**.

The addressing modes of any processor can be broadly classified as :

- Data addressing modes.
- Program memory addressing modes.
- Stack memory addressing modes.

6.5.1 Data Addressing Modes

May/June-08

The data addressing modes can be further classified as

1. Addressing modes for accessing immediate and register data (register and immediate modes).
2. Addressing modes for accessing data in memory (memory modes)
3. Addressing modes for accessing I/O ports (I/O modes)

6.5.1.1 Addressing Modes for Accessing Immediate and Register Data

1. Register Addressing Mode

This mode specifies the source operand, destination operand, or both to be contained in an 8086 register.

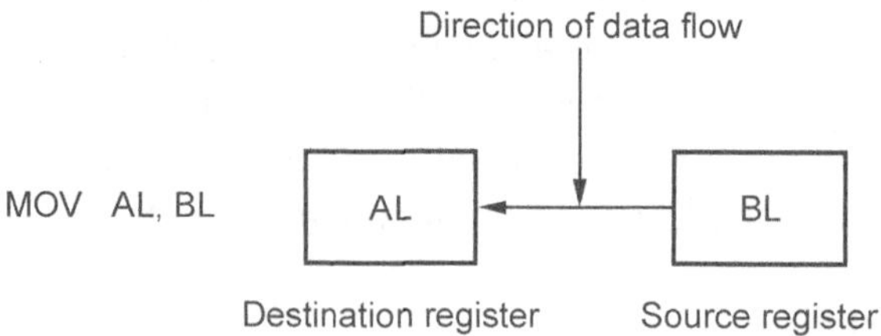

Note : Both source and destination operands are in 8086 register

Example :

MOV , CX ; Copies the 16-bit contents of CX into BX

MOV CL, BL ; Copies 8-bit contents of BL into CL.

2. Immediate Addressing Mode

In an immediate mode, 8 or 16-bit data can be specified as a part of instruction.

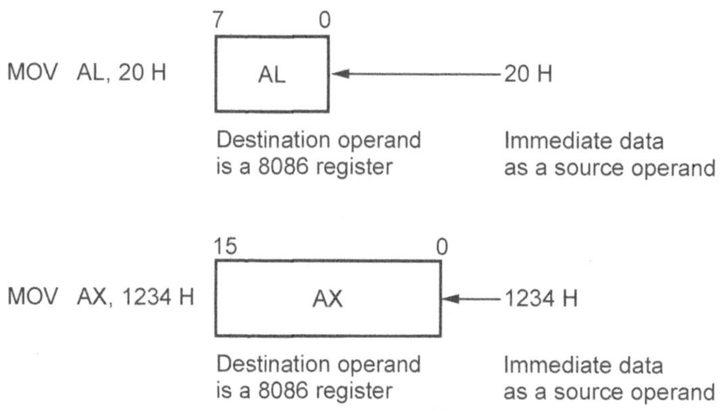

Note : Arrow indicates direction of data flow

Examples :

MOV BL, 26H ; Copies the 8-bit data 26H into BL

MOV , 4567H ; Copies the 16-bit data 4567H into CX.

6.5.1.2 Addressing Modes for Accessing Data in Memory

As mentioned before, the Execution Unit (EU) has direct access to all registers and data for register and immediate operands. However, the EU cannot directly access the memory operands. It must use the BIU segment registers to access memory operands. For example, when the EU needs to access a memory location, it sends an offset value to the BIU. This offset is also called the **Effective Address (EA).** Note that EA is displacement of the desired location from the segment base. As mentioned before, the BIU generates a

20-bit physical address after shifting the contents of the desired segment register four bits to the left and then adding the 16-bit EA to it.

There are six ways to specify effective address (EA) in the instruction.

a. Direct addressing mode
b. Register indirect addressing mode
c. Based addressing mode
d. Indexed addressing mode
e. Based indexed addressing mode
f. String addressing mode.

1. Direct Addressing Mode :

In this mode, the 16-bit effective address (EA) is taken directly from the displacement field of the instruction. The displacement (unsigned 16-bit or sign-extended 8-bit number) is stored in the location following the instruction opcode.

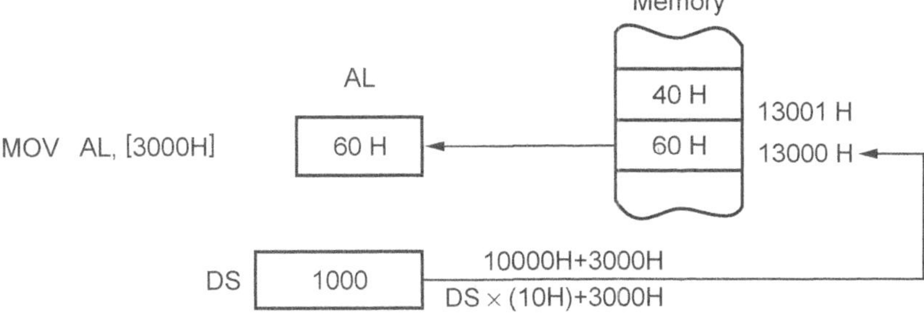

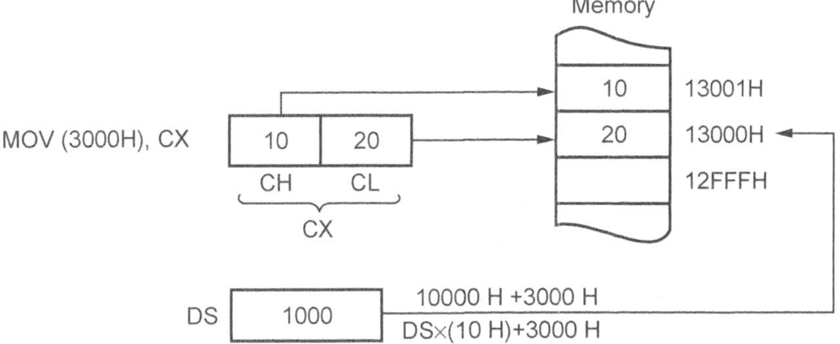

Note : 1. Assume DS = 1000

$\therefore$ Physical address = DS ×(10H)+ 3000H

= 1000[0] + 3000H = 13000H

2. Arrow indicates direction of data flow.

Example :

MOV CL, [9823H] ; This instruction will copy the contents of the
; memory location, at a displacement of 9823H from the
; data segment base, into the CL register. Here, 9823H is
; the effective address (EA) which is written
; directly in the instruction.

2. Register Indirect Addressing Mode

In this mode, the EA is specified in either a pointer register or an index register. The pointer register can be either base register BX or base pointer register BP and index register can be either Source Index (SI) register or Destination Index (DI) register. The 20-bit physical address is computed using DS and EA.

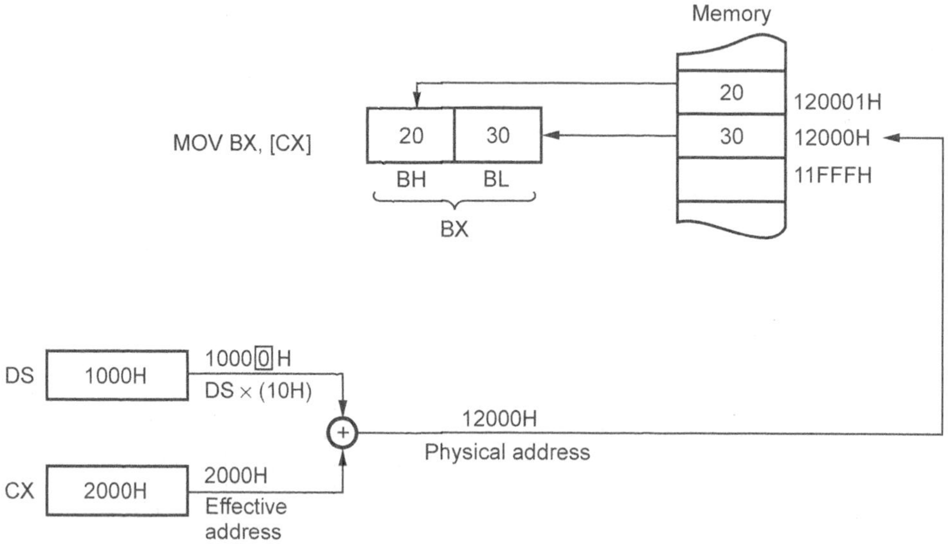

Example :

1. MOV [DI], BX ; The instruction copies the 16-bit contents of BX into a
; memory location offset by the value of EA specified in DI
; from the current contents in DS. Now, if [DS] = 7205H,
; [DI] = 0030H, and [] = 8765H, then after MOV [DI], BX,
; content of (8765H) is copied to memory locations
; 72080H and 72081H.

2. MOV DL, [BP] ; This instruction copies the 8-bit
; contents in DL from the memory location offset by the
; value of EA specified in BP from the contents of SS.
; Because data addressed by BP are by default located in
; stack segment (SS).

3. Base-Plus-Index-Addressing :

Base-plus-index addressing is similar to indirect addressing because it indirectly addresses memory data. This addressing uses one base register (BP or BX) and one index register (DI or SI) to indirectly address memory. The base register often holds the beginning location of a memory array, while the index register holds the relative position of an element in the array. Remember that whenever BP addresses the memory data, the contents of stack segment, BP and index register are used to generate physical address.

Locating data with base-pulse-index addressing :

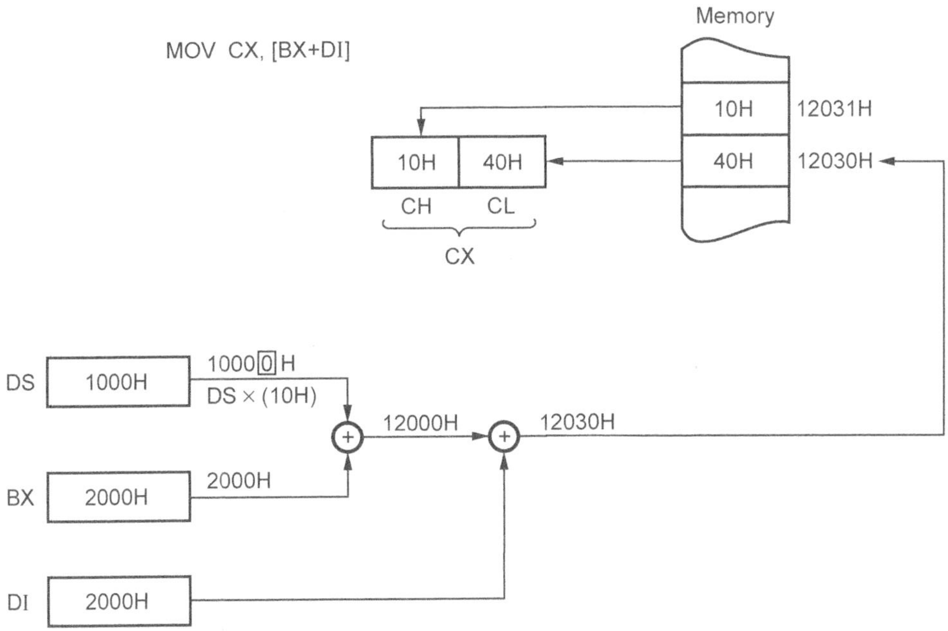

Locating array data using base-plus-index addressing :

A main use of the base-plus-index addressing mode is to address elements in a memory array. Suppose that the array is located in the data segment beginning from memory location ARRAY. To access a particular element within the array we have to load the BX register (base) with the beginning address of the array, and the DI register (index) with the element number to be accessed. This is illustrated in Fig. 6.10.

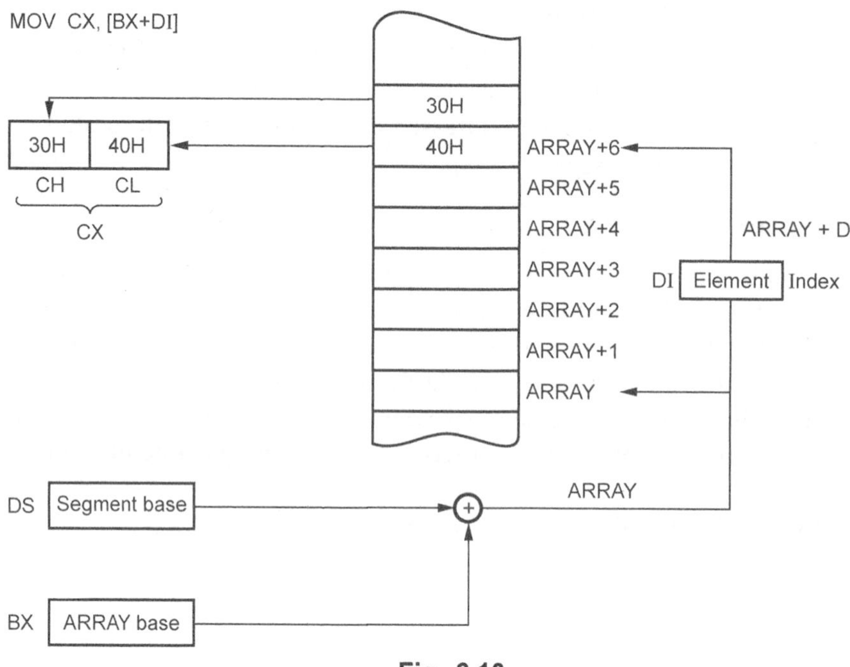

Fig. 6.10

4. Register Relative Addressing :

Register relative addressing is similar to base-plus-index addressing. Here, the data in a segment of memory are addressed by adding the displacement to the contents of a base or an index register (BP, BX, DI or SI). Remember that displacement should be added to the register within the [ ]. This is illustrated in the Fig. 6.11. Displacement can be any 8-bit or 16-bit number.

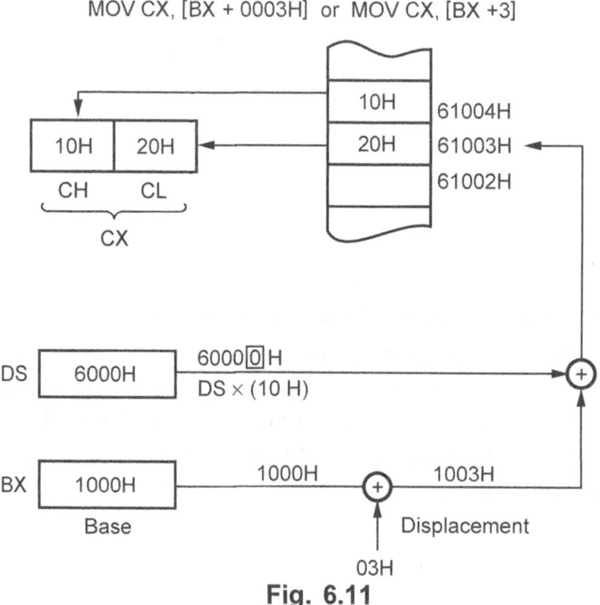

Fig. 6.11

Note :

- Displacement can be subtracted from the register : MOV AL, [DI–2].
- Displacement can be an offset address appended to the front of the [ ] : MOV AL, OFF_ADD [DI + 4].

Example : MOV AL, LAST [SI + 2] ; This instruction copies the contents of the 20-bit address computed from the displacement LAST, SI + 2 and DS into AL.

Addressing array data with register relative :

The Fig. 6.12 shows how to address data element within the array with register relative addressing.

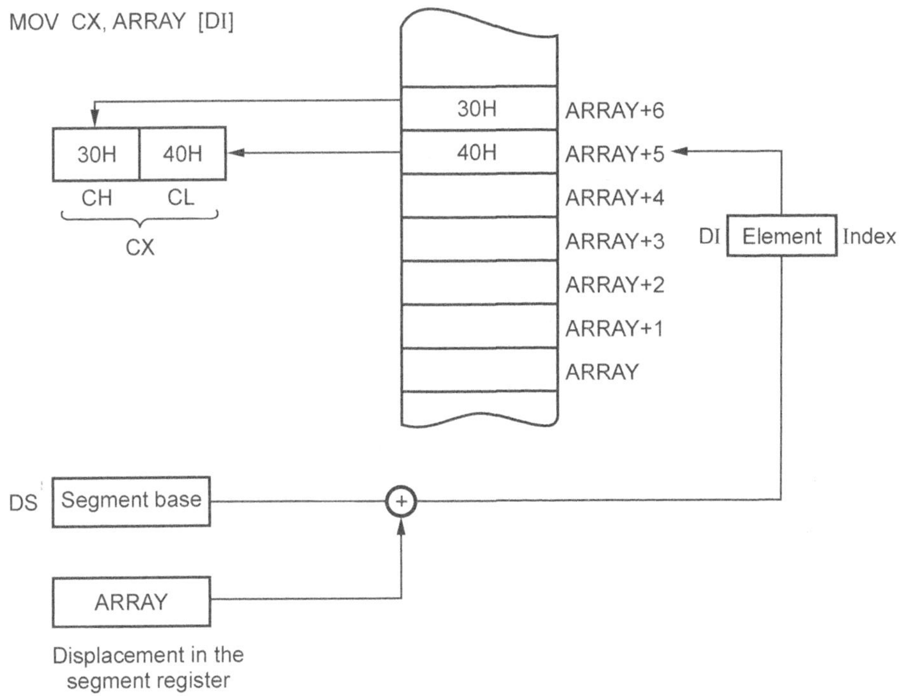

Fig. 6.12

5. Base Relative Plus Index Addressing :

The base relative plus index addressing mode is similar to the base plus index addressing mode, but it adds a displacement, besides using a base register and an index register to generate a physical address of the memory. This addressing mode is suitable to address data within the two dimensional array.

Addressing data with base relative plus index :

The Fig. 6.13 shows how data can be accessed with base relative plus index addressing mode.

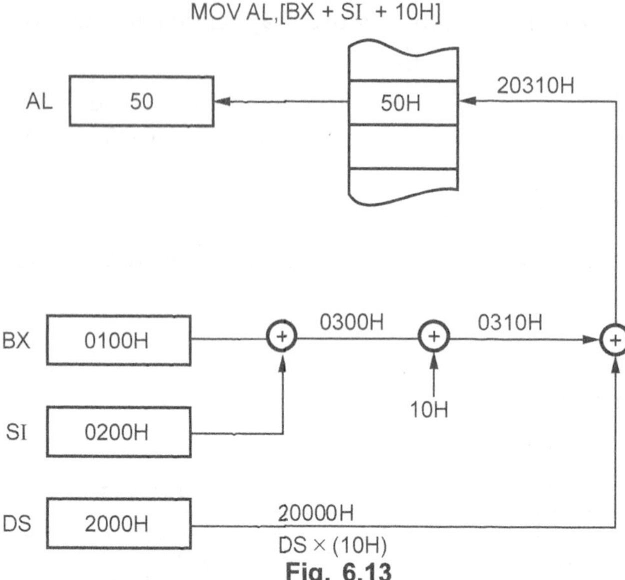

Fig. 6.13

Addressing arrays with base relative-plus-index :

As mentioned earlier this addressing mode is useful in addressing two dimensional array. Two dimensional array usually stores records. For example, student record such as its name, roll no etc. Therefore, each record contains number of data elements. To access

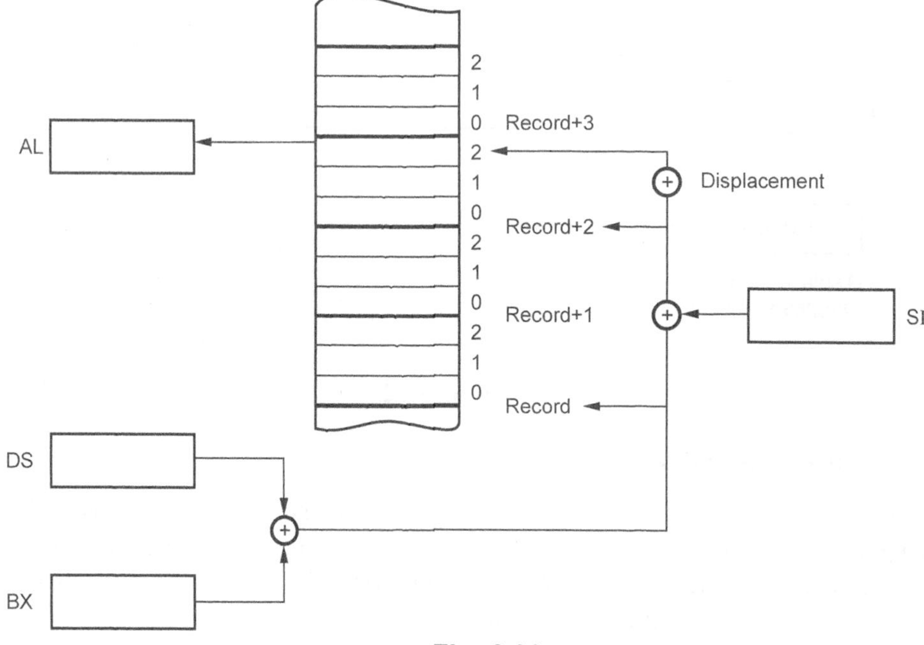

Fig. 6.14

data element from a particular record we use base register to hold the beginning address of the array of records, index register to point a particular record in the array of records and displacement to point a particular element in the record. This is illustrated in Fig. 6.14.

6. String Addressing Mode :

This mode uses index registers. The string instructions automatically assume SI to point to the first byte or word of the source operand and DI to point to the first byte or word of the destination operand. The contents of SI and DI are automatically incremented (by clearing DF to 0 by CLD instruction) or decremented (by setting DF to 1 by STD instruction) to point to the next byte or word. The segment register for the source is DS. The segment register for the destination must be ES.

Example :

```
MOVS BYTE          ; If [DF] = 0, [DS] = 3000H, [SI] = 0600H, [ES] = 5000H,
                   ; [DI] = 0400H, [30600H] = 38H, and [50400H] = 45H, then
                   ; after execution of the MOVS BYTE, [50400H] = 38H,
                   ; [SI] = 0601H, and [DI] = 0401H.
```

6.5.1.3 Addressing Modes for Accessing I/O Ports (I/O Modes) Nov./Dec.-08

Standard I/O devices uses port addressing modes. For memory-mapped I/O, memory addressing modes are used. There are two types of port addressing modes : direct and indirect.

In direct port mode, the port number is an 8-bit immediate operand. This allows fixed access to ports numbered 0 to 255.

Example :

```
OUT 05H, AL        ; Sends the contents of AL to 8-bit port 05H.
IN AX, 80H         ; Copies 16-bit contents of port 80H
```

In indirect port mode, the port number is taken from DX allowing 64 K 8-bit ports or 32 K 16-bit ports.

Example :

```
IN AL, DX     ; if [DX] = 7890H, then it copies 8-bit content of port 7890H
              ; into AL.
IN AX, DX     ; copies the 8-bit contents of ports 7890H and 7891H into AL
              ; and AH, respectively.
```

Note : The 8-bit and 16-bit I/O transfers must take place via AL and AX, respectively.

6.5.2 Program Memory-Addressing Modes

JMP (Jump) and CALL instructions use program memory addressing modes. These instruction have three distinct forms : direct, relative and indirect. Let us see these forms and corresponding addressing modes.

Direct program memory addressing :

In this addressing mode address where to transfer program control is specified within the instruction along with the opcode. The Fig. 6.15 shows the direct intersegment JMP instruction and the four bytes required to store the address 20000H. This JMP instruction loads CS with 2000H and IP with 0000H to jump to memory location 20000H for the next instruction. An **intersegment jump** is a jump where destination location is from a different segment; it can be any memory location within the entire memory locations. Therefore, intersection jump is also known as **far jump.**

Like JMP instruction, CALL instruction also uses direct program addressing with intersegment or far CALL instruction. Usually, in both instructions (JMP or CALL) the name of a memory address, called a **label** is specified in the instruction instead of address.

	Opcode	Offset (low)	Offset (high)	Segment (low)	Segment (high)
JMP 2000H	EA	00	00	00	00

Fig. 6.15

Relative program memory addressing :

In this addressing mode, the term relative is restricted to instruction pointer (IP). For example, if a JMP instruction skips the next 5 bytes of memory, the address in relation to the instruction pointer is a 5 that adds to the instruction pointer. This generates the address of the next program instruction. This is illustrated in Fig. 6.16.

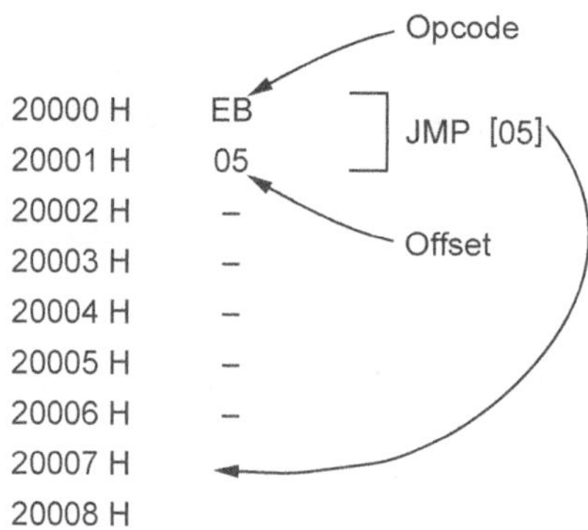

Fig. 6.16

It is important to note that in JMP instruction, opcode takes one byte and displacement may take one or two byte. When displacement is one byte (8-bit), it is called **short jump.** When displacement is two byte (16-bit), it is called **near jump.** In both (short and near) cases only contents of IP register are modified; contents of CS register are not modified. Such jumps are called **intrasegment jumps** because jumps are within the current code segment.

The relative JMP and CALL instructions can have either an 8-bit or a 16-bit signed displacement that allows a forward memory reference or a reverse memory reference.

Indirect program memory addressing :

The 8086 allows several forms of program indirect memory addressing for the JMP and CALL instructions. In this addressing mode, it is possible to use any 16-bit register (AX, BX, CX, DX, SP, BP, DI or SI); any relative register ([BP], [BX], [DI], or [SI]); and any relative register with displacement to specify the jump address. This is illustrated in Table 6.2.

Instruction	Operation
JMP BX	Jumps to memory location addressed by BX within current code segment. IP ← BX
JMP NEAR PTR [BX]	Jumps to memory location addressed by the contents of the data segment memory location addressed by BX within the current code segment. IP ← ([BX+ 1], [BX]) High byte Low byte
JMP NEAR PTR [DI + 2]	Jumps to memory location addressed by the contents of the data segment memory location addressed by DI plus 2 within the current code segment. IP ← ([DI + 3], [DI + 2]) High byte Low byte
JMP ARRAY [BX]	Jumps to memory location addressed by the contents of the data segment memory location addressed by ARRAY plus BX with the current code segment. IP ← ([ARRAY + BX + 1], [ARRAY + BX]) High byte Low byte

Table 6.2

6.5.3 Stack Memory Addressing Modes

Nov./Dec.-07

The stack is a portion of read/write memory set aside by the user for the purpose of storing information temporarily. When the information is written on the stack, the operation is called PUSH. When the information is read from stack, the operation is called a POP.

The microprocessor stores the information, much like stacking plates. Using this analogy of stacking plates it is easy to illustrate the stack operation.

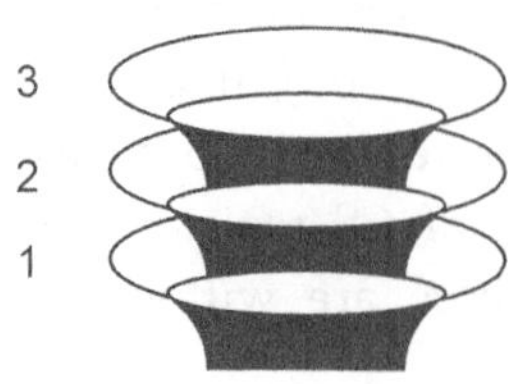

Fig. 6.17 Stacked plates

Fig. 6.17 shows the stacked plates. Here, we realize that if it is desired to take out the first stacked plate we will have to remove all plates above the first plate in the reverse order. This means that to remove first plate we will have to remove the third plate, then the second plate and finally the first plate. This means that, the first information pushed on to the stack is the last information popped off from the stack. This type of operation is known as a first in, last out (FILO). This stack is implemented with the help of special memory pointer register. The special pointer register is called the **stack pointer.** During PUSH and POP operation, stack pointer register gives the address of memory where the information is to be stored or to be read. The stack pointer's contents are automatically manipulated to point to stack top. The memory location currently pointed by stack pointer is called as **top of stack.**

6.5.3.1 Stack Structure of 8086/88

The 8086/88 has a special 16-bit register, SP to work as a stack pointer. The stack pointer (SP) register contains the 16-bit offset from the start of the segment to the top of stack. For stack operation, physical address is produced by adding the contents of stack pointer register to the segment base address in SS. To do this the contents of the stack segment register are shifted four bits left and the contents of SP are added to the shifted result. If the contents of SP are 9F20H and SS are 4000H then the physical address is calculated as follows. (Refer Fig. 6.18)

SS = 4000H after shifting four bits left SS = 40000H

Now

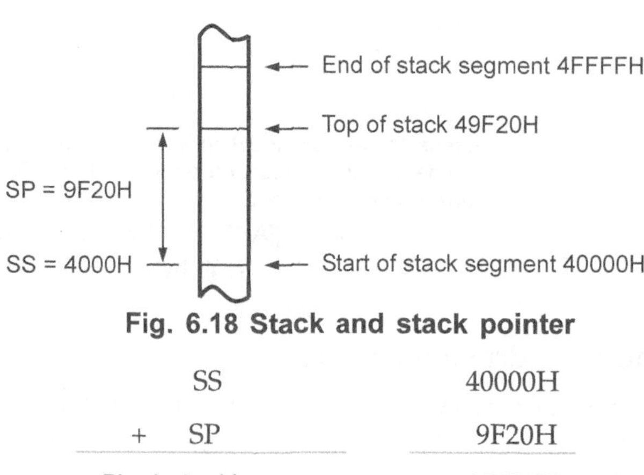

Fig. 6.18 Stack and stack pointer

SS	40000H
+ SP	9F20H
Physical address	49F20H

6.5.3.2 PUSH and POP Operations

Temporarily stores the contents of 16-bit register or memory location or program status word and retrieves when required. When programmer realizes the shortage of the registers, he stores the present contents of the registers in the stack with the help of PUSH instruction and then uses the registers for other function. After completion of other function programmer loads the previous contents of the register from the stack with the help of POP instruction.

PUSH Operation :

The PUSH instruction decrements stack pointer by two and copies a word from some source to the location in the stack where the stack pointer points. Here the source must be a **word** (16 bit). The source of the word can be a general purpose register, a segment register or memory. The Fig. 6.19 shows the map of the stack before and after execution of PUSH AX and PUSH CX instructions.

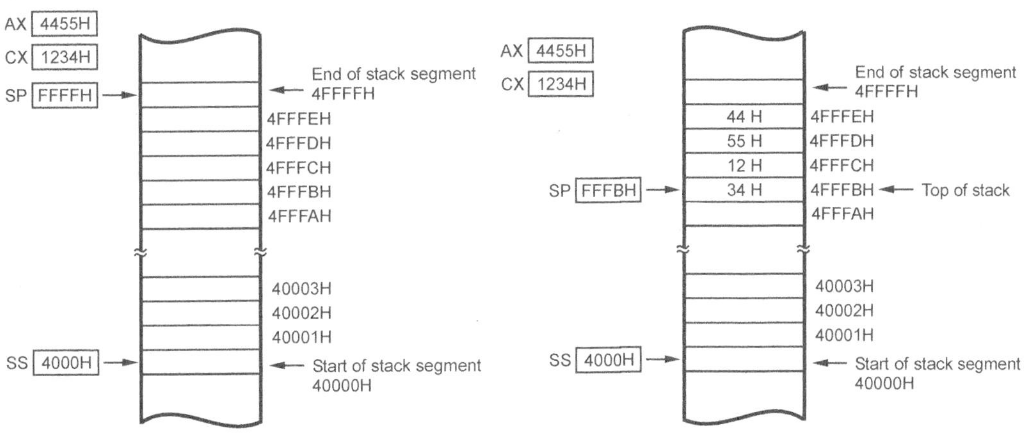

(a) Before execution **(b) After execution of PUSH AX and PUSH CX**

Fig. 6.19

POP Operation :

The POP instruction copies a word from the stack location pointed by the stack pointer to the destination. The destination can be a general purpose register, a segment register or a memory location. After the word is copied to the specified destination, the stack pointer is automatically incremented by 2. The Fig. 6.20 shows the map of the stack before and after execution of POP DX and POP BX instructions.

6.5.3.3 CALL Operation

The CALL instruction is used to transfer execution to a subprogram or procedure. There are two basic types of CALLs, near and far. A near CALL is a call to a procedure which is in the same code segment as the CALL instruction. When the 8086 executes a near CALL instruction it decrements the stack pointer by two and copies the offset of the next instruction after the CALL on the stack. It loads IP with the offset of the first instruction of the procedure in same segment.

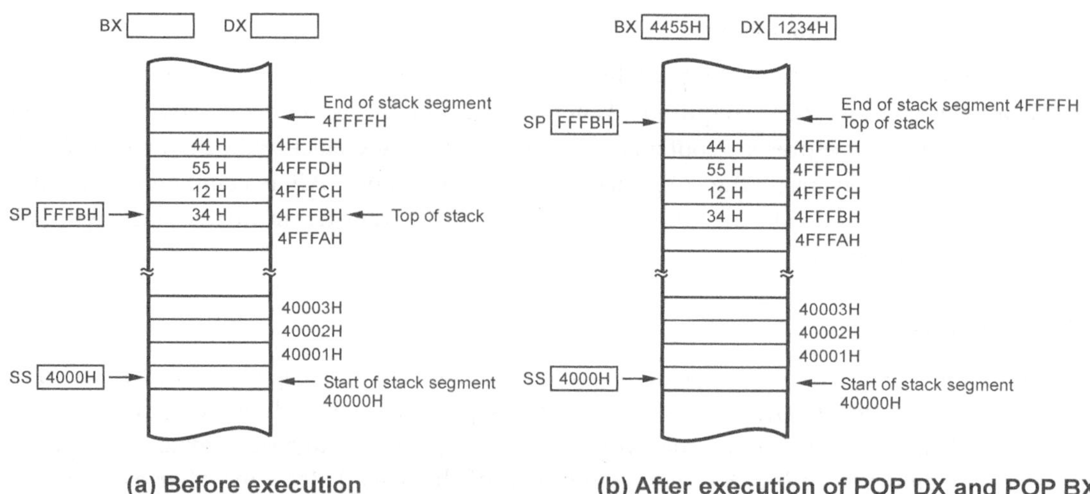

(a) Before execution (b) After execution of POP DX and POP BX

Fig. 6.20

A far CALL is a call to a procedure which is in a different segment from that which contains the CALL instruction. When the 8086 executes a far CALL it decrements the stack pointer by two and copies the contents of the CS register to the stack. It then decrements the stack pointer by two again and copies the offset of the instruction after the CALL to the stack. Finally, it loads CS with the segment base of the segment which contains the procedure and IP with the offset of the first instruction of the procedure in that segment.

6.5.3.4 RET Operation

The RET instruction will return execution from a procedure to the next instruction after the CALL instruction in the calling program. If the procedure is a near procedure (in the same code segment as the CALL instruction), then the return will be done by replacing the instruction pointer with a word from the top of the stack.

If the procedure is a far procedure (in a different code segment from the CALL instruction which calls it), then the instruction pointer will be replaced by the word at the top of the stack. The stack pointer will then be incremented by two. The code segment register is then replaced with a word from the new top of the stack. After the code segment word is popped off the stack, the stack pointer is again incremented by two. These words/word are the offset of the next instruction after the CALL. So 8086 will fetch the next instruction after the CALL.

6.5.3.5 Overflow and Underflow of Stack

We have seen the PUSH operation. During this operation stack pointer is decremented by two. We know that maximum length of stack segment is 64 K. If we go on performing PUSH operations successively, at one time the contents of SP will be 0000H. Any further attempt to PUSH data on the stack will result in **stack overflow**.

On the other hand, if we go on performing POP operations successively, at one time the contents of SP will be FFFFH. Any further attempt to POP data from the stack will result in **stack underflow**.

Review Questions

Section 6.2

Q.1 *List the features of 8086 microprocessor.*

Section 6.3

Q.1 *Name the various segment registers and their usage in 8086 processor.* **Dec.-06, Marks 4**

Section 6.4

Q.1 *Draw and explain in detail about the architecture of 8086.* **May-03, Dec.-03,04, Marks 16; May-05, Marks 10, Dec.-06,08, Marks 12**

Q.2 *Draw the internal block diagram of 8086 and explain the bus interface unit and execution unit.* **June-08, Dec.-11, Marks 8**

Q.3 *Give the significance of O flag, T flag and I flag, D flag of 8086.* **Dec.-06, Marks 4**

Q.4 *Write notes on status flag.* **June-07, Marks 6**

Q.5 *Draw and explain the flag register of 8086 in brief.* **Dec.-08, Marks 8**

Q.6 *Explain about the concept of effective address.* **Dec.-07, Marks 4**

Q.7 *If the stack segment register contains 3000h and stack pointer register contains 8434h, what is the physical address of the top of the stack in 8086 microprocessor ?* **Dec.-11, Marks 2**

Q.8 *What is the function of bus interface unit ?* **Dec.-08, Marks 2**

Q.9 *What are the advantages of using memory segmentation in 8086 ?* **Dec.-06, Marks 2**

Q.10 *List the advantages of using segment registers in 8086.* **June-08, Marks 2**

Section 6.5

Q.1 *Explain the addressing modes of 8086 with examples.* **June-06,07,09, Marks 16, Dec.-06,07,08, Marks 12**

Q.2 *Discuss in detail the data related addressing modes of 8086 with an example.* **June-08, Marks 10**

Q.3 *Explain in detail the stack structure of 8086. Write a simple program to illustrate the concept of programming the stack.* **Dec.-07, Marks 16**

Q.4 *Write notes on addressing input/output devices.* **Dec.-08, Marks 4**

Two Marks Questions with Answers

Q.1 *In 8086 processor the code segment contains 124BH and instruction pointer contains 341CH. Find the memory location addressed by the processor.* **May-04**

Ans. :

	1	2	4	B	0	H
+		3	4	1	C	H
	1	**5**	**8**	**C**	**C**	H

Q.2 *What is the role of TF and IF flags in the flag register of 8086 ?* **Dec.-04, May-05**

Ans. : Trap flag is used for single stepping through a program. If set, a trap is executed after execution of each instruction, i.e. interrupt service routine is executed which displays various registers and memory variable contents on the display after execution of each instruction. Thus programmer can easily trace and correct errors in the program.

IF flag is used to allow/prohibit the interruption of a program. If set, a certain type of interrupt (a maskable interrupt) can be recognized by the 8086; otherwise, these interrupts are ignored.

Q.3 *What is a function of D flag in 8086 ?* **May-05**

Ans. : D flag is used with string instructions. If DF = 0, the string is processed from its beginning with the first element having the lowest address. Otherwise, the string is processed from the high address towards the low address.

Q.4 *What do you mean by pipelining in an 8086 processor ?* **Dec.-06**

Ans. : Feature of fetching the next instruction while the current instruction is executing is called **pipelining**.

The 8086 BIU fetches six instruction bytes ahead of time from the memory and save prefetched instructions in queue to implement pipelining.

Q.5 *How the 20-bit effective address is calculated in an 8086 processor ?* **Dec.-06**

Ans. : The segment register contents are shifted by 4 position to the left by inserting 4 zero bits and then 16-bits offset is added to shifted contents to get 20-bit physical address.

Q.6 *What is the purpose of CLK signal in an 8086 system ?* **Dec.-06**

Ans. : Refer section 6.2.

Q.7 *What are the advantages of using memory segmentation in 8086 ?* **Dec.-06**

Ans. : Refer section 6.4.3.2.

Q.8 *What is queue ? How queue is implemented in 8086 ?*

Ans. : To speed up program execution, the BIU fetches **six instruction bytes** ahead of time from the memory. These prefetched instruction bytes are held for the execution unit in a group of six registers called **Queue**.

Q.9 *What is a segment override prefix ? Give an example.* **Dec.-06**

Ans. : The segment override prefix is an additional 8-bit code which is put in memory before the code for the rest of the instruction. This additional code selects the alternate segment register. The code byte for the segment override prefix as the format 001XX110. The XX represents a 2 bits which are as follows : ES = 00, CS = 01, SS = 10 and DS = 11

In this instruction, the CS: in front of [BX] indicates that we want BIU to add the effective address to the code segment (CS) to produce the physical address.

In this instruction, the CS: in front of [BX] indicates that we want BIU to add the effective address to the code segment (CS) to produce the physical address.

Example : MOV CS : [BX], AL

Q.10 *What is pipelined architecture ?* **May-07**

Ans. : The microprocessor architecture which allows fetching the next instruction while the current instruction is executing is called pipelined architecture.

Q.11 *What is the addressing mode of the following instruction ?*
MOV AX, 55H[BX][SI] **May-08**

Ans. : Base relative plus index addressing.

Q.12 *List the advantages of using segment registers in 8086.* **May-08**

Ans. : Refer section 6.4.3.2.

Q.13 *What is the function of bus interface unit ?* **Dec.-08**

Ans. : Refer section 6.4.1.

Q.14 *List out the segment registers of 8086.* **Dec.-08**

Ans. : The segment registers of 8086 are : CS (Code segment), DS (Data segment), ES (Extra segment) and SS (Stack segment)

Q.15 *What is the need of a flag register in 8086 ?* **May-09**

Ans. : A flag is a flip-flop which indicates some condition produced by the execution of an instruction or control certain operations of the EU. Such conditions are necessary for programmer to develop the desired program logic.

Q.16 ***Calculate how many devices can be addressed by 8086.*** Dec.-07

Ans. : The 8086 can generate 16-bit I/O address, hence it can access 2^{16} = 65536 I/O ports.

Q.17 ***How is the memory segment accessed by 8086 microprocessor identified ?*** May-11

Ans. : The segment register is identified by the contents of the segres field in the instruction code, as shown in the following table -

Segres	Code
CS	0 1
DS	1 1
ES	0 0
SS	1 0

❑❑❑

7 8086 CPU Hardware Design

Contents

7.1 8086 Signals

Nov./Dec.-03, 06, May/June-06, 07, 08, 09

Unlike 8085, 8086 and 8088 can be operated in two modes : Minimum mode and Maximum mode. In this chapter we study the topics related to Minimum mode and Maximum mode operation of 8086. Topics include clock generation, bus buffering, bus latching, timings, minimum mode operation and maximum mode operation.

In order to implement many situations in the microcomputer system the 8086 and 8088 has been designed to work in two operating modes :

1. Minimum mode 2. Maximum mode

The minimum mode is used for a small systems with a single processor and maximum mode is for medium size to large systems, which often include two or more processors. Fig. 7.1 shows the pin diagram of 8086 and 8088 in minimum as well as maximum mode. As a close comparison reveals, there is no much difference between two microprocessors - both are packaged in 40-pin dual-in-line package (DIPs). As mentioned in section 6.1, the 8086 is a 16-bit microprocessor with a 16-bit data bus, and the 8088 is a 16-bit microprocessor with an 8-bit data bus. The pin-out shows, the 8086 has pin connections AD_0-AD_{15}, and the 8088 has pin connections AD_0-AD_7. There is one more minor difference in one of the control signals. The 8086 has an $M/\overline{IO}$ pin and the 8088 has

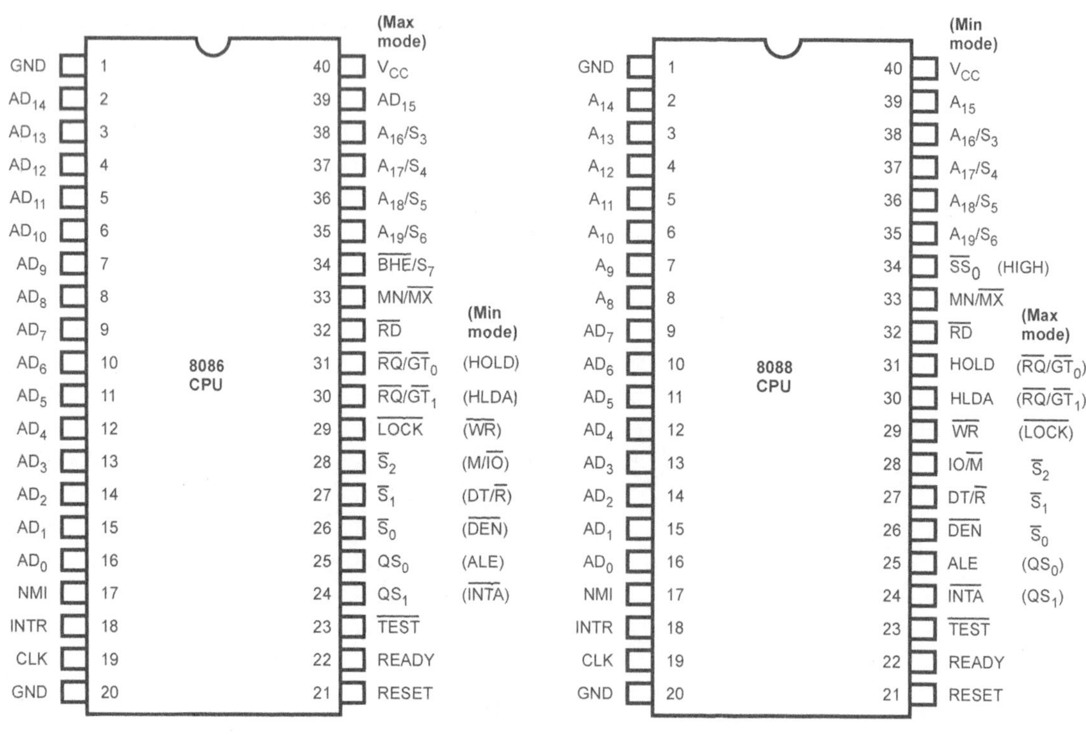

(a) Pin diagram of 8086 (b) Pin diagram of 8088

Fig. 7.1

an $IO/\overline{M}$ pin. The only hardware difference appears on pin 34 of both chips : on the 8086 it is a $\overline{BHE}/S_7$ pin, while on the 8088 it is a $\overline{SS_0}$ pin.

The 8086 signals can be categorized in three groups.

- Signals having common functions in both minimum and maximum modes.
- Signals having special functions for minimum mode.
- Signals having special functions for maximum mode.

7.1.1 Signals with Common Functions in both Modes

Nov./Dec.-06, 07, May/June-08

1. **AD_{15}-AD_0** : Acts as address bus during the first part of machine cycle and data bus for the remaining part of the machine cycle.
2. **A_{19}/S_6-A_{16}/S_3** : During the first part of machine cycle these are used to output upper 4-bits of address. During remaining part of the machine cycle these are used to output status, which indicates the type of operation to be performed in that cycle. S_3 and S_4 indicate the segment register being used as follows :

S_4	S_3	Register
0	0	ES
0	1	SS
1	0	CS or none
1	1	DS

S_5 gives the current setting of the interrupt flag (IF) and S_6 is always zero.

3. **$\overline{BHE}/S_7$** : BHE (Bus High Enable) : Low on this pin during first part of the machine cycle, indicates that at least one byte of the current transfer is to be made on higher order byte AD_{15}-AD_8; otherwise the transfer is made on lower order byte AD_7-AD_0.

$\overline{BHE}$	A_0	Data accesses
0	0	Word
0	1	Upper byte from odd address
1	0	Lower byte from even address
1	1	None

Status S_7 is output during the later part of the machine cycle, but, presently, S_7 has not been assigned a meaning.

4. : It is a positive edge triggered non-maskable interrupt request.

5. **INTR :** It is a level triggered maskable interrupt request. It is sampled during the last clock cycle of each instruction to determine if the processor should enter into an interrupt service routine.

6. **CLK :** 8086 requires clock signal (with 33 % duty cycle) from some external, crystal controlled generator to synchronize internal operations. Clock frequency depends on the version of 8086.

Processor	Required clock signal
8086	5 MHz
8086-2	8 MHz
8086-1	10 MHz

7. **RESET :** It clears , IP, DS, SS, ES, and the instruction queue. It then sets CS to FFFFH. This signal must be high for at least 4 clock cycles. When RESET is removed, 8086 will fetch its next instruction from physical address FFFF0H.

8. **READY :** If this signal is low the 8086 enters into wait state. This signal is used primarily to synchronize slower peripherals with the microprocessor.

9. **$\overline{\text{TEST}}$ (Input) :** This signal is only used by the WAIT instruction. The 8086 enters into a wait state after execution of the WAIT instruction until a LOW signal on the $\overline{\text{TEST}}$ pin. $\overline{\text{TEST}}$ signal is synchronized internally during each clock cycle on the leading edge of the clock cycle.

10. **$\overline{\text{RD}}$ (Output) :** $\overline{\text{RD}}$ is low whenever the 8086 is reading data from memory or an I/O device.

11. **MN/$\overline{\text{MX}}$ (Input) :** The 8086 can be configured in either minimum mode or maximum mode using this pin. This pin is tied high for minimum mode.

7.1.2 Signal Definitions (24 to 31) for Minimum Mode

INTA (Interrupt Acknowledge) Output : This indicates recognition of an interrupt request. It consists of two negative going pulses in two consecutive bus cycles. The first pulse informs the interface that its request has been recognized and upon receipt of the second pulse, the interface is to send the interrupt type to the processor over the data bus.

ALE (Address Latch Enable) output : This signal is provided by 8086 to demultiplex the AD_0-AD_{15} into A_0-A_{15} and D_0-D_{15} using external latches.

$\overline{\text{DEN}}$ (Data Enable) output : This signal informs the transceivers that the CPU is ready to send or receive data.

DT/$\overline{R}$ (Data transmit/Receive) output : This signal is used to control data flow direction. High on this pin indicates that the 8086 is transmitting the data and low indicates that the 8086 is receiving the data.

M/$\overline{IO}$ output : It is used to distinguish memory data transfer, (M/$\overline{IO}$ = HIGH) and I/O data transfer (M/$\overline{IO}$ = LOW).

$\overline{WR}$: Write output : $\overline{WR}$ is low whenever the 8086 is writing data into memory or an I/O device.

HOLD input, HLDA output : A HIGH on HOLD pin indicates that another master (DMA) is requesting to take over the system bus. On receiving HOLD signal processor outputs HLDA signal HIGH as an acknowledgment. At the same time, processor tristates the system bus. A low on HOLD gives the system bus control back to the processor. Processor then outputs low signal on HLDA.

7.1.3 Signal Definitions (24 to 31) for Maximum Mode

Nov./Dec.-06, May/June-08

1. **QS_1, QS_0 (output) :** These two output signals reflect the status of the instruction queue. This status indicates the activity in the queue during the previous clock cycle.

QS_1	QS_0	Status
0	0	No operation (queue is idle)
0	1	First byte of an
1	0	Queue is empty
1	1	Subsequent byte of an

2. **$\overline{S_2}$, $\overline{S_1}$, $\overline{S_0}$ (output) :** These three status signals indicate the type of transfer to be take place during the current bus cycle.

$\overline{S_2}$	$\overline{S_1}$	$\overline{S_0}$	Machine cycle
0	0	0	Interrupt Acknowledge
0	0	1	I/O Read
0	1	0	I/O Write
0	1	1	Halt

$\overline{S_2}$	$\overline{S_1}$	$\overline{S_0}$	Machine cycle
1	0	0	Instruction fetch
1	0	1	Memory read
1	1	0	Memory write
1	1	1	Inactive-Passive

3. **$\overline{LOCK}$:** This signal indicates that an instruction with a LOCK prefix is being executed and the bus is not to be used by another processor.

4. **$\overline{RQ}/\overline{GT_1}$ and $\overline{RQ}/\overline{GT_0}$** : In the maximum mode, HOLD and HLDA pins are replaced by $\overline{RQ}$ (Bus request)/$\overline{GT_0}$ (Bus Grant), and $\overline{RQ}/\overline{GT_1}$ signals. By using bus request signal another master can request for the system bus and processor communicate that the request is granted to the requesting master by using bus grant signal. Both signals are similar except the $\overline{RQ}/\overline{GT_0}$ has higher priority than $\overline{RQ}/\overline{GT_1}$.

7.2 Addressing Memory

Nov./Dec.-06, May/June-07

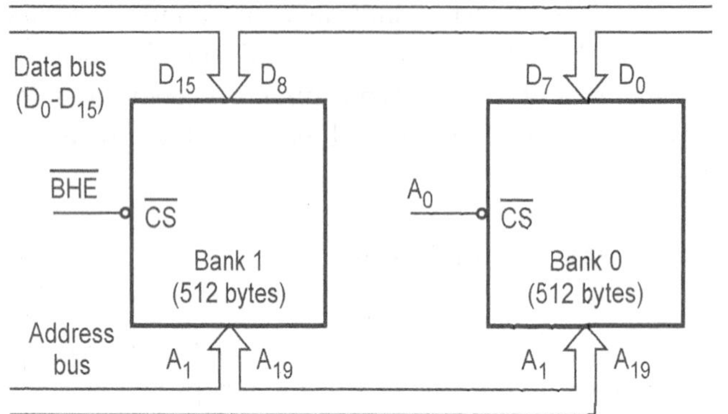

Fig. 7.2 Memory interfacing

Most of the memory ICs are byte oriented i.e. each memory location can store only one byte of data. The 8086 is a 16-bit microprocessor, it can transfer 16-bit data. So in addition to byte, word (16-bit) has to be stored in the memory. This is stored by using two consecutive memory locations, one for least significant byte and other for most significant byte. The address of word is the address of least significant byte. To implement this, the entire memory is divided into two memory banks : bank0 and bank1. Fig. 7.2 shows the interfacing diagram to these memory banks. Bank0 is selected only when A_0 is zero and $Bank_1$ is selected only when $\overline{BHE}$ is zero. A_0 is zero for all even addresses. So Bank0 is usually referred as **even addressed memory** bank. $\overline{BHE}$ is used to access higher order memory bank, referred to as **odd addressed memory** bank.

Together $\overline{BHE}$ and A_0 tell the interface how the data appears on bus. Four possible combinations are shown in the table.

No.	Operation	$\overline{BHE}$	A_0	Data Lines Used
1.	Read/Write a byte at an even address	1	0	D_7 - D_0
2.	Read/Write a byte at an odd address	0	1	D_{15} - D_8
3.	Read/Write a word at an even address	0	0	D_{15} - D_0
4.	Read/Write a word at an odd address	0	1	D_{15}-D_0 in first operation byte from odd bank is transferred.
		1	0	D_7-D_0 in second operation byte from even bank is transferred.

Note : To access odd addressed word two bus cycles are required.

Every microprocessor based system has a memory system. Almost all systems contain two basic types of memory, read-only memory (ROM) and random access memory (RAM) or read/write memory. Read only memory contains system software and permanent system data such as lookup tables, while Random Access Memory contains temporary data and application software. ROMs/PROMs/EPROMs are mapped to cover the CPU's reset address, since these are non-volatile. When the 8086 is reset, the next instruction is fetched from memory location FFFF0H. So in the 8086 systems, the location FFFF0H must be ROM location.

The Fig. 7.3 shows memory map for 8086. Certain locations in 1 Mbyte memory are reserved and some are dedicated for specific CPU operations. Locations from FFFF0H to FFFF5H are dedicated to the initialization procedure of the 8086, while locations FFFF6H to FFFFBH are dedicated to the initialization procedure of the 8089 input/output processor. Locations 00000H to 00013H are dedicated to store the vector addresses of the dedicated interrupts. The dedicated locations are used for processing of specific system initialization, interrupt and reset function.

Intel has also reserved several locations for future hardware and software products. Locations from 00014H to 0007FH and locations from FFFFCH to FFFFFH are reserved locations. The locations from 00000H to 003FFH are used for interrupt vector table (IVT). The interrupt vector table provides the starting location/address of the interrupt service routine for the interrupt supported by 8086.

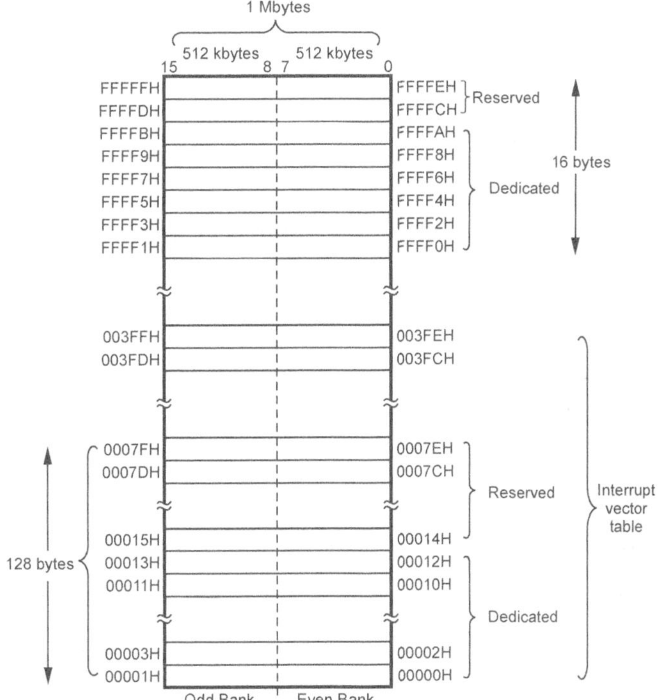

Fig. 7.3 Memory map for 8086

7.3 Addressing I/O

Nov./Dec.-07

The 8086 can generate 16-bit of I/O address. Thus it can address upto 64 kbyte I/O locations or 32 K word I/O locations. The 16-bit I/O address appears on A_0 to A_{15} address lines; A_{16} to A_{19} lines are at logic 0 during the I/O operations. The 16-bit DX register is used as 16-bit I/O address pointer to address upto 64 K devices in in-direct addressing mode. The I/O instructions with direct addressing mode can directly address one or two of the 256 I/O byte locations in page 0 of the I/O address space. See Fig. 7.4.

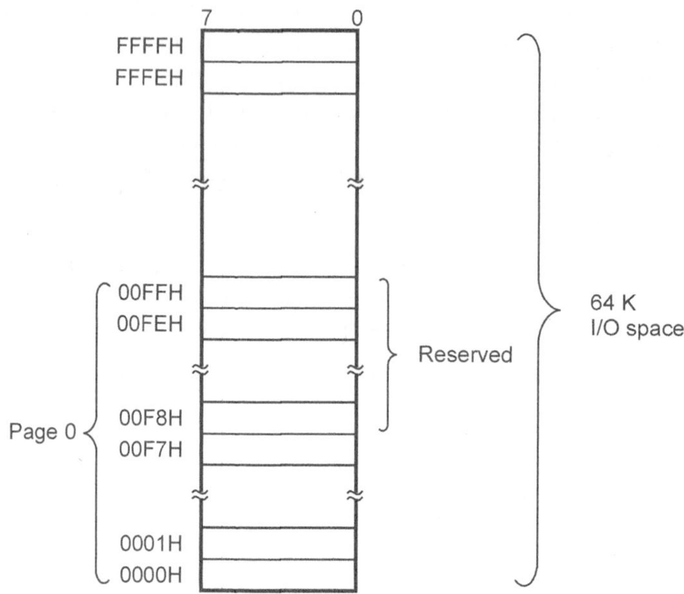

Fig. 7.4 I/O map for 8086

I/O ports are addressed in the same manner as memory locations. Even addressed bytes are transferred on the D_7-D_0 bus lines and odd addressed bytes on D_{15}-D_8. Care must be taken to assure that each register within an 8-bit peripheral located on the lower portion of the bus be addressed as even. In the I/O space, Intel has reserved 00F8H to 00FF locations.

7.4 Minimum Mode 8086 System and Timings

Nov./Dec.-06, 07, 08, May/June-06, 07, 08

7.4.1 Minimum Mode Configuration

Nov./Dec.-05, May/June-07

Latching

Fig. 7.5 shows the typical minimum mode configuration. As shown in the figure, (See Fig. 7.5 on next page). AD_0-AD_{15}, A_{16}/S_3-A_{19}/S_6, and $\overline{BHE}/S_7$ signals are multiplexed. These signals are demultiplexed by external latches and ALE signal generated by the processor. This is accomplished by using three latch ICs (Intel 8282/8283), two of them are

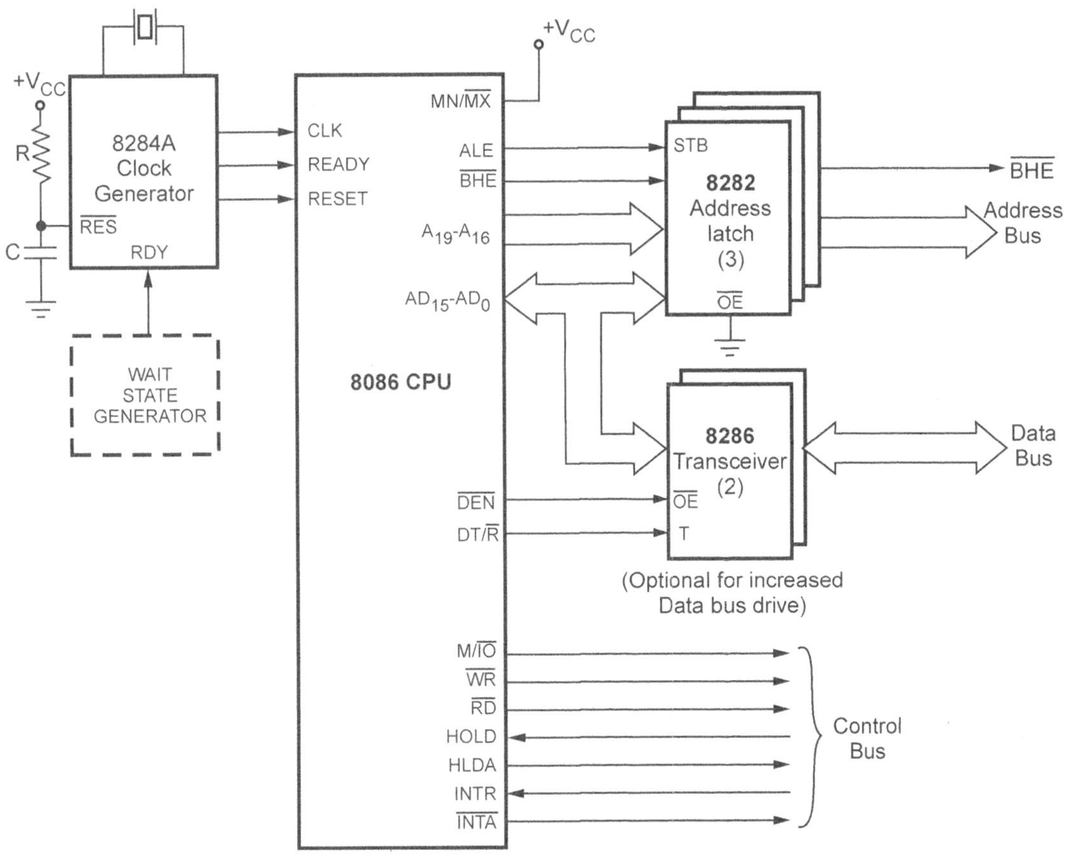

Fig. 7.5 Typical minimum mode configuration

required for a 16-bit address and three are needed if a full 20-bit address is used. In case of 8088, only two external latches are required. One for demultiplexing AD_0-AD_7 and other for demultiplexing A_{16}/S_3 and AD_{19}/S_6. Fig. 7.6 shows the internal block diagram of 8282/8283 latches (See Fig. 7.6 on next page). The 8282 provides noninverting outputs while the 8283 version inverts the input data. In addition to their demultiplexing function, these chips also buffer the address lines, providing increased output driving capability. The output low level is specified as 0.45 V maximum with a sink current of 32 mA maximum. The high level is specified as 2.4 V minimum while supplying a 5 mA maximum high level load current.

Buffering

If a system includes several interfaces then to increase current sourcing/sinking capacities it is necessary to use drivers and receivers (transceiver) for data bus also. The Intel 8286 device is used to implement the transceiver block shown in Fig. 7.5. The 8286 contains 16 tristate elements, eight receivers, and eight drivers. Therefore two 8286s are required to service 16 data lines of 8086. Fig. 7.7 shows the detailed connections of 8286.

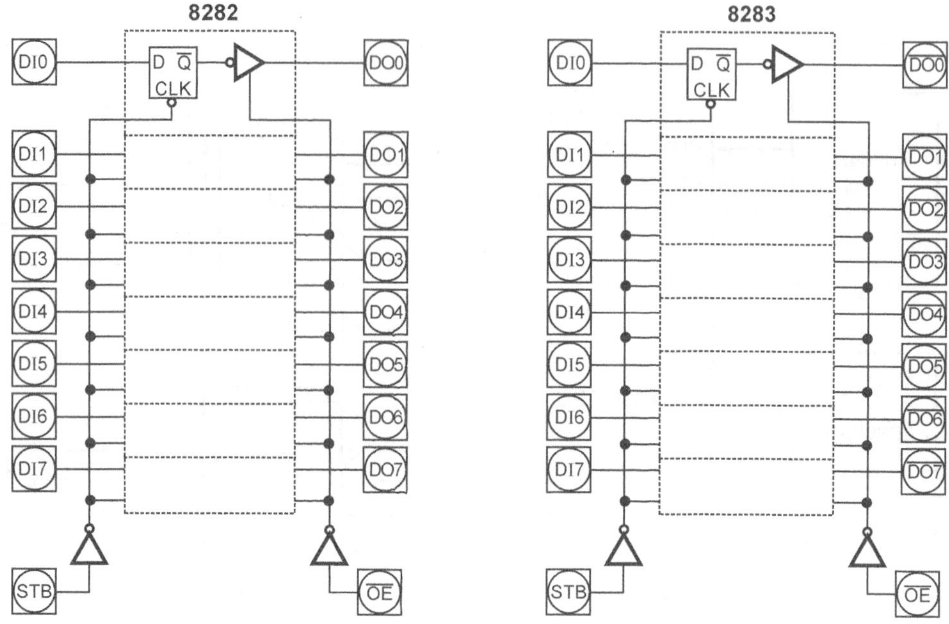

Fig. 7.6 Internal diagram of 8282 and 8283

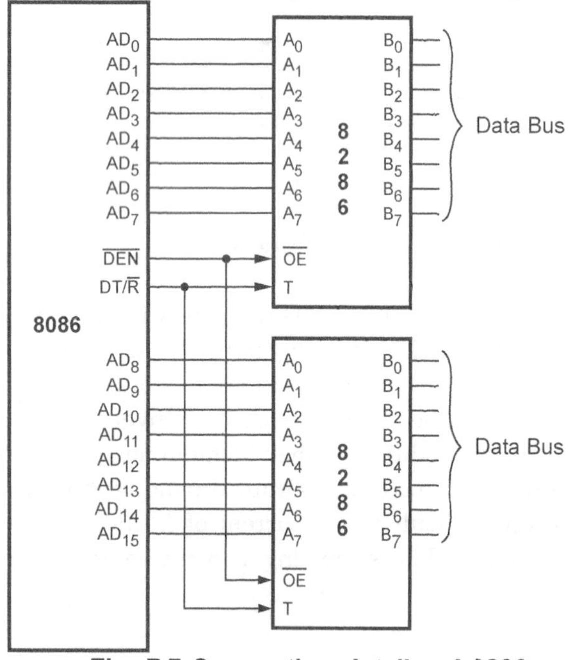

Fig. 7.7 Connection details of 8286

$DT/\overline{R}$ signal is connected to the T input, which controls the direction of the data flow. When this signal is low, receivers are enabled, so that 8086 can read data from memory or input device. To write data into memory or output device, the 8086's $DT/\overline{R}$ signal goes high. Due to this drivers are enabled to transfer data from 8086 to the memory or the output device. At the time of data transfer, to enable output of transceiver its $\overline{OE}$ should be low. This is accomplished by connecting $\overline{DEN}$ signal of 8086 to the $\overline{OE}$ pin of 8286, since $\overline{DEN}$ signal goes low when CPU is ready to send or receive data.

Clock generator

The third component, other than the processor that appears in Fig. 7.5 is an 8284 clock generator. The 8284 clock generator does the following functions :

- Clock generation
- RESET synchronization

- READY synchronization
- Peripheral clock generation.

The Fig. 7.8 shows the internal logic diagram of 8284.

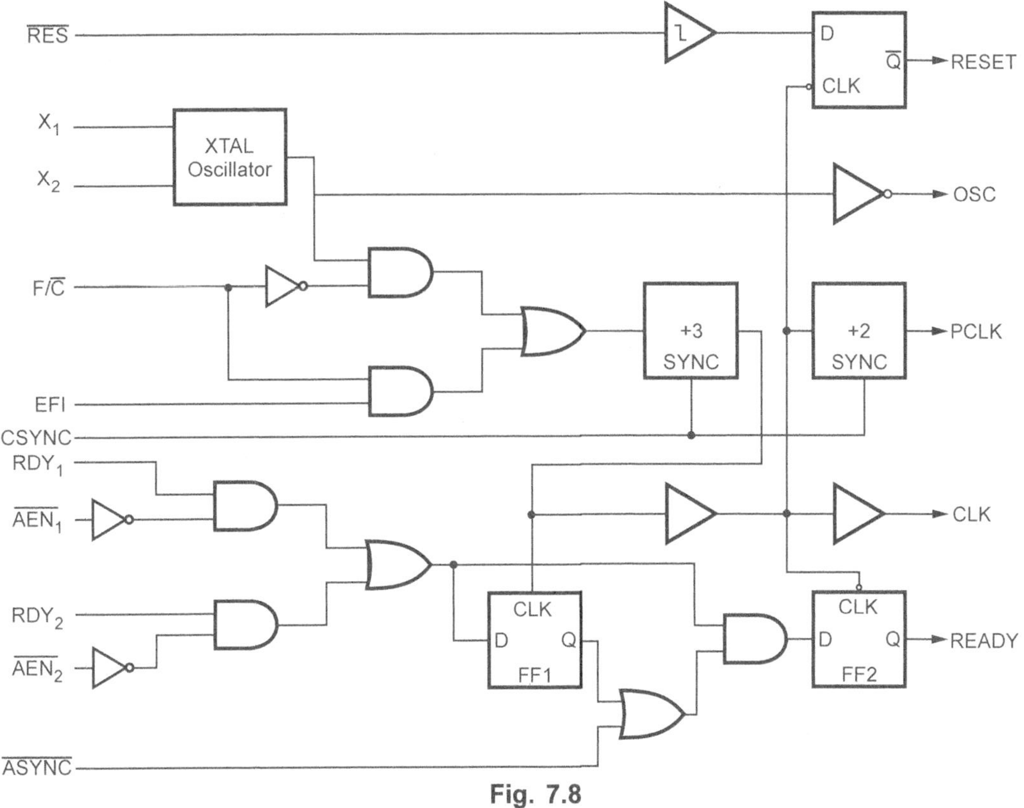

Fig. 7.8

The top half of the logic diagram represents the clock and reset synchronization section of the 8284 clock generator. As shown in the logic diagram, the crystal oscillator has two inputs : X_1 and X_2. If a crystal is attached to X_1 and X_2, the oscillator generates a square-wave signal at the same frequency as the crystal. The output of oscillator is fed to an AND gate and also to an inverter buffer that provides the OSC output signal. The $F/\overline{C}$ signal selects one of the oscillator inputs. When $F/\overline{C}$ input is 1, the EFI input determines the frequency; otherwise oscillator determines the frequency. When EFI input is used, CSYNC signal is used for multiple processor system synchronization. If the internal crystal oscillator is used, CSYNC signal is grounded. In both the cases the output clock frequency is one third of the input frequency. The CLK signal is also buffered before it leaves the clock generator. As shown in the Fig. 7.8, the output of the divide-by-3 counter generates the timing for ready synchronization, a signal for another counter (divide-by-2), and the CLK signal to the 8086/8088 microprocessors. The two cascaded counters (divide-by-3 and divide-by-2) provide the divide-by-6 output at PCLK, which can be used to provide clock input for peripherals. The address enable pins, $\overline{AEN_1}$ and $\overline{AEN_2}$ are provided to qualify the bus ready signals, RDY_1 and RDY_2, respectively.

The reset circuit of 8284 consists of a schmitt trigger buffer and a single D flip-flop circuit. The D flip-flop ensures that the timing requirements of the 8086/8088 RESET input are met. This circuit applies the RESET signal to the microprocessor on the negative edge (1 to 0 transition) of each clock. The 8086/8088 microprocessors sample RESET at the positive edge (0 to 1 transition) of the clocks; therefore, this circuit meets the timing requirements of the 8086/8088.

The Fig. 7.9 shows the circuit connection for 8284 clock generator. The RC circuit provides a logic 0 to the $\overline{RES}$ input pin when power is first applied to the system. After a short time, the $\overline{RES}$ input becomes a logic 1 because the capacitor charges toward + 5.0 V through the register. A push button switch allows the microprocessor to be reset by the operator.

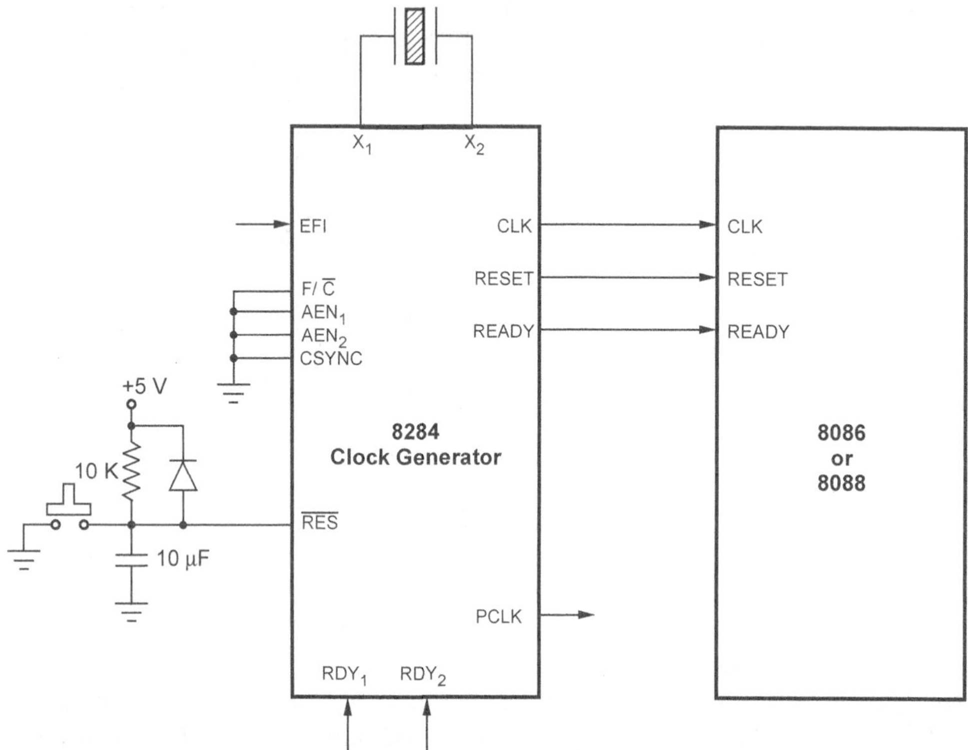

Fig. 7.9 Interfacing of 8284 clock generator with 8086 or 8088

Other signals

The status on the $M/\overline{IO}$, $\overline{RD}$, and $\overline{WR}$ lines decides the type of data transfer, as listed in the Table 7.1.

$M/\overline{IO}$	$\overline{RD}$	$\overline{WR}$	Operation
0	0	1	I/O read
0	1	0	I/O write
1	0	1	Memory read
1	1	0	Memory write

Table 7.1

HOLD and HLDA signals are used to interface other bus masters like DMA controller. Interrupt request (INTR) and interrupt acknowledge ($\overline{INTA}$) are used to extend the interrupt handling capacity of the 8086 with the help of interrupt controller.

7.4.2 Minimum Mode 8086 System

The Fig. 7.10 shows the typical minimum mode 8086 system. Here, interfacing of memory and I/O devices are shown with the basic minimum mode 8086 configuration.

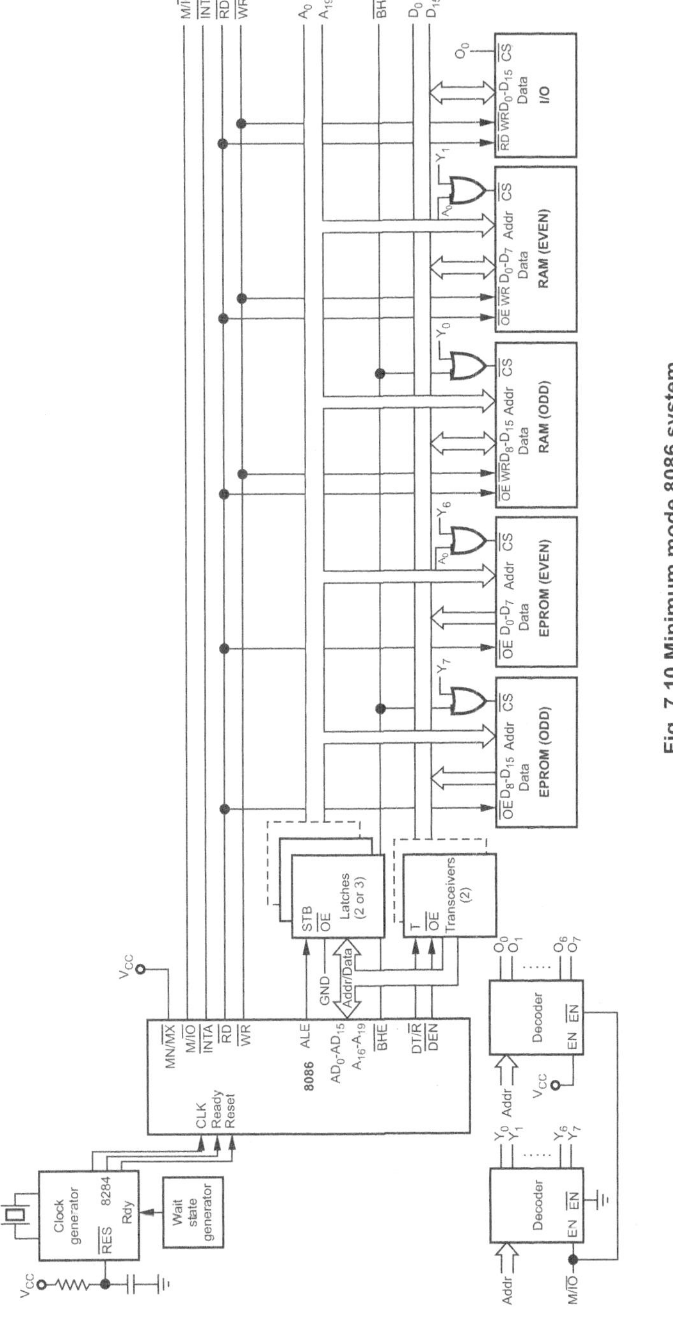

Fig. 7.10 Minimum mode 8086 system

For interfacing memory module to 8086, it is necessary to have odd and even memory banks. This is implemented by using two EPROMs and two RAMs. Data lines D_{15}-D_8 are connected to odd bank of EPROM and RAM, and data lines D_7-D_0 are connected to even bank of EPROM and RAM. Address lines are connected to EPROM and RAM as per their capacities. $\overline{RD}$ signal is connected to the output enable ($\overline{OE}$) signals of EPROMs and RAMs. $\overline{WR}$ signal is connected to $\overline{WR}$ signal of RAMs. Two separate decoders are used to generate chip select signals for memory and I/O devices. These chip select signals are logically ORed with either $\overline{BHE}$ or A_0 to generate final chip select signals. For generating final chip select signals for odd bank decoder outputs are logically ORed with $\overline{BHE}$ signal. On the other hand to generate final chip select signals for even bank decoder outputs are logically ORed with A_0 signal.

The 16-bit I/O interface is shown in the Fig. 7.10. $\overline{RD}$ and $\overline{WR}$ signals are connected to the $\overline{RD}$ and $\overline{WR}$ signals of I/O device. Data lines D_{15}-D_0 are connected to the data lines of I/O device. The chip select signal for I/O device is generated using separate decoder whose output is enabled only when M/$\overline{IO}$ signal is low.

7.4.3 Bus Timings for Minimum Mode

7.4.3.1 Timings for Read and Write Operations

The timing diagrams of input and output transfers for 8086 minimum mode are shown in the Fig. 7.11 (a) and (b) respectively.

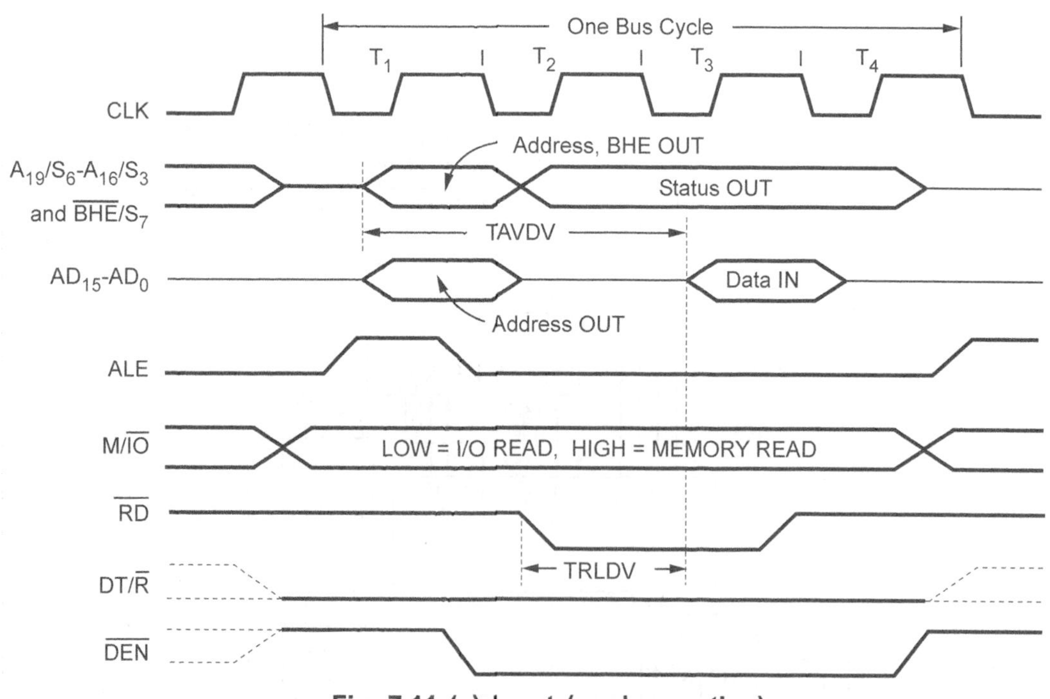

Fig. 7.11 (a) Input (read operation)

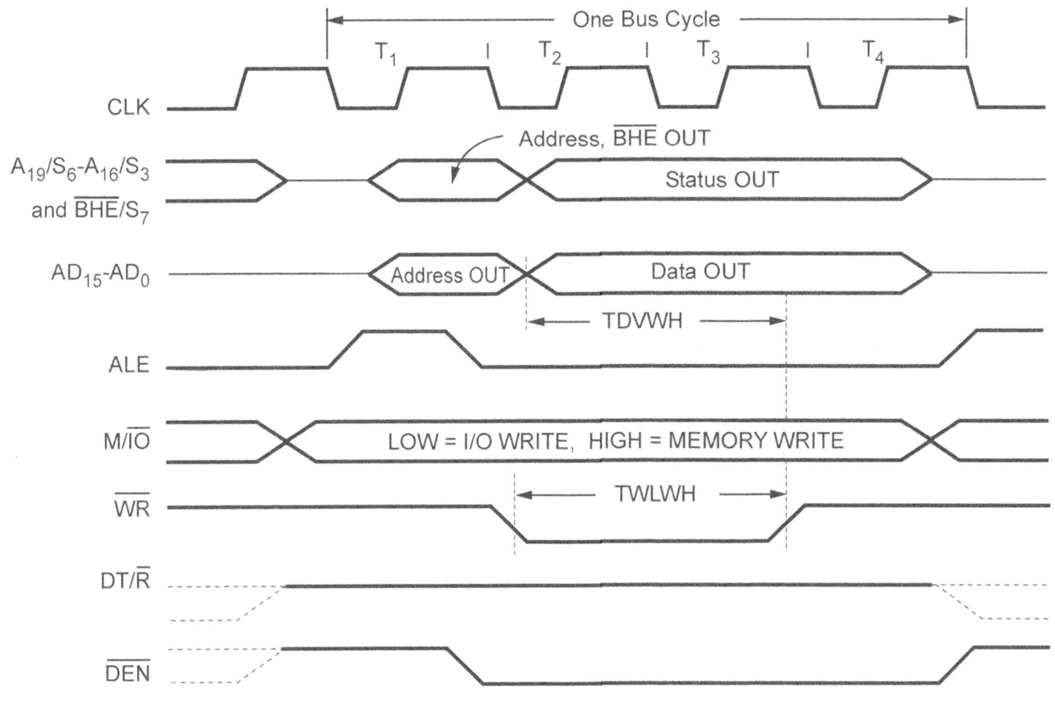

Fig. 7.11 (b) Output (write operation)

These are explained in steps.

1. When processor is ready to initiate the bus cycle, it applies a pulse to ALE during T_1. Before the falling edge of ALE, the address, $\overline{BHE}$, $M/\overline{IO}$, $\overline{DEN}$ and $DT/\overline{R}$ must be stable i.e. DEN = high and $DT/\overline{R} = 0$ for input or $DT/\overline{R} = 1$ for output.
2. At the trailing edge of ALE, ICs 74LS373 or 8282 latches the address.
3. During T_2 the address signals are disabled and S_3-S_7 are available on AD_{16}/S_3-AD_{19}/S_6 and $\overline{BHE}/S_7$. Also $\overline{DEN}$ is lowered to enable transceiver.
4. In case of input operation, $\overline{RD}$ is activated during T_2 and AD_0 to AD_{15} go in high impedance preparing for input.
5. If memory or I/O interface can perform the transfer immediately; there are no wait states and data is output on the bus during T_3.
6. After the data is accepted by the processor, $\overline{RD}$ is raised high at the beginning of T_4.
7. Upon detecting this transition during T_4, the memory or I/O device will disable its data signals.
8. For an output operation, processor applies $\overline{WR} = 0$ and then the data on the data bus during T_2.

9. In T_4, $\overline{WR}$ is raised high and data signals are disabled.
10. For either input or output operation, $\overline{DEN}$ is raised during T_4 to disable the transceiver. Also $M/\overline{IO}$ is set according to the next transfer at this time or during next T_1 state. Thus length of bus cycle in 8086 is four clock cycle. If the bus is to be inactive after completion of bus cycle, then the gap between the successive cycles is filled by ideal state clock cycles.

When the memory or I/O device is not able to respond quickly during transfer, wait states (T_W) are inserted between T_3 and T_4 by disabling the READY input of the 8086. The bus activity during wait state is same as during T_3.

7.4.3.2 HOLD Response Sequence

The Fig. 7.12 shows the HOLD and HLDA signal timings in minimum mode system. The HOLD pin is sampled at leading edge of each clock pulse. If it is sampled active by the 8086 before T_4 of the previous cycle or during T_1 state of the current cycle, the 8086 activates HLDA in the next clock cycle and for succeeding bus cycles. It relinquishes the control of all buses and the control of buses is handed over to the requesting master. The control of the bus is not regained by the 8086 until the requesting master does not inactivate the HOLD pin. After inactivation of HOLD signal, 8086 regains the control of buses and inactivates the HLDA signal.

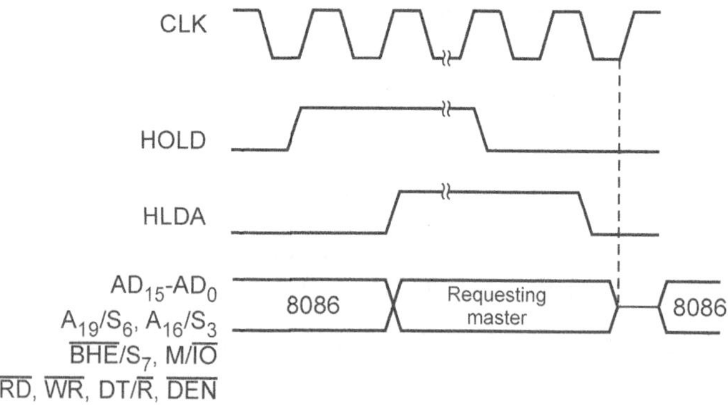

Fig. 7.12 HOLD and HLDA signal timings

7.5 Maximum Mode 8086 System and Timings

Nov./Dec.-06, 07, 09, May/June-06, 07, 09

7.5.1 Maximum Mode Configuration

Nov./Dec.-05, May/June-08

Fig. 7.13 shows the typical maximum mode configuration. In the maximum mode additional circuitry is required to translate the control signals. The additional circuitry converts the status signals ($\overline{S}_2$-$\overline{S}_0$) into the I/O and memory transfer signals. It also generates the control signals required to direct the data flow and for controlling 8282 latches and 8286 transceivers. The Intel 8288 bus controller is used to implement this control circuitry.

Fig. 7.14 shows that the 8288 is able to originate the address latch enable signal to the 8282's, the enable and direction signals to the 8286 transceivers, and the interrupt

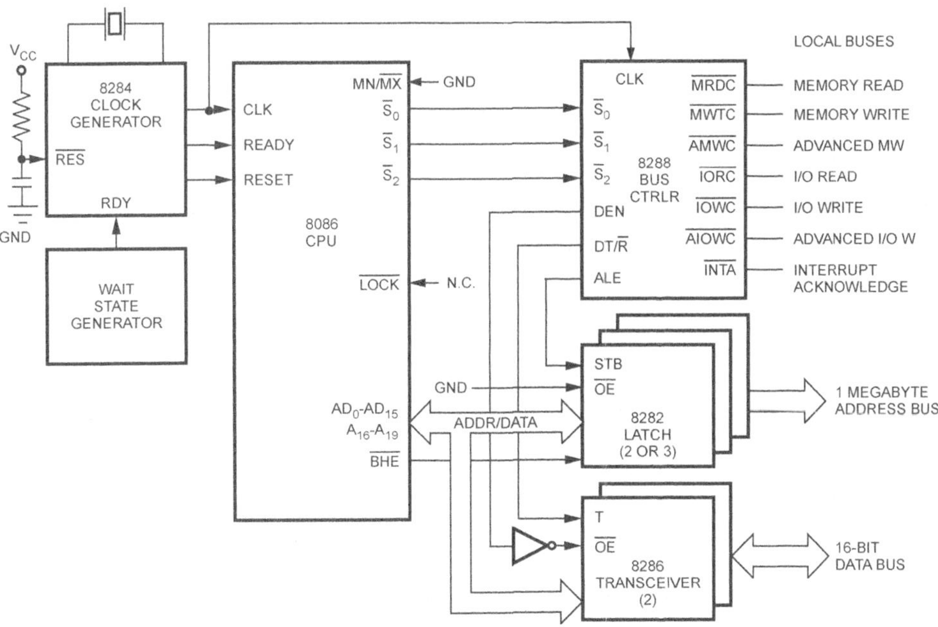

Fig. 7.13 Typical maximum mode configuration

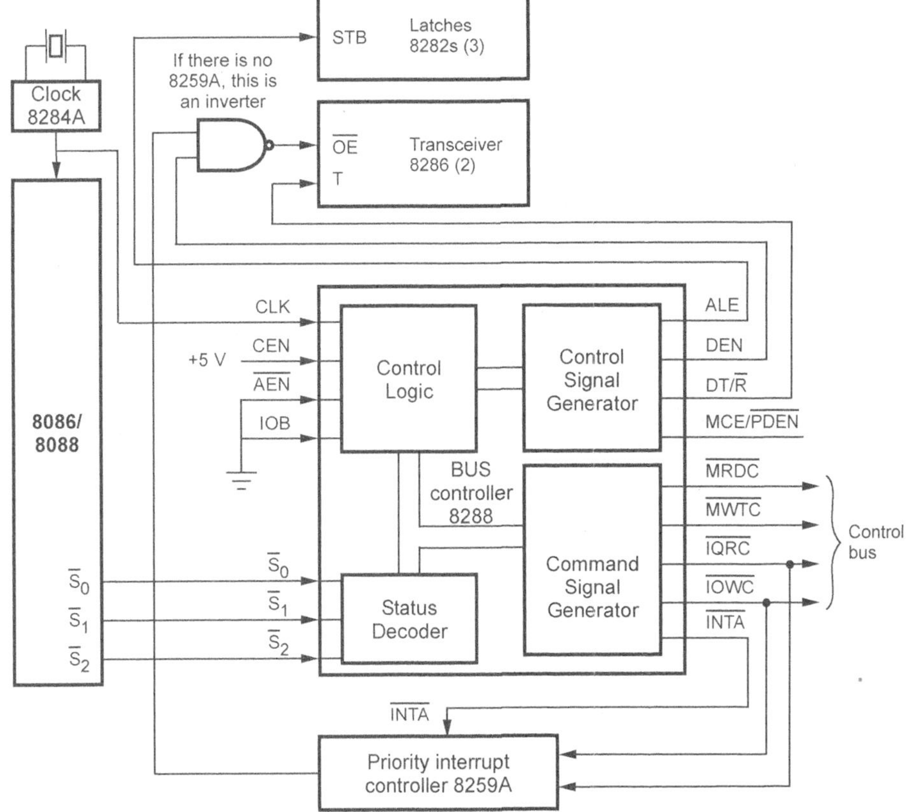

Fig. 7.14 8288 bus controller

acknowledge signal to the interrupt controller. It also decodes the $\overline{S_2}$-$\overline{S_0}$ signals to generate $\overline{\text{MRDC}}$, $\overline{\text{MWTC}}$, $\overline{\text{IORC}}$, $\overline{\text{IOWC}}$, MCE/$\overline{\text{PDEN}}$, $\overline{\text{AEN}}$, IOB, CEN, AIOWC, and AMWC signals.

$\overline{\text{MRDC}}$ (Memory Read Command) : It instructs the memory to put the contents of the addressed location on the data bus.

$\overline{\text{MWTC}}$ (Memory Write Command) : It instructs the memory to accept the data on the data bus and load the data into the addressed memory location.

$\overline{\text{IORC}}$ (I/O Read Command) : It instructs an I/O device to put the data contained in the addressed port on the data bus.

$\overline{\text{IOWC}}$ (I/O Write Command) : It instructs an I/O device to accept the data on the data bus and load the data into the addressed port.

MCE/$\overline{\text{PDEN}}$ (Master Cascade Enable/Peripheral Data Enable) : It controls the mode of operation of 8259. It selects cascade operation for 8259 (interrupt controller) if IOB signal is grounded and enables the I/O bus transceivers if IOB is tied high.

$\overline{\text{AEN}}$, IOB and CEN : These pins are used in multiprocessor system. With a single processor in the system, $\overline{\text{AEN}}$ and IOB are grounded and CEN is tied high. $\overline{\text{AEN}}$ causes the 8288 to enable the memory control signals. IOB (I/O bus mode) signal selects either the I/O bus mode or system bus mode operation. CEN (control enable) input enables the command output pins on the 8288.

$\overline{\text{AIOWC}}$/$\overline{\text{AMWC}}$ (Advance I/O Write Command/Advance Memory Write Command) : These signals are similar to IOWC and MWTC except that they are activated one clock pulse earlier. This gives slow interfaces an extra clock cycle to prepare to input the data.

7.5.2 Maximum Mode 8086 System

May/June-08

The Fig. 7.15 shows the typical maximum mode 8086 system. Here interfacing of memory and I/O devices are shown with the basic maximum mode configuration. The connections for memory and I/O devices are similar to that of minimum mode configuration. However, the generation of control signals from 8086 is done by external bus controller 8288.

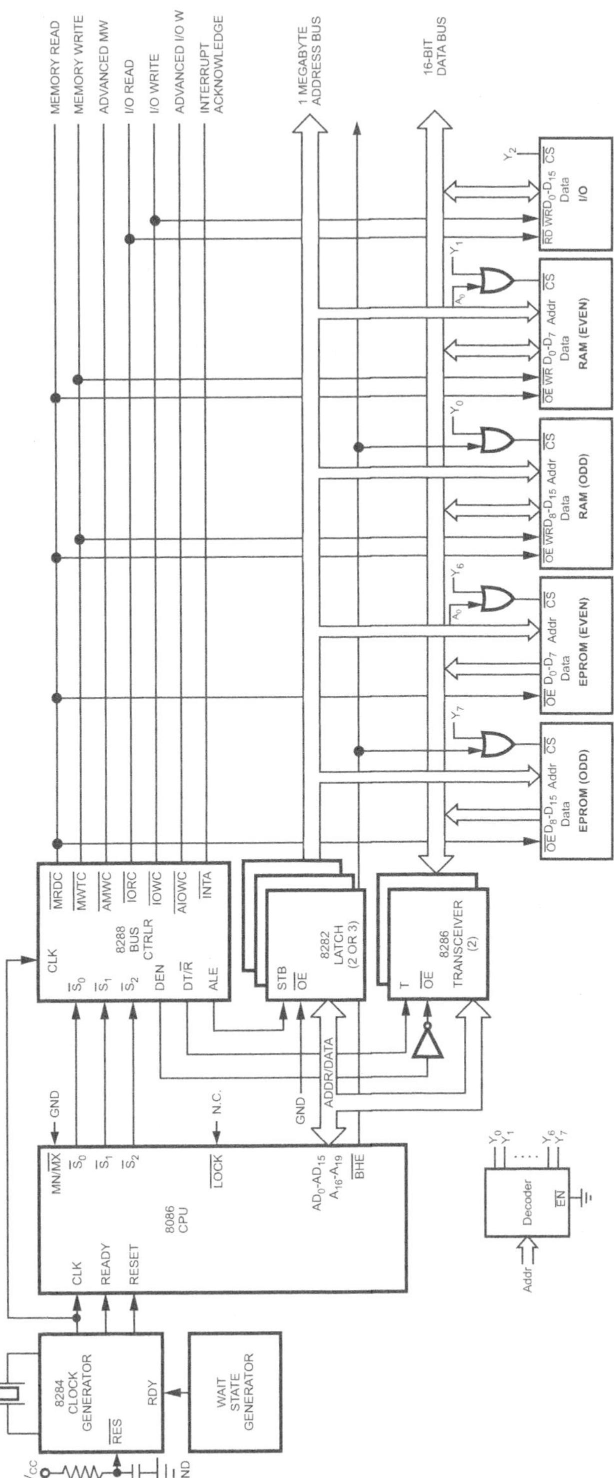
MEMORY READ
MEMORY WRITE
ADVANCED MW
I/O READ
I/O WRITE
ADVANCED I/O W
INTERRUPT ACKNOWLEDGE
1 MEGABYTE ADDRESS BUS
16-BIT DATA BUS
I/O
RAM (EVEN)
RAM (ODD)
EPROM (EVEN)
EPROM (ODD)
CLK
MRDC
MWTC
AMWC
IORC
IOWC
AIOWC
INTA
8288 BUS CTRLR
DEN
DT/R
ALE
STB
OE
8282 LATCH (2 OR 3)
T
8286 TRANSCEIVER (2)
GND
N.C.
ADDR/DATA
MN/MX
LOCK
BHE
8086 CPU
READY
RESET
8284 CLOCK GENERATOR
RES
RDY
WAIT STATE GENERATOR
Decoder
EN
Addr

Fig. 7.15

7.5.3 Bus Timings for Maximum Mode

May/June-08

7.5.3.1 Timings for Read and Write Operations

The timing diagrams of input and output transfers are shown in the Fig. 7.16 (a) and (b) respectively.

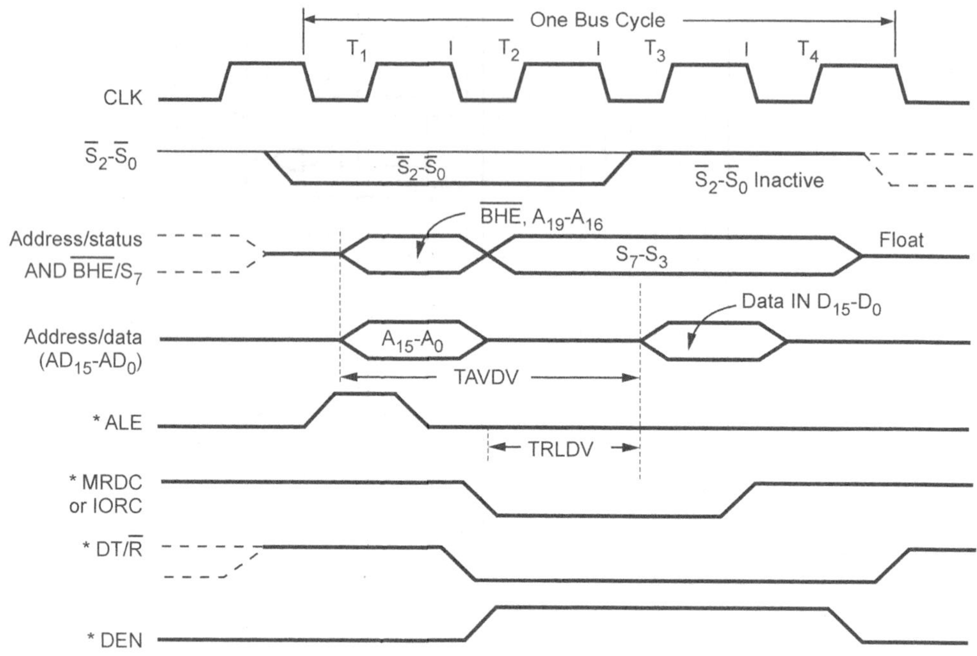

Fig. 7.16 (a) Input (read operation)

These are explained in steps.

1. S_0, $\overline{S}_1$, $\overline{S}_2$ are set at the beginning of bus cycle. On detecting the change on passive state $\overline{S}_0 = \overline{S}_1 = \overline{S}_2 = 1$, the 8288 bus controller will output a pulse on its ALE and apply a required signal to its DT/$\overline{R}$ pin during T_1.
2. In T_2, 8288 will set DEN = 1 thus enabling transceiver. For an input, 8288 it will activates $\overline{MRDC}$ or $\overline{IORC}$. These signals are activated until T_4. For an output, the $\overline{AMWC}$ or $\overline{AIOWC}$ is activated from T_2 to T_4 and $\overline{MWTC}$ or $\overline{IOWC}$ is activated from T_3 to T_4.
3. The status bits $\overline{S}_0$ to $\overline{S}_2$ remain active until T_3, and become passive during T_3 and T_4.
4. If ready input is not activated before T_3, wait state will be inserted between T_3 and T_4.

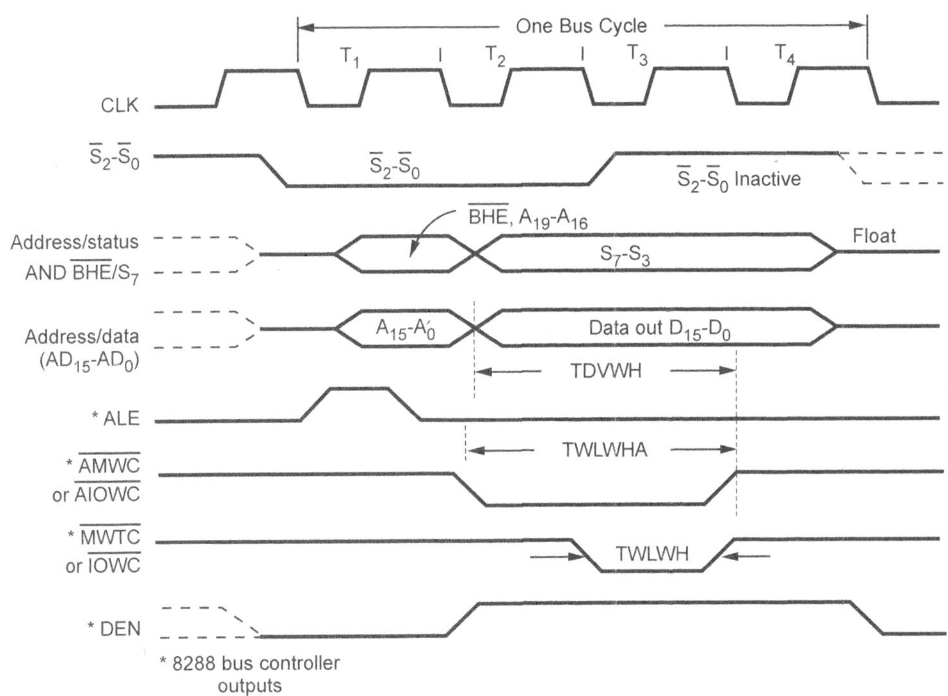

Fig. 7.16 (b) Output (write operation)

7.5.3.2 Timings for $\overline{RQ}/\overline{GT}$ Signals

The Fig. 7.17 shows the timing diagrams for bus request and bus grant pins of 8086. A bus request, grant and release is accomplished by a sequence of three pulses. The $\overline{RQ}/\overline{GT}$ pins are sampled at the rising edge of each clock pulse and if a request is detected the 8086 will apply a grant pulse to the $\overline{RQ}/\overline{GT}$ if the following conditions are met.

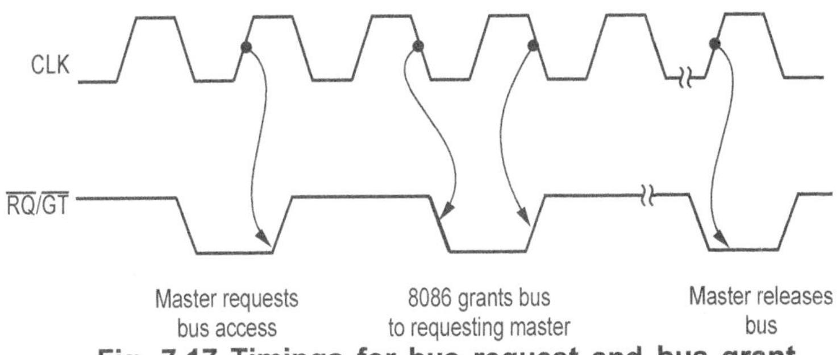

Fig. 7.17 Timings for bus request and bus grant signals

1. The previous bus transfer was not the low byte of a word to or from an odd address if the CPU is an 8086. For an 8088, regardless of the address alignment, the grant signal will not be sent until the second byte of a word reference is accessed.

2. The first pulse of an interrupt acknowledgement did not occur during the previous bus cycle.

3. An instruction with a LOCK prefix is not being executed.

If condition 1 and 2 is not met, then the grant will not be given until the next bus cycle, and if condition 3 is not met, the grant will wait until the locked instruction is completed.

After activation of grant pulse, requesting master takes the control of buses. This master may control the buses for only one bus cycle or for several bus cycles. When it is ready to relinquish the buses it will send the processor release pulse over the same line that it made its request.

Review Questions

Section 7.1

Q.1 *Explain Min/Max mode of 8086 microprocessor.* **Dec.-03, Marks 2; Dec.-06, Marks 10**

Q.2 *Explain the functions of following 8086 signals.*
1) HLDA 2) $\overline{RQ}/\overline{GT}0$ 3) $\overline{DEN}$ 4) ALE. **May-07, Marks 8**

Q.3 *Explain the pin configuration of 8086.* **May-09, Marks 16, May-11, Marks 2**

Q.4 *Show the pin configuration and function of signals of 8086 microprocessor.* **May-11, Marks 2**

Q.5 *Explain the function of following pins in 8086.*
1) NMI 2) BHE 3) $\overline{TEST}$ **Dec.-06, Marks 6**

Q.6 *Give the significance of $\overline{RQ}/\overline{GT}0$ and $IO/\overline{M}$ signals.* **Dec.-06, Marks 4**

Section 7.2

Q.1 *Explain in detail about the 8086 memory banks and associated signals for byte and word operations.* **Dec.-06, Marks 12**

Q.2 *Explain the memory organization in 8086.* **Dec.-06, Marks 8**

Q.3 *Explain in detail about memory access mechanism in 8086.* **May-07, Marks 8**

Q.4 *Show the memory organization and interfacing with 8086 microprocessor. Explain how the memory is accessed.* **May-11, Marks 2**

Section 7.3

Q.1 *Calculate how many devices can be addressed by 8086.* **Dec.-07, Marks 2**

Section 7.4

Q.1 *Describe the system design using 8086.* **May-06, Marks 16**

Q.2 *Describe the minimum mode 8086 system and its timing diagram.* **May-06,07,09, Dec.-06,07,08, Marks 16**

Section 7.5

Q.1 *Write a brief note on 8086 based maximum mode and minimum mode CPU module with a neat diagram.* **Dec.-05,06,07, May-06,08, Marks 16**

Q.2 *Draw and explain a block diagram showing 8086 in maximum mode configuration.* **May-07, Dec.-09, Marks 12**

Q.3 *Write a brief note on 8086 based multiprocessor system design/configuration.* **Dec.-05, Marks 16**

Q.4 *Explain the maximum mode of 8086 with the timing diagrams of memory read cycles, memory write cycle and $\overline{RQ}|\overline{GT}$ timing.* **May-08, Marks 16**

Two Marks Questions with Answers

Q.1 ***Name the signals used by 8086 to demultiplex the address/data bus and to control the data bus buffers.*** **Dec.-05**

Ans. : 8086 uses ALE signal to demultiplex the address/data bus and it uses $\overline{DEN}$ (Data Enable) and DT/$\overline{R}$ (Data Transmit/Receive) signals to control the data bus buffers.

Q.2 ***What are the two operating modes of 8086 ?*** **May-06,07**

Ans. : 1. Minimum mode 2. Maximum mode

Q.3 ***What is the use of latch signal on the AD_0-AD_{15} bus in an 8086 system ?*** **Dec.-06**

Ans. : The latch signal (ALE) is used to demultiplex (separate) the address bus and data bus of the 8086.

Q.4 ***What is the need for MN/$\overline{MX}$ pin in 8086 microprocessor ? or why we use MN / $\overline{MX}$ pin in 8086 ?*** **Dec.-06, 07**

Ans. : The 8086 provides MN/$\overline{MX}$ pin to select the mode of operation : MN/$\overline{MX}$ = 1 for minimum mode and MN/$\overline{MX}$ = 0 for maximum mode.

Q.5 ***What are the signals involved in memory bank selection in 8086 microprocessor ?*** **May-07**

Ans. : The signals $\overline{BHE}$ and A_0 are involved in memory bank selection in 8086 microprocessor. When $\overline{BHE}$ = 0 odd bank (Bank 1) is selected and when A_0 = 0 even bank (Bank 0) is selected.

Q.6 *How clock signal is generated in 8086? What is the maximum internal clock frequency of 8086 ?* **May-07**

Ans. : The clock signal of 8086 is generated using 8284 clock generator. The crystal is connected to the crystal oscillator inputs of 8284 to generate the clock signal. The maximum internal clock frequency of 8086 is 5 MHz.

Q.7 *Explain the $\overline{BHE}$ and $\overline{LOCK}$ signals of 8086.* **May-08**

Ans. : $\overline{\text{BHE}}$ (Bus High Enable) : Low on this pin during first part of the machine cycle, indicates that at least one byte of the current transfer is to be made on higher order byte AD_{15}-AD_8; otherwise the transfer is made on lower order byte AD_7-AD_0.

$\overline{\text{LOCK}}$: This signal indicates that an instruction with a LOCK prefix is being executed and the bus is not to be used by another processor.

Q.8 *What information is conveyed when* Qs1 Qs0 *bits are 01 ?* **May-08**

Ans. : When QS_1 QS_0 bits are 01, they indicate that the queue is loaded with the first byte of an opcode during the previous clock cycle.

Q.9 *What happen in 8086 when $\overline{DEN}$ = 0 and DT/$\overline{R}$ = 1 ?* **May-08**

Ans. : When $\overline{\text{DEN}}$ = 0, the transceivers are enabled to send or receive data. Since DT/$\overline{\text{R}}$ = 1, the transceivers are used to transmit data.

Q.10 *What is the advance signal name of write command of MAX mode 8086?* **May-09**

Ans. : The advance signal name of write command of MAX mode 8086 is $\overline{\text{AMWC}}$ for memory write and $\overline{\text{AIOWC}}$ for I/O write.

Q.11 *What do you understand by bit addressable RAM in 8051 microcontroller ?* **Dec.-10**

Ans. : The 8051 provides 16 bytes of a bit-addressable area. It occupies RAM byte addresses from 20H to 2FH, forming a total of 128 (16 × 8) addressable bits.

An addressable bit may be specified by its bit address of 00H to 7FH, or 8 bits may form any byte address from 20H to 2FH.

For example, bit address 4EH refers bit 6 of the byte address 29H.

❑❑❑

8 8086 Interrupts

Contents

8.1 Introduction

Nov./Dec.-05,07,08; May/June-08,09

Sometimes it is necessary to have the computer automatically execute one of a collection of special routines whenever certain conditions exists within a program or the microcomputer system e.g. It is necessary that microcomputer system should give response to devices such as keyboard, sensor and other components when they request for service.

The most common method of servicing such device is the **polled approach**. This is where the processor must test each device in sequence and in effect "ask" each one if it needs communication with the processor. It is easy to see that a large portion of the main program is looping through this continuous polling cycle. Such a method would have a serious and decremental effect on system throughput, thus limiting the tasks that could be assumed by the microcomputer and reducing the cost effectiveness of using such devices.

A more desirable method would be the one that allows the microprocessor to execute its main program and only stop to service peripheral devices when it is told to do so by the device itself. In effect, the method, would provide an external asynchronous input that would inform the processor that it should complete whatever instruction that is currently being executed and fetch a new routine that will service the requesting device. Once this servicing is completed, the processor would resume exactly where it left off. This method is called **interrupt method.** It is easy to see that system throughput would drastically increase, and thus enhance its cost effectiveness. Most microprocessors allow execution of special routines by interrupting normal program execution. When a microprocessor is interrupted, it stops executing its current program and calls a special routine which "services" the interrupt. The event that causes the interruption is called **interrupt** and the special routine executed to service the interrupt is called **interrupt service routine/procedure**. Normal program can be interrupted by three ways :

1. By external signal
2. By a special instruction in the program or
3. By the occurrence of some condition.

An interrupt caused by an external signal is referred as a **hardware interrupt**. Conditional interrupts or interrupts caused by special instructions are called **software interrupts**.

8.2 Sources of Interrupts in 8086

Nov./Dec.-07; May/June-08

An 8086 interrupt can come from any one the three sources :

- External signal
- Special Instruction in the program
- Condition produced by instruction

8.2.1 External Signal (Hardware Interrupt)

An 8086 can get interrupt from an external signal applied to the non-maskable interrupt (NMI) input pin, or the interrupt (INTR) input pin.

8.2.2 Special Instruction

8086 supports a special instruction, INT to execute special program. At the end of the interrupt service routine, execution is usually returned to the interrupted program.

8.2.3 Condition Produced by Instruction

An 8086 is interrupted by some condition produced in the 8086 by the execution of an instruction. For example divide by zero : Program execution will automatically be interrupted if you attempt to divide an operand by zero.

At the end of each instruction cycle 8086 checks to see if there is any interrupt request. If so, 8086 responds to the interrupt by performing series of actions (Refer Fig. 8.1).

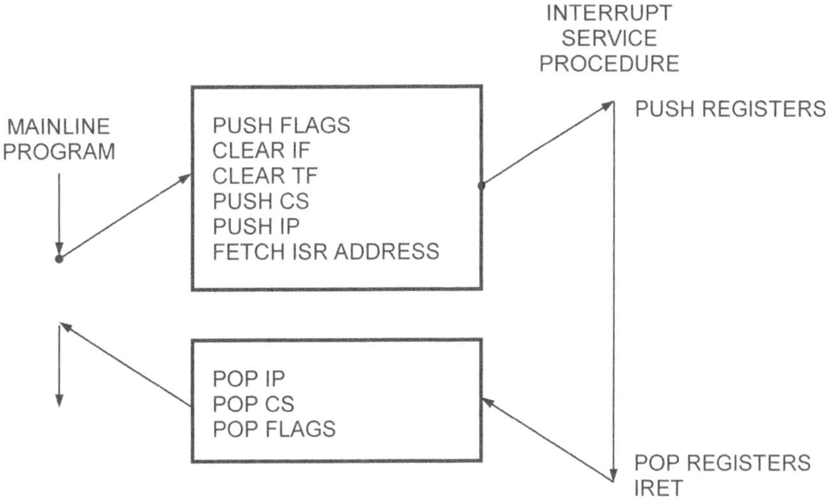

Fig. 8.1 8086 interrupt response

1. It decrements stack pointer by 2 and pushes the flag register on the stack .
2. It disables the INTR interrupt input by clearing the interrupt flag in the flag register.
3. It resets the trap flag in the flag register.
4. It decrements stack pointer by 2 and pushes the current code segment register contents on the stack.
5. It decrements stack pointer by 2 and pushes the current instruction pointer contents on the stack.

6. It does an indirect far jump at the start of the procedure by loading the CS and IP values for the start of the interrupt service routine (ISR).

An IRET instruction at the end of the interrupt service procedure returns execution to the main program.

Now the question is "How to get the values of CS and IP register ?" The 8086 gets the new values of CS and IP register from four memory addresses. When it responds to an interrupt, the 8086 goes to memory locations to get the CS and IP values for the start of the interrupt service routine. In an 8086 system the first 1 Kbyte of memory from 00000H to 003FFH is reserved for storing the starting addresses of interrupt service routines. This block of memory is often called the **interrupt vector table** or the **interrupt pointer table**. Since 4 bytes are required to store the CS and IP values for each interrupt service procedure, the table can hold the starting addresses for 256 interrupt service routines. Fig. 8.2 shows how the 256 interrupt pointers are arranged in the memory table. (See Fig. 8.2 on next page)

Each interrupt type is given a number between 0 to 255 and the address of each interrupt is found by multiplying the type by 4 e.g. for type 11, interrupt address is $11 \times 4 = 44_{10}$ = 0002CH

Only first five types have explicit definitions such as divide by zero and non maskable interrupt. The next 27 interrupt types, from 5 to 31, are reserved by Intel for use in future microprocessors. The upper 224 interrupt types, from 32 to 255, are available for user for hardware or software interrupts.

When the 8086 responds to an interrupt, it automatically goes to the specified location in the interrupt vector table to get the starting address of interrupt service routine. So user has to load these starting addresses for different routines at the start of the program.

8.3 8086 Interrupt Types

May/June-06,07,08; Nov./Dec.-06,08

8.3.1 Divide by Zero Interrupt (Type 0)

When the quotient from either a DIV or IDIV instruction is too large to fit in the result register; 8086 will automatically execute type 0 interrupt.

8.3.2 Single Step Interrupt (Type 1)

The type 1 interrupt is the single step trap. In the single step mode, system will execute one instruction and wait for further direction from user. Then user can examine the contents of registers and memory locations and if they are correct, user can tell the system to execute the next instruction. This feature is useful for debugging assembly language programs.

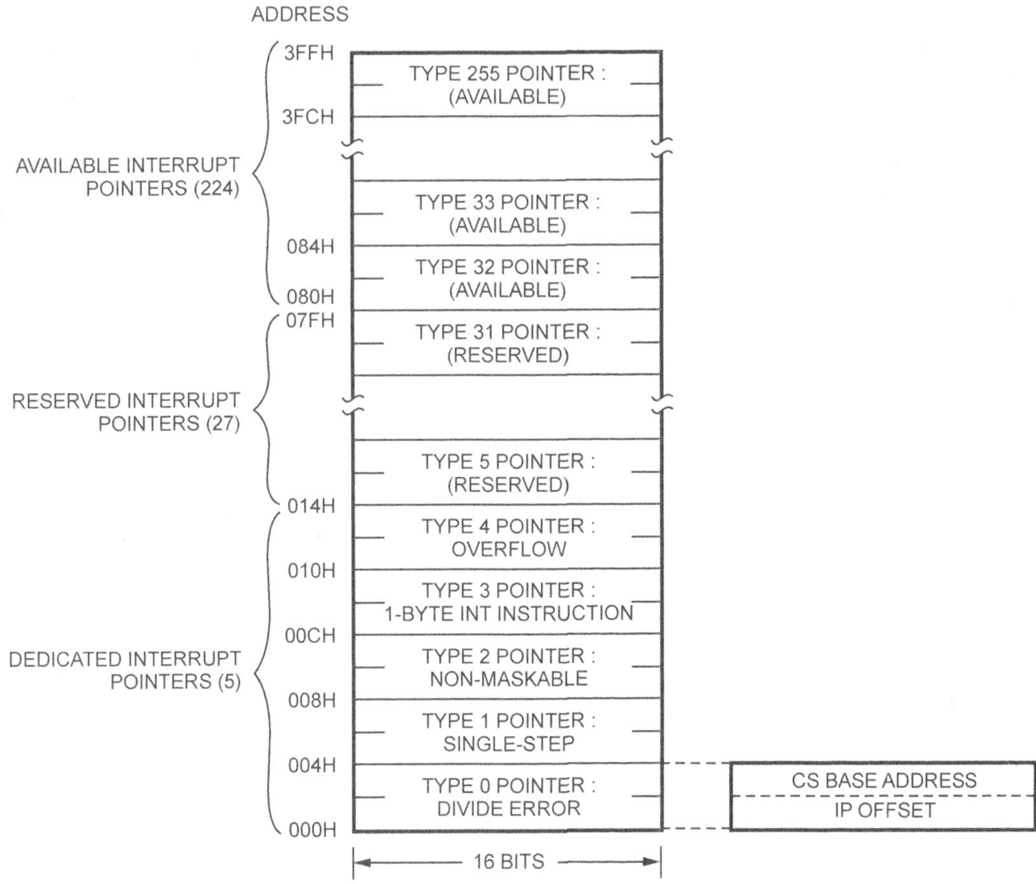

Fig. 8.2 8086 interrupt vector table

An 8086 system is used in the single step mode by setting the trap flag. If the trap flag is set, the 8086 will automatically execute a type 1 interrupt after execution of each instruction. But the 8086 has no such instruction to directly set or reset the trap flag. These operations can be performed by taking the flag register contents into memory, changing the memory contents so to set or reset trap flag and save the memory contents into flag register.

Assembly language program to set trap flag :

```
PUSHF               ; save the contents of trap flag in
                    ; stack memory
MOV BP, SP          ; copy SP to BP for use as index
OR [ BP + 0 ], 0100H  ; set the Bit 8 in the memory pointed
                    ; by BP i.e. set TF bit
POPF                ; Restore the flag register with TF = 1
```

To reset the trap flag we have to reset Bit 8. This can be done by using AND [BP + 0], 0FEFFH instruction instead of OR [BP + 0], 0100H.

8.3.3 Non Maskable Interrupt (Type 2)

As the name suggests, this interrupt cannot be disabled by any software instruction. This interrupt is activated by low to high transition on 8086 NMI input pin. In response, 8086 will do a type 2 interrupt.

8.3.4 Breakpoint Interrupt (Type 3)

The type 3 interrupt is used to implement **break point** function in the system. The type 3 interrupt is produced by execution of the INT 3 instruction. Break point function is often used as a debugging aid in cases where single stepping provides more detail than wanted. When you insert a breakpoint, the system executes the instructions upto the breakpoint, and then goes to the breakpoint procedure. In the break point procedure you can write a program to display register contents, memory contents and other information that is required to debug your program. You can insert as many breakpoints as you want in your program.

8.3.5 Overflow Interrupt (Type 4)

The type 4 interrupt is used to check overflow condition after any signed arithmetic operation in the system. The 8086 overflow flag, OF, will be represented in the destination register or memory location.

For example, if you add the 8-bit signed number 0111 1000 (+ 120 decimal) and the 8-bit signed number 0110 1010 (+ 106 decimal), result is 1110 0010 (–98 decimal). In signed numbers, MSB (Most significant Bit) is reserved for sign and other bits represent magnitude of the number. In the previous example, after addition of two 8-bit signed numbers result is negative, since it is too large to fit in 7–bits. To detect this condition in the program, you can put interrupt on overflow instruction, INTO, immediately after the arithmetic instruction in the program. If the overflow flag is not set when the 8086 executes the INTO instruction, the instruction will simply function as an NOP (no operation). However, if the overflow flag is set, indicating an overflow error, the 8086 will execute a type 4 interrupt after executing the INTO instruction.

Another way to detect and respond to an overflow error in a program is to put the jump if overflow instruction (JO) immediately after the arithmetic instruction. If the overflow flag is set as a result of arithmetic operation, execution will jump to the address specified in the JO instruction. At this address you can put an error routine which responds in the way you want to the overflow.

8.3.6 Software Interrupts

Type 0 - 255 :

The 8086 INT instruction can be used to cause the 8086 to do one of the 256 possible interrupt types. The interrupt type is specified by the number as a part of the instruction. You can use an INT2 instruction to send execution to an NMI interrupt service routine. This allows you to test the NMI routine without needing to apply an external signal to the NMI input of the 8086.

With the software interrupts you can call the desired routines from many different programs in a system. e.g. BIOS in IBM PC. The IBM PC has in its ROM collection of routines, each performing some specific function such as reading character from keyboard, writing character to CRT. This collection of routines referred to as **Basic Input Output System** or **BIOS**.

The BIOS routines are called with INT instructions. We will summarize interrupt response and how it is serviced by going through following steps.

1. 8086 pushes the flag register on the stack.
2. It disables the single step and the INTR input by clearing the trap flag and interrupt flag in the flag register.
3. It saves the current CS and IP register contents by pushing them on the stack.
4. It does an indirect far jump to the start of the routine by loading the new values of CS and IP register from the memory whose address calculated by multiplying 4 to the interrupt type. e.g. If interrupt type is 4 then memory address is $4 \times 4 = 16_{10}$ = 10H. So 8086 will read new value of IP from 00010H and CS from 00012H.
5. Once these values are loaded in the CS and IP, 8086 will fetch the instruction from the new address which is the starting address of interrupt service routine.
6. An IRET instruction at the end of the interrupt service routine gets the previous values of CS and IP by popping the CS and IP from the stack.
7. At the end the flag register contents are copied back into flag register by popping the flag register form stack.

8.3.7 Maskable Interrupt (INTR)

The 8086 INTR input can be used to interrupt a program execution. The 8086 is provided with a maskable handshake interrupt. This interrupt is implemented by using two pins - INTR and $\overline{\text{INTA}}$. This interrupt can be enabled or disabled by STI (IF = 1) or CLI (IF = 0), respectively. When the 8086 is reset, the interrupt flag is automatically cleared (IF = 0). So after reset INTR is disabled. User has to execute STI instruction to enable INTR interrupt.

The 8086 responds to an INTR interrupt as follows :

1. The 8086 first does two interrupt acknowledge machine cycles as shown in the Fig. 8.3 to get the interrupt type from the external device. In the first interrupt acknowledge machine cycle the 8086 floats the data bus lines AD_0-AD_{15} and sends out an $\overline{INTA}$ pulse on its $\overline{INTA}$ output pin. This indicates an interrupt acknowledge cycle in progress and the system is ready to accept the interrupt type from the external device. During the second interrupt acknowledge machine cycle the 8086 sends out another pulse on its $\overline{INTA}$ output pin. In response to this second $\overline{INTA}$ pulse the external device puts the interrupt type on lower 8-bits of the data bus.

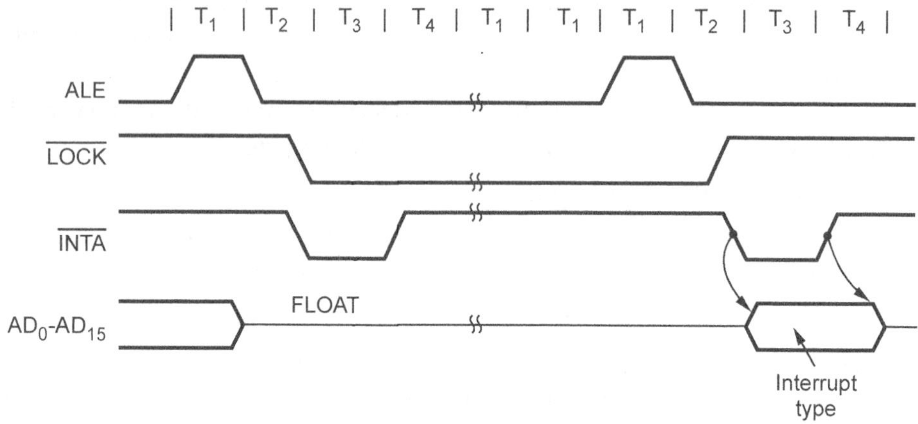

Fig. 8.3 Interrupt acknowledge machine cycle

2. Once the 8086 receives the interrupt type, it pushes the flag register on the stack, clears TF and IF, and pushes the CS and IP values of the next instruction on the stack.

3. The 8086 then gets the new value of IP from the memory address equal to 4 times the interrupt type (number), and CS value from memory address equal to 4 times the interrupt number plus 2.

8.4 Interrupt Priorities

May/June-06

As far as the 8086 interrupt priorities are concerned, software interrupts (All interrupts except single step, NMI and INTR interrupts) have the highest priority, followed by NMI followed by INTR. Single step has the least priority.

Interrupt	Priority
Divide Error, Int n, Int 0	HIGHEST
NMI	↓
INTR	↓
SINGLE - STEP	LOWEST

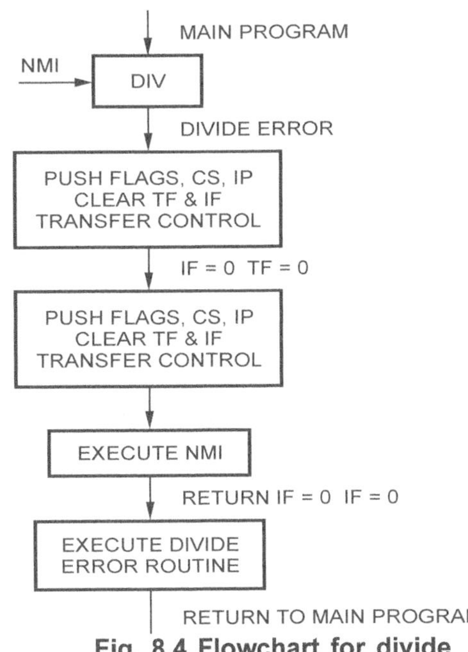

Fig. 8.4 Flowchart for divide error routine

The interrupt flag is automatically cleared as part of the response of an 8086 to an interrupt. This prevents a signal on the INTR input from interrupting a higher priority interrupt service routine. The 8086 allows NMI input to interrupt higher priority interrupt, for example suppose that a rising edge signal arrives at the NMI input while the 8086 is executing a DIV instruction, and that the division operation produces a divide error. Since the 8086 checks for internal interrupts before it checks for an NMI interrupt, the 8086 will push the flags on the stack, clear TF and IF, push the return address on the stack, and go to the start of the divide error service routine. The 8086 will then do an NMI interrupt response and execute non-maskable interrupt service routine. After completion of NMI service routine an 8086 will return to the divide error routine. It will execute divide error routine and then it will return to the main program (Refer Fig. 8.4).

Review Questions

Section 8.1

Q.1 *Write a short note on interrupts and interrupt service routines.* **Dec.-08, Marks 8**

Q.2 *Why is an interrupt driven I/O more efficient than programmed I/O for 8086 microprocessor ?* **Dec.-05, Marks 2**

Q.3 *What is an interrupt service routine?* **May-09 Marks 2**

Section 8.2

Q.1 *Discuss in detail the interrupts and interrupt service routine in 8086 processor.* **Dec.-07,08, May-08, Marks 8**

Q.2 *Describe the action taken by 8086 when INTR pin is activated.* **May-07, Marks 6**

Q.3 *What are the sources of interrupts in 8086 ?*

Q.4 *What is interrupt vector table ?*

Q.5 *Draw and explain the IVT for 8086.*

Section 8.3

Q.1 *Describe the action taken by 8086 when NMI pin is activated.* **Dec.-06, Marks 4**

Q.2 *Briefly describe the conditions which cause the 8086 to perform each of the following types of interrupts : Type 0, Type 1, Type 2, Type 3 and Type 4.*

Q.3 *Explain interrupt structure of 8086.*

Q.4 *What are software interrupt ? How 8086 responds to software interrupts ?*

Q.5 *Draw and explain the interrupt acknowledge cycle of 8086.*

Q.6 *What is the storage space required to store the interrupt vectors of 8086 ?* **May-08, Marks 2**

Q.7 *What do you mean by non-maskable interrupt ?* **Dec.-08, Marks 2**

Section 8.4

Q.1 *What do you mean by interrupt priorities ?*

Q.2 *State the interrupt priorities for 8086 interrupts.*

Two Marks Questions with Answers

Q.1 ***Why is an interrupt driven I/O more efficient than programmed I/O for 8086 microprocessor ?*** **Dec.-05**

Ans. : Refer section 8.1.

Q.2 ***An interrupt device based on 8086 microprocessor sends 03H onto AD_0 through AD_7 data bus when $\overline{INTA}$ is low. Where should the interrupt jump address located in the vector table?*** **Dec.-04**

Ans. : 03H $\times$ 4 $\rightarrow$ 000DH.

Q.3 ***What are the different types of interrupts in 8086 ?*** **May-06**

Ans. : Different types of interrupts in 8086 are :

1. Divide by zero interrupts
2. Single step interrupt
3. Non maskable interrupt (NMI)
4. Breakpoint interrupts
5. Overflow interrupt
6. Software interrupts Type 0-255
7. Maskable interrupt (INTR)

Q.4 *State the interrupt priorities of 8086.* **May-06**

Ans. :

Interrupt	Priority
Divide Error, Int n, Int 0	HIGHEST
NMI	↓
INTR	↓
SINGLE - STEP	LOWEST

Q.5 *What is meant by software interrupt in 8086 ?* **May-07**

Ans. : The 8086 INT instruction can be used to cause the 8086 to do one of the 256 possible interrupt types. The interrupt type is specified by the number as a part of the instruction. Such interrupts are called software interrupt in 8086.

Q.6 *How the interrupts can be masked/unmasked in 8086 ?* **May-07**

Ans. : The INTR interrupt of 8086 can be masked or unmasked by making IF flag equal to 0 or 1, respectively. IF can be set STI instruction and it can be reset by CLI instruction.

Q.7 *What is an interrupt service routine?* **May-09**

Ans. : Refer section 8.1.

Q.8 *What is the storage space required to store the interrupt vectors of 8086 ?* **May-08**

Ans. : Refer section 8.3.1.

Q.9 *What do you mean by non-maskable interrupt ?* **Dec.-08**

Ans. : Refer section 8.3.3.

Notes

9 Memory Interfacing

Contents

9.1 Introduction

Nov./Dec.-04,05; May/June-06, April/May-08

Memory is an integral part of a microprocessor system, and in this chapter, we will discuss how to interface a memory device with the microprocessor. The memory interfacing circuit is used to access memory quite frequently to read instruction codes and data stored in memory. This read/write operations are monitored by control signals. The microprocessor activates these signals when it wants to read from and write into memory. In this chapter we will see memory structure and its requirements, concepts in memory interfacing and interfacing examples.

9.2 Terminology and Operations

Memories are made up of registers. Each register in the memory is one storage location. Each location is identified by an **address**. The number of storage locations can vary from a few in some memories to hundreds of thousand in others. Each location can accommodate one or more bits. Generally, the total number of bits that a memory can store is its **capacity**. Most of the types the capacity is specified in terms of bytes (group of eight bits).

Each register consists of storage elements (flip-flops or capacitors in semiconductor memories and magnetic domain in magnetic storage), each of which stores one bit of data. A storage element is called a **cell**.

The data stored in a memory by a process called **writing** and are retrieved from the memory by a process called **reading**. Fig. 9.1 illustrates in a very simplified way the concept of write, read, address and storage capacity for a generalized memory.

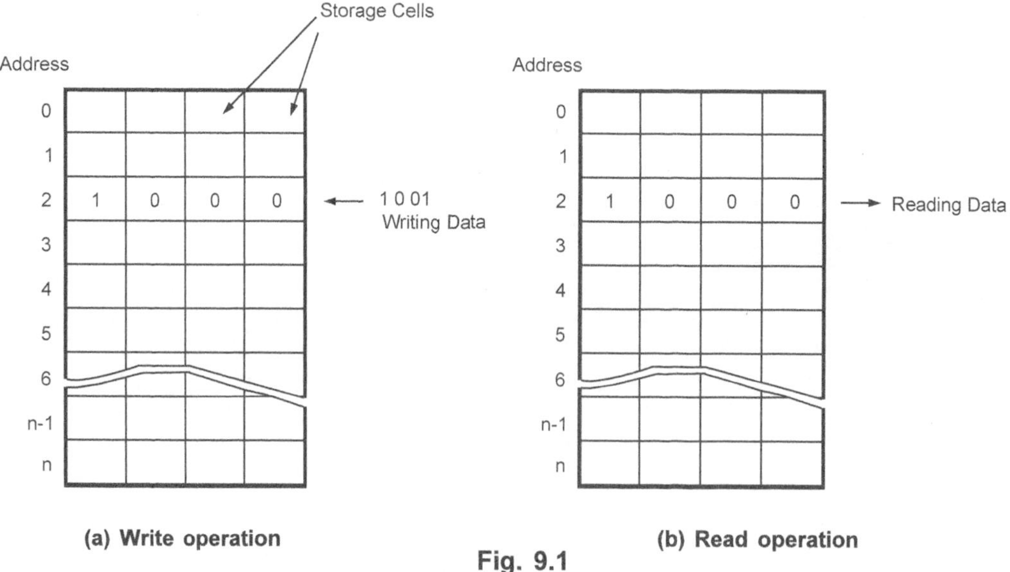

(a) Write operation (b) Read operation

Fig. 9.1

9.3 Memory Structure and its Requirements

As mentioned earlier, read/write memories consist of an array of registers, in which each register has unique address. The size of the memory is N × M as shown in Fig. 9.2 (a) where N is the number of registers and M is the word length, in number of bits.

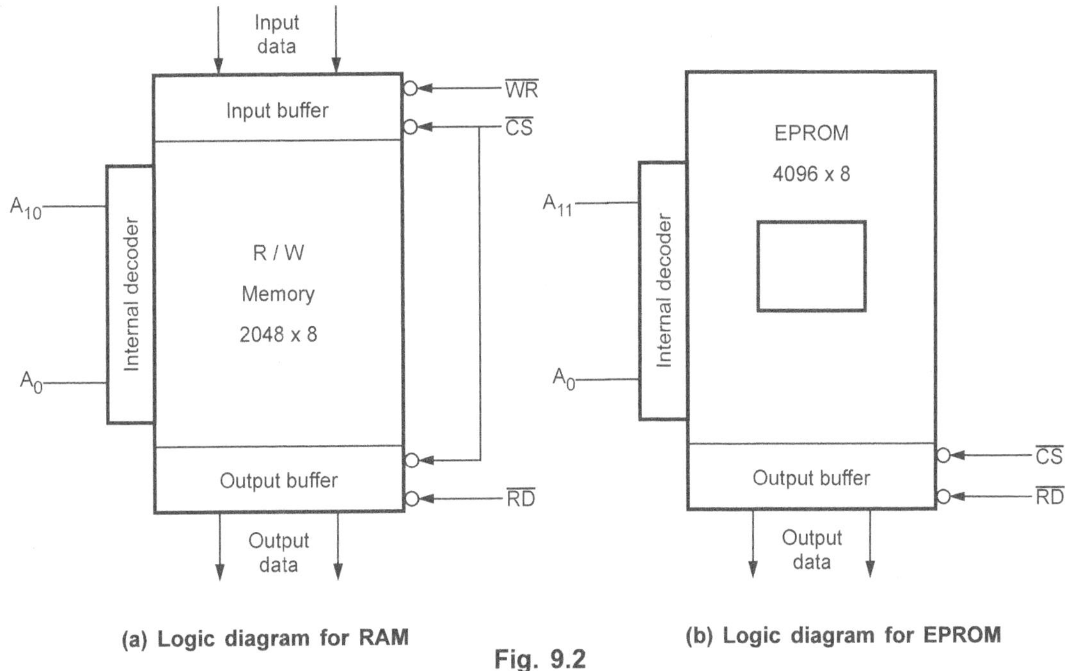

(a) Logic diagram for RAM **(b) Logic diagram for EPROM**

Fig. 9.2

Example 1 : If memory is having 12 address lines and 8 data lines, then

Number of registers/memory locations $= 2^N = 2^{12}$

$= 4096$

Word length = M-bit

= 8-bit

Example 2 : If memory has 8192 memory locations, then it has 13 address lines.

The Table 9.1 summarizes the memory capacity and address lines required for memory interfacing.

Memory capacity	Address lines required
1 K = 1024 memory locations	10
2 K = 2048 memory locations	11
4 K = 4096 memory locations	12
8 K = 8192 memory locations	13
16 K = 16384 memory locations	14
32 K = 32768 memory locations	15
64 K = 65536 memory locations	16

Table 9.1

As shown in the Fig. 9.2 (a) memory chip has 12 address lines A_0-A_{11}, one chip select ($\overline{CS}$), and two control lines, read ($\overline{RD}$) to enable output buffer and write ($\overline{WR}$) to enable the input buffer. The internal decoder is used to decode the address lines. Fig. 9.2 (b) shows the logic diagram of a typical EPROM (Erasable Programmable Read-Only Memory) with 4096 (4 K) registers. It has 12 address lines A_0-A_{11}, one chip select ($\overline{CS}$), one Read control signal. Since EPROM is a read only memory, it does not require the ($\overline{WR}$) signal.

9.4 Basic Concepts in Memory Interfacing with 8085

Nov./Dec.-07, April/May-10

For interfacing memory devices to microprocessor 8085, following important points are to be kept in mind.

1. Microprocessor 8085 can access 64 kbytes memory since address bus is 16-bit. But it is not always necessary to use full 64 kbytes address space. The total memory size depends upon the application.
2. Generally EPROM (or EPROMs) is used as a program memory and RAM (or RAMs) as a data memory. When both, EPROM and RAM are used, the total address space 64 kbytes is shared by them.
3. The capacity of program memory and data memory depends on the application.
4. It is not always necessary to select 1 EPROM and 1 RAM. We can have multiple EPROMs and multiple RAMs as per the requirement of application.

For example :

We have to implement 32 kbytes of program memory and 4 kbytes EPROMs are available. In this case, we can connect 8 EPROMs in parallel
(4 kbytes × 8 = 32 kbytes) with different chip select for each EPROM.

6. We can place EPROM/RAM anywhere in full 64 kbytes address space. But program memory (EPROM) should be located from address 0000H since reset address of 8085 microprocessor is 0000H.
7. It is not always necessary to locate EPROM and RAM in consecutive memory addresses. For example : If the mapping of EPROM is from 0000H to 0FFFH, it is not must to locate RAM from 1000H. We can locate it anywhere between 1000H and FFFFH. Where to locate memory component totally depends on the application.

The memory interfacing requires to :

- Select the chip
- Identify the register
- Enable the appropriate buffer.

Microprocessor system includes memory devices and I/O devices. It is important to note that microprocessor can communicate (read/write) with only one device at a time, since the data, address and control buses are common for all the devices. In order to communicate with memory or I/O devices, it is necessary to decode the address from the microprocessor. Due to this each device (memory or I/O) can be accessed independently. The following section describes common address decoding techniques.

Address Decoding Techniques :

- Absolute decoding/Full decoding
- Linear decoding/Partial decoding

Absolute decoding

In absolute decoding technique, all the higher address lines are decoded to select the memory chip, and the memory chip is selected only for the specified logic levels on these high-order address lines; no other logic levels can select the chip. Fig. 9.3 shows the memory interface with absolute decoding. This addressing technique is normally used in large memory systems.

Memory Map :

Memory ICs	A_{15}	A_{14}	A_{13}	A_{12}	A_{11}	A_{10}	A_9	A_8	A_7	A_6	A_5	A_4	A_3	A_2	A_1	A_0	Address
Starting address of EPROM	0	0	0	0	0	0	0	0	0	0	0	0	0	0	0	0	0000H

End address of EPROM	0	0	0	0	0	0	1	1	1	1	1	1	1	1	1	1	03FFH
Starting address of RAM	0	0	1	0	0	0	0	0	0	0	0	0	0	0	0	0	2000H
End address of RAM	0	0	1	0	0	0	1	1	1	1	1	1	1	1	1	1	23FFH

Table 9.2

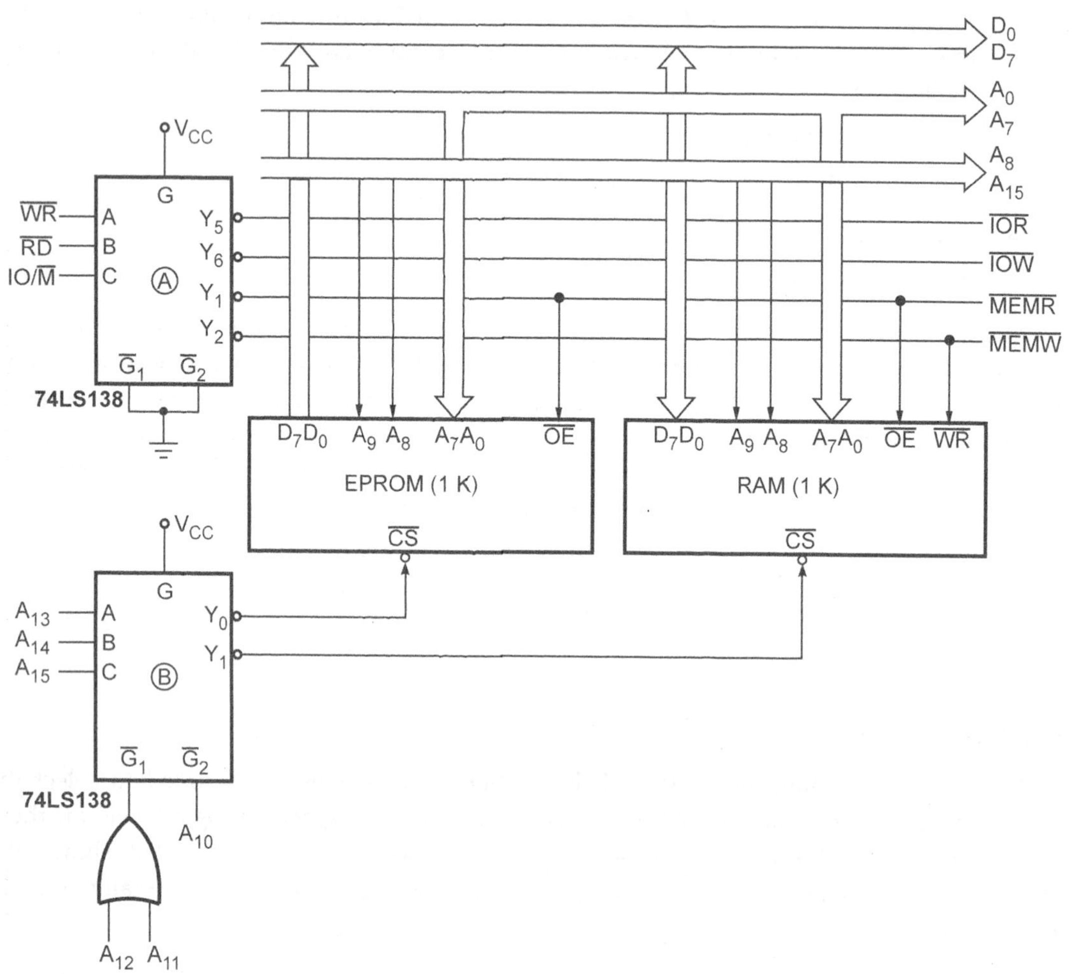

Fig. 9.3 Absolute decoding technique

Linear decoding

In small systems, hardware for the decoding logic can be eliminated by using individual high-order address lines to select memory chips. This is referred to as linear decoding. Fig. 9.4 shows the addressing of RAM with linear decoding technique. This technique is also called **partial decoding**. It reduces the cost of decoding circuit, but it has a drawback of multiple addresses (shadow addresses).

Fig. 9.4 shows the addressing of RAM with linear decoding technique. A_{15} address line, is directly connected to the chip select signal of EPROM and after inversion it is connected to the chip select signal of the RAM. Therefore, when the status of A_{15} line is 'zero', EPROM gets selected and when the status of A_{15} line is 'one' RAM gets selected. The status of the other address lines is not considered, since those address lines are not used for generation of chip select signals.

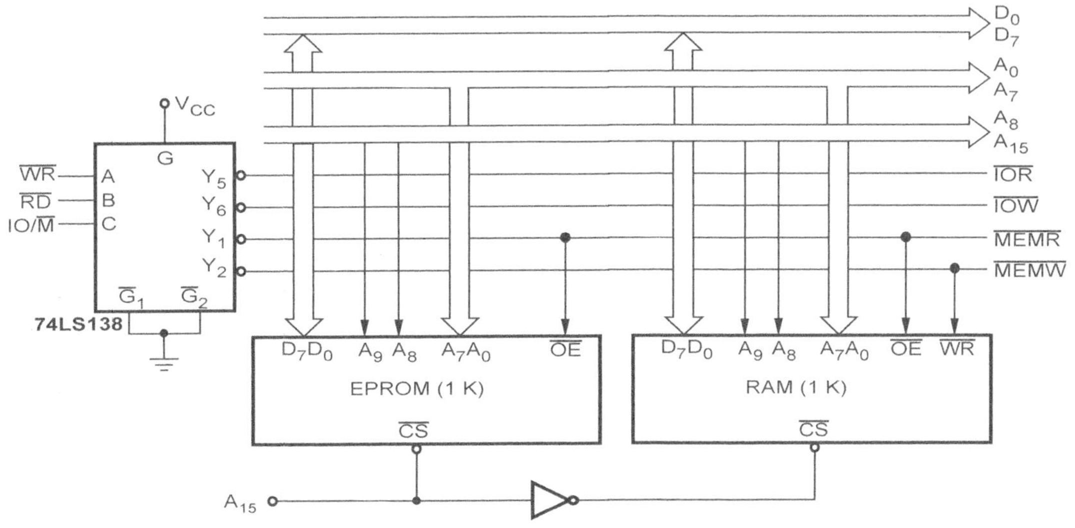

Fig. 9.4 Linear decoding

Memory Map :

Memory ICs	A_{15}	A_{14}	A_{13}	A_{12}	A_{11}	A_{10}	A_9	A_8	A_7	A_6	A_5	A_4	A_3	A_2	A_1	A_0	Address
Starting address of EPROM	0	X	X	X	X	X	0	0	0	0	0	0	0	0	0	0	0000H
End address of EPROM	0	X	X	X	X	X	1	1	1	1	1	1	1	1	1	1	03FFH
Starting address of RAM	1	X	X	X	X	X	0	0	0	0	0	0	0	0	0	0	8000H
End address of RAM	1	X	X	X	X	X	1	1	1	1	1	1	1	1	1	1	83FFH

Table 9.3

9.4.1 Interfacing Examples

Example 9.1 : *Design memory system for the 8085 microprocessor such that it should contain 8 kbyte of EPROM (Erasable Programmable Read Only Memory) and 8 kbyte of RAM (Read/Write Memory).*

Solution : Fig. 9.5 shows the desired memory system using IC 2764 (8 K) EPROM and 6264 (8 K) RAM. Memory requires 13 address lines (A_0-A_{12}) since 2^{13} = 8 K. The remaining address lines (A_{13} - A_{15}) are decoded to generate chip select ($\overline{CS}$) signals. IC 74LS138 is used as decoder. When (A_{15} - A_{13}) address lines are zero, the Y_0 output of decoder goes low and selects the EPROM. This means that A_{15} - A_{13} address lines must be zero to read data from EPROM. The address lines A_{12} - A_0 select the particular memory location in the EPROM when A_{15} - A_{13} lines are zero. Similarly, when address lines A_{15} - A_{13} are 001, the Y_1 output of decoder goes low and selects the RAM. The Table 9.4 shows the memory map for the designed circuit.

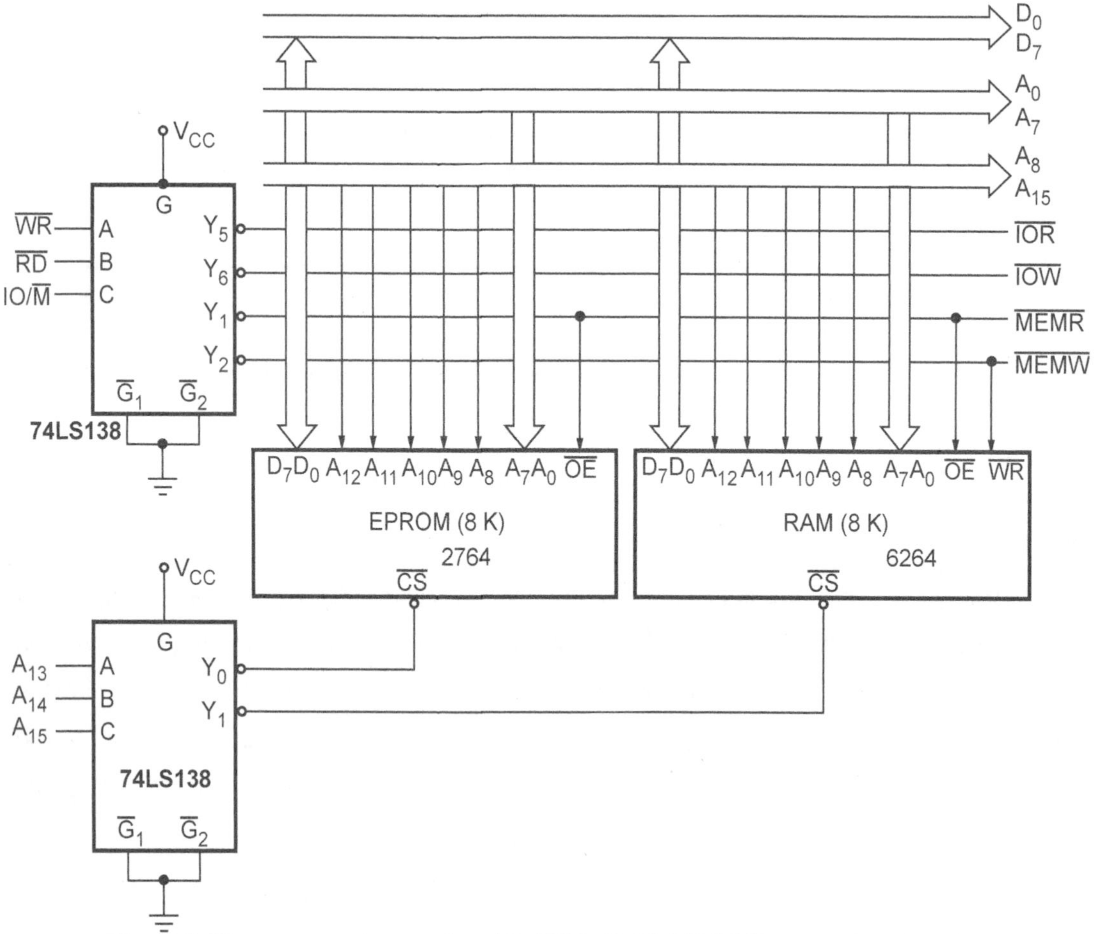

Fig. 9.5 Memory system using IC 2764 (8 K) EPROM and 6264 (8 K) RAM

Memory Map :

Memory ICs	A_{15}	A_{14}	A_{13}	A_{12}	A_{11}	A_{10}	A_9	A_8	A_7	A_6	A_5	A_4	A_3	A_2	A_1	A_0	Address
Starting address of EPROM	0	0	0	0	0	0	0	0	0	0	0	0	0	0	0	0	0000H
End address of EPROM	0	0	0	1	1	1	1	1	1	1	1	1	1	1	1	1	1FFFH
Starting address of RAM	0	0	1	0	0	0	0	0	0	0	0	0	0	0	0	0	2000H
End address of RAM	0	0	1	1	1	1	1	1	1	1	1	1	1	1	1	1	3FFFH

Table 9.4 Memory map

Example 9.2 : *Design a microprocessor system for the 8085 microprocessor such that it should contain 16 kbyte of EPROM and 4 kbyte of RAM using two 8 kbyte EPROMs (2764) and two 2 kbyte RAMs (6116).*

Solution : Fig. 9.6 (See on page no. 9 - 10) shows the desired memory system using two (8 K × 8) EPROM and two (2 K × 8) RAMs. EPROM memory is 8 K, so it requires 13 address lines (A_{12} - A_0) whereas RAM memory is 2 K, so it requires 11 address lines (A_{10} - A_0). The remaining higher address lines (A_{15} - A_{13}) are used to generate chip-select ($\overline{CS}$) signals. Table 9.5 shows the memory map for the designed circuit.

Memory Map :

Memory ICs	A_{15}	A_{14}	A_{13}	A_{12}	A_{11}	A_{10}	A_9	A_8	A_7	A_6	A_5	A_4	A_3	A_2	A_1	A_0	Address
Starting Address of EPROM 1	0	0	0	0	0	0	0	0	0	0	0	0	0	0	0	0	0000H
End Address of EPROM 1	0	0	0	1	1	1	1	1	1	1	1	1	1	1	1	1	1FFFH
Starting Address of EPROM 2	0	0	1	0	0	0	0	0	0	0	0	0	0	0	0	0	2000H
End Address of EPROM 2	0	0	1	1	1	1	1	1	1	1	1	1	1	1	1	1	3FFFH
Starting Address of RAM 1	0	1	0	X	X	0	0	0	0	0	0	0	0	0	0	0	4000H
End Address of RAM 1	0	1	0	X	X	1	1	1	1	1	1	1	1	1	1	1	47FFH
Starting Address of RAM 2	0	1	1	X	X	0	0	0	0	0	0	0	0	0	0	0	6000H
End Address of RAM 2	0	1	1	X	X	1	1	1	1	1	1	1	1	1	1	1	67FFH

Table 9.5 Memory map

Example 9.3 : *Interface 2 kbyte RAM to 8085 using 2114 (1 K × 4) chips, 74LS138 decoder and full address decoding and give the address map (memory map).*

Solution : 2114 RAM is 1 K × 4 i.e. it has 1 K (1024) memory locations, each of which is of 4 bits. 8085 is an 8 bit processor. To interface byte RAM, we require two nibble wide RAMs, connected together to form byte wide RAM. To form 2 K × 8 RAM we require two sets of 1 K × 4 + 1 K × 4 RAM chips. So in all we require four 1 K × 4 RAM chips.

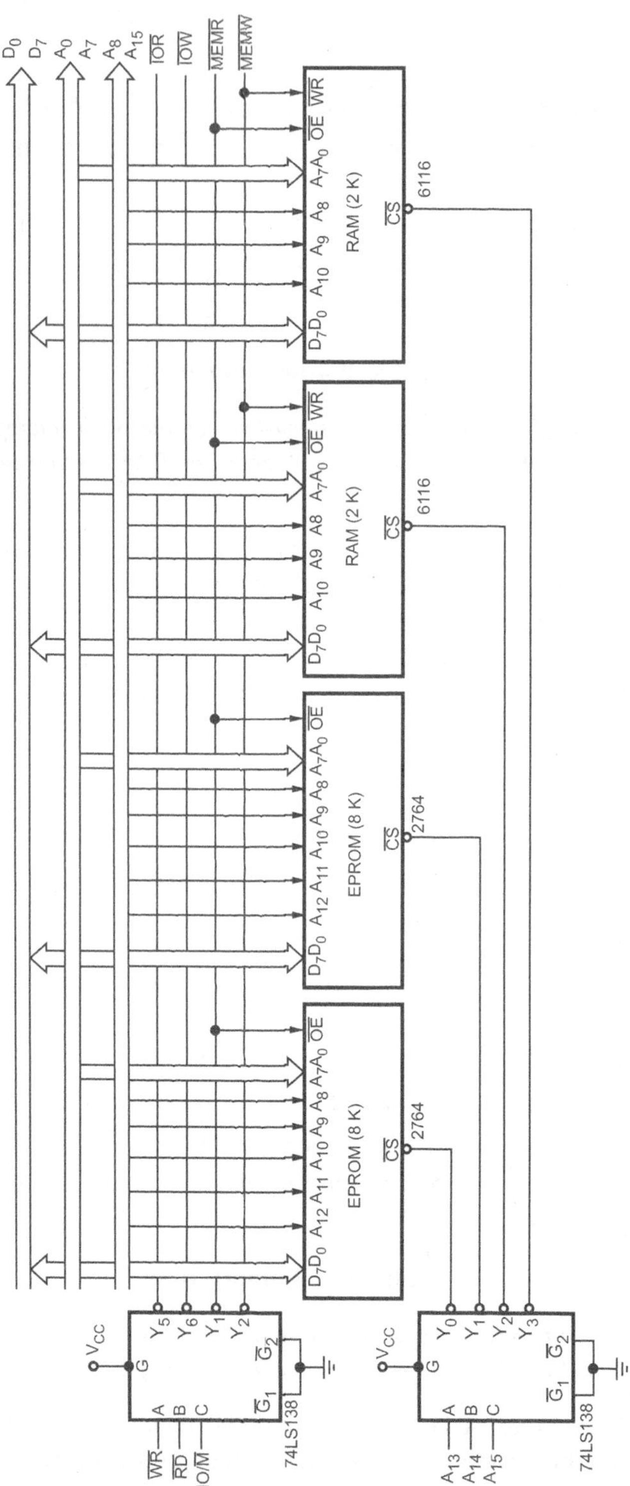

Fig. 9.6 Memory system using two (8 K × 8) EPROMs and two (2 K × 8) RAMs

(Fig. 9.7 see page no. 9 - 12) shows the interface. The IC 74LS138 is used to generate chip select ($\overline{CS}$) signals. Table 9.6 shows the memory map.

Memory Map :

Memory ICs	A_{15}	A_{14}	A_{13}	A_{12}	A_{11}	A_{10}	A_9	A_8	A_7	A_6	A_5	A_4	A_3	A_2	A_1	A_0	Address
Starting Address of RAM 1	0	0	0	0	0	0	0	0	0	0	0	0	0	0	0	0	0000H
End Address of RAM 1	0	0	0	0	0	0	1	1	1	1	1	1	1	1	1	1	03FFH
Starting Address of RAM 2	0	0	0	0	0	0	0	0	0	0	0	0	0	0	0	0	0000H
End Address of RAM 2	0	0	0	0	0	0	1	1	1	1	1	1	1	1	1	1	03FFH
Starting Address of RAM 3	0	0	1	0	0	0	0	0	0	0	0	0	0	0	0	0	2000H
End Address of RAM 3	0	0	1	0	0	0	1	1	1	1	1	1	1	1	1	1	23FFH
Starting Address of RAM 4	0	0	1	0	0	0	0	0	0	0	0	0	0	0	0	0	2000H
End Address of RAM 4	0	0	1	0	0	0	1	1	1	1	1	1	1	1	1	1	23FFH

Table 9.6 Memory map

Example 9.4 : *Design a microprocessor system for the 8085 microprocessor such that it should contain 2 kbyte of EPROM and 2 kbyte of RAM with starting addresses 0000H and 6000H respectively.*

Solution : Fig. 9.8 (See on page no 9 - 13) shows the desired memory system using 2 kbyte EPROM and 2 kbyte RAM. Both EPROM and RAM are 2 K, so they require 11 address lines (A_{10} - A_0). The remaining higher address lines (A_{15} - A_{11}) are used to generate chip select ($\overline{CS}$) signals.

The chip selection logic is designed to have starting address of EPROM, 0000H and starting address of RAM, 6000H. This is implemented by selecting EPROM only when higher address lines (A_{15} - A_{11}) are all zero, and selecting RAM only when higher address lines (A_{15} - A_{11}) are 01100 (Binary). The Table 9.7 shows the memory map for the designed circuit.

Memory Map :

Memory ICs	A_{15}	A_{14}	A_{13}	A_{12}	A_{11}	A_{10}	A_9	A_8	A_7	A_6	A_5	A_4	A_3	A_2	A_1	A_0	Address
Starting address of EPROM	0	0	0	0	0	0	0	0	0	0	0	0	0	0	0	0	0000H
End address of EPROM	0	0	0	0	0	1	1	1	1	1	1	1	1	1	1	1	07FFH
Starting address of RAM	0	1	1	0	0	0	0	0	0	0	0	0	0	0	0	0	6000H
End address of RAM	0	1	1	0	0	1	1	1	1	1	1	1	1	1	1	1	67FFH

Table 9.7 Memory map

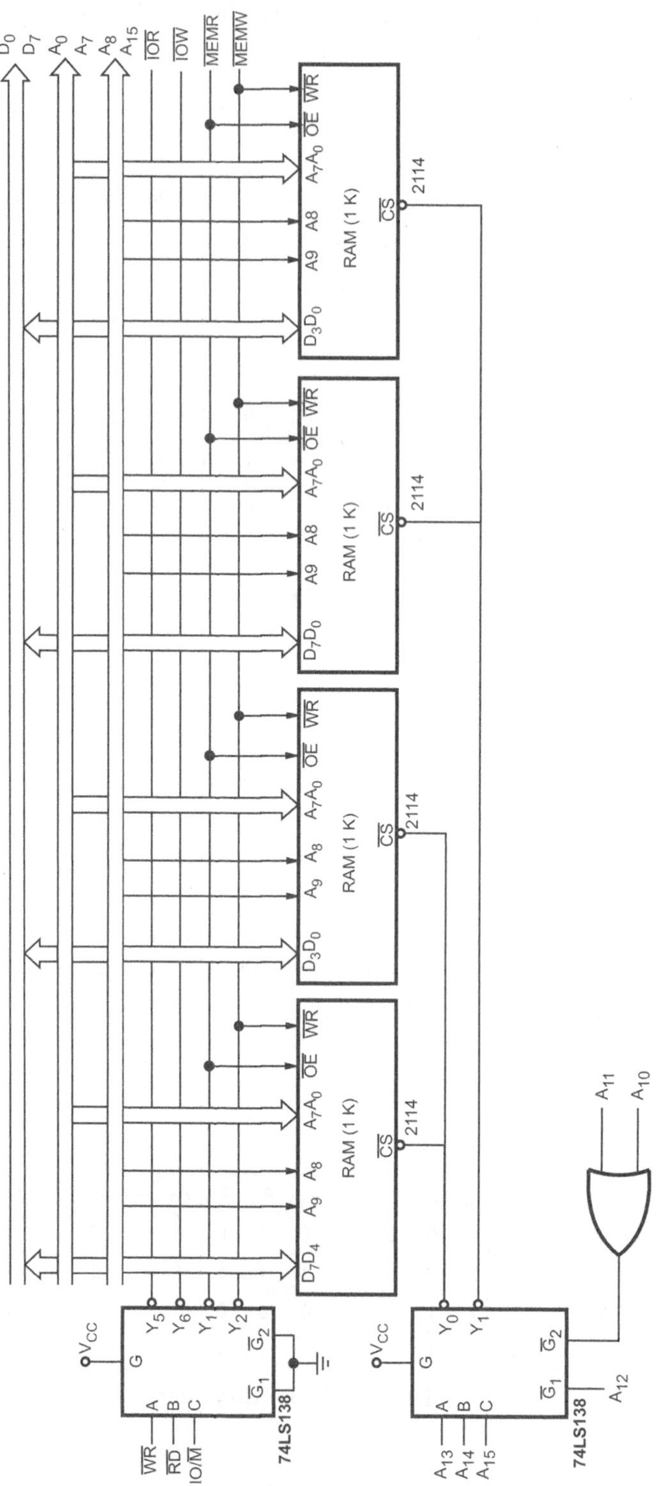

Fig. 9.7 Memory system using 2114 (1 K × 4) chips

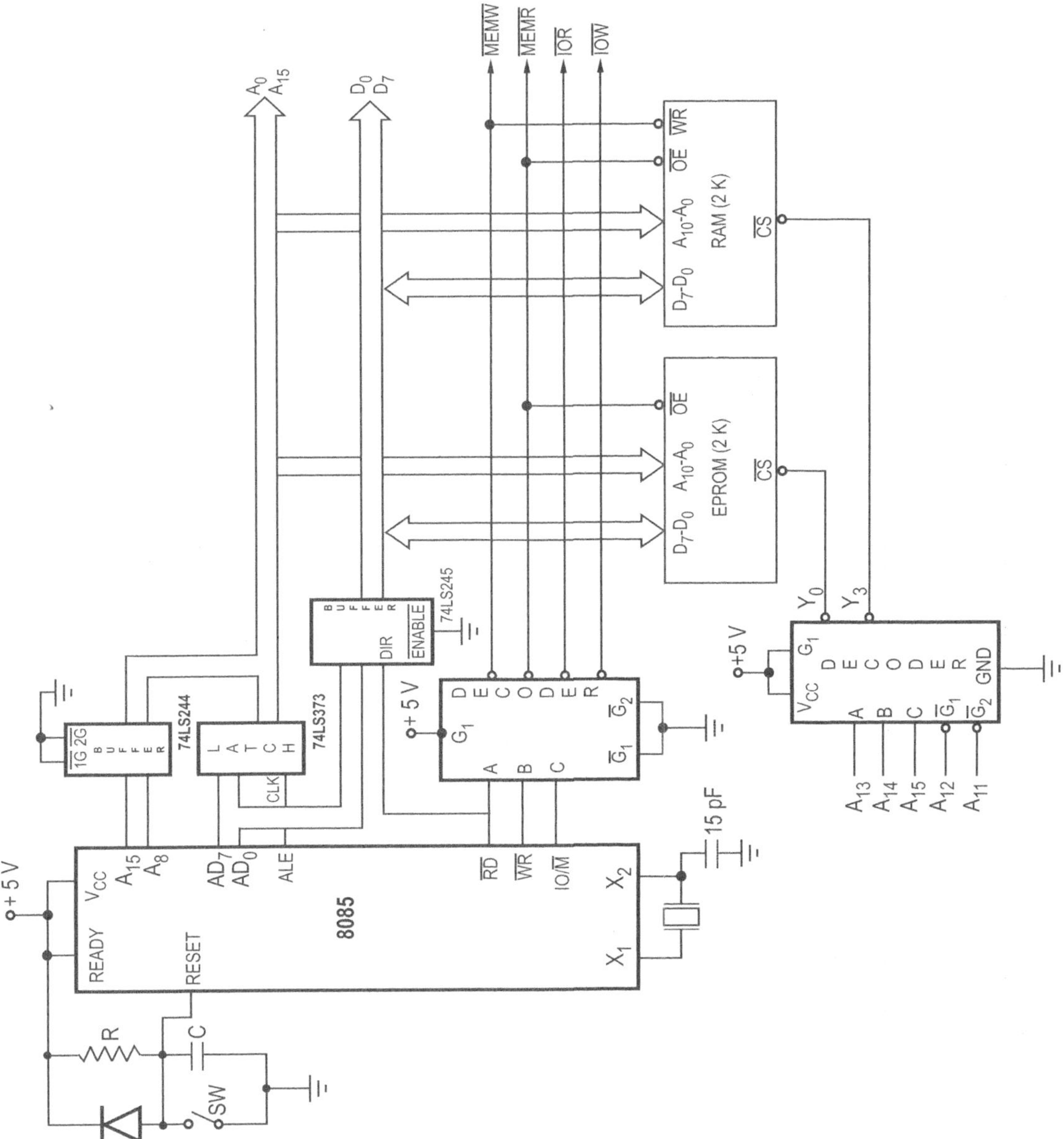

Fig. 9.8 Memory system using 2 kbyte EPROM and 2 kbyte RAM

Example 9.5 : *Design a microprocessor system for the 8085 microprocessor such that it should contain 4 kbyte of EPROM and 2 kbyte of RAM using two 2 kbytes of EPROMs and two 1 kbytes RAM. Draw the complete interfacing diagram with buffers, latches, and chip select logic used.*

Solution : Fig. 9.9 shows the desired memory system using two 2 kbyte EPROMs and two 1 kbyte RAMs.

The uni-directional buffer is used to drive the high order address bus and bi-directional buffer is used to drive the data bus. The direction pin of the bi-directional buffer is controlled by the $\overline{RD}$ signal from the microprocessor. EPROM memory is 2 kbyte, so it requires 11 address lines (A_{10}-A_0) whereas RAM memory is 1 K, so it requires 10 address lines (A_9-A_0). The remaining higher address lines (A_{15}-A_{11}) are used to generate chip-select ($\overline{CS}$) signals. Table 9.8 shows the memory map for the designed circuit.

Memory Map :

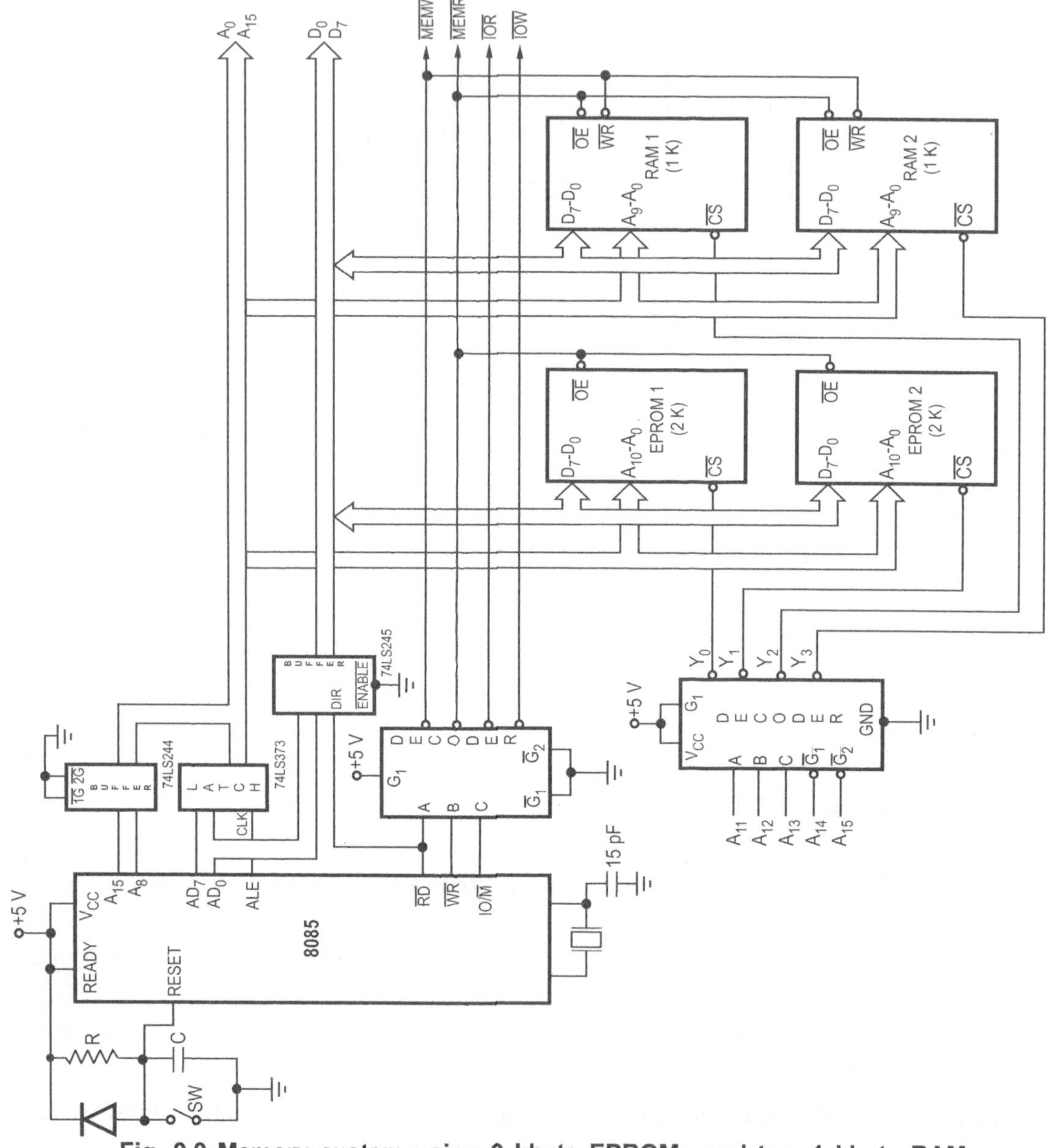

Fig. 9.9 Memory system using 2 kbyte EPROMs and two 1 kbyte RAMs

Memory ICs	A_{15}	A_{14}	A_{13}	A_{12}	A_{11}	A_{10}	A_9	A_8	A_7	A_6	A_5	A_4	A_3	A_2	A_1	A_0	Address
Starting Address of EPROM 1	0	0	0	0	0	0	0	0	0	0	0	0	0	0	0	0	0000H
End Address of EPROM 1	0	0	0	0	0	1	1	1	1	1	1	1	1	1	1	1	07FFH
Starting Address of EPROM 2	0	0	0	0	1	0	0	0	0	0	0	0	0	0	0	0	0800H
End Address of EPROM 2	0	0	0	0	1	1	1	1	1	1	1	1	1	1	1	1	0FFFH
Starting Address of RAM 1	0	0	0	1	0	0	0	0	0	0	0	0	0	0	0	0	1000H
End Address of RAM 1	0	0	0	1	0	0	1	1	1	1	1	1	1	1	1	1	13FFH
Starting Address of RAM 2	0	0	0	1	1	0	0	0	0	0	0	0	0	0	0	0	1800H
End Address of RAM 2	0	0	0	1	1	0	1	1	1	1	1	1	1	1	1	1	1BFFH

Table 9.8 Memory map

Example 9.6 : *Design a microprocessor system for the 8085 microprocessor such that it should contain 8 kbyte of EPROM and 8 kbyte of RAM. Use linear addressing technique and give the detailed address map.*

Solution : Fig. 9.10 shows the desired memory system using 8 kbyte EPROM and 8 kbyte RAM. Both EPROM and RAM are 8 K, so they require 13 address lines (A_{12}-A_0). As problem says to design microprocessor system using linear addressing technique, A_{15} address line is used to generate chip select ($\overline{CS}$) signals. When A_{15} address line is low, it selects EPROM and when it is high, it selects RAM. The table 9.9 shows the memory map for the designed circuit.

Memory Map :

Memory ICs	A_{15}	A_{14}	A_{13}	A_{12}	A_{11}	A_{10}	A_9	A_8	A_7	A_6	A_5	A_4	A_3	A_2	A_1	A_0	Address
Starting address of EPROM	0	X	X	0	0	0	0	0	0	0	0	0	0	0	0	0	0000H
End address of EPROM	0	X	X	1	1	1	1	1	1	1	1	1	1	1	1	1	1FFFH
Starting address of RAM	1	X	X	0	0	0	0	0	0	0	0	0	0	0	0	0	8000H
End address of RAM	1	X	X	1	1	1	1	1	1	1	1	1	1	1	1	1	9FFFH

Table 9.9 Memory map

Note : X represents the don't care condition and addresses are written taking don't cares as zeroes.

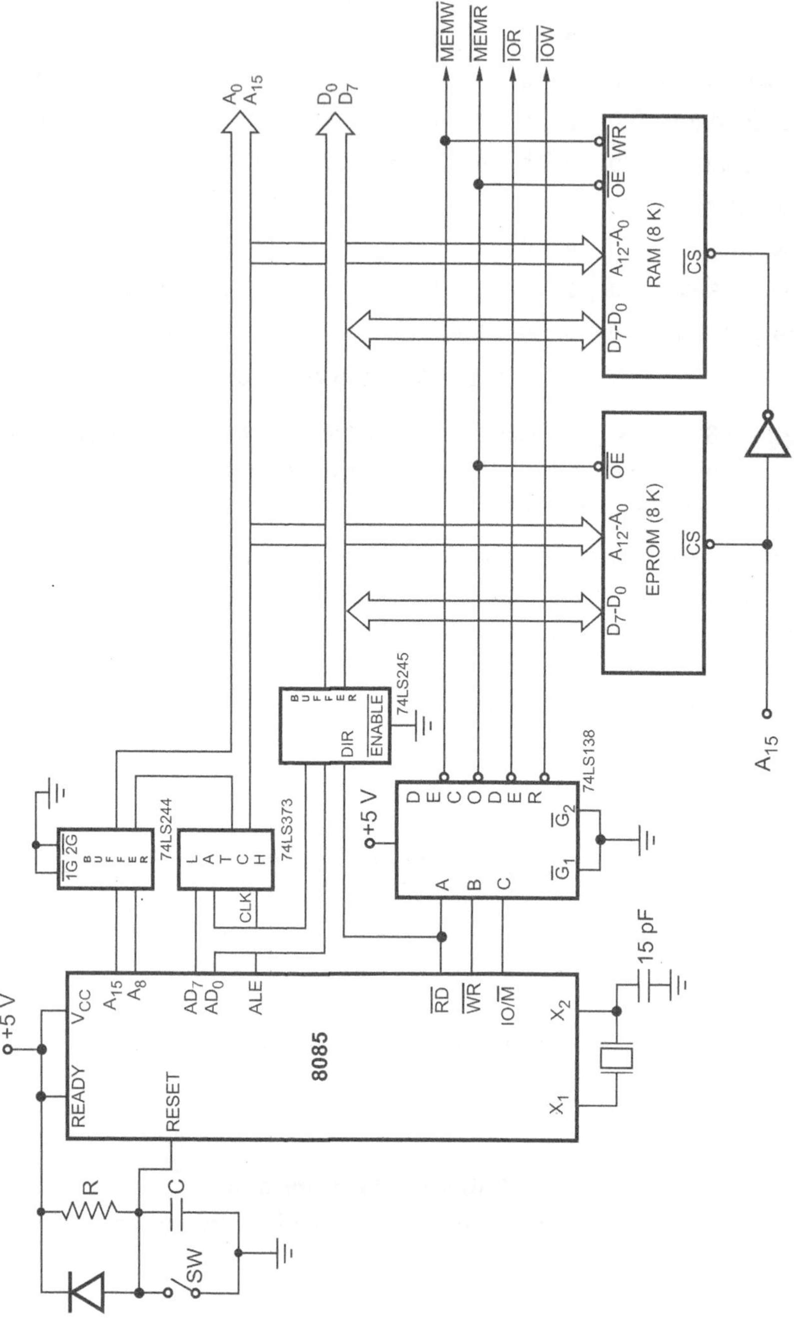

Fig. 9.10 Memory system using 8 kbyte EPROM and 8 kbyte RAM with linear address decoding

Sr. No.	Full address decoding	Partial address decoding
1.	All higher address lines are decoded to select the memory or I/O device.	Few higher address lines are decoded to select the memory or I/O device.
2.	More hardware is required to design decoding logic.	Hardware required to design decoding logic is less and sometimes it can be eliminated.
3.	Higher cost for decoding circuit.	Less cost for decoding circuit.
4.	No multiple addresses.	It has a disadvantage of multiple addresses (shadow addresses).
5.	Used in large systems.	Used in small systems.

Table 9.10

Review Questions

Section 9.2

Q.1 *What is address ?*

Q.2 *What is memory capacity.*

Section 9.3

Q.1 *Explain the memory structure and its requirements.*

Q.2 *How much address lines are required to interface 4 kbytes of memory.*

Section 9.4

Q.1 *With necessary diagrams, write short notes RAM memory interfacing and ROM memory interfacing* **May-08, Marks 16**

Q.2 *Design a microprocessor system to interface an 8K × 8 EPROM and 8K × 8 RAM.* **Dec.-05, Marks 8**

Q.3 *Explain the interfacing of memory with 8085 microprocessor.* **May-10, Marks 10**

Q.4 *Interface a 8KX8 EPROM IC and 2KX8 RAM IC with 8085 such that the starting address assigned to them are 0000H and 4000H respectively using address decoder having NAND gate and inverters.* **Dec.-07, Marks 8**

Q.5 *How address decoding is done in memory Interface.* **Dec.-11, Marks 8**

Q.6 *With necessary diagram, explain the interfacing of a RAM memory IC-6116 (2Kx8) with 8085.* **May-11, Marks 8**

Q.7 *List the steps involved in interfacing a memory to the 8085 microprocessor.* **Dec.-10, Marks 2**

Two Marks Questions with Answers

Q.1 *How many address lines are required to interface 4096 × 8 EPROM chip ?*

Ans. : 12 address lines.

Q.2 *Basic concepts in memory interfacing.*

Ans. : The primary function of memory interfacing is that the microprocessor should be able to read from and write into a given register of a memory chip. To perform these operations the microprocessor should

1) Be able to select the chip.

2) Identify the register.

3) Enable the appropriate buffer.

Q.3 *Define interfacing.* **Dec.-04**

Ans. : Interfacing is the method used to interconnect two separate electronic devices in such a way that their output and input voltages and currents are compatible.

Q.4 *What is the need for interfacing?* **May-06**

Ans. : To communicate with external world, microprocessor needs interfacing with peripheral storage devices, input and output devices and display devices.

Q.5 *Justify your choice between UV-EPROM and flash EPROM for an external ROM in an 8051 microcontroller application.*

Ans. : Flash EPROMS can be erased electrically with selective erase facility. However, UV-EPROMS cannot be erased electrically, they need ultraviolet light source. EPROMS need around 20 minutes to erase and entire EPROM is erased at a time. Thus Hash EPROM is more preferable during development stage. However, once the product is ready we can use EPROM as an external memory.

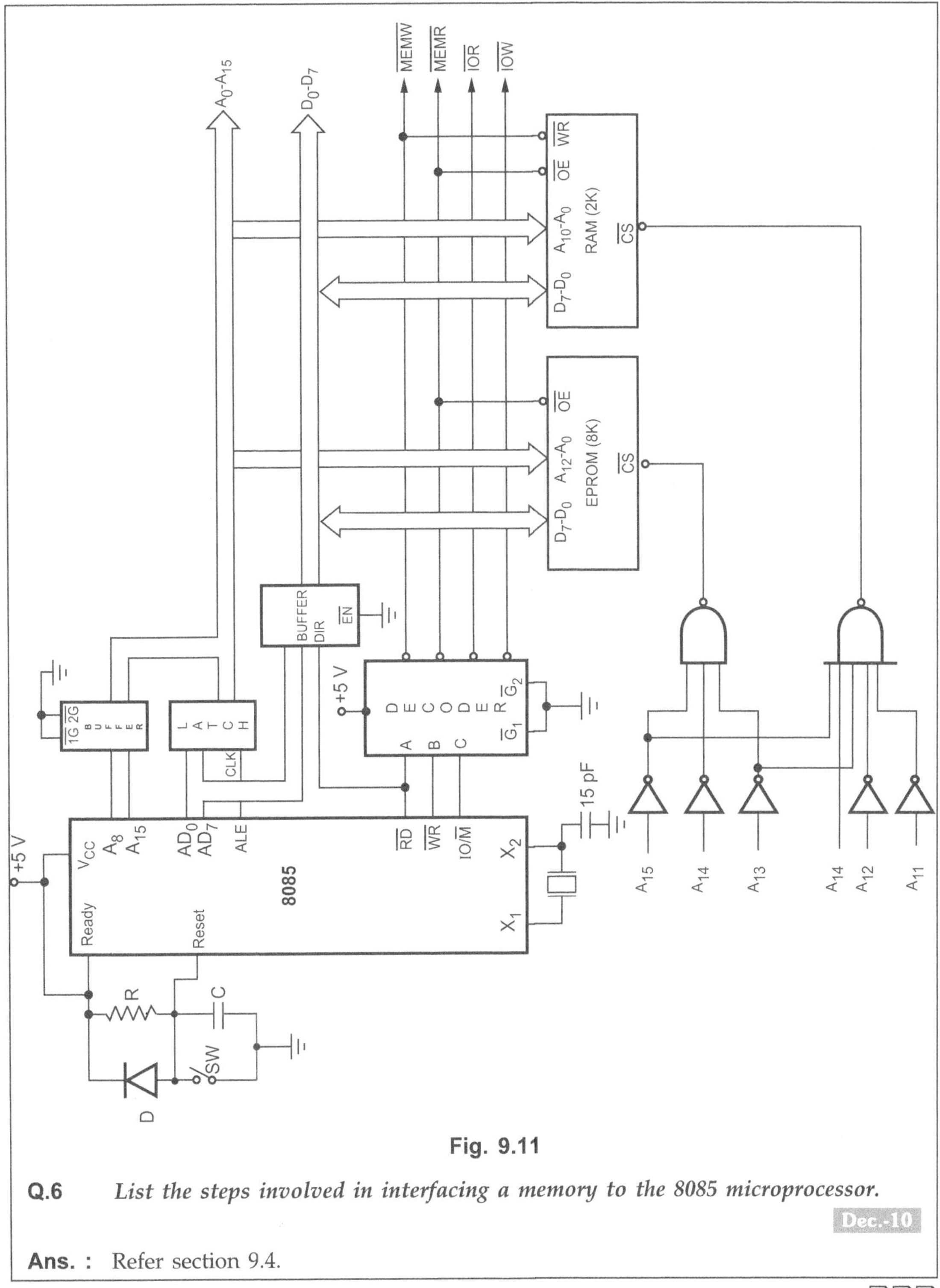

Fig. 9.11

Q.6 *List the steps involved in interfacing a memory to the 8085 microprocessor.* **Dec.-10**

Ans. : Refer section 9.4.

❑❑❑

Notes

10 I/O Interfacing

Contents

10.1 Introduction

April/May-08

Any application of a microprocessor based system requires the transfer of data between external circuitry to the microprocessor and microprocessor to the external circuitry. User can give information to the microprocessor based system using keyboard and user can see the result or output information from the microprocessor based system with the help of display device. The transfer of data between keyboard and microprocessor and microprocessor and display device is called input/output data transfer or I/O data transfer. This data transfer is done with the help of I/O ports.

Input port :

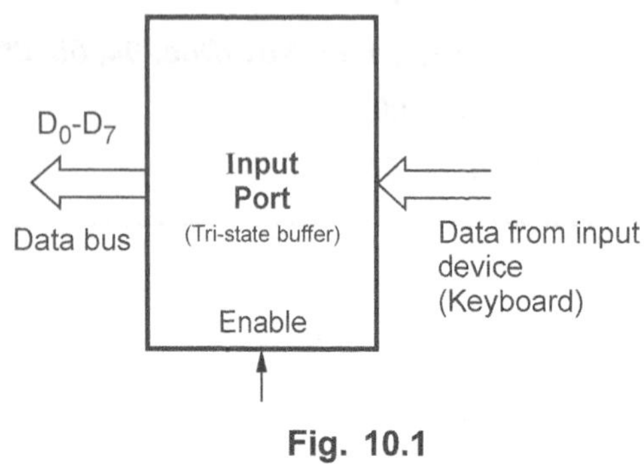

Fig. 10.1

It is used to read data from the input device such as keyboard. The simplest form of input port is a buffer. The input device is connected to the microprocessor through buffer, as shown in the Fig. 10.1. This buffer is a tri-state buffer and its output is available only when enable signal is active. When microprocessor wants to read data from the input device (keyboard), the control signals from the microprocessor activates the buffer by asserting enable input of the buffer. Once the buffer is enabled, data from the input device is available on the data bus. Microprocessor reads this data by initiating read command.

Output port : It is used to send data to the output device such as display from the microprocessor. The simplest form of output port is a latch. The output device is connected to the microprocessor through latch, as shown in the Fig. 10.2. When microprocessor wants to send data to the output device it puts the data on the data bus and activates the clock signal of the latch, latching the data from the data bus at the output of latch. It is then available at the output of latch for the output device.

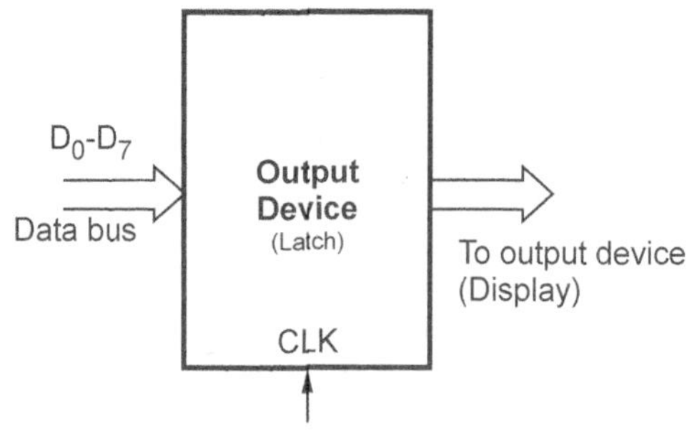

Fig. 10.2

In this chapter, we will see the interfacing concepts of these I/O devices and different methods of I/O transfer.

10.2 I/O Interfacing Techniques in 8085 April/May-04,05; Nov./Dec.-04

The most of the microprocessors support isolated I/O system. It partitions memory from I/O, via software, by having instructions that specifically access (address) memory, and others that specifically access I/O. When these instructions are decoded by the microprocessor, an appropriate control signal is generated to activate either memory or I/O operation. In 8085, $IO/\overline{M}$ signal is used for this purpose. The 8085 outputs a logic '1' on the $IO/\overline{M}$ line for an I/O operation and a logic '0' for memory operation. In 8085, it is possible to connect 64 kbyte memory and 256 I/O ports in the system since 8085 sends 16 bit address for memory and 8-bit address for I/O. I/O devices can be interfaced to an 8085A system in two ways :

1. I/O Mapped I/O 2. Memory mapped I/O

10.2.1 I/O Mapped I/O Nov./Dec.-05, May/June-06,07

In I/O mapped I/O, the 8085 uses $IO/\overline{M}$ signal to distinguish between I/O read/write and memory read/write operations. The 8085 has separate instructions IN and OUT for I/O data transfer. When 8085 executes IN or OUT instruction, it places device address (port number) on the demultiplexed low order address bus as well as the high order address bus. In other words, we can say that higher order address bus duplicates the contents of demultiplexed low-order address bus, when 8085 microprocessor executes an IN or OUT instruction. For example, if the device address is 60H then the contents on A_{15} to A_0 will be as follows :

A_{15}	A_{14}	A_{13}	A_{12}	A_{11}	A_{10}	A_9	A_8	A_7	A_6	A_5	A_4	A_3	A_2	A_1	A_0
0	1	1	0	0	0	0	0	0	1	1	0	0	0	0	0

Here, A_8 follows A_0, A_9 follows A_1 and so on, as shown below.

A_7	A_6	A_5	A_4	A_3	A_2	A_1	A_0	**Device Address**
A_{15}	A_{14}	A_{13}	A_{12}	A_{11}	A_{10}	A_9	A_8	
0	1	1	0	0	0	0	0	60H

The instruction IN inputs data from an input device (such as keyboard) into the accumulator and the instruction OUT sends the contents of the accumulator to an output device such as LED display. These are two byte instructions. The second byte of the instruction specifies the address or the port number of an I/O device. As it is a byte, the address or port number can be any of the 256 combinations of eight bits, from 00H to FFH. Therefore, the 8085 can communicate with 256 different I/O devices. When we want to interface an I/O device, it is necessary to assign a device address or a port number. Before going to see this device address logic, we will examine how the 8085 executes IN and OUT instructions.

IN and OUT instructions :

IN :

It is used to read 8-bit data from I/O device into the accumulator. This two byte instruction has, the first byte as an opcode and the second byte specifies the device address or a port number.

10.2.2 I/O Device Selection

Nov./Dec.-09

As mentioned earlier, the 8085 gives 8-bit I/O address. This means it can select one of the 256 I/O ports. To select an appropriate I/O device, it is necessary to do following things.

1. Decode the address to generate unique signal corresponding to the device address on the bus.
2. When device address signal and control signal ($\overline{IOR}$ or $\overline{IOW}$) both are low, generate device select signal.
3. Use device select signal to activate the interfacing device (I/O port).

Fig. 10.3 shows the absolute decoding circuit for the I/O device. The IC 74LS138, 3:8 decoder along with 3 input OR gate is used to generate device select signal. This signal is ORed with control signal ($\overline{IOR}$ or $\overline{IOW}$) to generate device enable signal.

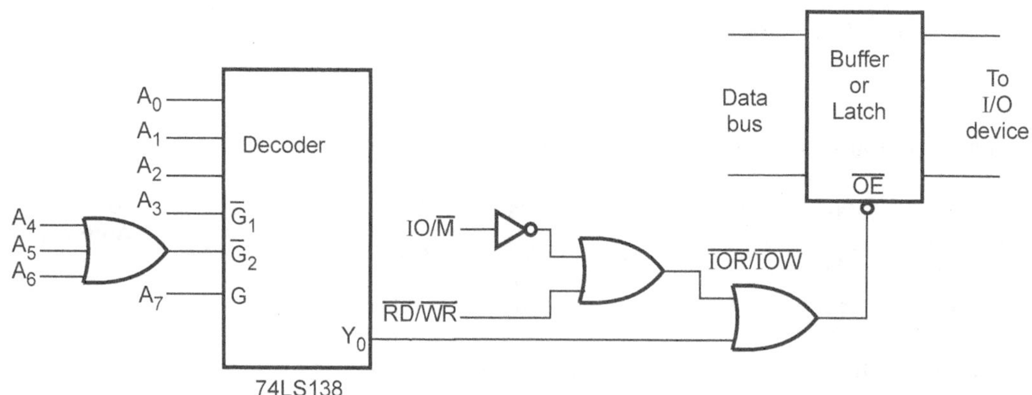

Fig 10.3 Absolute decoding circuit for the I/O device

To generate device select signal (Y_0) low, the address on the address bus must be as given below :

$A_2\ A_1\ A_0$ = 000H ; Activates Y_0 output

$A_3\ A_4\ A_5\ A_6$ = 0000H ; makes $\overline{G}_1$ and $\overline{G}_2$ low to enable output of decoder

A_7 = 1H ; Makes G high to enable output of decoder

Note : Decoder output is enabled only when control signals $\overline{G}_1$ and $\overline{G}_2$ are low and control signal G is high. Therefore the address of this I/O device is 80H as shown in the Table 10.1.

A_7	A_6	A_5	A_4	A_3	A_2	A_1	A_0	Address
1	0	0	0	0	0	0	0	80H

Table 10.1

10.2.3 Interfacing Input and Output Devices with Examples

Interfacing Input Device :

The microprocessor 8085 accepts 8-bit data from the input device such as keyboard, sensors, transducers etc. Fig. 10.4 shows the circuit diagram to interface input port (buffer) which is used to read the status of 8 switches. The address for this input device is 80H as device select signal goes low when address is 80H.

When the switch is in the released position, the status of line is high otherwise status is low. With this information microprocessor can check a particular key is pressed or not.

The following program checks whether the switch 2 is pressed or not.

Program :

```
IN 80H      ; Read status of all switches
ANI 02H     ; Mask bit positions for other switches
JZ NEXT     ; if program control is transferred to label
            ; NEXT, then switch 2 is pressed otherwise not.
```

Interfacing Output Device :

The microprocessor 8085 sends 8-bit data to the output device such as 7 segment displays, LEDs, printer etc. Fig 10.5 shows the circuit diagram to interface output port (latch) which is used to send the signal for glowing the LEDs. LED will glow when output pin status is low. The IC 74LS138 and 3 input OR gate is used to generate device select signal. The latch enable signal is active high. So NOR gate is used to generate latch enable signal, which goes high when Y_1 and $\overline{IOW}$ both are low.

The following program glows the LEDs L_1, L_3 and L_6.

L_8	L_7	L_6	L_5	L_4	L_3	L_2	L_1		
1	1	0	1	1	0	1	0	=	DAH

The code (data) DAH must be sent on the latch to glow LEDs L_1, L_3 and L_6.

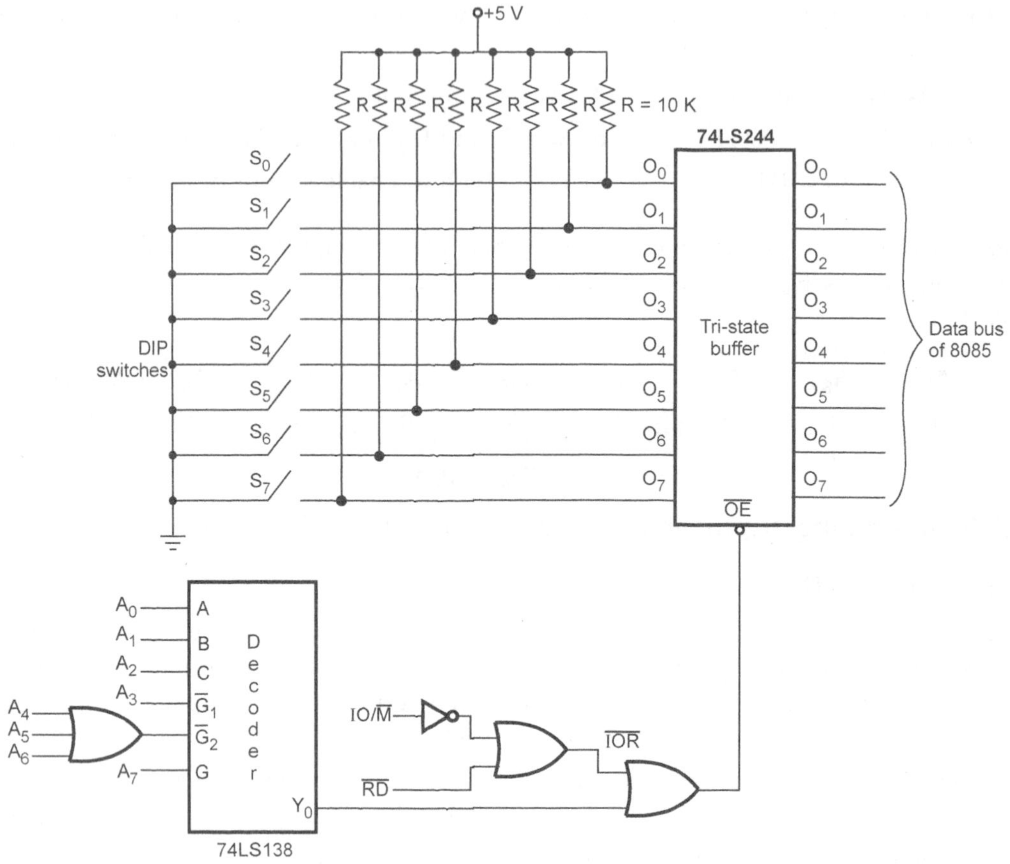

Fig. 10.4 Circuit diagram to interface input port

Decoder select					Decoder input			
A_7	A_6	A_5	A_4	A_3	A_2	A_1	A_0	
1	0	0	0	0	0	0	1	= 81 H

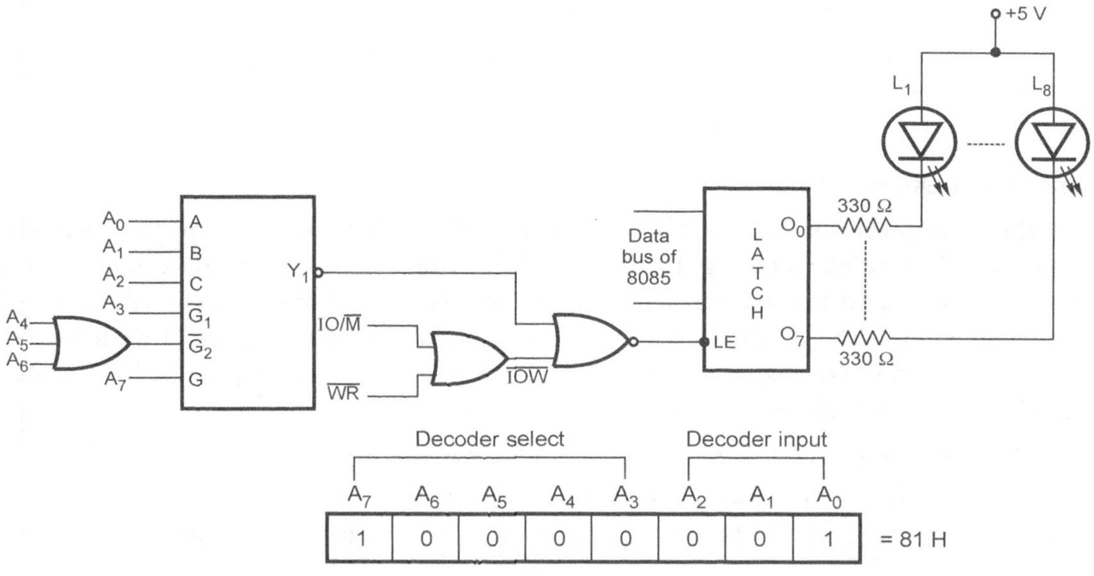

Fig. 10.5 Circuit diagram to interface output port

Program :

```
MVI A, DAH    ; Loads the data in the accumulator.
OUT 81H       ; sends the data on the latch.
```

The Fig. 10.6 shows the combined circuit for I/O interfacing. For this circuit the address of input port is 80H and address of output port is 81H. The following program displays the status of switches on the LEDs.

Program :

```
IN 80H        ; Read status of all switches.
OUT 81H       ; send status on the output port.
```

Example 10.1 : *Refer Fig. 10.6 and write a program that will check the switch1 status and do accordingly.*

1. SW1 = 0 : Blink lower nibble LEDs.

2. SW1 = 1 : Blink higher nibble LEDs.

Assume delay routine is available.

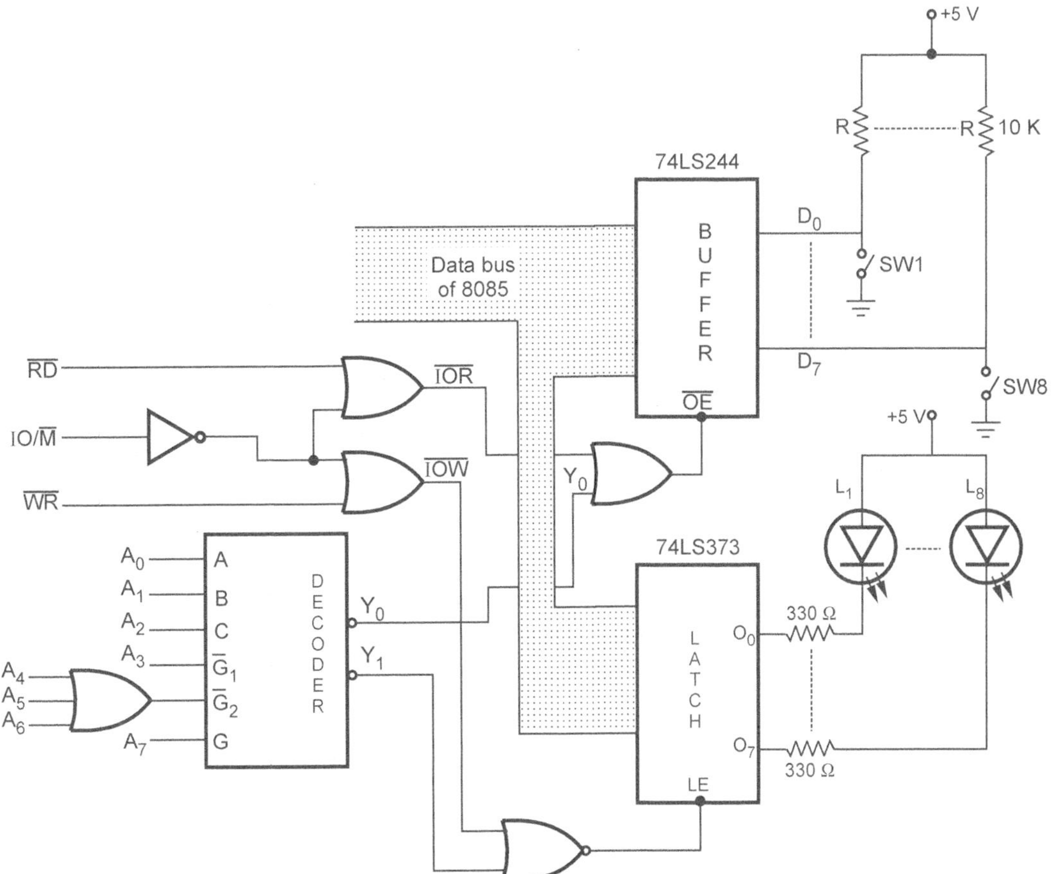

Fig. 10.6 I/O interfacing using I/O mapped I/O

Solution :

Input port address = 80H

Output port address = 81H

Flowchart :

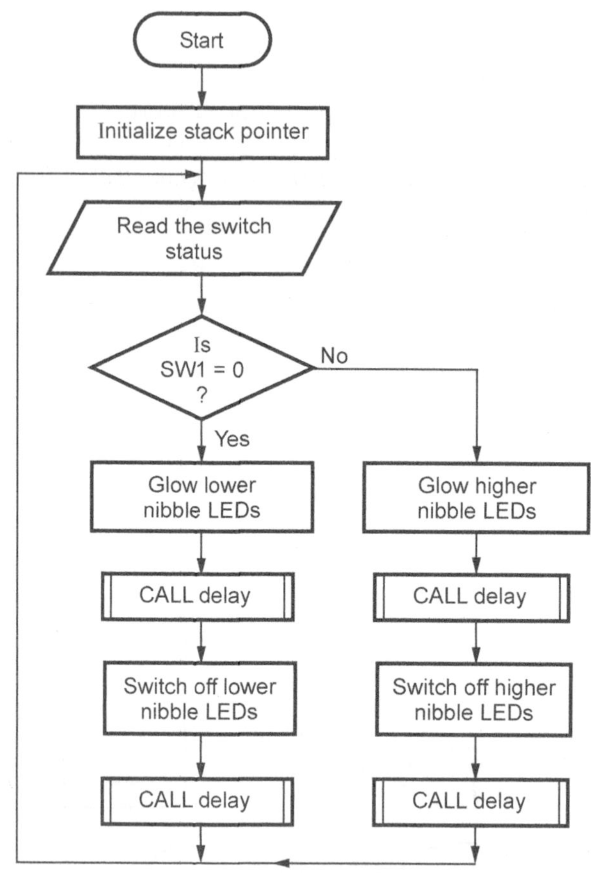

Source Program :

```
         LXI SP, 27FFH    ; Initialize stack pointer
START :  IN 80H           ; Read status of switches
         ANI 01H          ; Masks Bit 1 to Bit 7
         JNZ HIGHER       ; If sw1 status is not zero goto blink
                          ; higher nibble
         MVI A, F0H       ; Load bit pattern to glow lower nibble
                          ; LEDs
         OUT 81H          ; Send it to output port
         CALL Delay       ; Call delay subroutine
         MVI A, FFH       ; Load bit pattern to switch off all LEDs
```

```
          OUT 81H       ; Send it to output port
          CALL Delay    ; Call delay subroutine
          JMP START     ; JUMP to START
HIGHER :  MVI A, 0FH    ; Load bit pattern to glow higher nibble LEDs
          OUT 81H       ; Send it to output port
          CALL Delay    ; Call delay subroutine
          MVI A, FFH    ; Load bit pattern to switch off all LEDs
          OUT 81H       ; Send it to output port
          CALL Delay    ; Call delay subroutine
          JMP START     ; JUMP to START
```

10.2.4 Memory Mapped I/O

In memory mapped I/O, the I/O devices are assigned and identified by 16-bit addresses. The memory related instructions transfer the data between an I/O device and the microprocessor, as long as I/O port is assigned to the memory address space rather than to the I/O address space. The register associated with the I/O port is simply treated as a memory location. Thus I/O device becomes a part of the system's memory map and hence its name. In memory-mapped I/O every instruction that refers to a memory location can control I/O. The source and destination of the data is limited with I/O mapped I/O, since for an IN instruction the destination register is always the accumulator and for the OUT instruction the source register is always the accumulator. However, for memory mapped I/O there are number of sources and destinations.

Instructions	Interpretation for memory mapped I/O
MOV r, M	; Input from a port to specified register.
LDA addr	; Input from a port to accumulator.
LHLD addr	; Input from two ports to HL register pair.
ADD M	; Port contents are added into accumulator ; contents and result is stored in the accumulator.
ANA M	; Port contents are logically ANDed with the accumulator contents and result is stored in the accumulator.
ORA M	; Port contents are logically ORed with the accumulator contents and result is stored in the accumulator.
XRA M	; Port contents are logically XORed with the accumulator contents and result is stored in the accumulator.
CMP M	; Compares the port contents with the accumulator contents and updates the flag register contents accordingly.
MOV M, r	; Outputs specified register contents to the port.
STA addr	; Outputs accumulator contents to the port.
SHLD addr	; Outputs HL register contents to two ports.
MVI M, data	; Outputs immediate data to the port.

Interfacing of I/O port with memory mapped I/O

In memory mapped I/O, $\overline{MEMR}$ (memory read) and $\overline{MEMW}$ (memory write) control signals are required to control the data transfer between I/O device and microprocessor. As 8085 gives 16-bit memory address, it is necessary to decode 16-bit memory address to generate device select signal in case of memory mapped I/O. Fig. 10.7 shows the interfacing of I/O devices in memory mapped I/O mode.

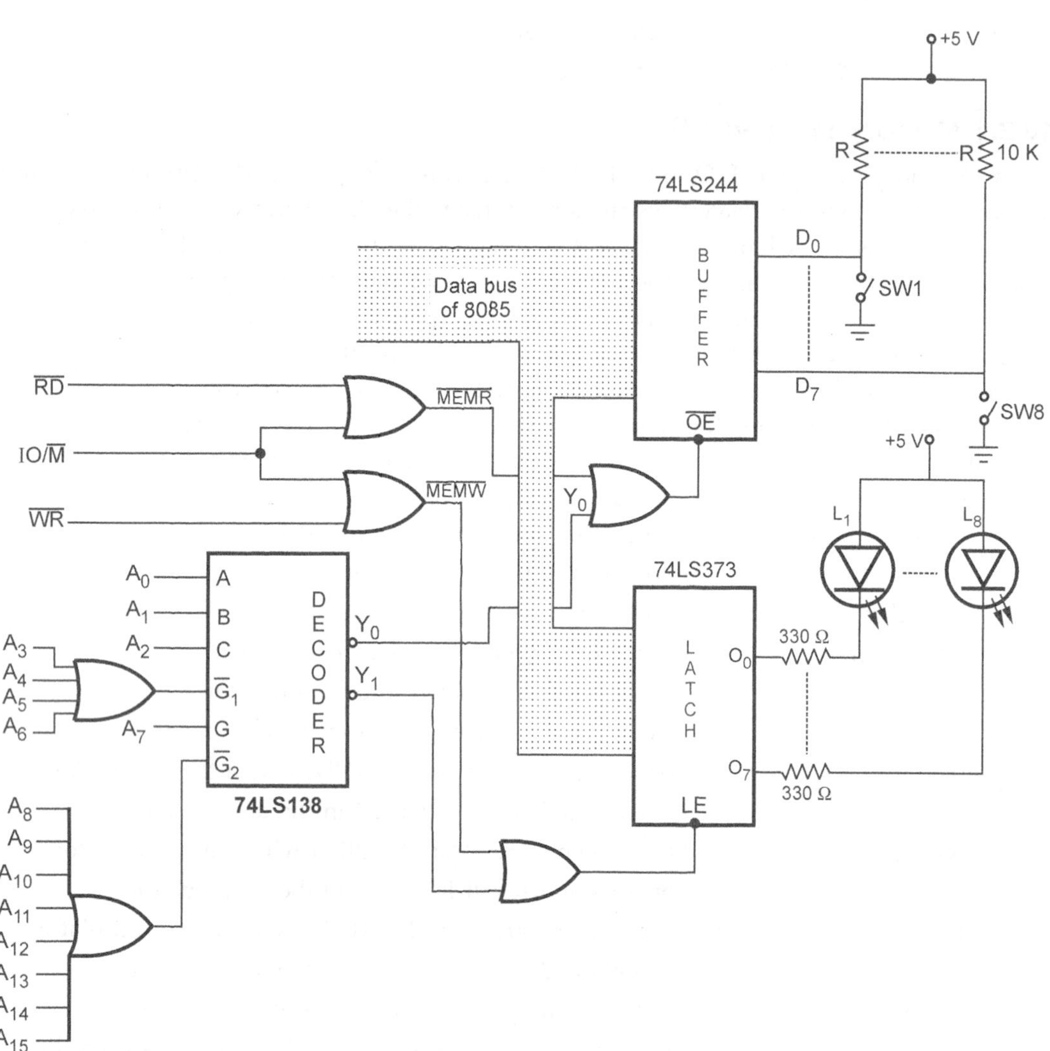

Fig. 10.7 I/O interfacing using memory mapped I/O

Example 10.2 : *Identify the port address and the mapping scheme for the Fig. 10.8 given below.*

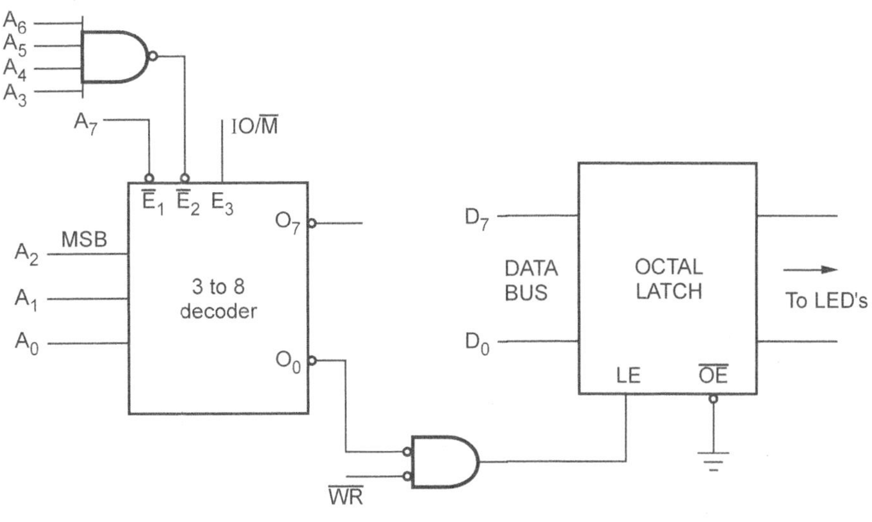

Note : $E_1 E_2$ are active low

Fig. 10.8

Solution :

Mapping scheme : I/O mapped I/O

10.2.4.1 Comparison between Memory Mapped I/O and I/O Mapped I/O in 8085

Sr. No.	Memory mapped I/O	I/O mapped I/O
1.	In this device address is 16-bit. Thus A_0 to $A1_5$ lines are used to generate device address.	In this I/O device address is 8-bit. Thus A_0 to A_7 or A_8 to A_{15} lines are used to generate device address.
2.	$\overline{MEMR}$ and $\overline{MEMW}$ control signals are used to control read and write I/O operations.	$\overline{IOR}$ and $\overline{IOW}$ control signals are used to control read and write I/O operations.
3.	Instructions available are LDA addr, STA addr, LDAX rp, STAX rp, MOV M,R, MOV R,M, ADD, CMP M etc.	Instructions available are IN and OUT.
4.	Data transfer is between any register and I/O device.	Data transfer is between accumulator and I/O device.
5.	Maximum number of I/O devices are 65536 (theoretically).	Maximum number of I/O devices are 256.

6.	Execution speed using LDA addr, STA addr is 13 T-state and 7 T-states for MOV M, r and MOV r, M instructions.	Execution speed is 10 T-states.
7.	Decoding 16-bit address may require more hardware.	Decoding 8-bit address will require less hardware.

10.3 Data Transfer Schemes

Dec.-08

In I/O data transfer, the system requires the transfer of data between external circuitry and the microprocessor. In this section, we will discuss different ways of I/O transfer.

a. Program controlled I/O or polling control.

b. Interrupt program controlled I/O or interrupt driven I/O.

c. Hardware controlled I/O.

d. I/O controlled by handshake signals.

e. I/O controlled by ready signal.

a. Program controlled I/O or polling control :

In program controlled I/O, the transfer of data is completely under the control of the microprocessor program. This means that the data transfer takes place only when an I/O transfer instructions executed. In most of the cases it is necessary to check whether the device is ready for data transfer or not. To check this, microprocessor polls the status bit associated with the I/O device.

b. Interrupt program controlled I/O or Interrupt driven I/O :

In interrupt program controlled approach, when a peripheral is ready to transfer data, it sends an interrupt signal to the microprocessor. This indicates that the I/O data transfer is initiated by the external I/O device. When interrupted, the microprocessor stops the execution of the program and transfers the program control to an interrupt service routine. This interrupt service routine performs the data transfer. After the data transfer, it returns control to the main program at the point it was interrupted.

c. Hardware controlled I/O :

To increase the speed of data transfer between memory and I/O, the hardware controlled I/O is used. It is commonly referred to as direct memory access (DMA). The hardware which controls this data transfer is commonly known as DMA controller. The DMA controller sends a HOLD signal to the microprocessor to initiate data transfer. In response to HOLD signal, microprocessor releases its data, address and control buses to the DMA controller. Then the data transfer is controlled at high speed by the DMA controller without the intervention of the microprocessor. After data transfer, DMA controller sends low on the HOLD pin, which gives the control of data, address and control buses back to the microprocessor. This type of data transfer is used for large data transfers.

d. I/O control by handshake signals :

The handshake signals are used to ensure the readiness of the I/O device and to synchronize the timing of the data transfer. In this data transfer, the status of handshaking signals are checked between the microprocessor and an I/O device and when both are ready, the actual data is transferred.

e. I/O control by READY signal :

This technique is used to transfer data between slower I/O device and the microprocessor. In some applications, speed of I/O system is not compatible with the microprocessor's timings. This means that it takes longer time to read/write data. In such situations, the microprocessor has to confirm whether a peripheral is ready to transfer data or not. If READY pin is high, the peripheral is ready otherwise 8085 enters WAIT state or WAIT states. These WAIT states elongate the read/write cycle timings and prepare 8085 microprocessor to communicate with slower I/O devices.

Review Questions

Section 10.1

Q.1 *What do you mean by input port and output port ?*

Section 10.2

Q.1 *With suitable examples explain how I/O devices are connected using memory mapped I/O and peripheral I/O.* **May-05, Marks 10**

Q.2 *Describe the comparision of I/O mapped and memory mapped I/O interfacing.* **May-04,12, Marks 8**

Q.3 *Distinguish peripheral mapped I/O and memory mapped I/O technique.* **May-07, Dec.-09, Marks 8**

Q.4 *Show the common anode seven segment LED configuration. How to switch it on and off ?* **May-04, Marks 2**

Q.5 *State the disadvantages of memory mapped I/O scheme.* **Dec.-05 Marks 2**

Q.6 *Write the difference between memory mapped I/O and peripheral mapped I/O.* **Dec.-04,10; May-06, Marks 2**

Section 10.3

Q.4 *With necessary diagrams, explain the different data transfer schemes in 8085.* **Dec.-08, Marks 10**

Two Marks Questions with Answers

Q.1 *What is memory mapping ?*

Ans. : The assignment of memory addresses to various registers in a memory chip is called memory mapping.

Q.2 *What is I/O mapping ?*

Ans. : The assignment of addresses to various I/O devices in the memory chip is called I/O mapping.

Q.3 *Show the common anode seven segment LED configuration. How to switch it on and off ?* **May-04**

Ans. : Refer section 10.2.

Q.4 *State the disadvantages of memory mapped I/O scheme.* **Dec.-05**

Ans. : Refer section 10.2.4.

Q.5 *Write the difference between memory mapped I/O and peripheral mapped I/O.* **Dec.-04,10; May-06**

Ans. : Refer section 10.2.4.1.

Q.6 *What is the significance of I/O ports ?* **May-08**

Ans. : I/O ports allow to transfer data from input devices such as keyboard to the microprocessor and from microprocessor to the output devices such as display devices.

Q.7 *What are the different data transfer schemes ?* **Dec.-08**

Ans. : Different data transfer schemes are :

- Programmed I/O or Polling control
- Interrupt driven I/O
- DMA transfer (Hardware Controlled I/O)
- I/O controlled by handshake signals
- I/O controlled by ready signal

Q.8 *What are the requirements to be met while interfacing I/O devices to microprocessor/microcontroller ?* **May-05**

Ans. : The requirements to be met while interfacing I/O devices to microprocessor/microcontroller are :

- I/O port and circuit to select I/O port
- Mechanism to synchronize data transfer
- Level translator if voltage levels are different
- Buffers if sourcing current requirements are beyond the limit of microprocessor/microcontrollers.

❑❑❑

11 PPI - 8255

Contents

The 8255 is a general purpose programmable I/O device used for parallel data transfer. It has 24 I/O pins which can be grouped in three 8-bit parallel ports : Port A, Port B and Port C. The eight bits of Port C can be used as individual bits or be grouped in two 4-bit ports : C_{upper} (C_U) and C_{lower} (C_L).

The 8255, primarily, can be programmed in two basic modes : Bit Set/Reset (BSR) mode and I/O mode. The BSR mode is used to set or reset the bits in Port C. The I/O mode is further divided into three modes :

Mode 0 : Simple Input/Output

Mode 1 : Input/Output with handshake

Mode 2 : Bi-directional I/O data transfer

The function of I/O pins (input or output) and modes of operation of I/O ports can be programmed by writing proper control word in the control word register. Each bit in the control word has a specific meaning and the status of these bits decides the function and operating mode of the I/O ports.

11.1 Features of 8255A

Nov./Dec.-04, May/June-06,09

1. The 8255A is a widely used, programmable, parallel I/O device.
2. It can be programmed to transfer data under various conditions, from simple I/O to interrupt I/O.
3. It is compatible with all Intel and most other microprocessors.
4. It is completely TTL compatible.
5. It has three 8-bit ports : Port A, Port B, and Port C, which are arranged in two groups of 12 pins. Each port has an unique address, and data can be read from or written to a port. In addition to the address assigned to the three ports, another address is assigned to the control register into which control words are written for programming the 8255 to operate in various modes.
6. Its bit set/reset mode allows setting and resetting of individual bits of Port C.
7. The 8255 can operate in 3 I/O modes : (i) Mode 0, (ii) Mode 1, and (iii) Mode 2.

a) In Mode 0, Port A and Port B can be configured as simple 8-bit input or output ports without handshaking. The two halves of Port C can be programmed separately as 4-bit input or output ports.

b) In Mode 1, two groups each of 12 pins are formed. Group A consists of Port A and the upper half of Port C while Group B consists of Port B and the lower half of Port C. Ports A and B can be programmed as 8-bit Input or Output ports with three lines of Port C in each group used for handshaking.

c) In Mode 2, only Port A can be used as a bidirectional port. The handshaking signals are provided on five lines of Port C (PC_3 - PC_7). Port B can be used in Mode 0 or in Mode 1.

8. All I/O pins of 8255 has 2.5 mA DC driving capacity (i.e. sourcing current of 2.5 mA).

11.2 Pin Diagram

Fig. 11.1 shows the pin diagram of 8255.

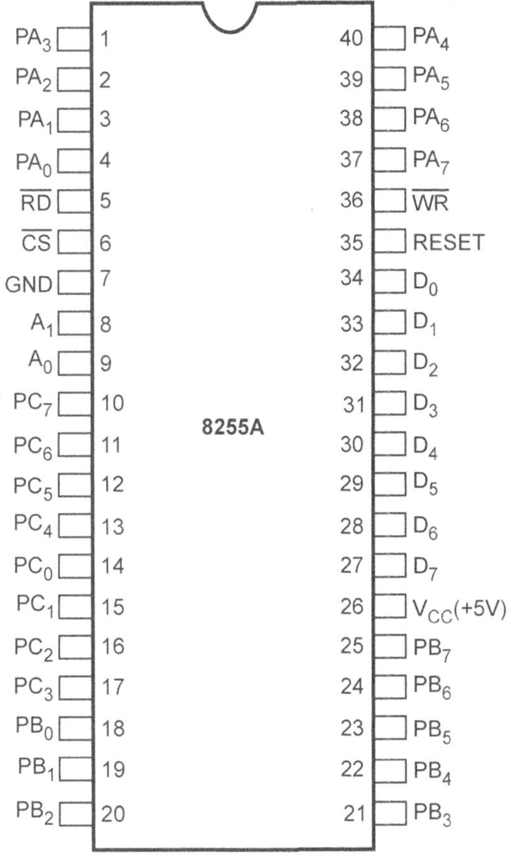

Fig. 11.1 Pin diagram of 8255A

Pin Symbols	Function
D_0-D_7 (Data Bus)	These bi-directional, tri-state data bus lines are connected to the system data bus. They are used to transfer data and control word from microprocessor (8085) to 8255 or to receive data or status word from 8255 to the 8085.
PA_0-PA_7 (Port A)	These 8-bit bi-directional I/O pins are used to send data to output device and to receive data from input device. It functions as an 8-bit data output latch/buffer, when used in output mode and an 8-bit data input buffer, when used in input mode.
PB_0-PB_7 (Port B)	These 8-bit bi-directional I/O pins are used to send data to output device and to receive data from input device. It functions as an 8-bit data, output latch/buffer when used in output mode and an 8-bit data input buffer, when used in input mode.
PC_0-PC_7	These 8-bit bi-directional I/O pins are divided into two groups PC_L (PC_3-PC_0) and PC_U (PC_7-PC_4). These groups individually can transfer data in or out when programmed for simple I/O, and used as handshake signals when programmed for handshake or bi-directional modes.
$\overline{RD}$ (Read)	When this pin is low, the CPU can read the data in the ports or the status word, through the data buffer.
$\overline{WR}$ (Write)	When this input pin is low, the CPU can write data on the ports or in the control register through the data bus buffer.
$\overline{CS}$ (Chip Select)	This is an active low input which can be enabled for data transfer operation between the CPU and the 8255.
RESET	This is an active high input used to reset 8255. When RESET input is high, the control register is cleared and all the ports are set to the input mode. Usually RESET OUT signal from 8085 is used to reset 8255.
A_0 and A_1	These input signals along with $\overline{RD}$ and $\overline{WR}$ inputs control the selection of the control/status word registers or one of the three ports. Table. 11.1 summarizes the status of A_0 , A_1, $\overline{CS}$, $\overline{RD}$ and $\overline{WR}$ to access the control word/ports. A_0 and A_1 are generally connected to the A_0, A_1 pins of the address bus; the 8255 therefore occupies four consecutive locations in the I/O space.

A_1	A_0	$\overline{RD}$	$\overline{WR}$	$\overline{CS}$	Operations
					Input (Read) Operation
0	0	0	1	0	Port A to Data Bus
0	1	0	1	0	Port B to Data Bus
1	0	0	1	0	Port C to Data Bus
					Output (Write) Operation
0	0	1	0	0	Data Bus to Port A
0	1	1	0	0	Data Bus to Port B
1	0	1	0	0	Data Bus to Port C
1	1	1	0	0	Data Bus to Control Register

					Disable Function
X	X	X	X	1	Data Bus Tri-stated
1	1	0	1	0	Illegal Condition
X	X	1	1	0	Data Bus Tri-stated

Table 11.1 Port and register select signals summary

11.3 Block Diagram

May/June-06,09

Fig. 11.2 shows the internal block diagram of 8255A. It consists of data bus buffer, control logic and Group A and Group B controls.

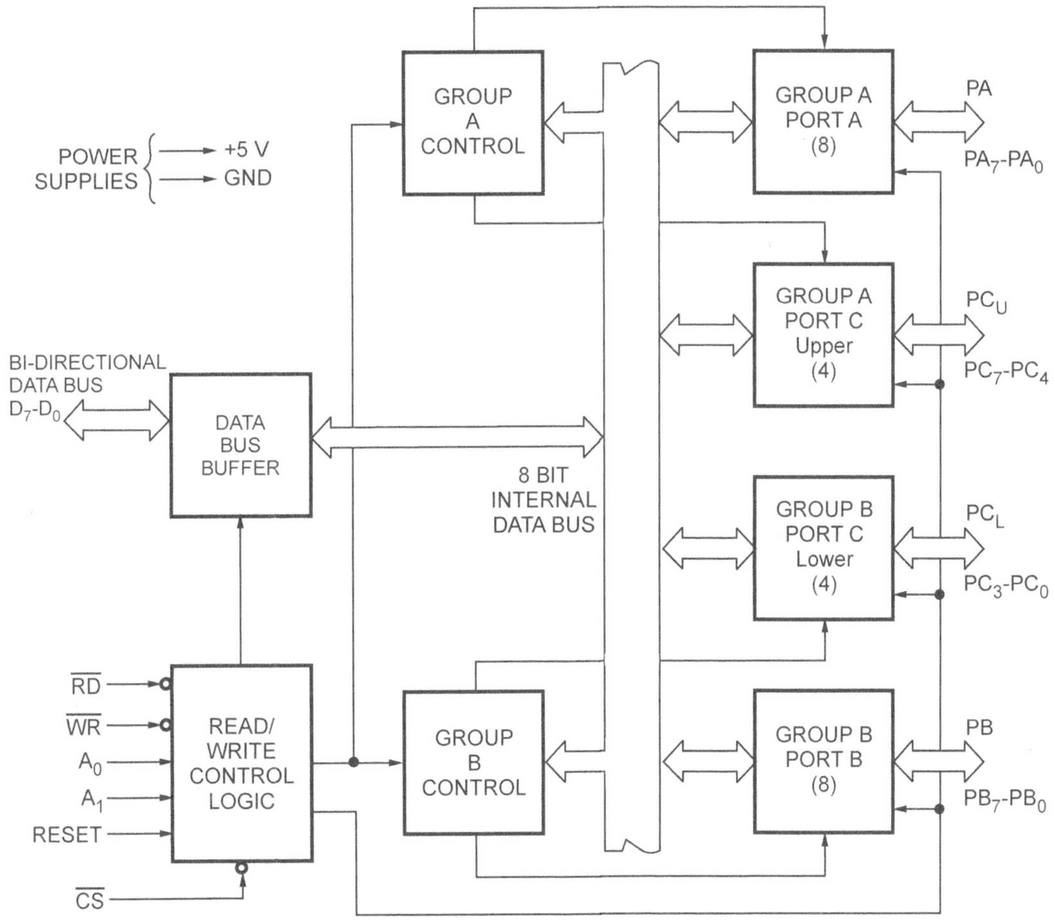

Fig. 11.2 Block diagram of 8255A

11.3.1 Data Bus Buffer

This tri-state bi-directional buffer is used to interface the internal data bus of 8255 to the system data bus. Input or Output instructions executed by the CPU either Read data from, or Write data into the buffer. Output data from the CPU to the ports or control register, and input data to the CPU from the ports or status register are all passed through the buffer.

11.3.2 Control Logic

The control logic block accepts control bus signals as well as inputs from the address bus, and issues commands to the individual group control blocks (Group A control and Group B control). It issues appropriate enabling signals to access the required data/control words or status word. The input pins for the control logic section are described here.

11.3.3 Group A and Group B Controls

Each of the Group A and Group B control blocks receives control words from the CPU and issues appropriate commands to the ports associated with it. The Group A control block controls Port A and PC_7-PC_4 while the Group B control block controls Port B and PC_3-PC_0.

Port A : This has an 8-bit latched and buffered output and an 8-bit input latch. It can be programmed in three modes: mode 0, mode 1 and mode 2.

Port B : This has an 8-bit data I/O latch/buffer and an 8-bit data input buffer. It can be programmed in mode 0 and mode 1.

Port C : This has one 8-bit unlatched input buffer and an 8-bit output latch/buffer. Port C can be separated into two parts and each can be used as control signals for ports A and B in the handshake mode. It can be programmed for bit set/reset operation.

11.4 Operation Modes

April/May-04,08, Nov./Dec.-04, May/June-07

11.4.1 Bit Set-Reset (BSR) Mode

Nov./Dec.-09

The individual bits of Port C can be set or reset by sending out a single OUT instruction to the control register. When Port C is used for control/status operation, this feature can be used to set or reset individual bits.

11.4.2 I/O Modes

Mode 0 : Simple input/output

In this mode, Ports A and B are used as two simple 8-bit I/O ports and Port C as two 4-bit ports. Each port (or half - port, in case of C) can be programmed to function as simply an input port or an output port. The input/output features in Mode 0 are as follows :

1. Outputs are latched.
2. Inputs are buffered, not latched.
3. Ports do not have handshake or interrupt capability.

Mode 1 : Input/Output with handshake

In this mode, input or output data transfer is controlled by handshaking signals. Handshaking signals are used to transfer data between devices whose data transfer speeds are not same. For example, computer can send data to the printer with large speed but printer can't accept data and print data with this rate. So computer has to send data with the speed with which printer can accept. This type of data transfer is achieved by using handshaking signals alongwith data signals. Fig. 11.3 shows data transfer between computer and printer using handshaking signals.

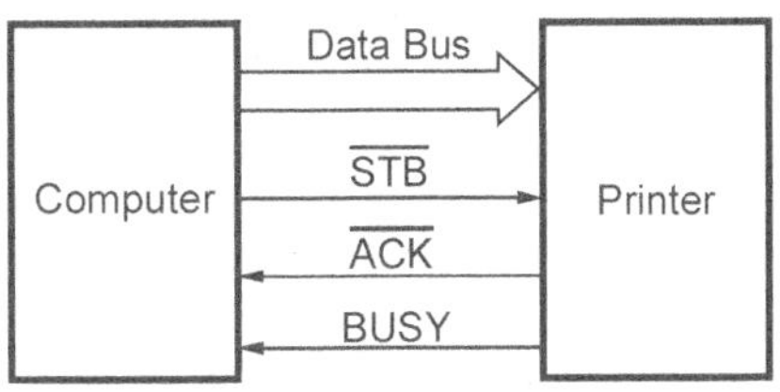

Fig. 11.3 Data transfer between computer and printer using handshaking signals.

These handshaking signals are used to tell computer whether printer is ready to accept the data or not. If printer is ready to accept the data then after sending data on data bus, computer uses another handshaking signal ($\overline{STB}$) to tell printer that valid data is available on the data bus.

The 8255 mode 1 which supports handshaking has following features.

1. Two ports (A and B) function as 8-bit I/O ports. They can be configured either as input or output ports.
2. Each port uses three lines from Port C as handshake signals. The remaining two lines of Port C can be used for simple I/O functions.
3. Input and output data are latched.
4. Interrupt logic is supported.

Mode 2 : Bi-directional I/O data transfer

This mode allows bi-directional data transfer (transmission and reception) over a single 8-bit data bus using handshaking signals. This feature is available only in Group A with Port A as the 8-bit bidirectional data bus; and PC_3 - PC_7 are used for handshaking purpose. In this mode, both inputs and outputs are latched. Due to use of a single 8-bit data bus for bi-directional data transfer, the data sent out by the CPU through Port A appears on the bus connecting it to the peripheral, only when the peripheral requests it. The remaining lines of Port C i.e. PC_0-PC_2 can be used for simple I/O functions. The Port B can be programmed in mode 0 or in mode 1. When Port B is programmed in mode 1, PC_0-PC_2 lines of Port C are used as handshaking signals.

11.5 Control Word Formats

April/May-04, Nov./Dec.-05,07,08

A high on the RESET pin causes all 24 lines of the three 8-bit ports to be in the input mode. All flip-flops are cleared and the interrupts are reset. This condition is maintained even after the RESET goes low. The ports of the 8255 can then be programmed for any other mode by writing a single control word into the control register, when required.

11.5.1 For Bit Set/Reset Mode

Fig. 11.4 shows bit set/reset control word format.

The eight possible combinations of the states of bits D_3 - D_1 (B_2 B_1 B_0) in the Bit

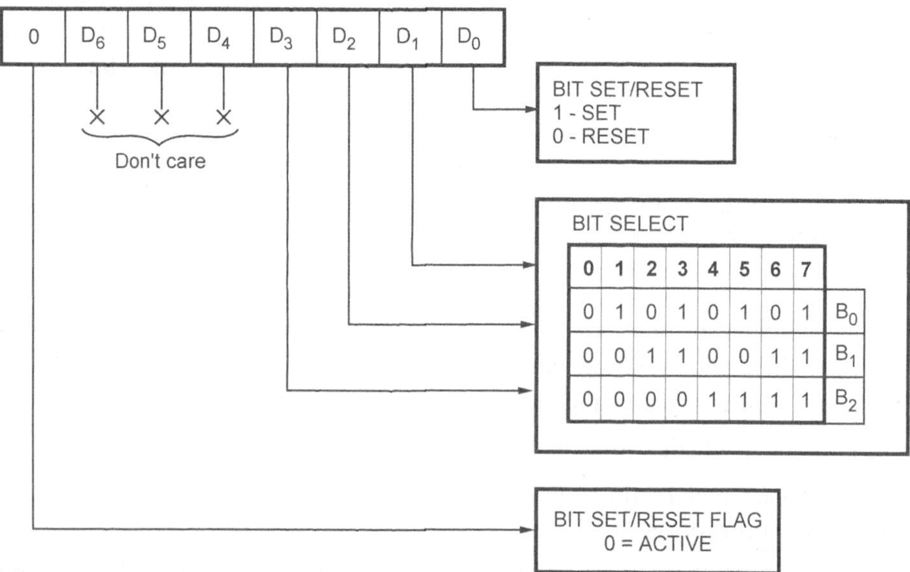

Fig. 11.4 Bit set/reset control word format

Set-Reset format (BSR) determine particular bit in PC_0 - PC_7 being set or reset as per the status of bit D_0. A BSR word is to be written for each bit that is to be set or reset. For example, if bit PC_3 is to be set and bit PC_4 is to be reset, the appropriate BSR words that will have to be loaded into the control register will be, 0XXX0111 and 0XXX1000, respectively, where X is don't care.

The BSR word can also be used for enabling or disabling interrupt signals generated by Port C when the 8255 is programmed for Mode 1 or 2 operation. This is done by setting or resetting the associated bits of the interrupts. This is described in detail in next section.

11.5.2 For I/O Mode

The mode definition format for I/O mode is shown in Fig. 11.5. The control words for both, mode definition and Bit Set-Reset are loaded into the same control register, with bit D_7 used for specifying whether the word loaded into the control register is a mode definition word or Bit Set-Reset word. If D_7 is high, the word is taken as a mode definition word, and if it is low, it is taken as a Bit Set-Reset word. The appropriate bits are set or reset depending on the type of operation desired, and loaded into the control register.

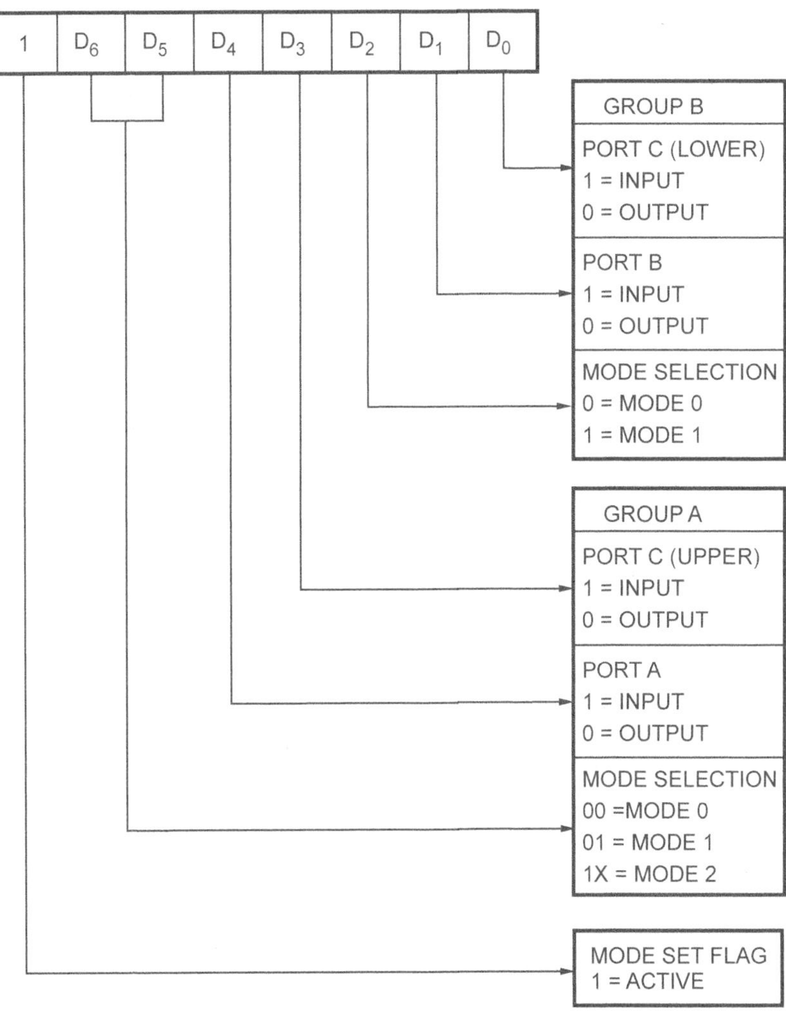

Fig. 11.5 8255 Mode definition format

Example 1 : Write a program to initialize 8255 in the configuration given below :

1. Port A : Simple input
2. Port B : Simple output
3. Port C_L : Output
4. Port C_U : Input

Assume address of the control word register of 8255 as 83H.

Solution :

Source program :

```
MVI A, 98H     ; Load control word
OUT 83H        ; Send control word
```

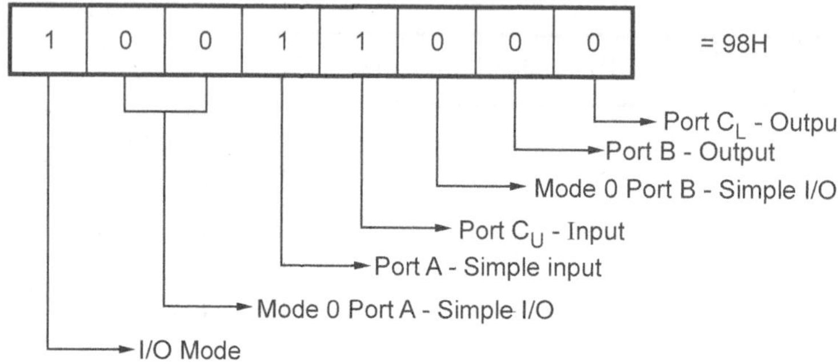

Example 2 : Write a program to initialize 8255 in the configuration given below :

1. Port A : Output with handshake
2. Port B : Input with handshake
3. Port C_L : Output
4. Port C_U : Input

Assume address of the control word register of 8255 as 23H.

Solution :

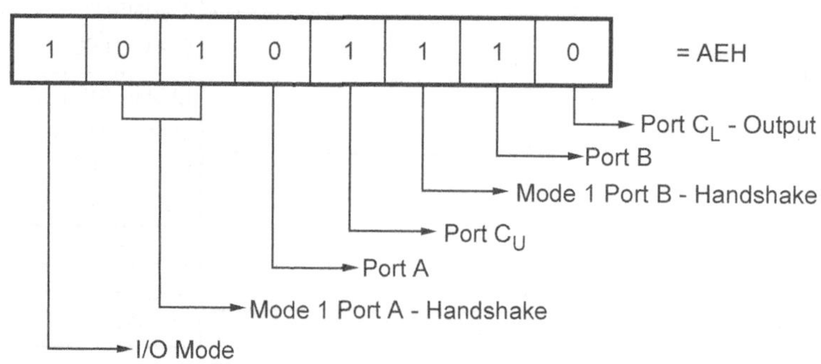

Source program :

```
        MVI A, AEH      ; Load control word
        OUT 23H         ; Send control word
```

Lab Experiment 64 : Blink port C bit 0 of 8255.

Statement : Write a program to blink Port C bit 0 of the 8255. Assume address of control word register of 8255 as 83H. Use Bit Set/Reset mode.

Solution : Control word to make bit 0 high.

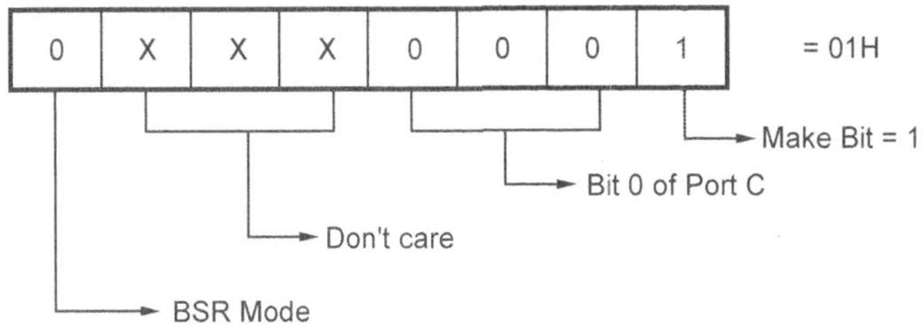

Control word to make Bit 0 low

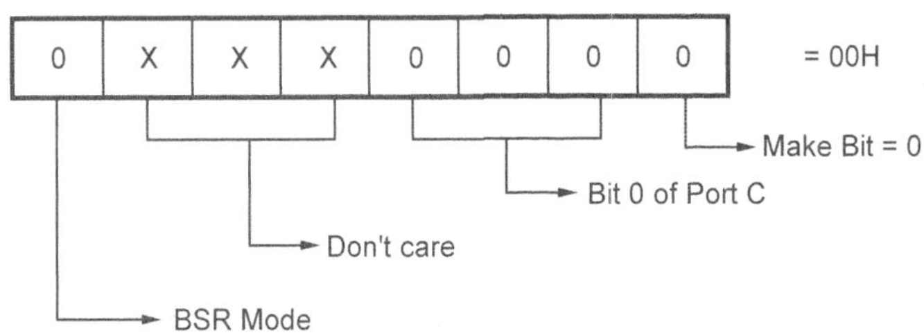

Flowchart :

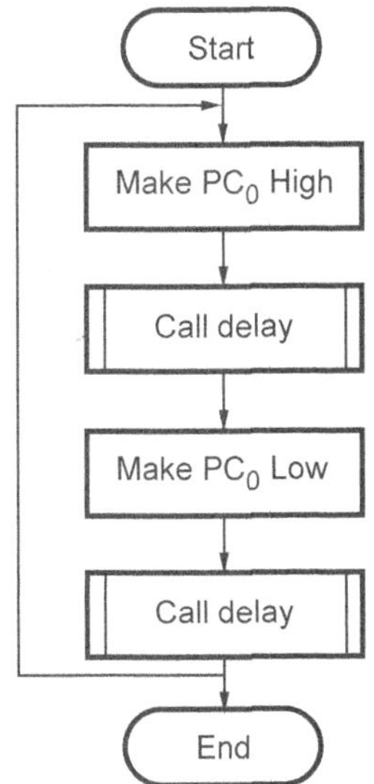

Source program :

```
BACK : MVI A, 01H     ; Load bit pattern to make PC0 high
       OUT 83H        ; Send it to control word register
       CALL DELAY     ; Call Delay subroutine
       MVI A, 00H     ; Load bit pattern to make PC0 Low
       OUT 83H        ; Send it to control word register
       CALL Delay     ; Call Delay subroutine
       JMP BACK       ; Repeat
```

11.6 8255 Programming and Operation

11.6.1 Programming in Mode 0

The Ports A, B and C can be configured as simple input or output ports by writing the appropriate control word in the control word register. In the control word, D_7 is set to '1' (to define a mode set operation) and D_6, D_5 and D_2 are all set to '0' to configure all the ports in Mode 0 operation. The status of bits D_4, D_3, D_1 and D_0 then determine (Refer to Fig. 11.5) whether the corresponding ports are to be configured as Input or Output.

For example in mode 0, if Port A and Port B are to operate as output ports with Port C lower as input, and Port C upper as output, the control word that will have to be loaded into the control register will be as follows.

D_7	D_6	D_5	D_4	D_3	D_2	D_1	D_0	
1	0	0	0	0	0	0	1	= 81H

As mentioned earlier, this mode provides simple input and output operations for each of the three ports. No handshaking is required, data is simply written to or read from a specified port.

Input Mode : Fig. 11.6 shows the timing diagram for mode 0 input mode.

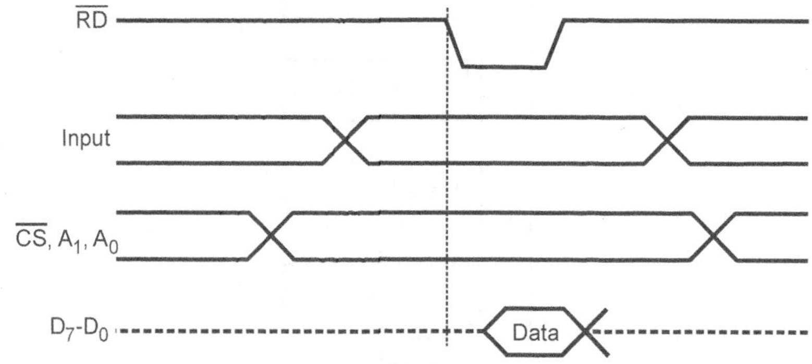

Fig. 11.6 Timing diagram for mode 0 input mode

After initialization of 8255 in the input mode 0, CPU can read data through the input port by initiating read command with proper port address. Read command activates $\overline{RD}$ signal. Upon activation of $\overline{RD}$ signal CPU reads the data from the selected input port into the CPU register.

Output Mode : Fig. 11.7 shows the timing diagram for mode 0 output mode.

After initialization of 8255 in the output mode 0, CPU can write data into the output port by initiating write command with proper port address. CPU sends data on the data bus and upon activation of $\overline{WR}$ signal, data on the data bus gets latched on the selected output port.

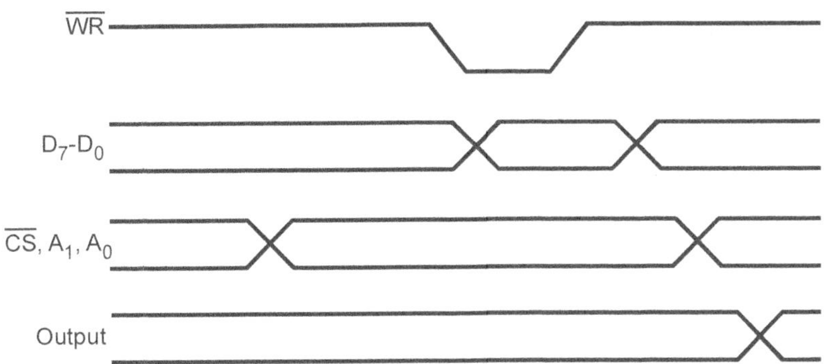

Fig. 11.7 Timing diagram for mode 0 output mode

Mode 0 Configurations :

A		B		GROUP A			GROUP B	
D_4	D_3	D_1	D_0	PORT A	PORT C (Upper)	#	PORT B	PORT C (Lower)
0	0	0	0	OUTPUT	OUTPUT	0	OUTPUT	OUTPUT
0	0	0	1	OUTPUT	OUTPUT	1	OUTPUT	INPUT
0	0	1	0	OUTPUT	OUTPUT	2	INPUT	OUTPUT
0	0	1	1	OUTPUT	OUTPUT	3	INPUT	INPUT
0	1	0	0	OUTPUT	INPUT	4	OUTPUT	OUTPUT
0	1	0	1	OUTPUT	INPUT	5	OUTPUT	INPUT
0	1	1	0	OUTPUT	INPUT	6	INPUT	OUTPUT
0	1	1	1	OUTPUT	INPUT	7	INPUT	INPUT

1	0	0	0	INPUT	OUTPUT	8	OUTPUT	OUTPUT
1	0	0	1	INPUT	OUTPUT	9	OUTPUT	INPUT
1	0	1	0	INPUT	OUTPUT	10	INPUT	OUTPUT
1	0	1	1	INPUT	OUTPUT	11	INPUT	INPUT
1	1	0	0	INPUT	INPUT	12	OUTPUT	OUTPUT
1	1	0	1	INPUT	INPUT	13	OUTPUT	INPUT
1	1	1	0	INPUT	INPUT	14	INPUT	OUTPUT
1	1	1	1	INPUT	INPUT	15	INPUT	INPUT

11.6.2 Programming in Mode 1 (Input / Output with Handshake)

Both Group A and Group B can operate in Mode 1, either together, or individually, with each port containing an 8-bit latched Input or Output data port, and a 4-bit port which is used for control and status of the 8-bit port.

When Port A is to be programmed as an input port, PC_3 , PC_4 and PC_5 are used for control. PC_6 and PC_7 are not used and can be Input or Output, as programmed by bit D_3 of the control word. When Port A is programmed as an output port, PC_3 , PC_6, and PC_7 are used for control and PC_4 and PC_5 can be Input or Output, as programmed by bit D_3, of the control word.

When Port B is to be programmed as an input or output port, PC_0, PC_1 and PC_2 are used for control.

Mode 1 : Input control signals :

1. $\overline{STB}$ (Strobe Input) : This is an active low input signal for 8255 and output signal for the input device. The input device activates this signal to indicate CPU that the data to be read is already sent on the port lines of 8255 port. Upon activation of this signal 8255 loads the data from the input port lines into the input buffer of that port.

2. IBF (Input Buffer Full) : This is an active high output signal for 8255 and an input signal for input device. This signal is generated by 8255 in response to $\overline{STB}$ signal as an acknowledgment to input device. It also indicates to the input device that the input buffer is full and it is not ready to accept next byte from the input device. Therefore input device sends data on the port lines only when IBF signal is not active. The IBF signal is deactivated when CPU reads the data from input buffer of the respective port by activation of $\overline{RD}$ signal.

3. INTR (Interrupt Request) : This is an active high output signal generated by 8255. A 'high' on this output can be used to interrupt the CPU when an input device is requesting service. The 8255 sets the INTR when $\overline{STB}$ signal is 'one', IBF signal is 'one' and INTE is 'one', indicating CPU that the data from the input device is available in the input buffer. This signal is reset by the falling edge of the $\overline{RD}$ signal i.e. immediately after reading the data from the input buffer.

INTE (Interrupt Enable) flip flop is used to enable or disable INTR (Interrupt request) signal. If INTE flip-flop is set, the interrupt request is generated depending on the status of $\overline{STB}$ and IBF signals. If INTE flip flop is reset, the interrupt request is not generated, allowing masking facility for the interrupt.

Mode 1 : Port A input operation

Fig. 11.8 (a) shows Port A as an input port along with the control word and control signals (for handshaking with a peripheral). When the control word (as in Fig. 11.8 (a) is loaded into the control register, Group A is configured in Mode 1 with Port A as an input port. Port A can accept parallel data from a peripheral (like a keyboard) and this data can be read by the CPU. The peripheral first loads data into Port by making the $\overline{STB_A}$ input low. This latches the data placed by the peripheral on the common data bus into Port A. Port A acknowledges reception of data by making IBF_A (Input Buffer Full) high. IBF_A is set when the $\overline{STB_A}$ input is made low, as shown in Fig. 11.8 (b).
(See Fig. 11.8 (b) on next page).

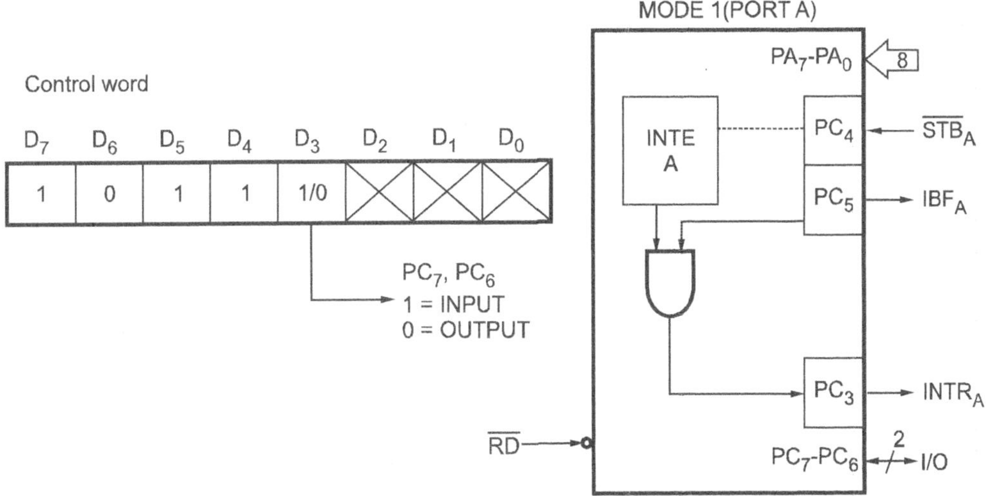

Fig. 11.8 (a) Port A in mode 1

$INTR_A$ is an active high output signal which can be used to interrupt the CPU so that the CPU can suspend its current operation and read the data written into Port A by the peripheral. $INTR_A$ can be enabled or disabled by the $INTE_A$ flip-flop which is controlled by Bit Set-Reset operation of PC_4. $INTR_A$ is set (if enabled by setting the $INTE_A$ flip-flop) after the $\overline{STB_A}$ has gone high again, and if IBF_A is high.

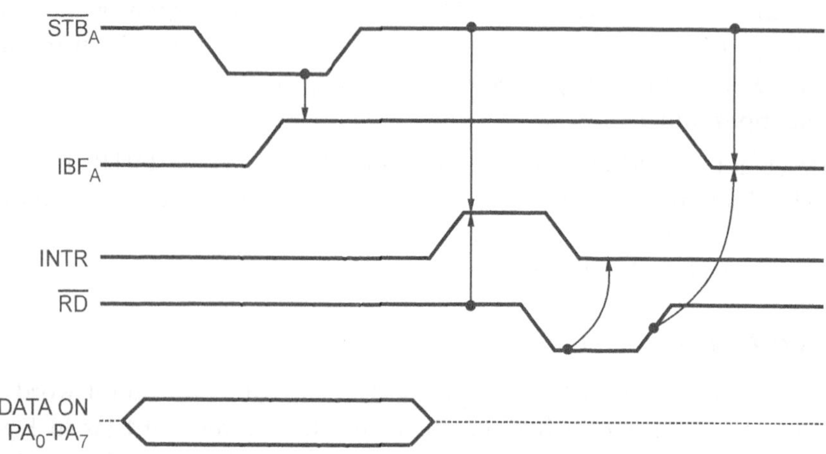

Fig. 11.8 (b) Timing diagram for port A in mode 1

On receipt of the interrupt, the CPU can be forced to read Port A. The falling edge of the $\overline{RD}$ input resets IBFA and it goes low. This can be used to indicate to the peripheral that the input buffer is empty and that data can again be loaded into it.

Mode 1 : Port B input operation.

Fig. 11.9 shows Port B as an input port (when in Mode 1). The timing diagram and operation of Port B is similar to that of Port A except that it uses different bits of Port C for control. $INTE_B$ is controlled by Bit Set/Reset of PC_2.

If the CPU is busy with other system operations, it can read data from the input port when it is interrupted. This is often called Interrupt driven I/O. However, if the CPU is

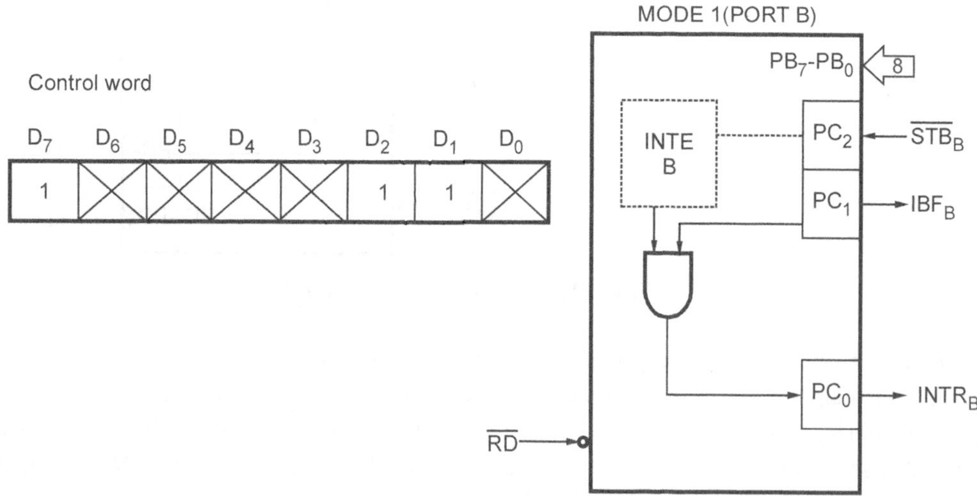

Fig. 11.9 Port B in mode 1

otherwise not busy with other jobs, it can continuously poll (read) the status word to check for an IBF_A. This is often called Program Controlled I/O. The status word is accessed by reading **Port C** (A_1A_0 must be 10, $\overline{RD}$ and $\overline{CS}$ must be low). The status word format when Ports A and B are input ports in Mode 1, is shown in Fig. 11.10.

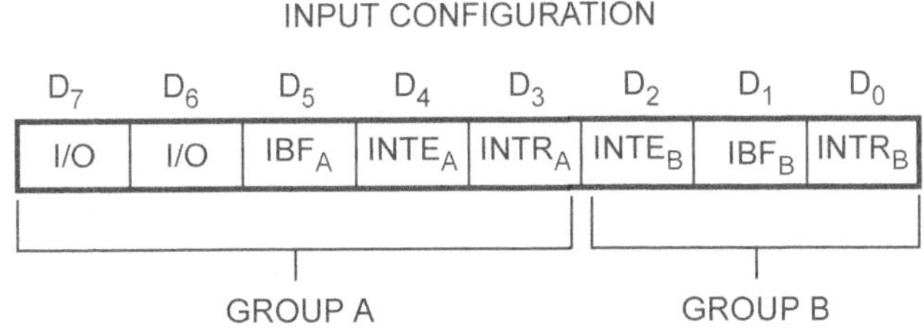

Fig. 11.10 Mode 1 status word (Input)

Mode 1 : Output control signals

1. $\overline{\text{OBF}}$ (Output Buffer Full) :

This is an active low output signal for 8255 and input signal for the output device. The 8255 activates this signal to indicate output device that data is available on the output port. Upon activation of $\overline{OBF}$ signal, output device reads data from the output port and acknowledges it by $\overline{ACK}$ signal. The $\overline{OBF}$ signal is activated at the rising edge of the $\overline{WR}$ signal and de-activated at the falling edge of the $\overline{ACK}$ signal.

2. $\overline{\text{ACK}}$ (Acknowledge Input) :

This is an active low input signal for 8255 and output signal for the output device. The output device generates this signal to indicate 8255 that the data from port A or Port B has been accepted.

3. INTR (Interrupt Request) :

This is an active high output signal generated by 8255. A 'high' on this output can be used to interrupt the CPU when an output device has accepted data transmitted by the CPU. The 8255 sets the INTR when $\overline{ACK}$ signal is 'one', $\overline{OBF}$ is 'one' and INTE is 'one', indicating that the output device is ready to accept next data byte. This signal is reset by the falling edge of the $\overline{WR}$ signal i.e. immediately after sending the data to the output port.

INTE (Interrupt Enable) flip flop is used to enable or disable INTR (Interrupt Request) signal. If INTE flip flop is set, the interrupt request is generated depending on the status of $\overline{ACK}$ and $\overline{OBF}$ signals. If INTE flip flop is reset, the interrupt request is not generated, allowing masking facility for the interrupt.

Mode 1 : Port A output operation.

Fig. 11.11 (a) shows Port A configured as an output port (when in Mode 1) along with the control word and control signals (for handshaking with a peripheral). When the control word (as in Fig. 11.11 (a)) is loaded into the control register, Group A is configured in Mode 1 with Port A as an output port. The CPU can send data to a peripheral (like a display device) through Port A of the 8255.

The $\overline{OBF_A}$ output (Output Buffer Full) goes low on the rising edge of the $\overline{WR}$ signal (when the CPU writes data into the 8255). The $\overline{OBF_A}$ output from 8255 can be used as a strobe input to the peripheral to latch the contents of Port A. The peripheral responds to

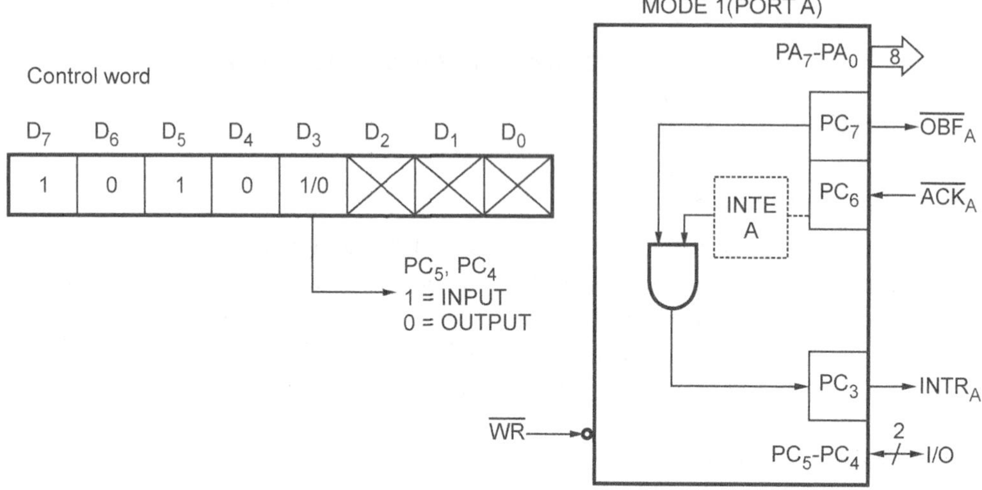

Fig. 11.11 (a) Port A in mode 1

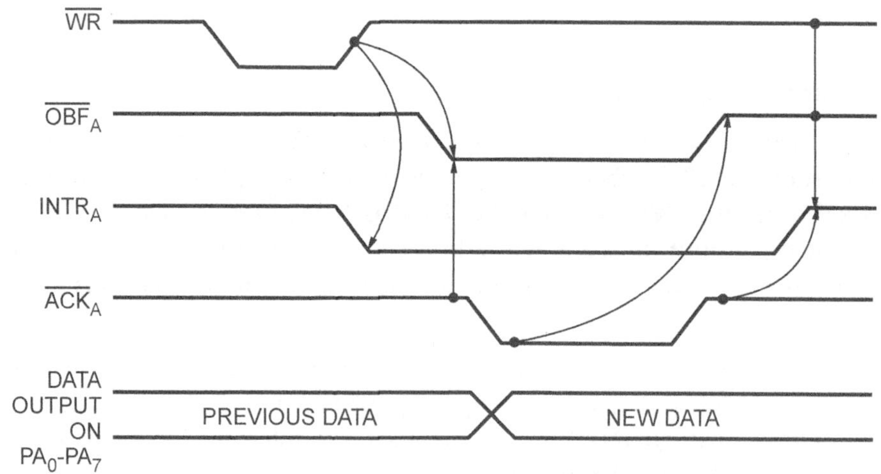

Fig. 11.11 (b) Port A in mode 1 (Output)

the receipt of data by making the $\overline{ACK_A}$ input of the 8255 low, thus acknowledging that it has received the data sent by the CPU through Port A. The $\overline{ACK_A}$ low sets the OBF_A signal, which can be polled by the CPU through $\overline{OBF_A}$ of the status word to load the next data when it is high again.

$INTR_A$ is an active high output of the 8255 which is made high (if the associated $INTE_A$ flip-flop is set) when $\overline{ACK_A}$ is made high again by the peripheral, and when $\overline{OBF_A}$ goes high again (See timing diagram in Fig. 11.11(b)). It can be used to interrupt the CPU whenever the output buffer is empty. It is reset by the falling edge of $\overline{WR}$ when the CPU writes data onto Port A. It can be enabled or disabled by writing a '1' or a'0' respectively to PC_6 in the BSR mode.

Mode 1 : Port B output operation.

Fig. 11.12 shows Port B as an output port when in Mode 1. The operation of Port B is similar to that of Port A. $INTR_A$ is controlled by writing a '1' or a '0' to PC_2 in the BSR mode. The status word is accessed by issuing a Read to Port C. The format of the status word when Ports A and B are Output ports in Mode 1 is shown in Fig. 11.13.

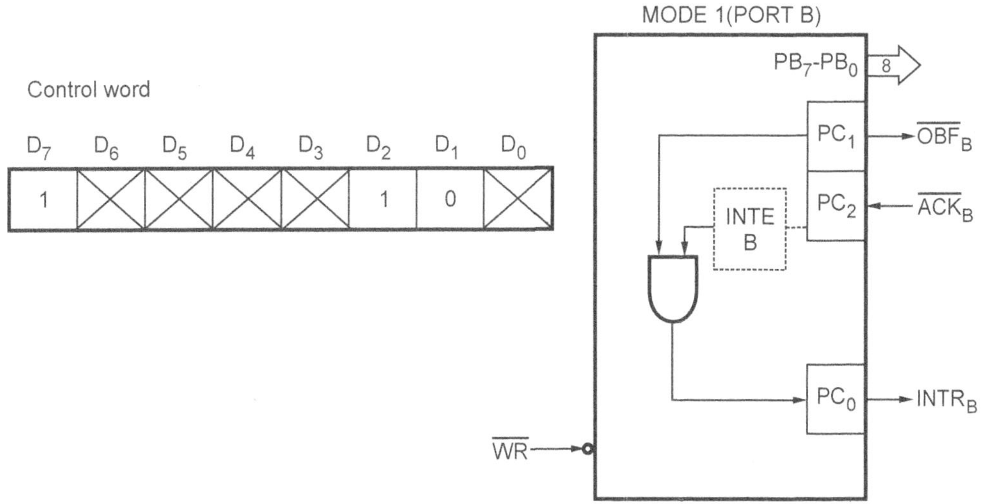

Fig. 11.12 Port B in mode 1 (Output)

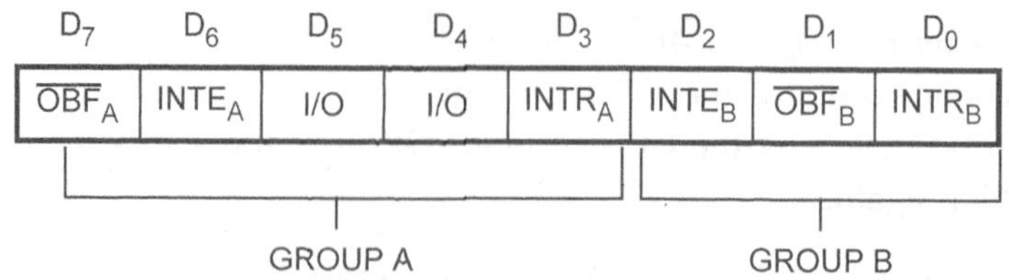

Fig. 11.13 Mode 1 status word (Output)

11.6.3 Programming in Mode 2 (Strobes Bi-directional Bus I/O)

When the 8255 is operated in Mode 2 (by loading the appropriate control word), Port A can be used as a bi-directional 8-bit I/O bus using for handshaking. Port B can be programmed in Mode 0 or in Mode 1. When Port B is programmed in mode 1, PC_0 - PC_2 lines of Port C are used as handshaking signals.

Fig. 11.14 shows the control word that should be loaded into the control port to configure 8255 in Mode 2.

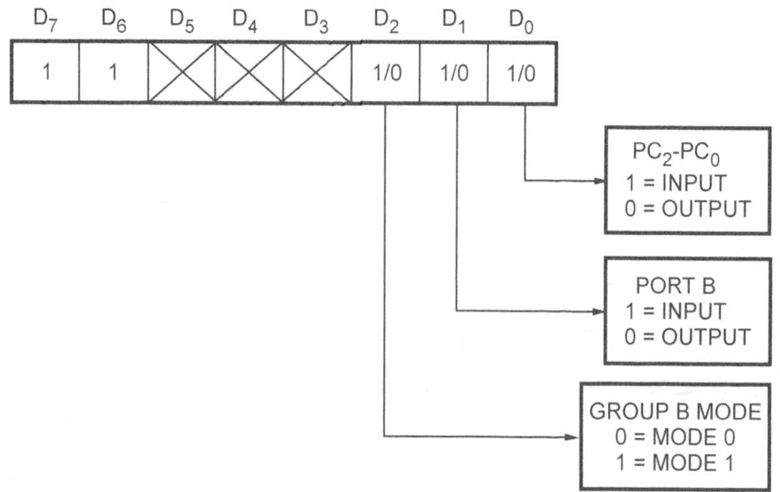

Fig. 11.14 Mode 2 control word

Mode 2 : Control signals

INTR (Interrupt Request) : A 'high' on this output can be used to interrupt the CPU for input or output operations.

Output Control Signals :

$\overline{OBF}_A$ (Output Buffer Full)

This is an active low output which indicates that the CPU has written data into Port A.

$\overline{ACK_A}$ (Acknowledge)

This is an active low input signal (generated by the peripheral) which enables the tri-state output buffer of Port A and makes Port A data available to the peripheral. In Mode 2, Port A outputs are in tri-state until enabled.

INTE 1

This is the flip-flop associated with Output Buffer Full. INTE 1 can be used to enable or disable the interrupt by setting or resetting PC_6 in the BSR Mode.

Input Control Signals :

$\overline{STB}$ (Strobe Input)

This is an active low input signal which enables Port A to latch the data available at its input.

IBF (Input Buffer Full Flip-Flop)

This is an active high output which indicates that data has been loaded into the input latch of Port A.

INTE 2

This is an Interrupt enable flip-flop associated with Input Buffer Full. It can be controlled by setting or resetting PC_4 in the BSR Mode.

Mode 2 : Port A operation.

Fig. 11.15 shows Port A and associated control signals when 8255 is in Mode 2. Interrupts are generated for both output and input operations on the same $INTR_A$ (PC_3) line.

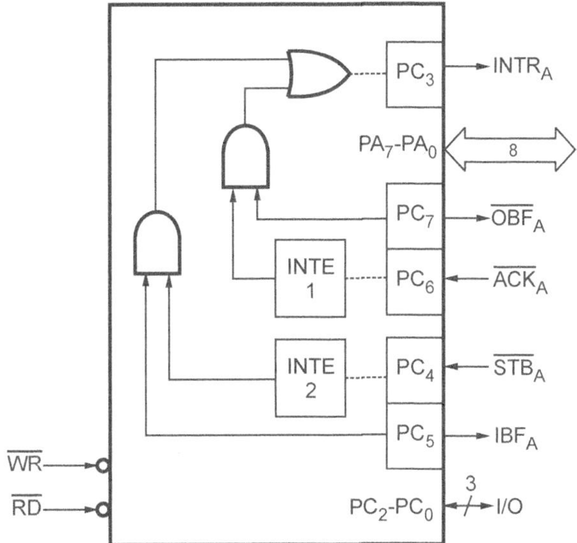

Fig. 11.15 Mode 2 operation

Status Word In Mode 2

The status word for Mode 2 (accessed by reading Port C) is shown in Fig. 11.15. D_7 - D_3 of the status word carry information about $\overline{OBF}_A$, $INTE_1$, IBF_A, $INTE_2$, $INTR_A$. The status of the bits D_2-D_0 depends on the mode setting of Group B. If B is programmed in Mode 0, D_2-D_0 are the same as PC_2-PC_0 (simple I/O); however if B is in Mode 1, D_2 - D_0 carry information about the control signals for Port B (as in Fig. 11.10, or Fig. 11.13), depending upon whether Port B is an Input port or Output port respectively.

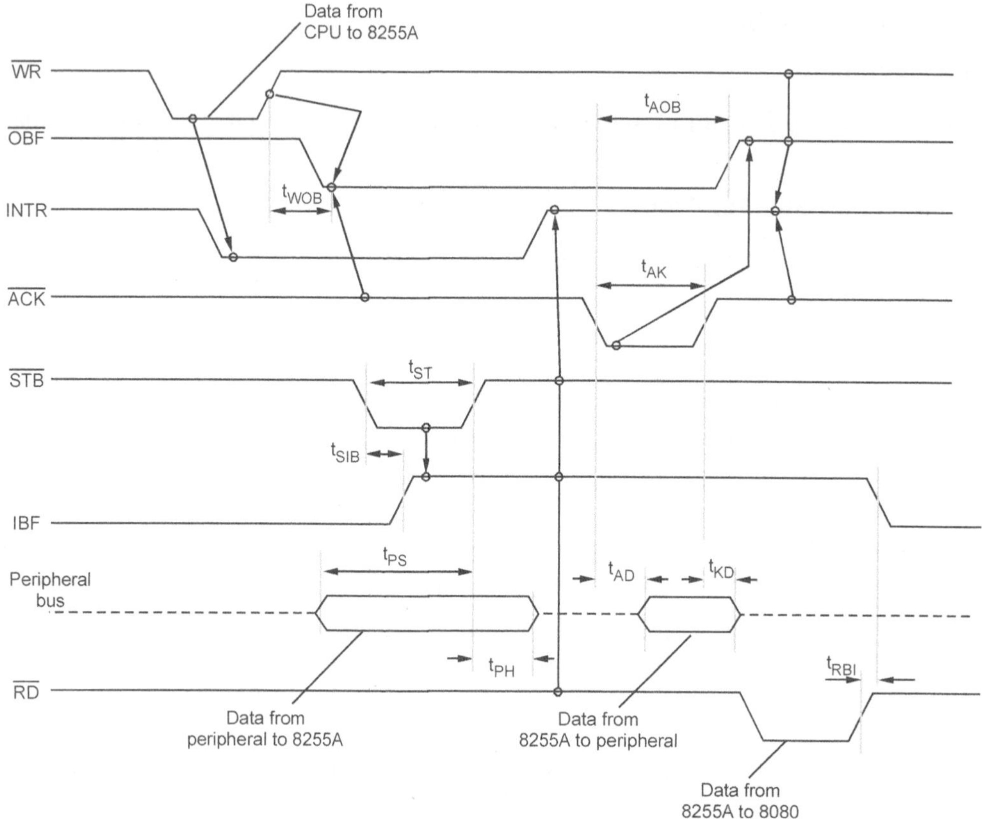

Fig. 11.16 Mode 2 waveform

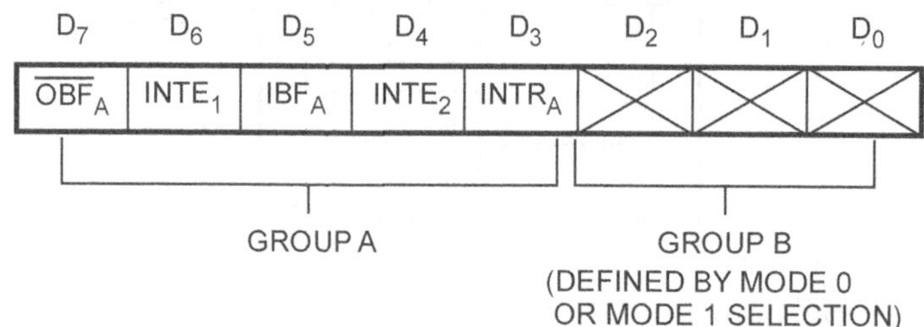

Fig. 11.17 Status word for mode 2

Mode Definition Summary

	MODE 0		MODE 1		MODE 2
	IN	OUT	IN	OUT	GROUP A ONLY
PA_0	IN	OUT	IN	OUT	↔
PA_1	IN	OUT	IN	OUT	↔
PA_2	IN	OUT	IN	OUT	↔
PA_3	IN	OUT	IN	OUT	↔
PA_4	IN	OUT	IN	OUT	↔
PA_5	IN	OUT	IN	OUT	↔
PA_6	IN	OUT	IN	OUT	↔
PA_7	IN	OUT	IN	OUT	↔

	MODE 0		MODE 1		MODE 2	
	IN	OUT	IN	OUT	GROUP A ONLY	
PB_0	IN	OUT	IN	OUT	–	Mode 0 or Mode 1 Only
PB_1	IN	OUT	IN	OUT	–	
PB_2	IN	OUT	IN	OUT	–	
PB_3	IN	OUT	IN	OUT	–	
PB_4	IN	OUT	IN	OUT	–	
PB_5	IN	OUT	IN	OUT	–	
PB_6	IN	OUT	IN	OUT	–	
PB_7	IN	OUT	IN	OUT	–	
PC_0	IN	OUT	$INTR_B$	$INTR_B$	I/O	
PC_1	IN	OUT	IBF_B	OBF_B	I/O	
PC_2	IN	OUT	STB_B	ACK_B	I/O	
PC_3	IN	OUT	$INTR_A$	$INTR_A$	$INTR_A$	
PC_4	IN	OUT	STB_A	I/O	STB_A	
PC_5	IN	OUT	IBF_A	I/O	IBF_A	
PC_6	IN	OUT	I/O	ACK_A	ACK_A	
PC_7	IN	OUT	I/O	OBF_A	OBF_A	

11.7 Interfacing 8255 in I/O Mapped I/O

Fig. 11.18 shows the interfacing of 8255 with 8085 in I/O mapped I/O technique. Here $\overline{RD}$ and $\overline{WR}$ signals are activated when $IO/\overline{M}$ signal is high, indicating I/O bus cycle. Reset out signal from 8085 is connected to the RESET signal of the 8255.

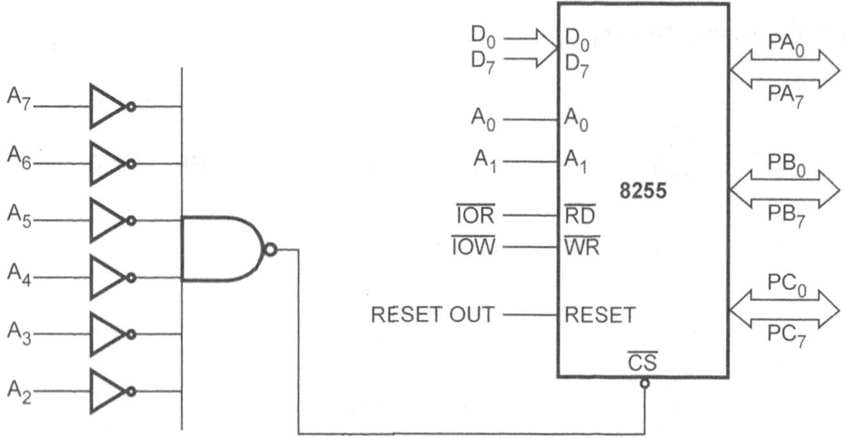

Fig. 11.18 Interfacing of 8255 in I/O mapped I/O

I/O Map :

Ports / Control Register	Address lines A_7 A_6 A_5 A_4 A_3 A_2 A_1 A_0	Address
Port A	0 0 0 0 0 0 0 0	00H
Port B	0 0 0 0 0 0 0 1	01H
Port C	0 0 0 0 0 0 1 0	02H
Control Register	0 0 0 0 0 0 1 1	03H

11.8 Parallel Communication between Two MP Kits using Mode 2 of 8255

May-05

The Fig. 11.19 shows a block diagram to implement the bidirectional communication between the master and the slave processors. As shown in the Fig. 11.28, the data buses of two processors are interconnected through the 8255, which servers as a peripheral device of the master processor. Here, 8255 is used in bidirectional I/O mode (mode 2), in which port A of the 8255 is used for bidirectional data transfer, and four signals from port C are used for handshaking.

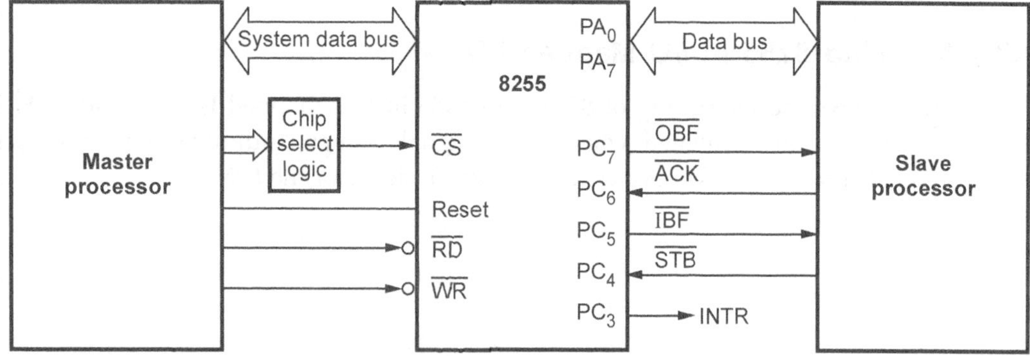

Fig.11.19 Block diagram of bidirectional communication between two processors using 8255 in mode 2

Transfer of data from master processor to slave processor

1. The master processor reads the status of $\overline{OBF}$ to verify whether the previous byte has been read by the slave processor.
2. If master processor finds output buffer empty it writes data into port A and informs slave processor by activating the $\overline{OBF}$ signal.
3. The slave processor checks the $\overline{OBF}$ signal from the master processor for the presence of data.
4. If it finds active $\overline{OBF}$ signal, it reads data from port A and acknowledges the reading at the same time by activating the $\overline{ACK}$ signal.

Transfer of data from slave processor to master processor

1. The slave processor checks the IBF (input buffer full) signal from 8255 to find out whether port A is available (empty) to transfer a data byte.
2. If slave processor confirms availability of port A it sends a data byte on the data bus and informs the 8255 by activating $\overline{STB}$ signal.
3. Since the data is loaded in the 8255 its IBF signal is activated and master processor reads this signal to check the presence of data.
4. If master processor finds IBF signal activated it reads the data byte from port A.

Hardware

The Fig. 11.20 shows the detail hardware required for bidirectional communication between two 8085 processors. It shows all the signals and the decoder circuitry for the communication (See Fig. 11.20 on next page).

The NAND gate acts as a chip-select logic for 8255. The 8255 is selected when A_2 through A_7 address lines are high. Thus, the port addresses for 8255 are :

Port / Control Register	A_7	A_6	A_5	A_4	A_3	A_2	A_1	A_0	Address
PORT A	1	1	1	1	1	1	0	0	FCH
PORT B	1	1	1	1	1	1	0	1	FDH
PORT C	1	1	1	1	1	1	1	0	FEH
Control Register	1	1	1	1	1	1	1	1	FFH

Port A of 8255 is configured in mode 2. Here, out off five control signal four control signals are used; INTR signal is not used and hence not shown. The master processor checks the $\overline{ACK}$ and the $\overline{STB}$ signals by reading the status of respective bits in port C. The other two control signals $\overline{OBF}$ and IBF are connected to bits D_7 and D_0 of the slave data bus, respectively, through tri-state buffer so that they can be read by the slave processor.

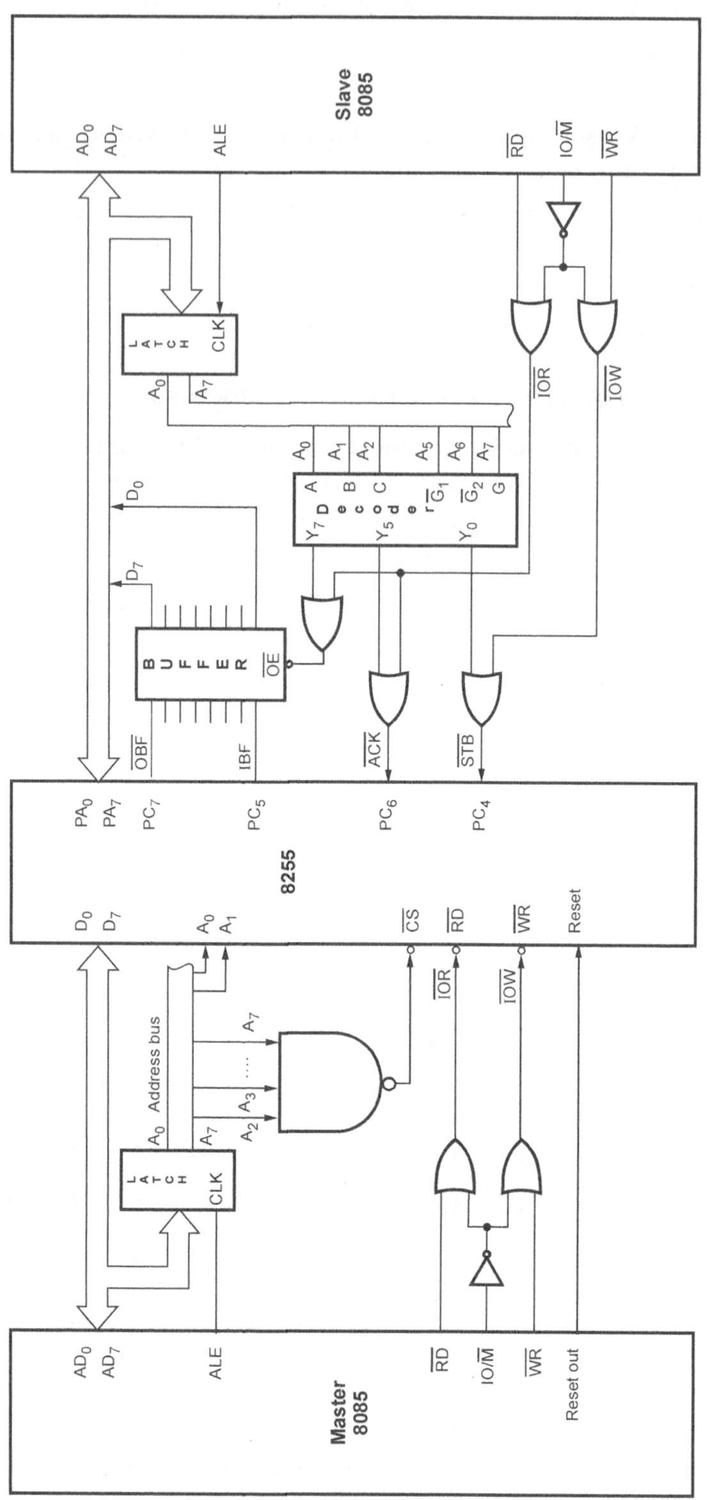
Slave
8085
AD_0
AD_7
ALE
$\overline{RD}$
$IO/\overline{M}$
$\overline{WR}$
LATCH
CLK
A_0
A_7
$\overline{IOR}$
$\overline{IOW}$
A_0 A_1 A_2 A_5 A_6 A_7
A B C $\overline{G_1}$ $\overline{G_2}$ G
Decoder
Y_7 Y_5 Y_0
D_0
D_7
BUFFER
$\overline{OE}$
$\overline{OBF}$
IBF
$\overline{ACK}$
$\overline{STB}$
PA_0 PA_7 PC_7 PC_5 PC_6 PC_4
8255
D_0 D_7 A_0 A_1 $\overline{CS}$ $\overline{RD}$ $\overline{WR}$ Reset
$\overline{IOR}$
$\overline{IOW}$
A_0 Address bus
A_7
A_7 A_3 A_2
LATCH
CLK
AD_0
AD_7
ALE
$\overline{RD}$
$IO/\overline{M}$
$\overline{WR}$
Reset out
Master
8085

Fig. 11.20

A 3 : 8 decoder is used to generate $\overline{ACK}$ and $\overline{STB}$ signals and the output enable signal for tri-state buffer with the help of external circuitry. Address lines A_0 through A_2 select the output of the decoder and address lines A_5, A_6 and A_7 decoder when $A_5 = A_6 = 0$ and $A_7 = 1$. Address lines A_3 and A_4 are don't care lines and are assumed at logic 0. Therefore the output Y_7 is selected when address is 87 H, the output Y_5 is selected when address is 85 H and the output Y_0 is selected when address is 80 H . This is illustrated in Table 11.2.

Address	A_7	A_6	A_5	A_4	A_3	A_2	A_1	A_0	Decoder output	$\overline{IOR}$	$\overline{IOW}$	$\overline{OE}$	$\overline{ACK}$	$\overline{STB}$
80H	1	0	0	X	X	0	0	0	$Y_0 = 0$	1	0	1	1	0
85H	1	0	0	X	X	1	0	1	$Y_5 = 0$	0	1	1	0	1
87H	1	0	0	X	X	1	1	1	$Y_7 = 0$	0	1	0	1	1

Table 11.2 Activation of control signals

As shown in the Table 11.2, the decoder line Y_0 is combined with $\overline{IOW}$ to generate $\overline{STB}$ signal, Y_5 is combined with $\overline{IOR}$ to generate $\overline{ACK}$ signal and Y_7 is combined with $\overline{IOR}$ to generate $\overline{OE}$ signal.

Control Word for Mode 2

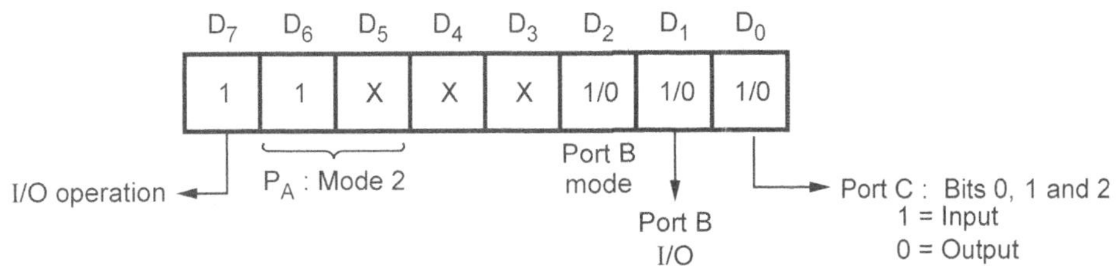

Fig. 11.21

Here, we are not using port B and port C bits 0, 1 and 2. Hence bits D_2 to D_0 are don't cares. Therefore, the required control word to configure port A in mode 2 is C0 H.

Status word in Mode 2

Looking at the status word format the master processor can check the $\overline{OBF}$ signal by reading the status of D_7 bit of status register and it can check the IBF signal by reading the status of D_5 bit of the status register.

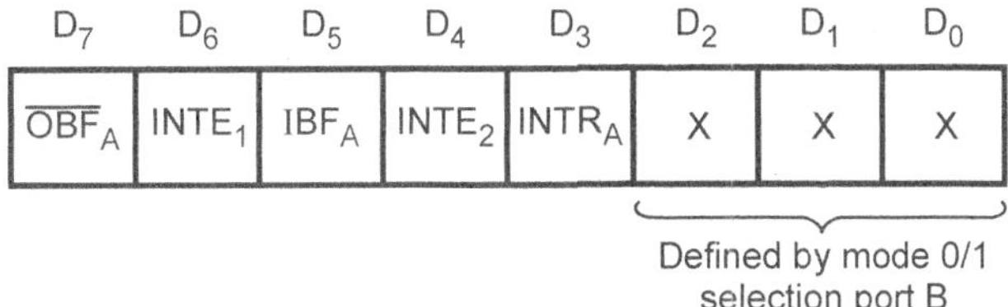

Fig. 11.22

Transfer of data from master 8085 to slave 8085

Let us see the flow chart; program and timing diagram for master and slave 8085s to transfer data bytes from master 8085 to slave 8085.

Flowchart

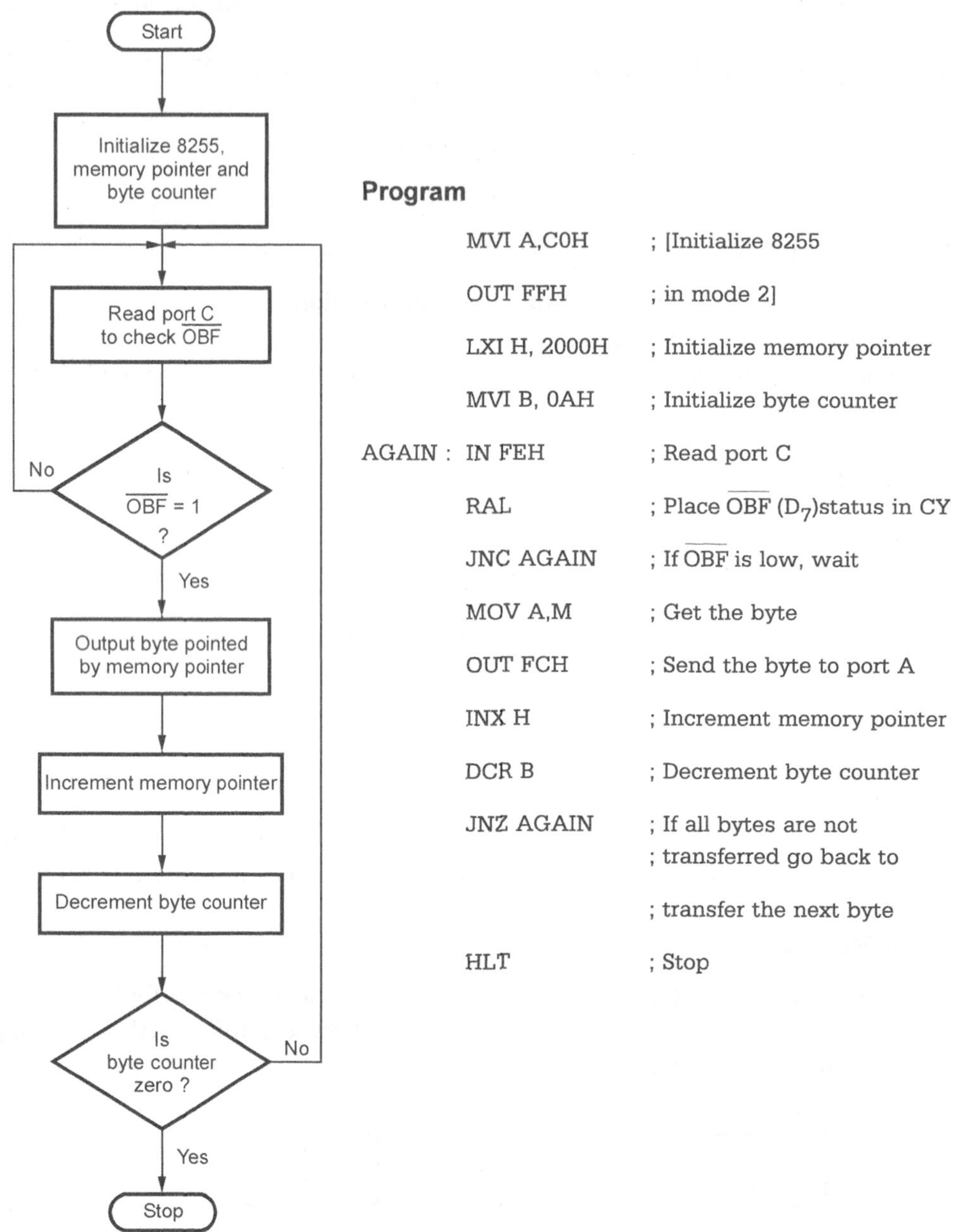

Program

```
        MVI A,COH       ; [Initialize 8255
        OUT FFH         ; in mode 2]
        LXI H, 2000H    ; Initialize memory pointer
        MVI B, 0AH      ; Initialize byte counter
AGAIN : IN FEH          ; Read port C
        RAL             ; Place OBF (D7)status in CY
        JNC AGAIN       ; If OBF is low, wait
        MOV A,M         ; Get the byte
        OUT FCH         ; Send the byte to port A
        INX H           ; Increment memory pointer
        DCR B           ; Decrement byte counter
        JNZ AGAIN       ; If all bytes are not
                        ; transferred go back to
                        ; transfer the next byte
        HLT             ; Stop
```

Fig. 11.23 Flowchart and program for master 8085 for transfer of data from master to slave

Flowchart

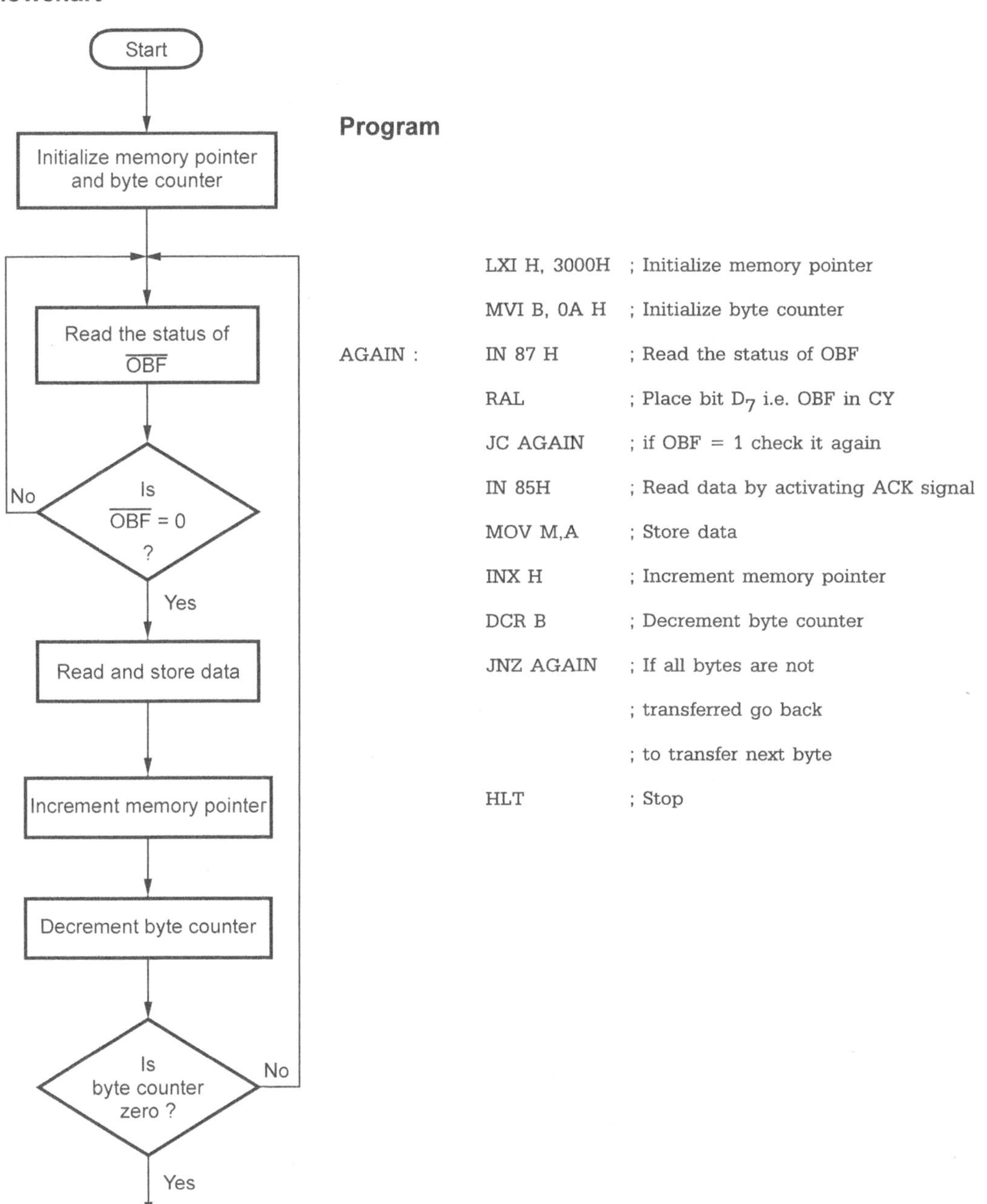

Program

```
        LXI H, 3000H  ; Initialize memory pointer
        MVI B, 0A H   ; Initialize byte counter
AGAIN : IN 87 H       ; Read the status of OBF
        RAL           ; Place bit D7 i.e. OBF in CY
        JC AGAIN      ; if OBF = 1 check it again
        IN 85H        ; Read data by activating ACK signal
        MOV M,A       ; Store data
        INX H         ; Increment memory pointer
        DCR B         ; Decrement byte counter
        JNZ AGAIN     ; If all bytes are not
                      ; transferred go back
                      ; to transfer next byte
        HLT           ; Stop
```

Fig. 11.24 Flowchart and program for slave 8085 for transfer of data from master to slave

Timing Diagram

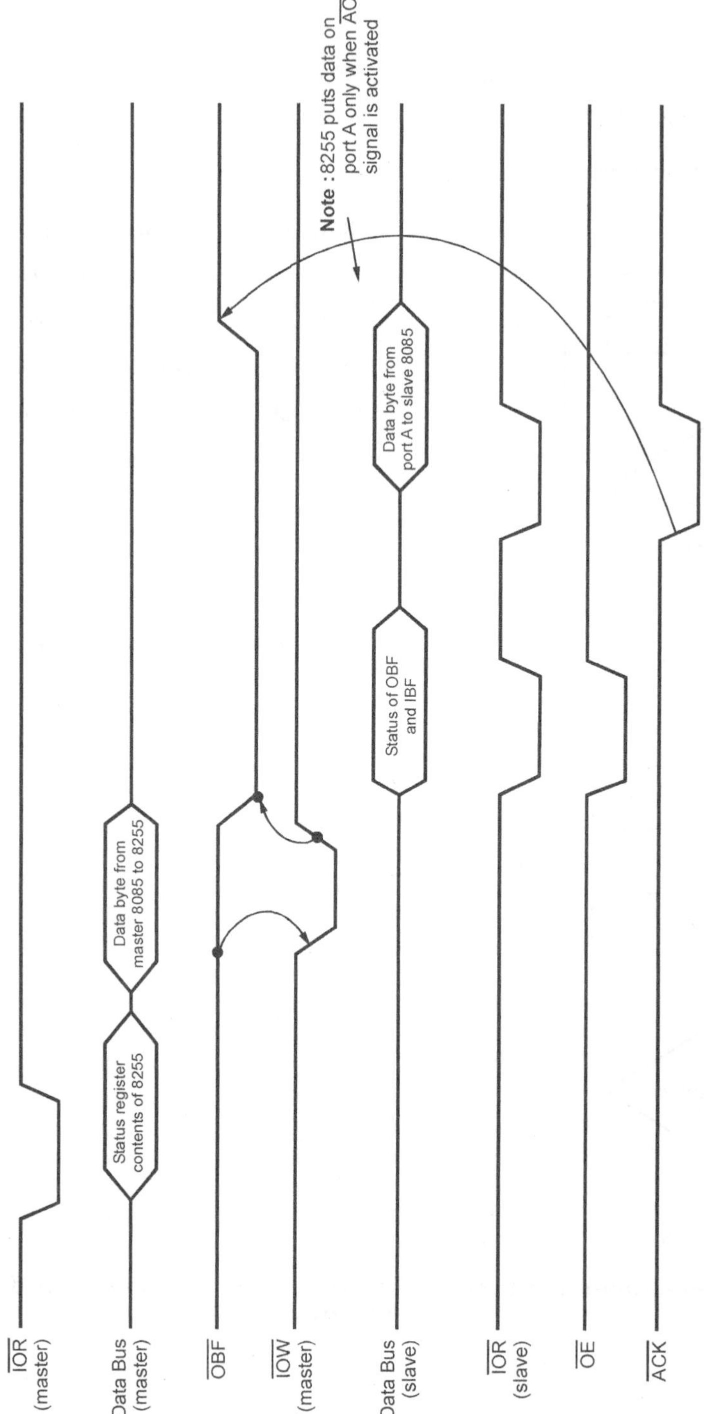

Fig. 11.25 Timing diagram for the transfer data from master to slave

Flowchart

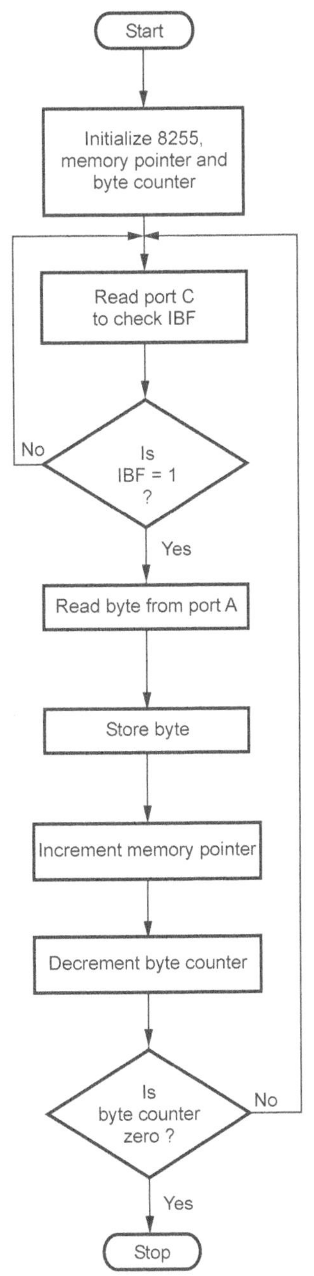

Transfer of data from slave 8085 to master 8085

Let us see the flowchart, program and timing diagram for master and slave 8085 to transfer data bytes from slave 8085 to master 8085.

Program

```
        MVI A, C0H      ; [Initialize 8255
        OUT FFH         ; in mode 2]
        LXI H, 2000H    ; Initialize memory pointer
        MVI B, 0AH      ; Initialize byte counter
AGAIN:  IN FEH          ; Read port C
        ANI 20H         ; Mask All bits except D5 i.e., IBF
        JZ AGAIN        ; if IBF = 0, check it again
        IN FCH          ; Read byte from port A
        INX H           ; Increment memory pointer
        DCR B           ; Decrement counter
        JNZ AGAIN       ; If all bytes are not
                        ; transferred go back to
                        ; transfer the next byte
        HLT             ; Stop
```

Fig. 11.26 Flowchart and program for master 8085 for transfer of data from slave to master

Flowchart

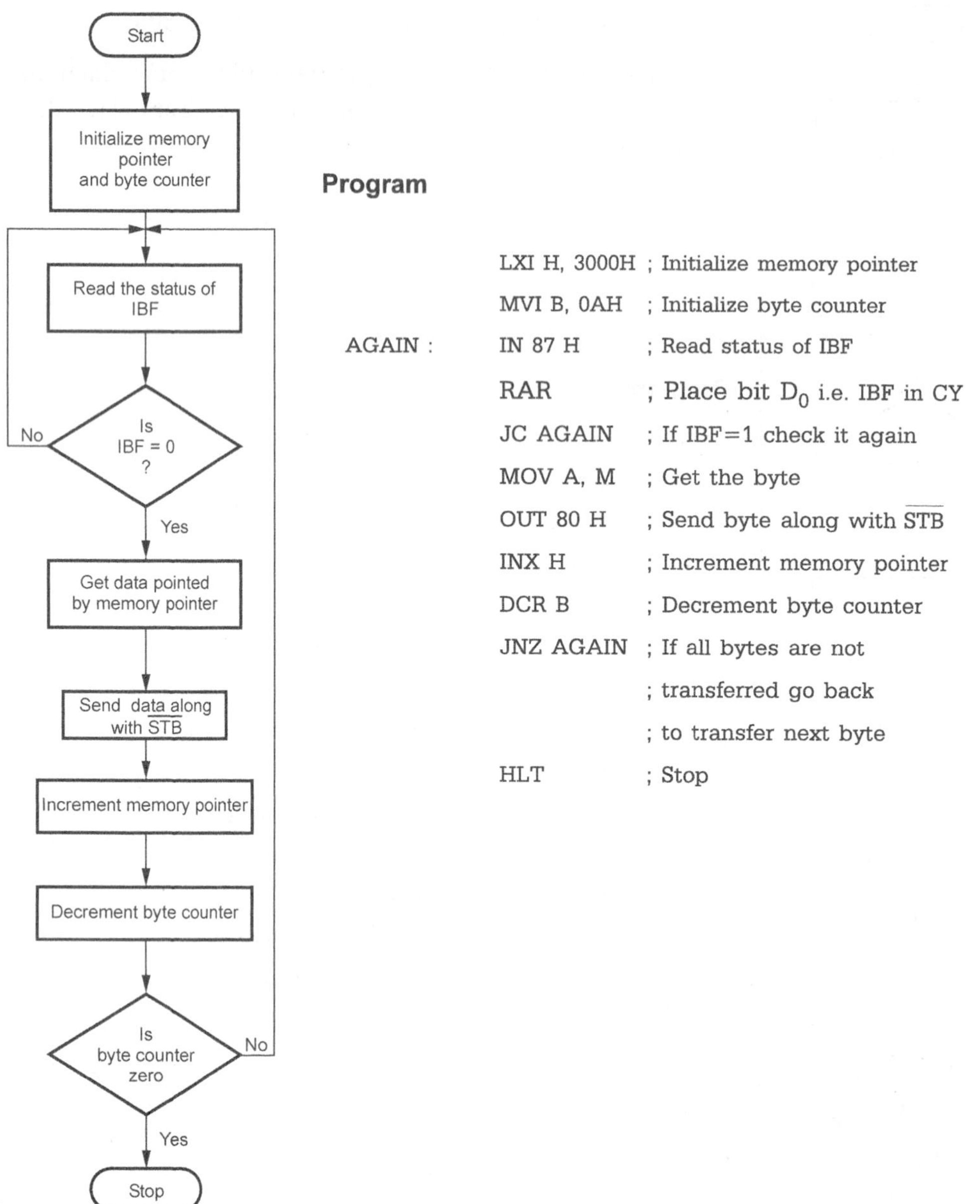

Program

```
         LXI H, 3000H ; Initialize memory pointer
         MVI B, 0AH   ; Initialize byte counter
AGAIN :  IN 87 H      ; Read status of IBF
         RAR          ; Place bit D0 i.e. IBF in CY
         JC AGAIN     ; If IBF=1 check it again
         MOV A, M     ; Get the byte
         OUT 80 H     ; Send byte along with STB
         INX H        ; Increment memory pointer
         DCR B        ; Decrement byte counter
         JNZ AGAIN    ; If all bytes are not
                      ; transferred go back
                      ; to transfer next byte
         HLT          ; Stop
```

Fig. 11.27 Flowchart and program for slave 8085 for transfer of data from slave to master

Timing diagram

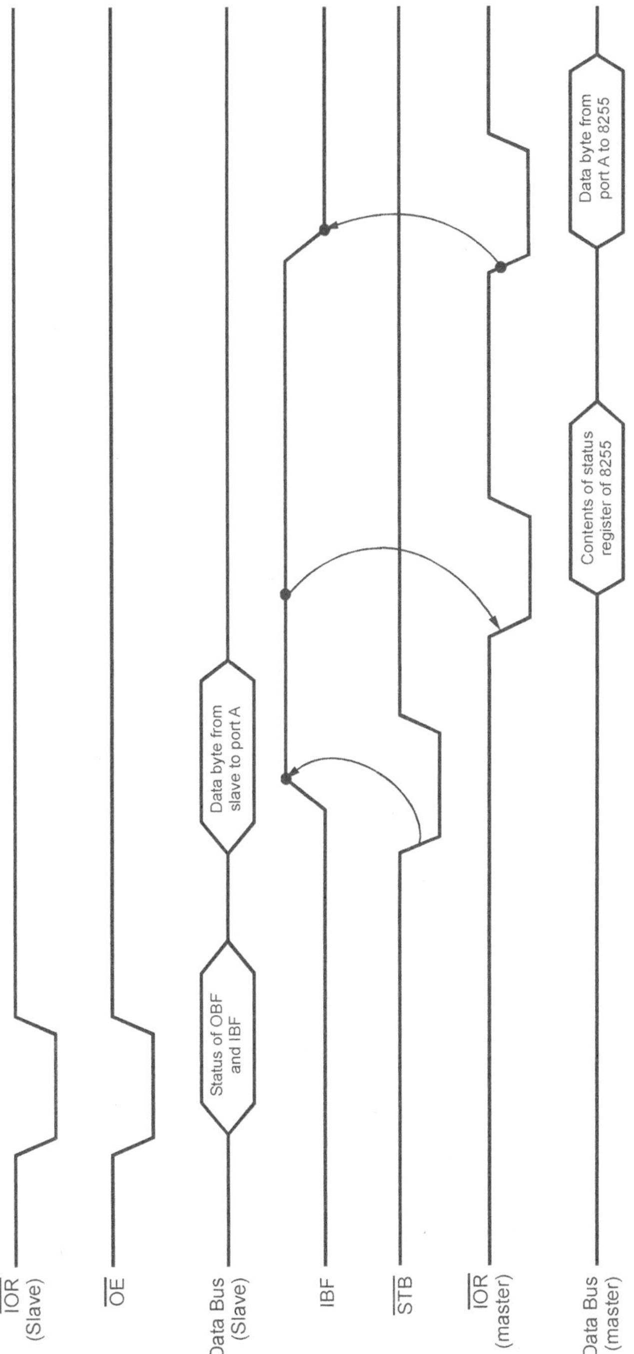

Fig. 11.28 Timing diagram for the transfer of data from slave to master

Review Questions

Section 11.1

Q.1 *What is known as PPI, what is the use of interfacing the same in 8085 ?*

May-09, Marks 4

Section 11.2

Q.1 *List the features of 8255.*

Q.2 *Explain the use of important signals of 8255.*

Section 11.3

Q.1 *Draw and explain the block diagram / architecture of 8255.* **May-06,09, Marks 12**

Section 11.4

Q.1 *Explain in detail about various operating modes of 8255 PPI.*

May-07, Marks 16, Dec.-11, Marks 8

Q.2 *Explain the mode 0 of 8255 in detail.* **Dec.-04, Marks 16**

Section 11.5

Q.1 *Show the control word format of 8255 and explain how each bit is programmed.*

May-04, Marks 4

Q.2 *Explain the bit set/reset mode of 8255.*

Q.3 *Write the format of control word for 8255 PPI.* **Dec.-08, Marks 2**

Section 11.6

Q.1 *Explain the mode 1 input mode operation of 8255 in detail.* **May-04, Marks 8**

Q.2 *With neat block diagram, explain the operating modes of 8255 PPI.*

May-11, Marks 8

Q.3 *Explain the operation of 8255 PPI Port A programmed as input and output in mode 1 with necessary handshaking signals.* **May-11, Marks 8**

Section 11.7

Q.1 *Explain how the 8255 A programmable peripheral interface chip can be used with the 8085 microprocessor for reading and writing parallel data from and to I/O devices.*

Dec.-10, Marks 16

Section 11.8

Q.1 *Using model, write a program to communicate between two microprocessors using 8255.* **May-05, Marks 10**

Two Marks Questions with Answers

Q.1 ***What are the basic modes of operation of 8255 ?***

Ans. : There are two basic modes of operation of 8255, They are :

1. I/O mode. 2. BSR mode.

Q.2 ***Write the features of mode 0 in 8255 ?***

Ans. :

1. Two 8-bit ports (port A and port B) and two 4-bit ports (port C upper and lower) are available. The two 4-bit ports can be combined used as a third 8-bit port.
2. Any port can be used as an input or output port.
3. Output ports are latched. Input ports are not latched.
4. A maximum of four ports are available so that overall 16 I/O configurations are possible.

Q.3 ***What are the features used mode 1 in 8255 ?***

Ans. : Two groups-group A and group B are available for strobed data transfer.

1. Each group contains one 8-bit data I/O port and one 4-bit control/data port.
2. The 8-bit data port can be either used as input or output port. The inputs and outputs both are latched.
3. Out of 8-bit port C, PC0-PC2 is used to generate control signals for port B and PC3 = PC5 are used to generate control signals for port A. The lines PC6, PC7 may be used as independent data lines.

Q.4 ***What are the signals used in input control signal and output control signal ?***

Ans. : **Input control signal** :

1. STB (Strobe input)
2. IBF (Input buffer full)
3. INTR(Interrupt request)

Output control signal

1. OBF (Output buffer full)
2. ACK (Acknowledge input)
3. INTR(Interrupt request)

Q.5 *What are the features used mode 2 in 8255 ?*

Ans. : The single 8-bit port in-group A is available.

1. The 8-bit port is bi-directional and additionally a 5-bit control port is available.
2. Three I/O lines are available at port C, viz PC2-PC0.
3. Inputs and outputs are both latched.
4. The 5-bit control port C (PC3=PC7) is used for generating/accepting handshake signals for the 8-bit data transfer on port A.

Q.6 *List the operation modes of 8255.*

Ans. : a) I/O Mode

i. Mode 0-Simple Input/Output.

ii. Mode 1-Strobed Input/Output (Handshake mode)

iii. Mode 2-Strobed bidirectional mode

b) Bit Set/Reset Mode.

Q.7 *What is a control word ?*

Ans. : It is a word stored in a register (control register) used to control the operation of a program digital device.

Q.8 *What is the purpose of control word written to control register in 8255 ?*

Ans. : The control words written to control register specify an I/O function for each I/O port. The bit D7 of the control word determines either the I/O function of the BSR function.

Q.9 *What is the size of ports in 8255 ?*

Ans. : Port-A : 8-bits

Port-B : 8-bits

Port-CU : 4-bits

Port-CL : 4-bits

Q.10 *What is the use of stepper motor ?*

Ans. : A stepper motor is a device used to obtain an accurate position control of rotating shafts. A stepper motor employs rotation of its shaft in terms of steps, rather than continuous rotation as in case of A.C. or D.C. motor.

Q.11 *Define PPI.* **Dec.-04, May-06**

Ans. : PPI means programmable parallel interface.

Q.12 *Write down the function of $\overline{OBF}$ in 8255.* **Dec.-05**

Ans. : $\overline{OBF}$ is an active low output which indicates that the CPU has written data into port.

Q.13 ***Write the BSR control words to set PC0 and to reset PC4 in 8255.*** **Dec.-07**

Ans. : **BSR control word to set PC0**

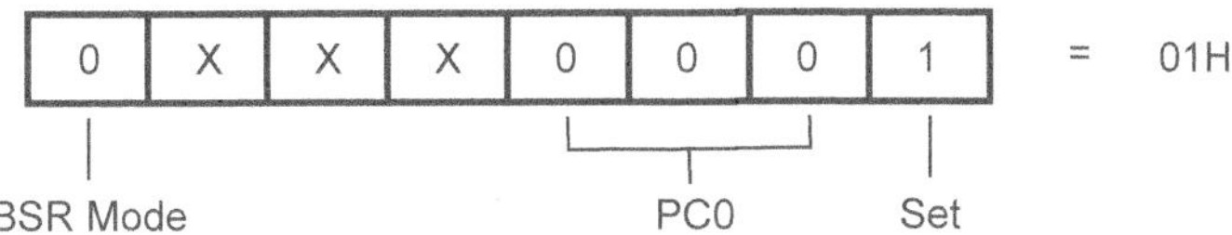

BSR control word to reset PC4

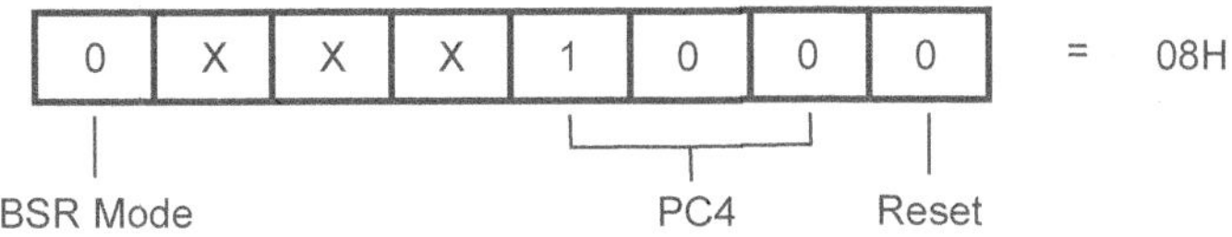

Q.14 ***What is the bit set reset mode of 8255 PPI ?*** **May-08, Dec.-09**

Ans. : The eight possible combinations of the states of bits D_3 - D_1 (B_2 B_1 B_0) in the Bit. Set-Reset format (BSR) determine particular bit in PC_0 - PC_7 being set or reset as per the status of bit D_0.

Q.15 ***Write the format of control word for 8255 PPI.*** **Dec.-08**

Ans. : Refer section 11.5.

Q.16 ***Write the sequence of bit pattern for a four phase stepper motor in half stepping mode of control.*** **Dec.-08**

Ans. : Refer sections 11.9.2 and 11.20.7.

Q.17 ***What are the ports available in 8255 ? What is the advantage of the third port ?*** **May-09**

Ans. : The ports available in 8255 are : Port A, Port B and Port C. The advantages of third port, Port C is that it can be programmed for bit set/reset operation.

Q.18 ***What is handshaking and what are handshake signals ?***

Ans. : Handshaking is the process of using signals to establish conditional data transfer. Devices provide signals called handshake signals to inform each other if they have any data available to send or if they are ready to accept data.

Q.19 ***Specify the bit of a control word for the 8255, which differentiates between I/O mode and the BSR mode.***

Ans. : Bit D_7 in the control word. D_7 = 0 indicates bit set/reset mode and D_7 = 1 indicates I/O mode.

Q.20 ***What is the importance of handshake signals ?***

Ans. : Handshake signals are used between two communicating devices to inform each other if they have any data available to send or if they are ready to accept data. These are very useful when two devices operate with different speed.

Q.21 ***What is the function of 8255 ?***

Ans. : The function of 8255 is to provide microprocessor three different ways of parallel data transfer :

- Simple input/output
- Input/output with handshake
- Bi-directional I/O data transfer.

❑❑❑

12 PIC - 8259

Contents

12.1 8259A Programmable Interrupt Controller

Interrupts can be used for a variety of applications. Each of these interrupt applications requires a separate interrupt input. If we are working with an 8085 microprocessor we get TRAP, RST7.5, RST6.5, RST5.5, and INTR interrupt inputs. For applications where we have multiple interrupt sources (more than five), we have to use external device called a Priority Interrupt Controller (PIC). By connecting such a device it is possible to increase the interrupt handling capacity of the microprocessor. Fig. 12.1 shows the connection between 8085 and 8259A. The 8259A is a commonly used priority interrupt controller, which is specifically designed for use with interrupt signals INTR and $\overline{\text{INTA}}$ of Intel series. It is packaged in a 28 pin DIP. It uses NMOS technology and requires a single + 5 V supply.

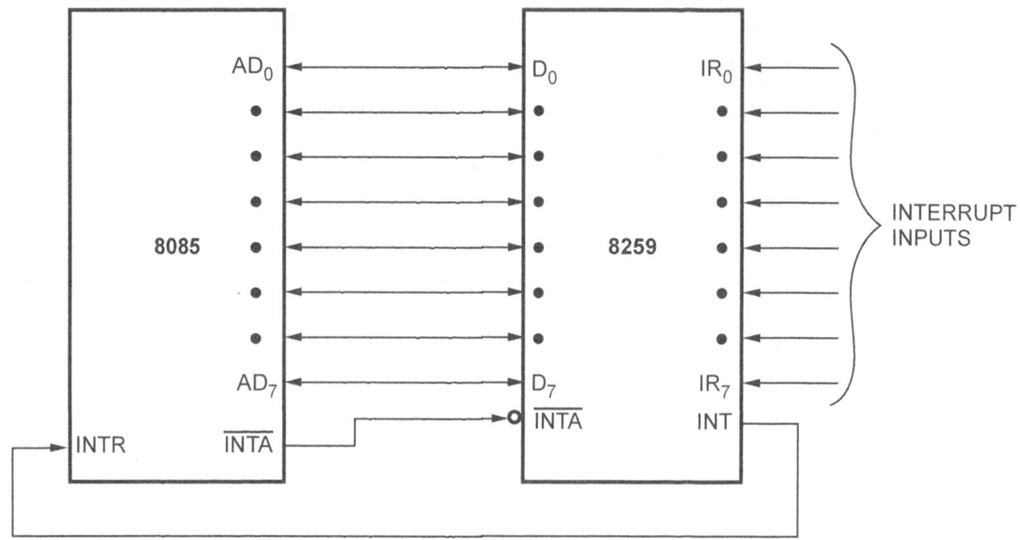

Fig. 12.1 Connection between 8085 and 8259A

12.2 Features of 8259A

1. It can manage eight priority interrupts. This is equivalent to providing eight interrupt pins on the processor in place of INTR pin.
2. It is possible to locate vector table for these additional interrupts any where in the memory map. However, all eight interrupts are spaced at the interval of either four or eight locations.
3. By cascading nine 8259s it is possible to get 64 priority interrupts.
4. Interrupt mask register makes it possible to mask individual interrupt request.
5. The 8259A can be programmed to accept either the level triggered or the edge triggered interrupt request.

6. With the help of 8259A user can get the information of pending interrupts, in-service interrupts and masked interrupts.
7. The 8259A is designed to minimize the software and real time overhead in handling multi-level priority interrupts.

12.3 Block Diagram of 8259A

Nov./Dec.-09

Fig. 12.2 shows the internal block diagram of the 8259A. It includes eight blocks : data bus buffer, read/write logic, control logic, three registers (IRR, ISR and IMR), priority resolver, and cascade buffer.

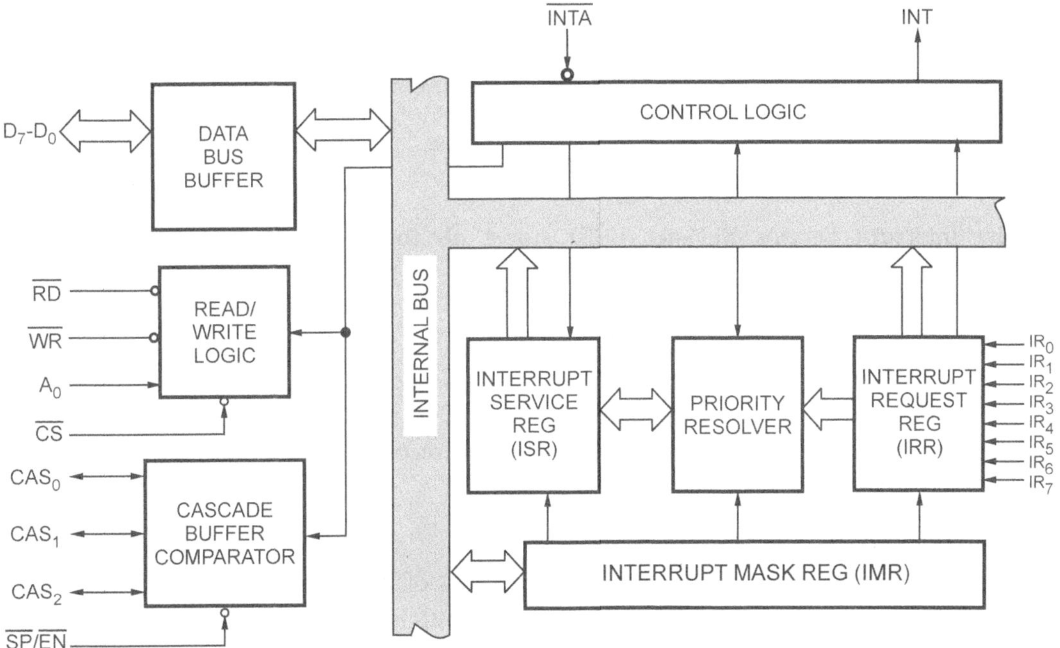

Fig. 12.2 Block diagram of 8259A

Data Bus Buffer

The data bus buffer allows the 8085 to send control words to the 8259A and read a status word from the 8259A. The 8-bit data bus buffer also allows the 8259A to send interrupt opcode and address of the interrupt service subroutine to the 8085.

Read/Write Logic

The $\overline{RD}$ and $\overline{WR}$ inputs control the data flow on the data bus when the device is selected by asserting its chip select ($\overline{CS}$) input low.

Control Logic

This block has an input and an output line. If the 8259A is properly enabled, the interrupt request will cause the 8259A to assert its INT output pin high. If this pin is connected to the INTR pin of an 8085 and if the 8085 Interrupt Enable (IE) flag is set, then this high signal will cause the 8085 to respond INTR as explained earlier.

Interrupt Request Register (IRR)

The IRR is used to store all the interrupt levels which are requesting the service. The eight interrupt inputs set corresponding bits of the Interrupt Request Register upon service request.

Interrupt Service Register (ISR)

The Interrupt Service Register (ISR) stores all the levels that are currently being serviced.

Interrupt Mask Register (IMR)

Interrupt Mask Register (IMR) stores the masking bits of the interrupt lines to be masked. This register can be programmed by an Operation Command Word (OCW). An interrupt which is masked by software will not be recognised and serviced even if it sets the corresponding bits in the IRR.

Priority Resolver

The priority resolver determines the priorities of the bits set in the IRR. The bit corresponding to the highest priority interrupt input is set in the ISR during the $\overline{INTA}$ input.

Cascade Buffer Comparator

This section generates control signals necessary for cascade operations. It also generates Buffer-Enable signals. As stated earlier, the 8259 can be cascaded with other 8259s in order to expand the interrupt handling capacity to sixty-four levels. In such a case, the former is called a **master**, and the latter are called **slaves**. The 8259 can be set up as a master or a slave by the $\overline{SP}/\overline{EN}$ pin.

CAS_0 - CAS_2

For a master 8259, the CAS_0-CAS_2 pins are output pins, and for slave 8259s, these are input pins. When the 8259 is a master (that is, when it accepts interrupt requests from other 8259s), the CALL opcode is generated by the master in response to the first $\overline{INTA}$. The vector address must be released by the slave 8259. The master sends an identification code of three-bits to select one out of the eight possible slave 8259s on the CAS_0-CAS_2 lines. The slave 8259s accept these three signals as inputs (on their CAS_0 - CAS_2 pins) and compare the code sent by the master with the codes assigned to them during initialisation. The slave thus selected (which had originally placed an interrupt request to the master 8259) then puts the address of the interrupt service routine during the second and third $\overline{INTA}$ pulses from the MPU.

$\overline{SP}$ / $\overline{EN}$ (Slave Program / Enable Buffer)

The $\overline{SP}/\overline{EN}$ signal is tied high for the master. However it is grounded for the slave.

In large systems where buffers are used to drive the data bus, the data sent by the 8259 in response to $\overline{INTA}$ cannot be accessed by the MPU (due to the data bus buffer being disabled). If an 8259 is used in the buffered mode (buffered or non-buffered modes of operation can be specified at the time of initialising the 8259), the $\overline{SP}/\overline{EN}$ pin is used as an output which can be used to enable the system data bus buffer whenever the data bus outputs of 8259 are enabled (i.e. when it is ready to send data).

Thus, in non-buffered mode, the $\overline{SP}/\overline{EN}$ pin of an 8259 is used to specify whether the 8259 is to operate as a master or as a slave, and in the buffered mode, the $\overline{SP}/\overline{EN}$ pin is used as an output to enable the data bus buffer of the system.

12.4 Interrupt Sequence with 8085

The events occur as follows in an 8085 system :

1. One or more of the INTERRUPT REQUEST lines (IR_0-IR_7) are raised high, setting the corresponding IRR bit(s).
2. The priority resolver checks three registers : The IRR for interrupt requests, the IMR for masking bits, and the ISR for the interrupt request being served. It resolves the priority and sets the INT high when it is appropriate to do so.
3. In response to the INTR signal, 8085 completes current instruction cycle and executes interrupt acknowledge cycle, thus giving an $\overline{INTA}$ pulse.
4. Upon receiving an $\overline{INTA}$ from the 8085, the highest priority ISR bit is set and the corresponding IRR bit is reset. Then 8259A places the opcode for CALL instruction on the data bus.
5. This CALL instruction initiates two more interrupt acknowledge cycles.
6. These two interrupt acknowledge cycles allow the 8259 to release **preprogrammed** subroutine address onto the data bus. In response to second interrupt acknowledge pulse, 8259 places a lower byte of interrupt subroutine address and in response to

third interrupt acknowledge pulse 8259 places a higher byte of the subroutine address.

7. This completes the interrupt cycle. In the AEOI (Automatic End of Interrupt) mode the ISR bit is reset at the end of the second $\overline{INTA}$ pulse. Otherwise, the ISR bit remains set until the issue of an appropriate EOI command at the end of the interrupt subroutine.

12.5 Priority Modes and Other Features

The various modes of operation of the 8259 are : **1.** Fully Nested Mode, **2.** Special Fully Nested Mode (SFNM) **3.** Rotating Priority Mode, **4.** Special Masked Mode, and **5.** Polled Mode.

1. Fully Nested Mode (FNM) :

After initialization, the 8259A operates in fully nested mode so it is called **default mode**. The 8259 continues to operate in the Fully Nested Mode until the mode is changed through Operation Command Words. In this mode, IR_0 has highest priority and IR_7 has lowest priority. When the interrupt is acknowledged, it sets the corresponding bit in ISR. This bit will inhibit all interrupts of the **same or lower level,** however it will accept higher priority interrupt requests. The vector address corresponding to this interrupt is then sent. The bit in the ISR will remain set until an EOI command is issued by the microprocessor at the end of interrupt service routine. But if AEOI (Automatic End of Interrupt) bit is set, the bit in the ISR resets at the trailing edge of the last $\overline{INTA}$.

End of Interrupt (EOI)

1. The ISR bit can be reset by an End of Interrupt command issued by the MPU, usually just before exiting from the interrupt routine.
2. In the Fully Nested Mode, the highest level in the ISR would necessarily correspond to the last interrupt acknowledged and serviced. In such a case, a non-specific EOI command may be issued by the MPU.
3. However, if the FNM is not used, the 8259 may not be able to determine the last interrupt acknowledged. In such a case, a specific EOI command will have to be issued by the MPU.
4. It should be noted that in the cascade mode, the EOI command must be issued twice, once for the master and once for the slave.

Automatic End of Interrupt (AEOI)

If the AEOI mode is set, the 8259 will perform a **non-specific EOI** on its own on the trailing edge of the third $\overline{INTA}$ pulse. The AEOI mode can only be used for a **master 8259** and not for a slave.

2. Special Fully Nested Mode (SFNM)

In the FNM, on the acknowledgement of an interrupt, further interrupts from the same level are disabled. Consider a large system which uses cascaded 8259s and where the interrupt levels within each slave have to be considered. An interrupt request input to a slave, in turn causes the slave to place an interrupt request to the master on one of the master's inputs. Further interrupts to the slave will cause the slave to place requests to the master on the same input to the master, but these will not be recognised because further interrupts on the same input level are disabled by the master.

The Special Fully Nested Mode (SFNM) is used to avoid this problem. The SFNM is set up by ICW4 during initialisation. It is similar to the FNM except for the following differences:

1. When an interrupt request from a slave is being serviced, the slave is allowed to place further requests if these requests are of a higher priority than the request currently being serviced. These interrupts are recognised by the master and it initiates interrupt requests to the MPU.
2. Before exiting from the interrupt service routine, a non-specific EOI must be sent to the slave and its ISR must be read to determine if it was the only interrupt to the slave. If the ISR is empty, a non-specific EOI command can be sent to the master. If it is not empty, it implies that the same IR level input to the master is to be serviced again due to more than one interrupts being presented to the slave, and an **EOI must not** be sent to the master.

3. Rotating Priority Mode

The Rotating Priority mode can be set in i) Automatic Rotation, and ii) Specific Rotation.

i) Automatic Rotation

In this mode, a device, after being serviced, receives the lowest priority. The device just been serviced, will receive the seventh priority. Here IR_3 has just been serviced.

IR_0	IR_1	IR_2	IR_3	IR_4	IR_5	IR_6	IR_7
4	5	6	7	0	1	2	3

ii) Specific Rotation

In the Automatic Rotation mode, the interrupt request last serviced is assigned the lowest priority, whereas in the Specific Rotation mode, the lowest priority can be assigned to any interrupt input (IR_0 to IR_7) thus fixes all other priorities.

For example if the lowest priority is assigned to IR_2, other priorities are as shown below.

IR_0	IR_1	IR_2	IR_3	IR_4	IR_5	IR_6	IR_7
5	6	7	0	1	2	3	4

4. Special Mask Mode

If any interrupt is in service, then the corresponding bit is set in ISR and the lower priority interrupts are inhibited. Some applications may require an interrupt service routine to dynamically alter the system priority structure during its execution under software control. For example, the routine may wish to inhibit lower priority requests for a portion of its execution but enable some of them for another portion. In these cases, we have to go for special mask mode. In the special mask mode it inhibits further interrupts at that level and enables interrupts from all other levels (lower as well as higher) that **are not masked.** Thus any interrupt may be selectively enabled by loading the mask register.

5. Poll Mode

In this mode the INT output is **not used.** The microprocessor checks the status of interrupt requests by issuing poll command. The microprocessor reads contents of 8259A after issuing poll command. During this read operation the 8259A provides **polled word** and sets ISR bit of highest priority active interrupt request FORMAT.

I	X	X	X	X	W_2	W_1	W_0

I = 1 → One or more interrupt requests activated.

I = 0 → No interrupt request activated.

W_2 W_1 W_0 → Binary code of highest priority active interrupt request.

12.6 Programming the 8259A

The 8259A requires two types of command words. Initialization Command Words (ICWs) and Operational Command Words (OCWs). The 8259A can be initialized with four ICWs; the first two are compulsory, and the other two are optional based on the modes being used. These words must be issued in a given sequence. After initialization, the 8259A can be set up to operate in various modes by using three different OCWs; however, they are not necessary to be issued in a specific sequence. Refer Fig. 12.3 for initialization flowchart.

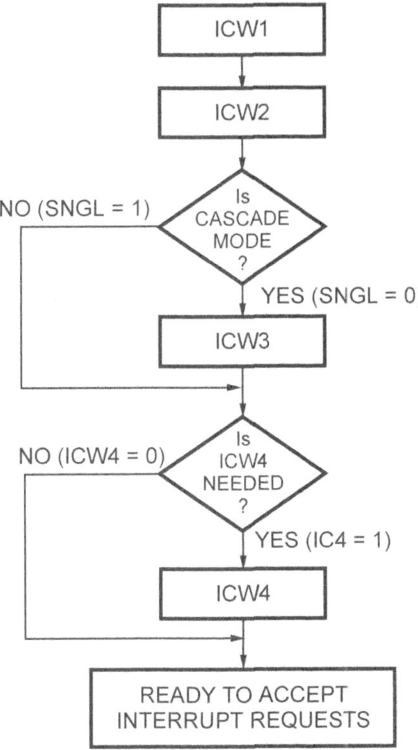

Fig. 12.3 Initialization flowchart

Initialization Command Word 1 (ICW1)

Fig. 12.4 shows the Initialization Command Word 1(ICW1). A write command issued to the 8259 with $A_0 = 0$ and $D_4 = 1$ is interpreted as ICW1, which starts the initialization sequence. It specifies,

1. Single or multiple 8259As in the system.
2. 4 or 8 bit interval between the interrupt vector locations.
3. The address bits A_7 - A_5 of the CALL instruction. (3 bits of lower byte address of CALL are given by user, rest bits are inserted by 8259A).
4. Edge triggered or level triggered interrupts.
5. ICW4 is needed or not.

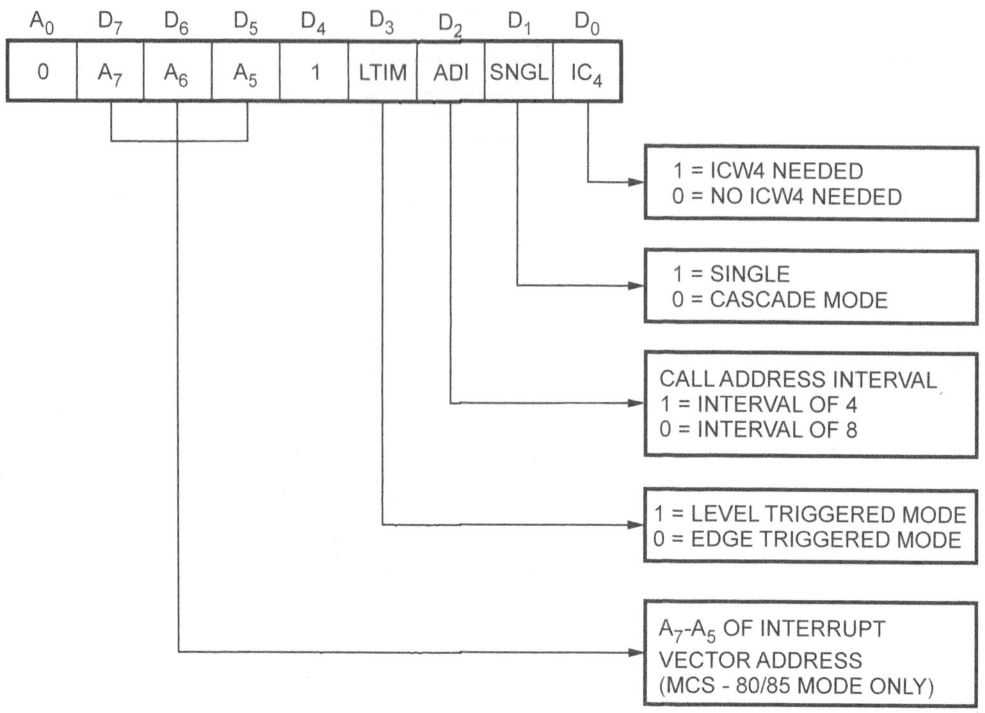

Fig. 12.4 Initialization command word 1 (ICW1)

Initialization Command Word 2 (ICW2)

Fig. 12.5 shows the Initialization Command Word 2 (ICW2).

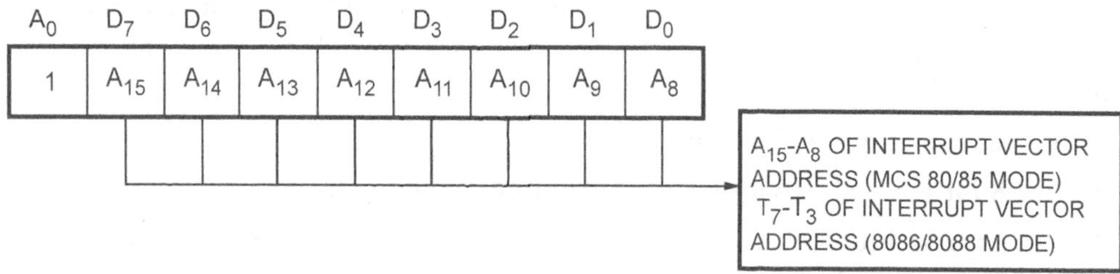

Fig. 12.5 Initialization command word 2 (ICW2)

A write command following ICW1, with A_0 = 1 is interpreted as ICW2. This is used to load the high order byte of the interrupt vector address of all the interrupts.

Initialization Command Word 3 (ICW3)

ICW3 is required only if there is more than one 8259 in the system and if they are cascaded. An ICW3 operation loads a slave register in the 8259. The format of the byte to be loaded as an ICW3 for a master 8259 or a slave is shown in the Fig. 12.6. For master, each bit in ICW3 is used to specify whether it has a slave 8259 attached to it on its corresponding IR (Interrupt Request) input. For slave, bits D_0 - D_2 of ICW3 are used to assign a slave identification code (slave ID) to the 8259.

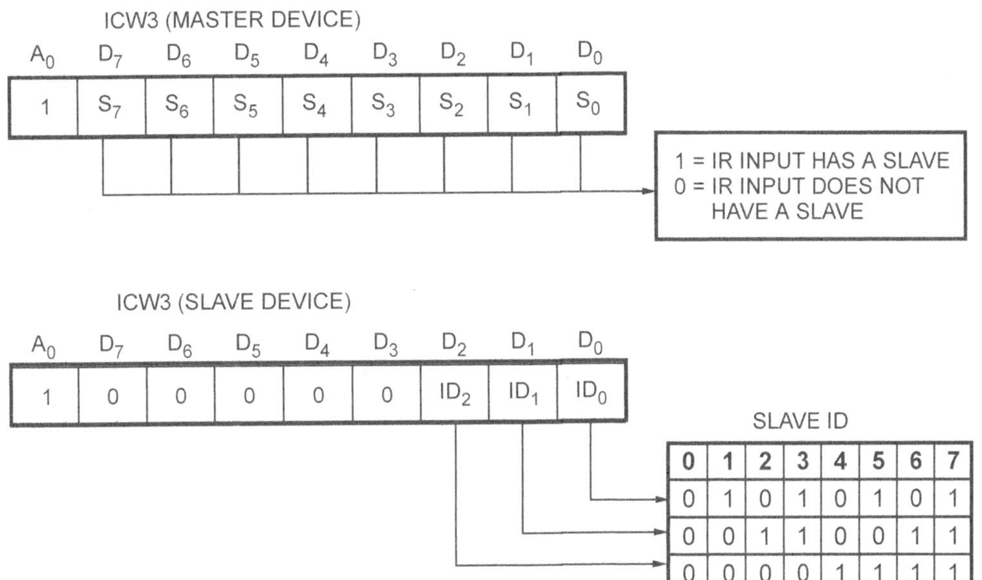

Fig. 12.6 Initialization command word 3 (ICW3)

Initialization Command Word 4 (ICW4)

It is loaded only if the D_0 bit of ICW1 is set. The format of ICW4 is shown in Fig. 12.7. It specifies,

1. Whether to use special fully nested mode or non special fully nested mode.
2. Whether to use buffered mode or non buffered mode.
3. Whether to use Automatic EOI or Normal EOI.
4. MPU used, 8086/8088 or 8085.

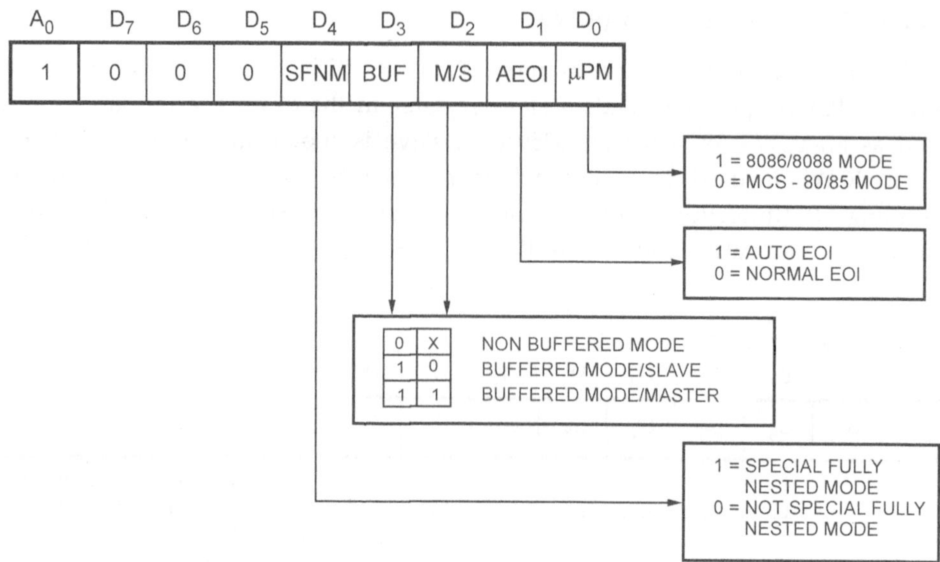

Fig. 12.7 Initialization command word 4 (ICW4)

Operation Command Words (OCWs)

After initialisation, the 8259 is ready to process interrupt requests. However, during operation, it might be necessary to change the mode of processing the interrupts. Operation Command Words (OCWs) are used for this purpose. They may be loaded anytime after the initialisation of 8259 to dynamically alter the priority modes.

Operation Command Word 1 (OCW 1)

A Write command to the 8259 with A_0 = 1 (after ICW2) is interpreted as OCW1. OCW1 is used for enabling or disabling the recognition of specific interrupt requests by programming the IMR.

M = 1 indicates that the interrupt is to be masked, and M = 0 indicates that it is to be unmasked as shown in Fig. 12.8.

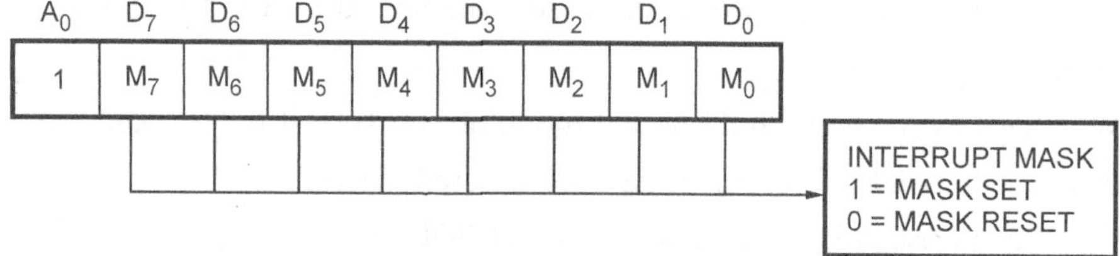

Fig. 12.8 Operation command word 1 (OCW 1)

Operation Command Word 2 (OCW2)

A Write command with A_0 = 1 and D_4 D_3 = 00 is interpreted as OCW2. The R (Rotate), SL (Select-Level), EOI bits control the Rotate and End of Interrupt Modes and combinations of the two. Fig. 12.9 shows the Operation Command Word format. L_2 - L_0 are used to specify the interrupt level to be acted upon when the SL bit is active.

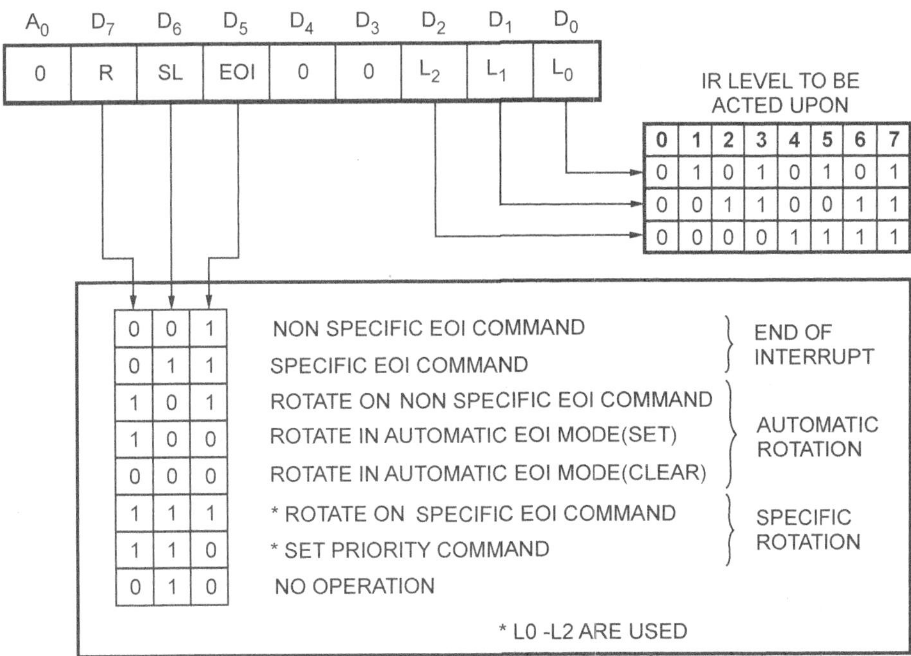

Fig. 12.9 Operation command word 2 (OCW2)

Operation Command Word 3 (OCW3)

OCW3 is used to read the status of the registers, and to set or reset the Special Mask and Polled modes. Fig. 12.10 shows format of operation command word 3.

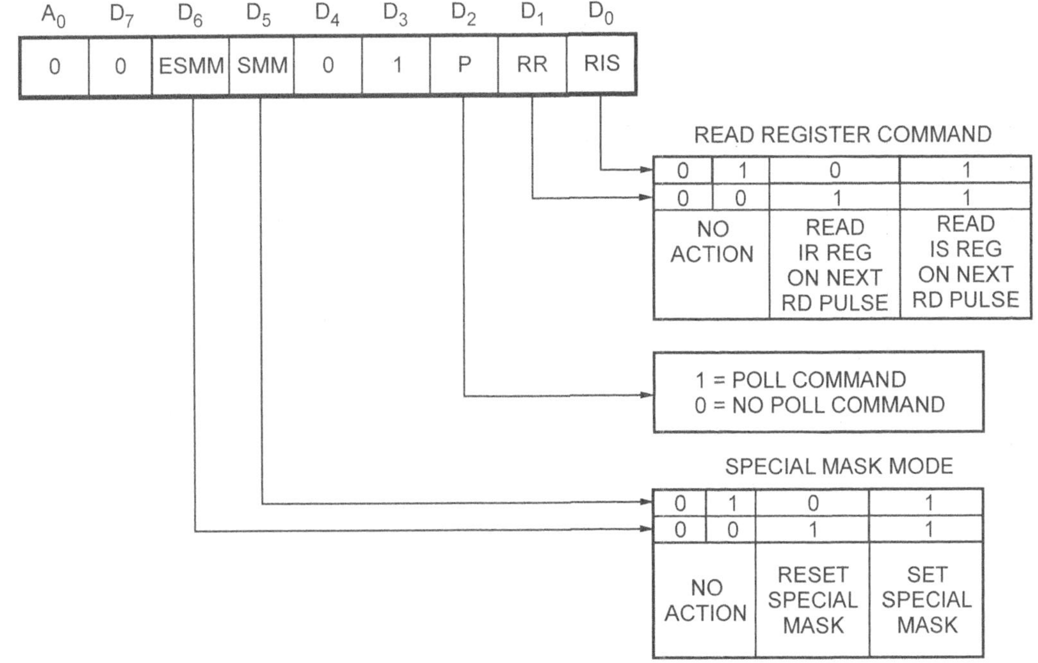

Fig. 12.10 Operation command word 3 (OCW3)

8259 Status Read Operations

The status of the Interrupt Request Register, the Interrupt-Service Register, and the Interrupt Mask Register of the 8259 may be read by issuing appropriate Read commands as described further.

IRR Status Read

An OCW3 with RR (Read Register) = 1 and RIS (Read ISR) = 0 set up the 8259 for a status read of the Interrupt Request Register.

When the 8259 is not in the Polled mode, after it is set up for an IRR status read operation, all Read commands with $A_0 = 1$ cause the 8259 to send the IRR status word.

ISR Status Read

An OCW3 with RR = 1 and ISR = 1 sets up the 8259 for a status read of the Interrupt-Service Register. A subsequent read command issued to the 8259 will cause the 8259 to send the contents of the ISR onto the data bus.

IMR Status Read

A Read command issued to the 8259 with $A_0 = 1$ (with $\overline{RD} = 0$, $\overline{CS} = 0$) causes the 8259 to put the contents of the Interrupt Mask Register on the data bus. OCW3 is not required for a status read of the IMR.

As described earlier, the sequence shown in flowchart must be followed to initialize 8259A. According to this flowchart, an ICW1 and an ICW2 must be sent to any 8259A in the system. If the system has any slave 8259As (cascade mode), then an ICW3 must be sent to the master, and a different ICW3 must be sent to the slave. If the system is an 8086, or if you want to specify certain special conditions, then you have to send an ICW4 to the master and to each slave. To have better understanding the initialisation sequences for different specifications are given in the next section.

Note : It is assumed that A_0 of the system bus is connected to the A_0 of the 8259A. So the internal addresses are correspond to 0 and 1. It is also assumed that the base address of the device is 40H. So the two system addresses for the 8259A are 40H and 41H.

Example 12.1 : *Write the initialization instructions for 8259A interrupt controller to meet the following specifications :*

1. Edge triggered, single and ICW4 are not needed.
2. Mask interrupts IR_1 and IR_3.
3. Interrupt vector address for IR_0 is 6280H and
4. Call address intervals are four bytes.

Solution :

ICW1

A_7	A_6	A_5	1	LTM	ADI	SNGL	IC_4	
1	0	0	1	0	1	1	0	= 96H

ICW2

In an 8085 system, ICW2 is used to tell the 8259A the higher byte of the interrupt service routine address to be sent in response to an interrupt signal on the IR0 input.

B_7	B_6	B_5	B_4	B_3	B_2	B_1	B_0	
0	1	1	0	0	0	1	0	= 62H

ICW3

Since we are not using a slave in our example, we don't need to send an ICW3.

OCW1

An OCW1 must be sent to an 8259A to unmask any IR inputs. For our example we want to mask IR_1 and IR_3, so we put 1s in these two bits and 0s in the rest of the bits.

M_7	M_6	M_5	M_4	M_3	M_2	M_1	M_0	
0	0	0	0	1	0	1	0	= 0AH

Program :

```
MVI A, 96H      ; Edge triggered, single, interval 4, ICW4 not needed
OUT 40H         ; Send ICW1
MVI A, 62H      ; Higher byte of ISR.
OUT 41H         ; Send ICW2
MVI A, 0AH      ; OCW1 to mask IR1 and IR3
OUT 41H         ; Send OCW1
```

Example 12.2 : *Write the initialization instructions for master and slave configuration to meet the following specifications :*

1. The INTR of slave is routed through IR_2 of the master 8259A to the 8085.
2. Master and slave are both level triggered.
3. Master Interrupt vector address for IR_0 is 6280H.
4. Slave Interrupt vector address for IR_0 is 7280H.
5. Modes : automatic rotation and auto end of interrupt.
6. Addresses of the master are 40H and 41H and the slave are 80H and 81H.
7. Buffers are not used.

Solution :

Initialization Command Words for Master

ICW1 (master)

A_7	A_6	A_5	1	LTM	ADI	SNGL	IC_4	
1	0	0	1	1	0	0	1	= 99H

ICW2 (master)

B_7	B_6	B_5	B_4	B_3	B_2	B_1	B_0	
0	1	1	0	0	0	1	0	= 62H

ICW3 (master)

S_7	S_6	S_5	S_4	S_3	S_2	S_1	S_0	
0	0	0	0	0	1	0	0	= 04H

ICW4 (master)

0	0	0	SFNM	BUF	M/S	AEIO	μPM	
0	0	0	0	0	0	1	0	= 02H

Program :

```
MVI A,99H      ; level triggered, cascaded, ICW4 needed
OUT 40H        ; send ICW1 (master)
MVI A,62H      ; Higher byte of ISR
OUT 41H        ; send ICW2 (master)
MVI A,04H      ; slave at IR2
OUT 42H        ; send ICW3 (master)
MVI A,02H      ; ICW4, 8085 mode, and set AEOI
OUT 41H        ; send ICW4 (master)
MVI A,99H      ; level triggered, cascaded, ICW4 needed
OUT 80H        ; send ICW1 (slave)
MVI A,72H      ; Higher byte of ISR
OUT 81H        ; send ICW2 (slave)
MVI A,02H      ; ID for slave connected to IR2
OUT 81H        ; send ICW3 (slave)
MVI A,02H      ; ICW4, 8085 mode
OUT 81H        ; send ICW4
MVI A,80H      ; OCW2 (rotate in auto
```

```
                    ; EOI mode set command)
      OUT 80H       ; send OCW2 (slave)
```

12.7 8259A Interfacing with 8085

Fig. 12.11 shows that how an 8259A can be interfaced with the 8085 microprocessor system.

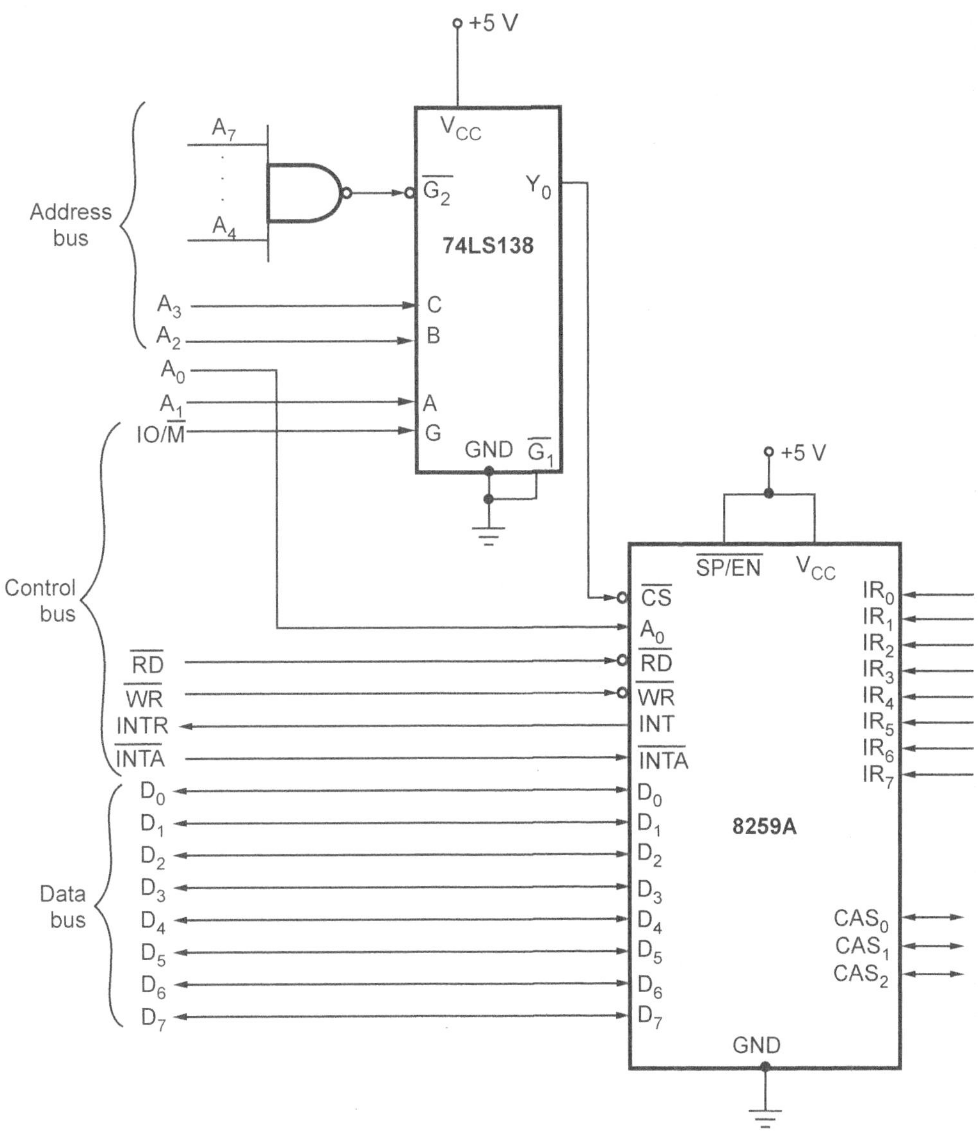

Fig. 12.11 Interface to 8085 system bus

Addressing of 8259A :

A_7	A_6	A_5	A_4	A_3	A_2	A_1	A_0
1	1	1	1	0	0	0	X
F				0/1			

= F0H

= F1H

The 74LS138 address decoder will assert the $\overline{CS}$ input of the 8259A when an I/O base address is F0H or F1H on the address bus. The A_0 input of the 8259A is used to select one of the two internal addresses in the device. A_0 of the 8259A is connected to system line A_0. So the system addresses for the two internal addresses are F0H and F1H. The data lines of an 8259A are connected to the AD_0-AD_7 of the system data bus, $\overline{RD}$ and $\overline{WR}$ signals are connected to the system $\overline{RD}$ and $\overline{WR}$ lines. The interrupt request signal INT from the 8259A is connected to the INTR input of the 8085 and $\overline{INTA}$ from the 8085 is connected to $\overline{INTA}$ of the 8259A. As we are using single 8259A in the system, $\overline{SP}/\overline{EN}$ pin is tied high and CAS_0-CAS_2 lines are left open. The eight IR inputs are available for interrupt signals.

Note : Unused IR inputs should be tied to ground so that a noise pulse cannot accidently cause an interrupt.

12.8 Cascading

April/May-10

The 8259A can be easily interconnected to get multiple interrupts. (See Fig. 12.12 on next page) Fig. 12.12 shows how 8259A can be connected in the cascade mode. In cascade mode one 8259A is configured in Master mode and other should be configured in the Slave mode. In this figure, 8259A-1 is in the master mode and others are in slave mode. Each slave 8259A is identified by the number which is assigned as a part of its initialization. Since the 8085 has only one INTR input, only one of the 8259A INT pins is connected to the 8085 INTR pin. The 8259A connected directly to the 8085 INTR pin is referred to as the master. The INT pins from other 8259As are connected to the IR inputs of the **master** 8259A. These cascaded 8259As are referred to as **slave**. The $\overline{INTA}$ signal is connected to both master and slave 8259A.

The cascade pins CAS_0 to CAS_2 are connected from the master to the corresponding pins of the slave. For the master these pins function as outputs, and for the slave these pins function as inputs. The $\overline{SP}/\overline{EN}$ signal is tied high for the master. However, it is grounded for the slave.

Each 8259A has its own addresses so that command words can be written to it and status bytes read from it.

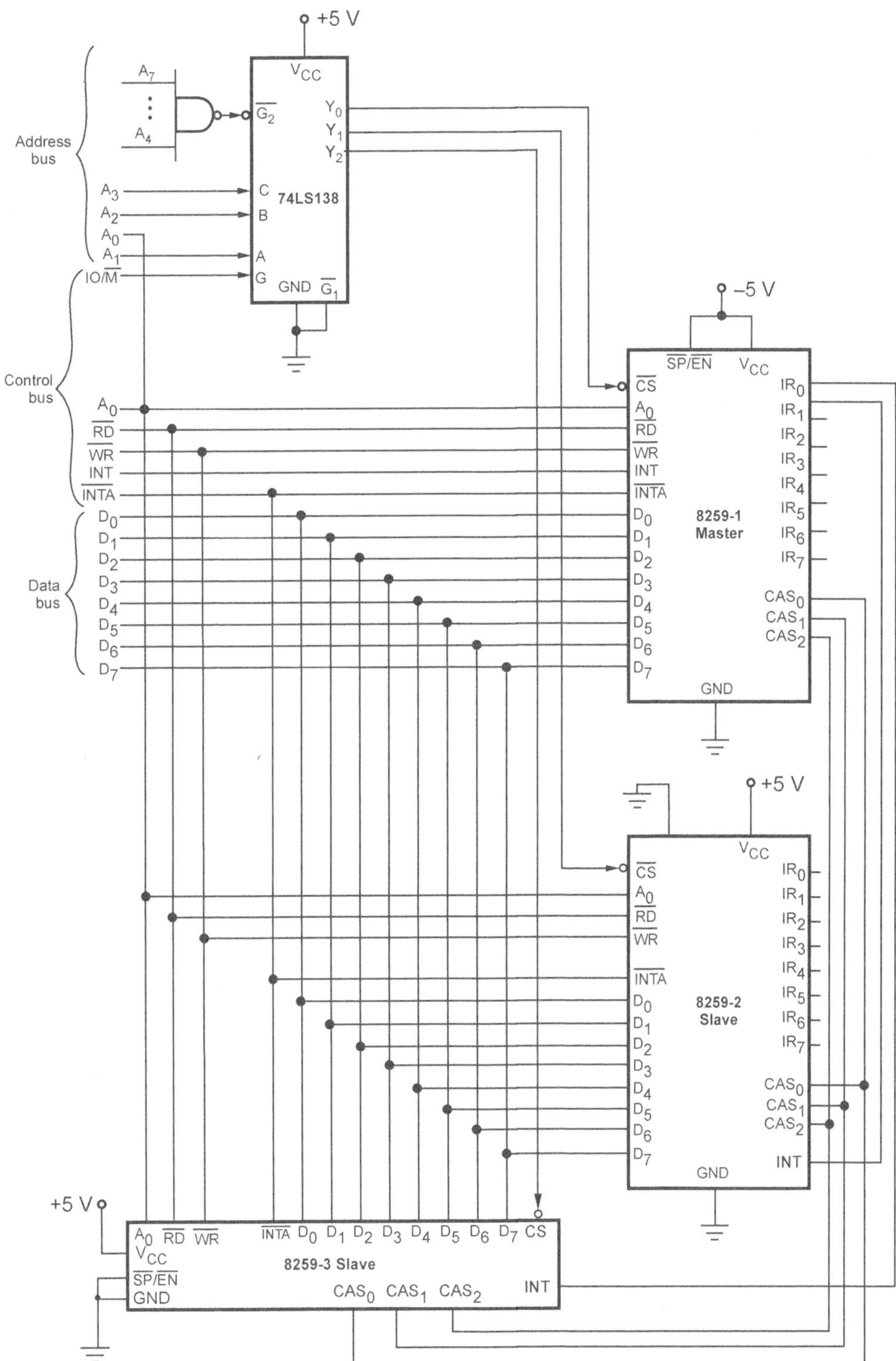

Fig. 12.12 Three 8259 in the cascade mode

Addresses for 8259As :

No	A_7	A_6	A_5	A_4	A_3	A_2	A_1	A_0	Address
8259A-1	1	1	1	1	0	0	0	X	F0H
			F				0/1		F1H
8259A-2	1	1	1	1	0	0	1	X	F2H
			F				2/3		F3H
8259A-3	1	1	1	1	0	1	0	X	F4H
			F				4/5		F5H

Master and Slave Operation :

When the slave receives an interrupt signal on one of its IR inputs, it checks mask condition and priority of the interrupt request. If the interrupt is unmasked and its priority is higher than any other interrupt level being serviced in the slave, then the slave will send an INT signal to the IR input of a master. If that IR input of the master is unmasked and if that input has higher priority than any other IR inputs currently being serviced, then the master will send an INT signal to the 8085 INTR input. If the INTR interrupt is enabled, the 8085 will go through its INTR interrupt procedure and sends three $\overline{INTA}$ pulses to both the master and the slave. In response to first interrupt acknowledge signal opcode for CALL instruction is put on the data bus and the master outputs a 3-bit slave identification number on the CAS_0-CAS_2 lines. Sending the 3-bit ID number enables the slave. When the slave receives the second $\overline{INTA}$ pulse from the 8085, the slave will send the low-order address byte of the ISR on the data bus. Finally, slave sends the high-order byte of the ISR on the data bus on receiving third $\overline{INTA}$ signal.

If an interrupt signal is applied directly to one of the IR inputs of the master, the master will send the opcode for CALL instruction to the 8085 when it receives the first $\overline{INTA}$ pulse from the 8085. It then sends low-order byte and high-order byte in successive interrupt acknowledge cycles (second and third).

Review Questions

Section 12.1

Q.1 *List the interrupt related signals of 8085 that are connected to 8259 IC.*

June-11, Marks 2

Section 12.2

Q.1 *List the features of 8259.*

Section 12.3

Q.1 *With a neat diagram, discuss the functional organization of a programmable interrupt controller.*

Dec.-09,11 Marks 16

Q.2 *State the use of ISR and PR registers in 8259 PIC.* **Dec.-11, Marks 2**

Section 12.4

Q.1 *Explain the processing of interrupt using 8259.*

Section 12.5

Q.1 *What are the different ways to end the interrupt execution in 8259 programmable interrupt controller ?* **May-11, Marks 2**

Q.2 *Explain the operating modes of 8259.*

Section 12.6

Q.1 *Explain the ICWs and OCWs with the help of example.*

Section 12.7

Q.1 *Draw and explain the interfacing of 8259 with 8085.*

Section 12.8

Q.1 *Draw and explain the interfacing of cascaded 8259s with 8085.*

Two Marks Questions with Answers

Q.1 ***Give the different types of command words used in 8259A ?***

Ans. : The command words of 8259A are classified in two groups

1. Initialization command words (ICWs) 2. Operation command words (OCWs)

Q.2 ***Give the operating modes of 8259A ?***

Ans. :

(a) Fully nested mode
(b) End of interrupt (EOI)
(c) Automatic rotation
(d) Automatic EOI mode
(e) Specific rotation
(f) Special mask mode
(g) Edge and level Triggered mode
(h) Reading 8259 status
(i) Poll command
(j) Special fully nested mode
(k) Buffered mode
(l) Cascade mode

Q.3 ***What is the cascaded mode of 8259 programmable interrupt controller?*** May-10

Ans. : The mode in which 8259s are interconnected to get multiple interrupt is called cascaded mode.

In cascade mode one 8259A is configured in Master mode and other should be configured in the Slave mode. The 8259A connected directly to the 8085 INTR pin is referred to as the master. The INT pins from other 8259As are connected to the IR inputs of the **master** 8259A. These cascaded 8259As are referred to as **slave**.

Q.4 ***What are the different ways to end the interrupt execution in 8259 programmable interrupt controller ?*** May-11

Ans. : Refer section 12.5.

❑❑❑

13 Serial Data Transfer (USART) 8251

Contents

Most of the microprocessors are designed for parallel communication. In parallel communication number of lines required to transfer data depend on the number of bits to be transferred. For example, to transfer a byte of data, 8 lines are required and all 8 bits are transferred simultaneously. Thus for transmitting data over a long distance, using parallel communication is impractical due to the increase in cost of cabling. Parallel communication is also not practical for devices such as cassette tapes or a CRT terminal. In such situations, serial communication is used. In serial communication one bit is transferred at a time over a single line.

13.1 Serial Communication Supported by 8085

The 8085 microprocessor communicates serially using two lines : SOD and SID. The Serial Output Data (SOD) line is used to send 1-bit data on the SOD Pin of 8085 and RIM instruction is used to receive 1-bit data on the SID pin of 8085.

Lab Experiment 65 : Output byte from SOD pin.

Statement : Write a program to output contents of B register LSB to MSB on the SOD pin.

Flowchart

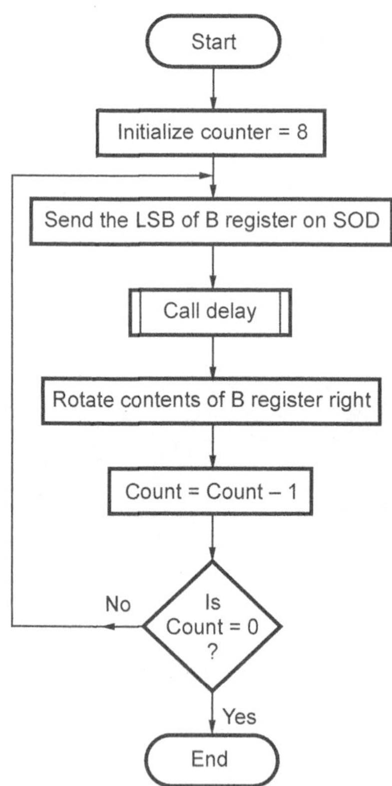

Source program

```
          MVI C, 08H     ; Initialize count with 8
BACK :    MOV A,B        ;
          RRC            ; Rotate B register contents right
          MOV B,A        ; Save contents of register B
          JNC SKIP       ; If no carry skip
          MVI A,C0H
          SIM            ; If carry, send high on SOD
          JMP NEXT
SKIP:     MVI A,40H
          SIM            ; If no carry, send low on SOD
NEXT:     CALL DELAY     ; Wait for specific time
          DCR C          ; Decrement count by 1
          JNZ BACK       ; if count = 0, if not repeat
          HLT            ; Stop program execution
```

Note : Refer section 3.2 for delay subroutine

Lab Experiment 66 : Output square wave from SOD pin.

Statement : Write a program to output square wave of 1 kHz frequency on the SOD pin of 8085 for 5 seconds. Operating frequency of 8085 is 2 MHz.

Flowchart (See flowchart on next page).

Source program

```
          LXI SP,27FFH   ; Initialize stack pointer
          LXI B,1388H    ; Initialize counter with count 5000.
BACK:     MVI A,C0H
       SIM            ; Send high on SOD pin
       CALL DELAY     ; Wait for 0.5 msec (Refer delay program of program 46)
       MVI A, 40H     ; Send low on SOD pin
       CALL DELAY     ; Wait for 0.5 msec
```

```
DCX B        ; Decrement count by 1
MOV A,C
ORA B        ; Check if count = 0
JNZ BACK     ; If not, repeat
HLT          ; Stop program execution
```

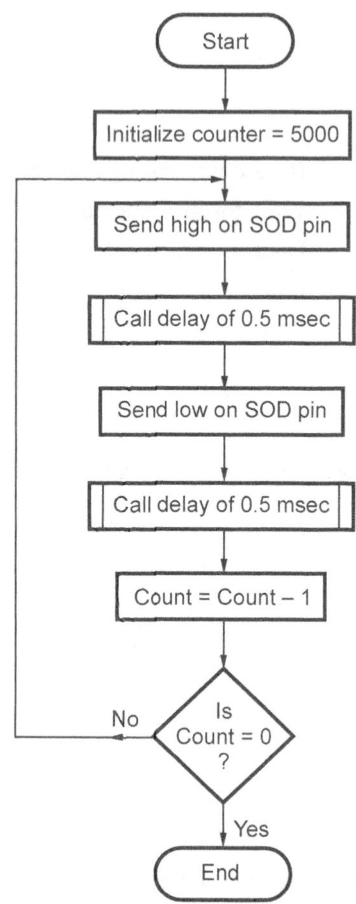

Lab Experiment 67 : Receive ASCII character through SID pin.

Statement : An ASCII character is being received on SID pin of 8085. Write a program in assembly language of 8085 to assemble this character and store it in memory. Write comment for each instruction.

Flowchart

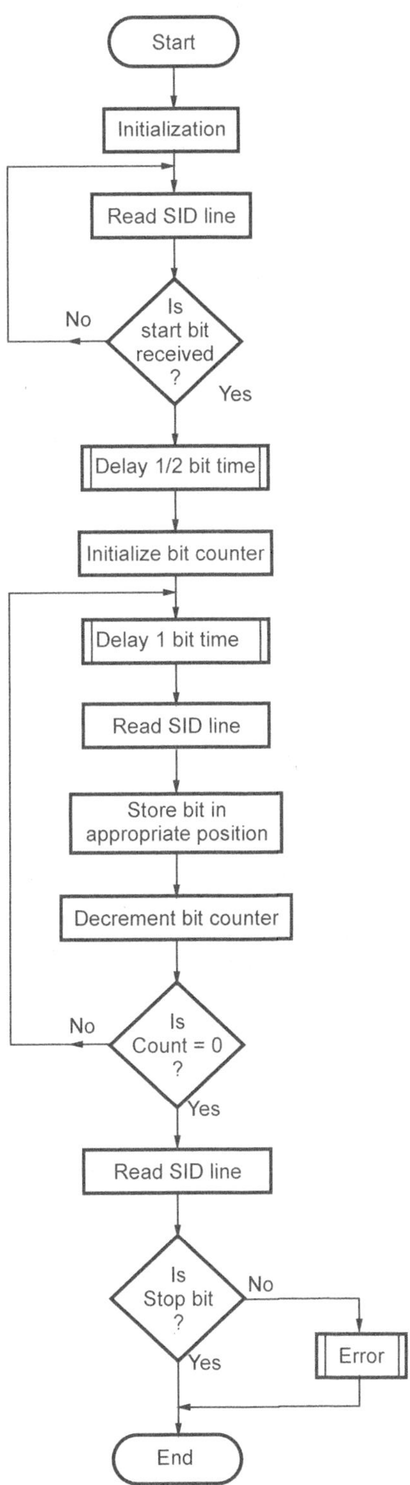
Start
Initialization
Read SID line
Is start bit received ?
No
Yes
Delay 1/2 bit time
Initialize bit counter
Delay 1 bit time
Read SID line
Store bit in appropriate position
Decrement bit counter
Is Count = 0 ?
No
Yes
Read SID line
Is Stop bit ?
No
Yes
Error
End

Source program

```
      LXI SP, 27FFH
      LXI H, 2000H   ; Memory pointer
      RIM            ; Read SID
      ANI 80H        ; Check D7 bit of Accumulator
      CALL Delay     ; 1/2 bit time delay for stop bit
      MVI B,08H      ; Initialize bit counter
      MVI D,00H      ; Clear data register
UP1:  ALL Delay      ; 1bit time
      RIM            ; Read SID line
      ANI 80H        ; Mask bits B6 -B0
      ORA D          ; OR data bit with previous bits
      RRC
      MOV D,A        ; Store data bit at appropriate position
      DCR B
      JNZ UP1
      RLC            ; Shift left to correct result
      MOV M,A        ; Store result
      RIM            ; Read stop bit
      ANI 80H
      CZ error       ; If not stop bit  call error
      HLT            ; Terminate program.
```

From above examples it is clear that 8085 has two pins for serial communication. However, it does not support built-in serial to parallel converter and parallel-to-serial converter. To transmit byte data it is necessary to convert byte into eight serial bits. This can be done by using the parallel to serial converter. Similarly at the reception these serial bits must be converted into parallel 8 bit data. The serial to parallel converter is used to convert serial data bits into the parallel data.

In 8085, we have to achieve this with the help of programming as done in previous examples.

The Intel has designed special devices for this purpose are called Universal Asynchronous Receiver-Transmitter (UART). The devices which provide synchronous as well as asynchronous transmission and reception are called Universal Synchronous Asynchronous Receiver-Transmitter. A good example of UART is 8250 and USART is 8251. These devices are software programmable for number of data bits, parity and number of stop bits. In the next section we discuss IC 8251 (USART).

13.2 Features of 8251A (USART)

April/May-04, Nov./Dec.-05

1. The Intel 8251A is an universal synchronous and asynchronous communication controller.
2. It supports standard asynchronous protocol with :
   a) 5 to 8 Bit character format
   b) odd, even or no parity generation and detection
   c) Baud rate from DC to 19.2 Kbaud
   d) False start bit detection
   e) Automatic break detect and handling
   f) Break character generation.
3. It has built in baud rate generator.
4. It supports standard synchronous protocol with :
   a) 5 to 8 Bit character format
   b) Internal or external character synchronization
   c) Automatic sync insertion
   d) Baud rate from DC to 64 Kbaud
5. It allows full duplex transmission and reception.
6. It provides double buffering of data both in the transmission section and in the receiver section.
7. It provides error detection logic, which detects parity, overrun and framing errors.
8. It has Modem Control Logic, which supports basic data set control signals.
9. It provides separate clock inputs for receiver and transmitter sections, thus providing an option of fixing different baud rates for the transmitter and receiver section.
10. It is compatible with an extended range of Intel microprocessors.
11. It is fabricated in 28 pin DIP package and its all inputs and outputs are TTL compatible.
12. It is available in standard as well as extended temperature range.

13.3 Pin Diagram of 8251A

Fig. 13.1 shows the pin diagram of 8251A.

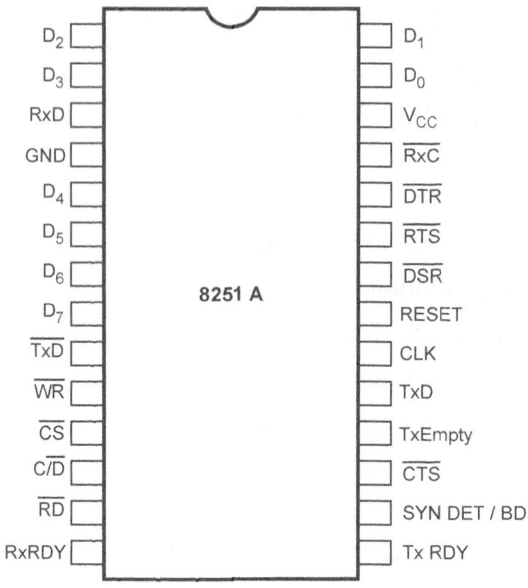

Fig. 13.1 Pin diagram of 8251A

Data Bus : Bi-directional, tri-state, 8-bit Data Bus. This pin allow transfer of bytes between the CPU and the 8251A.

$\overline{RD}$ (Read) : A low on this input allows the CPU to read data or status bytes from 8251A.

$\overline{WR}$ (Write) : A low on this input allows the CPU to write data or command word to the 8251A.

CLK (Clock) : The CLK input is used to generate internal device timing. The frequency of CLK must be greater than 30 times the receiver or transmitter data bit rates.

RESET : A high on this input forces the 8251A into an "Idle" mode. The device will remain at "Idle" until a new set of control words is written into the 8251A to program its functional definition.

$C/\overline{D}$ (Control /Data) : This input in conjunction with the $\overline{WR}$ and $\overline{RD}$ inputs, informs the 8251A that the word on the Data Bus is either a data character, control word or status information as shown in table.

C/$\overline{D}$	$\overline{RD}$	$\overline{WR}$	Operation
0	0	1	CPU reads data from USART
0	1	0	CPU writes data to USART
1	0	1	CPU reads status from USART
1	1	0	CPU writes command to USART
X	1	1	USART Bus floating

$\overline{CS}$ (Chip Select) : A low on this input allows communication between CPU and 8251A

Modem Control Signals

The 8251A has a set of control inputs and outputs that can be used to simplify the interface to almost any modem.

$\overline{DSR}$ (Data Set Ready) : This input signal is used to test modem conditions such as Data Set Ready.

$\overline{DTR}$ (Data Terminal Ready) : This output signal is used to tell modem that Data Terminal is ready.

$\overline{RTS}$ (Request to Send) : This output signal is asserted to begin transmission.

$\overline{CTS}$ (Clear to Send) : A low on this input enables the 8251A to transmit serial data if the TxE bit in the command byte is set to a "one".

Note : The modem control signals are general purpose in nature and can be used for functions other than modem control, if necessary. The $\overline{DSR}$ can be used as an inverted input port and $\overline{DTR}$ can be used as an inverted output port.

Transmitter Signals

TxD : (Transmit data) : This output signal outputs a composite serial stream of data on the falling edge of $\overline{TxC}$.

TxRDY (Transmitter Ready) : This output signal indicates the CPU that the transmitter is ready to accept a data character.

TxE (Transmitter Empty) : This output signal indicates that the transmitter has no character to transmit.

TxC (Transmitter Clock) : This clock input controls the rate at which the character is to be transmitted.

Receiver Signals

RxD (Receiver data) : This input receives a composite serial stream of data on the rising edge of $\overline{RxC}$.

RxRDY (Receiver Ready) : This output indicates that the 8251A contains a character that is ready to be input to the CPU.

$\overline{RxC}$ (Receiver Clock) : This clock input controls the rate at which the character is to be received.

SYNDET (Sync Detect) / BRKDET (Break Detect)

This pin is used in synchronous mode for detection of synchronous characters and may be used as either input or output.

In asynchronous mode this pin goes high if receiver line stays low for more than 2 character times. It then indicates a break in the data stream.

When used as an input (external sync detect mode) a positive signal will cause the 8251A to start receiving data characters on the rising edge of the next $\overline{RxC}$.

13.4 Block Diagram

Nov./Dec.-07, April/May-08, 10

Fig. 13.2 shows the block diagram of IC 8251A. It includes : Data bus buffer, Read/Write control logic, Modem control, Transmit buffer, Transmit Control, Receiver Buffer and Receiver control.

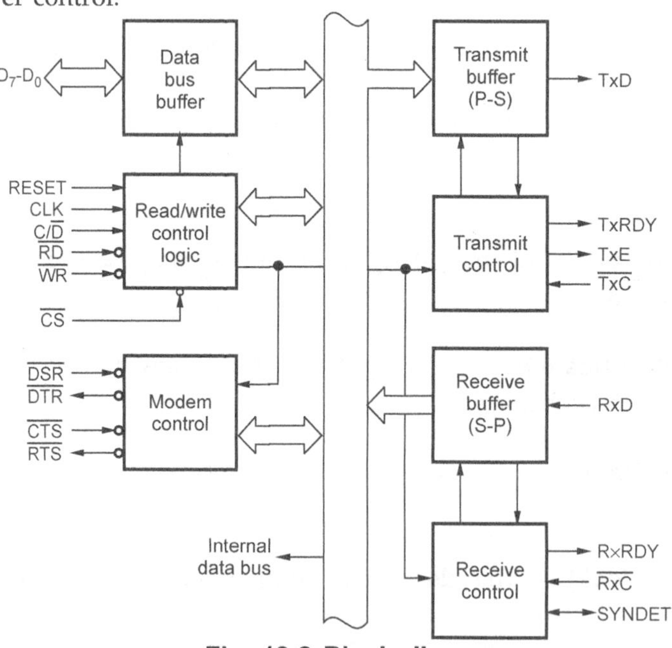

Fig. 13.2 Block diagram

Data Bus Buffer : This tri-state, bi-directional, 8-bit buffer is used to interface 8251 to the system data bus. Along with the data, control word, command words and status information are also transferred through the Data Bus Buffer.

Read/Write control logic : This functional block accepts inputs from the system control bus and generates control signals for overall device operation. It decodes control signals on the 8085 control bus into signals which controls the internal and external I/O bus. It contains the control word register and command word register that stores the various control formats for the device functional definition.

Transmit Buffer : The transmit buffer accepts parallel data from the CPU, adds the appropriate framing information, serializes it, and transmits it on the TxD pin on the falling edge of $\overline{\text{TxC}}$.

It has two registers : A buffer register to hold eight bits and an output register to convert eight bits into a stream of serial bits. The CPU writes a byte in the buffer register, which is transferred to the output register when it is empty. The output register then transmits serial data on the TxD pin.

In the asynchronous mode the transmitter always adds START bit; depending on how the unit is programmed, it also adds an optional even or odd parity bit, and either 1, $1\frac{1}{2}$, or 2 STOP bits. In synchronous mode no extra bits (other than parity, if enable) are generated by the transmitter.

Transmit Control

It manages all activities associated with the transmission of serial data. It accepts and issues signals both externally and internally to accomplish this function.

TxRDY (Transmit Ready) : This output signal indicates CPU that buffer register is empty and the USART is ready to accept a data character. It can be used as an interrupt to the system or, for polled operation, the CPU can check TxRDY using the status read operation. This signal is reset when a data byte is loaded into the buffer register.

TxE (Transmitter Empty) : This is an output signal. A high on this line indicates that the output buffer is empty. In the synchronous mode, if the CPU has failed to load a new character in time, TxE will go high momentarily as SYNC characters are loaded into the transmitter to fill the gap in transmission.

$\overline{\text{TxC}}$ (Transmitter Clock) : This clock controls the rate at which characters are transmitted by USART. In the synchronous mode $\overline{\text{TxC}}$ is equivalent to the baud rate, and is supplied by the modem. In asynchronous mode $\overline{\text{TxC}}$ is 1, 16, or 64 times the baud rate. The clock division is programmable. It can be programmed by writing proper mode word in the mode set register.

Receiver Buffer : The receiver accepts serial data on the RxD line, converts this serial data to parallel format, checks for bits or characters that are unique to the communication technique and sends an "assembled" character to the CPU.

When 8251A is in the asynchronous mode and it is ready to accept a character, it looks for a low level on the RxD line. When it receives the low level, it assumes that it is a START bit and enables an internal counter. At a count equivalent to one-half of a bit time, the RxD line is sampled again. If the line is still low, a valid START bit is detected and the 8251A proceeds to assemble the character. After successful reception of a START bit the 8251A receives data, parity and STOP bits, and then transfers the data on the receiver input register. The data is then transferred into the receiver buffer register.

In the synchronous mode the receiver simply receives the specified number of data bits and transfers them to the receiver input register and then to the receiver buffer register.

Receiver Control

It manages all receiver-related activities. Along with data reception, it does false start bit detection, parity error detection, framing error detection, sync detection and break detection.

RxRDY (Receiver Ready) : This is an output signal. It goes high (active), when the USART has a character in the buffer register and is ready to transfer it to the CPU. This line can be used either to indicate the status in the status register or to interrupt the CPU. This signal is reset when a data byte from receiver buffer is read by the CPU.

$\overline{\text{RxC}}$ (Receiver Clock) : This clock controls the rate at which the character is to be received by USART in the synchronous mode. $\overline{\text{RxC}}$ is equivalent to the baud rate, and is supplied by the modem. In asynchronous mode $\overline{\text{RxC}}$ is 1, 16, or 64 times the baud rate. The clock division is programmable. It can be programmed by writing proper mode word in the mode set register.

Modem Control

The 8251 has a set of control inputs and outputs that can be used to simplify the interface to almost any modem. It provides control circuitry for the generation of $\overline{\text{RTS}}$ and $\overline{\text{DTR}}$ and the reception of $\overline{\text{CTS}}$ and $\overline{\text{DSR}}$. In addition, a general purpose inverted output and a general purpose input are provided. The output is labeled $\overline{\text{DTR}}$ and the input is labeled $\overline{\text{DSR}}$. $\overline{\text{DTR}}$ can be asserted by setting bit 2 of the command instruction; DSR can be sensed as bit 7 of the status register. When used as a modem control signal $\overline{\text{DTR}}$ indicates that the terminal is ready to communicate and $\overline{\text{DSR}}$ indicates that it is ready for communication.

13.5 8251A Control Words

Nov./Dec.-07

The control words defines the complete functional definition of 8251A and they must be loaded before any transmission or reception. The control words of 8251A are split into two formats :

1. Mode instruction 2. Command instruction

Mode Instruction : Fig. 13.3 shows the mode instruction format.

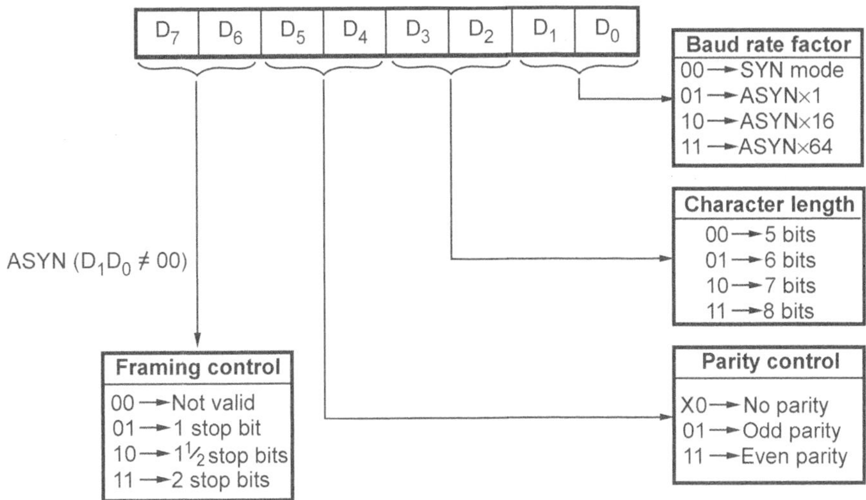

Fig. 13.3 Mode instruction format

The instruction can be considered as four 2-bit fields. The first 2-bit field (D_1-D_0) determines whether the USART is to operate in the synchronous (00) or asynchronous mode. In the asynchronous mode, this field determines the division factor for clock to decide the baud rate. For example, if D_1 and D_0 are both ones, the $\overline{RxC}$ and $\overline{TxC}$ will be divided by 64 to establish the baud rate.

The second 2-bit field (D_3-D_2) determines number of data bits in one character. With this 2-bit field we can set character length from 5-bits to 8 bits.

The third 2-bit field, (D_5-D_4), controls the parity generation. The parity bit is added to the data bits only if parity is enabled.

The last field, (D_7-D_6), has two meanings depending on whether operation is to be in the synchronous or asynchronous mode. For asynchronous mode, (i.e. $D_1D_0 \neq 00$), it controls the number of STOP bits to be transmitted with the character. In synchronous mode, (i.e. $D_1D_0 = 00$) this field controls the synchronizing process. It decides whether to operate with external synchronization or internal synchronization and whether to transmit single synchronizing character or two synchronizing characters.

Command Instruction

After the mode instruction, command character should be issued to the USART. It controls the operation of the USART within the basic frame work established by the mode instruction. Fig. 13.4 shows command instruction format.

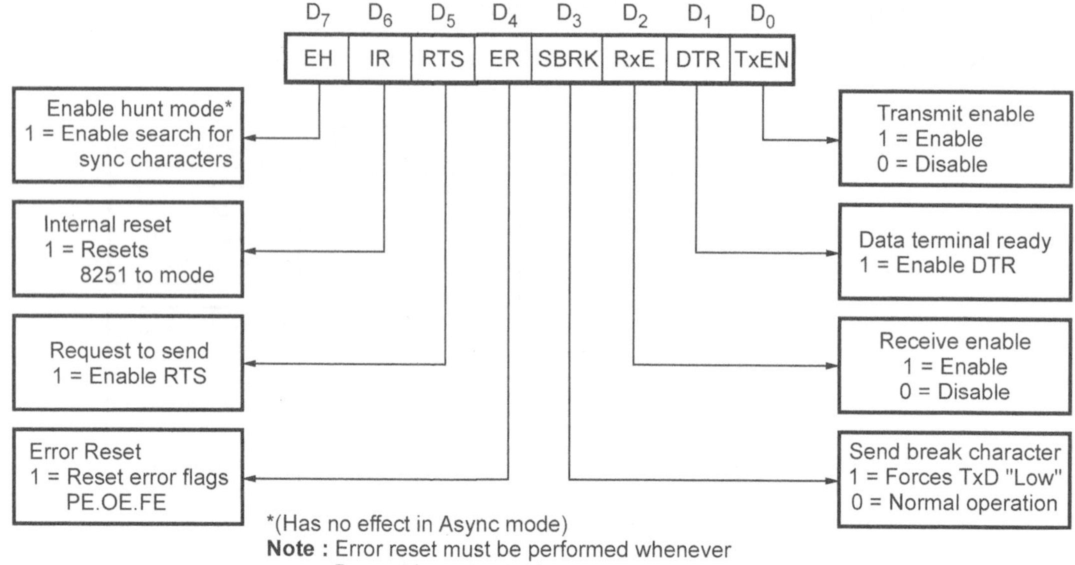

Fig. 13.4 Command instruction format

It does function such as : Enable Transmit/Receive, Error Reset and Modem Control.

13.6 8251A Status Word

Nov./Dec.-07

In the data communication systems it is often necessary to examine the "status" of the transmitter and receiver. It is also necessary for CPU to know if any error has occurred during communication. The 8251A allow the programmer to read above mentioned information from the status register any time during the functional operation. Fig. 13.5 shows the format of status register. (See Fig. 13.5 on next page)

Error Definitions

Parity Error : At the time of transmission of data an even or odd parity bit is inserted in the data stream. At the receiver end, if parity of the character does not match with the pre-defined parity, parity error occurs.

Overrun Error : In the receiver section received character is stored in the receiver buffer. The CPU is supposed to read this character before reception of the next character. But if CPU fails in reading the character loaded in the receiver buffer, the next received character replaces the previous one and the OVERRUN error occurs.

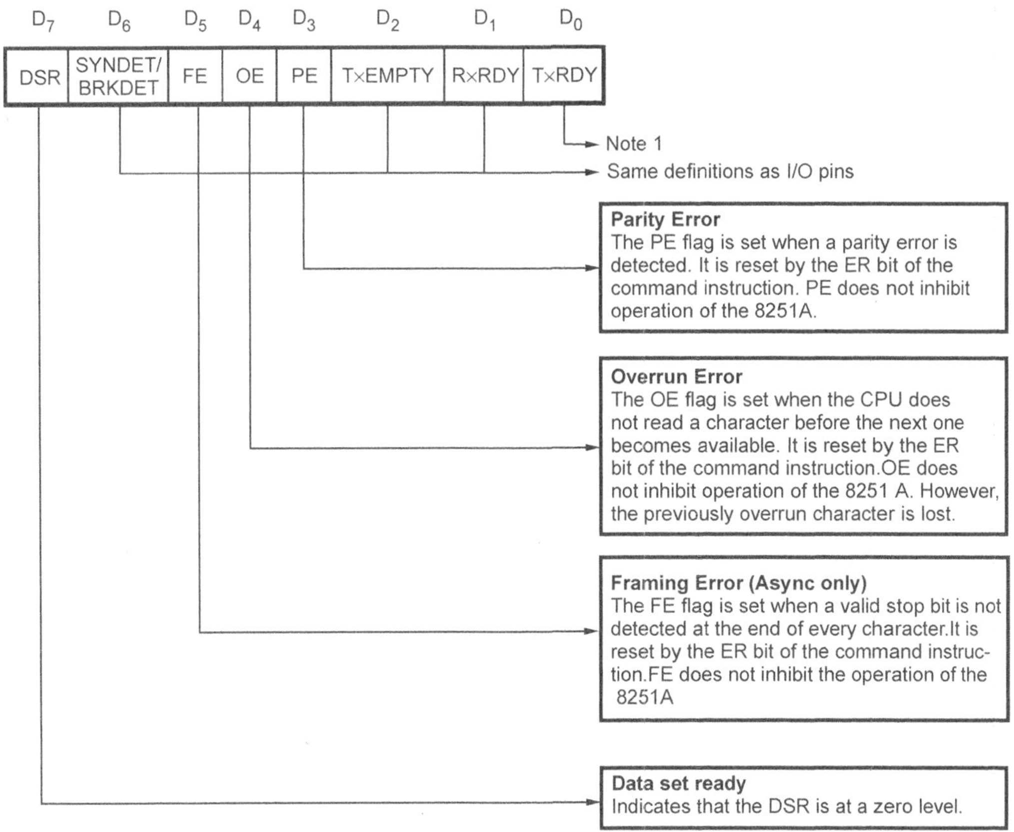

Fig. 13.5 Status register format

Framing Error : If valid stop bit is not detected at the end each character framing error occurs.

All these errors, when occur, set the corresponding bits in the status register. These error bits are reset by setting ER bit in the command instruction.

13.7 Data Communication Types

April/May-04, 05, Nov./Dec.-07

We know that, 8251A is Universal Synchronous, Asynchronous, Receiver, and Transmitter. Therefore communication can take place with four different ways.

1. Asynchronous transmission
2. Asynchronous reception
3. Synchronous transmission
4. Synchronous reception

These communication modes can be enabled by writing proper mode and command instructions. The mode instruction defines the baud rate (in case of asynchronous mode), character length, number of stop bit(s) and parity type. After writing proper mode instruction it is necessary to write appropriate command instruction depending on the communication type.

13.7.1 Asynchronous Transmission

Transmission can be enabled by setting transmission enable bit (bit 0) in the command instruction. When transmitter is enabled and $\overline{CTS}$ = 0 the transmitter is ready to transfer data on TxD line.

Operation :

When transmitter is ready to transfer data on TxD line, CPU sends data character and it is loaded in the transmit buffer register. The 8251A then automatically adds a start bit (low level) followed by the data bits (least significant bit first), and the programmed number of STOP bit(s) to each character. It also adds parity information prior to STOP bit(s), as defined by the mode instruction. The character is then transmitted as a serial data stream on the TxD output at the falling edge of $\overline{TxC}$. The rate of transmission is equal to 1, $1/16$ or $1/64$ that of the $\overline{TxC}$, as defined by the mode instruction. Fig. 13.6 shows the transmitter output in the asynchronous mode.

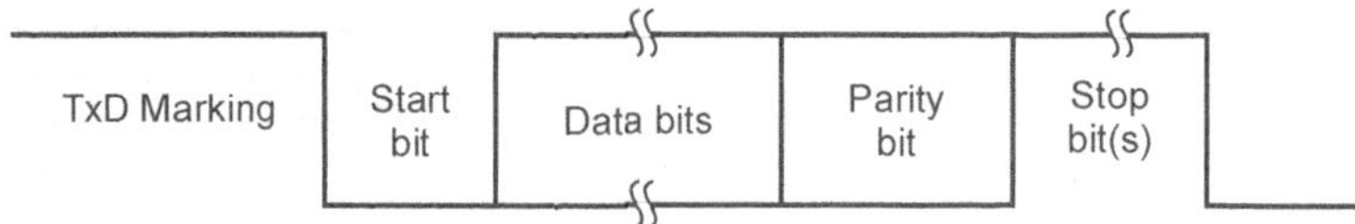

Fig. 13.6 Transmitter output in asynchronous mode

13.7.2 Asynchronous Reception

Reception can be enabled by setting receive enable bit (bit 2) in the command instruction.

Operation :

The RxD line is normally high. 8251A looks for a low level on the RxD line. When it receives the low level, it assumes that it is a START bit and enables an internal counter. At a count equivalent to one-half of a bit time, the RxD line is sampled again. If the line is still low, a valid START bit is detected and the 8251A proceeds to assemble the character. After successful reception of a START bit the 8251A receives data, parity, and STOP bits and then transfers the data on the receiver input register. The data is then transferred into the receiver buffer register. Fig. 13.7 shows the receiver input in the asynchronous mode.

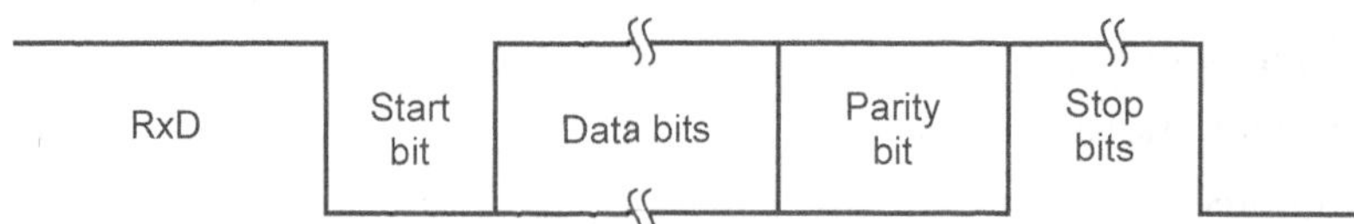

Fig. 13.7 Receiver input in asynchronous mode

13.7.3 Synchronous Transmission

Transmission can be enabled by setting transmission enable bit (bit 0) in the command instruction. When transmitter is enabled and $\overline{CTS}$ = 0, the transmitter is ready to transfer data on TxD line.

Operation :

When transmitter is ready to transfer data on TxD line, 8251A transfers characters serially out on the TxD line at the falling edge of the $\overline{TxC}$. The first character usually is the SYNC character.

Once transmission has started, the data stream at the TxD output must continue at the $\overline{TxC}$ rate. If CPU does not provide 8251A with a data character before transmitter buffers become empty, the SYNC characters will be automatically inserted in the TxD data stream, as shown in the Fig. 13.8. In this case, the TxEMPTY pin is raised high to indicate CPU that transmitter buffers are empty. The TxEMPTY pin is internally reset when CPU writes data character in the transmitter buffer.

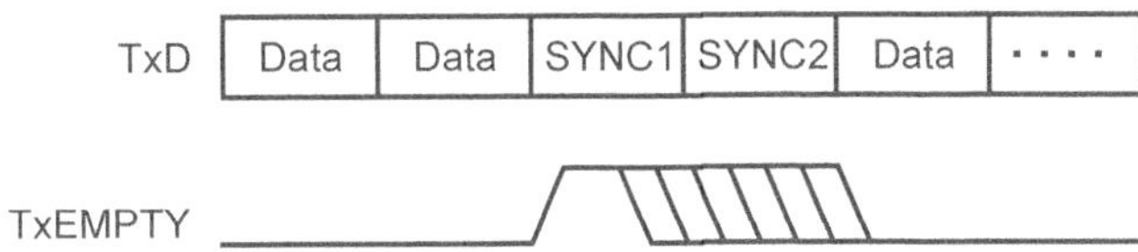

Fig. 13.8 Insertion of SYNC characters

13.7.4 Synchronous Reception

Reception can be enabled by setting receive enable bit (bit 2) in the command instruction.

Operation :

In this mode character synchronization can be achieved internally or externally.

Internal SYNC

To detect the SYNC character 8251A should be programmed in the 'Enter HUNT' mode by setting bit 7 in the command instruction. Once 8251A enters in the 'Enter HUNT' mode it starts sampling data on the RxD pin on the rising edge of the $\overline{RxC}$. The content of the receiver buffer is compared at every bit boundary with the first SYNC character until a match occurs. If the 8251A has been programmed for two SYNC characters, the subsequent SYNC characters are compared until the match occurs. Once 8251A detects SYNC character(s) it enters from 'HUNT' mode to character synchronization mode, and starts receiving the data characters on the rising edge of the next $\overline{RxC}$. To indicate that the synchronization is achieved 8251A sets the SYNDET pin high. It is reset automatically when CPU reads the status register.

External SYNC

In the external SYNC mode, synchronization is achieved by applying a high level on the SYNDET pin, thus forcing the 8251A out of the HUNT mode.

13.8 Interfacing 8251A in I/O Mapped I/O

Fig. 13.9 shows the interfacing of 8251 with 8085 in I/O mapped I/O technique. Here, $\overline{RD}$ and $\overline{WR}$ signals are activated by CPU when IO/$\overline{M}$ signal is high, indicating I/O bus cycle.

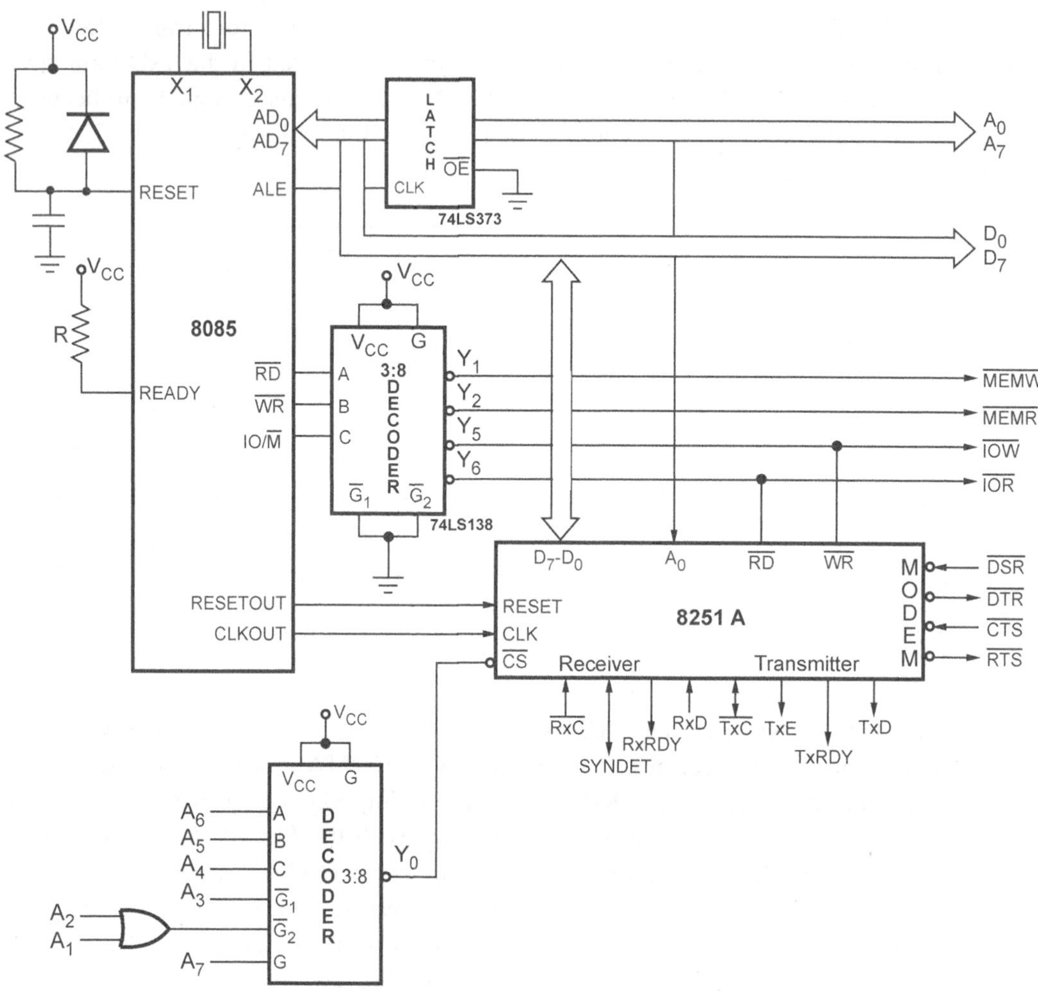

Fig. 13.9 Interfacing of 8251 with 8085 in I/O mapped I/O

The address line A_0 is connected to the C/$\overline{D}$ input of the 8251A. The RESET and CLK signals are driven from the RESETOUT and CLKOUT signals of the 8085, respectively.

I/O MAP :

Register	Address lines								Address
	A_7	A_6	A_5	A_4	A_3	A_2	A_1	A_0	
Data Register	1	0	0	0	0	0	0	0	80H
Control Register	1	0	0	0	0	0	0	1	81H

13.9 Programming 8251A

To implement serial communication the CPU must inform the 8251A all details such as mode, baud rate (in case of asynchronous mode), stop bits, parity etc. Therefore, prior to data transfer, a set of control words must be loaded into the mode instruction and control instruction registers of 8251A.

Example 1 : Write the sequence of instructions required to initialize 8251A at address 80H and 81H for the configuration given below

i) Character length - 6 bits

ii) Parity even

iii) Stop bit 1

iv) Baud rate 64 X

v) DTR and RTS asserted

vi) Error flag reset

vii) Transmitter enable

Solution : In the example, number of stop bits and baud rate is specified, therefore, it is necessary to initialize 8251A in the asynchronous mode.

Mode word for given specification is as follows :

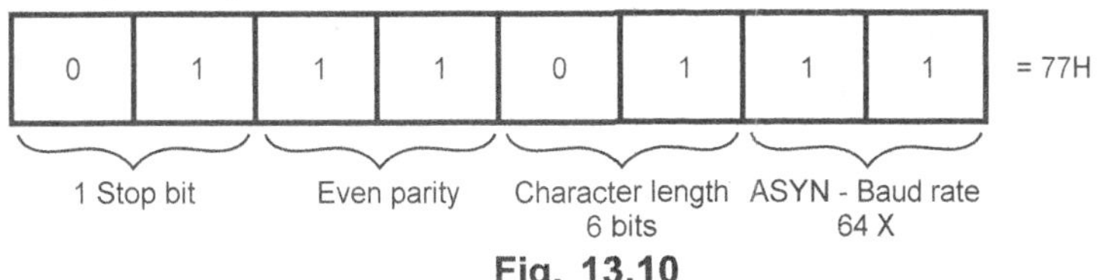

Fig. 13.10

Command word for given specification is as follows :

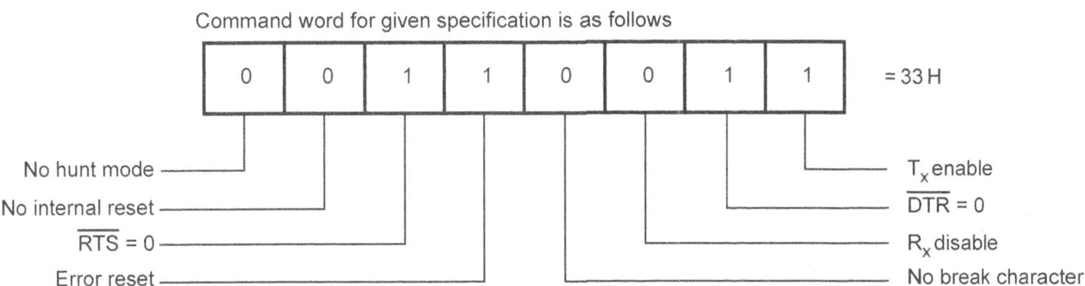

Fig. 13.11

Program :

```
MVI A, 00H
OUT 81H          ; Dummy mode word
OUT 81H
OUT 81H
MVI A, 40H       ; Reset command word
OUT 81H          ; Reset 8251A
MVI A, 77H       ; Mode Word initialization
OUT 81H
MVI A, 33H       ; Command word initialization
OUT 81H
```

Note : Before initialization of the 8251A, the dummy mode word and the reset command are sent to the control register. Initially control register may have any random word; therefore, it is a good practice to reset the 8251A. However, it expects the instruction as a mode word followed by the command word. Therefore, the reset command is sent after sending three dummy mode words, which are recommended to avoid problems when it is turned on.

Lab Experiment 68 : Transmit message using 8251.

Statement : Draw interfacing diagram and write a assembly program to transmit a message from an 8085 to a CRT terminal for the following requirements.

i) A message of 50 characters is stored as ASCII characters (without parity) in memory locations starting at 2200H.

ii) Baud rate × 16

iii) Stop bits 2

Solution : CRT terminal uses normal RS 232C standard serial communication interface. Therefore to transmit data to CRT it is necessary to have RS 232C interface at the sending end. Fig. 13.12 shows the interfacing of 8251 with RS 232C to 8085.

As shown in the Fig. 13.12 three RS-232C signals (TxD, RXD are Ground) are used for serial communication between the CRT terminal and the 8085 system. Line drivers and receivers are used to transfer logic levels from TTL logic to RS-232C logic. For RS-232C the voltage level +3 V to +15 V is defined as logic 0 and voltage level from –3 V to –15 V is defined as logic 1. The line driver, MC 1488, converts logic 1 of TTL to approximately –9 V and logic 0 of TTL to approximately +9 V. These levels at the receiving end are again converted by the line receiver, MC1489, into TTL compatible logic.

I/O Map :

Register	Address lines								Address
	A_7	A_6	A_5	A_4	A_3	A_2	A_1	A_0	
Data Register	1	1	1	1	1	1	1	0	FEH
Control Register	1	1	1	1	1	1	1	1	FFH

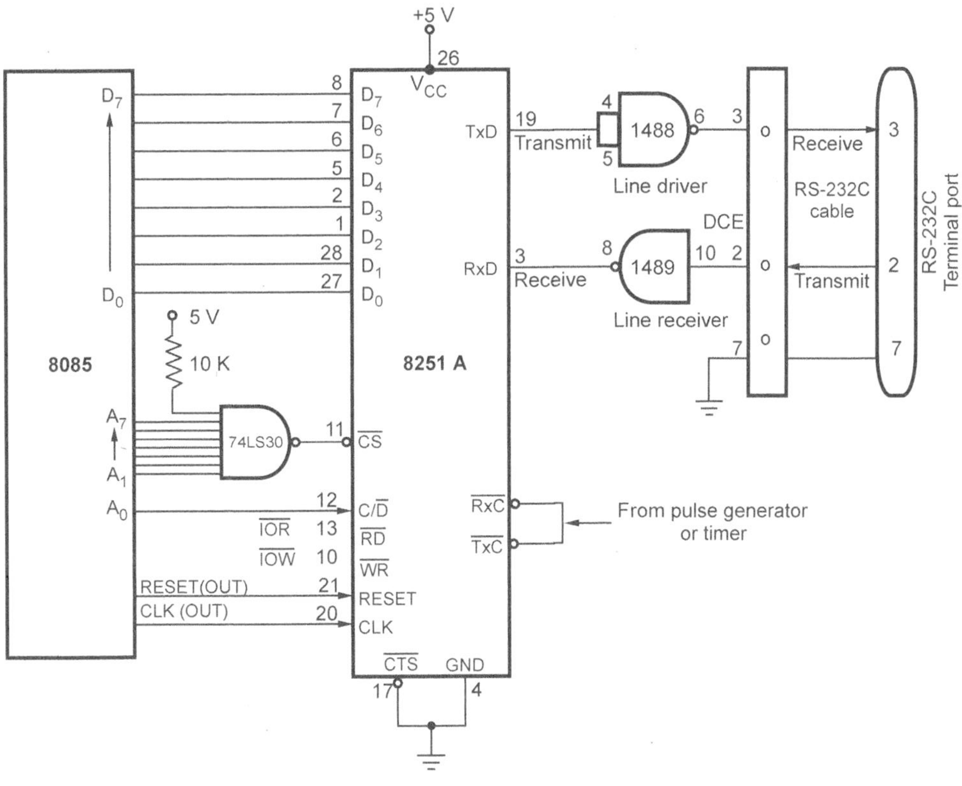

Fig. 13.12 Schematic of interfacing an RS-232C terminal with an 8085 system using the 8251A

Mode word necessary for the given specification is as follows :

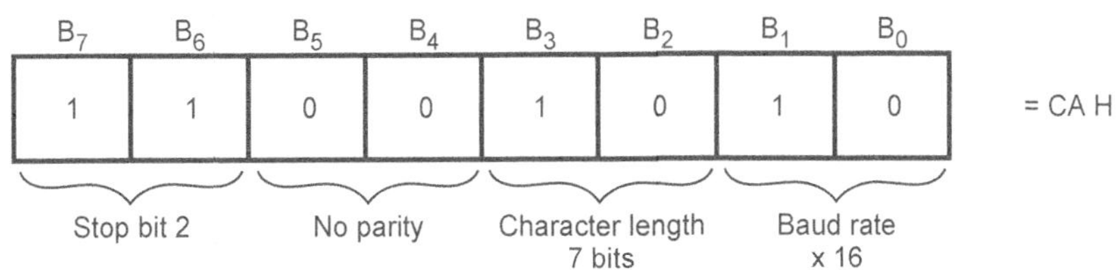

Fig. 13.13

Command word necessary for the given specification is as follows :

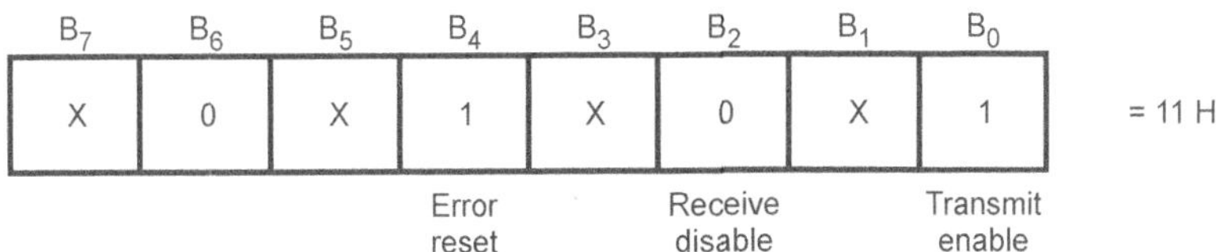

Fig. 13.14

To transmit characters on the TxD line it is necessary for 8085 check whether transmitter is ready or not. This can be checked by reading status word as shown in the Fig. 13.15.

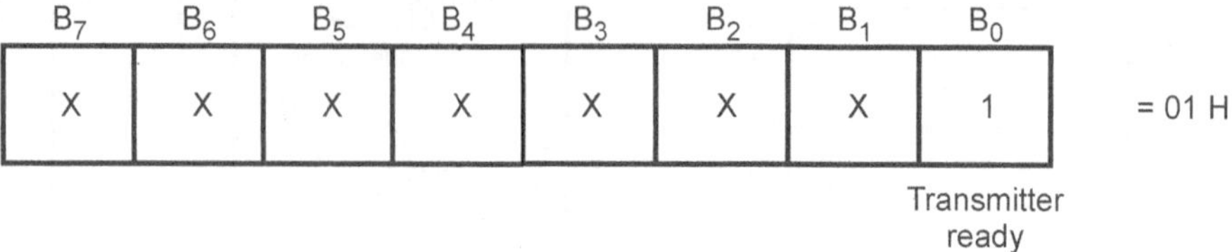

Fig. 13.15 Status word

If bit 0 of the status word is logic '1' then transmitter is ready to accept the character.

Flowchart :

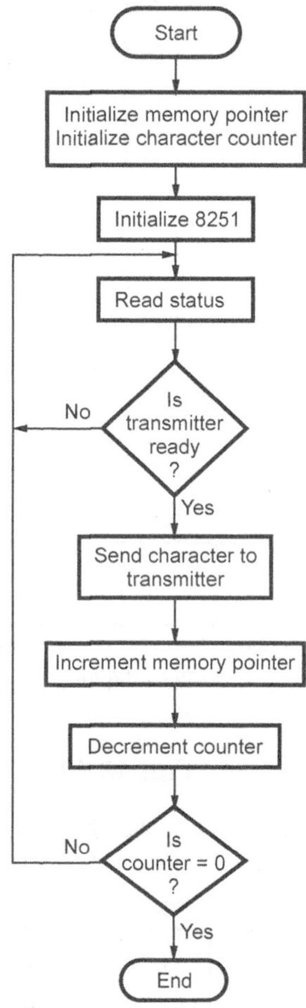

Program :

```
LXI H, 2200H   ; Initialize memory pointer to point the message
MVI C, 32H     ; Initialize counter to send 50 characters
```

```
        MVI A, 00H
        OUT FFH
        OUT FFH       ; Dummy  mode word
        OUT FFH
        MVI A, 40H    ; Reset command word
        OUT FFH       ; Reset 8251A
        MVI A, CAH    ; Mode word initialization
        OUT FFH
        MVI A, 11H    ; Command word initialization
        OUT FFH
CHECK : IN FFH
        ANI 01H       ; Check TxRDY
        JZ CHECK      ; Is TxRDY 1 ?  if not, check again
        MOV A, M      ; Get the character in accumulator
        OUT FEH       ; Send character to the transmitter
        INX H         ; Increment memory pointer
        DCR C         ; Decrement counter
        JNZ CHECK     ; if not zero, send next character
        HLT           ; Stop program execution
```

Lab Experiment 69 : Receive message using 8251.

Statement : For the interfacing in lab experiment 66, write an assembly language program to receiver 25 bytes from the CRT terminal.

Solution : Mode word necessary for the given specification is as follows :

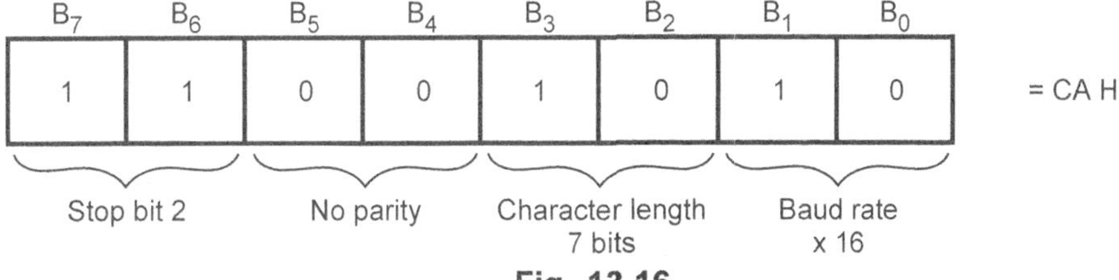

Fig. 13.16

Command word necessary for the given specification is as follows :

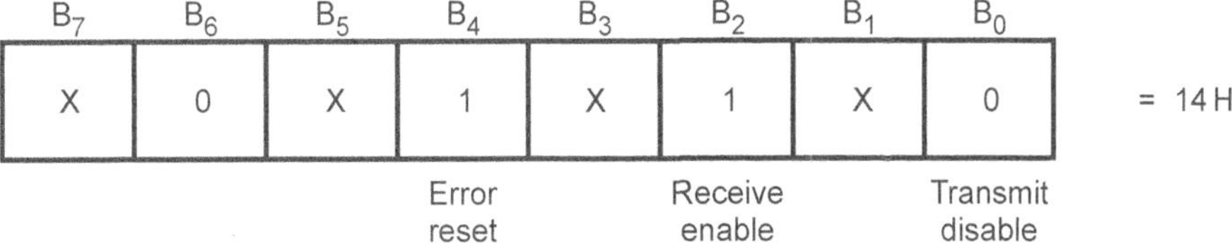

Fig. 13.17

To receive characters from RxD line it is necessary for 8085 to check whether receiver is ready to give data or not. This can be checked by reading status word as shown in the Fig. 13.18.

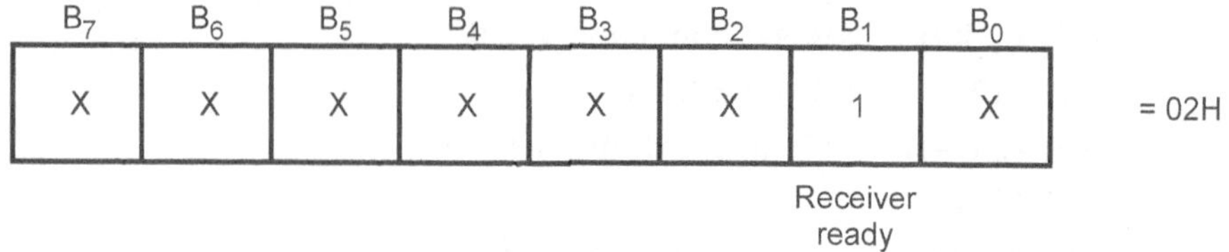

Fig. 13.18

If bit 1 of the status word is logic '1' then receiver is ready to give the character.

Flowchart :

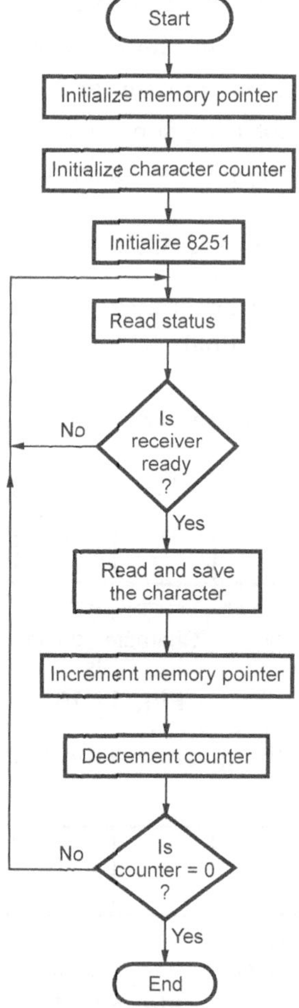

Program :

```
         LXI H, 2300 H    ; Initialize memory pointer
         MVI C, FFH       ; Initialize counter to accept 25 characters
         MVI A, 00H
         OUT FFH
         OUT FFH          ; Dummy mode word
         OUT FFH
         MVI A, 40H       ; Reset command word
         OUT FFH          ; Reset 8251A
         MVI A, CAH       ; Mode word initialization
         OUT FFH
         MVI A, 14H       ; Command word initialization
         OUT FFH
CHECK :  IN FFH
         ANI 02H          ; Check RxRDY
         JZ CHECK         ; Is RxRDY 1 ? If not, check again
         IN FEH           ; Get the character
         MOV M, A         ; save the character
         INX H            ; Increment memory pointer
         DCR C            ; Increment memory pointer
         OUT FEH          ; Send character to the transmitter
         JNZ CHECK        ; if not zero, accept next character
         HLT              ; Stop program execution
```

Review Questions

Section 13.1

Q.1 *Compare parallel and serial type of data transfer.*

Q.2 *Write a short note on serial communication supported by 8085.*

Section 13.2

Q.1 *Explain the advantages of using the following chip in microprocessor based systems : USART.* **May-04, Marks 5**

Q.2 *Bring about the features of 8251.* **Dec.-05, Marks 4**

Section 13.3

Q.1 *Explain the important signals and 8251.*

Section 13.4

Q.1 *With neat block diagram, explain the architecture of 8251 USART.*

Dec.-07, May-08,11, Marks 16

Section 13.5

Q.1 *Draw the 'Mode Word' and command word format of 8251 USART.*

Dec.-11, Marks 2

Section 13.6

Q.1 *Describe the status control words in 8251.* **Dec.-07, Marks 8**

Section 13.7

Q.1 *Explain the data communication types supported by 8251.*

Q.2 *Discuss how 8251 is used for serial communication of data.* **May-05, Marks 6**

Section 13.8

Q.1 *Explain with a neat diagram the interfacing of 8251 to 8085 microprocessor.*

June-12, Marks 8

Section 13.9

Q.1 *Explain the operation and programming of 8251 USART in detail.*

May-10,11, Marks 16

Two Marks Questions with Answers

Q.1 ***What is an USART ?***

Ans. : USART stands for universal synchronous/Asynchronous Receiver/Transmitter. It is a programmable communication interface that can communicate by using either synchronous or asynchronous serial data.

Q.2 ***What is the use of 8251 chip ?***

Ans. : 8251 chip is mainly used as the asynchronous serial interface between the processor and the external equipment.

Q.3 ***What is the use of modem control unit in 8251?***

Ans. : The modem control unit handles the modem handshake signals to coordinate the communication between the modem and the USART.

Q.4 *What is TXD ?*

Ans. : TXD - Transmitter Data Output. This output pin carries serial stream of the transmitted data bits along with other information like start bit, stop bits and priority bit.

Q.5 *What is RxD ?*

Ans. : RxD - Receive Data Input. This input pin of 8251A receives a composite stream of the data to be received by 8251A.

Q.6 *Explain the working of receiver part of USART.* May-04

Ans. : USART receives data through RxD line. It can receive that in two basic modes : asynchronous reception and synchronous reception. Data reception can be enabled by setting receive command instruction.

Q.7 *Write the format in which data is transmitted in asynchronous mode by 8251.* Dec.-07

Ans. : The format in which data is transmitted in asynchronous mode by 8251 is as shown in the Fig. 13.19.

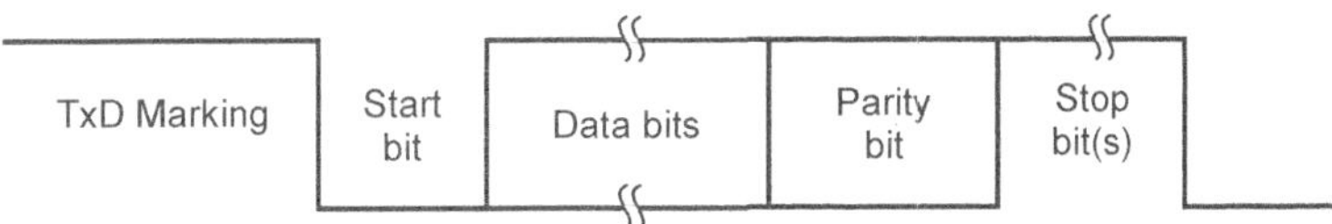

Fig. 13.19 Transmitter output in asynchronous mode

Q.8 *Name the peripheral ICs used for parallel and serial data transfer.* May-10

Ans. : 8255 and 8251.

Q.9 *What is baud rate ?*

Ans. : The baud rate is the number of distinct symbol changes made to the transmission medium per second in a digitally modulated signal. It is used to identify that how much of the data had been transferred but at how much speed.

❑❑❑

Notes

14 Keyboard and Display Controller - 8279

Contents

We have seen that keyboard and display devices are the two main components of microprocessor based system. Using them user can give and receive information from the microprocessor based system. In this chapter we will discuss keyboard and display interfacing in detail and study the programmable keyboard/display interface, 8279.

14.1 Keyboard Interfacing

May/June-06, Nov./Dec.-07

For interfacing keyboard to the microprocessor based systems, usually push button keys are used. These push button keys when pressed, bounces a few times, closing and opening the contacts before providing a steady reading, as shown in the Fig. 14.1. Reading taken during bouncing period may be faulty. Therefore, microprocessor must wait until the key reach to a steady state; this is known as **key debounce**.

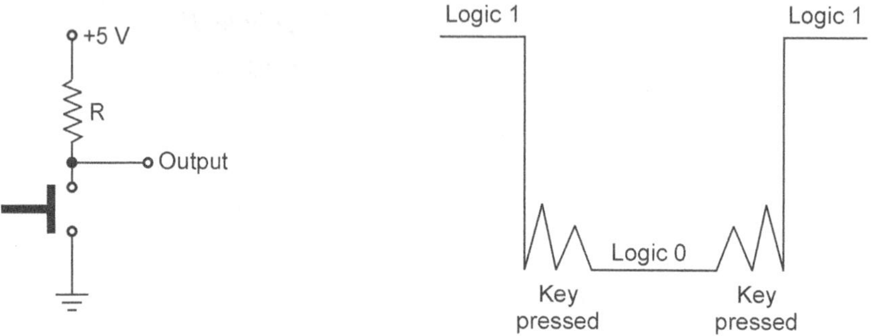

Fig. 14.1 Bouncing of key switch

The problem of key bounce can be eliminated using key debounce technique, either hardware or software.

14.1.1 Key Debounce using Hardware

Key position	a	b	Y	c	d	$\overline{Y}$
A	0	0	1	1	1	0
B	1	1	0	0	0	1
Between A and B	1	$\overline{Y}$	No change	Y	1	No change

Table 14.1

Fig. 14.2 shows the circuit diagram of key debounce. It consists of flip-flop. The output of flip-flop shown in Fig. 14.2 is logic 1 when key is at position A (unpressed) and it is logic 0 when key is at position B, as shown in Table 14.1. It is important to note that, when key is in between A and B, output does not change, preventing bouncing of key output. In other words we can say that output does not change during transition period, eliminating key debouncing.

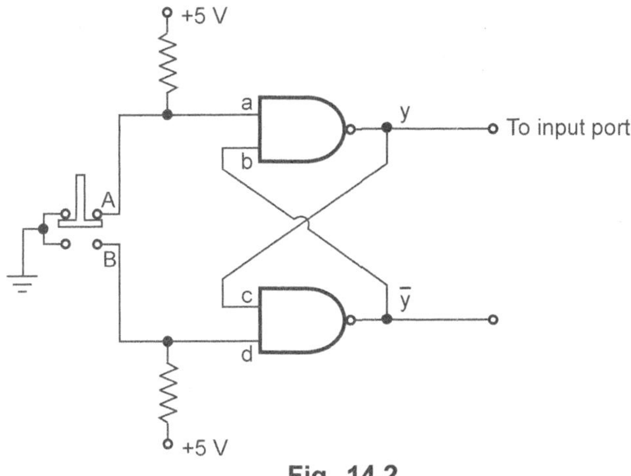

Fig. 14.2

14.1.2 Key Debouncing using Software

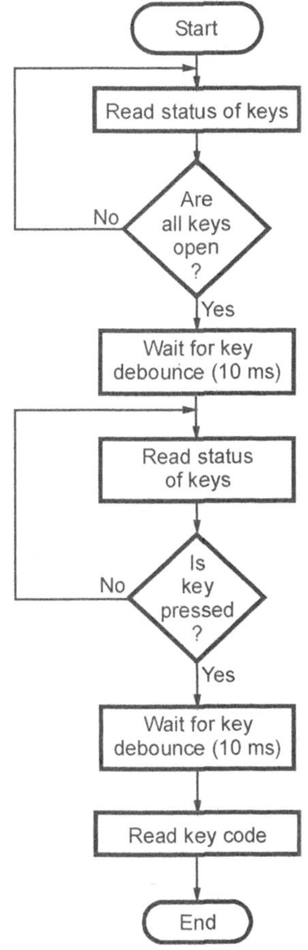

Fig. 14.3 Flowchart of key input with debounce

In the software technique, when a key press is found, the microprocessor waits for at least 10 ms before it accepts the key as an input. This 10 ms period is sufficient to settle key at steady state. Fig. 14.3 shows the flowchart with key debounce technique.

14.1.3 Simple Keyboard Interface

Fig. 14.4 shows simple keyboard interface.

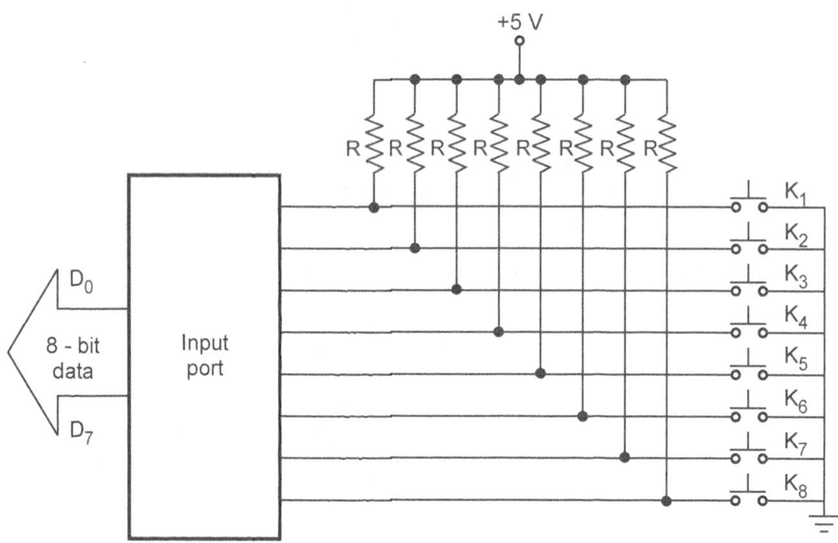

Fig. 14.4 Simple keyboard interface

Here eight keys are individually connected to specific pins of input port. Each port pin gives the status of key connected to that pin. When port pin is logic 1, key is open, otherwise key is closed.

Software routine to get keycode with key debounce.

```
START : IN IN_PORT              ; Read key status
        CPI FFH                 ; check if keys are open
        JNZ START               ; if no, goto start otherwise  continue
        CALL DEBOUNCE_DELAY     ; call debounce delay
AGAIN : IN IN_PORT              ; Read key status
        CPI FFH                 ; check if any key is pressed
        JZ AGAIN                ; if no, goto AGAIN; otherwise  continue
        CALL DEBOUNCE_DELAY     ; call debounce delay
        IN IN_PORT              ; Get key code
        RET                     ; Return from subroutine
```

This program reads status of all keys by getting data through port IN_PORT and compares it with FFH to check whether all keys are open. If all keys are open, instruction CPI sets the zero flag, and the program waits for key debounce. After waiting about 10 ms, program checks the IN_PORT for key press. If key press is found, program waits for another 10 ms as a key debounce period. After key debounce period, program reads the keycode from port IN_PORT.

Key	Keycode							
	D_7	D_6	D_5	D_4	D_3	D_2	D_1	D_0
K_1	1	1	1	1	1	1	1	0
K_2	1	1	1	1	1	1	0	1
K_3	1	1	1	1	1	0	1	1
K_4	1	1	1	1	0	1	1	1
K_5	1	1	1	0	1	1	1	1
K_6	1	1	0	1	1	1	1	1
K_7	1	0	1	1	1	1	1	1
K_8	0	1	1	1	1	1	1	1

Table 14.2

14.1.4 Matrix Keyboard Interface

In simple keyboard interface one input line is required to interface one key and this number will increase with number of keys. Therefore, such technique is not suitable when it is necessary to interface large number of keys. To reduce number of connections keys are arranged in the matrix form as shown in the Fig. 14.5.

Fig. 14.5 shows sixteen keys arranged in four rows and four columns. When keys are open, row and column do not have any connection. When a key is pressed, it shorts corresponding one row and one column. This matrix keyboard requires eight lines to make all the connections instead of the sixteen lines required if the keys are connected individually, as shown in Fig. 14.4.

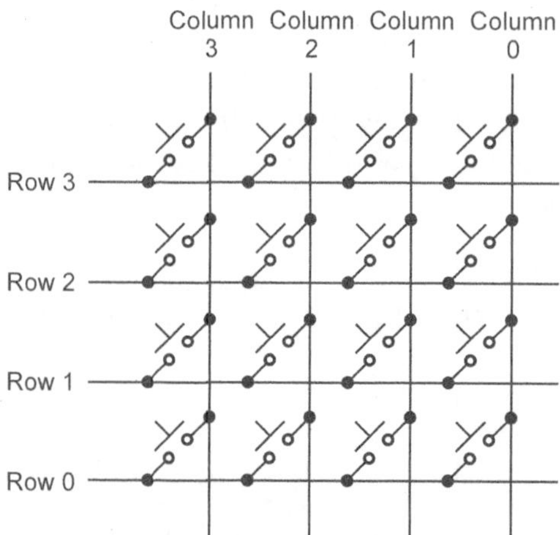

Fig. 14.5 Matrix keyboard

Fig. 14.6 shows the interfacing of matrix keyboard. It requires two ports : an input port and an output port. Rows are connected to the input port referred to as returned lines, and columns are connected to the output port referred to as scan lines. We know that, when all keys are open, row and column do not have any connection. When any key is pressed it shorts corresponding row and column. If the output line of this column is low, it makes corresponding row line low; otherwise the status of row line is high. The key is identified by data sent on the output port and input code received from the input port. The following section explains the steps required to identify pressed key.

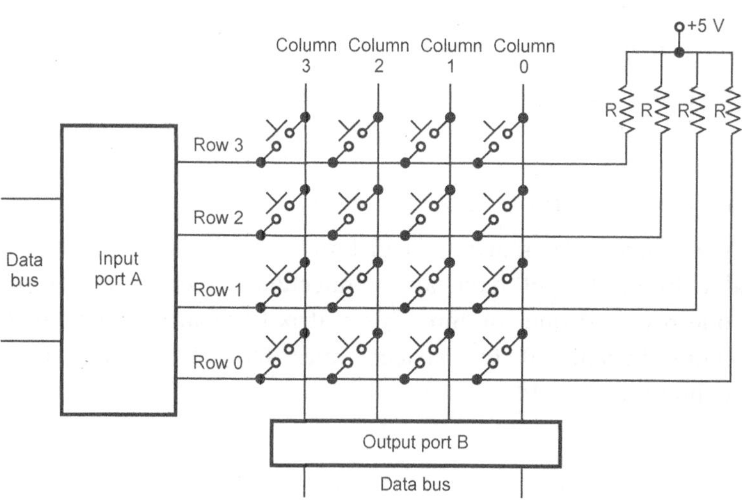

Fig. 14.6 Matrix keyboard connections

Check 1 : Whether any key is pressed or not

1. Make all column lines zero by sending low on all output lines. This activates all keys in the keyboard matrix. (**Note** : When scan lines are logic high, the status on the return lines do not change, it will remain logic high.)
2. Read the status of return lines. If the status of all lines is logic high, key is not pressed; otherwise key is pressed.

Check 2 :

1. Activate keys from any one column by making any one column line zero.
2. Read the status of return lines. The zero on any return line indicates key is pressed from the corresponding row and selected column. If the status of all lines is logic high, key is not pressed from that column.
3. Activate the keys from the next column and repeat 2 and 3 for all columns.

Lab Experiment 70 : Hardware and software for 64-key matrix keyboard interface

Statement : Interface 64-key matrix keyboard to the 8085 microprocessor using 8255. Write an 8085 assembly language program to initialize 8255 and to read the key code.

Hardware : Fig. 14.7 shows a matrix keyboard with 64 keys connected to the 8085 microprocessor using 8255. A matrix keyboard reduces the number of connections, thus the number of interfacing lines. In this example, the keyboard with 64 keys, is arranged in 8×8 (8 rows and 8 columns) matrix. This requires sixteen lines from the microprocessor to make all the connections instead of 64 lines if the keys are connected individually. The interfacing of matrix keyboard requires two ports : one input port and other output port. Rows are connected to the input port, port A and columns are connected to the output port, port B.

Source program :

```
          MVI A, 90H     ; Initialize Port A as input and Port B as
          OUT CR         ; Output
START :   MVI A, 00
          OUT PB         ; Make all scan lines zero
BACK :    IN PA
          CPI FF         ; Check for key release
          JNZ BACK       ; If not, wait for key release
          CALL DELAY     ; Wait for key debounce
BACK_1 :  IN PA
          CPI FF         ; Check for key press
          JZ BACK_1      ; If not, wait for key press
          CALL DELAY     ; Wait for key debounce
          MVI L, 00H     ; Initialize key counter
          MVI C, 08H
```

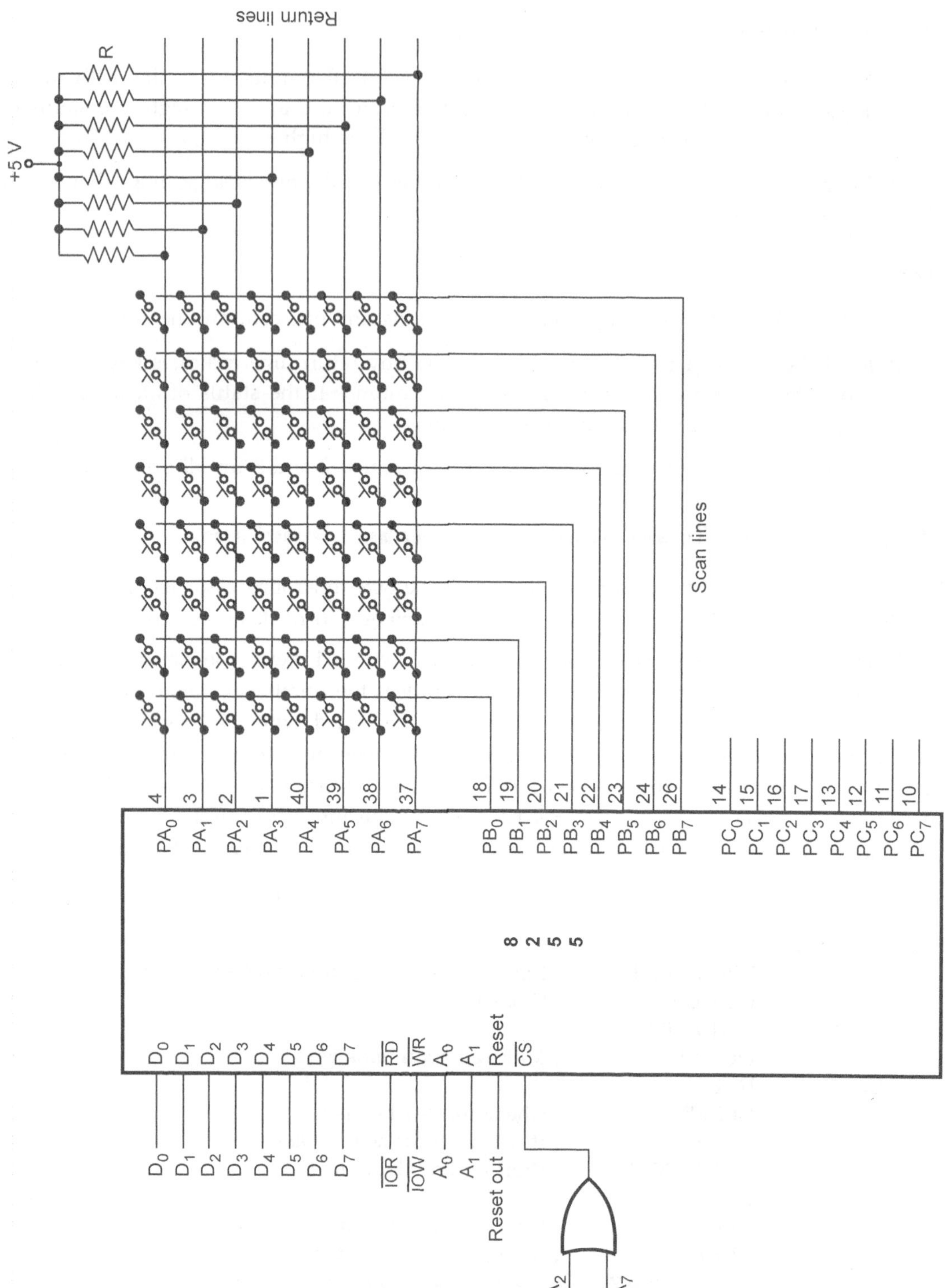

Fig. 14.7 Interfacing of matrix keyboard with 64 keys using 8255

Flowchart

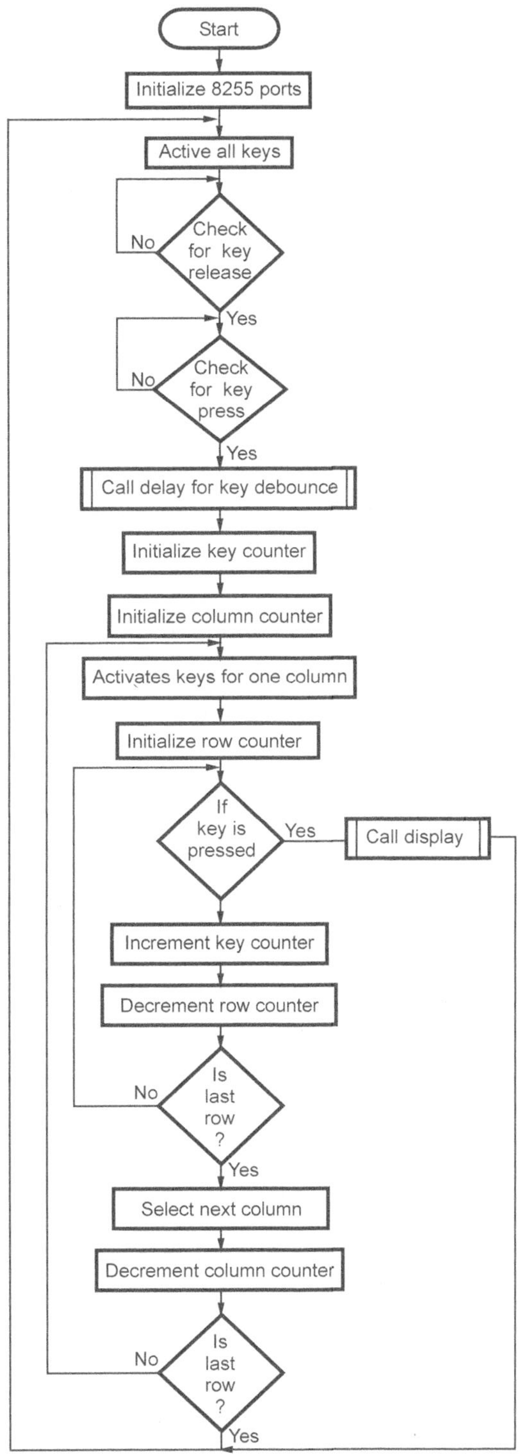

Fig. 14.8 Flowchart

```
            MVI B, FEH     ; Make one column low
NEXTCOL :   MOV A, B
            OUT PB
            MVI D,08H      ; Initialize row counter
            IN PA          ; Read return line status
NEXTROW :   RRC            ; Check for one row
            JNC DISPLAY    ; If zero, goto display otherwise continue
            INR L          ; Increment key counter
            DCR D          ; Decrement row counter
            JNZ NEXTROW    ; Check for next row
            MOV A,B
            RLC            ; Select the next column
            MOV B,A
            DCR C          ; Decrement column count
            JNZ NEXTCOL    ; Check for last column if not repeat
            JMP START      ; Goto start
```

14.2 Display Interfacing

Nov./Dec.-04,05, April/May-05, May/June-06

Most of the microprocessor-controlled instruments and machines need to display letters of the alphabet and numbers to give directions or data values to users. This information can be displayed using CRT, LED or LCD displays. CRT displays are used when a large amount of data is to be displayed. In systems where only a small amount of data is to be displayed, simple LED and LCD displays are used.

14.2.1 Interfacing Static LED Display

Fig. 14.9 shows a circuit to drive a single, seven segment, common anode LED display. For common anode, when anode is connected to positive supply, a low voltage is applied to a cathode to turn it on. Here, BCD to seven segment decoder, IC 7447 is used to apply low voltages at cathodes according to BCD input applied to 7447. To limit the current through LED segments resistors are connected in series with the segments. This circuit connection is referred to as a static display because current is being passed through the display at all times.

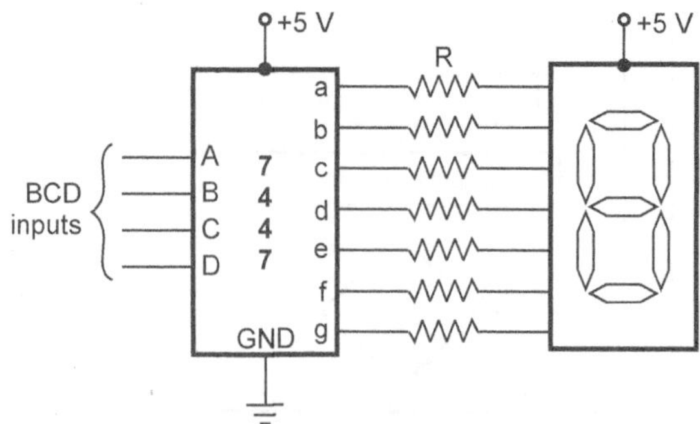

Fig. 14.9 Circuit for driving single seven segment LED display

The value of the resistor in series with the segment can be calculated as follows :

We know, V_{CC} – drop across LED segment – IR = 0

Drop across LED segment is nearly 1.5 V.

$$\therefore \quad IR = V_{CC} - 1.5 \text{ V}$$
$$= 5 - 1.5 \text{ V}$$
$$= 3.5 \text{ V}$$

Each LED segment requires a current of between 5 and 30 mA to light. Let's assume that current through LED segment is 15 mA.

$$\therefore \quad R = \frac{3.5\text{V}}{15\text{mA}}$$
$$= 233\ \Omega$$

In practice, the voltage drop across the LED and the output of 7447 are not exactly predictable and the exact current through the LED is not critical as long as we don't exceed its maximum current rating. Therefore, a standard value 220 Ω can be used.

The static display circuits work well for driving just one or two LED digits. However, these circuits are not suitable for driving more LED digits, say 8 digits. When there are more number of digits, the first problem is power consumption. For worst-case calculations, assume that all eight digits with all segments are lit. Therefore, worst case current required is

$$I = 8 \text{ (digits)} \times 7 \text{ (segment)} \times 15 \text{ mA (current per segment)}$$
$$= 840 \text{ mA}$$

A second problem of the static approach is that each display digit requires a separate BCD to 7 segment decoder.

14.2.2 Interfacing Multiplexed Display

To solve the problems of the static display approach, multiplexed display method is used. Fig. 14.10 shows the 4 seven segment displays connected using multiplexed method. Here, common anode seven segment LEDs are used.

Anodes are connected to +5 V through transistors. Cathodes of all seven segments are connected in parallel and then to the output of 7447 IC through resistors. Looking at the Fig. 14.10, the question may occur in our mind that,"Aren't all of the digits going to display the same number?" The answer is that they would show the same number only if all the digits are turned on at the same time. However, in multiplexed display the segment information is sent for all digits on the common lines (output lines of 7447), but only one display digit is turned on at a time. The PNP transistors connected in series with the common anode of each digit act as an ON and OFF switch for that digit. Here's how the multiplexing process works.

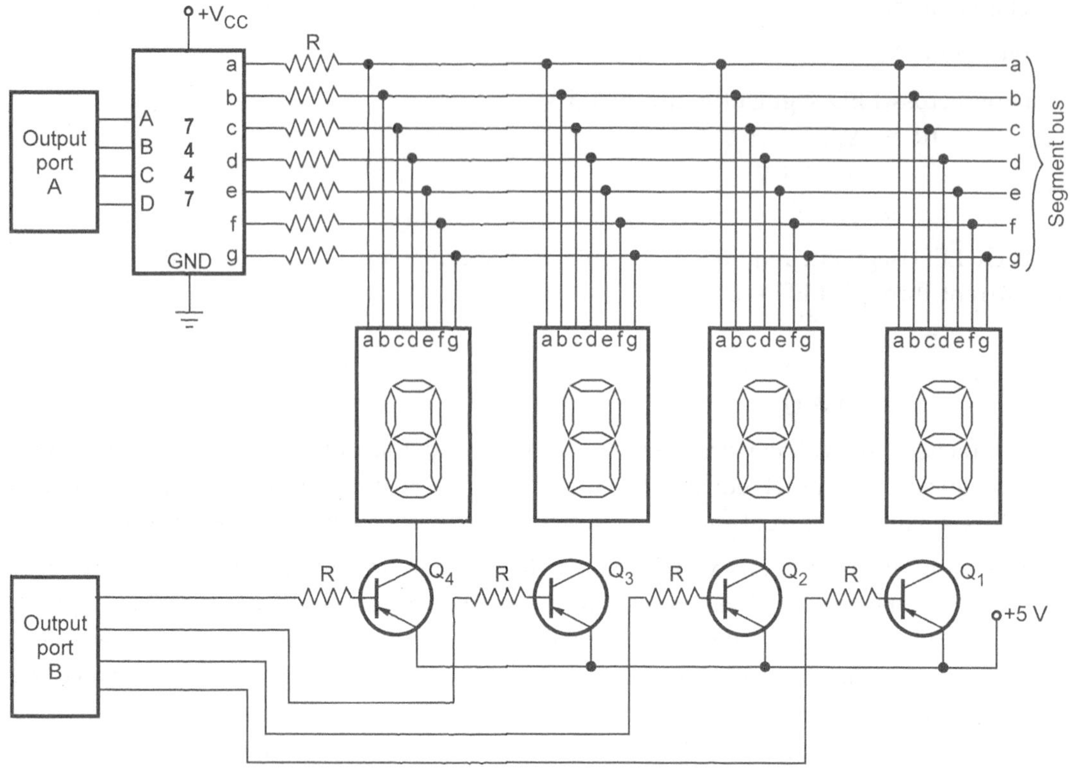

Fig. 14.10 Seven segment display in multiplexed connection

The BCD code for digit 1 is first output from port A, to the 7447. The 7447, BCD to seven segment decoder outputs the corresponding seven segment code on the segment bus lines. The transistor Q_1 connected to digit 1 is then turned on by outputting a low to that bit of port B. All of the rest of the bits of port B are made high to ensure no other digits are turned on. After 2 ms, digit 1 is turned OFF outputting all highs to port B. The BCD code for digit 2 is then output to the port A, and bit pattern to turn on digit 2 is output on port B. After 2 ms, digit 2 is turned off and the process is repeated for digit 3 and digit 4. After completion of turn for each digit, all the digits are lit again in turn.

With 4 digits and 2 ms per digit we get back to digit 1 every 8 ms or about 125 times a second. This refresh rate is fast enough that, to our eye and due to persistence of vision all digits will appear to be lit all the time.

In multiplexed display, the segment current is kept in between 40 mA to 60 mA so that they will appear as bright as they would if not multiplexed. Even with this increased segment current, multiplexing gives a large saving in power and hardware components.

Lab Experiment 71 : Hardware and software for interfacing 8-digit 7-segment display.

Statement : Interface an 8-digit 7-segment LED display using 8255 to the 8085 microprocessor system and write an 8085 assembly language routine to display message on the display.

Hardware : Fig. 14.11 (See Fig. 14.11 on next page) shows the multiplexed eight 7-segment display connected in the 8085 system using 8255. In this circuit port A and port B are used as simple latched output ports. Port A provides the segment data inputs to the display and port B provides a means of selecting a display position at a time for multiplexing the displays. A_0-A_7 lines are used to decode the addresses for 8255. For this circuit different addresses are :

PA = 00H PC = 02H

PB = 01H CR = 03H.

The register values are chosen in Fig. 14.11 such that the segment current is 80 mA. This current is required to produce an average of 10 mA per segment as the displays are multiplexed. In this type of display system, only one of the eight display position is 'ON' at any given instant. Only one digit is selected at a time by giving low signal on the corresponding control line. Maximum anode current is $(7 - \text{segments} \times 80 \text{ mA} = 560 \text{ mA})$ but the average anode current is 70 mA.

Software : Before going to write the software we must know the control word to program 8255 according to hardware connections. For 8255 Port A and B are used as output ports.

BSR	Mode A		P_A	P_{CU}	Mode B	P_B	P_{CL}	
1	0	0	0	X	0	0	X	= 80H

Fig. 14.12 Control word format for 8255

```
; Software to initialize 8255
    MVI A, 80H      ; Load control word in AL
    OUT CR          ; Load control word in CR
; Subroutine to display message on multiplexed LED display
; set up registers for display
    MVI B, 08H      ; load count
    MVI C, 7FH      ; load select pattern
    LXI H, 6000H    ; starting address of message
; display message
DISP_1 : MOV A, C   ; select digit
         OUT  PB
         MOV A, M   ; get data
      OUT  PA       ; display data
```

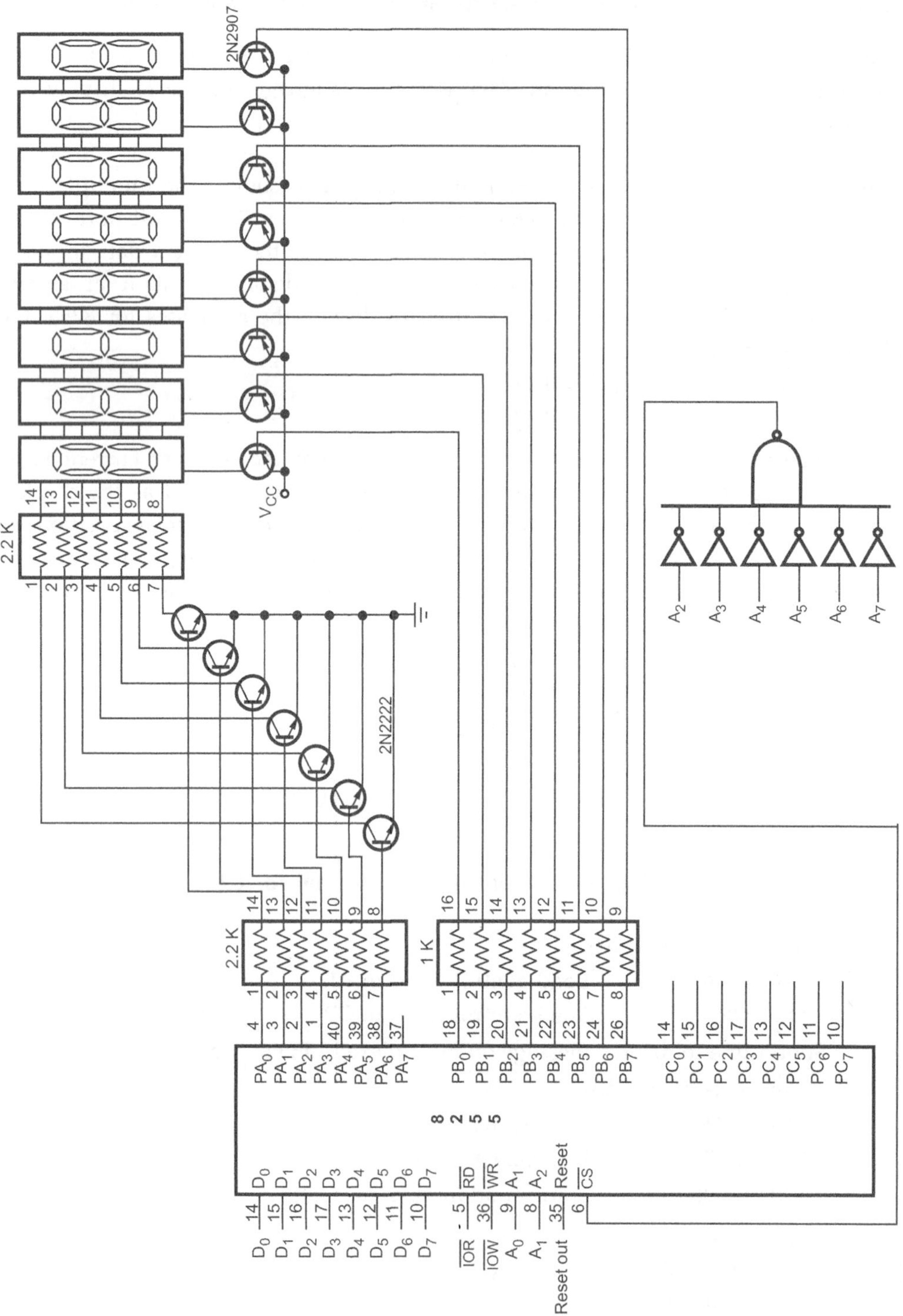

Fig. 14.11 Interfacing of multiplexed eight 7-segment display using 8255

```
CALL DELAY  ; wait for some time
MOV A, C
RRC
MOV C, A    ; adjust selection pattern
INX H
DCR B       ; Decrement count
JNZ  DISP_1 ; repeat 8 times
RET
```

Note : This subroutine must be called continuously to display the 7-segment coded message stored in the memory from address 6000H.

Disadvantage of software approach

In the last example, we have seen the software approach to drive multiplexed displays. In software approach CPU has to look after digit selection in synchronism with the data for specific digit. In other words, CPU has to give digit data on one port and then the digit selection bit pattern on the another port in synchronism. The process of refreshing has to be repeated all the time, which puts an additional burden on the CPU. This is a major disadvantage of the software multiplexing approach. Another disadvantage of software multiplexing approach is that, if CPU gets involved in going some lengthy task which cannot be interrupted to refresh the display, only one digit of the display will be left lit.

An alternative approach to interface multiplexed displays to microprocessor systems is to use a dedicated keyboard and display controller 8279, designed by Intel. IC 8279 independently keeps display refresh and scans the matrix keyboard. In the next section, we will see the details of 8279 and its interfacing with 8085 microprocessor.

14.3 Features of 8279

April/May-04

1. IC 8279 provides a scanned interface to a 64-contact key matrix, with two more keys CONTROL and SHIFT.
2. It provides three input modes for keyboard interface.
   (i) Scanned Keyboard Mode (ii) Scanned Sensor Matrix Mode
   (iii) Strobed Input Mode
3. It has built-in hardware to provide key debounce.
4. It allows key depressions in 2 key lockout or N-key rollover mode, which eliminates software required to implement 2 key lockout and N-key rollover modes.
5. The interrupt output of 8279 can be used to tell CPU that the keypress is detected. This eliminates the need of software polling.
6. It provides 8 byte FIFO RAM to store keycodes. This allows to store 8 key board inputs when CPU is busy in performing his own computation.
7. It provides multiplexed display interface with blanking and inhibit options.

8. It provides sixteen byte display RAM to store display codes for 16 digits, allowing to interface 16 digits.
9. In autoincrement mode, address of display RAM and FIFO RAM is incremented automatically which eliminates extra command after each read/write operation to access successive locations of display RAM and FIFO RAM.
10. It provides two output modes for display interface.

    (i) Left Entry (typewriter type) (ii) Right Entry (calculator type)

11. Simultaneous keyboard and display operation facility allows to interleave keyboard and display software.

14.4 Pin Description

Fig. 14.13 shows functional and pin diagram of 8279. It is a 40 pin device and looking at Fig. 14.13 (a) we can see that these pins are divided in four functional groups :

- CPU interface
- Key data
- Display data
- Scan

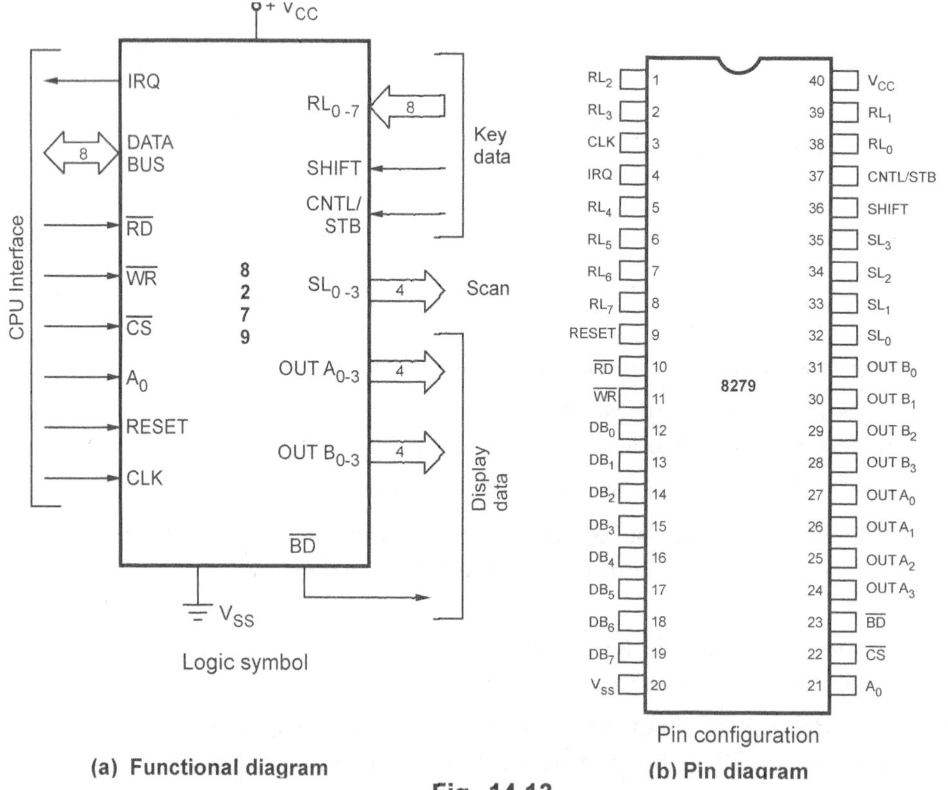

(a) Functional diagram (b) Pin diagram

Fig. 14.13

14.4.1 CPU Interface Pins

As shown in Fig. 14.13 (a), it consists of 8-bit data bus, $\overline{RD}$, $\overline{WR}$, A_0, $\overline{CS}$, RESET, CLK and IRQ lines.

DB_0-DB_7 : Bi-directional data bus

All data, commands and status information between the CPU and the 8279 are transmitted on these bi-directional 8-bit data bus.

$\overline{RD}$: Read

It is an active low signal. When $\overline{RD}$ signal is low CPU reads the contents of selected register (display RAM, status register or FIFO RAM) from 8279; depending on the type of command and the status of the A_0 signal.

$\overline{WR}$: Write

It is an active low signal. When $\overline{WR}$ signal is low, CPU loads the data into selected register (control register or display register) depending on the status of A_0 signal.

A_0 : Address line

When A_0 is high, signals are interpreted as a command or status. When A_0 is low signals are interpreted as a data.

$\overline{CS}$: Chip select

It is an active low signal. When low, enables the communication between CPU and 8279.

RESET : A high signal on this pin resets 8279. After being reset 8279 is configured in the following mode.

1. Sixteen 8-bit character display-left entry
2. Encoded scan keyboard- 2 key lockout
3. The program clock prescaler is set to 31.

CLK : This signal is usually driven by the system clock and used to generate internal timings.

IRQ : Interrupt Request

This signal is used to implement interrupt driven input system. In scanned keyboard mode, the interrupt line goes low when there is data in the FIFO/sensor RAM. The interrupt line goes low with each FIFO/sensor RAM read and returns high if there is still information in the RAM. In sensor matrix mode, the interrupt line goes high whenever a change in a sensor is detected. The IRQ line is cleared by the first data read operation if the autoincrement flag is set to zero, or by the End interrupt command if the auto-increment flag is set to one. The interrupt feature of 8279 eliminates the need of polling the keyboard.

14.4.2 Keyboard Data

This group consists of return, SHIFT and CNTL/STB lines.

RL_0-RL_7 : Return lines : These input lines are used to interface matrix keyboard. These lines have active internal pullups which keep their status high. When the key from the matrix keyboard is pressed corresponding return line goes low. In the strobed input mode these lines are used as 8 input lines.

SHIFT : It is a special key input line. Its status is stored along with the key position on the key closure in the scanned keyboard modes. It has an active internal pullup to keep it high until a switch closure pulls it low.

CNTL/STB : Control/strobe

For scanned keyboard mode this line is used as a control input. Like SHIFT key, its status is stored along with the key position on the key closure. It also has an active internal pullup to keep it high until a switch closure pulls it low.

In the strobed input mode this line is used as a strobe input. When activated, loads the status of keyboard into the FIFO RAM.

14.4.3 Display Data

This group consists of OUT A_3-A_0, OUT B_3-B_0 and $\overline{BD}$ lines.

OUT A_3-A_0 and OUT B_3-B_0 : These two four bit output ports, which can be considered as an one 8-bit port. These are used for sending data to display drivers from display RAM and connected to the segment inputs of 7 segment display or row inputs of dot matrix displays. These lines are synchronized to the scan lines (SL_0-SL_3) for multiplexed digit display. In other words we can say that when the data on the scan lines is 0000, ports will have data from register 0 of display RAM and when the data on the scan lines is 1111, ports will have data from register 15 of display RAM. The two 4-bit ports can be blanked independently.

$\overline{BD}$: Blank Display

This is an active low output used to blank the display during digit switching or by a display blanking command.

14.5 Block Diagram

Nov./Dec.-09

Fig. 14.14 shows the block diagram of 8279. It consists of four main sections :

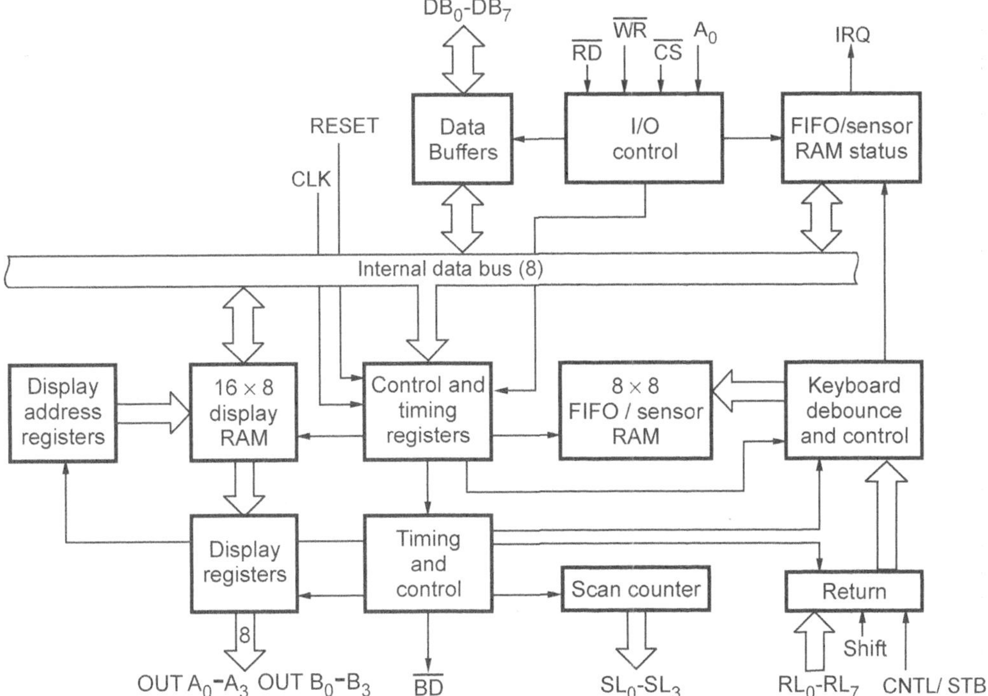

Fig. 14.14

- CPU interface and control section
- Scan section
- Keyboard section
- Display section

14.5.1 CPU Interface and Control Section

This section consists of data buffers, I/O control, control and timing registers, and timing and control logic.

Data Buffers

The data buffers are 8-bit bi-directional buffers that connect the internal data bus to the external data bus.

I/O Control

The I/O control section uses the A_0, $\overline{CS}$, $\overline{RD}$ and $\overline{WR}$ signals to control data flow to and from the various internal registers and buffers. The data flow to and from the 8279 is enabled only when $\overline{CS}$ = 0; otherwise the 8279 signals are in a high impedance state. The 8279 interprets the data given or desired by the CPU with the help of A_0, $\overline{RD}$ and $\overline{WR}$ signals, as shown in Table 14.3. When A_0 is logic 0 data is transferred and when A_0 is logic 1 command word or status word is transferred. $\overline{RD}$ and $\overline{WR}$ determine the direction of data flow through the data buffers.

A_0	$\overline{RD}$	$\overline{WR}$	Interpretation
0	1	0	Data from CPU to 8279
0	0	1	Data to CPU from 8279
1	1	0	Command word from CPU to 8279
1	0	1	Status word to CPU from 8279

Table 14.3

Control and Timing Registers

The control and timing registers store the keyboard and display modes and other operating conditions programmed by the CPU. The modes are programmed by sending the proper command on the data lines with A_0 = 1. The command is latched on the rising edge of $\overline{WR}$. The command is then decoded and the appropriate mode/function is set.

Timing Control

The timing control consists of the basic timing counter chain. The first counter is divided by N prescaler that can be programmed to give an internal frequency of 100 kHz. The other counters divide down the basic internal frequency to provide the proper key scan, row scan, keyboard matrix scan, and display scan times. The internal frequency of 100 kHz gives the internal timings as shown in the Table 14.4.

Parameter	Timings
Keyboard scan time	5.1 msec
Keyboard debounce time	10.3 msec
Key scan time	80 μsec
Display scan time	10.3 msec
Digit ON time	480 μsec
Blanking time	160 μsec
Internal clock cycle	10 μsec

Table 14.4 Internal timings of 8279

14.5.2 Scan Section (Scan Counter)

The scan section has a scan counter which has two modes : Encoded mode and Decoded mode.

Encoded mode

In the encoded mode, the scan counter provides a binary count from 0000 to 1111 on the four scan lines $(SC_3 - SC_0)$ with active high outputs. This binary count must be externally decoded to provide 16 scan lines.

Display can use all 16 scan lines to interface 16 digit 7-segment display, but keyboard can use only 8 scan lines out of 16 scan lines.

Decoded mode

In the decoded mode, the internal decoder decodes the least significant 2 bits of binary count and provides four possible combinations on the scan lines $(SC_3 - SC_0)$: 1110, 1101, 1011 and 0111. Thus the output of decoded scan is active low. These four active low output lines can be used directly to interface 4 digit 7 segment display, 8×4 matrix keyboard, eliminating the external decoder.

14.5.3 Keyboard Section

This section consists of return buffers, keyboard debounce and control, FIFO/sensor RAM and FIFO/sensor RAM status. There functions depend on selected keyboard mode out of three keyboard input modes : scanned keyboard, sensor matrix and strobed input.

Return buffers

The 8 return lines $(RL_7 - RL_0)$ are buffered and latched by the return buffers during each row scan in scanned keyboard or sensor matrix mode. In strobed input mode, the contents of the return lines are transferred to the FIFO RAM on the rising edge of the CNTL/STB line pulse.

Keyboard debounce and control

Keyboard and debounce control is enabled only when scanned keyboard mode is selected. In the scanned keyboard mode, return lines are scanned, looking for key closures in that row. If the debounce circuit detects a close switch, it waits about 10 msec to check if the switch remains closed. If it does, the address of the switch in the matrix plus the status of SHIFT and CONTROL keys are transferred to the FIFO RAM.

FIFO/Sensor RAM

This is a dual function 8×8 RAM. In scanned keyboard and strobed input modes, it is a FIFO. Each new entry is written into successive RAM positions and then read in order of entry. In sensor matrix mode, the memory is referred to as sensor RAM. Each row of the sensor RAM is loaded with the status of the corresponding row of sensor in the sensor matrix.

FIFO/sensor RAM status

FIFO RAM status keeps track of the number of characters in the FIFO and whether it is full or empty. The status logic also makes IRQ signal high when the FIFO is not empty, which can be used to interrupt CPU telling that key press is detected and keycode is available in FIFO RAM.

14.5.4 Display Section

The display section consists of display RAM, display address registers and display registers.

Display RAM

It is 16×8 RAM, which stores the display codes for 16 digits. It can be accessed directly by CPU. In decoded mode, 8279 uses only first four locations of display RAM. In encoded mode, 8279 uses first eight locations for 8 digit display and all 16 locations for 16 digits display.

Display address registers

The display address registers hold the address of the byte currently being written or read by the CPU and scan count value. The read/write addresses are programmed by CPU command. If set in autoincrement mode, address in the address register is incremented for each read or write.

Display registers

Display registers are two 4-bit registers A and B. They hold the bit pattern of character to be displayed. The contents of display registers A and B can be blanked and inhibited individually.

14.6 Operating Modes

April/May-05

14.6.1 Input Modes

The 8279 provides 3 basic input modes :

- Scanned keyboard
- Scanned sensor matrix
- Strobed input

Scanned Keyboard

In this mode, keyboard can be scanned in two ways : **Encoded scan and Decoded scan.**

Encoded scan : In the encoded scan, scan lines $(SL_2 - SL_0)$ are decoded externally to provide 8 scan lines. We know that 8279 provides 8 returns lines. Therefore, the maximum size of keyboard matrix is 8×8 = 64. When the key is pressed, 8279 stores the encoded status of scan lines and return lines along with the status of SHIFT and CNTL/STB keys into the FIFO RAM, as shown in the Fig. 14.15.

B_7	B_6	B_5	B_4	B_3	B_2	B_1	B_0
CNTL	SHIFT	SCAN			RETURN		

Fig. 14.15 Scanned keyboard data format

CNTL is the MSB of the character and SHIFT is the next most significant bit. The next three bits are from the scan counter. The last three bits indicate to which return line the key is connected. With this 8-bit key code 8279 can recognize 256 (2^8) different characters.

Example 14.1 : *Find the key code for condition given below :*
CNTL/STB SHIFT keys are open.
The pressed key is connected to scan line 2 and return line 4.

Solution :

B_7	B_6	B_5	B_4	B_3	B_2	B_1	B_0
1	1	0	1	0	1	0	0

CNTL = 1
SHIFT = 1
Scan Code = 0 1 0 (scan line 2)
Return Code = 1 0 0 (return line 4)
∴ Key code = D4H

Decoded scan : In the decoded mode, the internal decoder decodes the least significant 2 bits of scan lines internally to provide four possible combinations on the scan lines $(SC_3 - SC_0)$: 1110, 1101, 1011 and 0111. Therefore maximum size of keyboard matrix is 8×4 = 32. In this mode, keycode is generated in similar way as in the encoded mode, only bit 5 of keycode is always 0. Therefore, 8279 can recognize only 128 (2^7) characters.

The scanned keyboard mode allows key depressions in 2-key lockout or N-key rollover mode with key debounce.

2-key lockout : In this mode, simultaneous key depression is not allowed. When any key is depressed, the debounce logic is set and 8279 checks for any other key depress during next two scans. Now we will see how this mode reacts with three possible conditions that can occur during debounce scanning.

Condition 1 : If other key depress not found during next two scans, it is a single key depression and the key code is entered into FIFO RAM along with the status of CNTL and SHIFT lines. If the FIFO was empty, IRQ will be set to signal the CPU that there is an entry in the FIFO RAM. If the FIFO RAM was full, the key will not be entered and the error flag will be set.

Condition 2 : If another key depress is encountered, no entry to the FIFO can occur. If all other keys are released before first one, then it will be entered to the FIFO. If first key is released before any other, it will be entirely ignored.

Condition 3 : If two keys are depressed within the debounce cycle, it is a simultaneous depression. Neither key will be recognized until one key remains depressed alone. The last key will be treated as a single key depression.

N-Key Rollover : In N-Key rollover, each key depression is treated independently from all others. When a key is depressed, the debounce logic is set and 8279 checks for key depress during next two scans. Now we will see how this mode reacts with three possible conditions that can occur during debounce scanning.

Condition 1 : If key is still pressed then key is entered into the FIFO.

Condition 2 : If other keys are pressed, they are recognized and entered into the FIFO.

Condition 3 : If a simultaneous depression occurs, the keys are recognized and entered according to the keyboard scan found them.

Scanned Sensor Matrix : In the sensor matrix mode, image of the sensor matrix is kept in the sensor RAM. The status of the sensor switches are input directly to the sensor RAM. 8279 scans rows one by one and stores the status of each row in the corresponding location in the sensor RAM. For example, when 8279 scans first row of sensor matrix it stores the status of first row in the location 0 of the sensor RAM. At the end of sensor matrix scan if any sensor value change is detected then 8279 sets 'S' bit in the status register and activates the IRQ signal. In the autoincrement mode, the IRQ line is cleared by issuing End of Interrupt command, otherwise it is cleared by the first data read operation. When multiple changes in the sensor matrix occurs, multiple interrupts are generated. In sensor matrix mode, the debounce logic is inhibited. Although it is inhibited, sensor matrix mode has the advantage that CPU knows how long the sensor was closed and when it was released. The scanned keyboard mode can only indicate validated key closure.
In encoded mode, size of sensor matrix is 8×8 whereas in decoded mode size of sensor matrix is 8×4. In both the modes CNTL and SHIFT lines are ignored.

Strobed input mode

In the strobed input mode, data is entered to the FIFO RAM from the returned lines. The data is entered at the rising edge of the CNTL/STB signal.

14.6.2 Display Modes

The 8279 provides 2 basic output modes

- Left Entry (type writer type)
- Right Entry (calculator type)

14.6.2.1 Left Entry

In the left entry mode, 8279 displays characters from left to right in the multiplexed displays like a typewriter. In this, each display position directly corresponds to a byte (or nibble) in the display RAM. Address 0 in the RAM is the left-most display character and address 15 (or address 7 in 8 character display) is the right most display character, as shown in the Fig. 14.16.

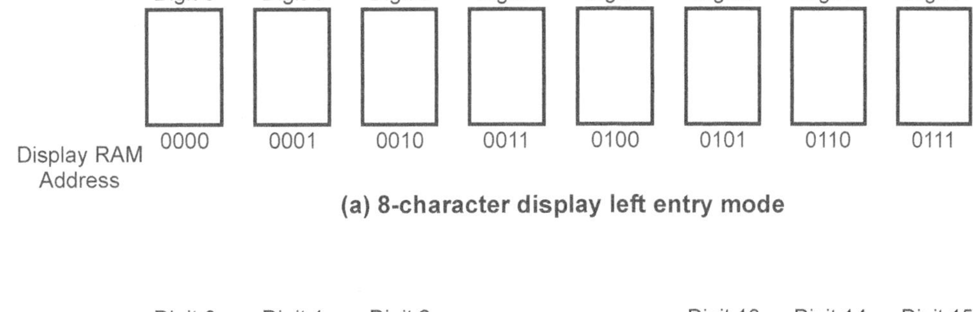

(a) 8-character display left entry mode

(b) 16-character display left entry mode

Fig. 14.16

Entering characters from possible zero causes the display to fill from the left. The 17th (9th in case 8 character display) character is entered back in the left most position and filling again proceeds from there, as shown in the Fig. 14.17. The characters can be displayed on the specific digit by loading character code in the corresponding location in the display RAM.

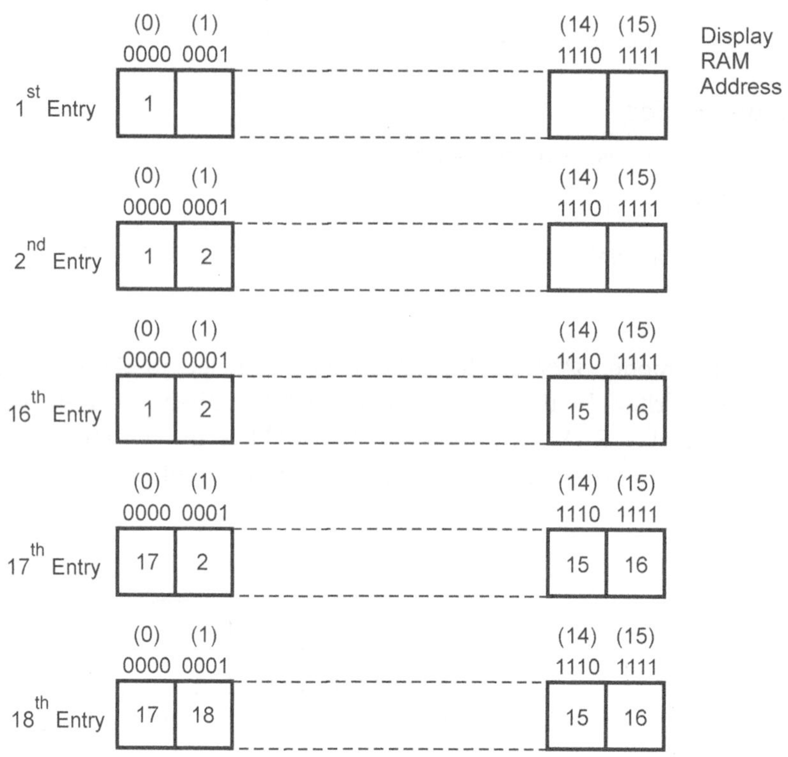

Fig. 14.17 16-characters left entry mode

Autoincrement in Left Entry

In left entry mode, if autoincrement flag is set to 1 after each write operation display RAM address is incremented by one so that it will point the next location in the display RAM. This autoincrement facility allows user to load display RAM in a sequential manner, and it is not necessary to specify display RAM address for each write operation.

14.6.2.2 Right Entry

In the right entry mode, 8279 displays characters from right to left in the multiplexed display like a calculator. The first entry is displayed on the right most display. The next entry is also displayed on the right most display after the display is shifted left one character, as shown in the Fig. 14.18.

When new character is entered, it shifts all previous characters left by one position and displays new entry on the right most display.

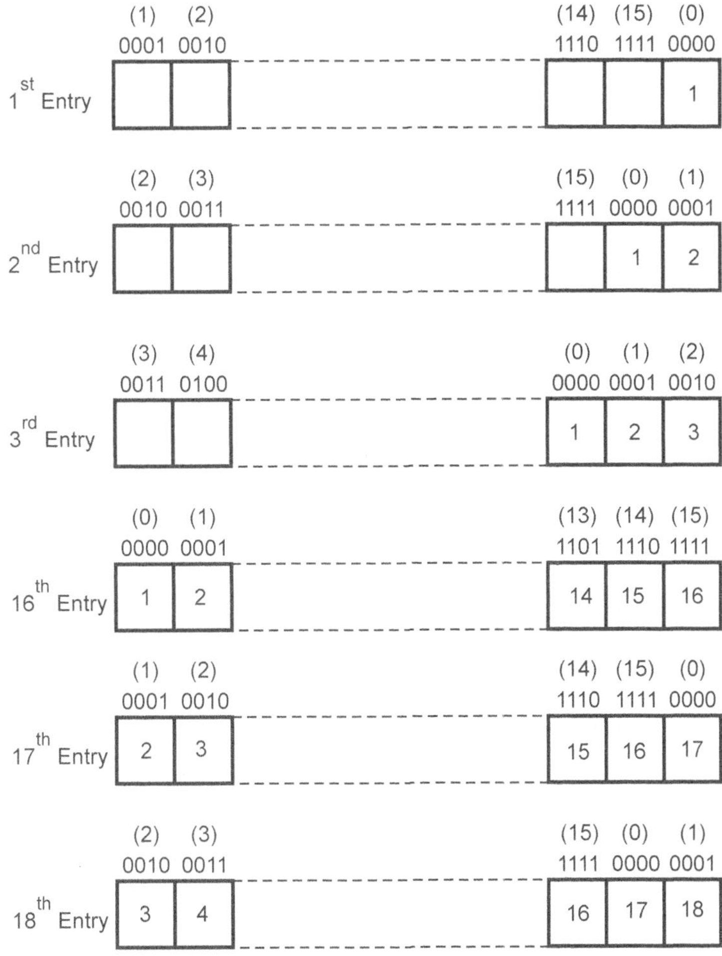

Fig. 14.18 16-characters right entry mode with autoincrement

Autoincrement in Right Entry

In the right entry mode, autoincrementing and non autoincrementing have the same effect as in the left entry except if the address sequence is changed. Some examples with changed address sequence.

First character is displayed on the right most digit of the display. After second entry, first character is shifted left and second character is displayed on the right most digit of the display. In the third entry, address of display RAM is changed to 5, displaying the third character at fifth digit after shifting the previous characters 1 digit left. In the 4th entry the new character is displayed at 5th digit after shifting all previous characters 1 digit left, and this sequence is continued.

14.7 8279 Commands

In the last sections we have seen various operating modes of 8279. To program 8279 in the desired mode it provides eight command words. The command words are sent on the data bus with $\overline{CS}$ low and A_0 high and are loaded to the 8279 on the rising edge of $\overline{WR}$. 8279 differentiate these commands by checking 3 most significant bits of the command word.

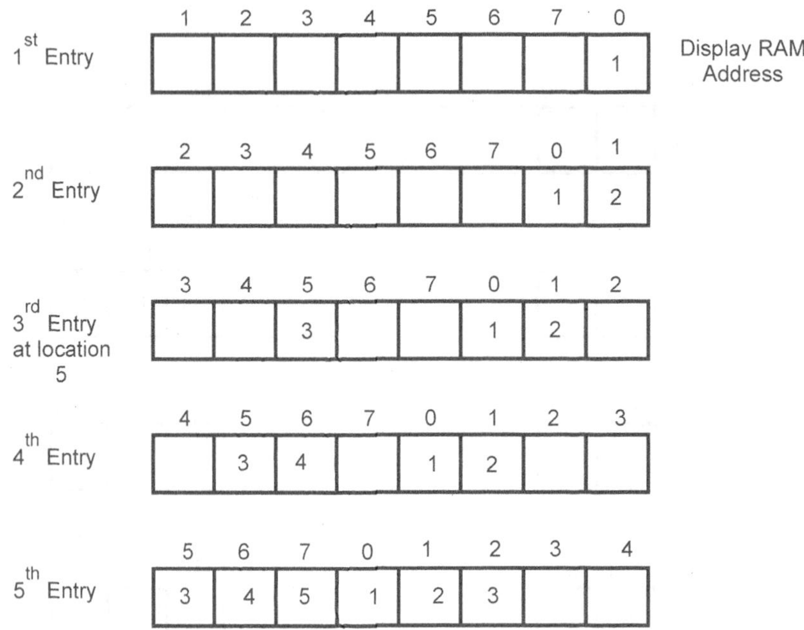

Fig. 14.19 8-characters right entry with autoincrement

14.7.1 Keyboard / Display Mode Set Command (000)

This command is used to program operating modes of keyboard and display. Three least significant bits decide the keyboard mode and next two bits decide the display mode, as shown in the tables.

Command Word Format

B_7	B_6	B_5	B_4	B_3	B_2	B_1	B_0
0	0	0	D	D	K	K	K

Fig. 14.20 Keyboard / display command word format

K	K	K	Keyboard Modes
0	0	0	Encoded Scan Keyboard-2 key lockout
0	0	1	Decoded Scan Keyboard-2 key lockout
0	1	0	Encoded Scan Keyboard-N key rollover
0	1	1	Decoded Scan Keyboard-N key rollover
1	0	0	Encoded Scan Sensor Matrix
1	0	1	Decoded Scan Sensor Matrix
1	1	0	Strobed Input, Encoded Display Scan
1	1	1	Strobed Input, Decoded Display Scan

Table 14.5 Keyboard modes

D	D	Display Modes
0	0	8 8-bit character display - Left Entry
0	1	16 8-bit character display - Left Entry
1	0	8 8-bit character display - Right Entry
1	1	16 8-bit character display - Right Entry

Table 14.6 Display modes

Example 14.2 : *Give the command word to set keyboard / display mode for the following configuration.*

Encoded scan keyboard - N key rollover

16 8-bit character display - Right Entry

Solution : **Command word :**

0	0	0	D	D	K	K	K	
0	0	0	1	1	0	1	0	= 1AH

Example 14.3 : *The microprocessor system has a configuration given below. Find the keyboard / display command word.*

8×4 *matrix keyboard - 2 key lockout*

4 Digit 7-segment display left entry

Solution : The system has 8×4 matrix keyboard and 4 digit display. Hence, only 4 scan lines are sufficient. The decoded mode of 8279 provides 4 scan lines directly and these lines can be used directly to interface 8×4 matrix keyboard and 4 digit display without external decoder. Therefore, we should select keyboard and display modes as:

Keyboard mode : Decoded scan keyboard - 2 key lockout

Display mode : 8-bit character display left entry

Command word :

0	0	0	D	D	K	K	K	
0	0	0	0	0	0	0	1	= 01H

14.7.2 Program Clock Command (001)

All timing and multiplexing signals for the 8279 are generated by an internal prescaler. This prescaler divides the external clock by a programmable integer value given in the program clock command word, to generate internal frequency. Fig. 14.21 shows format for program clock command word.

B_7	B_6	B_5	B_4	B_3	B_2	B_1	B_0
0	0	1	P	P	P	P	P

Fig. 14.21 Program clock command word format

Bits PPPPP determine the value of this integer which ranges from 2 to 31. To give proper scan and key debounce times the internal frequency should be 100 kHz. Therefore, prescaler integer value should be selected to get 100 kHz internal frequency.

$$\text{Prescaler value} = \frac{\text{External clock}}{100 \text{ kHz}}$$

Example 14.4 : *Find the program clock command word if external clock frequency is 2 MHz.*

Solution :

$$\text{Prescaler value} = \frac{2 \times 10^6}{100 \times 10^3} = 20 = (10100)_2$$

$$\therefore \text{ Command word} = (00110100)_2 = 34\text{H}$$

14.7.3 Read FIFO / Sensor RAM Command (010)

To read data from FIFO/Sensor RAM, it is necessary to set 8279 in read FIFO/sensor RAM mode. Read FIFO/Sensor RAM command is used for this purpose. Fig. 14.22 shows the format for Read FIFO/Sensor RAM command.

B_7	B_6	B_5	B_4	B_3	B_2	B_1	B_0
0	1	0	AI	X	A	A	A

Fig. 14.22 Read FIFO / Sensor RAM command word format

Here, three least significant bits, (AAA) specify the address of the sensor RAM and bit B_4, if 1 enables autoincrement mode. In the scan keyboard mode, the autoincrement flag (AI) and the FIFO RAM address bits (AAA) are irrelevant. In this mode, 8279 provides data for each subsequent read in the same sequence in which the data first entered in the FIFO RAM.

In the sensor matrix mode, the sensor RAM address bits AAA select one of the 8 rows of the sensor RAM. If the autoincrement flag is set (AI = 1), each successive read will be from the subsequent row of the sensor RAM.

Example 14.5 : *Write a command word to read data from FIFO RAM.*

Solution : We know that, in scan keyboard mode, the autoincrement flag (AI) and the FIFO RAM address bits (AAA) are irrelevant. Therefore, command word to read data from FIFO RAM is as given below.

			AI	D	A	A	A	
0	1	0	X	X	X	X	X	= 40H

Note : X = Don't care. Taking don't cares equal to zeros we get command word to read data from FIFO RAM is 40H.

Example 14.6 : *Write a command word to read third location with autoincrement of the sensor RAM in sensor matrix mode.*

Solution : Command word :

			AI		A	A	A	
0	1	0	1	X	0	1	1	= 53H

14.7.4 Read Display RAM Command (011)

To read data from display RAM, it is necessary to set 8279 in read display RAM mode. Read display RAM command is used for this purpose. Fig. 14.23 shows the format for Read Display RAM command.

B_7	B_6	B_5	B_4	B_3	B_2	B_1	B_0
0	1	1	AI	A	A	A	A

Fig. 14.23 Read display RAM command word format

Here, four least significant bits (AAAA) specify the address of the 16 byte display RAM and bit B_4, if 1, enables autoincrement mode. If the bit B_4 (AI) is set, display RAM address is incremented after each read command to display RAM.

Example 14.7 : *Write a command word to read fourth location with autoincrement of the display RAM.*

Solution : Command word :

			AI	A	A	A	A	
0	1	1	1	0	1	0	0	= 74H

14.7.5 Write Display RAM Command (100)

To write data into display RAM, it is necessary to set 8279 in write display RAM mode. Write display RAM command is used for this purpose. Fig. 14.24 shows the format for Write display RAM command.

B_7	B_6	B_5	B_4	B_3	B_2	B_1	B_0
1	0	0	AI	A	A	A	A

Fig. 14.24 Write display RAM command word format

Here, four least significant bits (AAAA) specify the address of the 16 byte display RAM and bit B_4, if 1, enables autoincrement mode. If the bit B_4 (AI) is set, display RAM address is incremented after each write command to display RAM.

Example 14.8 : *Write a command word to write fifth location without autoincrement of the display RAM.*

Solution : Command word :

			AI	A	A	A	A	
1	0	0	0	0	1	0	1	= 85H

14.7.6 Display Write Inhibit / Blanking Command (101)

We know that, display RAM data is sent on the two 4-bit ports (B_3-B_0 and A_3-A_0) This two 4-bit pots can be individually inhibited or blanked with Display Write Inhibit/Blanking command. Fig. 14.25 shows the format for Display Write Inhibit/Blanking Command.

B_7	B_6	B_5	B_4	B_3	B_2	B_1	B_0
1	0	1	X	IW A	IW B	BL A	BL B

Fig. 14.25 Display write Inhibit / blanking command word format

The IW bits are used to mask nibble. A (4-bit port A) and nibble B (4-bit port B) in applications requiring separate 4-bit display ports. By setting the IW flag (I/W = 1) for one of the ports, the port can be masked so that entries to the display RAM from the CPU do not affect other port.

The BL bits are used to blank the individual nibbles. This command loads the blank code (All zeros, 20H, or All ones) determined by the last issued clear command, in the display RAM to blank the display.

Note : After reset blank code is set to all zeros.

Example 14.9 : *Write a command word to inhibit nibble A of the display.*

Solution : Command word :

				IW A	IW B	BL A	BL B	
1	0	1	X	1	0	0	0	= A8H

14.7.7 Clear Command (110)

Clear command is used to clear all the rows of the display RAM with a selectable blanking code, to clear status of FIFO RAM and to reset interrupt output line. Fig. 14.26 shows the format of clear command.

1	1	0	CD_2	CD_1	CD_0	CF	CA

Fig. 14.26 Clear command word format

CD bits (CD_0 - CD_1) are used to select the blanking code as given below

CD_1	CD_0	Blanking Code
0	X	All zeros (for common cathode displays)
1	0	20H (for alphanumeric displays)
1	1	All ones (for common anode displays)

Bit CD_2, when set to one, enables clear display.

Bit CF, when set to one, clears the status of the FIFO, resets the interrupt output line and sets the sensor RAM address to 000.

CA, the clear all bit, has the combined effect of CD and CF; it uses the CD clearing code on the displays RAM and also clears FIFO status. It also resynchronizes the internal timing chain.

Example 14.10 : *Write a command word to set blanking code for common anode display and to clear the FIFO status.*

Solution : Blanking code for common anode display is all ones and which can be set by writing CD_1 = 1 and CD_2

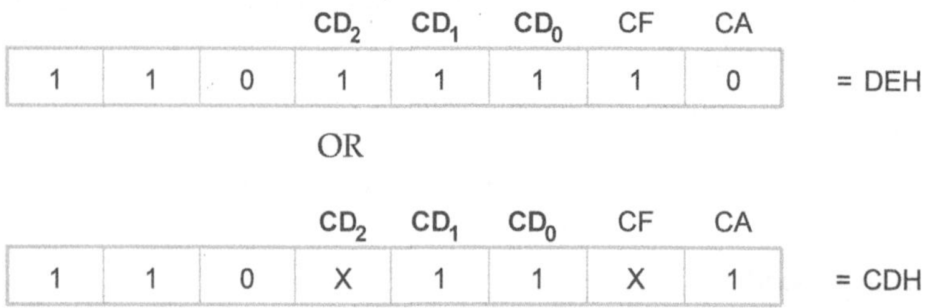

			CD_2	CD_1	CD_0	CF	CA	
1	1	0	1	1	1	1	0	= DEH

OR

			CD_2	CD_1	CD_0	CF	CA	
1	1	0	X	1	1	X	1	= CDH

14.7.8 End Interrupt / Error Mode Set Command (111)

In the sensor matrix mode, if any change in sensor value is detected, IRQ line goes high at the end of a sensor matrix scan. The IRQ line is cleared by the first data read operation if the autoincrement flag is set to zero. But if autoincrement flag is set to one then it is necessary to issue End Interrupt Command to clear the IRQ line. Fig. 14.27 shows the format for End Interrupt/Error mode set command.

B_7	B_6	B_5	B_4	B_3	B_2	B_1	B_0
1	1	1	E	X	X	X	X

Fig. 14.27 End interrupt / Error mode set command word format

For the N key rollover mode, if the E bit is programmed to '1', the 8279 will operate in the Special Error Mode. In the special error mode, if two keys are depressed during single debounce, the error flag in the FIFO status word is set.

Example 14.11 : *Write a command word to clear IRQ line in a sensor matrix mode.*

Solution : Command word :

			E					
1	1	1	X	X	X	X	X	= E0H

Note : Status of E bit can be 0 or 1.

FIFO STATUS REGISTER

It is used in the keyboard and strobed input modes to indicate the number of characters in the FIFO and to indicate whether an error has occurred. Fig. 14.28 shows the format of FIFO status word. (See Fig. 14.28 on next page.)

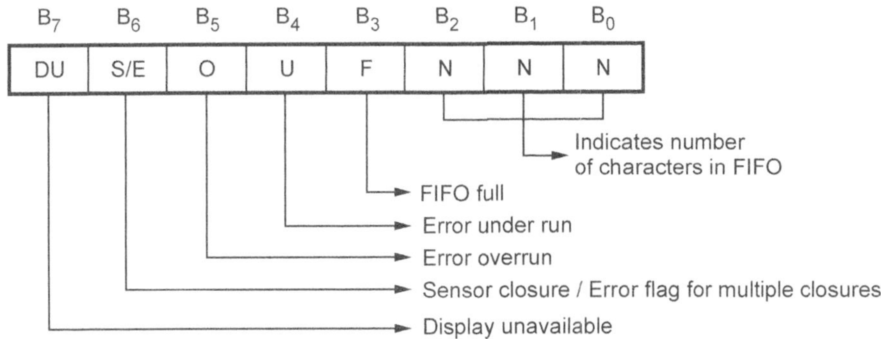

Fig. 14.28 FIFO status word

As shown in the Fig. 14.28, there are two types of possible errors : Overrun and underrun. Overrun error occurs when the entry of another character into a full FIFO is attempted. Underrun occurs when the CPU tries to read an empty FIFO.

During clear display or clear all command, display RAM is not available for user. This is indicated DU bit in the FIFO status register.

In the sensor matrix mode, a S/E bit is set in the FIFO status word to indicate that at least one sensor closure indication is contained in the sensor RAM.

In the special error mode, a S/E bit is set in the FIFO status word to indicate that a simultaneous multiple closure error has occurred.

14.8 Interfacing 8279 in I/O Mapped I/O

Fig. 14.29 shows the interfacing of 8279 with 8085 in I/O mapped I/O technique. Here $\overline{RD}$ and $\overline{WR}$ signals are activated when IO/$\overline{M}$ signal is high, indicating I/O bus cycle. Reset out signal from 8085 is connected to the Reset signal of the 8279. CLK input of 8279 is driven from the clock out of 8085. A_0 signal from the 8085 is connected to the A_0 input of 8279. The chip select signal, $\overline{CS}$ is generated using decoding circuit. Interrupt signal from the 8279 is connected to the RST 7.5 input of the 8085. It can also be connected to the RST 5.5, RST 6.5 or Trap input of 8085.

I/O Map :

Data/Control Register	Address lines								Address
	A_7	A_6	A_5	A_4	A_3	A_2	A_1	A_0	
Data Register	0	0	0	0	0	0	0	0	00H
Control Register	0	0	0	0	0	0	0	1	01H

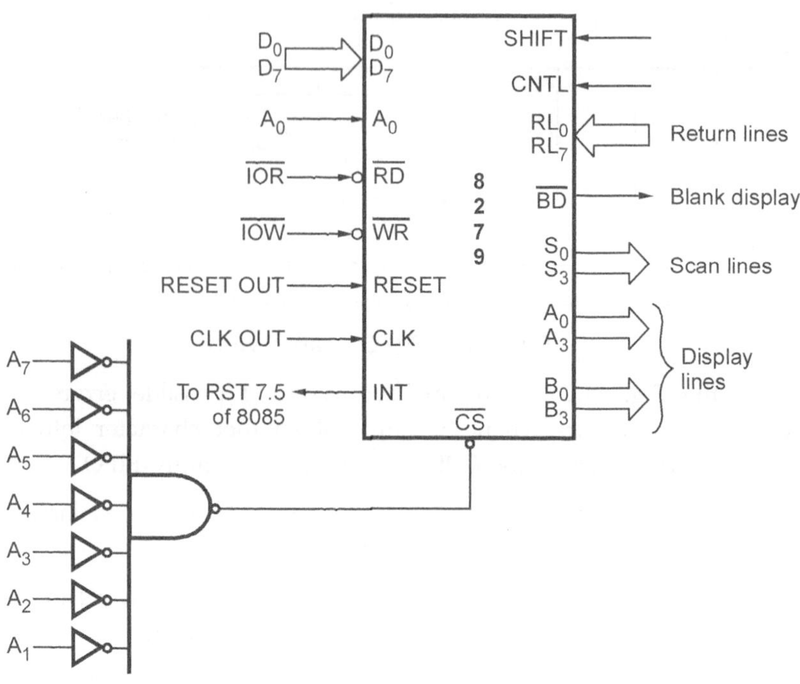

Fig. 14.29 Interfacing of 8279 in I/O mapped I/O

14.9 Applications

In this section we will discuss many useful applications with different modes of keyboard and display interfacing. In addition to this we are going to see the software requirement to control the interfacing circuits. All these applications are illustrated using different examples.

Lab Experiment 72 : Hardware and software for 8 × 8 keyboard interface using 8279.

Statement : Interface an 8 × 8 matrix keyboard to 8085 through 8279 in 2-key lockout mode and write an assembly language program to read keycode of the pressed key. The external clock frequency is 2 MHz. Use I/O mapped I/O technique.

Solution : The 8 × 8 matrix keyboard can be interfaced to 8085 through 8279 in two ways.

1. Without interrupt signal
2. With interrupt signal (Interrupt driven Input)

We will see both the ways one by one.

1. Without interrupt signal

Hardware : Fig. 14.30 shows the interfacing of 8 × 8 matrix keyboard.

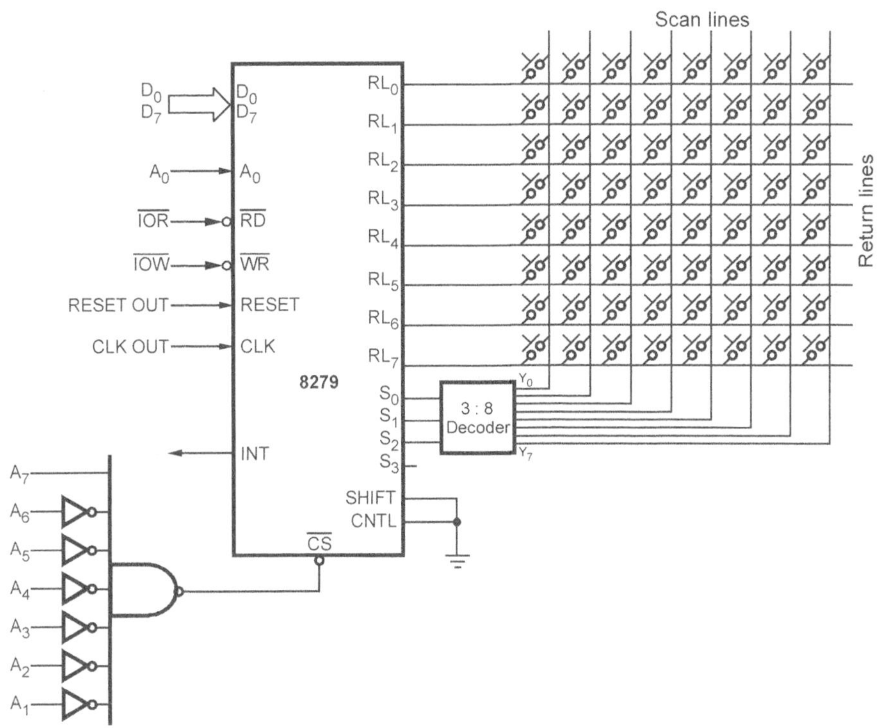

Fig. 14.30 Interfacing of 8 × 8 matrix keyboard

I/O Map :

Data/Control Register	Address lines								Address
	A_7	A_6	A_5	A_4	A_3	A_2	A_1	A_0	
Data Register	1	0	0	0	0	0	0	0	80H
Control Register	1	0	0	0	0	0	0	1	81H

Software :

Step 1 : Find keyboard/display command word. To interface 8 × 8 matrix keyboard we need 8 scan lines and 8 return lines. To get 8 scan lines. We have to select encoded scan keyboard mode. Therefore, the keyboard/display command word for above keyboard configuration is given as follows :

0	0	0	D	D	K	K	K	
0	0	0	X	X	0	0	0	= 00H

Note : 000 → Encoded scan keyboard - 2 key lockout
X → don't care

Step 2 : Find program clock command word

External clock frequency is 2 MHz

$$\therefore \quad \text{Prescaler value} = \frac{2\,\text{MHz}}{100\,\text{kHz}}$$

$$= 20 = (10100)_2$$

Therefore, the program clock command word is as given below :

			P	P	P	P	P	
0	0	1	1	0	1	0	0	= 34H

Step 3 : Find Read FIFO/sensor RAM command word we want to read first entry from the FIFO RAM. Therefore command word is as given below.

			AI		A	A	A	
0	1	0	0	X	0	0	0	= 40H

Flowchart :

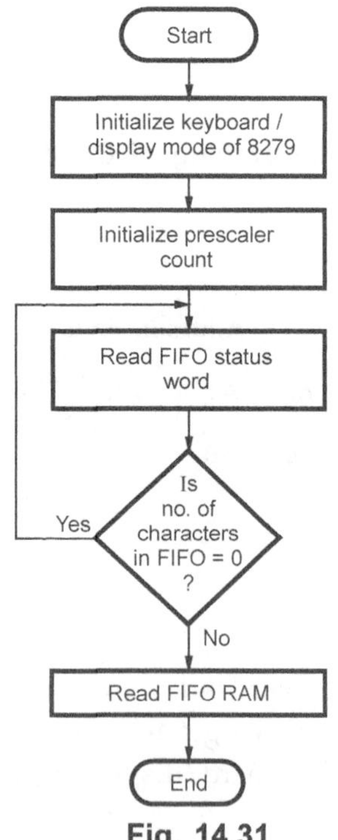

Fig. 14.31

Program :

```
        MVI A, 00H
        OUT 81H      ; Initialize keyboard/display
                     ; in encoded scan keyboard-2 keylockout mode
        MVI A 34H
        OUT 81H      ; Initialize prescaler count
BACK :  IN 81H       ; Read FIFO status word
        ANI 07H      ; Mask bit B3 to B7
        JZ BACK      ; If 0, key is not pressed wait for key press
                     ; otherwise read FIFO RAM
        MVI A, 40H   ; Initialize 8279 in read
        OUT 81H      ; FIFO RAM mode
        IN 80H       ; Read FIFO RAM (keycode)
        HLT          ; Stop program execution.
```

2. With Interrupt Signal

Hardware : Fig. 14.32 shows the interfacing of 8×8 matrix keyboard in interrupt driven keyboard mode.

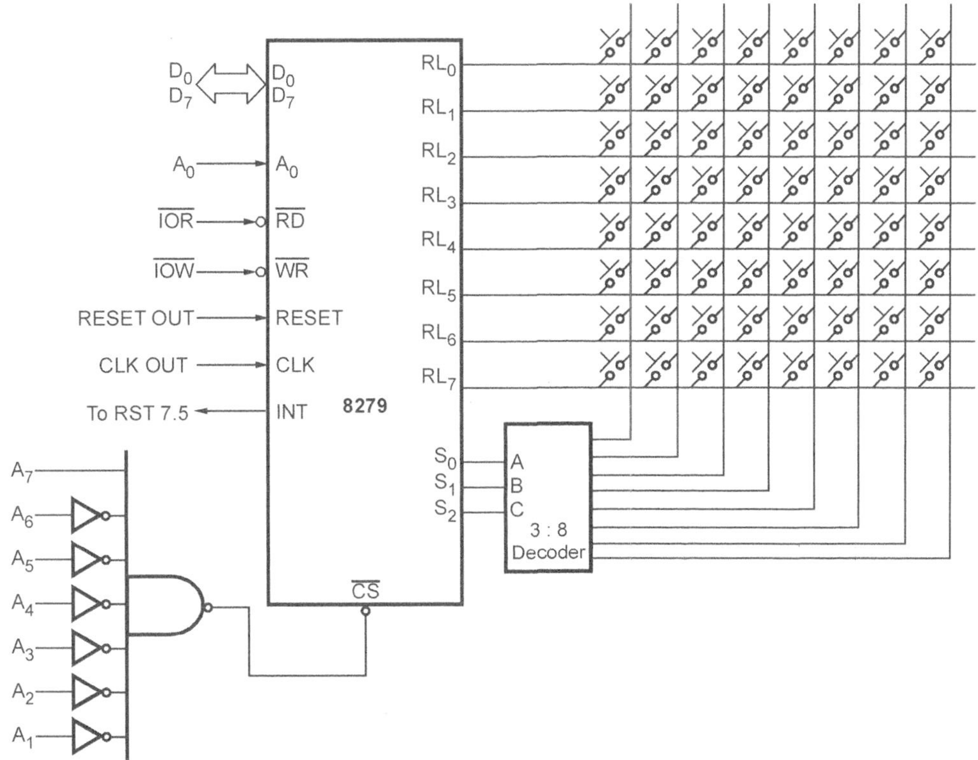

Fig. 14.32 Interfacing of 8×8 matrix keyboard in interrupt driven keyboard mode

In the interrupt driven mode interrupt line from 8279 is connected to the one of the interrupt input of 8085 except INTR. Here, INT line from 8279 is connected to the interrupt RST 7.5 of 8085. Other signal connections are same as in the non interrupt mode.

Software : All the command words required to initialize 8279 are same as in the non interrupt mode.

Flowchart :

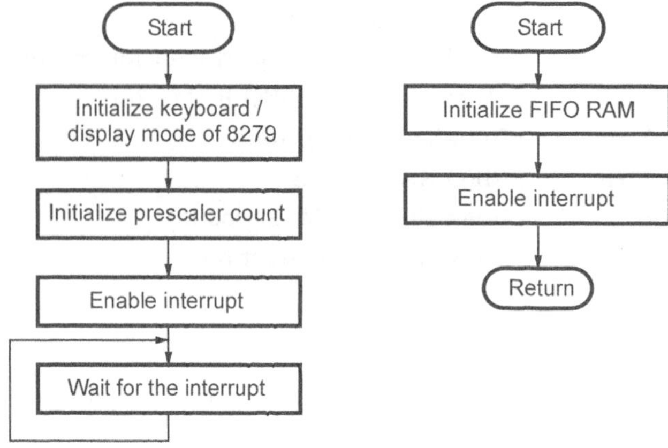

Fig. 14.33

Main Program :

```
        MVI A, 00H
        OUT 81H       ; Initialize keyboard/display in encoded
                      ; scan keyboard 2 key lockout mode
        MVI A, 34H
        OUT 81H       ; Initialize prescaler count
        MVI A, 0BH    ; Load mask pattern to enable RST 7.5 and mask other interrupts
        SIM
        EI            ; Enable Interrupt
HERE : JMP HERE       ; Wait for the interrupt
```

Interrupt Subroutine :

```
        MVI A, 40H    ; Initialize 8279 in read FIFO
        OUT 81H       ; RAM mode
        IN 80H        ; Read FIFO RAM (keycode)
        EI            ; Enable Interrupt
        RET           ; Return to main program
```

In the interrupt driven keyboard, when key is pressed, key code is loaded into FIFO RAM and interrupt is generated. This interrupt signal is used to tell CPU that there is a keycode in the FIFO RAM. CPU then initiates read command with in the interrupt service routine to read keycode from the FIFO RAM.

Lab Experiment 73 : Hardware and software to interface 8×4 matrix keyboard using 8279

Statement : Interface an 8×4 matrix keyboard to 8085 through 8279.

Solution : Fig. 14.34 shows interfacing of an 8×4 matrix keyboard to 8085 through 8279.

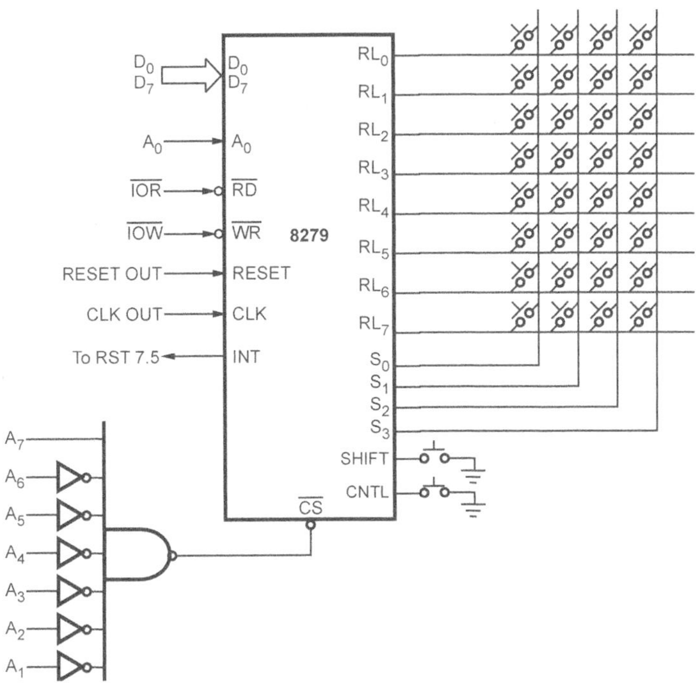

Fig. 14.34 Interfacing 8 × 4 keyboard matrix in decoded scan keyboard mode

As keyboard is having 8 rows and 4 columns, only 4 scan lines are required and we can avoid external decoder to generate scan lines by selecting decoded scan keyboard mode.

Main Program :

```
        MVI A, 00H
        OUT 81H         ; Initialize keyboard/display in encoded
                        ; scan keyboard 2 key lockout mode
        MVI A, 34H
        OUT 81H         ; Initialize prescaler count
        MVI A, 0BH      ; Load mask pattern to enable RST 7.5
                        ; and mask other interrupts
        SIM
        EI              ; Enable Interrupt
HERE : JMP HERE         ; Wait for the interrupt
```

Interrupt Subroutine :

```
MVI A, 40H    ; Initialize 8279 in read FIFO
OUT 81H       ; RAM mode
IN 80H        ; Read FIFO RAM (keycode)
EI            ; Enable Interrupt
RET           ; Return to main program
```

Lab Experiment 74 : Hardware and software to interface eight 7-segment digits using 8279.

Statement : Interface 8/7-segment digits (common cathode) to 8085 through 8279 and write an 8085 assembly language program to display 1 to 8 on the eight seven segment digits. External clock frequency is 3 MHz.

Solution : Fig. 14.35 (see Fig. 14.35 on next page) shows the interfacing of eight 7-segment digits to 8085 through 8279.

As shown in the Fig. 14.35, eight display lines (B_0-B_3 and A_0-A_3) are buffered with the help of transistor and used to drive display digits. These buffered lines are connected in parallel to all display digits. S_0, S_1 and S_2 lines are decoded and decoded lines are used for selection of one of the eight digits.

Software : To display 1 to 8 numbers on the eight 7-segment digits we have to load 7-segment codes for 1 to 8 numbers in the corresponding display locations.

Number	h	g	f	e	d	c	b	a	Code
1	0	0	0	0	0	1	1	0	06
2	0	1	0	1	1	0	1	1	5B
3	0	1	0	0	1	1	1	1	4F
4	0	1	1	0	0	1	1	0	66
5	0	1	1	0	1	1	0	1	6D
6	0	1	1	1	1	1	0	1	7D
7	0	0	0	0	0	1	1	1	07
8	0	1	1	1	1	1	1	1	7F

Table 14.7 7-Segment codes for common cathode display

Step 1 : Find keyboard/display command word. To interface 8 digit 7 segment display we need 8/8-bit character display mode with left entry. For selection of 8 digits we need encoded scan mode. Therefore, the keyboard/display command word is as given below.

			D	D	K	K	K	
0	0	0	0	0	0	0	0	= 00H

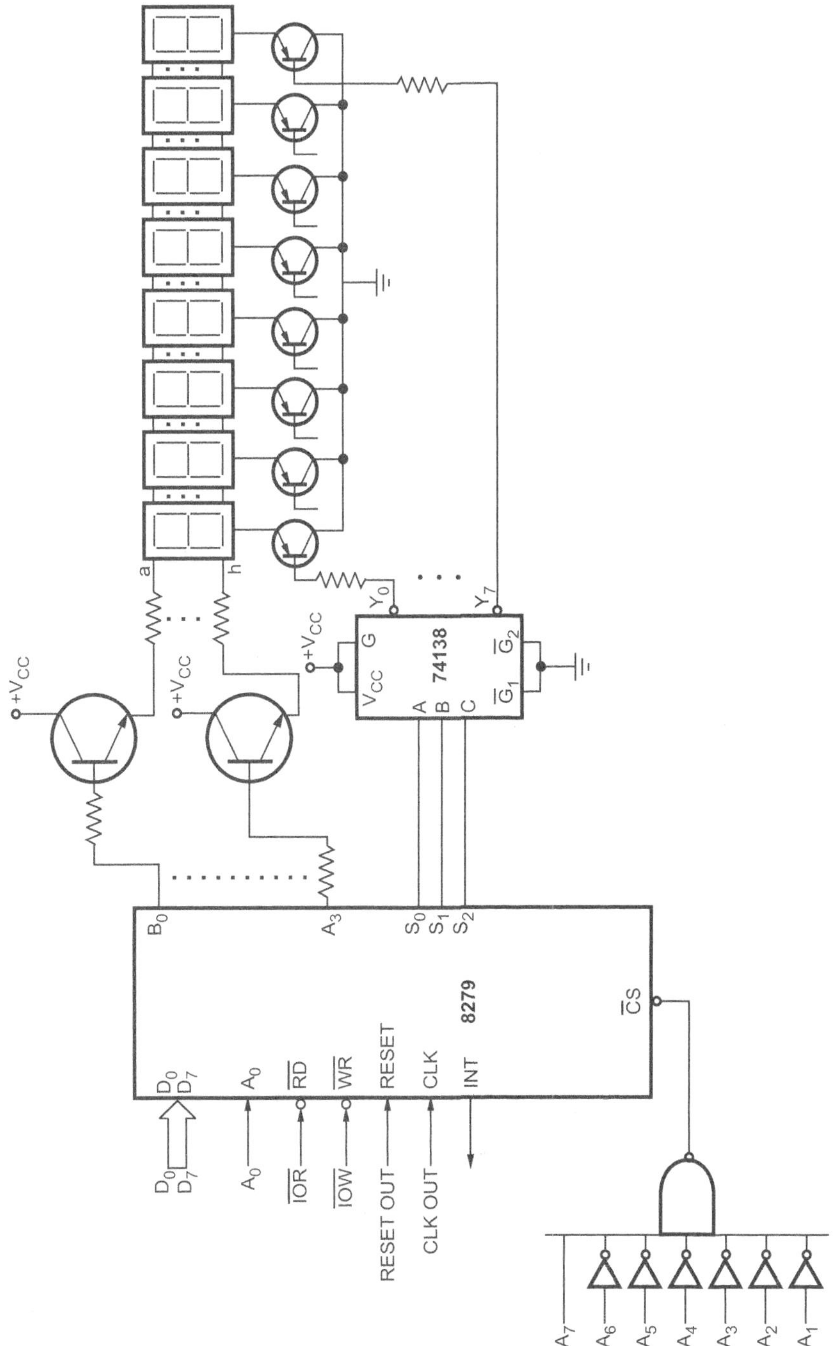

Fig. 14.35

Step 2 : Find program clock command word. External clock frequency is 3 MHz.

$\therefore$ Prescaler value $= \dfrac{3 \text{ MHz}}{100 \text{ MHz}} = 30 = (11110)_2$

Therefore, the program clock command word is as given below

			P	P	P	P	P	
0	0	1	1	1	1	1	0	= 3EH

Step 3 : Find write display RAM command word. We want to write first eight locations of display RAM with corresponding 7 segment codes. So we start from first location with autoincrement mode by command word given below.

			AI	A_3	A_2	A_1	A_0	
1	0	0	1	0	0	0	0	= 90H

Flowchart :

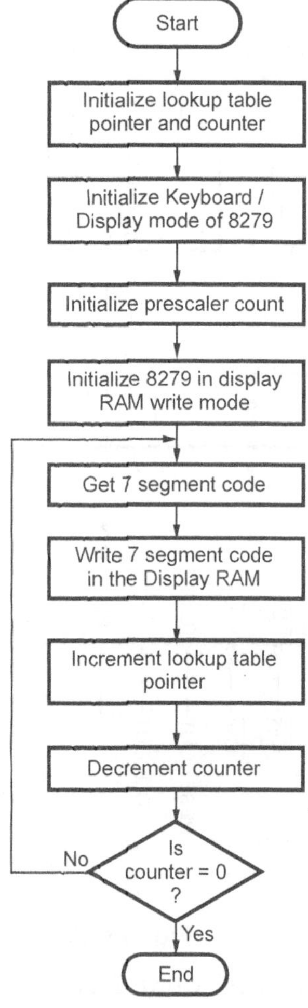

Fig. 14.36

Program :

```
        LXI H, 6200H   ; Initialize lookup table pointer
        MVI C, 08H     ; Initialize counter
        MVI A, 00H     ; Initialize keyboard/display
        OUT 81H        ; Mode
        MVI  A, 3EH    ; Initialize prescaler count
        OUT 81H
        MVI  A, 90H    ; Initialize 8279 in write Display
        OUT 81H        ; RAM mode
BACK :  MOV A,M        ; Get the 7-segment code
        OUT 80H        ; Write 7-segment code in display RAM
        INX H          ; Increment lookup table pointer
        DCR C          ; Decrement counter
        JNZ BACK       ; if count = 0 stop otherwise go to back
        HLT            ; Stop program execution
```

Lookup Table :

Memory Address	Contents
6200	66
6201	5B
6202	4F
6203	66
6204	6D
6205	7D
6206	07
6207	7F

Lab Experiment 75 : Write an assembly language program to roll message 'HELLO123'.

Statement : Using hardware same as in the example 3, write an assembly language program to roll message 'HELLO123' from right to left.

Solution : To roll above message we have to load 7-segment codes for characters within the message and it is necessary to configure 8279 in right entry mode.

Character	h	g	f	e	d	c	b	a	Code
H	0	1	1	1	0	1	1	0	76H
E	0	1	1	1	1	0	0	1	79H
L	0	0	1	1	1	0	0	0	38H
L	0	0	1	1	1	0	0	0	38H
0	0	0	1	1	1	1	1	1	3FH
1	0	0	0	0	0	1	1	0	06H
2	0	1	0	1	1	0	1	1	5BH
3	0	1	0	0	1	1	1	1	4FH

Table 14.8 7-segment codes for given message

Step 1: Find keyboard/display command word

			D	D	K	K	K	
0	0	0	1	0	0	0	0	= 10H

Note : DD= 10 = 8 8-bit character display right entry.

Program clock command word and write display RAM command word are same as in the previous example.

Clear command word

			CD_2	CD_1	CD_0	CF	CA	
1	1	0	1	0	0	0	0	= D0H

CD_0 - CD_1 = 00 (Blanking code)

Flowchart :

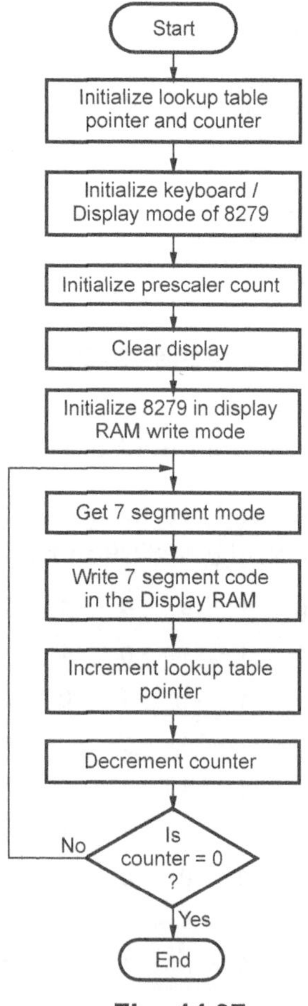

Fig. 14.37

Program :

```
        LXI H,6200H   ; Initialize lookup table pointer
        MVI C,08H     ; Initialize counter
        MVI A,10H     ; Initialize keyboard/display in right entry mode.
        OUT 81H       ; Mode
        MVI A,34H     ; Initialize prescaler count
        OUT 81H
        MVI A, D0H    ; Clear display
        OUT 81H
        MVI A, 90H    ; Initialize 8279 in write display
        OUT 81H       ; RAM mode
BACK :  MOV A,M       ; Get the 7-segment code
        OUT 80H       ; Write 7 segment code in display RAM
        INX H         ; Increment lookup table pointer
        DCR C         ; Decrement counter
        JNZ BACK      ; If count-0 stop; otherwise goto BACK
        HLT           ; Stop program execution.
```

Lookup table :

Memory address	Contents
6200H	76H
6201H	79H
6202H	38H
6203H	38H
6204H	3FH
6205H	06H
6206H	58H
6207H	4FH

Lab Experiment 76 : Interface 4×4 matrix keyboard and 4 digit 7-segment display using 8279

Statement : Interface 4 × 4 matrix keyboard and 4 digit 7-segment display and write an assembly language program to read keycode of the pressed key and display same key on the 7 segment display.

Solution : Fig. 14.38 shows interfacing diagram. Here, only 4 scan lines are sufficient to scan matrix keyboard and to select display digits. Hence decoded mode is used.

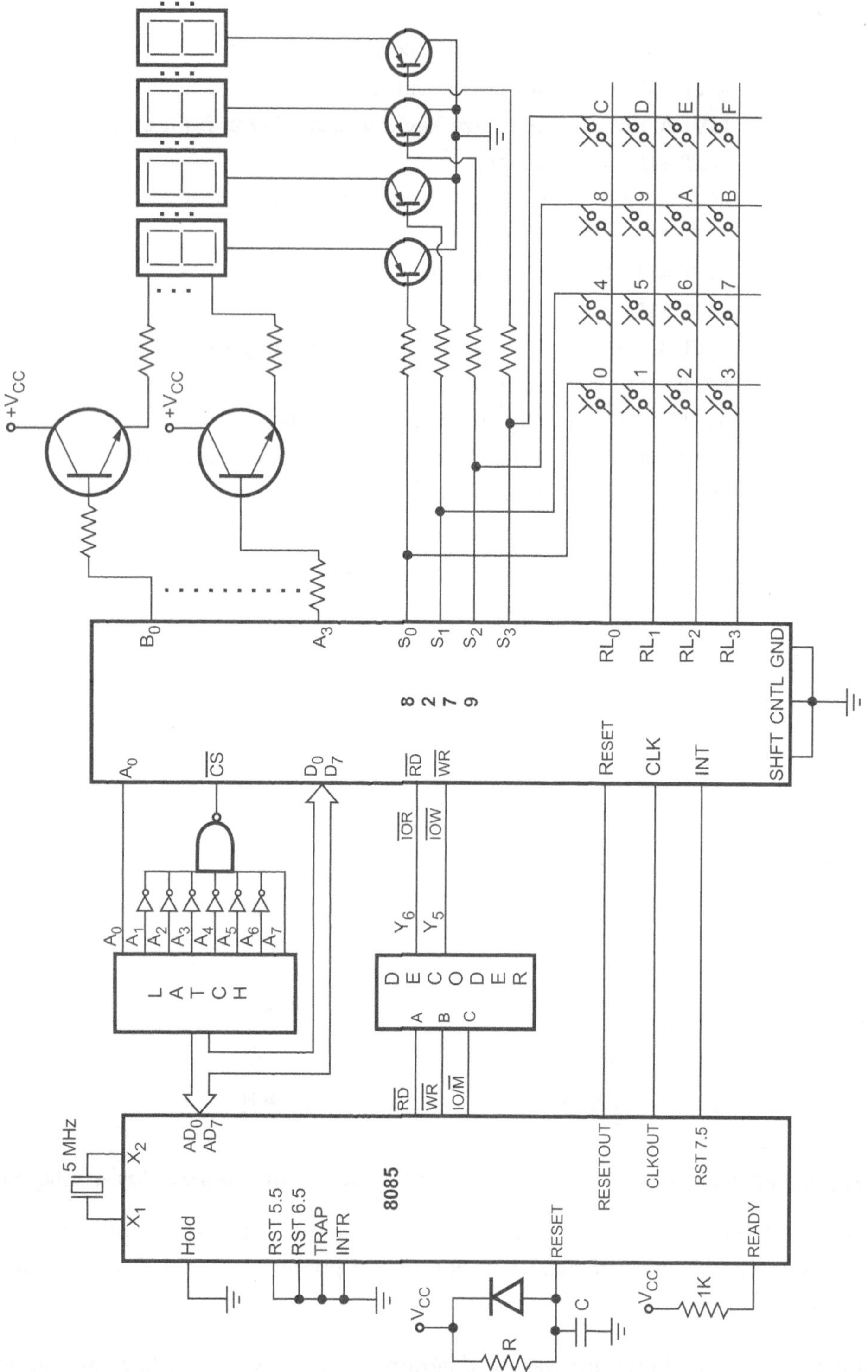

Fig. 14.38 Keyboard and display interfacing in decoded mode using 8279

Software :

Step 1 : Find keyboard / display command word.

			D	D	K	K	K	
0	0	0	0	0	0	0	1	= 01H

DD = 00 8/8-bit character display left entry

KKK = 001-Decoded scan keyboard-2 key lockout

Step 2 : Find program clock command word.

External clock frequency is 2.5 MHz

$$\therefore \quad \text{Prescaler value} = \frac{2.5\,\text{MHz}}{100\,\text{kHz}} = 25\ (11001)_2$$

Therefore, the program clock command word is as given below

			P	P	P	P	P	
0	0	1	1	1	0	0	1	= 39H

Step 3 : Find Read FIFO RAM command word. We want to read first entry from the FIFO RAM. Therefore command word is as given below.

			A	AI	A	A	A	
0	1	0	0	X	0	0	0	= 40H

Step 4 : Find Write FIFO RAM command word.

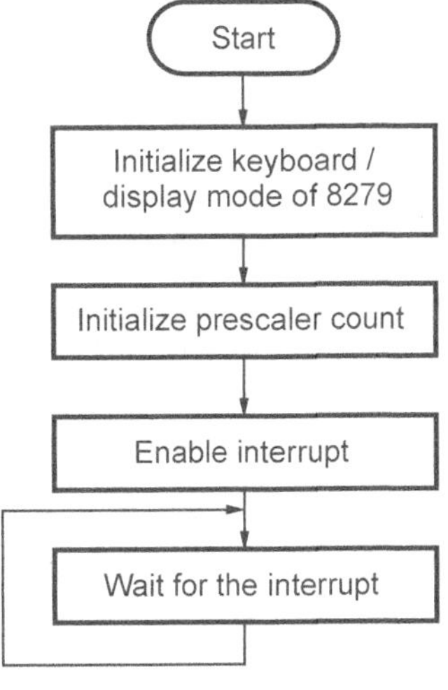

Fig. 14.39

We have to display at a time only single key number. Here mode is not required.

			AI	A_3	A_2	A_1	A_0	
1	0	0	0	0	0	0	0	= 80H

Flowchart : (See on previous page)

Interrupt Service Routine :

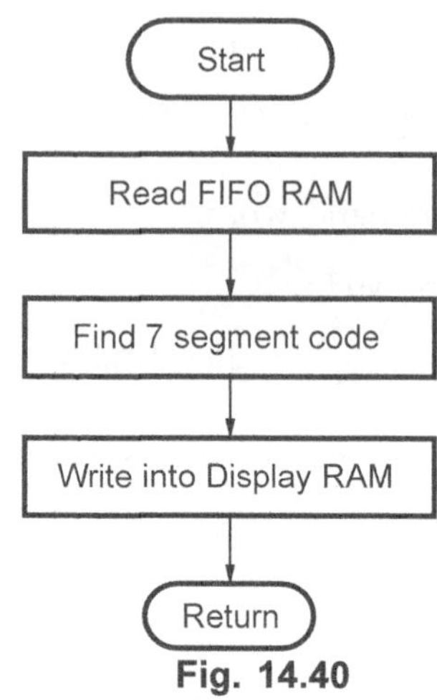

Fig. 14.40

Program :

```
        MVI A, 00H    ; Initialize keyboard / display in
        OUT 81H       ; encoded scan keyboard 2-key lockout mode.
        MVI A, 39H    ; Initialize prescaler count
        OUT 81H
        MVI A, 0BH    ; load mask pattern to enable RST 7.5
        SIM           ; and mask other interrupts
        EI            ; Enable interrupt
HERE :  JMP HERE      ; Wait for the interrupt
```

Interrupt service routine :

```
MVI A, 40H    ; Initialize 8279 in read FIFO RAM mode  OUT 81H
IN 80H        ; Get
MVI H, 62H    ; Initialize memory pointer to point
MOV L,A       ; 7-Segment code
MVI A, 80H    ; Initialize 8279 in write display RAM mode
OUT 81H
MOV A,M       ; Get the 7-segment code
OUT 80H       ; Write 7-segment code in display RAM
EI            ; Enable interrupt
RET           ; Return to main program
```

Review Questions

Section 14.1

Q.1 *What is keyboard interfacing ?* **May-12, Marks 2**

Section 14.2

Q.1 *Explain the seven segment LED interface with microprocessor.* **Dec.-04, May-06, Marks 16**

Q.2 *Design an interface circuit needed to connect DIP switch as an input device and display the value of the key pressed using a 7 segment LED display. Using 8085 system, write a program to implement the same.* **Dec.-05, Marks 16**

Section 14.3

Q.1 *Explain the advantages of using the following chips in microprocessor based systems : i) Keyboard and ii) Display controller.* **May-04, Marks 6**

Section 14.4

Q.1 *Explain important signals of 8279.*

Section 14.5

Q.1 *Explain the operation of the keyboard/display controller with a neat diagram.* **Dec.-09,11, Marks 8**

Q.2 *What is the function of scan section in 8279 programmable keyboard/display controller ?* **May-11, Marks 2**

Section 14.6

Q.1 *What do you mean by encoded scan and decoded scan ?*

Q.2 *Explain the input modes provided by 8279.*

Q.3 *Explain the terms 2-key lockout and N-key rollover.*

Q.4 *Why maximum size of keyboard matrix is $8 \times 8 = 64$, when interfaced with 8279 ?*

Q.5 *Explain the display modes provided by 8279.*

Section 14.7

Q.1 *Explain various command word formats of 8279.*

Section 14.8

Q.1 *Draw and explain the interfacing of 8279 with 8085.*

Section 14.9

Q.1 *Write a program using RST 5.5 interrupt to get an input from keyboard and display it on the display system.* **May-05, Marks 6**

Q.2 *Using peripheral mapped I/O, design a seven segment LED output port with device address of F2h using necessary control ICs. Draw the schematic and write 8085 ALP for displaying digit 8.* **May-07, Marks 8**

Two Marks Questions with Answers

Q.1 ***Define scan counter.***

Ans. : The scan counter has two modes to scan the key matrix and refresh the display. In the encoded mode, the counter provides binary count that is to be externally decoded to provide the scan lines for keyboard and display. In the decoded scan mode, the counter internally decodes the least significant 2 bits and provides a decoded 1 out of 4 scan on SL0-SL3. The keyboard and display both are in the same mode at a time.

Q.2 ***What is the output modes used in 8279?***

Ans. : 8279 provides two output modes for selecting the display options.

1. **Display scan :** In this mode, 8279 provides 8 or 16 character-multiplexed displays those can be organized as dual 4-bit or single 8-bit display units.
2. **Display entry** : 8279 allows options for data entry on the displays. The display data is entered for display from the right side or from the left side.

Q.3 ***What are the modes used in keyboard modes ?***

Ans. : 1. Scanned keyboard mode with 2 Key lockout. 2. Scanned keyboard with N-key rollover. 3. Scanned keyboard special error mode. 4. Sensor matrix mode.

Q.4 ***What are the modes used in display modes ?***

Ans. : 1. **Left entry mode :** In the left entry mode, the data is entered from the left side of the display unit.

2. **Right entry mode :** In the right entry mode, the first entry to be displayed is entered on the rightmost display.

Q.5 ***What is 8279?***

Ans. : The 8279 is a programmable keyboard/display interface.

Q.6 *List the major components of the keyboard/display interface.*

Ans. : a. Keyboard section b. Scan section c. Display section d. CPU interface section

Q.7 *What is key bouncing ?* May-06

Ans. : Mechanical switches are used as keys in most of the keyboards. When a key is pressed the contact bounce back and forth and settle down only after a small time delay (about 10 ms). Even though a key is actuated once, it will appear to have been actuated several times. This problem is called key bouncing.

Q.8 *How much current is needed to drive an LED? Draw a typical driver circuit for it.* May-05

Ans. : Around 15 mA current is needed to drive LED. The typical driver circuit for LED is

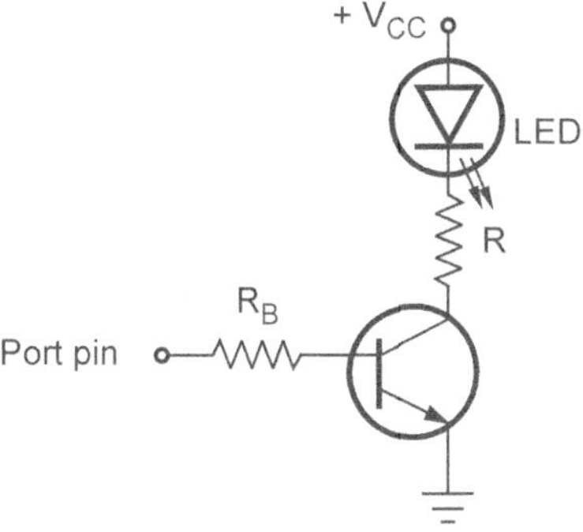

Fig. 14.41

Q.9 *How keyboard debouncing is done by software ?* Dec.-07

Ans. : In the software technique, when a key press is found, the microprocessor waits for at least 10 ms before it accepts the key as an input. This 10 ms period is sufficient to settle key at steady state. In this way key debouncing is done by software.

Q.10 *What is the difference between two key lockout and N-key rollover modes in 8279 ?* Dec.-10

Ans. : **2-key lockout :** In this mode, simultaneous key depression is not allowed.

N-key rollover : In N-key rollover, each key depression is treated independently from all others.

Q.11 *List the functions performed by 8279.*

Ans. : The functions performed by 8279 are :

1. It independently keeps display refresh with its multiplexed display interface in right entry mode or left entry mode.
2. It scans the matrix keyboard upto 64 keys with three input modes : scanned keyboard mode, scanned sensor matrix mode and stored input mode.

Q.12 ***What is the internal operating frequency of 8279 ? How can you derive it from any available clock signal ?***

Ans. : The internal operating frequency of 8279 is 100 kHz. We can derive the internal operating frequency from any available clock signal using internal prescaler.

This prescaler divides the external clock by a programmable integer value given in the program clock command word, to generate internal frequency.

Q.13 ***Describe the three major tasks needed to get meaningful information from matrix keyboard.***

Ans. :

1. Initialize keyboard in proper mode.
2. Initialize prescaler count.
3. Read keyboard entry from FIFO RAM.

Q.14 ***What is the necessity for a separate 8279 keyboard display controller ?***

Ans. : In software approach, to drive multiplexed displays CPU has to look after digit selection in synchronism with the data for specific digit and these displays need continuous refreshing. This puts a lot of burden on the CPU. In keyboard interface to provide facilities such as 2-key lockout, N-key Rollover CPU needs to execute necessary programs which further increases the burden on CPU and hence it is necessary to have separate 8279 keyboard/display controller.

Q.15 ***How a keyboard matrix is formed in keyboard interface using 8279 ?***

Ans. : Refer lab experiment 69.

Q.16 ***What is the function of scan section in 8279 programmable keyboard/display controller ?***

Ans. : Refer section 14.5.2.

❑❑❑

15 Programmable Interval Timer/Counter 8253/8254

Contents

The 8253/54 solves one of the most common problem in any microcomputer system - the generation of accurate time delays under software control. Instead of setting up timing loops in system software, the programmer configures the 8253/54 to match his requirements, initializes one of the counters of the 8253/54 with the desired quantity, then upon command the 8253/54 will count out the delay and interrupt the CPU when it has completed its tasks. It is easy to see that the software overhead is minimum and that multiple delays can be easily be maintained by assignment of priority levels.

The 8253/54 includes three identical 16 bit counters that can operate independently. To operate a counter, a 16-bit count is loaded in its register and, on command, it begins to decrement the count until it reaches 0. At the end of the count, it generates a pulse that can be used to interrupt the CPU. The counter can count either in binary or BCD. In addition, a count can be read by the CPU while the counter is decrementing. In this chapter, we are going to study two timer ICs 8253 and 8254. The 8254 is a superset of 8253. The functioning of these two ICs are almost similar along with the pin configuration. Only the differences are :

Sr. No.	8253	8254
1.	Operating frequency 0 - 2.6 MHz.	Operating frequency 0 - 10 MHz.
2.	Uses N-MOS technology.	Uses H-MOS technology.
3.	Read-Back command not available.	Read-Back command available.
4.	Reads and writes of the same counter cannot be interleaved.	Reads and writes of the same counter can be interleaved.

In this chapter, where the things are common 8253/54 is mentioned and 8254 is mentioned specifically for giving only information about 8254.

15.1 Features

1) Three independent 16-bit down counters.
2) 8254 can handle inputs from DC to 10 MHz (5 MHz 8254-5 8 MHz 8254 10 MHz 8254-2) where as 8253 can operate upto 2.6 MHz.
3) Three counters are identical, presettable and can be programmed for either binary or BCD count.

4) Counter can be programmed in six different modes.

5) Compatible with all Intel and most other microprocessors.

6) 8254 has powerful command called READ BACK command which allows the user to check the count value, programmed mode and current mode and current status of the counter.

15.2 Block Diagram

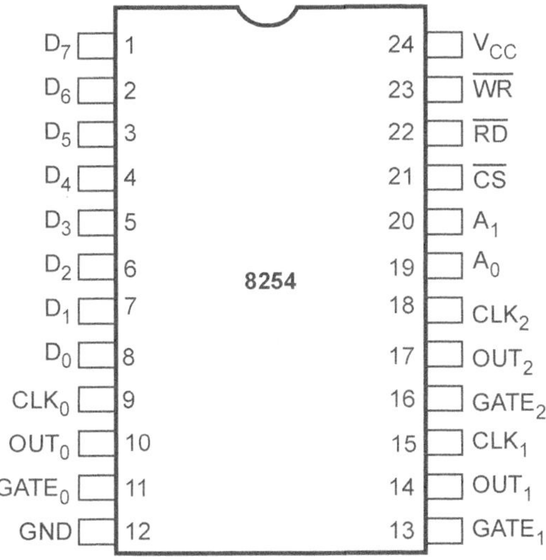

Fig. 15.1 Pin diagram of 8254

Fig. 15.1 and Fig. 15.2 show the pin diagram and block diagram of 8253/54. The block diagram of 8253/54 includes three counters, a data bus buffer, Read/Write control logic, and a control register. Each counter has two input signals CLOCK and GATE and one output signal OUT.

Data Bus Buffer : This tri-state, bi-directional, 8-bit buffer is used to interface the 8253/54 to the system data bus. The Data bus buffer has three basic functions.

1. Programming the 8253/54 in various modes.
2. Loading the count registers.
3. Reading the count values.

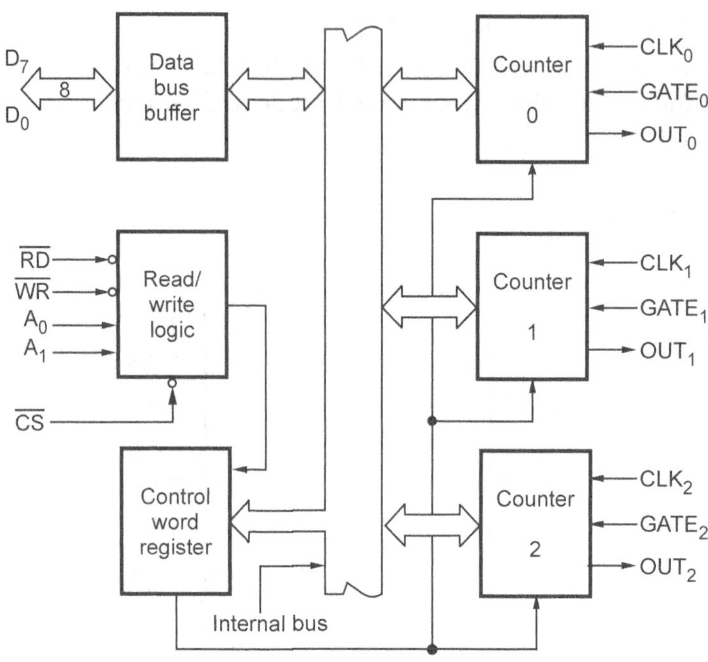

Fig. 15.2 Block diagram of 8254

Read/Write Logic : The Read/Write logic has five signals : $\overline{RD}$, $\overline{WR}$, $\overline{CS}$ and the address lines A_0 and A_1. In the peripheral I/O mode, the $\overline{RD}$, and $\overline{WR}$ signals are connected to $\overline{IOR}$ and $\overline{IOW}$, respectively. In memory-mapped I/O, these are connected to $\overline{MEMR}$ and $\overline{MEMW}$. Address lines A_0 and A_1 of the CPU are usually connected to lines A_0 and A_1 of the 8253/54, and $\overline{CS}$ is tied to a decoded address. The control word register and counters are selected according to the signals on lines A_0 and A_1.

A_1	A_0	Selection
0	0	Counter 0
0	1	Counter 1
1	0	Counter 2
1	1	Control word Register

Control Word Register : This register is accessed when lines A_0 and A_1 are at logic 1. It is used to write a command word which specifies the counter to be used (binary or BCD), its mode and either a read or write operation.

Counters : These three functional blocks are identical in operation. Each counter consists of a single, 16 bit, pre-settable, down counter. The counter can operate in either binary or BCD and its input, gate and output are configured by the selection of modes stored in the control word register. The counters are fully independent. The programmer can read the contents of any of the three counters without disturbing the actual count in process.

15.3 Operational Description

The complete functional definition of the 8253/54 is programmed by the system software. Once programmed, the 8253/54 is ready to perform whatever timing tasks it is assigned to accomplish.

Programming the 8253/54 :

Each counter of the 8253/54 is individually programmed by writing a control word into the control word register (A_0 A_1 = 11). The Fig. 15.3 shows the control word format. Bits SC_1 and SC_0 select the counter, bits RW_1 and RW_0 select the read, write or latch command, bits M_2, M_1 and M_0 select the mode of operation and bit BCD decides whether it is a BCD counter or binary counter.

D_7	D_6	D_5	D_4	D_3	D_2	D_1	D_0
SC_1	SC_0	RW_1	RW_0	M_2	M_1	M_0	BCD

SC - Select counter

SC_1	SC_0	
0	0	Select counter 0
0	1	Select counter 1
1	0	Select counter 2
1	1	Illegal for 8253 Read -Back command for 8254 (See Read operations)

M - Mode

M_2	M_1	M_0	
0	0	0	Mode 0
0	0	1	Mode 1
×	1	0	Mode 2
×	1	1	Mode 3
1	0	0	Mode 4
1	0	1	Mode 5

RW - Read /Write

RW_1	RW_0	
0	0	Counter latch command (See Read operations)
0	1	Read / Write least significant byte only
1	0	Read / Write most significant byte only
1	1	Read / write least significant byte first, then most significant byte

BCD :

0	Binary counter 16 - bits
1	Binary coded decimal (BCD) Counter (4 Decades)

Note : Don't care bits (×) should be 0 to ensure compatibility with future Intel products

Fig. 15.3 Control word format

WRITE Operation :

1. Write a control word into control register.
2. Load the low-order byte of a count in the counter register.
3. Load the high-order byte of count in the counter register.

READ Operation :

In some applications, especially in event counters, it is necessary to read the value of the count in process. This can be done by three possible methods :

1. Simple Read : It involves reading a count after inhibiting the counter by controlling the gate input or the clock input of the selected counter, and two I/O read operations are performed by the CPU. The first I/O operation reads the low-order byte, and the second I/O operation reads the high order byte.

2. Counter Latch Command : In the second method, an appropriate control word is written into the control register to latch a count in the output latch, and two I/O read operations are performed by the CPU. The first I/O operation reads the low-order byte, and the second I/O operation reads the high order byte.

3. Read-Back Command (Available only for 8254) : The third method uses the Read-Back command. This command allows the user to check the count value, programmed Mode, and current status of the OUT pin and Null count flag of the selected counter(s). Fig. 15.4 shows the format of the control word register for Read-Back command.

$A_0, A_1 = 11$ $\overline{CS} = 0$ $\overline{RD} = 1$ $\overline{WR} = 0$

D_7	D_6	D_5	D_4	D_3	D_2	D_1	D_0
1	1	$\overline{\text{COUNT}}$	$\overline{\text{STATUS}}$	CNT_2	CNT_1	CNT_0	0

D_5 : 0 = Latch count of selected counter(s)

D_4 : 0 = Latch status of selected counter(s)

D_3 : 1 = Select counter 2

D_2 : 1 = Select counter 1

D_1 : 1 = Select counter 0

D_0 : Reserved for future expansion : must be 0.

Fig. 15.4 Control word register for read-back command

The Read-Back command may be used to latch multiple counter output latches by setting the $\overline{\text{COUNT}}$ bit $D_5 = 0$ and selecting the desired counter(s). Each counter's latch count in held until it is read (or the counter is reprogrammed). That counter is automatically unlatched when read.

Other Features of Read - Back Command (Available only for 8254) :

The Read-Back command may also be used to latch status information of selected counter(s) by setting STATUS bit $D_4 = 0$. The contents of the counter must be latched before reading. The status of a counter is then accessed by a read from that counter. The Fig. 15.5 shows the counter status format.

D_7	D_6	D_5	D_4	D_3	D_2	D_1	D_0
OUTPUT	NULL COUNT	RW_1	RW_0	M_2	M_1	M_0	BCD

D_7 1 = OUT pin is 1.
0 = OUT pin is 0.

D_6 1 = NULL count.
0 = Count available for reading.

D_5-D_0 = Counter programmed mode. (see Fig. 15.3)

Fig. 15.5 Counter status format

Bit D_5 - D_0 contains the counter's programmed mode exactly as written in the last mode control word. Bit D_7 contains the current status of the output pin. In 8254, it is not possible to read count from the counter, if the count is not loaded into the counting element (CE). The Bit D_6 indicates whether the counting element has count or not. If $D_6 = 0$, counting element has count otherwise null count.

Interleaved Read and Write :

Another feature of the 8254 is that reads and writes of the same counter may be interleaved. For example, if the counter is programmed for the two byte counts, the following sequence is valid.

1. Read least significant byte.
2. Write new least significant byte.
3. Read most significant byte.
4. Write new most significant byte.

15.4 Mode Definition

May/June-07

Mode 0 : Interrupt on terminal count

a) Normal Operation :

1) The output will be initially low after the mode set operation. 2) After the count is loaded into the selected count Register the output will remain low and the counter will count. 3) When the terminal count is reached the output will go high and remain high until the selected count is reloaded.

b) Gate Disable :

1) Gate = 1 enables counting.

2) Gate = 0 disables counting.

Note : Gate has no effect on OUT.

c) New Count :

If a new count is written to the counter, it will be loaded on the next CLK pulse and counting will continue from the new count

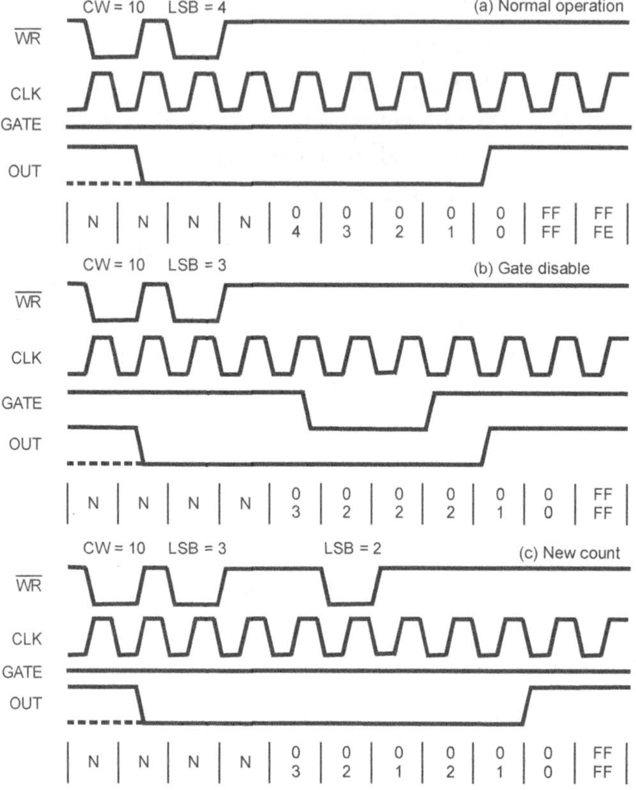

Fig. 15.6 Mode 0: interrupt on terminal count

In case of two byte count :

1) Writing the first byte disables counting.

2) Writing the second byte loads the new count on the next CLK pulse and counting will continue from the new count.

MODE 1 : Hardware Retriggerable One-shot

a) Normal operation :

1) The output will be initially high.

2) The output will go low on the CLK pulse following the rising edge at the gate input.

3) The output will go high on the terminal count and remain high until the next rising edge at the gate input.

b) Retriggering :

The one shot is retriggerable, hence the output will remain low for the full count after any rising edge of the gate input.

c) New count :

If the counter is loaded during one shot pulse, the current one shot is not affected unless the counter is retriggered. If retriggered, the counter is loaded with the new count and the one-shot pulse continues until the new count expires.

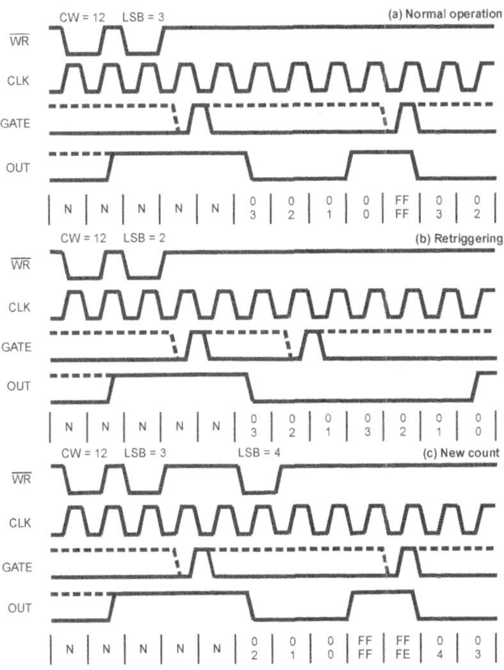

Fig. 15.7 Mode 1 : hardware retriggerable one-shot

MODE 2 : Rate generator

This mode functions like a divide by-N counter.

a) Normal operation :

1) The output will be initially high.
2) The output will go low for one clock pulse before the terminal count.
3) The output then goes high, the counter reloads the initial count and the process is repeated.
4) The period from one output pulse to the next equals the number of input counts in the count register.

b) Gate disable :

1) If Gate = 1 it enables a counting otherwise it disables counting (Gate = 0).
2) If Gate goes low during an low output pulse, output is set immediately high. A trigger reloads the count and the normal sequence is repeated.

c) New count :

The current counting sequence does not affect when the new count is written. If a trigger is received after writing a new count but before the end of the current period, the new count will be loaded with the new count on the next CLK pulse and counting will continue from the new count. Otherwise, the new count will be loaded at the end of the current counting cycle.

Note : In mode 2, a count of 1 is illegal.

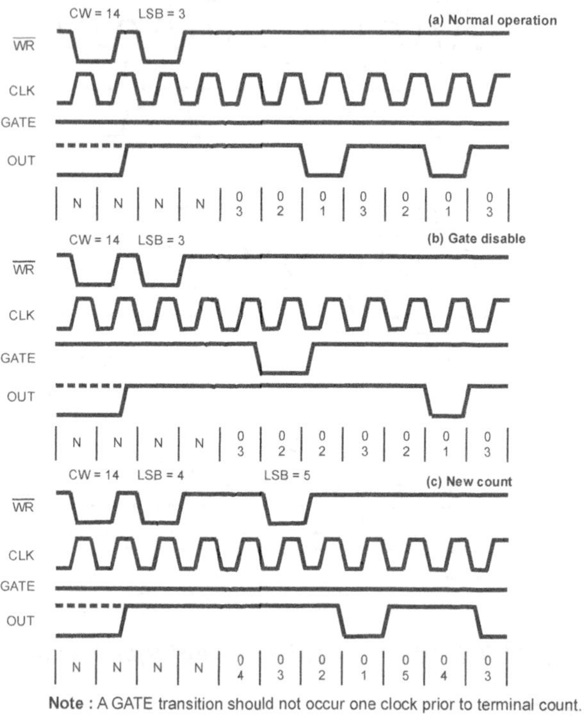

Fig. 15.8 Mode 2 : rate generator

MODE 3 : Square Wave Rate Generator

a) Normal operation :

1) Initially output is high.
2) For even count, counter is decremented by 2 on the falling edge of each clock pulse. When the counter reaches terminal count, the state of the output is changed and the counter is reloaded with the full count and the whole process is repeated.

3) If the count is odd and the output is high the first clock pulse (after the count is loaded) decrements the count by 1. Subsequent clock pulses decrement the clock by 2. After timeout, the output goes low and the full count is reloaded. The first clock pulse (following the reload) decrements the count by 3 and subsequent clock pulse decrement the count by two. Then the whole process is repeated. In this way, if the count is odd, the output will be high for (n+1)/2 counts and low for (n-1)/2 counts.

b) Gate disable: If Gate is 1 counting is enabled otherwise it is disabled. If Gate goes low while output is low, output is set high immediately. After this, When Gate goes high, the counter is loaded with the initial count on the next clock pulse and the sequence is repeated.

c) New count : The current counting sequence does not affect when the new count is written. If a trigger is received after writing a new count but before the end of the current half-cycle of the square wave, the counter will be loaded with the new count on the next CLK pulse and counting will continue from the new count. Otherwise, the new count will be loaded at end of the current half-cycle.

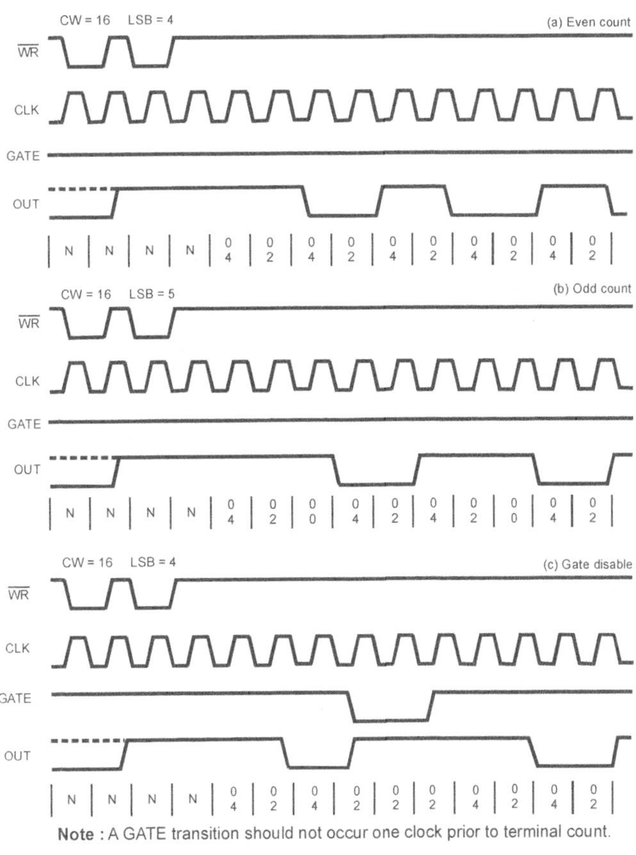

Note : A GATE transition should not occur one clock prior to terminal count.

Fig. 15.9 Mode 3 : Square wave rate generator

MODE 4 : Software Triggered Strobe.

a) Normal operation :

1) The output will be initially high.

2) The output will go low for one CLK pulse after the terminal count (TC).

b) Gate Disable : If Gate is one the counting is enabled otherwise it is disabled. The Gate has no effect on the output.

c) New count : If a new count is written during counting, it will be loaded on the next CLK pulse and counting will continue from the new count. If the count is two byte then

1) Writing the first byte has no effect on counting.

2) Writing the second byte allows the new count to be loaded on the next CLK pulse.

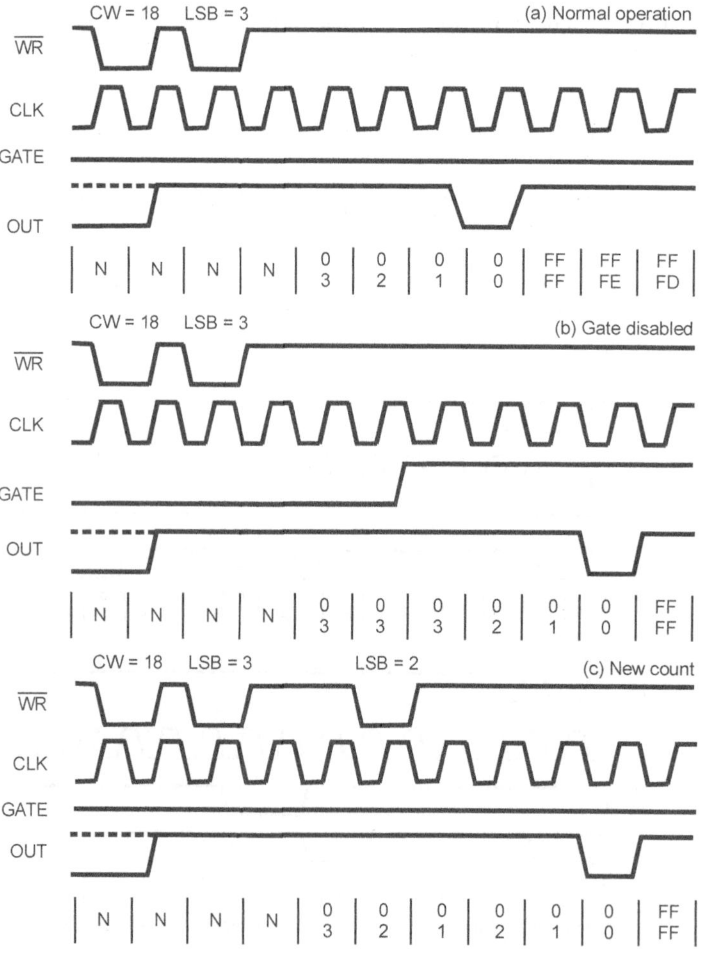

Fig. 15.10 Mode 4 : Software triggered strobe

MODE 5 : Hardware triggered strobe (Retriggerable).

a) Normal operation :

1) The output will be initially high.

2) The counting is triggered by the rising edge of the Gate.

3) The output will go low for one CLK pulse after the terminal count (TC).

b) Retriggering : If the triggering occurs on the Gate input during the counting, the initial count is loaded on the next CLK pulse and the counting will be continued until the terminal count is reached.

c) New count : If a new count is written during counting, the current counting sequence will not be affected. If the trigger occurs after the new count is written but before the terminal count, the counter will be loaded with the new count on the next CLK pulse and counting will continue from there.

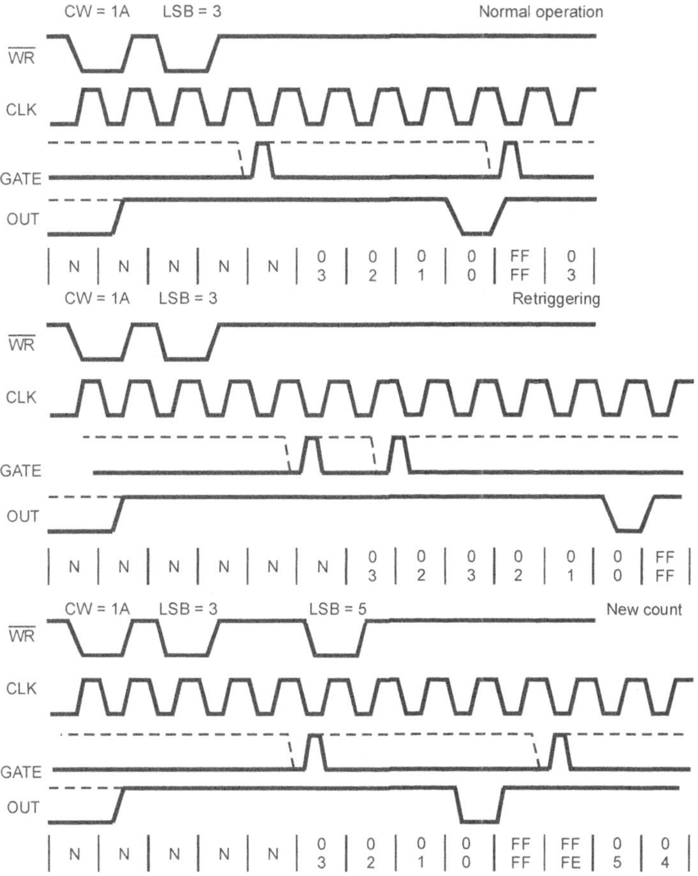

Fig. 15.11 Mode 5 hardware triggered strobe

Table 15.1 shows the gate pin operations.

Signal Status Modes	Low or Going Low	Rising	High
0	Disables counting	—	Enables counting
1	—	i) Initiates counting ii) Resets output after next clock	—
2	i) Disables counting ii) Sets output immediately high	Initiates counting	Enables counting
3	i) Disables counting ii) Sets output immediately high	Initiates counting	Enables counting
4	Disables counting	—	Enables counting
5	—	Initiates counting	—

Table 15.1 Gate pin operations

15.5 Programming Examples

Example 1 : *Write a program to initialize counter 2 in mode 0 with a count of C030H. Assume address for control register = 0BH, counter 0 = 08H, counter 1 = 09H and counter 2 = 0AH.*

Solution : **Control word :**

D_7	D_6	D_5	D_4	D_3	D_2	D_1	D_0	
SC_1	**SC_2**	**RW_1**	**RW_0**	**M_2**	**M_1**	**M_0**	**BCD**	
1	0	1	1	0	0	0	0	= B0H

Source Program :

```
MVI A, B0H
OUT 0BH                   ; Loads control word (B0H)in the control register.
MVI A, lowbyte (30H)
OUT 0AH                   ; Loads lower byte of the count.
MVI A, higher byte (C0H)  ; Loads higher byte of the count.
OUT 0AH
```

Example 2 : *Write a program to generate a square wave of 1kHz frequency on OUT 1 pin of 8253/54. Assume CLK1 frequency is 1MHz and address for control register = 0BH, counter 1 = 09H and counter 2 = 0AH.*

Solution : To get square wave mode 3 is selected count should be $\frac{1\ \text{MHz}}{1\ \text{kHz}} = 1000$

Control word :

D_7	D_6	D_5	D_4	D_3	D_2	D_1	D_0		
SC_1	SC_2	RW_1	RW_0	M_2	M_1	M_0	BCD		
0	1	1	1	0	1	1	1	=	77H

Source program :

```
MVI A, 77H
OUT 0BH                  ; Loads control word (77H) in the control register.
MVI A, Lowerbyte(00)     ; Loads lower byte of the count
OUT 09H
MVI A, Higherbyte(10)    ; Loads higher byte of the count
OUT 09H
```

15.6 Interfacing of 8253/54 in I/O Mapped I/O

We know that, 8253/54 has separate address and data lines. Therefore it is necessary to separate A_0-A_7 and D_0-D_7 lines from AD_0-AD_7 with the help of external decoder and ALE signal. 8253/54 IC decodes A0 and A1 lines internally to select one of its ports or control register. In I/O mapped I/O, higher byte address bus duplicates the address of lower address bus, therefore A_8 and A_9 lines are also indirectly involved in the selection of

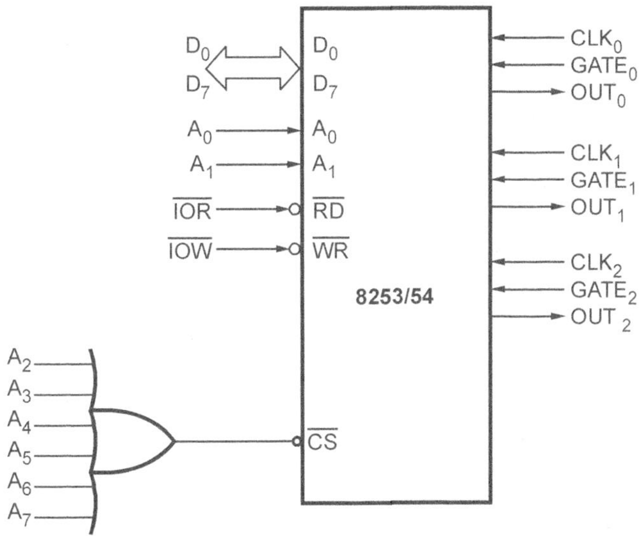

Fig. 15.12 Interfacing of 8253/54 in I/O mapped I/O

ports or control register. The remaining address lines (A_7-A_2 or A_{15}-A_{10}) can be used to generate chip select signal. Fig. 15.12 (See Fig. 15.12 on previous page) shows the interfacing of 8253/54 with 8085. The 74LS138 IC (3:8 decoder) is used to generate chip select signal. Another decoder can be used to generate $\overline{IOR}$, $\overline{IOW}$, and $\overline{MEMW}$ signals from the $\overline{RD}$, $\overline{WR}$ and IO/$\overline{M}$ signals of 8085.

Address Map :

Ports / control Register	Address lines								Address
	A_7	A_6	A_5	A_4	A_3	A_2	A_1	A_0	
Counter 0	0	0	0	0	0	0	0	0	00H
Counter 1	0	0	0	0	0	0	0	1	01H
Counter 2	0	0	0	0	0	0	1	0	02H
Control Register	0	0	0	0	0	0	1	1	03H

Review Questions

Section 15.1

Q.1 *What is the necessity of the programmable interval timer?*

Q.2 *List the features of any programmable interval timer.*

Q.3 *List the differences between 8253 and 8254.*

Section 15.2

Q.1 *Draw and explain the functional block diagram of IC 8253/54.*

Section 15.3

Q.1 *Draw the control word of 8253 timer/counter and explain.* **Dec.-11, Marks 8**

Section 15.4

Q.1 *Discuss various operating modes of 8253 timer with necessary control words.* **June-07, Dec.-11, Marks 16**

Section 15.6

Q.1 *Draw and explain the interfacing of 8253 with 8085.*

Two Marks Questions with Answers

Q.1 *What are the modes of operations used in 8253?*

Ans. : Each of the three counters of 8253 can be operated in one of the following six modes of operation.

1. Mode 0 (Interrupt on terminal count)
2. Mode 1 (Programmable monoshot)
3. Mode 2 (Rate generator)
4. Mode 3 (Square wave generator)
5. Mode 4 (Software triggered strobe)
6. Mode 5 (Hardware triggered strobe)

Q.2 *What are the different types of write operations used in 8253?*

Ans. : There are two types of write operations in 8253

1) Writing a control word register

2) Writing a count value into a count register

Q.3 *8253's out signal is to be used as a clock input of the desired frequency to a particular device. Is it possible ? How ?*  Dec.-09

Ans. : It is possible to use the out signal of 8253 as a clock input of the desired frequency to a particular device. Because we can program 8253 to generate continuous square wave signal of desired frequency on the out signal of it.

Q.4 *What is the function of gate signal in 8252 timer ?*

Ans. : The function of gate signal is to control the counter. Gate = 1 enables counting and Gate = 0 disables counting.

Q.5 *Mention the applications of 8253.*

Ans. : The applications of 8253 are :

1. Clock generator
2. Pulse generator
3. Square wave generator
4. Programmable timer
5. Programmable counter
6. Rate generator

❑❑❑

Notes

16 A/D and D/A Converter Interfacing

Contents

16.1 Digital to Analog Converter

A DAC (Digital to Analog Converter) accepts an n-bit input word $b_1, b_2, b_3, \ldots b_n$ in binary and produce an analog signal proportional to it. Fig. 16.1 (a) shows circuit symbol and input-output characteristics of a 4-bit DAC. There are four digital inputs, indicating 4-bit DAC. Each digital input requires an electrical signal representing either a logic 1 or a logic 0. The b_n is the least significant bit, LSB, whereas b_1 is the most significant bit, MSB.

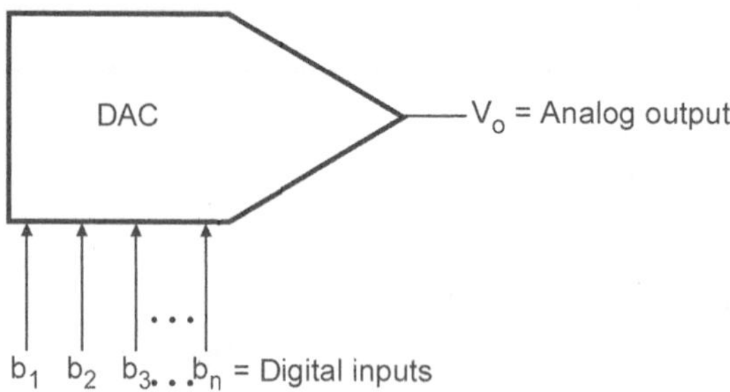

Fig. 16.1 (a) DAC circuit symbol

Fig. 16.1 (b) shows analog output voltage V_o is plotted against all 16 possible digital input words.

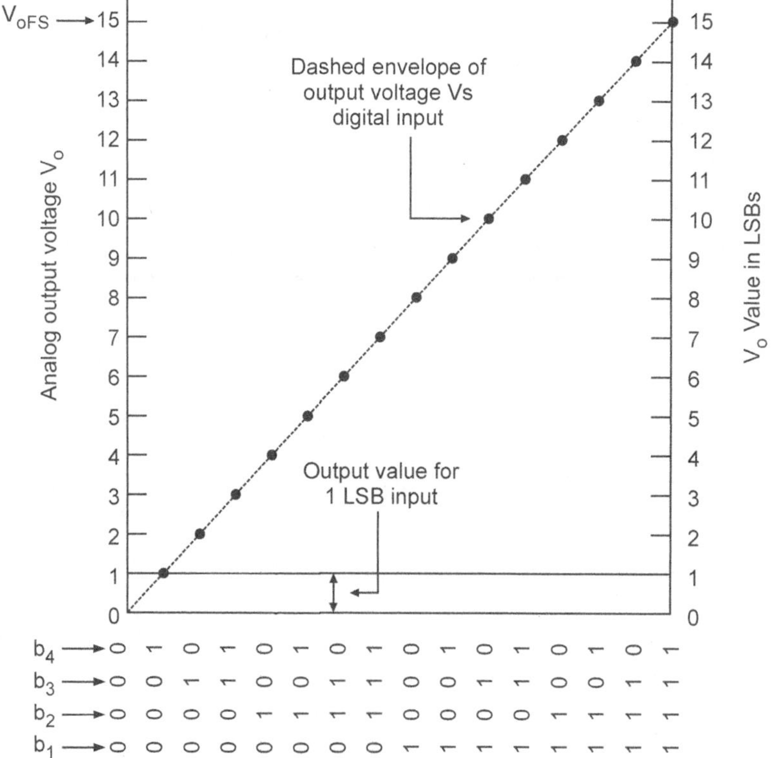

Fig. 16.1 (b)

16.2 DAC 1408

In this section we will see how we can interface IC 1408 (8-bit R/2R ladder type D/A converter) to the 8085 system using 8255. Before going to see interfacing details we see the details of IC 1408.

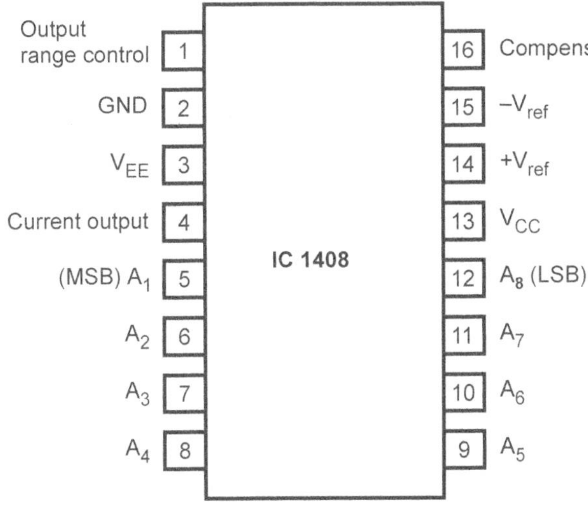

Fig. 16.2 (a) Pin diagram

Fig. 16.2 shows the pin diagram and block diagram for IC 1408 DAC.

The IC 1408 consists of a reference current amplifier, an R/2R ladder and eight high speed current switches. It has eight input data lines A_1 (MSB) through A_8 (LSB) which control the positions of current switches.

It requires 2 mA reference current for full scale input and two power supplies V_{CC} = + 5 V and V_{EE} = – 15 V (V_{EE} can range from – 5 V to – 15 V).

The voltage V_{ref} and resistor R_{14} determines the total reference current source and R_{15} is generally equal to R_{14} to match the input impedance of the reference current amplifier.

Fig. 16.2(b) shows a typical circuit for IC 1408.

The output current I_o can be given as

$$I_o = \frac{V_{ref}}{R_{14}}\left(\frac{A_1}{2}+\frac{A_2}{4}+\frac{A_3}{8}+\frac{A_4}{16}+\frac{A_5}{32}+\frac{A_6}{64}+\frac{A_7}{128}+\frac{A_8}{256}\right) \quad \ldots(1)$$

Note : Input A_1 through A_8 can be either 0 or 1. Therefore, for typical circuit full scale current can be given as,

$$I_o = \frac{5}{2.5\text{ K}}\left(\frac{1}{2}+\frac{1}{4}+\frac{1}{8}+\frac{1}{16}+\frac{1}{32}+\frac{1}{64}+\frac{1}{128}+\frac{1}{256}\right)$$

$$= \frac{2\text{ mA} \times 255}{256}$$

$$= 1.992\text{ mA}$$

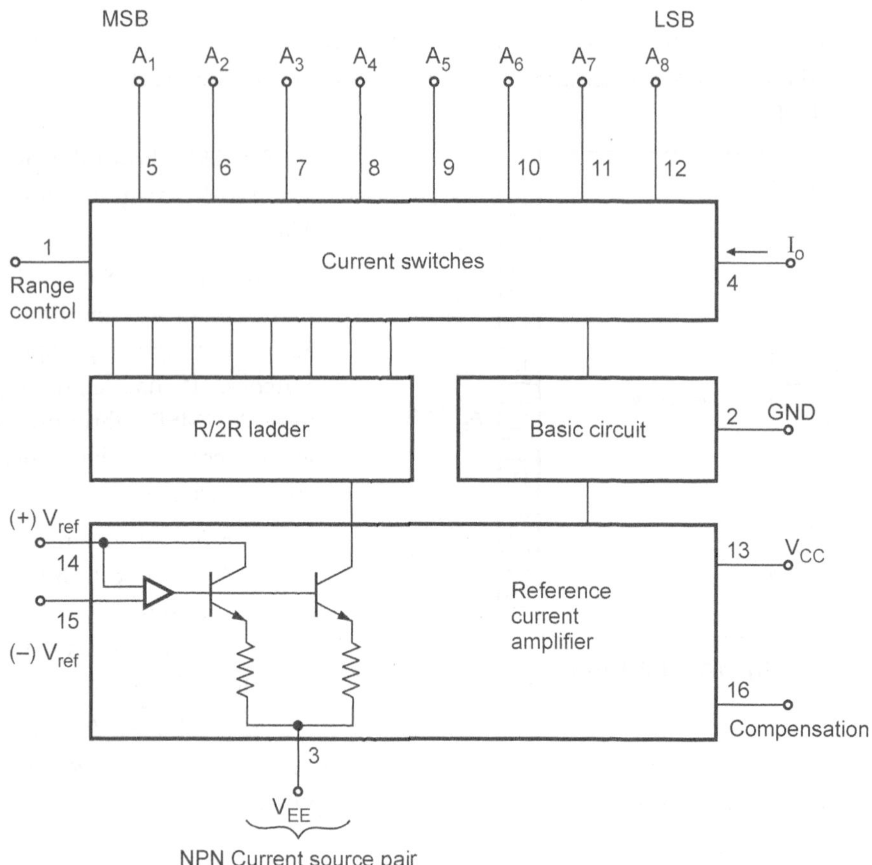

Fig. 16.2 (b) Block diagram

It shows that the full scale output current is always 1 LSB less than the reference current source of 2 mA. This output current is converted into voltage by I to V converter. The output voltage for full scale input can be given as

$$V_o = 1.992 \times 2.5 \text{ K}$$

$$= 4.98 \text{ V}$$

Note : The arrow on the pin 4 shows the output current direction. It is inward. This means that IC 1408 sinks current. At $(0000\,0000)_2$ binary input it sinks zero current and at $(1111\,1111)_2$ binary input it sinks 1.992 mA.

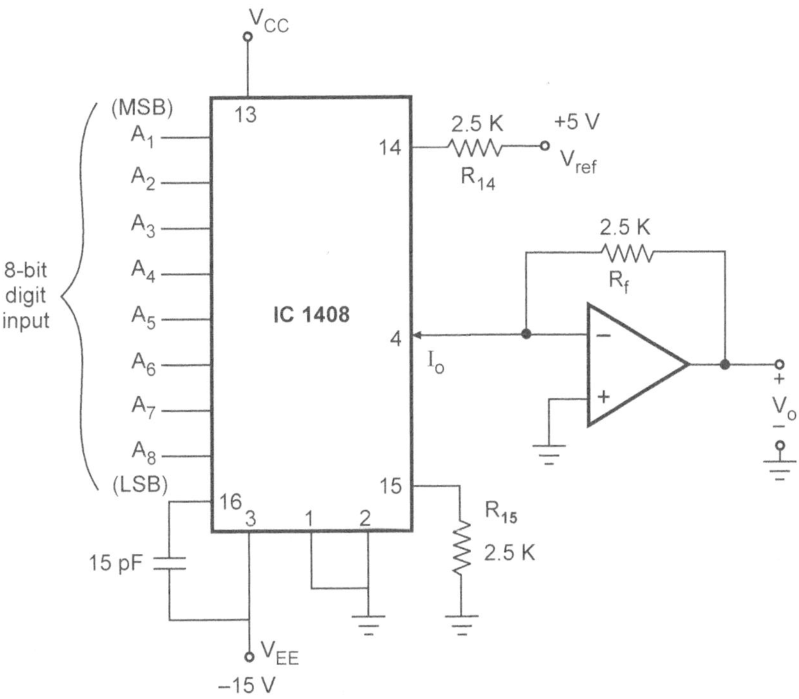

Fig. 16.3 Typical circuit for IC 1408

The circuit shown in the Fig. 16.4 gives output in the unipolar range. When digital input is 00H, the output voltage is 0 V and when digital input is FFH $(1111\,1111)_2$, the output voltage is + 5 V. This circuit can be modified to give bipolar output.

Fig. 16.4 shows the circuit for giving output in the bipolar range. Here, resistor R_B (5 K) is connected between V_{ref} and the output terminal of IC 1408. This gives a constant current source of 1 mA.

The circuit operation can be observed for three conditions :

Condition 1 : For binary input (00H)

When binary input is 00H, the output current I_o at pin 4 is zero. Due to this current flowing through R_B (1 mA) flows through R_f giving $V_o = -5$ V.

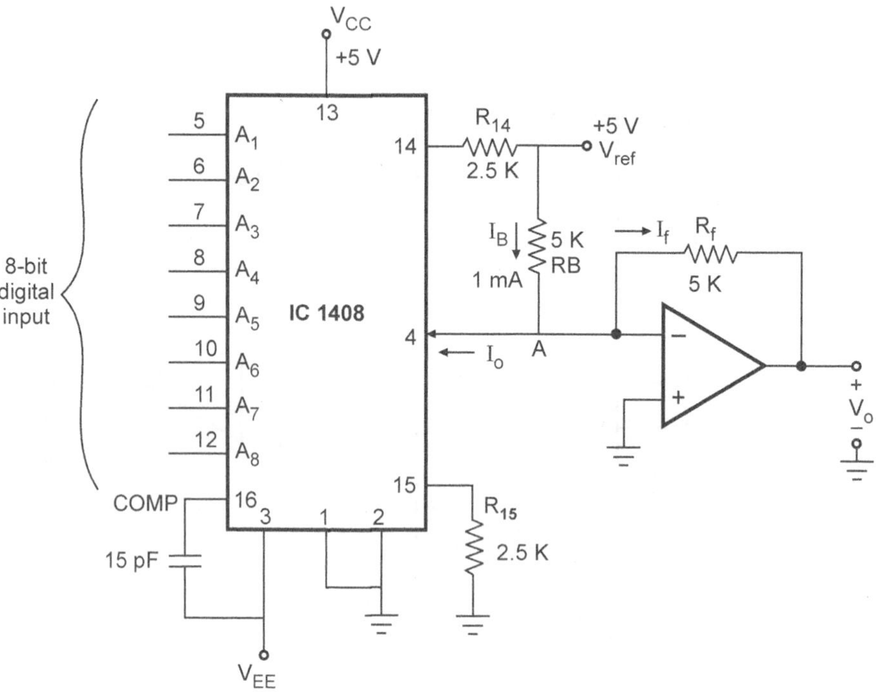

Fig. 16.4 Interfacing DAC in the bipolar range

Condition 2 : For binary input 80H

When binary input is 80H, the output current I_o at pin 4 is 1 mA. By applying KCL at node A we get,

$$-I_B + I_o + I_f = 0$$

Substituting values of I_B and I_o we get,

$$-(1 \text{ mA}) + (1 \text{ mA}) + I_f = 0$$

$$\therefore \quad I_f = 0$$

and therefore the output voltage is zero.

Condition 3 : For binary input FFH

When binary input is FFH, the output current I_o at pin 4 is 2 mA. By applying KCL at node A we get,

$$-I_B + I_o + I_f = 0$$

Substituting values of I_B and I_o we get,

$$-(1 \text{ mA}) + (2 \text{ mA}) + I_f = 0$$

$$\therefore \quad I_f = -1 \text{ mA}$$

Therefore, the output voltage is + 5 V. In this way, circuit shown in the Fig. 16.4 gives output in the bipolar range.

16.3 Interfacing DAC 1408 / 0808 with Microprocessor using 8255

Nov./Dec.-07, April/May-10

Fig. 16.5 shows the interfacing of DAC 0808 with microprocessor 8085. Here, programmable peripheral interface, 8255 is used as parallel port to send the digital data to DAC.

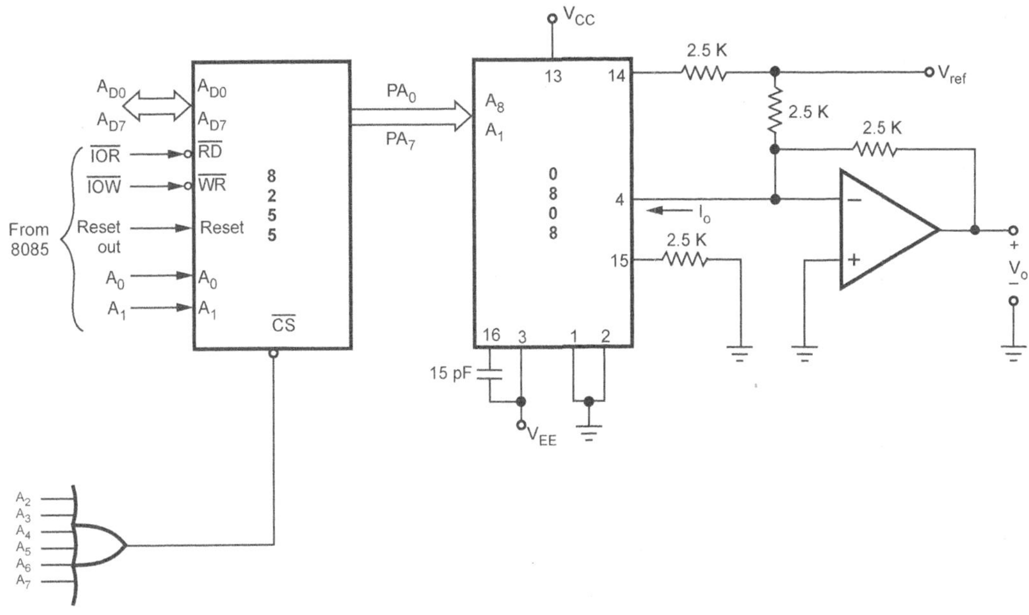

Fig. 16.5 Interfacing of 0808 with microprocessor

I/O Map for 8255

Port/Register	Address
Port A	0 0
Port B	0 1
Port C	0 2
Control register	0 3

Program :

```
MVI A, 80H    ; Initialization control word for 8255 to
OUT 03        ; Configure all ports as output ports
MVI A, data   ; Load 8-bit data to be sent at the input
              ; of 0808 DAC
OUT 00        ; Send data on port A.
```

We now see how different waveforms can be generated using this circuit.

Example 16.1 : *Generate square wave using DAC 0808.*

Solution : To generate square wave first we have to output FF and then 00 an Port A of 8255. The output of 8255 (Port A) connected to DAC 0808. According to frequency requirement delay is provided in between the two outputs.

Program

```
        LXI SP, 27FFH   ; Initialize Stack Pointer
        MVI A, 80H      ; Initialize 8255 to configure all
        OUT 03          ; ports as output ports
LOOP :  MVI A, 00       ; Load A with digital data
                        ; corresponds
                        ; to – 2.5 V output
        OUT 00          ; Send digital data to the input of
                        ; DAC 0808
        CALL DELAY      ; Wait for specified time.
        MVI A, FF       ; Load A with digital data
                        ; corresponds
                        ; to + 2.5 V output
        OUT 00          ; Send digital data to the input of
                        ; DAC 0808.
        CALL DELAY      ; Wait for specified time
        JMP LOOP        ; Repeat
```

Delay Program

```
DELAY :    MVI B,08      ; Load delay count in register
BACK :     DCR B         ; Decrement count
           JNZ BACK      ; Check if count = 0
                         ; otherwise repeat
           RET
```

Example 16.2 : *Generate triangular wave using DAC0808.*

Solution : To generate triangular wave we have to output data from 00 initially, and it should be incremented upto FF. When it reaches FF it should be decremented upto 00.

```
           LXI SP, 27FFH ; Initialize Stack Pointer
           MVI A, 80H    ; Initialize 8255 to configure all
                         ; ports as output ports
           OUT 03
           MVI A, 00     ; Load accumulator with digital data
                         ; corresponds to – 2.5 V output
           OUT 00        ; Send digital to the input
                         ; of DAC 0808.
LOOP_1:    INR A         ; Increment digital data in the
                         ; accumulator
           OUT 00        ; Send digital data to the input
                         ; of DAC 0808.
           CPI FF        ; Check digital data for Peak output
           JNZ LOOP_1    ; If no repeat,
LOOP_2:    DCR A         ; Decrement digital data in the
                         ; accumulator
           OUT 00        ; Send digital data to the input of
                         ; DAC 0808.
           JNZ LOOP_2
           JMP LOOP_1
```

Example 16.3 : *Generate sine wave using DAC 0808.*

Solution : To generate sine wave we have to output digital equivalent values which will represent sine wave as shown in the Fig. 16.6. Digital data 00H represents – 2.5 V. 7FH represents 0 V and FFH represents + 2.5 V.

The digital equivalent for sine wave can be calculated as follows.

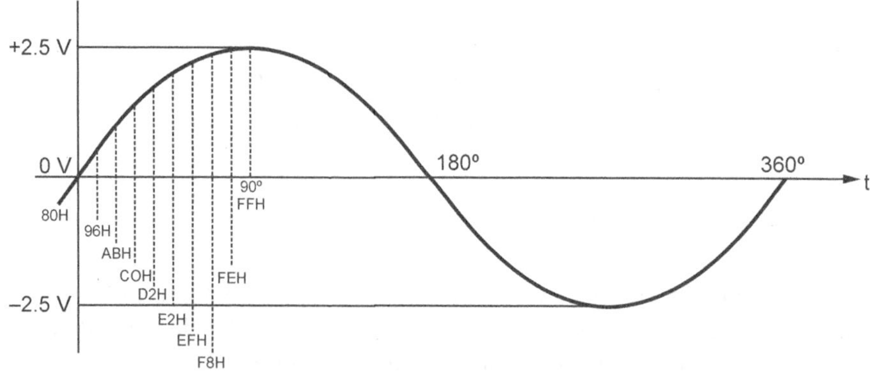

Fig. 16.6

We know that sin 0° = 0 and sin 90° = 1. The range sin 0° to sin 90° is distributed over digital range of 7FH to FFH i.e. (FFH – 7FH) 128 decimal steps. Therefore, taking 128 as a offset we can write,

Digital equivalent value (DEV) for $\sin\theta = (128 + 128 \times \sin\theta)$
where θ is a angle in degrees and digital value is in decimal.

Lookup table shows the digital equivalent values for sine wave.

Degrees	Equation	Digital equivalent in decimal	Digital equivalent in hex
0°	(128 + 128 × sin 0)	128	80H
10°	(128 + 128 × sin 10)	150	96H
20°	(128 + 128 × sin 20)	171	ABH
30°	(128 + 128 × sin 30)	192	COH
40°	(128 + 128 × sin 40)	210	D2H
50°	(128 + 128 × sin 50)	226	E2H
60°	(128 + 128 × sin 60)	239	EFH
70°	(128 + 128 × sin 70)	248	F8H
80°	(128 + 128 × sin 80)	254	FEH
90°	(128 + 128 × sin 90)	256 → 255	FFH
100°	(128 + 128 × sin 100)	254	FEH
110°	(128 + 128 × sin 110)	248	F8H
120°	(128 + 128 × sin 120)	239	EFH
130°	(128 + 128 × sin 130)	226	E2H
140°	(128 + 128 × sin 140)	210	D2H
150°	(128 + 128 × sin 150)	192	COH
160°	(128 + 128 × sin 160)	171	ABH
170°	(128 + 128 × sin 170)	150	96H

180°	(128 + 128 × sin 180)	128	80H
190°	(128 + 128 × sin 190)	106	6AH
200°	(128 + 128 × sin 200)	84	54H
210°	(128 + 128 × sin 210)	64	40H
220°	(128 + 128 × sin 220)	46	2EH
230°	(128 + 128 × sin 230)	30	1EH
240°	(128 + 128 × sin 240)	17	11H
250°	(128 + 128 × sin 250)	08	08H
260°	(128 + 128 × sin 260)	02	02H
270°	(128 + 128 × sin 270)	00	00H
280°	(128 + 128 × sin 280)	02	02H
290°	(128 + 128 × sin 290)	08	08H
300°	(128 + 128 × sin 300)	17	11H
310°	(128 + 128 × sin 310)	30	1EH
320°	(128 + 128 × sin 320)	46	2EH
330°	(128 + 128 × sin 330)	64	40H
340°	(128 + 128 × sin 340)	84	54H
350°	(128 + 128 × sin 350)	106	6AH
360°	(128 + 128 × sin 360)	128	80H

Program :

```
        LXI SP, 27FFH       ; Initialize Stack Pointer
        MVI A, 80H          ; Initialize 8255 to configure
                            ; all
        OUT 03H             ; Ports as output ports
START:  MVI C, 25H          ; Initialize counter
        LXI H, Lookup table ; Initialize HL pointer to point

                            ; to lookup table
BACK:   MOV A, M            ; Get the digital equivalent
                            ; data
                            ; from lookup table
        OUT 00              ; Send digital data to DAC
        INX H               ; Increment lookup table pointer
        DCR C               ; Decrement counter
        JNZ BACK            ; If not zero, go to BACK
        JMP START           ; Repeat
```

16.4 Analog to Digital Converter

May/June-06

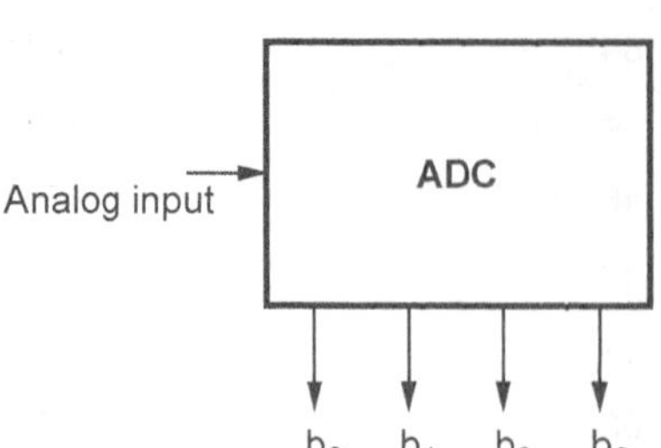

Fig. 16.7 Symbol for 4-bit ADC

The A/D conversion is a quantizing process whereby an analog signal is converted into equivalent binary word. Thus the A/D converter is exactly opposite function that of the D/A converter.

Fig. 16.7 shows symbol for A/D converter.

The Fig. 16.8 shows the digital output of an ideal 3-bit ADC plotted against the analog input voltage

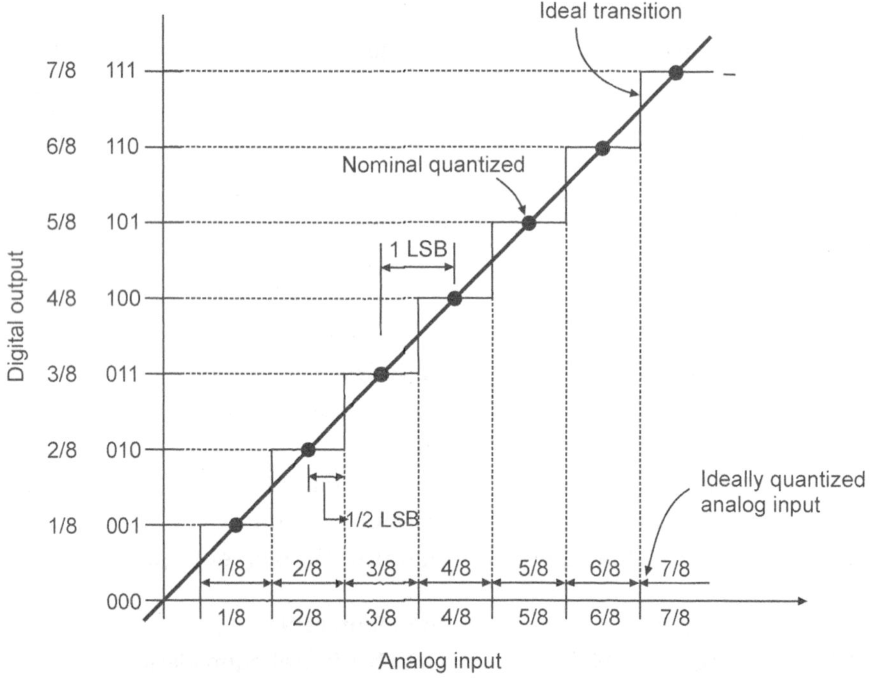

Fig. 16.8 Analog input Vs Digital output

16.5 ADC 0808/0809 Family

The ADC 0808 and ADC 0809 are monolithic CMOS devices with an 8-channel multiplexer. These devices are also designed to operate from common microprocessor control buses, with tri-state output latches driving the data bus.

The main features of these devices are :

Features

- 8-bit successive approximation ADC.
- 8-channel multiplexer with address logic.
- Conversion time 100 μs.
- It eliminates the need for external zero and full-scale adjustments.
- Easy to interface to all microprocessors.
- It operates on single 5 V power supply.
- Output meet TTL voltage level specifications.

Fig. 16.9 shows pin diagram of 0808/0809 ADC.

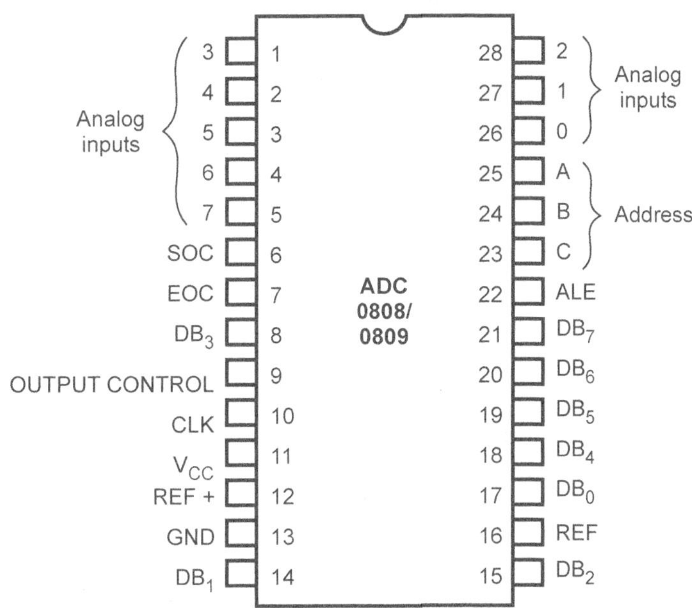

Fig. 16.9 Pin diagram of 0808/0809

ADC 0808/0809 has eight input channels, so to select desired input channel, it is necessary to send 3-bit address on A, B and C inputs. The address of the desired channel is sent to the multiplexer address inputs through port pins. After at least 50 ns, this address must be latched. This can be achieved by sending ALE signal. After another 2.5 μs, the start of conversion (SOC) signal must be sent high and then low to start the conversion process. To indicate end of conversion ADC 0808/0809 activates EOC signal. The microprocessor system can read converted digital word through data bus by enabling the output enable signal after EOC is activated. This is illustrated in Fig. 16.10.

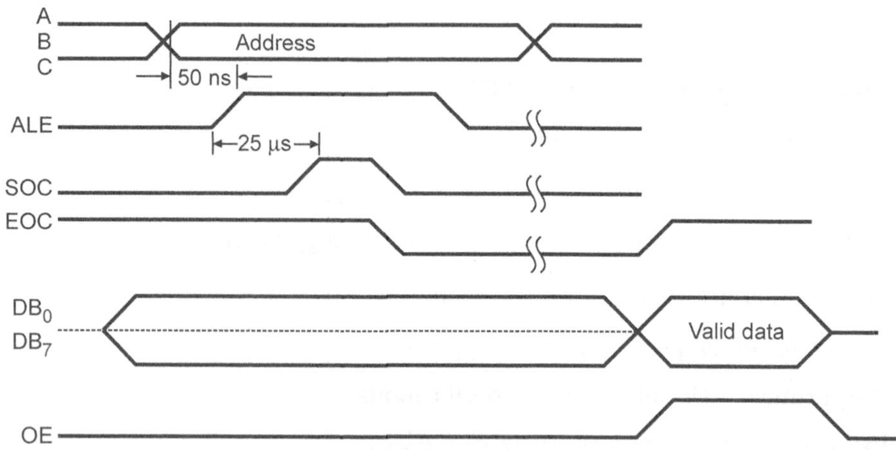

Fig. 16.10 Timing waveforms for ADC 0808

16.6 ADC 7109

The ADC 7109 is a high performance, low power integrating (Dual slope) A/D converter designed to easily interface with microprocessor.

Features

1. IC 7109 is a 12-bit dual slope A/D converter.
2. It has polarity and over range bits.
3. It has byte organized TTL compatible three-state outputs and UART handshake mode for simple parallel or serial interfacing to microprocessor systems.
4. It has $\overline{\text{RUN}}$/HOLD input and STATUS output, which can be used to monitor and control conversion timing.
5. It has true differential input and differential reference
6. It has low noise-typically 15 μV_{p-p}.
7. It has very low input current - 1 pA.
8. It operates at 30 conversions per second.
9. All inputs are fully protected against static discharge.

Pin Configuration and Test Circuit

Fig. 16.11 shows typical circuit and pin configuration for 7109.

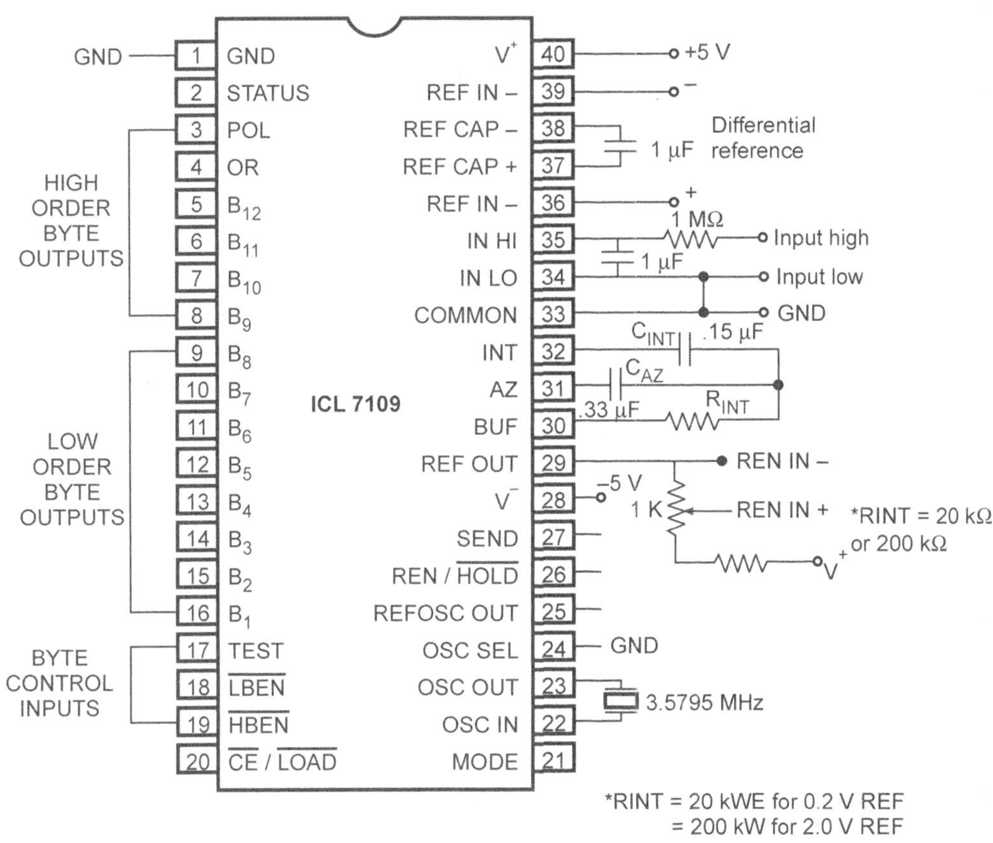

Fig. 16.11 Pin diagram of ICL 7109

16.7 Interfacing ADC 0808 with 8085

April/May-04, 05, 08, 10; Nov./Dec.-04, 05, 08, 09

Fig. 16.12 shows interfacing of ADC 0808 with 8085 using 8255. ADC 0808 has eight input channels, so to select desired input channel, it is necessary to send 3-bit address on ADC, ADB and ADA inputs. The address of the desired channel is sent to the multiplexer address inputs through PB_0 to PB_2 lines.

After at least 50 ns, this address must be latched. This is achieved by sending ALE signal using port line PB_3. After another 2.5 μs the start of conversion signal (SOC) must be sent high and then low. Port line PB4 is used for this purpose. The end of conversion (EOC) is detected by port line PC0. The Fig. 16.13 shows timing waveforms for the ADC 0808. Schmitt-trigger inverter circuitry generates 300 kHz clock which is required to operate ADC 0808. The zener diode and LM 308 amplifier circuitry is used to produce a V_{CC} and $+V_{REF}$ of 5.12 V for the A/D converter. With this reference voltage the A/D converter will have 256 steps of 20 mV each. (See Fig. 16.13 on page 16-17)

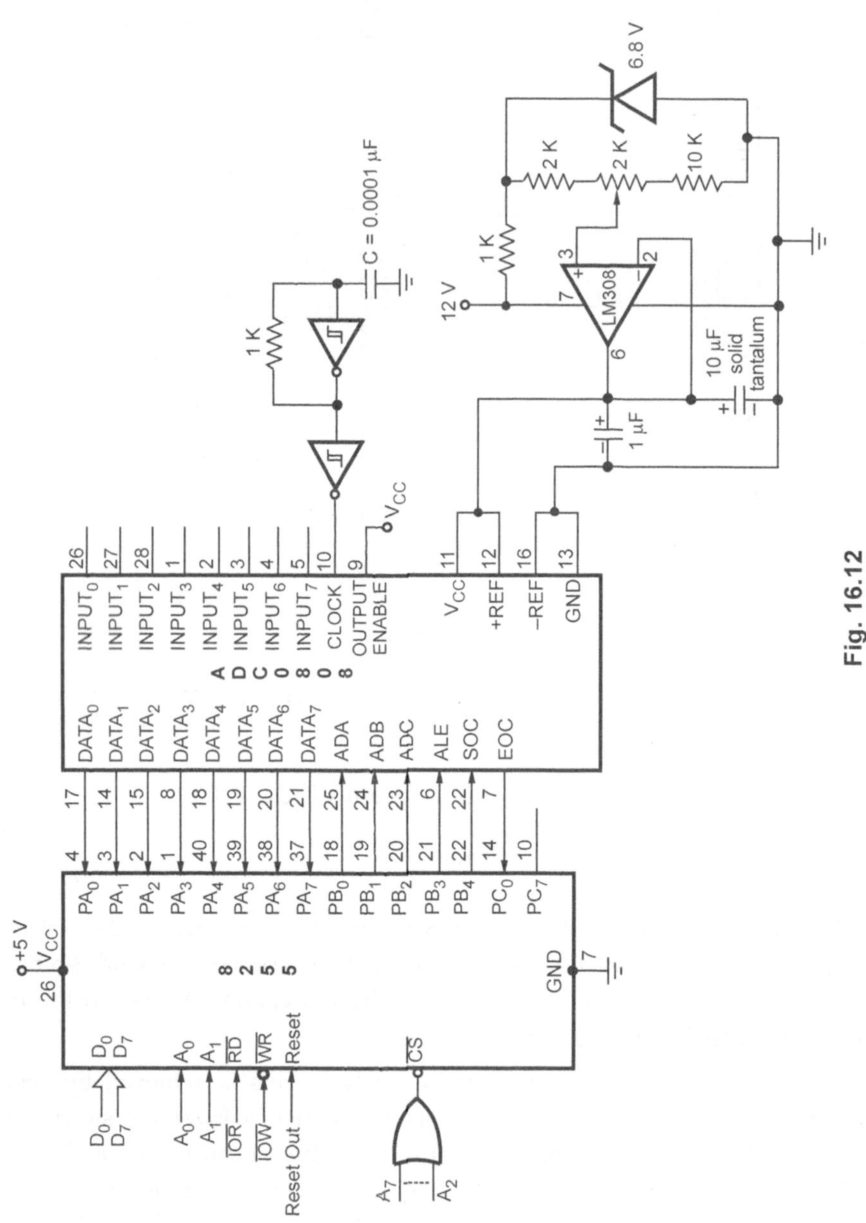
8255
ADC 0808
+5 V
V_{CC}
GND
PA_0 PA_1 PA_2 PA_3 PA_4 PA_5 PA_6 PA_7
PB_0 PB_1 PB_2 PB_3 PB_4
PC_0 PC_7
D_0 D_7
A_0 A_1
$\overline{RD}$ $\overline{WR}$ Reset $\overline{CS}$
$\overline{IOR}$ $\overline{IOW}$ Reset Out
A_7 A_2
$DATA_0$ $DATA_1$ $DATA_2$ $DATA_3$ $DATA_4$ $DATA_5$ $DATA_6$ $DATA_7$
ADA ADB ADC ALE SOC EOC
$INPUT_0$ $INPUT_1$ $INPUT_2$ $INPUT_3$ $INPUT_4$ $INPUT_5$ $INPUT_6$ $INPUT_7$
CLOCK
OUTPUT ENABLE
+REF
−REF
1 K
C = 0.0001 μF
12 V
LM308
2 K
10 K
6.8 V
1 μF
10 μF solid tantalum

Fig. 16.12

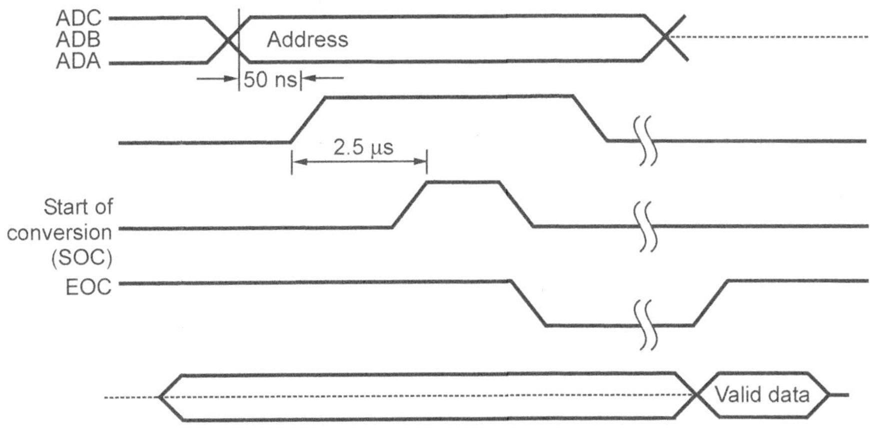

Fig. 16.13

I/O Map

Ports/CR	Address lines								Address
	A_7	A_6	A_5	A_4	A_3	A_2	A_1	A_0	
Port A	0	0	0	0	0	0	0	0	00H
Port B	0	0	0	0	0	0	0	1	01H
Port C	0	0	0	0	0	0	1	0	02H
Control register	0	0	0	0	0	0	1	1	03H

Control Word

I/O	Mode	A	PA	PC_U	Mode B	PB	PC_L	
1	0	0	1	1	0	0	1	= 99H

Routine does the conversion and reads the digital data

```
MVI A, 99H      ; initialize 8255
OUT CR
MVI A, 00H
OUT PB          ; Send address to select channel 0
MVI A, 08H
OUT PB          ; Latch the given address by sending
                ; ALE high
Call Delay      ; Wait for at least 2.5 µs
MVI A, 18H
OUT PB          ; Make SOC high
NOP             ; Wait for at least 05 µs
MVI A, 08H
OUT PB          ; Make SOC low
```

```
CHECK :    IN PC         ; Check for EOC
           ANI 01
           JZ CHECK      ; If no, repeat
           IN PA         ; Read digital input
           RET           ; Return
```

16.8 Interfacing ADC 7109 with 8085

The ADC 7109 can be interfaced directly or indirectly (with the help of 8255) to 8085.

Direct Mode : Fig. 16.14 shows direct interfacing of IC7109 to 8085.

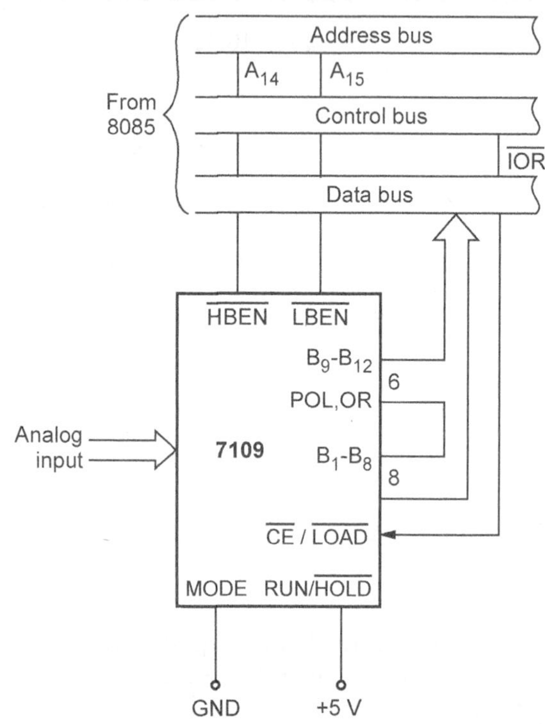

Fig. 16.14 Direct interfacing of IC7109 to 8085

Here, $\overline{CE/LOAD}$ signal serves as a chip select signal which is controlled by microprocessor $\overline{IOR}$ signal. The low order byte output and higher order byte output is enabled by $\overline{LBEN}$ and $\overline{HBEN}$ signals, respectively. These signals are driven by A_{15} and A_{14} signals, respectively. Microprocessor can read data (high order byte or low byte) by executing I/O read cycle.

Indirect Mode : Fig. 16.15 shows indirect interfacing of IC7109 to 8085.

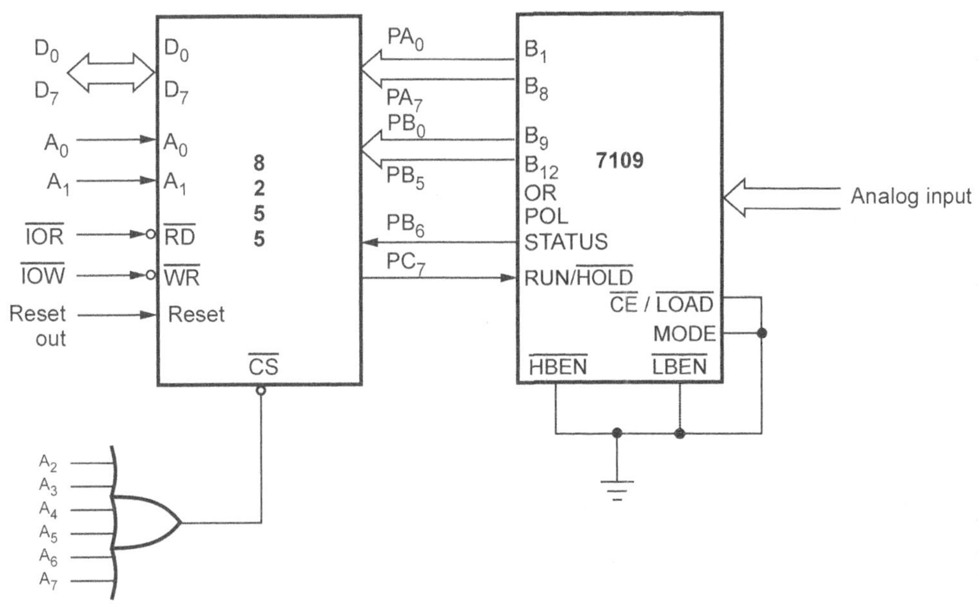

Fig. 16.15 Interfacing 7109 to 8085 using 8255

I/O Map :

Port/Register	A_7	A_6	A_5	A_4	A_3	A_2	A_1	A_0	Address
Port A	0	0	0	0	0	0	0	0	00
Port B	0	0	0	0	0	0	0	1	01
Port C	0	0	0	0	0	0	1	0	02
Control Register	0	0	0	0	0	0	1	1	03

Control Word for 8255

I/O	Mode	A	PA	PC_U	Mode B	PB	PC_L	
1	0	0	1	0	0	1	0	= 92H

Flowchart

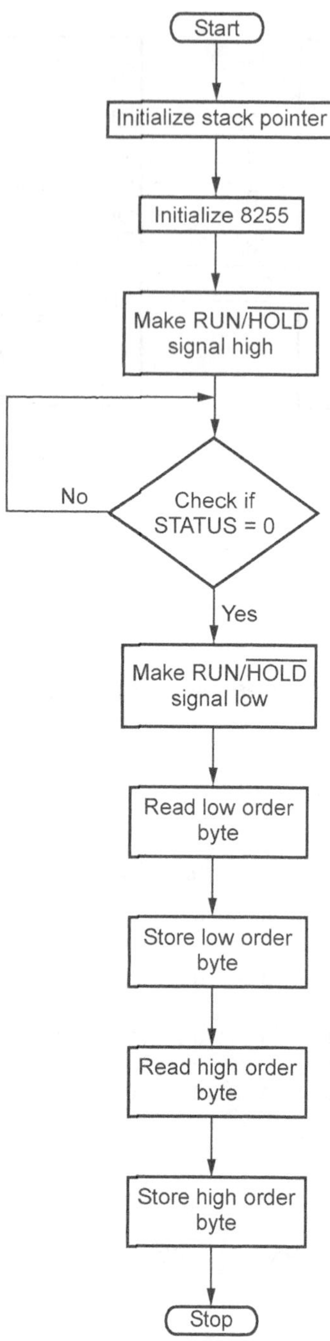
Start
Initialize stack pointer
Initialize 8255
Make RUN/$\overline{HOLD}$ signal high
No
Check if STATUS = 0
Yes
Make RUN/$\overline{HOLD}$ signal low
Read low order byte
Store low order byte
Read high order byte
Store high order byte
Stop

A/D conversion routing using 7109

```
        LXI SP,  Address ; Initialize Stack Pointer
        MVI A, 92H       ; Initialize 8255 as Port-A input
        OUT 03 (CR)      ; Port B input and Port C output
        MVI A, 80H
        OUT 02 (PC)      ; Send the RUN signal to 7109
BACK :  IN 01 (PB)       ; Check for STATUS signal
        ANI 40
        JNZ BACK         ; If it is high check again
        MVI A, 00        ; [Make RUN/HOLD
        OUT 02           ; Signal low]
        IN PA            ; If low, read lower byte
        MOV E, A         ; Save lower byte
        IN PB            ; Get higher nibble
        ANI 0FH
        MOV D, A         ; Save higher nibble
        HLT              ; Stop
```

After execution of above program 12-bit digital data is available in the DE register pair.

16.9 Temperature Control System

April/May-04,05

Before going to study the temperature control system, let us see the block diagram of microprocessor based process control system. It is capable of controlling more than one physical parameter. Such systems are commonly known as **data acquisition and control systems**. In these system, analog signals from various sensors are converted into digital values. These digital values are read in and processed by the microcomputer. The keyboard and display in the system allow the user to enter set point values, to read the current values of process variables, and to issue commands. Relays, D/A converters, solenoid valves, and other actuators are used to control process variables under program direction.

As an example, let us study the microcomputer based temperature control system to control the temperature between 0-100° C with ON/OFF control. The Fig. 16.16 shows the temperature sensing and heater control circuitry using ON/OFF control. It includes

1. Sensing circuitry
2. Analog to digital converter
3. Circuit required to drive the controller.

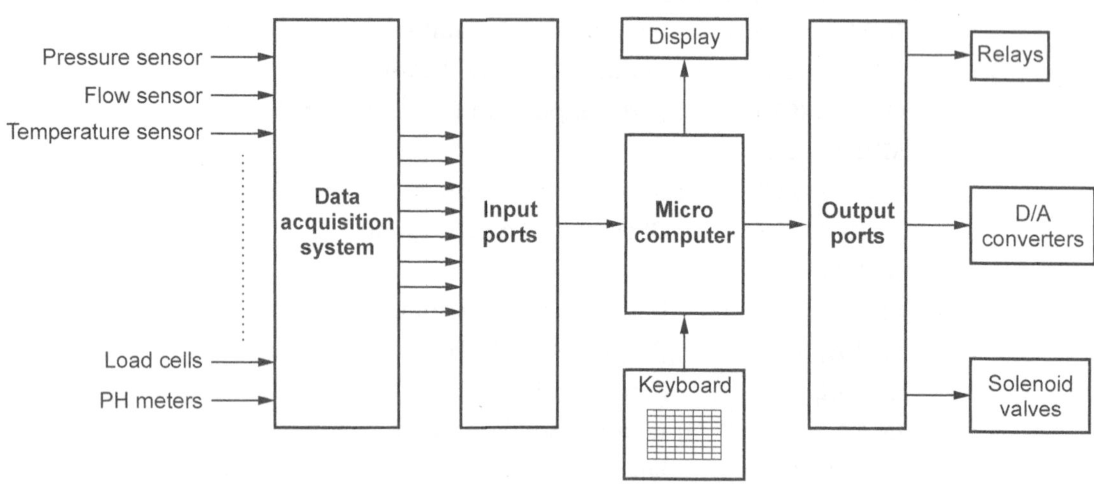

Fig. 16.16 Block diagram of microprocessor based process control system

1. Sensing circuitry :

The sensing circuitry consists of instrumentation amplifier using transducer bridge. RTD (Resistance Temperature Dependent) is used as transducer whose resistance is changed as a function of temperature.

$$R_t = R_0 \ (1 + \alpha \Delta t)$$

Where R_t is the resistance of RTD at temperature t.

R_0 is the resistance of RTD at 0° C

α is temperature coefficient of RTD (0.0039)

Δ t is difference in temperature $(t - t_0)$

At 0° C resistance of RTD is 100 Ω and at 100° C resistance of RTD is

$$R_{100} = 100 \ (1 + 0.0039 \ (100)\ ) = 139 \ \Omega$$

At 0° C, bridge is balanced so output of bridge (V_{ab}) is 0 V and at 100° C.

$$V_{ab} = V_{dc}\left(\frac{R_3}{R_1 + R_3}\right) - V_{dc}\left(\frac{R_4}{R_2 + R_4}\right)$$

$$= 5 \times \frac{1000}{1100} - 5\left(\frac{1000}{1139}\right)$$

$$= 0.1556 \text{ V}$$

Now the instrumentation amplifier gain $\left(\frac{R_f}{R_1}\right)$ must be chosen to get 5.12 V at 100° C

$$\frac{R_f}{R_1} = \frac{5.12 \text{ V}}{0.1556} = 32.89$$

If R_1 = 1 K the R_f = 32.89 K. This value of R_f is not available as a standard value so it is necessary to get this value by adjusting trimpot.

2. Analog to Digital converter

To convert analog signal into digital signal 8-bit ADC 0808 is used. ADC 0808 has eight input channels, so to select desired input channel it is necessary to send 3-bit address on ADC, ADB and ADA inputs. Port lines PB_0 to PB_2 are used for this purpose. Schmitt-trigger inverter circuitry generates 300 kHz clock which is required to operate ADC 0808. The zener diode and LM 308 amplifier circuitry is used to produce a V_{CC} and + V_{REF} of 5.12 V for the A/D converter. With this reference voltage the A/D converter will have 256 steps of 20 mV each.

After at least 50 ns, this address must be latched. This (SOC) is achieved by sending ALE signal using port line PB_4. After another 2.5 μs the start of conversion must be sent high and then low. Port line PB_3 is used for this purpose. The end of conversion (EOC) is detected by port line PC_0. The Fig. 16.17 show timing waveforms for the ADC 0808.

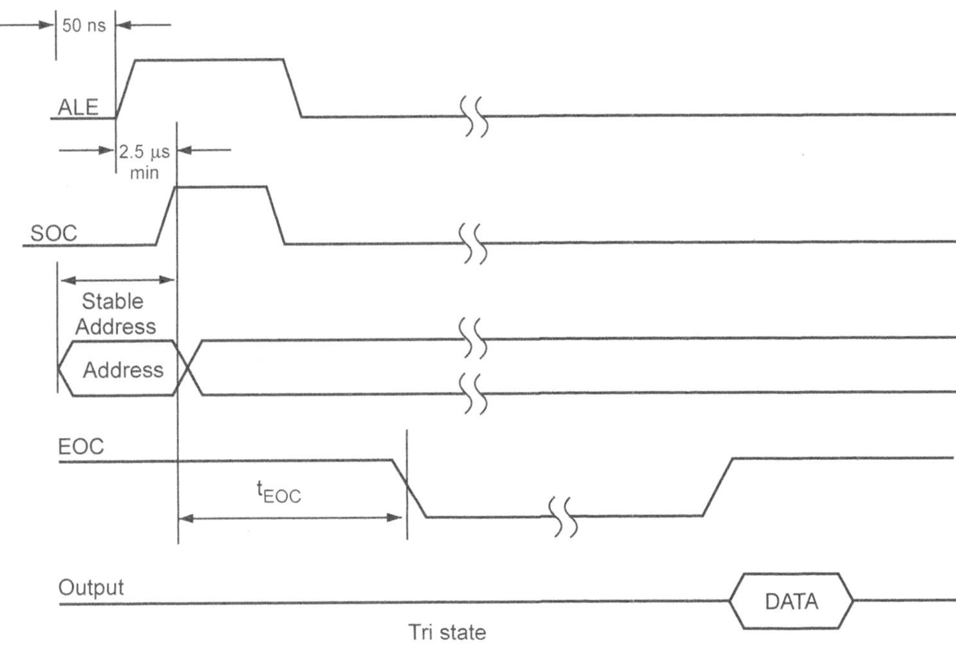

Fig. 16.17 Timing waveforms for the ADC 0808

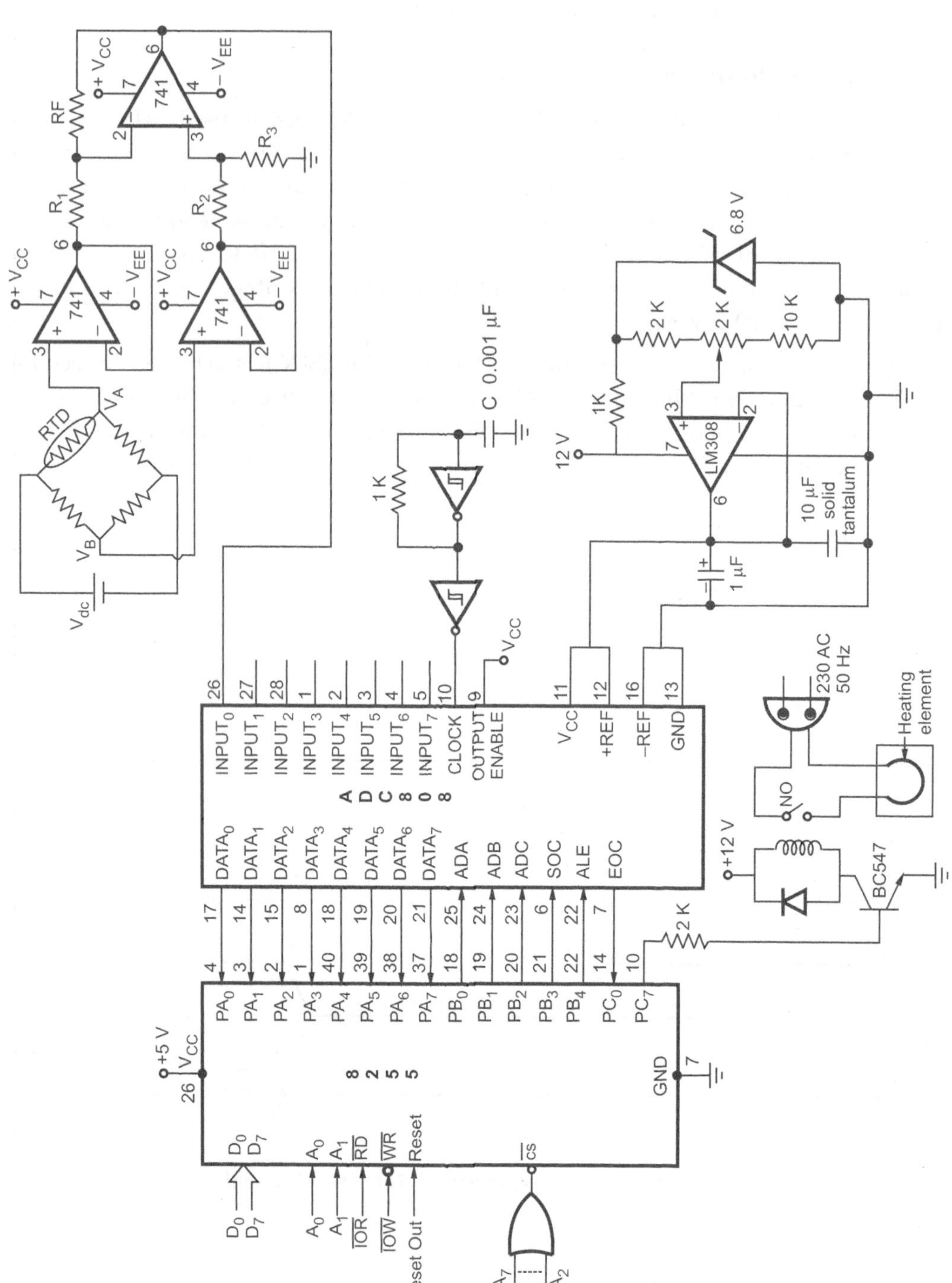

Fig. 16.18 Temperature sensing and heater control circuitry using ON/OFF control

3. Circuit required to drive the controller

As shown in the Fig. 16.18 solid state relay is used to switch ON/OFF heating element. Relay is energised and deenergised using transistor switch which is controlled by port line PC_7. When PC_7 is high, there is a sufficient base drive to run transistor in saturation (ON) and when PC_7 is low, transistor is in cut off (OFF).

Software :

It includes

1. Initialization of 8255
2. A/D conversion routine
3. Software required to take control action.

Flowchart :

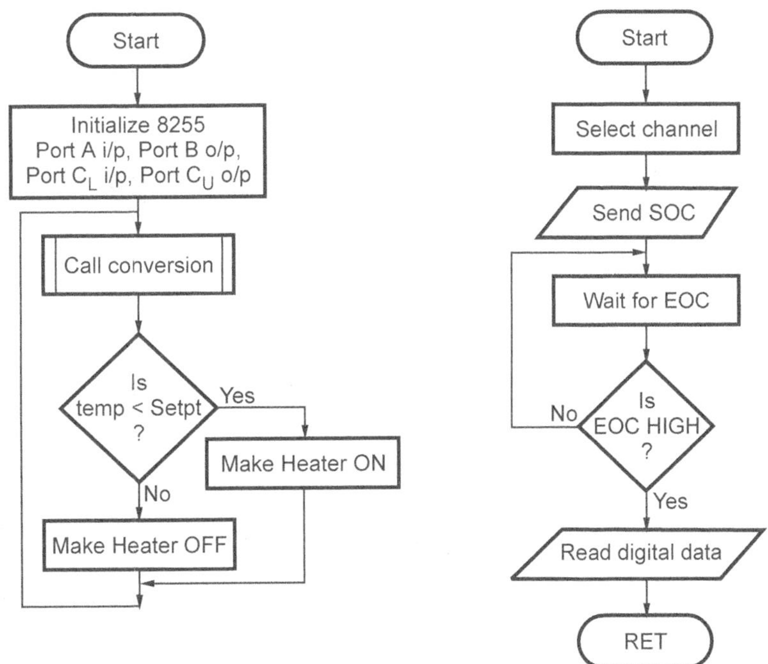

Control Word :

I/O	Mode A		PA	PC_U	Mode B	PB	PC_L	
1	0	0	1	0	0	0	1	= 91H

I/O map :

A_7	A_6	A_5	A_4	A_3	A_2	A_1	A_0	Address	Port
0	0	0	0	0	0	0	0	0 0 H	Port A
0	0	0	0	0	0	0	1	0 1 H	Port B
0	0	0	0	0	0	1	0	0 2 H	Port C
0	0	0	0	0	0	1	1	0 3 H	Port CR

Program :

```
        MVI  A, 91H         ;
        OUT  CR             ; Initialize 8255
BEGIN : CALL CONVERSION     ; Call conversion subroutine
        CPI 80H             ; compare with SETPT (80H)
        JC NEXT
        MVI  A,0EH          ; Reset bit PC7 to switch off heater with
        OUT CR              ; Bit Set/Reset Mode
        JMP  BEGIN
NEXT :  MVI  A,0FH          ; Set bit PC7 to switch ON heater with
        OUT CR              ; Bit Set/Reset Mode
        JMP  BEGIN
```

Subroutine Conversion

```
        MVI  A,00H
        OUT PB              ; Send address to select input 0
        MVI  A,08H
        OUT  PB             ; Latch the given address by sending ALE high
        MVI  C,0AH
BACK :  DCR C
        JNZ  BACK           ; Give delay greater than 2.5 µs
        MVI  A,18H
        OUT  PB             ; Make SOC high
        MVI  A,08H          ; Make SOC low
        OUT  PB
        MVI  A,00H
        OUT  PB             ; Make ALE low
```

```
AGAIN : IN PC
        ANI   01
        JZ AGAIN        ; Wait for EOC
        IN PA
        RET
```

16.10 Asynchronous, Synchronous and Interrupt Modes of Interfacing ADC

Asynchronous Mode

In asynchronous type interface, microprocessor starts the conversion process by activating the start of conversion (SOC) signal of the ADC. Microprocessor then continuously checks the end of conversion signal from the ADC. ADC activates this signal when conversion process is over. On receiving end of conversion signal, the microprocessor reads the data present at the output of ADC. This is illustrated in Fig. 16.19.

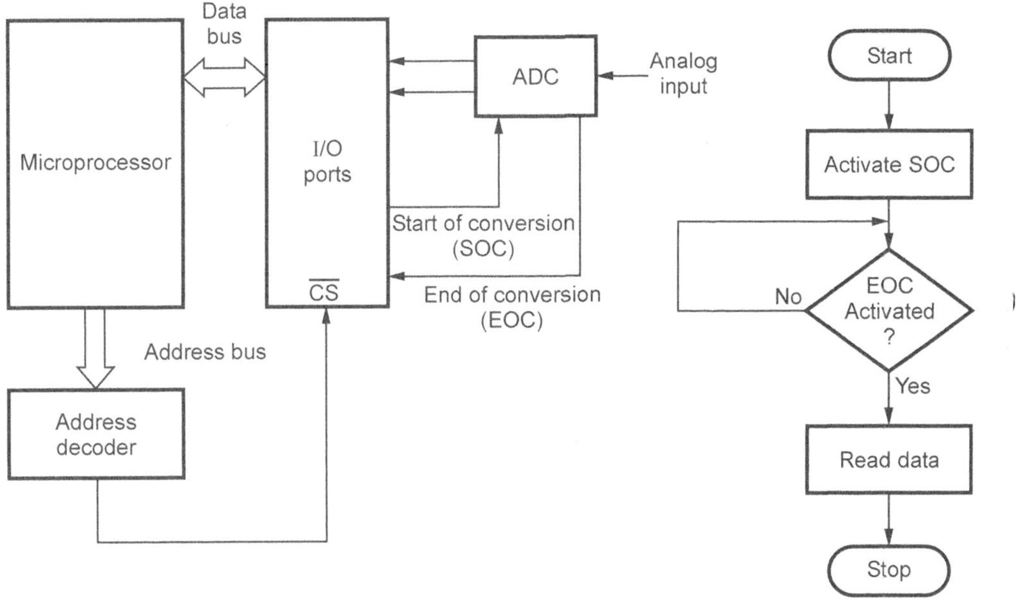

(a) ADC interface in asynchronous mode

(b) Flowchart for asynchronous mode interface

Fig. 16.19

Synchronous Mode

In asynchronous mode, the microprocessor waste time by waiting for the end of conversion signal. The conversion time of ADCs is in the range of hundreds of microseconds. Thus for every conversion cycle, this much time of the microprocessor is wasted. In synchronous mode, microprocessor executes certain instructions so that execution time of instructions is greater or equal to the conversion time, during conversion process. After execution of these instructions, microprocessor reads data from ADC without checking end of conversion signal. Here, microprocessor utilizes conversion time in executing a part of the program, thus increasing throughput.

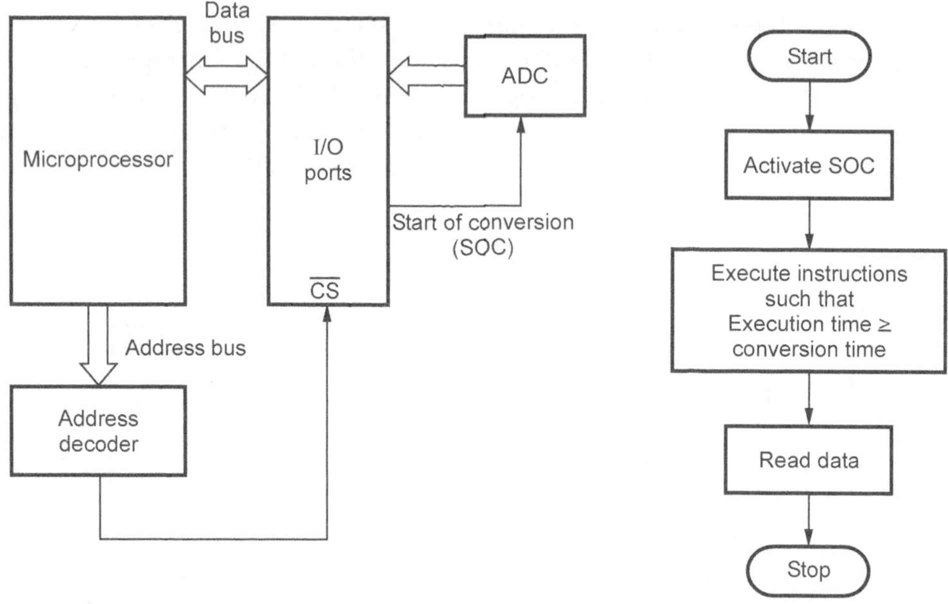

(a) ADC interface in synchronous mode

(b) Flowchart for synchronous mode interface

Fig. 16.20

Interrupt Mode

Many times, it is inconvenient to write instructions whose execution time is nearly equal to the conversion time. To overcome this difficulty we can use interrupt mode of interfacing ADC. Here, end of conversion signal from ADC is connected as an interrupt input of microprocessor. In this case, microprocessor continues instruction execution after initiating the conversion process. Whenever conversion process is completed, ADC activates EOC signals and microprocessor is interrupted. Microprocessor suspends its program execution, saves the program status and then executes the interrupt service routine (ISR). The interrupt service routine reads the data from ADC and returns program control to the main program.

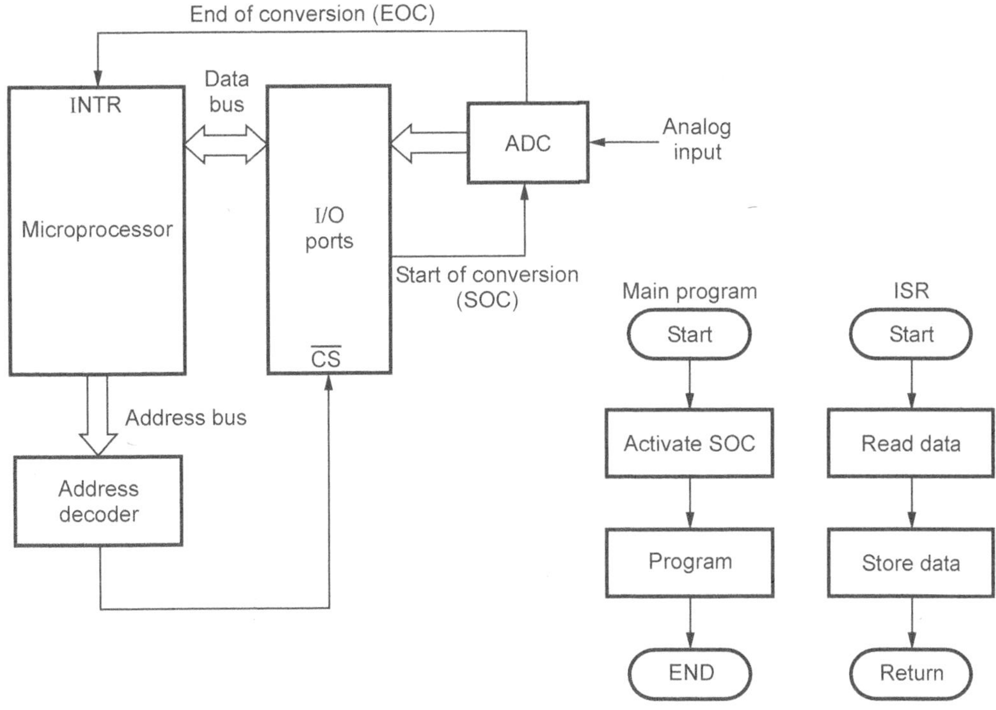

(a) ADC interface in interrupt mode (b) Flowchart for interrupt mode interface

Fig. 16.21

16.11 Sample and Hold Circuit and Multiplexer

April/May-04, 05

A **sample and hold** circuit is used to interface real-world signals. The purpose of this circuit is to hold the analog value steady for a short time while the converter or other following system performs some operation that takes a little time.

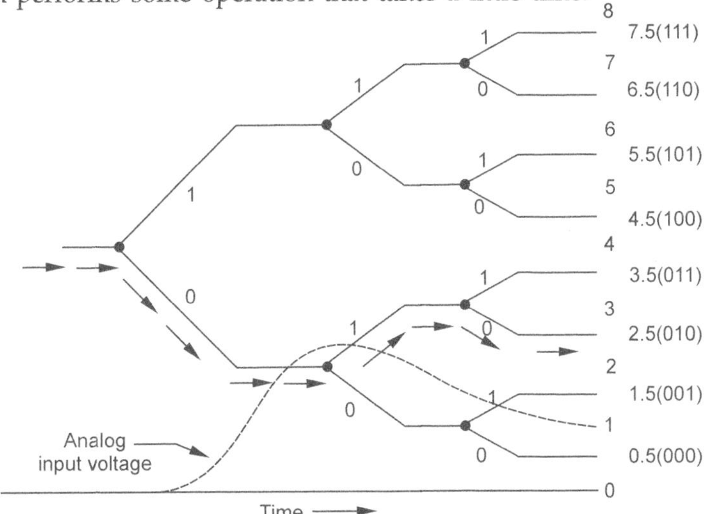

Fig. 16.22 Effect of changing input voltage

For accurate analog to digital conversion the analog input voltage should be held constant during the conversion cycle. If the analog input voltage changes by more than ± 1/2 LSB an error can occur in the digital output code. To illustrate the effect of a changing analog input voltage on the conversion processor, let us consider a situation of a successive approximation ADC with an analog input voltage that is initially zero, but there happen to be a large change in voltage amplitude occurring during the conversion process. Fig. 16.22 shows the changing input voltage and its effect on the successive approximation conversion process.

As shown in Fig. 16.22 analog input voltage at start of conversion process is zero volts and at the end of conversion process it is near to 1.5 volts, and the conversion process result is 010_2, i.e. 2.5 V. This result does not corresponds to the analog voltage at the start of conversion or at the end of conversion. To minimise the occurrence of these errors it is necessary to hold the value of the analog input voltage constant during the conversion process. The sample and hold circuit does this task.

As its name implies, the sample and hold (S/H) circuit samples the value of the input signal in response to a sampling command and hold it at the output until arrival of the next command. It samples an analog input voltage in a very short period, generally in the range of 1 to 10 μs, and holds the sampled voltage level for an extended period, which can range from a few millisecond to several seconds. Fig. 16.23(b) shows input and output response of the sample and hold circuit.

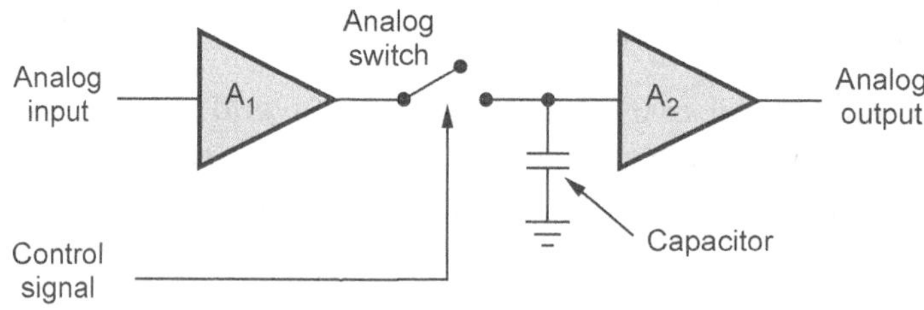

(a) Sample and hold circuit

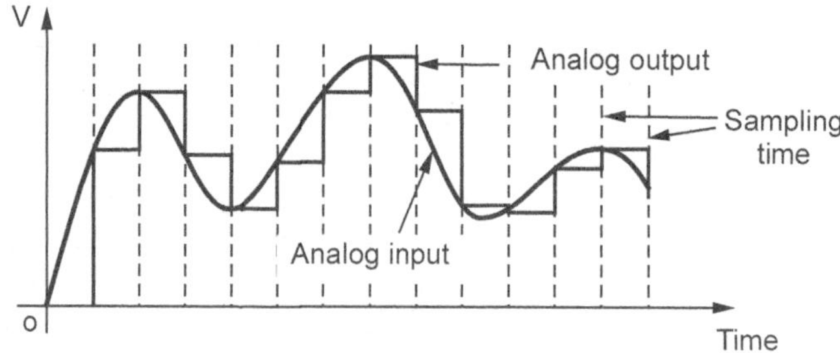

(b) Input and output response of sample and hold circuit

Fig. 16.23

The sample and hold circuit uses to basic components analog switch and capacitor. The Fig. 16.23(a) shows the basic sample and hold circuit. The circuit tracks the analog signal until the sample command causes the digital switch to isolate the capacitor from the signal, and the capacitor holds this analog voltage during A/D conversion.

The Fig. 16.24(a) illustrates a practical data acquisition system using an analog multiplexer, a sample and hold circuit and an A/D converter. In such system, microprocessor selects one of the input channels through multiplexer address lines. When the $\overline{\text{Sample}}$ / hold signal is low, the sample and hold circuit tracks the analog input; otherwise the sample and hold circuit holds the analog input. The stable analog signal is then converted into its digital equivalent using A/D converter. Microprocessor reads this output using input port.

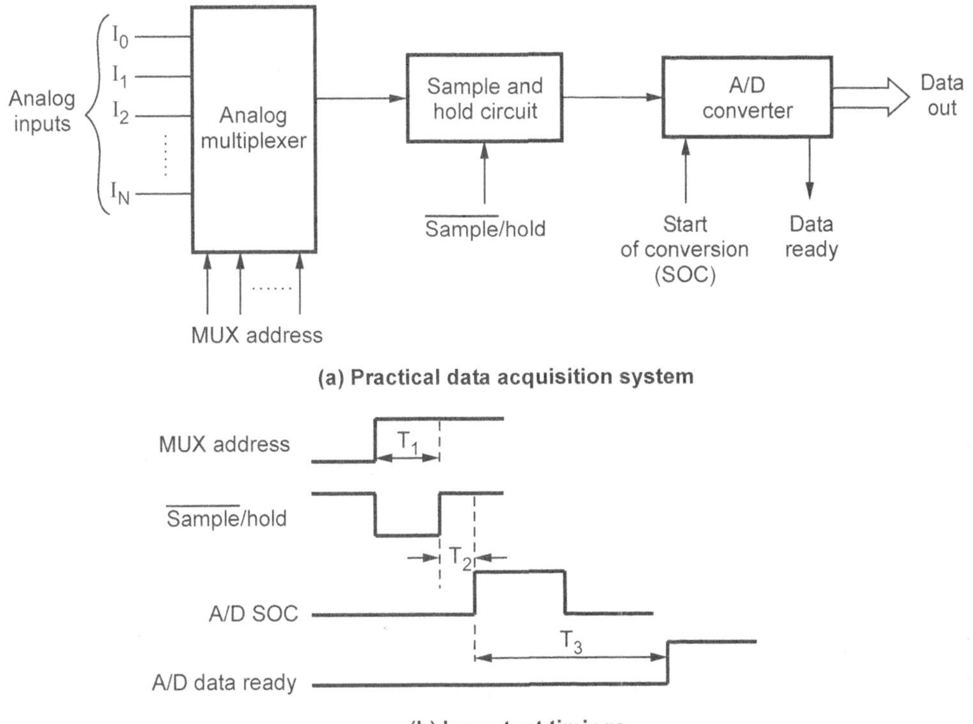

(a) Practical data acquisition system

(b) Important timings

Fig. 16.24

16.11.1 Data Acquisition System using 8085

Nov./Dec.-05

The Fig. 16.25 shows the data acquisition system using 8085 and 8255. Here 8255 is used to generate required control signals and accept data from A/D converter.

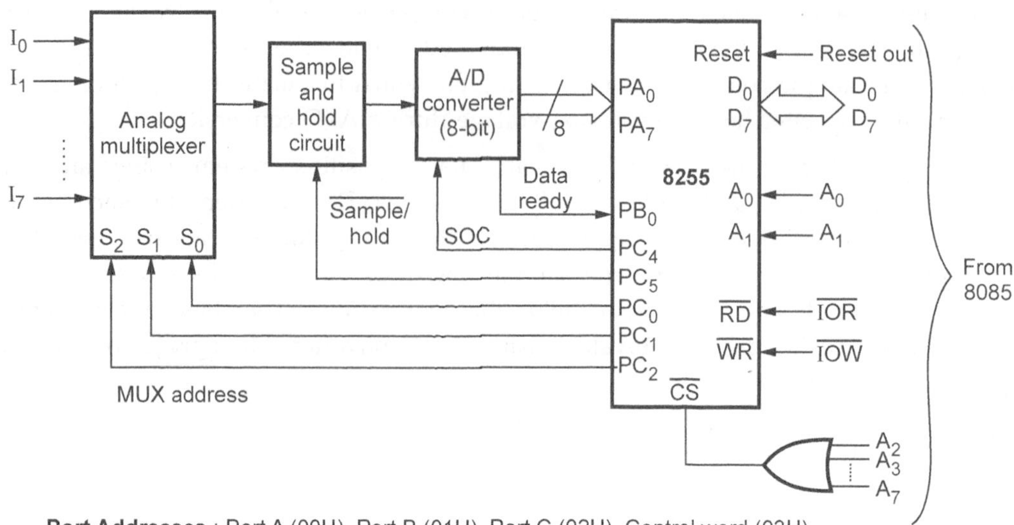

Port Addresses : Port A (00H), Port B (01H), Port C (02H), Control word (03H)

Fig. 16.25

According to ports used we require to configure 8255 as follows :

- Port A : input (mode 0)
- Port B : input (mode 0)
- Port C : output

Control Word

I/O	Mode	P_A	P_A	P_{CU}	Mode P_B	P_B	P_{CL}	
1	0	0	1	0	0	1	0	= 92 H

Program : To take sample from analog channel 2.

```
MVI A, 92H   ; Configure 8255 by
OUT 03H      ; Sending control word to control register
MVI A, 22H   ; Send MUX address, make sample/hold
OUT 02H      ; line HIGH and make SOC low
MVI A, 0AH   ; Make sample/hold Low using BSR mode
OUT 03H
MVI A, 0BH   ; Make sample/hold High using BSR mode
OUT 03H
MVI A, 09H   ; Make SOC High using BSR mode
OUT 03H
MVI A, 08H   ; Make SOC low using BSR mode
```

```
        OUT 03H
BACK :  IN 01H      ;  Read port B
        ANI 01H     ;  Check PB0
        JZ Back     ;  if zero wait for Data Ready
        IN 00H      ;  Read data through port A
        HLT         ;  Stop
```

16.11.2 Another Way of Connecting MUX and SH Circuits

In the previous examples we have seen that sample and hold circuit is connected after the multiplexer. Here, we have to select analog signal turn by turn and then sample it. Thus, we can not sample all the channels at the same time. If it is required to read values from all the channels at the same time then we need separate sample and hold circuit for each channel. This is illustrated in Fig. 16.26. With this configuration we can sample analog signals from all channels at a time. The microprocessor then selects channel one by one and read the respective values one by one with the help of multiplexer and A/D converter.

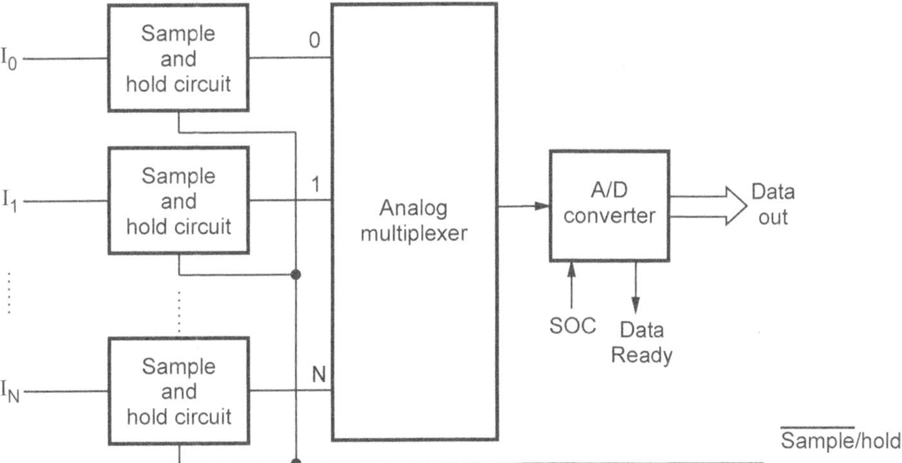

Fig. 16.26 SH and MUX connections for sampling all channels at the same time

Review Questions

Section 16.1

Q.1 *What is digital to analog converter ?*

Section 16.3

Q.1 *Explain the interfacing of D/A converter with microprocessor.*

Q.2 *Interface an 8-bit DAC with 8085 microprocessor using 8255 and write assembly language programs to generate square wave of 1 kHz and triangular wave of 100 Hz. The crystal frequency connected to 8085 is 6 MHz.* **Dec.-07, Marks 16**

Q.3 *With neat sketches, Explain the interfacing of D/A converter with 8085 Microprocessor.* **May-10,11, Dec.-11, Marks 8**

Section 16.4

Q.1 *What is analog to digital converter ?*

Q.2 *Explain how to convert an analog signal into digital signal.* **June-06, Marks 16**

Q.3 *Why do we need A/D converter and D/A converter ?* **Dec.-11, Marks 2**

Section 16.7

Q.1 *Explain the interfacing of A/D converter with microprocessor.*

Q.2 *Interface a ADC chip with 8085 processor through 8255 ports and write and ALP to use BSR mode to START conversion and STATUS CHECK mode to read output data. Explain the complete circuit and programs. Use I/O mapped I/O configuration.* **May-04, Marks 16**

Q.3 *With neat diagram explain the ADC interface to microprocessor.* **Dec.-04,10,11, May-08,11, Marks 16**

Q.4 *Using peripheral mapped I/O, design an interface circuit to connect an ADC 0808 to a microprocessor.* **May-05, Marks 6**

Q.5 *Explain how 8085 can be connected to an A/D convertor. Describe the signals involved in the process of conversion.* **Dec.-05, Marks 12**

Q.6 *What are the steps involved in interfacing an ADC with 8085.* **Dec.-09, Marks 4**

Section 16.9

Q.1 *Describe any typical automatic process control system using 8085. Use necessary block diagrams, flow charts, algorithms and program to explain the whole system operation.* **May-04, Marks 16**

Q.2 *Write a note on automatic process control.* **May-05, Marks 8**

Section 16.10

Q.1 *Discuss different modes of interfacing ADC to microprocessor.*

Section 16.11

Q.1 *What is sample and hold circuit ? Explain the purpose of it.*

Q.2 *Explain the use of sample and hold circuit with multiplexer.*

Q.3 *Draw and explain the data acquisition system.*

Q.4 *Draw and explain the operation of a sample and hold circuit.* **May-04,05, Marks 4**

Q.5 *Explain the sample and hold IC.* **Dec.-05, Marks 12**

Two Marks Questions with Answers

Q.1 ***Name any two type of ADCs.*** **May-04**

Ans. : ADC 0808, ADC 7109.

Q.2 ***Calculate the values of LSB, MSB and full scale output for 8-bit DAC for 0 to 10 V range.*** **June-07**

Ans. : Given : $n = 8, \ V_{oFS} = 10\ V$

$$\text{Resolution} = \frac{V_{oFS}}{2^n - 1} = \frac{10}{2^8 - 1}$$

$$= 39.21\ mV$$

$$\therefore \quad \text{LSB} = 39.21\ mV$$

$$\text{MSB (128)} = 128 \times 39.21 = 5\ V$$

Q.3 ***Draw the basic block diagram of ADC interfacing with 8085.*** **Dec.-08**

Ans. : Refer section 16.7.

Q.4 ***What are the signals handled in ADC interfacing ?***

Ans. : The signals handled in ADC interfacing are :

SOC : Start of conversion - Send to start conversion process.

EOC : End of conversion - Indicate the end of conversion.

ALE : In case of multi-channel ADC if is used to latch the address of channel to be selected.

Address : In case of multi-channel ADC address signals are sent to select the desired channel.

Q.5 ***What is the significance of end of conversion signal while interfacing A/D converter to a microprocessor ?***

Ans. : End of conversion signal from ADC indicates that the conversion is completed. So that microprocessors can read converted digital word through data bus by enabling the output enable signal after EOC is activated.

Q.6 ***Why ADC and DAC is used in the microprocessor bused system ?***

Ans. : Most of the information carrying signals such as voltage, current, charge, temperature, pressure and time are available in the analog form. However, for processing, transmission and storage purposes, it is often more convenient to express such signals in the digital form. When expressed in the digital form, they provide better accuracy and reduce noise.

Moreover, the development in the microprocessor technology has made it compulsory to process data in the digital form and hence ADC is used in the microprocessor based systems.

On the other hand, a digital to analog (D/A) converter is used when a binary output from a digital system must be converted to some equivalent analog voltage or current. For example, if in a particular system a computer is used as a controller, the controlling signal produced by the computer is always digital. The system to be controlled requires the analog signal. Hence in between the computer and the system to be controlled the digital to analog converter is must.

Q.7 ***What are the commonly used ADC's and DAC's ?***

Ans. : i) Commonly used ADC's are : ADC 0808/0809, ADC 0804, ADC 7109.

ii) Commonly used DAC's are : DAC 0808, DAC 0830.

Q.8 ***Draw the basic block diagram of ADC interfacing with 8085.*** Dec.-08

Ans. : Refer sections 16.7 and 16.10.

❑❑❑

17 8051 Microcontroller

Contents

17.1 Introduction to 8051 Microcontroller

To make a complete microcomputer system, only microprocessor is not sufficient. It is necessary to add other peripherals such as Read Only Memory (ROM), read/write memory (RAM), decoders, drivers, number of input/output devices to make a complete microcomputer system. In addition, special purpose devices, such as interrupt controller, programmable timers, programmable I/O devices, DMA controllers may be added to improve the capability and performance and flexibility of a microcomputer system.

The microcontroller incorporates all the features that are found in microprocessor. However, it has also added features to make a complete microcomputer system on its own. The microcontroller has built-in ROM, RAM, parallel I/O, serial I/O, counters and a clock circuit.

The advantages of built-in peripheral devices of microcontroller are :

- Built-in peripherals have smaller access times hence speed is more.
- Hardware reduces due to single chip microcomputer system.
- Less hardware, reduces PCB size and increases reliability of the system.

Sr. No.	Microprocessor	Microcontroller
1.	Microprocessor contains ALU, control unit (clock and timing circuit), different register and interrupt circuit.	Microcontroller contains microprocessor, memory (ROM and RAM), I/O interfacing circuit and peripheral devices such as A/D converter, serial I/O, timer etc.
2.	It has many instructions to move data between memory and CPU.	It has one or two instructions to move data between memory and CPU.
3.	It has one or two bit handling instructions.	It has many bit handling instructions.
4.	Access times for memory and I/O devices are more.	Less access times for built-in memory and I/O devices.
5.	Microprocessor based system requires more hardware.	Microcontroller based system requires less hardware reducing PCB size and increasing the reliability.
6.	Microprocessor based system is more flexible in design point of view.	Less flexible in design point of view.
7.	It has single memory map for data and code.	It has separate memory map for data and code.
8.	Less number of pins are multifunctioned.	More number pins are multifunctioned.

Table 17.1 Comparison between microprocessor and microcontroller

17.2 Features of 8051 and 8051 Family Microcontrollers

The 8051 is an 8-bit microcontroller designed by Intel. It was optimized for 8-bit math and single bit Boolean operations. Its family includes 8031, 8051, 8052 and 8751 microcontrollers. Let us see the features of 8051 microcontroller.

The features of the 8051 family are as follows :

1. 4096 bytes on - chip program memory.
2. 128 bytes on - chip data memory.
3. Four register banks.
4. 128 user-defined software flags.
5. 64 kilobytes each program and external RAM addressability.
6. One microsecond instruction cycle with 12 MHz crystal.
7. 32 bidirectional I/O lines organized as four 8-bit ports (16 lines on 8031).
8. Multiple mode, high-speed programmable serial port.
9. Two multiple mode, 16-bit timers/counters.
10. Two-level prioritized interrupt structure.
11. Full depth stack for subroutine return linkage and data storage.
12. Direct byte and bit addressability.
13. Binary or decimal arithmetic.
14. Signed-overflow detection and parity computation.
15. Hardware multiple and divide in 4 μsec.
16. Integrated boolean processor for control applications.
17. Upwardly compatible with existing 8084 software.

The Table 17.2 gives the comparison of MCS-51 family microcontrollers.

Feature	8031	8051	8052	8751
Program memory (in bytes)	None	4 K ROM	8 K ROM	4 K EPROM
Data memory (in Bytes)	128 RAM	128 RAM	256 RAM	128 RAM
Timers / Counters (16-bit)	2	2	3	2
I/O pins	32	32	32	32
Serial Port	1	1	1	1
Interrupt Sources (Reset not included)	5	5	6	5

Table 17.2 Comparison of MCS-51 family microcontrollers

As shown in the Table 17.2, the 8052 has an extra 128 bytes of RAM, 4 K extra ROM, extra timer and one more interrupt source than the 8051 microcontroller. The 8052 maintains the source compatibility with 8051. This means that all programs written for the 8051 will run on 8052; however, reverse is not true.

The 8751 microcontroller has 4 K of EPROM instead of ROM. This allows to erase and reprogram the contents of program memory within 8751. It takes around 20 minutes to erase the 8751 before it can be programmed again. This feature is very useful in the program development stage.

17.3 Architecture of 8051

The Fig. 17.1 shows the internal block diagram of 8051. It consists of a CPU, two kinds of memory sections (data memory - RAM and program memory - EPROM/ROM), input/output ports, special function registers and control logic needed for a timer / counter serial port and interrupt functions. These elements communicate through an eight bit data bus which runs throughout the chip referred as internal data bus. This bus is buffered to the outside world through an I/O port when memory or I/O expansion is desired. (Refer Fig. 17.1 on next page).

17.3.1 Central Processing Unit (CPU)

The CPU of 8051 consists of eight-bit arithmetic and logic unit with associated registers like A, B, PSW, SP, the sixteen bit program counter and "Data pointer" (DPTR) registers. Along with these registers it has a set of special function registers.

The unique feature of the 8051 architecture is that the ALU can also manipulate one bit as well as eight-bit data types.

17.3.2 A and B CPU Registers

Register A (Accumulator)

It is an 8-bit register called **accumulator**. It holds a source operand and receives the result of the arithmetic instructions (addition, subtraction, multiplication and division).

Several functions apply exclusively to the accumulator : Rotate, parity computation, testing for zero and so on.

Register B

In addition to accumulator, an 8-bit B-register is available as a general purpose register. It is used for the hardware multiply/divide operation.

17.3.3 Data Pointer (DPTR)

The data pointer (DPTR) consists of a high byte (DPH) and a low byte (DPL). Its function is to hold a 16-bit address. It may be manipulated as a 16-bit data register or as two independent 8-bit registers. It serves as a base register in indirect jumps, lookup table

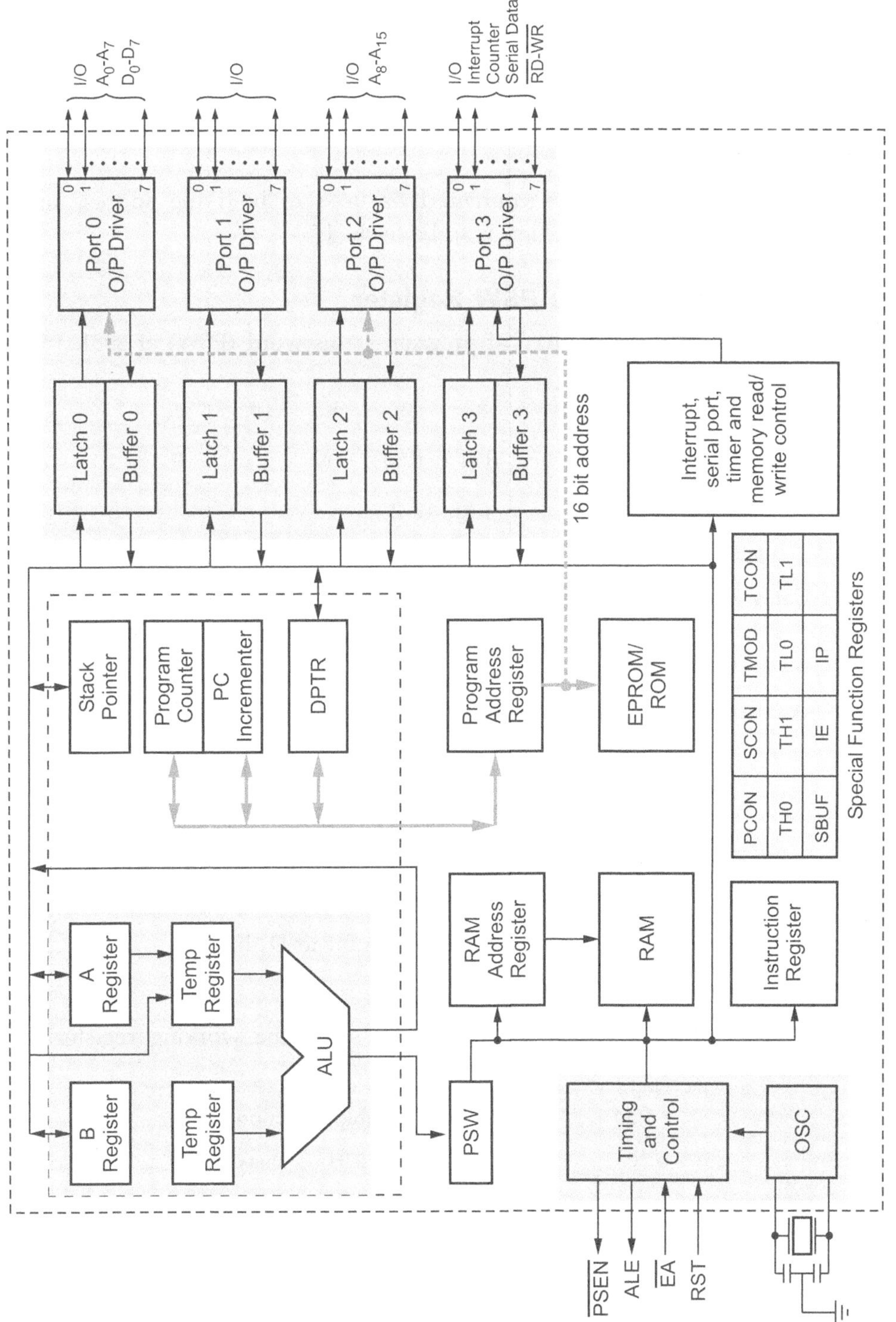

Fig. 17.1 Block diagram of 8051

instructions and external data transfer. The DPTR does not have a single internal address; DPH (83H) and DPL (82H) have separate internal addresses.

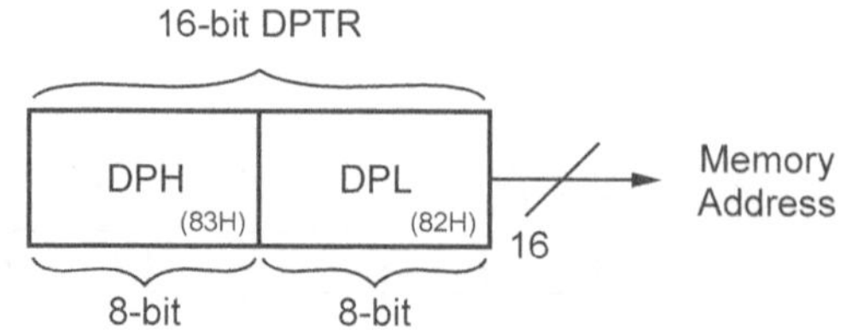

17.3.4 The Program Counter

The 8051 has a 16-bit program counter. It is used to hold the address of memory location from which the next instruction is to be fetched.

17.3.5 8051 Flag Bits and the PSW Register

The Fig. 17.2 shows the bit pattern of program status word (PSW) of 8051. PSW is also known as **flag register**.

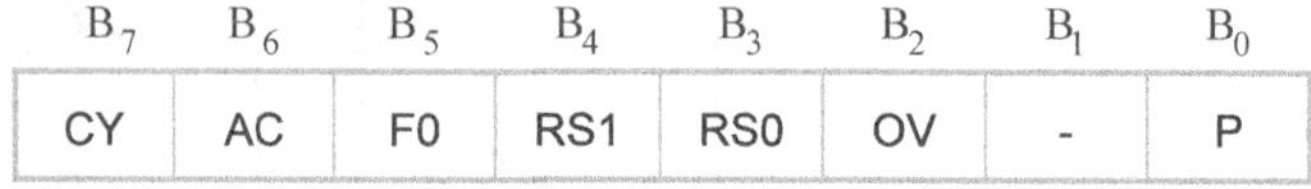

Fig. 17.2

The 8051 consists of following flags.

- **CY-Carry Flag :** This flag is set if there is an overflow out of bit 7. The carry flag also serves as a borrow flag for subtraction. In both the examples shown below, the carry flag is set.
- **AC-Auxiliary Carry Flag :** This flag is set if there is an overflow out of bit 3 i.e.,

ADDITION / **SUBTRACTION**

```
          9B H        1001 1011              89 H        1000 1001
      +   75 H      + 0111 0101         –    AB H      – 1010 1011
Carry [1] 10 H    [1] 0001 0000   Borrow [1] DE H    [1] 1101 1110
```

carry from lower nibble to higher nibble (D_3 bit to D_4 bit).

- **FO** - Available for user for general purpose.
- **RS1 - RS0 (Register Bank Select) :** They select the working register bank as follows :

RS1	RS0	Bank Selection	
0	0	00H - 07H	Bank 0
0	1	08H - 0FH	Bank 1
1	0	10H - 17H	Bank 2
1	1	18H - 1FH	Bank 3

- **OV-Over Flow Flag :** This flag is set whenever the result of a signed number operation is too large, causing the high-order bit to overflow into the sign bit.
- **P-Parity Flag :** Parity is defined by the number of ones present in the accumulator. P = 0, if number of ones are even and P = 1, if number of ones are odd.

Example : The status of CY, AC and P flags after the addition of 9BH and 65H is as follows :

		1	1	1	1	1	1	1		Carry
9 BH		1	0	0	1	1	0	1	1	
+ 65 H		0	1	1	0	0	1	0	1	
	1	**0**	**0**	**0**	**0**	**0**	**0**	**0**	**0**	

|← Accumulator →|

CY = 1, AC = 1 and P = 0

There are instructions in 8051, that tests the condition of flags in the PSW register and make decision based on the status of flags. Thus, programmer use these flags to perform some arithmetic operations which involves carry or borrow, or to change the program control (using conditional branching).

As mention earlier, programmer can select register bank by setting corresponding bits in PSW.

17.3.6 Special Function Register of 8051

The group of registers, implemented to perform special functions and are located immediately above the 128 bytes of RAM are called **special function registers.** All access to the four I/O ports, the CPU registers, interrupt control registers, the timer/counter, UART and power control are performed through registers between 80H and FFH.

Special Function Registers (SFRs) are a sort of control table used for running and monitoring the operation of the microcontroller. Each of these registers as well as each bit they include, has its name, address in the scope of RAM and precisely defined purpose such as timer control, interrupt control, serial communication control etc.

Even though there are 128 memory locations intended to be occupied by them, the basic core, shared by all types of 8051 microcontrollers, has only 21 such registers. Rest of locations are intentionally left unoccupied in order to enable the manufacturers to further develop microcontrollers keeping them compatible with the previous versions.

Fig. 17.3 shows special function bit addresses.

Direct byte address	(MSB)	Bit address						(LSB)	Hardware register symbol
0FFH									
0F0H	F7	F6	F5	F4	F3	F2	F1	F0	B
0E0H	E7	E6	E5	E4	E3	E2	E1	E0	ACC
0D0H	D7	D6	D5	D4	D3	D2	D1	D0	PSW
0B8H	---	---	---	BC	BB	BA	B9	B8	IP
0B0H	B7	B6	B5	B4	B3	B2	B1	B0	P3
0A8H	AF	---	---	AC	AB	AA	A9	A8	IE
0A0H	A7	A6	A5	A4	A3	A2	A1	A0	P2
98H	9F	9E	9D	9C	9B	9A	99	98	SCON
90H	97	96	95	94	93	92	91	90	P1
88H	8F	8E	8D	8C	8B	8A	89	88	TCON
80H	87	86	85	84	83	82	81	80	P0

Fig. 17.3 SFR bit address

Table 17.3 contains a list of all the SFRs and their addresses and their value in binary at reset.

Symbol	Name	Address	Value in Binary
*ACC	Accumulator	0E0H	0000 0000
*B	B Register	0F0H	0000 0000
*PSW	Program Status Word	0D0H	0000 0000
SP	Stack Pointer	81H	0000 0111
DPTR	Data Pointer 2 Bytes		
DPL	Low Byte	82H	0000 0000
DPH	High Byte	83H	0000 0000
*P0	Port 0	80H	1111 1111
*P1	Port 1	90H	1111 1111
*P2	Port 2	0A0H	1111 1111
*P3	Port 3	0B0H	1111 1111
*IP	Interrupt Priority Control	0B8H	8051 XXX0 0000 8052 XX00 0000
*IE	Interrupt Enable Control	0A8H	8051 0XX0 0000 8052 0X00 0000
TMOD	Timer/Counter Mode Control	89H	0000 0000
*TCON	Timer/Counter Control	88H	0000 0000
* + T2CON	Timer/Counter 2 Control	0C8H	0000 0000
TH0	Timer/Counter 0 High Byte	8CH	0000 0000
TL0	Timer/Counter 0 Low Byte	8AH	0000 0000
TH1	Timer/Counter 1 High Byte	8DH	0000 0000
TL1	Timer/Counter 1 Low Byte	8BH	0000 0000
+ TH2	Timer/Counter 2 High Byte	0CDH	0000 0000
+ TL2	Timer/Counter 2 Low Byte	0CCH	0000 0000
+ RCAP2H	T/C 2 Capture Reg. High Byte	0CBH	0000 0000
+ RCAP2L	T/C 2 Capture Reg. Low Byte	0CAH	0000 0000
* SCON	Serial Control	98H	0000 0000
SBUF	Serial Data Buffer	99H	Indeterminate
PCON	Power Control	87H	HMOS 0XXX XXXX CHMOS 0XXX 0000

Table 17.3 List of all SFRs (* – Bit addressable, + – 8052 only)

* before register name indicates that it is a bit addressable.

+ before register name indicates that it is supported by only 8052.

17.4 Pin Description of 8051

The 8051 is packaged in a 40-pin DIP. The Fig. 17.4 shows the pin diagram of 8051. It is important to note that many pins of 8051 are used for more than one function. The alternative functions of pins are shown in bold letters.

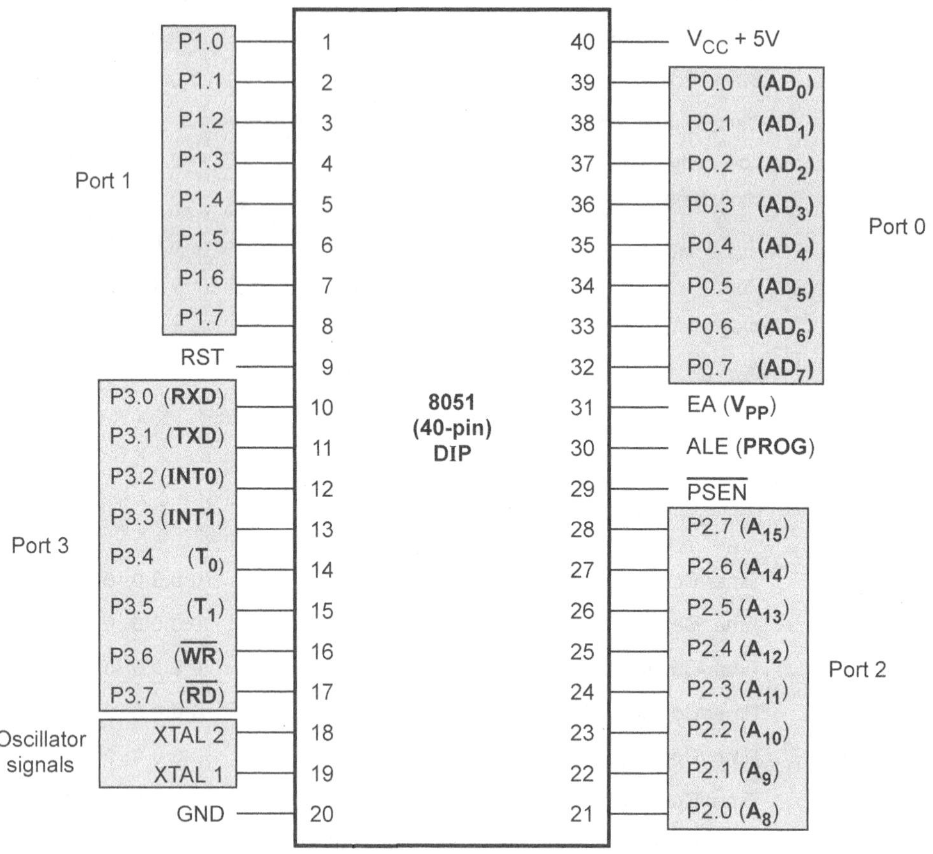

Fig. 17.4 Pin-out of 8051

The 8051 has 32 I/O pins configured as four eight-bit parallel ports (P0, P1, P2 and P3). All four ports are bidirectional i.e. each pin will be configured as input or output (or both). All port-pins are multiplexed except the pins of port 1. Each port consists of a latch, an output driver and an input buffer.

Port 0 (Pins 32 - 39)

Port 0 pins can be used as I/O pins. The output drives and input buffers of port 0 are used to access external memory. Port 0 outputs the low order byte of the external memory address, time multiplexed with the data being written or read. Thus, port 0 can be used as a multiplexed address/data bus.

Port 1 (Pins 1 - 8)

Port 1 pins can be used only as I/O pins.

Port 2 (Pins 21 - 28)

The output drives of port 2 are used to access external memory. Port 2 outputs the high order byte of the external memory address when the address is 16 bits wide. Otherwise, port 2 is used as an I/O port.

Port 3 (Pins 10 - 17)

All port pins of port 3 are multifunctional. Therefore, each pin of port 3 can be programmed to use as I/O or as one of the alternate function. They have special functions as shown below including two external interrupts, two counter inputs, two special data lines and two timing control strobes.

Symbol	Position	Alternate Use
$\overline{RD}$	P3.7	External memory read signal.
$\overline{WR}$	P3.6	External memory write signal.
T1	P3.5	External timer 1 input.
T0	P3.4	External timer 0 input.
$\overline{INT1}$	P3.3	External interrupt 1 input.
$\overline{INT0}$	P3.2	External interrupt 0 input.
TXD	P3.1	Serial data output.
RXD	P3.0	Serial data input.

Table 17.4

Power-supply Pins V_{CC} (Pin 40) and V_{SS} (Pin 20)

8051 operates on d.c. power supply of +5 V with respect to ground. The +5 V is to be connected to pin V_{CC} and ground to pin V_{SS} with rated power supply current of 125 mA.

Oscillator Pins XTAL2 (Pin 18) and XTAL1 (Pin 19)

For generating an internal clock signal, the external oscillator is connected at these two pins.

ALE (Address Latch Enable, Pin 30)

AD_0 to AD_7 lines are multiplexed. To demultiplex these lines and for obtaining lower half of an address, an external latch and ALE signal of 8051 is used.

RST (Reset, Pin 9)

This pin is used to reset 8051. For proper reset operation, reset signal must be held high at least for two machine cycles, while oscillator is running.

$\overline{\text{PSEN}}$ (Program Store Enable, Pin 29)

It is the active low output control signal used to activate the enable signal of the external ROM/EPROM. It is activated every six oscillator periods while reading the external memory. Thus, this signal acts as the read strobe to external program memory.

$\overline{\text{EA}}$ (External Access, Pin 31)

When the $\overline{\text{EA}}$ pin is high (connected to V_{CC}), program fetches to addresses 0000H through 0FFFH are directed to the internal ROM and program fetches to addresses 1000H through FFFFH are directed to external ROM/EPROM. When $\overline{\text{EA}}$ is low (grounded), all addresses (0000H to FFFFH) fetched by program are directed to the external ROM/EPROM.

17.5 Internal and External Memories

Fig. 17.5 shows the basic memory structure for 8051. It can access up to 64 K program memory and 64 K data memory. The 8051 has 4 K bytes of internal program memory and 256 bytes of internal data memory.

17.5.1 Internal RAM Organization

The 8051 has 128-byte internal RAM. It is accessed using RAM address register. The Fig. 17.6 (see on 17-14 page) shows the organization of internal RAM. As shown in the Fig. 17.6 internal RAM of 8051 is organized into three distinct areas :

- Register bank
- Bit addressable
- General purpose.

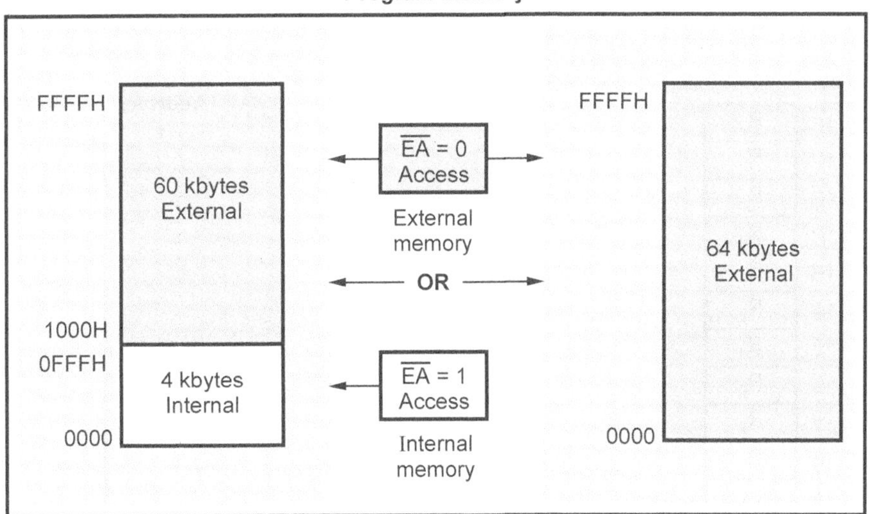
Program memory
FFFFH
60 kbytes
External
1000H
0FFFH
4 kbytes
Internal
0000
$\overline{EA}$ = 0
Access
External
memory
OR
$\overline{EA}$ = 1
Access
Internal
memory
FFFFH
64 kbytes
External
0000

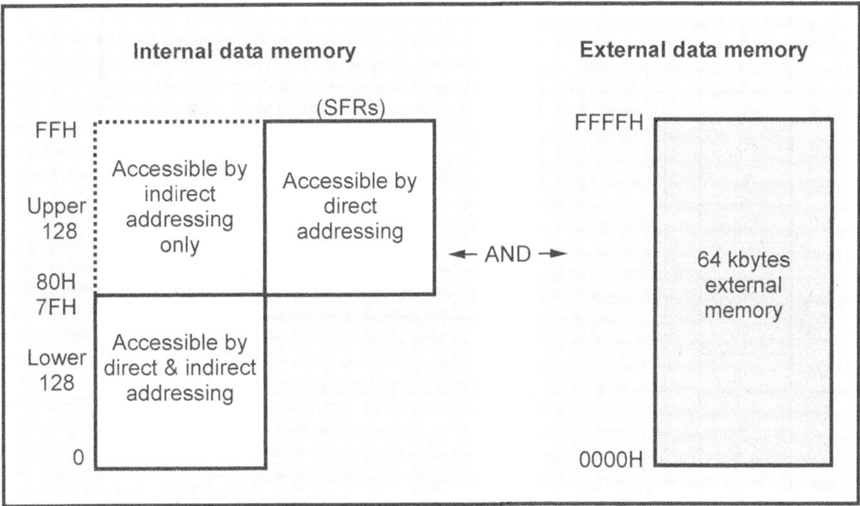
Data memory
Internal data memory
(SFRs)
FFH
Upper
128
80H
7FH
Lower
128
0
Accessible by
indirect
addressing
only
Accessible by
direct
addressing
Accessible by
direct & indirect
addressing
AND
External data memory
FFFFH
64 kbytes
external
memory
0000H

Fig. 17.5

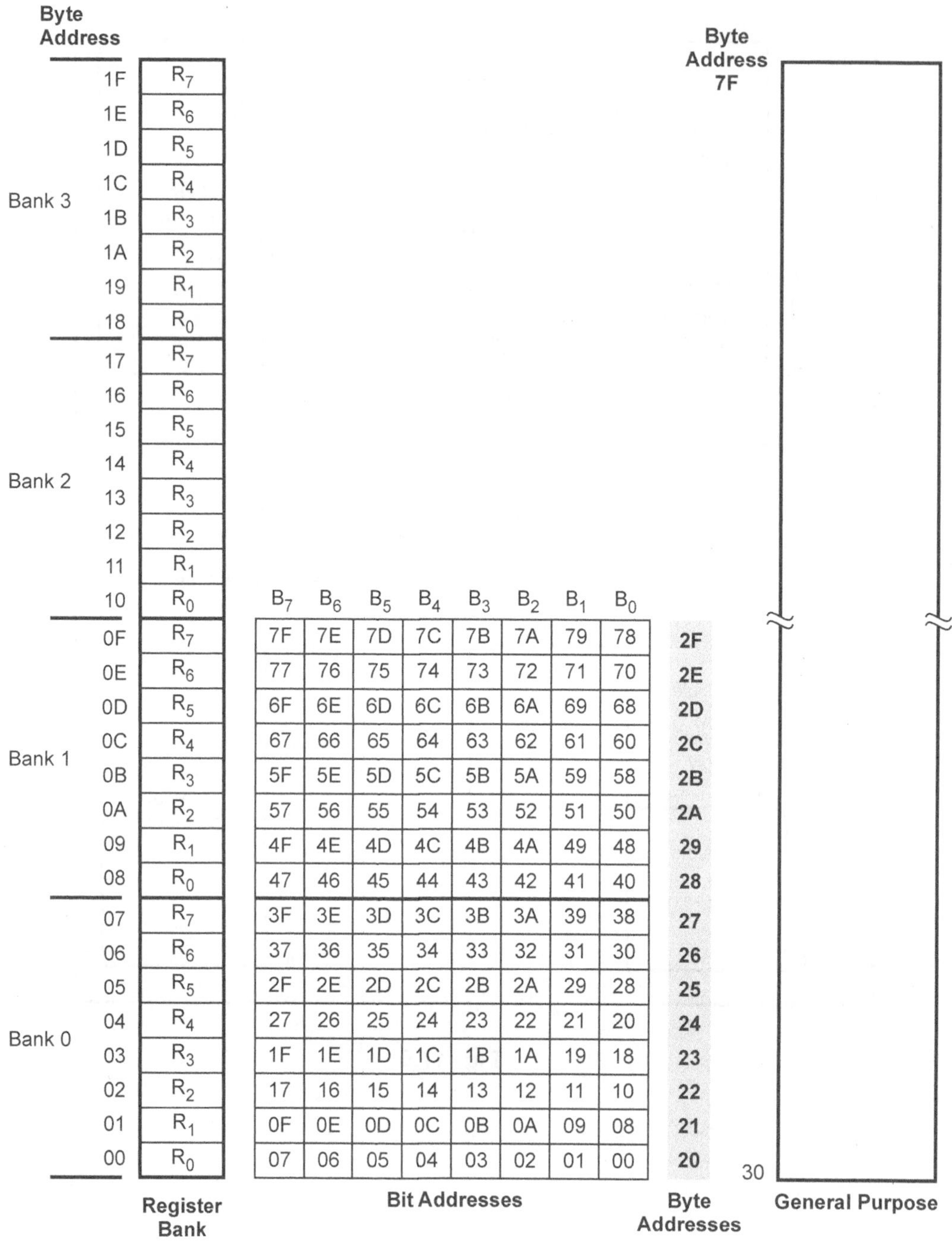

Fig. 17.6 Organization of internal RAM of 8051

17.5.1.1 8051 Register Banks (Working Registers)

The first 32-bytes from address 00H to 1FH of internal RAM constitute 32 working registers. They are organized into four banks of eight registers each. The four register banks are numbered 0 to 3 and are consists of eight registers named R_0 to R_7.

Each register can be addressed by name or by its RAM address.

Only one register bank is in use at a time. Bits RS0 and RS1 in the PSW determine which bank of registers is currently in use.

RS1 (PSW.4)	RS0 (PSW.3)	Bank selection
0	0	Bank 0
0	1	Bank 1
1	0	Bank 2
1	1	Bank 3

On reset, the bank 0 is selected and hence it is a default register bank. Register banks when not selected can be used as general purpose RAM.

17.5.1.2 Bit / Byte Addressable

The 8051 provides 16 bytes of a bit-addressable area. It occupies RAM byte addresses from 20H to 2FH, forming a total of 128 (16 × 8) addressable bits.

An addressable bit may be specified by its bit address of 00H to 7FH, or 8 bits may form any byte address from 20H to 2FH.

For example, bit address 4EH refers bit 6 of the byte address 29H.

17.5.1.3 General Purpose RAM

The RAM area above bit addressable area from 30H to 7FH is called general purpose RAM. It is addressable as byte.

17.5.2 ROM Space in the 8051

The 8051 has 4 kbyte of internal ROM with address space from 0000H to 0FFFH. It is programmed by manufacturer when the chip is built. This part cannot be erased or altered after fabrication. This is used to store final version of the program. It is accessed using program address register.

17.6 Interfacing and Timing Diagrams for Memory Interfacing

We have seen that 8051 has internal data and code memory with limited memory capacity. This memory capacity may not be sufficient for some applications. In such situations, we have to connect external ROM/EPROM and RAM to 8051 microcontroller to increase the memory capacity. We also know that ROM is used as a program memory and RAM is used as a data memory. Let us see how 8051 accesses these memories.

17.6.1 External Program Memory

Fig. 17.7 shows a map of the 8051 program memory.

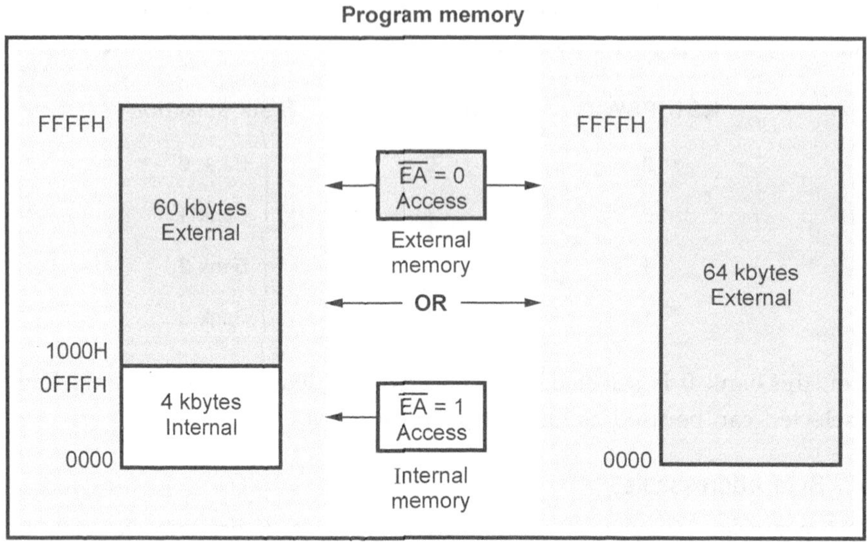

Fig. 17.7 The 8051 program memory

In 8051, when the $\overline{EA}$ pin is connected to V_{CC}, program fetches to addresses 0000H through 0FFFH are directed to the internal ROM and program fetches to addresses 1000H through FFFFH are directed to external ROM/EPROM. On the other hand when $\overline{EA}$ pin is grounded, all addresses (0000H to FFFFH) fetched by program are directed to the external ROM/EPROM. The $\overline{PSEN}$ signal is used to activate output enable signal of the external ROM/EPROM, as shown in the Fig. 17.8.

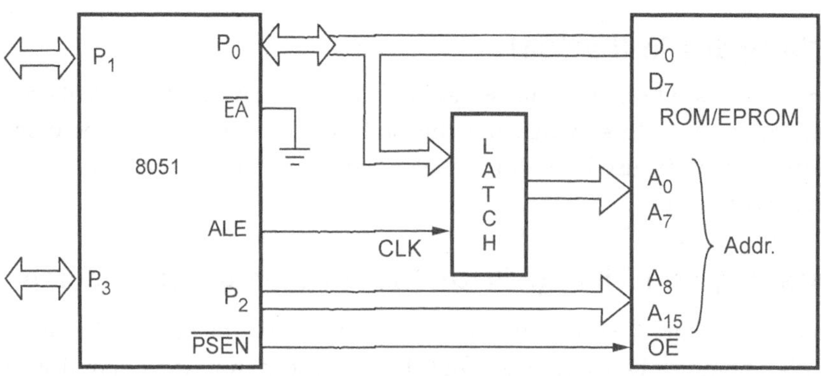

Fig. 17.8 Accessing external program memory

As shown in the Fig. 17.8, the port 0 is used as a multiplexed address/bus. It gives lower order 8-bit address in the initial T-cycle and later it is used as a data bus. The 8-bit address is latched using external latch and ALE signal generated by 8051. The port 2 provides the higher order 8-bit address. Fig. 17.9 shows the timing waveforms for external program memory read cycle.

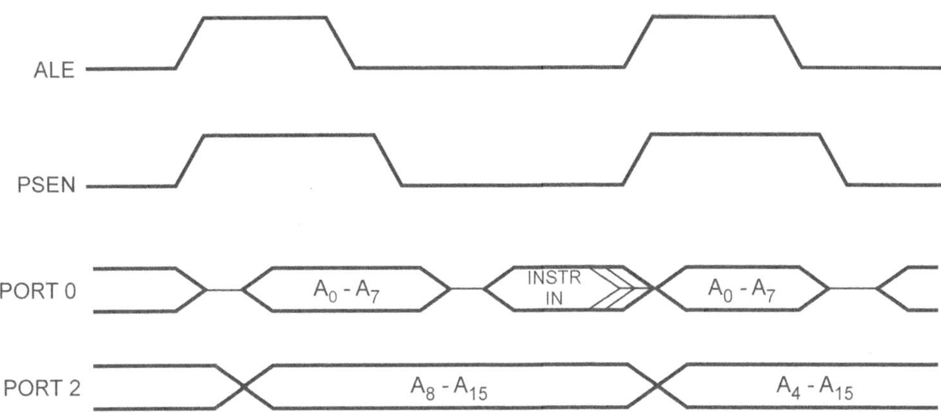

Fig. 17.9 Timing waveforms for external program memory read cycle

The lower part of program memory stores the vector addresses for various interrupt service routines. Fig. 17.10 shows the vector address map. Each interrupt is assigned with a fixed location in program memory. For example, external interrupt 0 is assigned to location 0003H. The interrupt service locations are spaced at 8-byte intervals such as 0003H for External Interrupt 0, 000BH for Timer 0, 0013H for External Interrupt 1, 001BH for Timer 1, etc. If interrupt is going to be used, its service routine must begin at

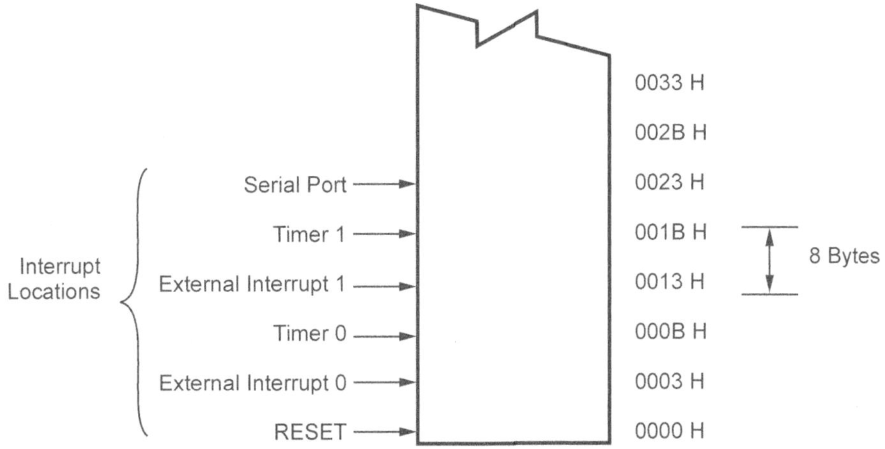

Fig. 17.10 Interrupt/Vector locations in the lower part of program memory

corresponding location. If the interrupt is not going to be used, its service location is available as general purpose program memory.

Instructions to Access External ROM / Program Memory

The Table 17.5 explains the instructions to access external ROM/program memory.

Mnemonic	Operation
MOVC A, @ A + DPTR	Copy the contents of the external ROM address formed by adding A and the DPTR, to A.
MOVC A, @ A + PC	Copy the contents of the external ROM address formed by adding A and the PC, to A.

Table 17.5

17.6.2 External Data Memory

Fig. 17.11 shows a map of the 8051 data memory.

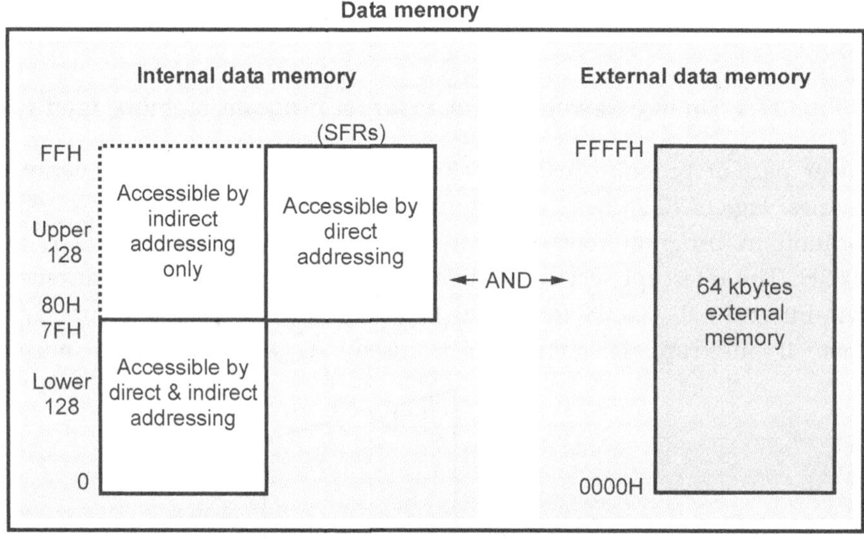

Fig. 17.11 A map of the 8051 data memory

The 8051 can address upto 64 kbytes of external data memory. The "MOVX" instruction is used to access the external data memory. The internal data memory space for 8051 is divided into three blocks : Lower 128 bytes, Upper 128 bytes and SFRs. The upper addresses and SFRs occupy the same block of address space, 80H through FFH, although they are physically separate entities. As shown in the Fig. 17.11, the upper address space is accessible by indirect addressing only and SFRs are accessible by direct addressing only. On the other hand, lower address space can be accessed either by direct addressing or by indirect addressing.

Fig. 17.12 shows the circuit diagram for connecting external data memory. The multiplexed address/data bus provided by port 0 is demultiplexed by external latch and ALE signal. Port 2 gives the higher order address bus. The $\overline{RD}$ and $\overline{WR}$ signals from 8051 selects the memory read and memory write operation, respectively.

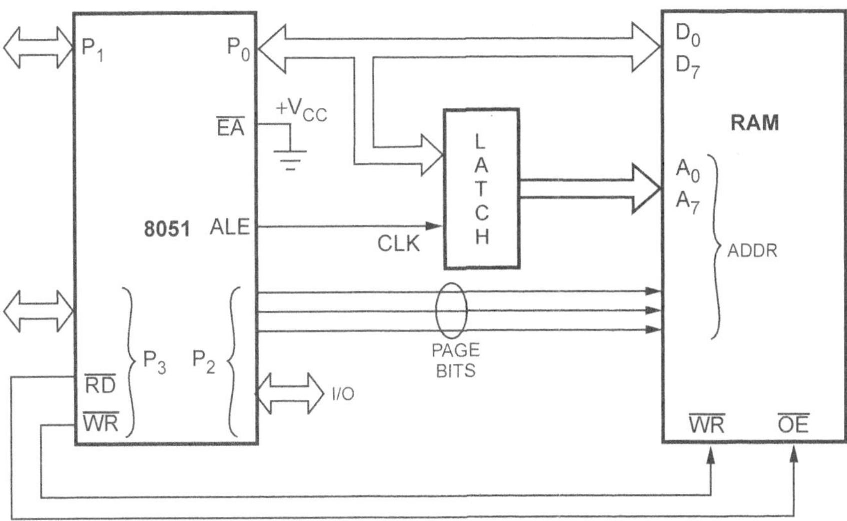

Fig. 17.12 Accessing external data memory

Fig. 17.13 (a) and (b) show the timing waveforms for external data memory read and write cycles, respectively.

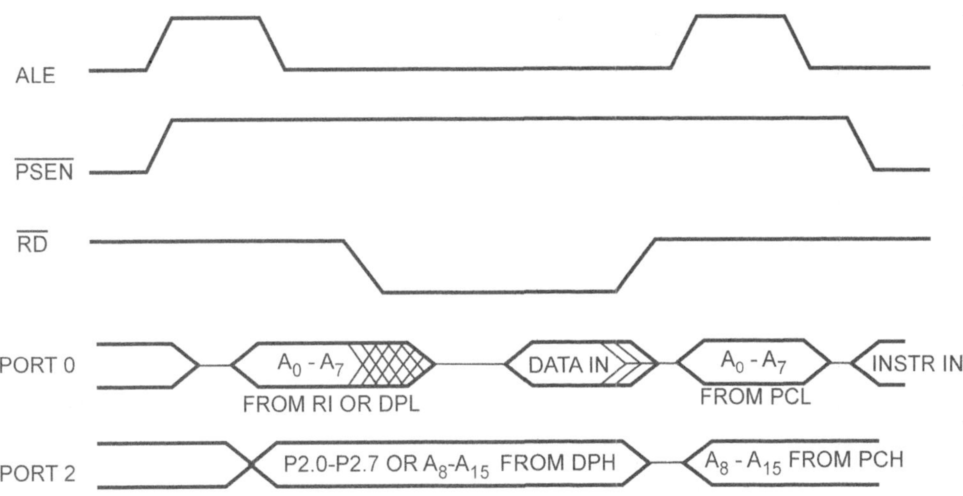

Fig. 17.13 (a) Timing waveforms for external data memory read cycle

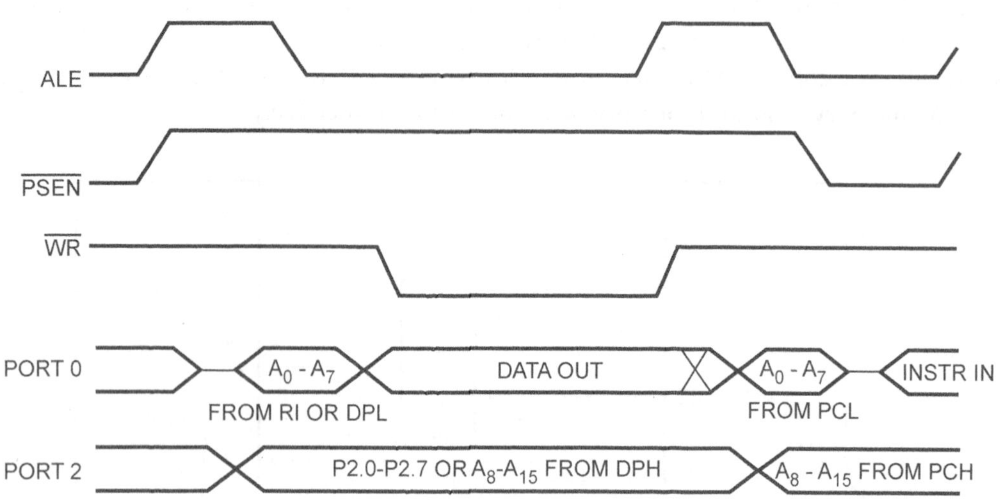

Fig. 17.13 (b) Timing waveforms for external data memory write cycle

Instructions to Access External Data Memory

The Table 17.6 explains the instruction to access external data memory.

Mnemonic	Operation
MOVX A, @Rp	Copy the contents of the external address in Rp to A.
MOVX A, @DPTR	Copy the contents of the external address in DPTR to A.
MOVX @ Rp, A	Copy data from A to the external address in Rp.
MOVX @DPTR, A	Copy data from A to the external address in DPTR.

Table 17.6

17.6.3 Important Points to Remember in Accessing External Memory

- All external data moves with external ROM or external RAM involve the A register.
- While accessing external memory, R_p can address 256 bytes and DPTR can address 64 kbytes.
- MOVX instruction is used to access external RAM or I/O addresses.

When PC is used to access external ROM, it is incremented by 1 (to point to the next instruction) before it is added to A to form the physical address of external ROM.

17.6.4 Interfacing Examples

We know that read/write memories consist of an array of registers, in which each register has unique address. The size of the memory is $N \times M$ as shown in Fig. 17.14(a). Where N is the number of registers and M is the word length in number of bits.

For Example : If memory is having 12 address lines and 8 data lines, then

Number of registers/memory locations = $2^N = 2^{12}$ = 4096.

Word length = Mbit = 8-bit .

For Example : If memory has 8192 memory locations, then it has 13 address lines.

The Table 17.7 summarizes the memory capacity and address lines required for memory interfacing.

Memory Capacity	Address Lines Required
1 K = 1024 memory locations	10
2 K = 2048 memory locations	11
4 K = 4096 memory locations	12
8 K = 8192 memory locations	13
16 K = 16384 memory locations	14
32 K = 32768 memory locations	15
64 K = 65536 memory locations	16

Table 17.7

As shown in the Fig. 17.14 (a) memory chip has 11 address lines A_{10}-A_0, one chip select ($\overline{CS}$) and two control lines. Read ($\overline{RD}$) to enable output buffer and write ($\overline{WR}$) to enable the input buffer. The internal decoder is used to decode the address lines. Fig. 17.14 (b) shows the logic diagram of a typical EPROM (Erasable Programmable Read Only Memory) with 4096 (4 K) registers. It has 12 address lines A_{11}-A_0, one chip select ($\overline{CS}$), one read control signal. Since EPROM is a read only memory, it does not require the ($\overline{WR}$) signal.

The memory interfacing requires to :

- Select the chip.
- Identify the register.
- Enable the appropriate buffer.

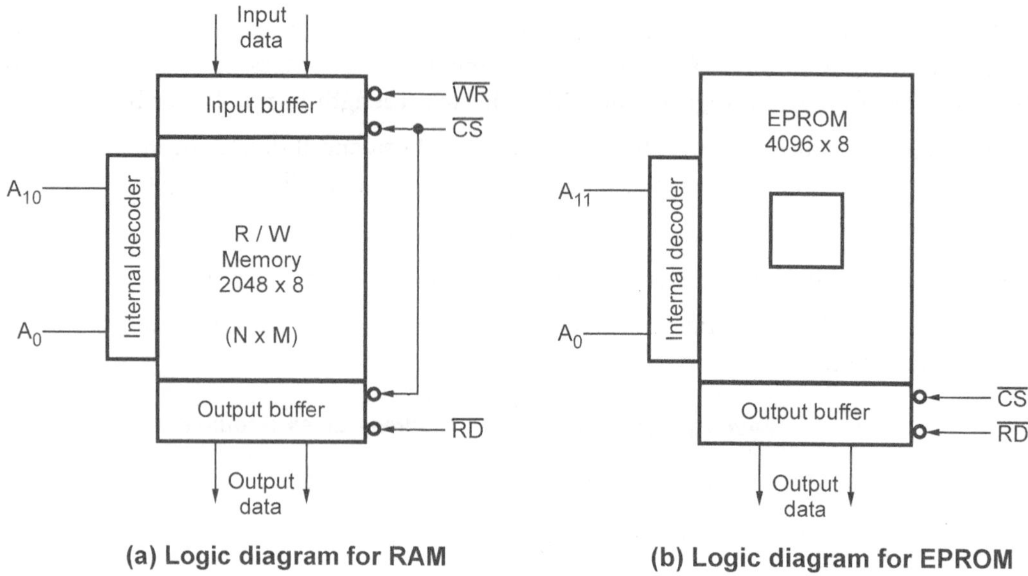

(a) Logic diagram for RAM **(b) Logic diagram for EPROM**

Fig. 17.14

Microprocessor/microcontroller system includes memory devices and I/O devices. It is important to note that microprocessor can communicate (read/write) with only one device at a time, since the data, address and control buses are common for all the devices. In order to communicate with memory or I/O devices, it is necessary to decode the address from the microprocessor/microcontroller. The following section describes common address decoding techniques.

Address Decoding Techniques :

- Absolute decoding/Full decoding
- Linear decoding/Partial decoding

Absolute decoding

In absolute decoding technique, all the higher address lines are decoded to select the memory chip, and the memory chip is selected only for the specified logic levels on these high-order address lines; no other logic levels can select the chip. Fig. 17.15 shows the memory interface with absolute decoding. This addressing technique is normally used in large memory systems.

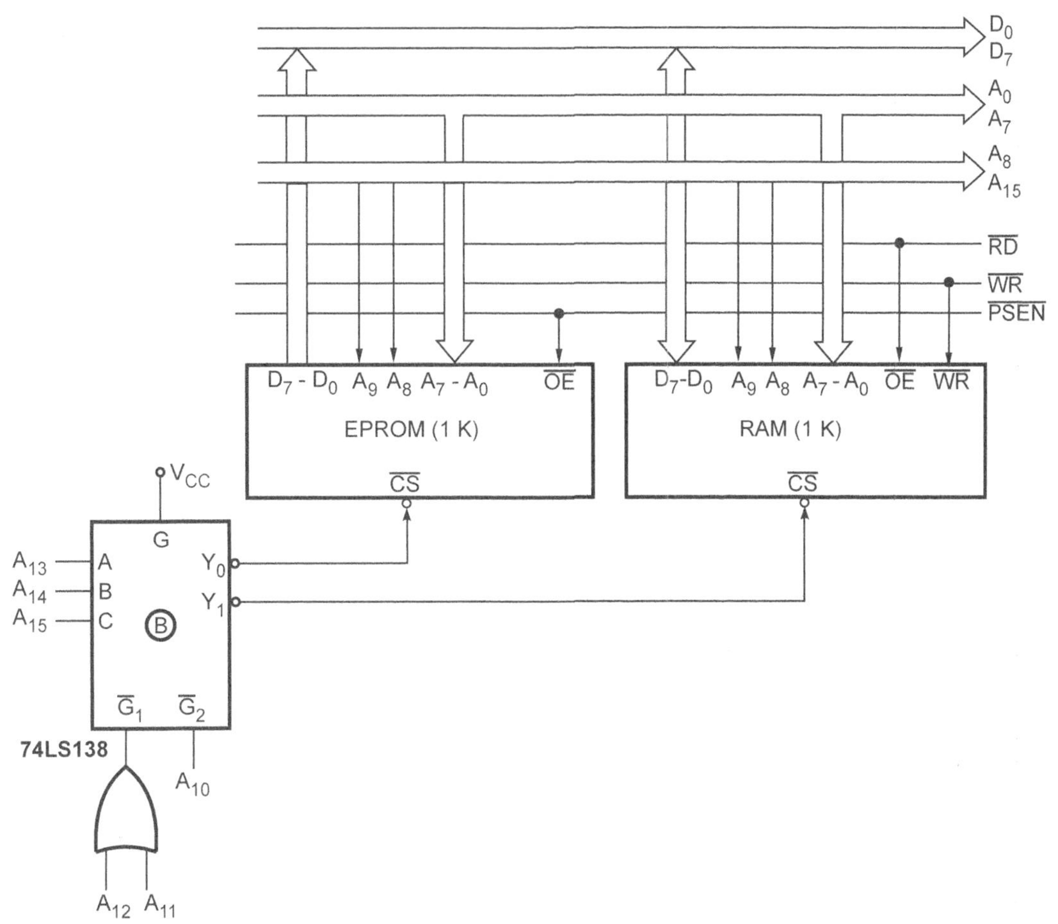

Fig. 17.15 Absolute decoding technique

Memory Map

Memory ICs	A_{15}	A_{14}	A_{13}	A_{12}	A_{11}	A_{10}	A_9	A_8	A_7	A_6	A_5	A_4	A_3	A_2	A_1	A_0	Address
Starting address of EPROM	0	0	0	0	0	0	0	0	0	0	0	0	0	0	0	0	0000H
End address of EPROM	0	0	0	0	0	0	1	1	1	1	1	1	1	1	1	1	03FFH
Starting address of RAM	0	0	1	0	0	0	0	0	0	0	0	0	0	0	0	0	2000H
End address of RAM	0	0	1	0	0	0	1	1	1	1	1	1	1	1	1	1	23FFH

Table 17.8

Linear decoding

In small systems, hardware for the decoding logic can be eliminated by using individual high-order address lines to select memory chips. This is referred to as linear decoding. Fig. 17.16 shows the addressing of RAM with linear decoding technique. This technique is also called **partial decoding**. It reduces the cost of decoding circuit, but it has a drawback of multiple addresses (shadow addresses).

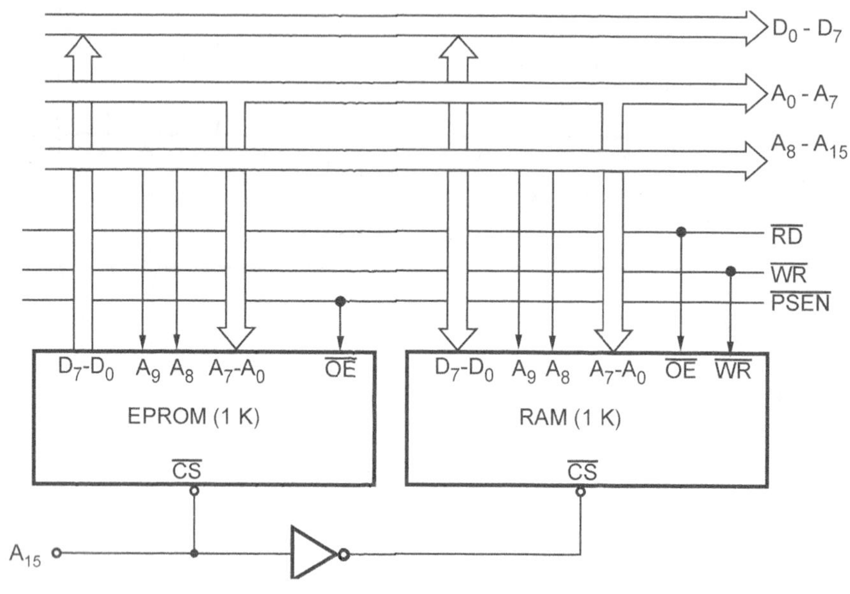

Fig. 17.16 Linear decoding

Fig. 17.16 shows the addressing of RAM with linear decoding technique. A_{15} address line, is directly connected to the chip select signal of EPROM and after inversion it is connected to the chip select signal of the RAM. Therefore, when the status of A_{15} line is 'zero', EPROM gets selected and when the status of A_{15} line is 'one' RAM gets selected. The status of the other address lines is not considered, since those address lines are not used for generation of chip select signals.

Memory Map :

Memory ICs	A_{15}	A_{14}	A_{13}	A_{12}	A_{11}	A_{10}	A_9	A_8	A_7	A_6	A_5	A_4	A_3	A_2	A_1	A_0	Address
Starting address of EPROM	0	X	X	X	X	X	0	0	0	0	0	0	0	0	0	0	0000H
End address of EPROM	0	X	X	X	X	X	1	1	1	1	1	1	1	1	1	1	03FFH
Starting address of RAM	1	X	X	X	X	X	0	0	0	0	0	0	0	0	0	0	8000H
End address of RAM	1	X	X	X	X	X	1	1	1	1	1	1	1	1	1	1	83FFH

Table 17.9

Example 17.1 : *An 8051 based system requires external memory of four 4 kbytes of SRAM each and two chips of EPROM of size 2 kbytes. The EPROM starts at address 2000H. SRAM address map follows EPROM map. Give the complete interface.*

Solution :

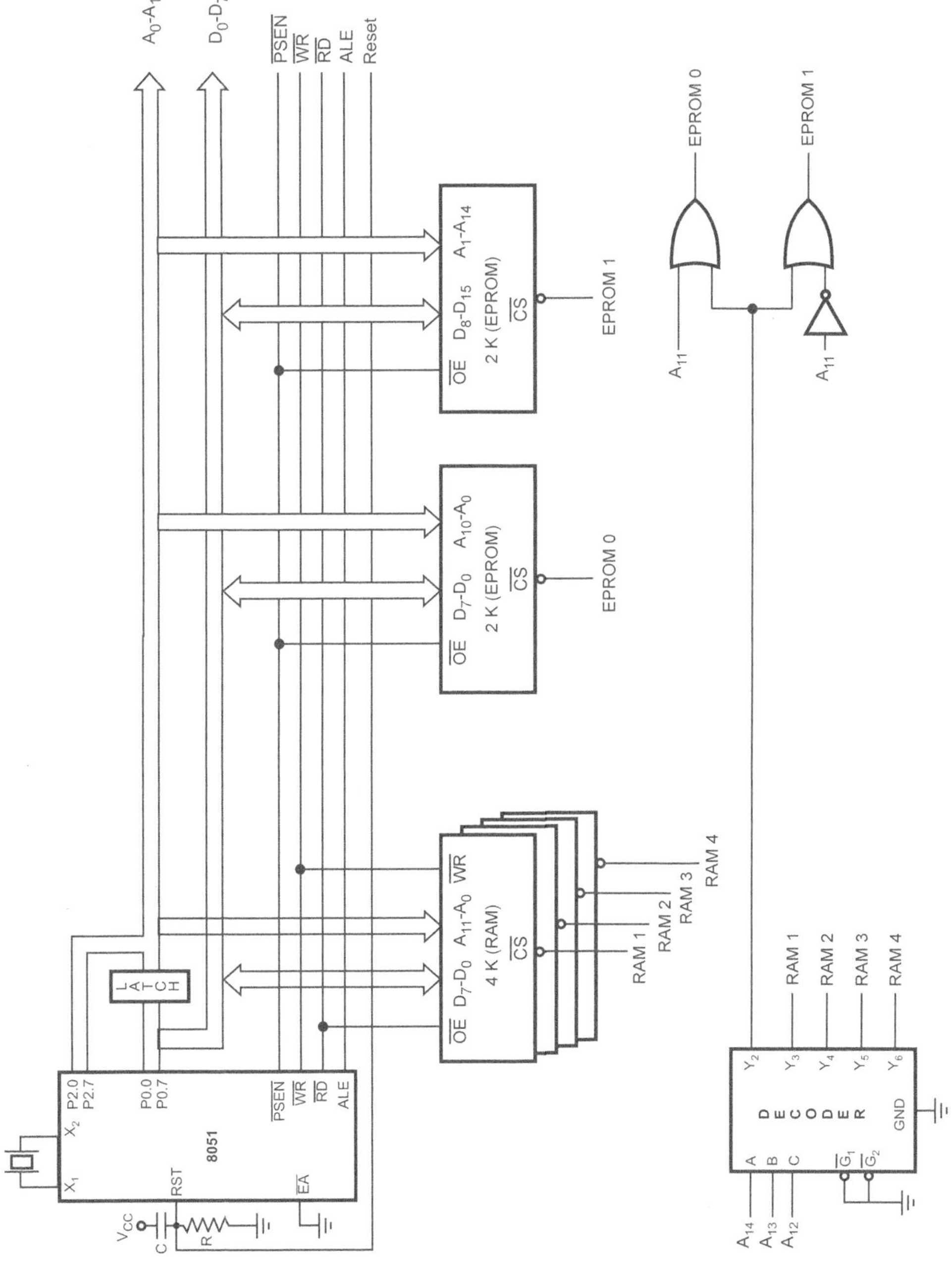

Fig. 17.17

A_{15}	A_{14}	A_{13}	A_{12}	A_{11}	A_{10}	A_9	A_8	A_7	A_6	A_5	A_4	A_3	A_2	A_1	A_0	Address	
0	0	1	0	0	0	0	0	0	0	0	0	0	0	0	0	2000H	EPROM0
0	0	1	0	0	1	1	1	1	1	1	1	1	1	1	1	27FFH	
0	0	1	0	1	0	0	0	0	0	0	0	0	0	0	0	2800H	EPROM1
0	0	1	0	1	1	1	1	1	1	1	1	1	1	1	1	2FFFH	
0	0	1	1	0	0	0	0	0	0	0	0	0	0	0	0	3000F	RAM0
0	0	1	1	1	1	1	1	1	1	1	1	1	1	1	1	3FFFH	
0	1	0	0	0	0	0	0	0	0	0	0	0	0	0	0	4000H	RAM1
0	1	0	0	1	1	1	1	1	1	1	1	1	1	1	1	4FFFH	
0	1	0	1	0	0	0	0	0	0	0	0	0	0	0	0	5000H	RAM2
0	1	0	1	1	1	1	1	1	1	1	1	1	1	1	1	5FFFH	
0	1	1	0	0	0	0	0	0	0	0	0	0	0	0	0	6000H	RAM3
0	1	1	0	1	1	1	1	1	1	1	1	1	1	1	1	6FFFH	

Example 17.2 : *Interface two 8255's to 8051 with stating address of 0F000H. Show the hardware design. Write the instruction sequence to initialize all ports of first 8255 as output ports in mode 0 and in the second 8255 port A as input in mode 1 and other ports as input in mode 0.*

Solution : See Fig. 17.18 on next page.

Address Map :

Ports	8255 (0) First	8255 (1) Second
Port A	0F000H	0F004H
Port B	0F001H	0F005H
Port C	0F002H	0F006H
CR	0F003H	0F007H

For 8255 (0) first :

```
MOV A, # 80H             ; Load control word
MOV DPTR, # 0F003H       ; Initialize DPTR with address of CR
MOVX@DPTR, A             ; Send the control word
```

For 8255 (1) second :

```
MOV A, # BBH             ; Load control word
MOV DPTR, # 0F007H       ; Initialize DPTR with address of CR
MOVX @ DPTR, A           ; Send the control word
```

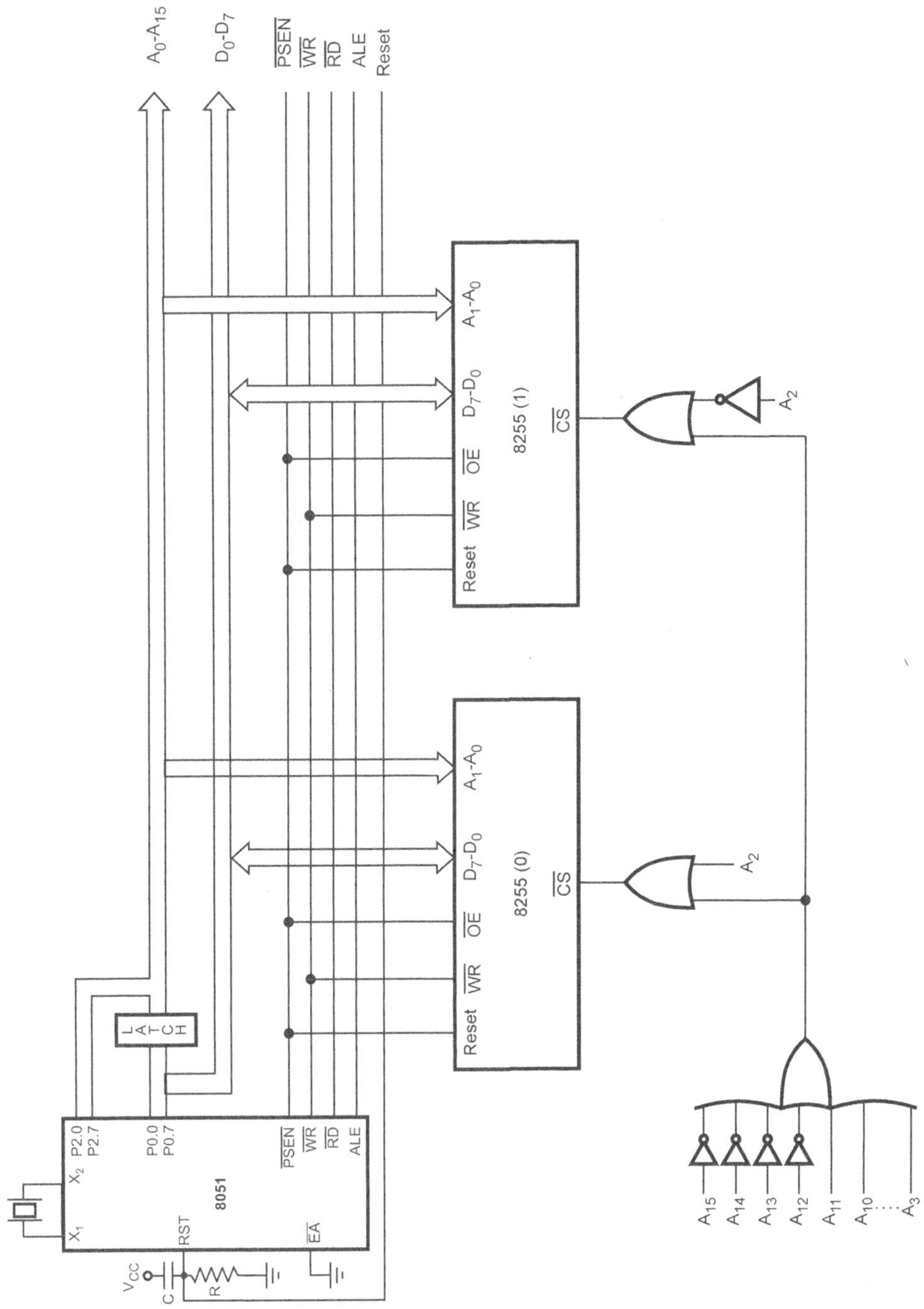
A0-A15
D0-D7
PSEN
WR
RD
ALE
Reset
A1-A0
D7-D0
OE
WR
Reset
8255 (1)
CS
A2
A1-A0
D7-D0
OE
WR
Reset
8255 (0)
CS
A2
LATCH
X2
X1
P2.0
P2.7
P0.0
P0.7
8051
RST
PSEN
WR
RD
ALE
EA
VCC
C
R
A15
A14
A13
A12
A11
A10
A3

Fig. 17.18

Example 17.3 : *Give the complete block schematic of an 8051 based system having following specifications.*

64 kB of program memory.

64 kB of data memory.

Make use of 16 K × 8-bit memory chips and 74 LS 138 decoders.

Indicate clearly, the addresses selected for the memory chips.

Solution : See Fig. 17.19 on next page.

Memory Map :

Memory	A_{15}	A_{14}	A_{13}	A_{12}	A_{11}	A_{10}	A_9	A_8	A_7	A_6	A_5	A_4	A_3	A_2	A_1	A_0	Address
EPROM1 Start	0	0	0	0	0	0	0	0	0	0	0	0	0	0	0	0	0000H
EPROM1 End	0	0	1	1	1	1	1	1	1	1	1	1	1	1	1	1	3FFFH
EPROM2 Start	0	1	0	0	0	0	0	0	0	0	0	0	0	0	0	0	4000H
EPROM2 End	0	1	1	1	1	1	1	1	1	1	1	1	1	1	1	1	7FFFH
EPROM3 Start	1	0	0	0	0	0	0	0	0	0	0	0	0	0	0	0	8000H
EPROM3 End	1	0	1	1	1	1	1	1	1	1	1	1	1	1	1	1	BFFFH
EPROM4 Start	1	1	0	0	0	0	0	0	0	0	0	0	0	0	0	0	C000H
EPROM4 End	1	1	1	1	1	1	1	1	1	1	1	1	1	1	1	1	FFFFH
RAM1 Start	0	0	0	0	0	0	0	0	0	0	0	0	0	0	0	0	0000H
RAM1 End	0	0	1	1	1	1	1	1	1	1	1	1	1	1	1	1	3FFFH
RAM2 Start	0	1	0	0	0	0	0	0	0	0	0	0	0	0	0	0	4000H
RAM2 End	0	1	1	1	1	1	1	1	1	1	1	1	1	1	1	1	7FFFH
RAM3 Start	1	0	0	0	0	0	0	0	0	0	0	0	0	0	0	0	8000H
RAM3 End	1	0	1	1	1	1	1	1	1	1	1	1	1	1	1	1	BFFFH
RAM4 Start	1	1	0	0	0	0	0	0	0	0	0	0	0	0	0	0	C000H
RAM4 End	1	1	1	1	1	1	1	1	1	1	1	1	1	1	1	1	FFFFH

Table 17.10

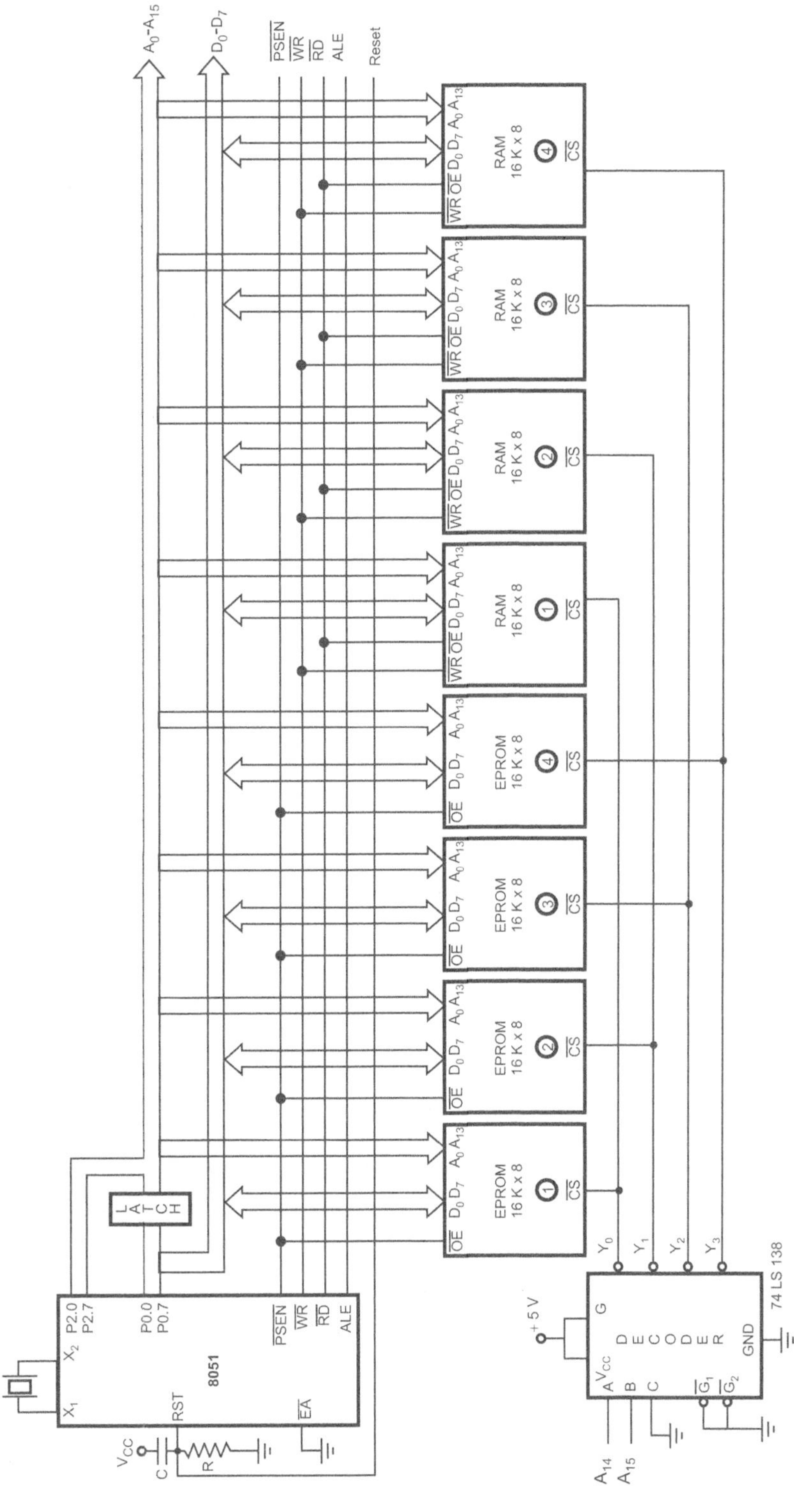
A_0-A_{15}
D_0-D_7
PSEN
WR
RD
ALE
Reset
RAM 16 K x 8 4
RAM 16 K x 8 3
RAM 16 K x 8 2
RAM 16 K x 8 1
EPROM 16 K x 8 4
EPROM 16 K x 8 3
EPROM 16 K x 8 2
EPROM 16 K x 8 1
WR OE D_0 D_7 A_0 A_{13} CS
OE D_0 D_7 A_0 A_{13} CS
LATCH
8051
X_1
X_2
P2.0
P2.7
P0.0
P0.7
PSEN
WR
RD
ALE
RST
EA
V_{CC}
C
R
+5 V
74 LS 138
Y_0 Y_1 Y_2 Y_3
G
DECODER
GND
V_{CC}
A B C
G_1 G_2
A_{14}
A_{15}

Fig 17.19

17.7 Stack and Stack Pointer

The stack refers to an area of internal RAM that is used to store and retrieve data quickly. The stack pointer register is used by the 8051 to hold an internal RAM address that is called **top of stack.** The stack pointer register is 8-bit wide. It is increased **before** data is stored during PUSH and CALL instructions and decremented **after** data is restored during POP and RET instructions.

The stack array can reside anywhere in on-chip RAM. The stack pointer is initialized to 07H after a reset. This causes the stack to begin at location 08H. The operation of stack and stack pointer is illustrated in Fig. 17.20.

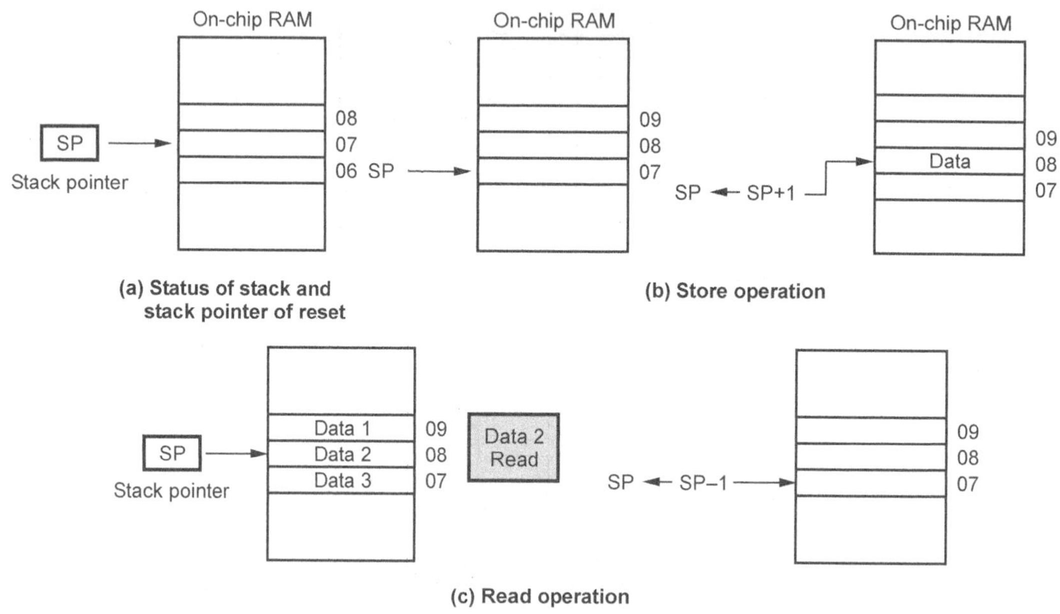

Fig. 17.20

The stack may overwrite data in the register banks, bit-addressable RAM and scratch-pad RAM. Thus to avoid conflict with the register, bit-addressable RAM and scratch-pad RAM data, the stack is initialized at a higher location in the internal RAM.

Review Questions

Section 17.1

Q.1 *Distinguish between microprocessor and microcontroller.*

Section 17.2

Q.1 *List the features of 8051 microcontroller ?*

Q.2 *Compare the 8051, 8031 and 8751 microcontroller.*

Q.3 *List out the hardware resources available in 8051.* **Dec.-04**

Q.4 *What are the main features of 8051 microcontroller ?* **May-12, Marks 2**

Section 17.3

Q.1 *Give the details of PSW of 8051.* **May-10**

Q.2 *Quantify the number of register banks in 8051 and say how the CPU knows which bank is currently in use.* **Dec.-10**

Q.3 *Explain the functional block diagram of 8051 in detail.* **Dec.-04,09, May-09,10 Marks 10**

Q.4 *Describe the architecture of 8051 with neat diagram.* **May-06,08,11,12, Marks 16**

Q.5 *List the on-chip peripherals of 8051 microcontroller.* **Dec.-11, Marks 2**

Q.6 *Mention the size of DPTR and stack pointer in 8051 microcontroller.* **May-11, Marks 2**

Q.7 *What is program status word of 8051 ?* **May-12, Marks 2**

Section 17.4

Q.1 *Draw the pin diagram of 8051 microcontroller and explain its port structure.* **Dec.-11, Marks 8**

Q.2 *List the alternative functions assigned to Port 3 pins of 8051 microcontroller.* **May-11, Marks 2**

Section 17.5

Q.1 *What do you understand by bit addressable RAM in 8051 microcontroller ?* **Dec.-10**

Q.2 *Discuss the internal memory organization of the 8051 microcontroller.* **Dec.-10, Marks 16**

Q.3 *Discuss about the organization of internal RAM and special function registers of 8051 microcontroller in detail.* **May-11, Marks 8**

Q.4 *What is the internal memory capacity of microcontroller 8051 ?* **May-11, Marks 8**

Q.5 *Explain the program memory and data memory structure of 8051 microcontroller.* **Dec.-11, Marks 8**

Section 17.6

Q.1 *Explain program memory interfacing in 8051 microcontroller.* **May-12, Marks 8**

Q.2 *Design an 8051 based system with 16 kbytes of program ROM and 16 kbytes of data ROM.* **Dec.-10, Marks 16**

Q.3 *Explain in detail the different methods of memory address decoding in 8051.* **Dec.-10, Marks 8**

Section 17.7

Q.1 *Explain the operation of stack in 8051.*

Q.2 *Define SP.*

Two Marks Questions with Answers

Q.1 ***Name any four additional hardware features available in microcontrollers when compared to microprocessors.*** **May-04**

Ans. : The microcontroller has built-in ROM, RAM, parallel I/O, serial I/O, timer/counters and a clock circuit.

Q.2 ***Write the memory capacity of microcontroller 8051.*** **Dec.-08**

Ans. : The memory capacity of microcontroller 8051 is 64 kbytes.

Q.3 ***What are the flags available in 8051.*** **May-09**

Ans. : The flags available in 8051 are : CY (Carry flag), AC (Auxiliary carry flag), OV (over flow flag) and P (Parity flag).

Q.4 ***What is meant by SFR in 8051 ? Give an example.*** **May-09**

Ans. : The group of registers, implemented to perform special function and are located immediately above the 128 bytes of RAM are called special function registers for example, all port registers, TCOM, SCON, IE, IP, and so on.

Q.5 ***Give the memory size of 8051 Microcontroller.*** **May-10**

Ans. : The 8051 can access upto 64 kbyte program memory and 64 kbytes of data memory.

Q.6 ***Give the details of PSW of 8051*** **May-10**

Ans. : Refer section 17.3.5.

Q.7 ***Distinguish between microprocessor and microcontroller.***

Ans. : Refer section 17.1.

Q.8 *What are the applications of 8051 microcontroller.* **May-12**

Ans. : Microcontrollers are more preferred in embedded products. Some applications of microcontroller are :

- Calculators
- Accounting systems
- Game machines
- Data acquisition systems
- Mobile systems
- Complex industrial controllers
- Traffic light control systems
- Military applications
- Communication systems

Q.9 *Explain the significance of SFRs in 8051 microcontroller.*

Ans. : The group of registers, implemented to perform special function and are located immediately above the 128 bytes of RAM are called special function registers. They are responsible for operation of ALU, timer, serial port, parallel ports and interrupt control.

Q.10 *What is mean by microcontroller ?*

Ans. : A device which contains the microprocessor with integrated peripherals like memory, serial ports, parallel ports, timer/counter, interrupt controller, data acquisition interfaces like ADC, DAC is called microcontroller.

Q.11 *List the features of 8051 microcontroller ?*

Ans. : Refer section 17.2.

Q.12 *State the function of RS1 and RS0 bits in the flag register of Intel 8051 microcontroller ?*

Ans. : RS1 and RS0 are bank selection bits. They are used to select working register bank of 8051 as given below :

- 0 0 Bank 0
- 0 1 Bank 1
- 1 0 Bank 2
- 1 1 Bank 3

Q.13 *Give the alternate functions for the port pins of port3 ?*

Ans. : Refer Table 17.4.

Q.14 ***Explain the function of the $\overline{PSEN}$ pin of 8051.***

Ans. : $\overline{PSEN}$: $\overline{PSEN}$ stands for program store enable. In 8051 based system in which an external ROM holds the program code, this pin is connected to the $\overline{OE}$ pin of the ROM.

Q.15 ***Explain the function of the $\overline{EA}$ pin of 8051.***

Ans. : $\overline{EA}$: It stands for external access. When the EA pin is connected to Vcc, program fetched to addresses 0000H through 0FFFH are directed to the internal ROM and program fetches to addresses 1000H through FFFFH are directed to external ROM/EPROM. When the $\overline{EA}$ pin is grounded, all addresses fetched by program are directed to the external ROM/EPROM.

Q.16 ***Explain the 16-bit registers DPTR of 8051 or what is a function of DPTR ?***

Ans. : DPTR : It stands for data pointer. DPTR consists of a high byte (DPH) and a low byte (DPL). Its function is to hold a 16-bit address. It may be manipulated as a 16-bit data register or as two independent 8-bit registers. It serves as a base register in indirect jumps, lookup table instructions and external data transfer.

Q.17 ***Explain the function of the SP register of 8051.***

Ans. : SP : It stands for stack pointer. SP is a 8- bit wide register. It is incremented before data is stored during PUSH and CALL instructions. The stack array can reside anywhere in on-chip RAM. The stack pointer is initialised to 07H after a reset. This causes the stack to begin at location 08H.

Q.18 ***Name the special function registers available in 8051.***

Ans. : The special function registers available in 8051 are :

- Accumulator B Register
- Program Status Word.
- Stack Pointer.
- Data Pointer.
- Port 0
- Port 1
- Port 2
- Port 3
- Interrupt priority control register.
- Interrupt enable control register.

Q.19 ***How is stack implemented in 8051 ?***

Ans. : The 8051 LIFO : Stack can reside anywhere in the internal RAM. It has 8 bit stack pointer to indicate the top of the stack using PUSH and POP instructions. During PUSH the SP is incremented by one and POP the SP is decremented by one.

Q.20 ***What is the maximum frequency of the clock signal that can be counted by 8051 counter ?***

Ans. : The maximum frequency of the clock signal that can be counted by 8051 counter is $1/12 \times$ crystal frequency.

Q.21 ***What are the features of ROM and RAM in 8051 microcontroller ?***

Ans. : The 8051 has 128-byte internal RAM. It is accessed using RAM address register. The internal RAM of 8051 is organized into three distinct areas :

- Register Bank
- Bit addressable
- General purpose.

The 8051 has 4 kbyte of internal ROM with address space from 0000H to 0FFFH. It is programmed by manufacturer when the chip is built. This part cannot be erased or altered after fabrication. This is used to store final version of the program. It is accessed using program address register.

Q.22 ***What is the function of program counter in 8051 ?***

Ans. : The 8051 has a 16-bit program counter. It is used to hold the address of memory location from which the next instruction is to be fetched.

Q.23 ***List the advantages of microcontroller over microprocessor.***

Ans. : The advantages of microcontroller over microprocessor are :

- Because of built-in peripheral support they provide single chip microcontroller system.
- Less hardware required.
- Less hardware increases reliability.
- Supports internal memory which reduces access time.

Q.24 ***Which ports of 8051 are bit addressable ?***

Ans. : All ports of 8051 - port 0, port 1, port 2 and port 3 are bit addressable.

Q.25 ***A given 8051 chip has a speed of 16 MHz. What is the range of frequency that can be applied to the XTAL 1 and XTAL 2 pins ?***

Ans. : The range of frequencies that can be applied to the XTAL 1 and XTAL 2 pins is 1 MHz to 16 MHz.

Q.26 ***Compare the 8051, 8031 and 8751 microcontroller.***

Ans. : Refer Table 17.2.

Q.27 ***What happens in power down mode of 8051 microcontroller ?***

Ans. : In the Power Down Mode (PD = 0), the CPU puts the whole chip to sleep by turning off the oscillator. In case if it is running from an external oscillator, it also gates off the path to the internal phase generators, so no internal clock is generated even if the external oscillator is still running. The on-chip RAM, however, saves its data, as long as V_{CC} is maintained. In this mode the only I_{CC} that flows is leakage, which is normally in the micro-amp range.

Q.28 ***What are on-chip resources ? List those available in the 8051 microcontroller.*** Dec.-10

Ans. : The advance microcontrollers are supported with on-chip peripherals such as program memory, data memory, parallel ports, PWM output, ADC, RTC (Real time clock), Timers/counters, Serial ports, I^2C interface and so on. These are known as on-chip resources. The resources available in 8051 are :

- 4096 byte on-chip program memory
- 128 bytes on chip data memory
- 32-bit bi-directional I/O lines
- Multi-mode serial port
- Two multi-mode 16-bit timers/counters

Q.29 ***Quantify the number of register banks in 8051 and say how the CPU knows which bank is currently in use.*** Dec.-10

Ans. : Refer section 17.3.5.

Q.30 ***Justify your choice between UV-EPROM and flash EPROM for an external ROM in an 8051 microcontroller application.*** Dec.-10

Ans. : Flash EPROMS can be erased electrically with selective erase facility. However, UV-EPROMS cannot be erased electrically, they need ultraviolet light source. EPROMS need around 20 minutes to erase and entire EPROM is erased at a time. Thus flash EPROM is more preferable during development stage. However, once the product is ready we can use EPROM as an external memory.

Q.31 ***What do you understand by bit addressable RAM in 8051 microcontroller ?*** Dec.-10

Ans. : Refer section 17.5.1.2.

❑❑❑

18 8051 Instruction Set and Programming

Contents

18.1 8051 Addressing Modes

The way, using which the data sources or destination addresses are specified in the instruction mnemonic for moving the data, is called '**addressing mode'.** This section explains addressing modes used in 8051 with examples.

18.1.1 Register Addressing

The 8051 can access eight "working registers" (R0-R7). Three bit code within the instruction selects one of the eight registers from the selected register bank. The programmer can select a register bank by modifying bits 4 and 3 in the PSW.

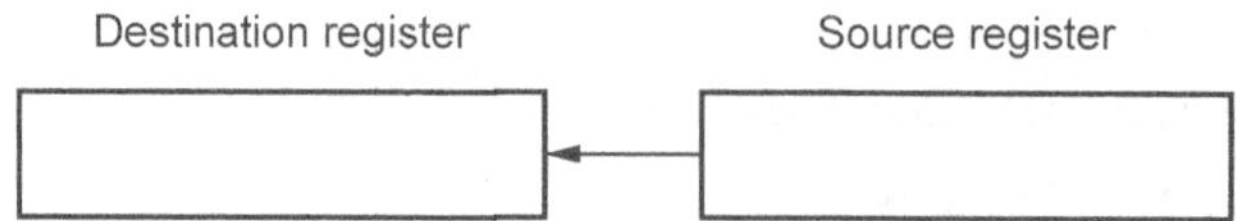

Example : Add the contents of register R3 and R4 from bank 2

Step 1 : Select register bank.

```
MOV PSW, #00001000B ; select register Bank 2
```

Step 2 : Add the contents of R3 and R4

```
MOV  A, R3
ADD  A, R4
```

18.1.2 Direct Byte Addressing

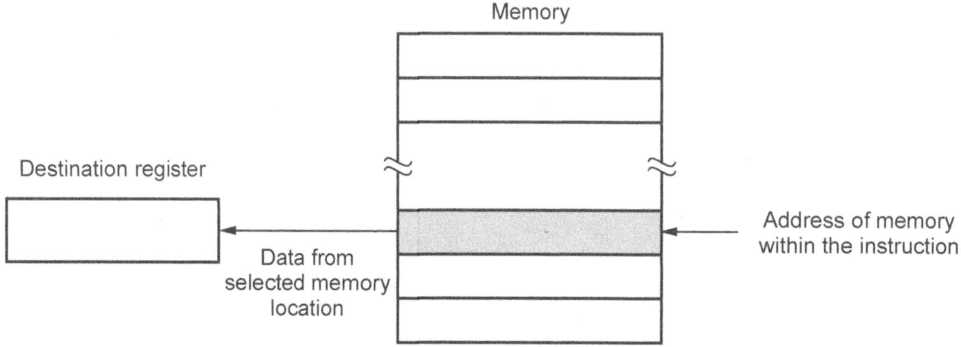

Direct addressing can access any on-chip variable or hardware register. i.e. on-chip RAM and special function register. The most significant bit of the address decides whether it is a location within on-chip RAM (MSB = 0) or in special function register (MSB = 1).

Example : Add the contents of locations 50H and 51H

```
MOV  A, 50H     ; load byte from address 50H into A
ADD  A, 51H     ; Add the contents of A and the contents at
                ; memory location 51H.
```

18.1.3 Register Indirect Addressing

In this addressing mode R0 and R1 of each register bank can be used as an index or pointer register. R0 and R1 point to the contents in the RAM. The instruction with indirect addressing uses the '@' sign.

Indirect addressing accesses data in dynamic manner rather than static manner. Looping is not possible in direct addressing mode. In indirect addressing we can increment the index or pointer register to access successive locations.

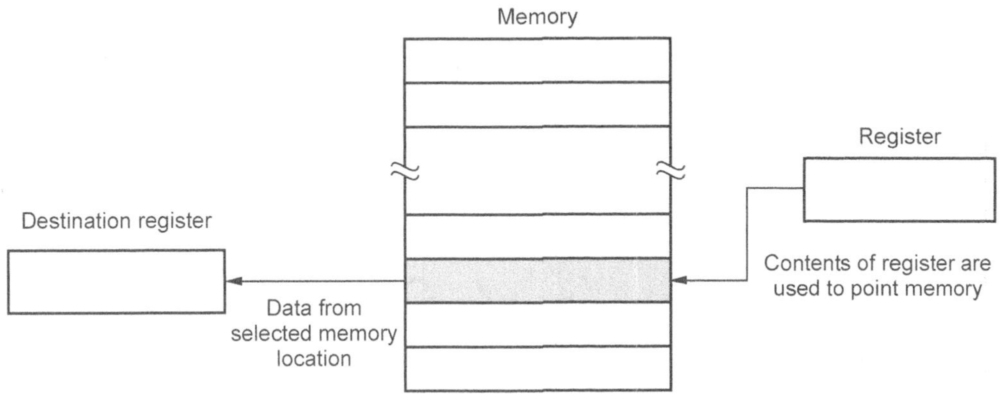

R0 and R1 are the only registers that can be used for pointers in register indirect addressing mode.

Example : ADD the contents of memory location addressed by register 1 to the contents of RAM location pointed by register 0.

```
MOV A, @R0   ; load the contents pointed by R0 in A
ADD A, @R1   ; Add the contents of A and the contents pointed by R1
```

18.1.4 Immediate Addressing

In this addressing mode source operand is a constant rather than a variable. So the constant can be incorporated in the instruction. Sign "#" indicates it is a immediate addressing mode.

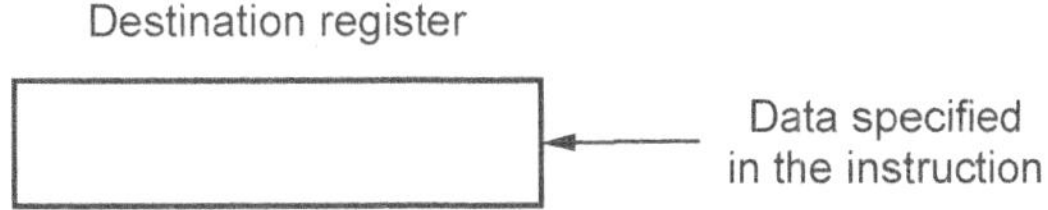

Example : Add the constant 52 decimal in accumulator.

```
MOV A, #52
```

18.1.5 Register Specific

Inherent in the instruction, these refer to a specific register such as accumulator or DPTR.

Example :

SWAP A ; Swap nibbles within the Accumulator

18.1.6 Index

Only program memory can be accessed in the index addressing. Either the DPTR or PC can be used as an index register.

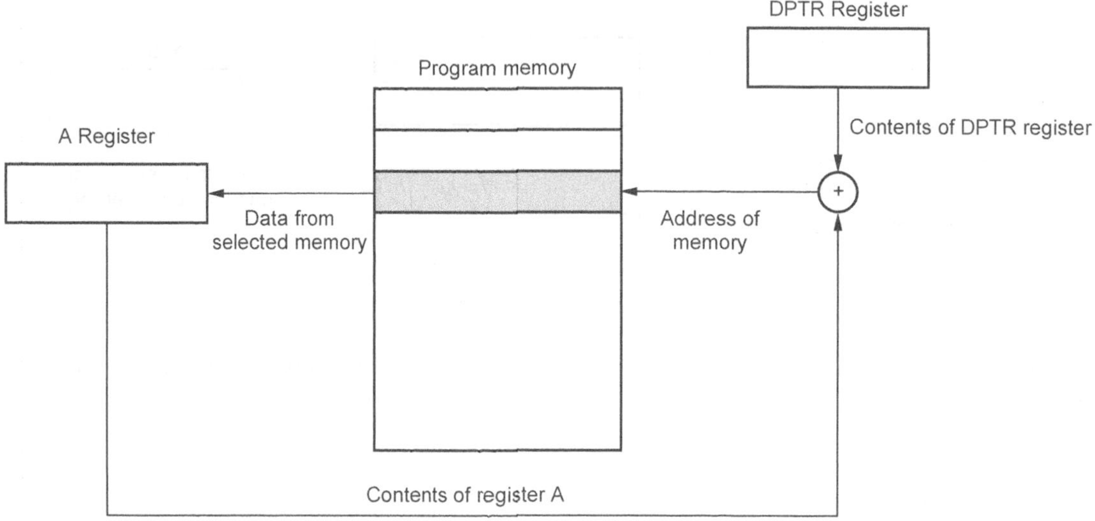

Example : Read data from the program memory.

```
MOVC A, @A+DPTR; This instruction adds the unsigned 8-bit
               ; and accumulator contents into sixteen bit
               ; Data pointer, and uses the sum as an address
               ; from which byte to be moved into accumulator
```

18.1.7 Stack Addressing Mode

It is subtype of direct addressing mode in which stack instructions (PUSH and POP) are used. Instruction such as 'PUSH A' is invalid. Here, we have to specify the address of register A. Thus, PUSH 0E0H is a valid instruction; it pushes/stores the contents of accumulator on the stack.

Examples :

```
PUSH 04   ;  Push R4 onto stack
PUSH 06   ;  Push R6 onto stack
```

```
POP 02      ; Pop top of stack into R2
POP 0F0H    ; Pop top of stack into register B
```

18.2 Classification of Instruction Set of 8051

An instruction is a single operation of a processor defined by an instruction set architecture. According to type of operations, the instruction set of 8051 is classified as,

- Data Transfer Instructions
- Byte Level Logical Instructions
- Bit Level Logical Instructions
- Arithmetic Instructions
- Jump and CALL Instructions

18.3 Data Transfer Instructions

An immediate, direct, register and indirect addressing modes are used in different MOVE instructions. Table 18.1 lists all types of data moving (data transfer) instructions.

Mnemonic	Operation
MOV <dest-byte>, <src-byte>	Copy the byte variable indicated by 'src-byte' into the 'dest-byte' location
MOV A, Rn	Copy the contents of register Rn of selected register bank to A.
MOV A, direct	Copy the contents of address specified with instruction to A.
MOV A, @ Ri	Copy the contents of the address in Ri to A.
MOV A, # data	Load data given in the instruction to A.
MOV Rn, A	Copy the contents of A to register Rn of selected register bank.
MOV Rn, direct	Copy the contents of address to register Rn of selected register bank.
MOV Rn, # data	Load data given in the instruction to register Rn of selected register bank.
MOV direct, A	Copy the contents A to the address specified within instruction.
MOV direct, Rn	Copy the contents of register Rn of selected bank register to the address specified within instruction.
MOV direct, direct	Copy the contents of the address specified within instruction to the address specified within instruction.

MOV direct, @Ri	Copy the contents of the address given by register Ri of selected register bank to the address specified within instruction.
MOV direct, #data	Load data given within instruction to the address specified within instruction.
MOV @Ri, A	Copy the contents of A to the address given by register Ri of selected register bank.
MOV @Ri, direct	Copy the contents of address specified within instruction to the address specified by register Ri of selected register bank.
MOV @Ri, #data	Load the data specified within instruction to the address specified by register Ri of selected register bank.
MOV DPTR, #data 16	Load data pointer with a 16-bit constant.

Table 18.1 MOV instructions

The MOV instructions can be explained completely with example as given below.

MOV <dest-byte>, <src-byte> **Bytes : 1/2/3 Cycles :1/2**

Function : Move byte variable

Description : The byte variable indicated by the second operand is copied into the location specified by the first operand. The source byte is not affected. No other register or flag is affected.

This is by far the most flexible operation. Fifteen combinations of source and destination addressing modes are allowed.

MOV A, Rn

Operation : (A) ← (Rn)

Example : **MOV A, R0 ;** This instruction copies the contents of the register R0 of selected register bank to the accumulator.

MOV A, direct

Example : **MOV A, 30H ;** This instruction copies the contents of memory location whose address is 30H to the accumulator.

Operation : (A) ← (direct)

Example : **MOV A, 30H ;** This instruction copies the contents of memory location whose address is 30H to the accumulator.

MOV A, @Ri

Operation : (A) ← ((Ri))

Example : **MOV A, @R1 ;** This instruction copies the contents of memory location whose address is specified in the register R1 from selected register bank.

MOV A, #data

Operation : (A) ← # data

Example : **MOV A, # 30H ;** This instruction copies data given within instruction (30H) into the accumulator.

MOV Rn, A

Operation : (Rn) ← (A)

Example : **MOV R2, A ;** This instruction copies the contents of accumulator in R2 register of selected register bank.

MOV Rn, direct

Operation : (Rn) ← (direct)

Example : **MOV R1, 40H ;** This instruction copies the contents at memory address 40H into the R1 register of the selected register bank.

MOV Rn, #data

Operation : (Rn) ← #data

Example : **MOV R2, #20H ;** This instruction loads 20H in the registers R2 of selected register bank.

MOV direct, A

Operation : (direct) ← (A)

Example : **MOV 20H, A ;** This instruction copies the contents of accumulator to the direct memory address specified in the instruction (20H)

MOV direct, Rn

Operation : (direct) ← (Rn)

Example : **MOV 30H, R2 ;** This instruction copies the contents of register R2 of selected register bank to the direct memory address specified in the instruction (30H).

MOV direct, direct

Operation : (direct) ← (direct)

Example : **MOV 20H, 40H ;** This instruction copies the contents of memory location whose address is 40H to the memory location whose address is 20H.

MOV direct, @Ri

Operation : (direct) ← ((Ri))

Example : **MOV 20H, @R3 ;** This instruction copies the contents of memory location whose address is given by register R3 of selected register bank into the memory location whose address is 20H.

MOV direct, #data

Operation : (direct) ← #data

Example : **MOV 30H, #12H ;** This instruction copies data given within instruction (12H) into the memory location whose address is 30H.

MOV @Ri, A

Operation : ((Ri)) ← (A)

Example : **MOV @R1, A ;** This instruction copies the contents of accumulator to the memory location whose address is given by register R1 of selected register bank.

MOV @Ri, direct

Operation : (Ri) ← (direct)

Example : **MOV @ R2, 30H ;** This instruction copies the contents of memory location whose address is given within the instruction (30H) into the memory location whose address is specified by register R2 of selected register bank.

MOV @Ri, #data

Operation : ((Ri)) ← #data

Example : **MOV @R2, #30H ;** This instruction loads 30H into the memory location whose address is specified by register R2 of selected register bank.

MOV A, ACC is not a valid instruction.

MOV DPTR, #data16 **Bytes : 3** **Cycles : 2**

Function : Load data pointer with a 16-bit constant

Description : The data pointer is loaded with the 16-bit constant indicated. The 16-bit constant is loaded into the second and third bytes of the instruction. The second byte (DPH) is the high-order byte, while the third byte (DPL) holds the low-order byte. No flags are affected.

This is the only instruction which moves 16 bits of data at once.

Example : The instruction,

MOV DPTR, #1234H

will load the value 1234H into the Data Pointer: DPH will hold 12H and DPL will hold 34H.

Operation : MOV

(DPTR) ← #data 15-0

DPH ← #data15-8 DPL ← #data7 - 0

18.3.1 Instructions to Access External Data Memory

The Table 18.2 explains the instruction to access external data memory.

Mnemonic	Operation
MOVX A, @Ri	Copy the contents of the external address in Ri to A.
MOVX A, @DPTR	Copy the contents of the external address in DPTR to A.
MOVX @ Ri, A	Copy data from A to the external address in Ri.
MOVX @DPTR, A	Copy data from A to the external address in DPTR.

Table 18.2

Some examples of the instructions listed in Table 18.2 are given below.

Example 1 : MOVX A, @ R0

This instruction copies data from the 8-bit address in R0 to A.

Example 2 : MOVX A, @ DPTR

This instruction copies data from the 16-bit address in DPTR to A.

Example 3 : MOVX @ R1, A

This instruction copies data from A to the 8-bit address in R1.

Example 4 : MOVX @ DPTR, A

This instruction copies data from A to the 16-bit address in DPTR.

The MOVX instructions can be explained completely with example as given below.

MOVX <dest-byte>,<src-byte> Function : Move External Bytes : 1 Cycles : 2

Description : The MOVX instructions transfer data between the Accumulator and a byte of external data memory, hence the "X" appended to MOV.

No flags are affected.

MOVX A, @Ri This instruction copies the contents of external memory whose address is given by register into the accumulator.

Operation : (A) ← ((Ri))

MOVX A, @DPTR : This instruction copies the contents of external memory whose address is given by DPTR register into the accumulator.

Operation : (A) ← ((DPTR))

MOVX @Ri, A : This instruction copies the contents of accumulator into the external memory whose address is given by the register.

Operation : ((Ri)) ← (A)

MOVX @DPTR, A : This instruction copies the contents of accumulator into the external memory whose address is given by the DPTR register.

Operation : ((DPTR)) ← (A)

Important Points to Remember in Accessing External Data Memory

- All external data moves with external RAM involve the A register.
- While accessing external RAM, Rp can address 256 bytes and DPTR can address 64 kbytes.
- MOVX instruction is used to access external RAM or I/O addresses.

18.3.2 Instructions to Access External ROM / Program Memory

The Table 18.3 explains the instructions to access external ROM/program memory.

Mnemonic	Operation
MOVC A, @A + DPTR	Copy the contents of the external ROM address formed by adding A and the DPTR, to A.
MOVC A, @A + PC	Copy the contents of the external ROM address formed by adding A and the PC, to A.

Table 18.3

Example 1 : Let the contents of DPTR are 1200 and the contents of A are 61H. MOVC A, @A + DPTR

This instruction copies the code byte found at the external ROM address formed by adding A and the DPTR, i.e. at an address (1200H + 61H) 1261H to A.

Example 2 : Let the contents of PC are 4000H and contents of A are 50H.

MOVC A, @A + PC

This instruction copies the code byte found at the external ROM address formed by adding A and the PC, i.e. at an address (4000H + 50H) 4050H to A.

The MOVC instructions can be explained completely with example as given below.

MOVC A,@A+<base-reg> Function : Move Code byte Bytes : 1 Cycles : 2

Description : The MOVC instructions load the Accumulator with a code byte, or constant from program memory. The address of the byte fetched is the sum of the original unsigned eight-bit Accumulator contents and the contents of a sixteen-bit base register, which may be either the Data Pointer or the PC. In the latter case, the PC is incremented to the address of the following instruction before being added with the Accumulator; otherwise the base register is not altered. No flags are affected.

MOVC A,@A + DPTR : This instruction loads the accumulator from the contents of program memory whose address is given by the sum of the contents of accumulator and contents of DPTR register.

Operation : (A) $\leftarrow$ ((A) + (DPTR))

MOVC A,@A + PC This instruction loads the accumulator from the contents of program memory whose address is given by the sum of the contents of accumulator and the contents of program counter. The current contents of program counter are incremented by 1 before summation.

Operation : (PC) ← (PC) + 1

(A) ← ((A) + (PC))

Important Points to Remember in Accessing External Read Only Memory

- When PC is used to access external ROM, it is incremented by 1 (to point to the next instruction) before it is added to A to form the physical address of external ROM.
- All external data moves with external ROM involve the A register.
- MOVC is used with internal or external ROM and can address 4 K of internal code or 64 K of external code.
- The DPTR and the PC are not changed.

18.3.3 Data Transfer with Stack (PUSH and POP) Instructions

PUSH direct	Function : Push onto stack	Bytes : 2	Cycles : 2

Description : The Stack Pointer is incremented by one. The contents of the indicated variable is then copied into the internal RAM location addressed by the Stack Pointer. Otherwise no flags are affected.

Example : PUSH B

This instruction increments the stack pointer by one and stores the contents of register B to the internal RAM location addressed by the stack pointer (SP).

Operation : (SP) ← (SP) + 1

((SP)) ← (direct)

POP direct	Function : Pop from stack	Bytes : 2	Cycles : 2

Description : The contents of the internal RAM location addressed by the Stack Pointer is read, and the Stack Pointer is decremented by one. The value read is then transferred to the directly addressed byte indicated. No flags are affected.

Example : POP ACC

This instruction copies the contents of the internal RAM location addressed by the stack pointer to the accumulator. Then the stack pointer is decremented by one.

Operation : (direct) ← ((SP))

(SP) ← (SP) – 1

Important Points to Remember during PUSH and POP

- When the SP contents become FFH, for the next PUSH, the SP rolls over to 00H.
- The top of the internal RAM, i.e. it's end address is 7FH. So next PUSHes after 7FH result in errors.
- Generally the SP is set at address above the register banks.
- The PUSH and POP operations may be applied to the stack pointer (SP).
- When PUSH and POP operations are used for the registers from the register banks (bank 0 - bank 3), specify direct addresses within the instructions. Do not use register name from register bank since the register name does not specify the bank in use.

18.3.4 Data Exchange Instructions

- When 8051 executes MOV, PUSH or POP instruction, the '**copy operation**' takes place. The data from the source address is copied to the destination address. The data at the source address remains unchanged. The **Exchange** instructions move data from source address to destination address and vice versa.
- Table 18.4 lists all types of exchange instructions in 8051.

Mnemonic	Operation
XCH A, <byte>	Exchange accumulator with byte variable.
XCH A, Rn	Exchange data bytes between register Rn and A.
XCH A, direct	Exchange data bytes between address directly given within instruction and A.
XCH A, @ Ri	Exchange data bytes between A and address in Ri.
XCHD A, @ Ri	Exchange lower nibble between A and address in Ri.

Table 18.4 Exchange instructions

- All the instructions given in the Table 18.4 are explained completely with example as follows.

XCH A,<byte> Bytes : 1/2 Cycles : 1 Function : Exchange Accumulator with byte variable

Description : XCH loads the Accumulator with the contents of the indicated variable, at the same time writing the original Accumulator contents to the indicated variable. The source/destination operand can use register, direct, or register-indirect addressing.

XCH A, Rn

Operation : $(A) \rightleftarrows (R_n)$

Example : **XCH A, R0 ;** This instruction exchanges contents of accumulator with the contents of register R0 of selected register bank.

XCH A, direct

Operation : $(A) \rightleftarrows (direct)$

Example : **XCH A, 20H ;** This instruction exchanges contents of accumulator with the contents of memory whose address is given within the instruction (20H)

XCH A, @Ri

Operation : $(A) \rightleftarrows (R_i)$

Example : **MOV A, #R2 ;** This instruction exchanges the contents of accumulator with the contents of memory location whose address is given by the contents of register R2 of selected register bank.

XCHD A, @Ri Function : Exchange Digit Bytes : 1 Cycles : 1

Description : XCHD exchanges the low-order nibble of the Accumulator (bits 3-0), generally representing a hexadecimal or BCD digit, with that of the internal RAM location indirectly addressed by the specified register. The high-order nibbles (bits 7-4) of each register are not affected. No flags are affected.

Example : R0 contains the address 20H. The Accumulator holds the value 36H (00110110B). Internal RAM location 20H holds the value 75H (01110101B). The instruction,

XCHD A, @R0

will leave RAM location 20H holding the value 76H (01110110B) and 35H (00110101B) in the Accumulator.

Operation : $(A_{3-0}) \rightleftarrows (R_{i3-0})$

Important Points to Remember in Exchange Instructions

- All exchanges involve the A register.
- All exchanges take place internally within 8051.
- When XCHD A, @Ri instruction is executed, the upper nibble of A and the upper nibble of the address in Ri do not change.
- Immediate addressing mode cannot be used in the exchange instructions.

18.4 Byte Level Logical Instructions

- The instructions ANL, ORL, and XRL perform the logical functions AND, OR , and/or Exclusive-OR on the two byte variables indicated, leaving the results in the first. No flags are affected.
- The byte-level logical operations use all four addressing modes for the source of a data byte. Here, directly addressed bytes may be used as the destination with either the accumulator or a constant as the source. These instructions are useful for clearing (ANL), setting (ORL) or complementing (XRL) one or more bits in a RAM, output ports, or control registers.
- This is illustrated in Fig. 18.1.

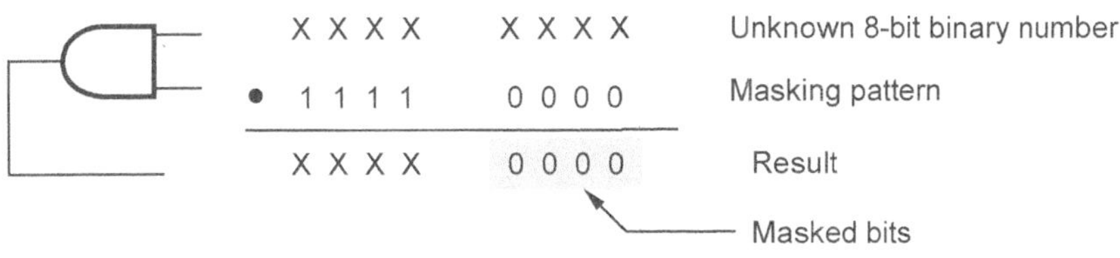

Fig. 18.1 Masking using AND operation

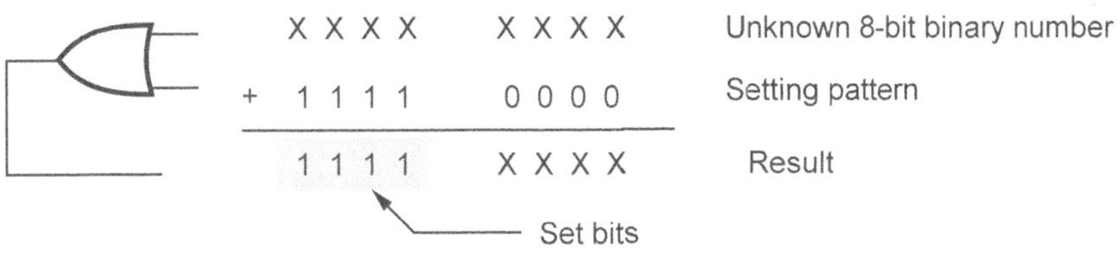

Fig. 18.2 Setting bit/s using OR operation

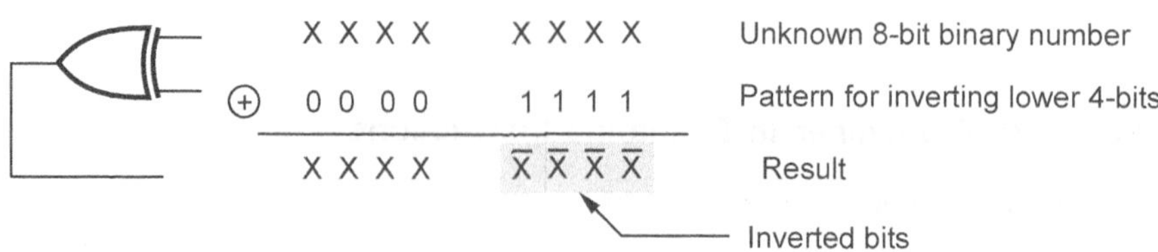

Fig. 18.3 Inversion of part of a number using XOR operation

- The Table 18.5 gives the list of byte level logical operations.

Mnemonic		Destination	Byte	Cycle
ANL	A, Rn	AND register to Accumulator	1	1
ANL	A, direct	AND direct byte to Accumulator	2	1
ANL	A, @Ri	AND indirect RAM to Accumulator	1	1
ANL	A, #data	AND immediate data to Accumulator	2	1
ANL	direct, A	AND Accumulator to direct byte	2	1
ANL	direct, #data	AND immediate data to direct byte	3	2
ORL	A, Rn	OR register to Accumulator	1	1
ORL	A, direct	OR direct byte to Accumulator	2	1
ORL	A, @Ri	OR indirect RAM to Accumulator	1	1
ORL	A, #data	OR immediate data to Accumulator	2	1
ORL	direct, A	OR Accumulator to direct byte	2	1
ORL	direct, #data	OR immediate data to direct byte	3	2
XRL	A, Rn	Exclusive-OR register to Accumulator	1	1
XRL	A, direct	Exclusive-OR direct byte to Accumulator	2	1
XRL	A, @Ri	Exclusive-OR indirect RAM to A	1	1
XRL	A, #data	Exclusive-OR immediate data to A	2	1
XRL	direct, A	Exclusive-OR Accumulator to direct byte	2	1
XRL	direct, #data	Exclusive-OR immediate data to direct	3	2
CLR	A	Clear Accumulator	1	1
CPL	A	Complement Accumulator	1	1

Table 18.5 Logical operations

Byte Level Logical Instructions with Examples

ANL<dest-byte>, <src-byte> Function : Logical-AND Bytes : 1/2/3 Cycles : 1

Description : ANL performs the bitwise logical-AND operation between the variables indicated and stores the result in the destination variable. No flags are affected.

ANL A, Rn

Operation : (A) ← (A) Λ (Rn)

Example : **ANL A, R2 ;** Logically ANDs A and R2 and store result in A.

ANL A, direct

Operation : (A) ← (A) Λ (direct)

Example : **ANL A, 20H ;** Logically ANDs contents of A and memory location whose address is 20H and stores result in A.

ANL A, @R1

Operation : (A) ← (A) Λ ((R_i))

Example : **ANL A, @R2 ;** Logically ANDs contents of A and memory location whose address is given by R2 and stores result in A.

ANL A, #data

Operation : (A) ← (A) Λ #data

Example : **ANL A, # 50H ;** logically ANDs contents of A with 50H and stores result in A.

ANL direct, A

Operation : (direct) ← (direct) Λ (A)

Example : **ANL 20H, A ;** Logically ANDs contents of A with the contents of memory location 20H and stores result at memory location 20H.

ANL direct, #data

Operation : (direct) ← (direct) Λ #data

Example : **ANL 20H, #20H ;** Logically ANDs the contents of memory location 20H with data 20H and stores result in memory location 20H.

ORL <dest-byte> <src-byte> **Bytes : 1/2/3** **Cycles : 1/2**

Function : Logical-OR for byte variables

Description : ORL performs the bitwise logical-OR operation between the indicated variables, storing the results in the destination byte. No flags are affected.

ORL A, Rn

Operation : (A) ← (A) V (Rn)

Example **ORL A, R2 ;** Logically ORs the contents of A and R2 and stores result in A.

ORL A, direct

Operation : (A) ← (A) V (direct)

Example **ORL A, 20H ;** logically ORs the contents of A and memory location 20H and stores result in A.

ORL A, @Ri

Operation : (A) ← (A) V ((Ri))

Example **ORL A, @R2 ;** Logically ORs the contents of A and memory location whose address is given by register R2 and stores result in A.

ORL A, #data

Operation : (A) ← (A) V #data

Example **ORL A, #32H ;** Logically ORs the contents of A with 32H and stores result in A.

ORL direct, A

Operation : (direct) ← (direct) V (A)

ORL direct, #data

Operation : (direct) ← (direct) V #data

Example **ORL 20H, #30H ;** Logically ORs the contents of memory location 20H and data 30H and stores result at memory location 20H.

XRL <dest-byte>,<src-byte> Bytes : 1/2 Cycles : 1

Function : Logical Exclusive-OR for byte variables

Description : XRL performs the bitwise logical Exclusive-OR operation between the indicated variables, storing the results in the destination. No flags are affected.

XRL A, Rn

Operation : (A) ← (A) ⊻ (Rn)

Example **XRL A, R2 ;** logically XOR the contents of A and R2 and stores result in A.

XRL A, direct

Operation : (A) ← (A) ⊻ (direct)

Example **XRL A, 20H ;** Logically XORs the contents of A with memory location 20H and stores result in A.

XRL A, @Ri

Operation : (A) ← (A) ⊻ ((Ri))

Example **XRL A,@R2 ;** Logically XORs the contents of A and the memory location whose address is given by R2 and stores result in A.

XRL A, #data

Operation : (A) ← (A) ⊻ # data

Example **XRL A, #40H ;** Logically XORs the contents of A with data 40H and stores result in A.

XRL direct, A

Operation : (direct) ← (direct) ⊻ (A)

Example **XRL 20H, A ;** Logically XORs the contents at 20H and the A and stores the result at 30H.

XRL direct, #data

Operation (direct) ← (direct) ⊻ #data

Example **XRL 30H, #40H ;** Logically XORs the contents at 30H and data 40H and stores the result at 30H.

CLR A **Function : Clear Accumulator** **Bytes : 1** **Cycles : 1**

Description : The Accumulator is cleared (all bits set on zero). No flags are affected.

Example : The Accumulator contains 95H (10010101B). The instruction,

CLR A

will leave the Accumulator set to 00H (00000000B).

Operation : (A) ← 0

CPL A **Function : Complement Accumulator** **Bytes : 1** **Cycles : 1**

Description : Each bit of the Accumulator is logically complemented (one's complement). Bits which previously contained a one are changed to a zero and vice-versa. No flags are affected.

Example : The Accumulator contains 55H (01010101B). The instruction,

CPL A

will leave the Accumulator set to AAH (10101010B).

Operation : $(A) \leftarrow \overline{(A)}$

18.5 Arithmetic Instructions

- The arithmetic operations of 8051 include increment, decrement, addition, subtraction, multiplication, division and decimal operations.

18.5.1 Incrementing and Decrementing

- Incrementing and decrementing instructions allow addition and subtraction of 1 from a given number. These instructions not affect C, AC and OV flags. The Table 18.6 lists the increment and decrement instructions.

Mnemonic	Operand	Description	Byte	Cycle
INC	A	Increment Accumulator	1	1
INC	Rn	Increment register	1	1
INC	direct	Increment direct byte	2	1
INC	@Ri	Increment indirect RAM	1	1
DEC	A	Decrement Accumulator	1	1
DEC	Rn	Decrement register	1	1
DEC	direct	Decrement direct byte	2	1
DEC	@Ri	Decrement indirect RAM	1	1
INC	DPTR	Increment data pointer	1	2

Table 18.6

Incrementing and Decrementing Instructions

INC <byte> **Function : Increment** **Bytes : 1/2** **Cycles : 1**

Description : INC increments the indicated variable by 1. An original value of 0FFH will overflow to 00H. No flags are affected.

INC A

Operation : (A) ← (A) + 1

INC Rn

Operation : (Rn) ← (Rn) + 1

Example **INC R2 ;** increments contents of R2 by 1

INC direct

Operation : (direct) ← (direct) + 1

Example **INC 20H ;** increments contents of memory location whose address is given within the instruction (20H).

INC @Ri

Operation : ((Ri)) ← ((Ri)) + 1

Example **INC @R2 ;** increment contents of memory location whose address is given by register R2 by 1.

INC DPTR	**Function : Increment Data Pointer**	**Bytes : 1**	**Cycles : 2**

Description : Increment the 16-bit data pointer by 1. A 16-bit increment (modulo 2^{16}) is performed; an overflow of the low-order byte of the data pointer (DPL) from FFH to 00H will increment the high-order byte (DPH). No flags are affected.

This is the only 16-bit register which can be incremented.

Operation : (DPTR) ← (DPTR) + 1

DEC byte	**Function : Decrement**	**Bytes : 1/2**	**Cycles : 1**

Description : The variable indicated is decremented by 1. An original value of 00H will underflow to 0FFH. No flags are affected.

DEC A

Operation : (A) ← (A) – 1

DEC Rn

Operation : (Rn) ← (Rn) – 1

Example **DEC R3 ;** Decrements contents of R3 by 1

DEC direct

Operation : (direct) ← (direct) – 1

Example **DEC 20H ;** Decrements the contents of memory location whose address is 20H by 1.

DEC @Rn

Operation : ((Ri)) ← ((Ri)) – 1

Example **DEC @R2 ;** Decrements the contents of memory location whose address is given by register R2 by 1.

18.5.2 Addition

The table shows the list of addition instructions supported by 8051.

Mnemonic	Operand	Description	Byte	Cycle
ADD	A, Rn	Add register to Accumulator	1	1
ADD	A, direct	Add direct byte to Accumulator	2	1
ADD	A, @Ri	Add indirect RAM to Accumulator	1	1
ADD	A, #data	Add immediate data to Accumulator	2	1
ADDC	A, Rn	Add register to Accumulator with carry	1	1
ADDC	A, direct	Add direct byte to A with carry flag	2	1
ADDC	A, @Ri	Add indirect RAM to A with carry flag	1	1
ADDC	A, #data	Add immediate data to A with carry flag	2	1

Addition Instructions

ADD A,<src-byte> Function : Add Bytes : 1/2 Cycles : 1

Description : ADD adds the byte variable indicated to the Accumulator, leaving the result in the Accumulator. The carry and auxiliary-carry flags are set, respectively, if there is a carry-out from bit 7 or bit 3, and cleared, otherwise.

When adding signed integers, OV indicates a negative number produced as the sum of two positive operands, or a positive sum from two negative operands.

ADD A, Rn

Operation : (A) ← (A) + (Rn)

Example **ADD A, R2 ;** Adds contents of A and R2 and store result in A.

ADD A, direct

Operation : (A) ← (A) + (direct)

Example **ADD A, 20H ;** Adds contents of A and memory whose address is 20H and store result in A.

ADD A, @Ri

Operation : (A) ← (A) + ((Ri))

Example **ADD A, @R2;** Adds contents of A and memory whose address is given by register R2 and store result in A

ADD A, #data

Operation : (A) ← (A) + #data

Example **ADD A, #20H ;** Adds the contents of A and 20H

ADDC A,<src-byte> Function : Add with Carry Bytes : 1/2 Cycles : 1

Description : ADDC simultaneously adds the byte variable indicated, the carry flag and the Accumulator. respectively, if there is a carry-out from bit 7 or bit 3, and cleared otherwise.

Precaution : When we use ADDC in loop to add 8-bit numbers carry flag should be cleared before first 8-bit addition.

ADDC A, Rn

Operation : (A) ← (A) + (C) + (Rn)

Example **ADDC A, R2 :** Adds the contents of A, R2 and carry flag, and stored result in A.

ADDC A, direct

Operation : (A) ← (A) + (C) + (direct)

Example **ADDC A, 20H ;** Adds the contents of A, memory location whose address is 20H and the carry flag and stores result in A.

ADDC A, @Ri

Operation : (A) ← (A) + (C) + ((R_i))

Example **ADDC A, @R2 ;** Adds the contents of A, memory location whose address is given by register R2 and the carry flag and stores result in the A.

ADDC A, #data

Operation : (A) ← (A) + (C) + #data

Example **ADDC A, #20H ;** Adds the contents of A and carry flag and 20H and stores result in A.

18.5.3 Subtraction

The table shows the list of subtraction instructions supported by 8051.

Mnemonic	Operand	Description	Byte	Cycle
SUBB	A,Rn	Subtract register from A with borrow	1	1
SUBB	A,direct	Subtract direct byte from A with borrow	2	1
SUBB	A,@Ri	Subtract indirect RAM from A with borrow	1	1
SUBB	A,#data	Subtract immediate data from A with borrow	2	1

Subtraction Instructions

SUBB A, <src-byte> Function : Subtract with borrow Bytes : 2 Cycles : 1

Description : SUBB subtracts the indicated variable and the carry flag together from the Accumulator, leaving the result in the Accumulator. SUBB sets the carry (borrow) flag if a borrow is needed for bit 7, and clears otherwise. AC is set if a borrow is needed for bit 3, and cleared otherwise. OV is set if a borrow is needed into bit 6, but not into bit 7, or into bit 7, but not bit 6.

Precaution : **If the state of the carry is not known before starting a single or multiple-precision subtraction, it should be explicitly cleared by a CLR C instruction.**

Example :

SUBB A, Rn

Operation : (A) ← (A) – (C) – (Rn)

Example **SUBB A, R3 ;** Subtracts contents of R3 and carry together from A and stores results in A.

SUBB A, direct

Operation : (A) ← (A) – (C) – (direct)

Example **SUBB A, 20H ;** subtracts the contents of memory location 20H and carry together from A stores result in A.

SUBB A, @Ri

Operation : (A) ← (A) – (C) – ((Ri))

Example **SUBB A, @R2** ; Subtracts the contents of memory location whose address is given by R2 and carry together from A and stores result in A.

SUBB A, #data

Operation : (A) ← (A) – (C) – #data

Example **SUBB A, #20H** ; Subtracts 20H from A and stores result in A.

18.5.4 Multiplication and Division

Multiplication Instruction

MUL AB	**Function : Multiply**	**Bytes : 1**	**Cycles : 4**

Description : MUL AB multiplies the unsigned eight-bit integers in the Accumulator and register B. The low-order byte of the sixteen-bit product is left in the Accumulator, and the high-order byte in B. If the product is greater than 255 (FFH) the overflow flag is set; otherwise it is cleared. The carry flag is always cleared.

Example : Originally the Accumulator holds the value 80 (50H). Register B holds the value 160 (0A0H). The instruction,

MUL AB

will give the product 12,800 (3200H), so B is changed to 32H (00110010B) and the Accumulator is cleared. The overflow flag is set, carry is cleared.

Operation : $(A)_{7-0} \leftarrow (A) \times (B)$

$(B)_{15-8}$

Division Instruction

DIV AB	**Function : Divide**	**Bytes : 1**	**Cycles : 4**

Description : DIV AB divides the unsigned eight-bit integer in the Accumulator by the unsigned eight-bit integer in register B. The Accumulator receives the integer part of the quotient; register B receives the integer remainder. The carry and OV flags will be cleared.

Exception : If B had originally contained 00H, the values returned in the Accumulator and B-register will be undefined and the overflow flag will be set. The carry flag is cleared in any case.

Example : The Accumulator contains 250 (0FBH or 11111010B) and B contains 18 (12H or 00010010B). The instruction,

DIV AB

will leave 13 in the Accumulator (0DH or 00001101B) and the value 16 (10H or 00010000B) in B, since 250 = $(13 \times 18) + 16$. Carry and OV will both be cleared.

Operation : DIV

$(A)_{15-8} \leftarrow (A)/(B)$

$(B)_{7-0}$

18.5.5 Decimal Arithmetic

DA A Function : Decimal-adjust Accumulator for addition Bytes : 1 Cycles : 1

Description : DA A adjusts the eight-bit value in the Accumulator resulting from the earlier addition of two variables (each in packed-BCD format), producing two four-bit digits.

Example : The Accumulator holds the value 55H (01010101B) representing the packed BCD digits of the decimal number 55. Register 3 contains the value 68H (01101000B) representing the packed BCD digits of the decimal number 68. The carry flag is set. The instruction sequence.

ADDC A, R3

DA A

will first perform a standard two's-complement binary addition, resulting in the value BEH (10111110) in the Accumulator. The carry and auxiliary carry flags will be cleared.

The Decimal Adjust instruction will then alter the Accumulator to the value 24H (00100100B), indicating the packed BCD digits of the decimal number 24, the low-order two digits of the decimal sum of 55, 68, and the carry-in. The carry flag will be set by the Decimal Adjust instruction, indicating that a decimal overflow occurred. The true sum 55, 68 and 1 is 124.

Operation DA

IF $[[(A_{3-0}) > 9] \text{ OR } [(AC)] = 1]]$

THEN $(A_{3-0}) \leftarrow (A_{3-0}) + 6$

AND

IF $[\,[(A_{7-4}) > 9] \text{ OR } [(C) = 1]]$

THEN $(A_{7-4}) \leftarrow (A_{7-4}) + 6$

18.6 Bit Level Logical Instructions

Bit level manipulations are very convenient when it is necessary to set or reset a particular bit in the internal RAM or SFRs. The internal RAM of 8051 from address 20H through 2FH is both byte addressable and bit addressable. However, byte and bit addresses are different. The Table 18.7 shows the correspondence between byte and bit addresses.

Byte Address in Hex	Bit Address in Hex
20	00-07
21	08-0F
22	10-17
23	18-1F
24	20-27
25	28-2F
26	30-37
27	38-3F
28	40-47
29	48-4F
2A	50-57
2B	58-5F
2C	60-67
2D	68-6F
2E	70-77
2F	78-7F

Table 18.7 Bit and byte addresses of internal RAM

As shown in the Table 18.7, addresses of bit 0 and bit 7 of internal RAM byte address 20H are 00H and 07H respectively. From Table 18.7 we can easily interpolate addresses of bit 1 and bit 6 of internal RAM byte address 26H as 31H and 36H, respectively.

Like internal RAM, some SFRs are bit addressable. The Table 18.8 shows the bit addressable SFR and the corresponding bit addresses.

SFR	Direct Address in Hex	Bit Address in Hex
A	E0	E0-E7
B	F0	F0-F7
IE	A8	A8-AF
IP	B8	B8-BF
P0	80	80-87
P1	90	90-97

P2	A0	A0-A7
P3	B0	B0-B7
PSW	D0	D0-D7
TCON	88	88-8F
SCON	98	98-9F

Table 18.8 Bit and byte addresses of SFRs

The Table 18.9 gives the list of bit level operations.

Mnemonic	Operands	Description	Byte	Cycle
CLR	C	Clear Carry flag	1	1
CLR	bit	Clear direct bit	2	1
SETB	C	Set Carry flag	1	1
SETB	bit	Set direct bit	2	1
CPL	C	Complement Carry flag	1	1
CPL	bit	Complement direct bit	2	1
ANL	C, bit	AND direct bit to Carry flag	2	2
ANL	C, /bit	AND complement of direct bit to Carry	2	2
ORL	C, bit	OR direct bit to Carry flag	2	2
ORL	C, /bit	OR complement of direct bit to Carry	2	2
MOV	C, bit	Move direct bit to Carry flag	2	1
MOV	bit, C	Move Carry flag to direct bit	2	2

Table 18.9 Boolean variable manipulation

Bit Level Instructions with Examples

CLR bit **Function : Clear bit** **Bytes : 1** **Cycles : 1**

Description : The indicated bit is cleared (reset to zero). No other flags are affected. CLR can operate on the carry flag or any directly addressable bit.

Example : Port 1 has previously been written with FFH (11111111B). The instruction,

CLR P1.2

will leave the port set to FBH (11111011B)

CLR C

Operation : (C) ← 0

CLR bit

Operation : CLR

(bit) ← 0

SETB <bit>	Function : Set bit	Bytes : 1/2	Cycles : 1

Description : SETB sets the indicated bit to one. SETB can operate on the carry flag or any directly addressable bit. No other flags are affected.

Example : The carry is cleared. Output Port 1 has been written with the value 34H (00110100B). The instruction,

SETB C

SETB P1.0

will leave the carry flag set to 1 and change the data output on Port 1 to 35H (00110101B).

SETB C

Operation : (C) ← 1

SETB bit

Operation : (bit) ← 1

CPL bit	Function : Complement bit	Bytes : 1/2	Cycles : 1

Description : The bit variable specified is complemented. No other flags are affected.

Example : Port 1 has previously been written with FFH (11111111B). The instruction

CPL P1.1

will leave the port set to FDH (11111101B)

CPL C

Operation : $(C) \leftarrow \overline{(C)}$

CPL bit

Operation : $(bit) \leftarrow \overline{(bit)}$

ANL C,<src-bit> Function : Logical-AND for bit variables Bytes : 2 Cycles : 2

Description : If the Boolean value of the source bit is a logical 0 then clear the carry flag; otherwise leave the carry flag in its current state. A slash ("/") preceding the operand in the assembly language indicates that the logical complement of the addressed bit is used as the source value, but the source bit itself is not affected. No flags are affected.

Only direct addressing is allowed for the source operand.

Example : Set the carry flag if, and only if, P1.0 = 1, ACC.7 = 1, and OV = 0:

```
MOV C, P1.0   ; LOAD CARRY WITH INPUT PIN STATE
ANL C, ACC.7 ; AND CARRY WITH ACCUMULATOR BIT 7
ANL C,/OV     ; AND WITH INVERSE OF OVERFLOW FLAG
```

ANL C, bit

Operation : $(C) \leftarrow (C) \wedge (bit)$

ANL C/ bit

Operation : $(C) \leftarrow (C) \wedge \overline{(bit)}$

ORL C, <src-bit> Bytes : 2 Cycles : 2
Function : Logical-OR for bit variables

Description : Set the carry flag if the Boolean value is a logical 1; leave the carry in its current state otherwise slash ("/") preceding the operand in the assembly language indicates that the logical complement of the addressed bit is used as the source value, but the source bit itself is not affected. No other flags are affected.

Example : Set the carry flag if and only if P1.0 = 1, ACC.7 = 1, or OV = 0:

```
MOV   C, P1.0    ; LOAD CARRY WITH  INPUT PIN P10
ORL   C, ACC.7 ; OR CARRY WITH THE ACC.BIT7
ORL   C, /OV    ; OR CARRY WITH THE INVERSE OF OV.
```

ORL C, bit

Operation : (C) ← (C) V (bit)

ORL C,/bit

Operation : (C) ← (C) V $(\overline{bit})$

MOV <dest-bit>, <src-bit> Function : Move bit data Bytes : 2 Cycles : 1/2

Description : The Boolean variable indicated by the second operand is copied into the location specified by the first operand. One of the operands must be the carry flag; the other may be any directly addressable bit. No other register or flag is affected.

Example : The carry flag is originally set. The data present at input Port 3 is (11000101B). The data previously written to output Port 1 is C5H (00110101B).

MOV P1.3, C

MOV C, P3.3

MOV P1.2, C will leave the carry cleared and change Port 1 to 39H (00111001B).

MOV C, bit

Operation : (C) ← (bit)

MOV bit, C

Operation : (C) ← (bit)

18.7 Rotate and Swap Instructions

- The Table 18.10 gives the list of rotate and swap operations supported by 8051.

Mnemonic	Operand	Destination	Byte	Cycle
RL	A	Rotate Accumulator left	1	1
RLC	A	Rotate A left through the carry flag	1	1
RR	A	Rotate Accumulator right	1	1
RRC	A	Rotate A Right through carry flag	1	1
SWAP	A	Swap nibbles within the accumulator	1	1

Table 18.10 List of rotate and swap operations

Rotate and Swap Instructions with Examples

RL A	Function : Rotate Accumulator Left	Bytes : 1	Cycles : 1

Description : The eight bits in the Accumulator are rotated one bit to the left. Bit 7 is rotated into the bit 0 position. No flags are affected.

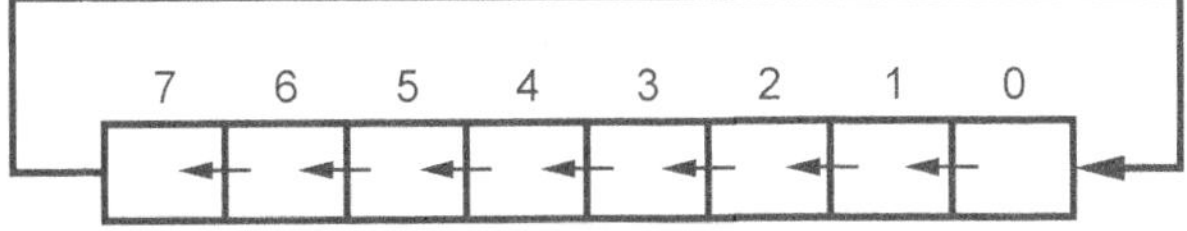

Example : The Accumulator holds the value C5H (11000101B). The instruction,

RL, A

leaves the Accumulator holding the value 8BH (10001011B) with the carry unaffected.

Operation : (An + 1) ← (An) n = 0 – 6

(A0) ← (A7)

RLC A	Bytes : 1	Cycles : 1	Function : Rotate Accumulator Left through the Carry flag

Description : The eight bits in the Accumulator and the carry flag are together rotated one bit to the left. Bit 7 moves into the carry flag; the original state of the carry flag moves into the bit 0 position. No other flags are affected.

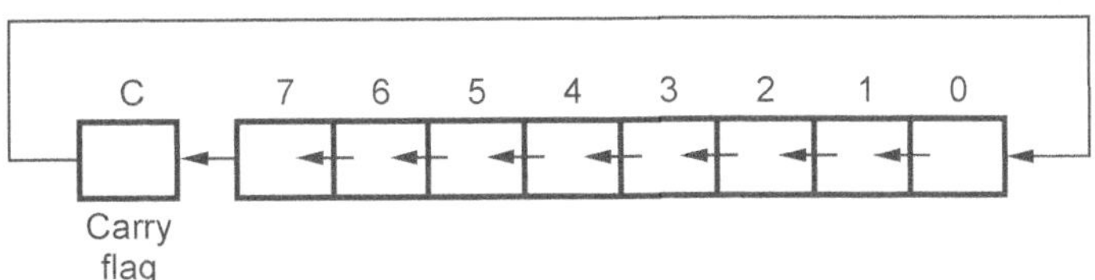

Example : The Accumulator holds the value C5H (11000101B), and the carry is zero. The instruction,

RLC A

leaves the Accumulator holding the value 8BH (10001010B) with the carry set.

Operation : (An + 1) ← (An) n = 0 – 6

(A0) ← (C)

(C) ← (A7)

RR A Function : Rotate Accumulator Right Bytes : 1 Cycles : 1

Description : The eight bits in the Accumulator are rotated one bit to the right. Bit 0 is rotated into the bit 7 position. No flags are affected.

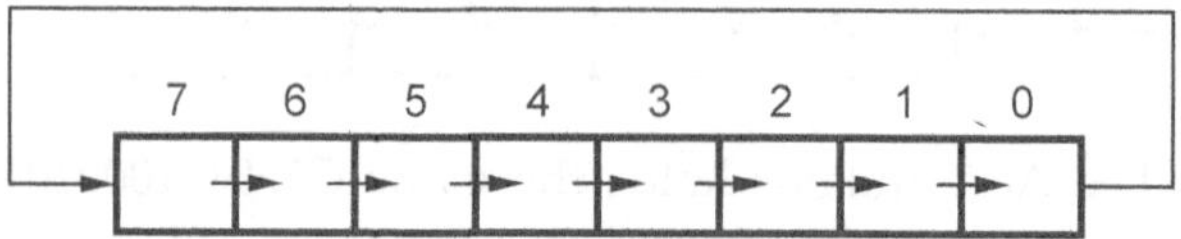

Example : The Accumulator holds the value C5H (11000101B). The instruction,

RR A

leaves the Accumulator holding the value E2H (11100010B) with the carry unaffected.

Operation : (An) ← (A_n + 1) = 0 – 6

(A7) ← (A0)

RRC A Bytes : 1 Cycles : 1 Function : Rotate Accumulator Right through Carry Flag

Description : The eight bits in the Accumulator and the carry flag are together rotated one bit to the right. Bit 0 moves into the carry flag; the original value of the carry flag moves into the bit 7 position. No other flags are affected.

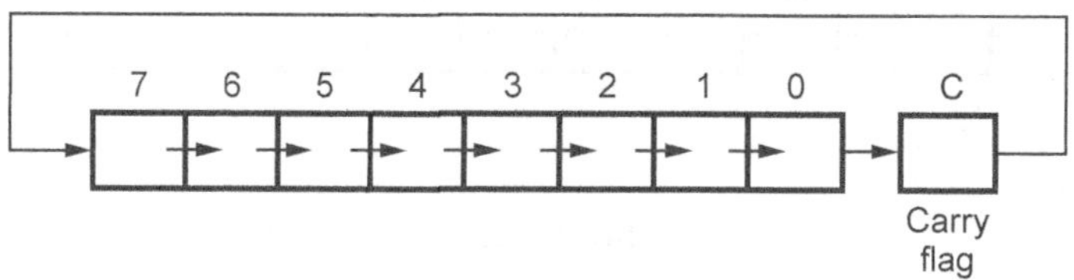

Example : The Accumulator holds the value C5H (11000101B), the carry is zero. The instruction

RRC A

leaves the Accumulator holding the value 62 (01100010B) with the carry set.

Operation : (An) ← (An + 1) n = 0 – 6

(A7) ← (C)

(C) ← (A0)

SWAP A Function : Swap nibbles within the Accumulator Bytes : 1 Cycles : 1

Description : Swap A interchanges the low and high-order nibbles (four-bit fields) of the Accumulator (bits 3-0 and bits 7-4). The operation can also be thought of as a four-bit rotate instruction. No flags are affected.

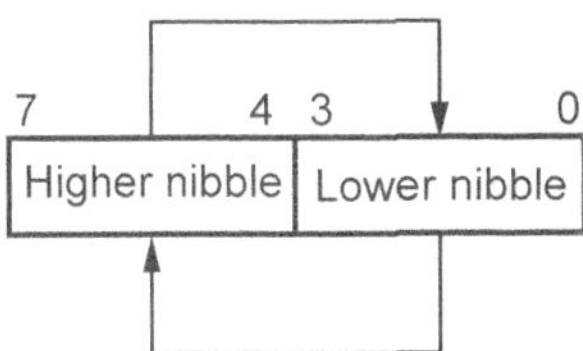

Example : The Accumulator holds the value C5H (11000101B). The instruction

SWAP A

leaves the Accumulator holding the value 5CH (01011100B)

Operation : SWAP

$(A_{3-0}) \rightleftarrows (A_{7-4})$

18.8 Jump and CALL Instructions

Jump and CALL instructions change the flow of the program by changing the contents of program counter. A jump permanently changes the program flow whereas call temporarily changes the program flow to allow another part of the program to run. There are jump instructions which change the program flow if certain condition exists. For example, CJNE (compare and jump if not equal). This instruction compares the magnitude of the first two operands, and changes program flow if their values are not equal.

The following types of instructions change the program flow :

- Jump on bit conditions.
- Compare byte and jump if not equal.
- Decrement byte and jump if zero.
- Jump unconditionally.
- Call a subroutine.
- Return from a subroutine.

18.8.1 Jump and Call Program Range

We know that a jump and call instructions replace the contents of the program counter with a new program address. The new address can be specified either by specifying the difference between the new address and the current program counter contents or by specifying the entire new address. The difference, in bytes, of the new address from the address in the program counter is called the **range of the jump** or **call**. For example, if a jump instruction is located at program address 0200H, and the jump causes the program counter to become 0230H, then the range of the jump is 30H bytes. Jump and CALL instructions may have one of the three ranges.

- Relative (short) range : +127 to – 128 (+7FH to – 80H)
- Absolute range : 0000H to 07FFH
- Long range : 0000H to FFFFH

18.8.2 Jump

The Table 18.11 shows the list of jump instructions supported by 8051.

Mnemonic	Operand	Description	Byte	Cycle
AJMP	addr11	Absolute Jump	2	2
LJMP	addr16	Long Jump	3	2
SJMP	rel	Short Jump (relative addr)	2	2
JMP	@A+DPTR	Jump indirect relative to the DPTR	1	2
JZ	rel	Jump if Accumulator is zero	2	2
JNZ	rel	Jump if Accumulator is not zero	2	2
JC	rel	Jump if carry flag is set	2	2
JNC	rel	Jump if no carry flag	2	2
JB	bit, rel	Jump if direct bit set	3	2
JNB	bit, rel	Jump if direct bit not set	3	2
JBC	bit, rel	Jump if direct bit is set and clear bit	3	2

Table 18.11

Jump Instructions

AJMP addr11 Function : Absolute Jump Bytes : 2 Cycles : 2

Description : AJMP transfers program execution to the indicated address. Since address is 11-bit the destination must therefore be within the same 2 K block of program memory as the first byte of the instruction following AJMP. No flags are affected.

LJMP addr16 **Function : Long Jump** **Bytes : 3** **Cycles : 2**

Description : LJMP causes an unconditional branch to the indicated address by loading the high-order and low-order bytes of the PC(respectively) with the second and third instruction bytes. The destination may therefore be anywhere in the full 64 K program memory address space. No flags are affected.

SJMP rel **Function : Short Jump** **Bytes : 2** **Cycles : 2**

Description : Program control branches unconditionally to the address indicated. The branch destination is computed by adding the signed displacement in the second instruction byte to the PC, after incrementing the PC twice. Therefore, the range of destinations allowed is from 128 bytes preceding this instruction to 127 bytes following it.

JMP @A + DPTR **Function : Jump Indirect** **Bytes : 1** **Cycles : 2**

Description : Add the eight-bit unsigned contents of the Accumulator with the sixteen-bit data pointer, and load the resulting sum to the program counter. This will be the address for subsequent instruction fetches.

Neither the accumulator nor the data pointer is altered. No flags are affected.

JZ rel **Function : Jump if Accumulator Zero** **Bytes : 2** **Cycles : 2**

Description : If all bits of the Accumulator are zero, branch to the address indicated; otherwise proceed with the next instruction. The accumulator is not modified. No flags are affected.

JNZ rel **Function : Jump if Accumulator Not Zero** **Bytes : 2** **Cycles : 2**

Description : If any bit of the Accumulator is a one, branch to the indicated address; otherwise proceed with the next instruction. The accumulator is not modified. No flags are affected.

JC rel **Function : Jump if Carry is set** **Bytes : 2** **Cycles : 2**

Description : If the carry flag is set branch to the address indicated; otherwise proceed with the next instruction. No flags are affected.

JNC rel **Function : Jump if Carry not set** **Bytes : 2** **Cycles : 2**

Description : If the carry flag is a zero, branch to the address indicated; otherwise proceed with the next instruction. The carry flag is not modified.

JB bit, rel **Function : Jump if Bit set** **Bytes : 3** **Cycles : 2**

Description : If the indicated bit is one, jump to the address indicated; otherwise proceed with the next instruction. The bit tested is not modified. No flags are affected.

JNB bit, rel **Function : Jump if Bit Not set** **Bytes : 3** **Cycles : 2**

Description : If the indicated bit is a zero, branch to the indicated address; otherwise proceed with the next instruction. The bit tested is not modified. No flags are affected.

JBC bit, rel **Function : Jump if Bit is set and Clear bit** **Bytes : 3** **Cycles : 2**

Description : If the indicated bit is one, branch to the address indicated; otherwise proceed with the next instruction. The bit will not be cleared if it is already a zero.

CJNE <dest-byte>,<scr-byte>, rel **Bytes : 3** **Cycles : 2**
Function : Compare and Jump if Not Equal

Description : CJNE compares the magnitudes of the first two operands, and branches if their values are not equal. The carry flag is set if the unsigned integer value of <dest-byte> is less than the unsigned integer value of <src-byte>; otherwise, the carry is cleared. Neither operand is affected.

DJNZ <byte>, <rel-addr> **Bytes : 2/3** **Cycles : 2**

Function : Decrement and Jump if Not Zero

Description : DJNZ decrements the location indicated by 1, and branches to the address indicated by the second operand if the resulting value is not zero. An original value of 00H will underflow to 0FFH. No flags are affected.

NOP **Function : No Operation** **Bytes : 1** **Cycles : 1**

Description : Execution continues at the following instruction. Other than the PC, no registers or flags are affected.

18.8.3 CALL and Subroutines

- There are two subroutine-call instructions. LCALL (Long Call) and ACALL (Absolute Call). Each increments the PC to the first byte of the following instruction, then pushes it onto the stack (low byte first). Saving both bytes increment the stack pointer by two. The subroutine's starting address is encoded in the same ways as LJMP and AJMP. The generic form of the call operation is the mnemonic CALL, which 8051 will translate into LCALL or ACALL as appropriate.
- The return instruction RET pops the high and low-order bytes of the program counter successively from the stack, decrementing the stack pointer by two. Program execution continues at the address previously pushed : the first byte of the instruction immediately following the call.

CALL and Return Instructions

ACALL addr11 **Function : Absolute Call** **Bytes : 2** **Cycles : 2**

Description : ACALL unconditionally calls a subroutine located at the indicated address. The instruction increments the PC twice to obtain the address of the following instruction, then pushes the 16-bit result onto the stack (low-order byte first) and increments the Stack Pointer twice. Since address is 11-bit the subroutine called must therefore start within the same 2 K block of the program memory as the first byte of the instruction following ACALL. No flags are affected.

LCALL addr16 Function : Long Call Bytes : 3 Cycles : 2

Description : LCALL calls a subroutine located at the indicated address. The instruction adds three to the program counter to generate the address of the next instruction and then pushes the 16-bit result onto the stack (low byte first), incrementing the stack pointer by two. The high-order and low-order bytes of the PC are then loaded, respectively, with the second and third bytes of the LCALL instruction. Program execution continues with the instruction at this address. The subroutine may therefore begin anywhere in the full 64 kbyte program memory address space. No flags are affected.

RET Function : Return from subroutine Bytes : 1 Cycles : 2

Description : RET pops the high and low-order bytes of the PC successively from the stack, decrementing the Stack Pointer by two program execution continues at the resulting address. No flags are affected.

RETI Function : Return from interrupt Bytes : 1 Cycles : 2

Description : RETI pops the high and low-order bytes of the PC successively from the stack, and restores the interrupt logic to accept additional interrupts at the same priority level as the one just processed. The Stack Pointer is left decremented by two. No other registers are affected; the PSW is not automatically restored to its per-interrupt status. Program execution continues at the resulting address, which is generally the instruction immediately after the point at which the interrupt request was detected. If a lower-level or same-level interrupt had been pending interrupt is processed.

18.9 Time Delay for 8051

Many times, it is necessary to generate time delays. For example, to generate a square wave we have to generate a delay of T/2 period so that we can make output 1 for T/2 period and make output 0 for T/2 period. Let us see how to calculate exact delays for 8051.

For 8051 operating frequency is one-twelfth (1/12) of the crystal frequency. Therefore, one machine cycle lasts for 12 oscillator periods.

$$\therefore \text{ Machine cycle period} = \frac{12}{\text{Crystal frequency}}$$

For crystal frequency 11.0592 MHz,

$$\text{Machine cycle period} = \frac{12}{11.0592 \times 10^6} = \mathbf{1.085\ \mu s}$$

For 8051, we know that how much machine cycle/s are required to execute the particular instruction. Therefore, we can calculate the exact time for execution of that instruction, as shown below.

Instruction	Machine cycle	Time to execute
MOV R2, #40	1	$1 \times 1.085\ \mu s = 1.085\ \mu s$
DJNZ R1, SKIP	2	$2 \times 1.085\ \mu s = 2.17\ \mu s$
MUL AB	4	$4 \times 1.085\ \mu s = 4.34\ \mu s$

Example 18.1 : *Calculate the time delay produced by the following subroutine.*

```
Delay : MOV R1, #30
HERE :  DJNZ R1, HERE
        NOP
        NOP
        RET
```

Solution : Let us assume the crystal frequency of 8051 is 11.0592 MHz. Therefore, the period of the machine cycle will be

$$T = \frac{12}{11.0592 \times 10^6} = 1.085\ \mu\text{sec}$$

	Instruction	Machine cycle
Delay :	MOV R1, #30	1
HERE :	DJNZ R1, HERE	2
	NOP	1
	NOP	1
	RET	1

$$\text{Time delay} = [1 + (2 \times 30) + 1 + 1 + 1] \times 1.085\ \mu\text{sec}$$

$$= \mathbf{69.44\ \mu s}$$

Here, (2×30) indicates that the instruction DJNZ R1, HERE is executed 30 times.

18.10 Introduction to Assembly Language Programming

Machine Language

A program which has simply a sequence of the binary codes for the instructions is called machine level language program. This binary form of the program is referred to as machine language because it is the form required by the machine. However, to write a program in machine language, programmer has to memorize the thousands of binary instruction codes for a processor. This task is difficult and error prone.

Assembly Language

To make programming easier, usually programmers write programs in assembly language. They then translate the assembly language program to machine language so that it can be loaded into memory and executed. Assembly language uses two, three or four letter words to represent each instruction types. These words are referred to as **mnemonics**. The letters in an assembly language mnemonic are usually initials or a shortened form of the English word(s) for the operation performed by the instruction. For example, the mnemonic for addition is ADD, the mnemonic for logic AND operation is AND, and the mnemonic for the instruction for copy data from one location to another is MOV. Therefore, the meaning expressed by mnemonics help us to remember the operation performed by the instruction.

Assembly language statements are usually written in a standard form and assembly language has its own unique syntactical structure, such as requiring upper case or lower case, or requiring colons after label definitions. Here we discuss the common features that assembler shares.

The assembly text is usually divided into fields, separated by spaces and tabs. A format for a typical line from assembly language program can be given as

Label : Mnemonic Operand1, Operand2 ; Comment

The first field, which is optional, is the label field, used to specify symbolic labels. A label is an identifier that is assigned to the address of the first byte of the instruction in which it appears. As mentioned earlier, the presence of a label is optional, but if present, the label provides a symbolic name that can be used in branch instructions to branch to the instruction.

The second field is mnemonic, which is compulsory. All instructions must contain a mnemonic. The third and following fields are operands. The presence of the operands depends on the instruction. Some instructions have no operands, some have one, and some have two. If there are two operands, they are separated by a comma.

The last field is a comment field. It begins with a delimiter such as the semicolon and continues to the end of the line. The comments are for our benefits, they tell us what the program is trying to accomplish. The Fig. 18.4 shows a typical 8051 assembly language instruction.

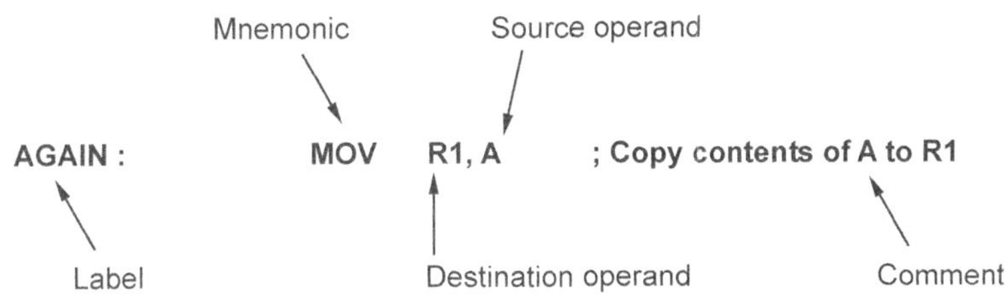

Fig. 18.4 Typical assembly language instruction

18.10.1 Comparison between Assembly Language and Machine Language

The Table 18.12 gives the comparison between assembly language and machine language.

Sr. No.	Machine language	Assembly language
1.	Language consists of binary codes which specify the operation.	Language consists of mnemonics which specify the operation.
2.	Processor dependent and hence requires knowledge of internal details of processor to write a program.	Processor dependent hence requires knowledge of internal details of processor to write a program.
3.	Programs require less memory.	Programs require less memory.
4.	Programs have less execution time.	Programs have less execution time.
5.	Program development is difficult.	Program development is simpler than machine language.
6.	It is not user friendly.	It is less user friendly.

Table 18.12 Comparison between assembly and machine language

18.10.2 Assembly Language Programming Tools

The development tools used frequently in microcontroller based systems are :

1. **Editor :** The editor is a program, which is used to create and modify source programs/text, (letters, numbers, punctuation marks, assembly language programs, higher level language programs such as PASCAL, C, FORTRAN etc). The editor has commands to change, delete or insert lines or characters.
2. **Assembler :** Assembler translates an assembly language source file that was created using the editor into machine language such as binary or object code.
3. **Cross Assembler :** A cross assembler is an assembler that generates machine language code for a different type of computer than the one the assembler is running in. For example, ASM 51 is a cross assembler since it runs on a IBM-PC,

i.e. the CPU chip other than the 8051 to convert assembly language program to machine language program.

4. **Macro Assembler :** A very useful facility provided by many assemblers is the use of macro. A macro is a sequence of instructions to which a name is assigned. When the macro is referenced by specifying its name, the macro assembler replaces the macro call by the sequence of instructions that define the macro. The macro assembler functions in a similar manner to the assembler described earlier. However, it has to perform an additional task of macro expansion before the assembly program is translated into an equivalent machine language program.
5. **Compiler :** A compiler is a program used to translate higher level language program (program written using BASIC, Pascal or C) to machine code which can be loaded into memory and executed.
6. **Cross Compiler :** A cross compiler is a compiler capable of creating executable code for a platform other than the one on which the compiler is run. It is used to generate executables for embedded system or multiple platforms.
7. **Linker :** A linker is a program used to join together several object files into one large object file and produce a link file which contains the binary codes for all the combined files.
8. **Loader :** A loader is a program that transfers the program to be executed from secondary memory into the memory accessed by microprocessor or microcontroller.

18.10.3 Assembling and Running an 8051 Program

The steps to create, assemble and run assembly language program are :

1. The first step in the process is to write an assembly language program. The assembly language program can be written / typed with a text editor such as MS-DOS EDIT or Notepad in Windows. This program must be saved with a file extension .asm.
2. The .asm source file containing the program code created in the first step is fed to an 8051 assembler. The assembler translates assembly language instructions into machine code and it will produce an object file and a list file. The extension of object file is **obj** and extension of the list file is **lst**.
   The lst file is an optional file. It is useful to the programmer because it lists all the opcodes and addresses as well as errors that the assembler detected.
3. The third step is called **linking**. In this step, the link program takes one or more object files and produces an absolute object file with the extension **abs**. This file is used by 8051 trainers that have a monitor program.
4. Finally, the **abs** file is fed into a program called object to hex converter (0H program) to produce a file with an extension **hex**. This file is an executable file and is ready to burn into ROM.

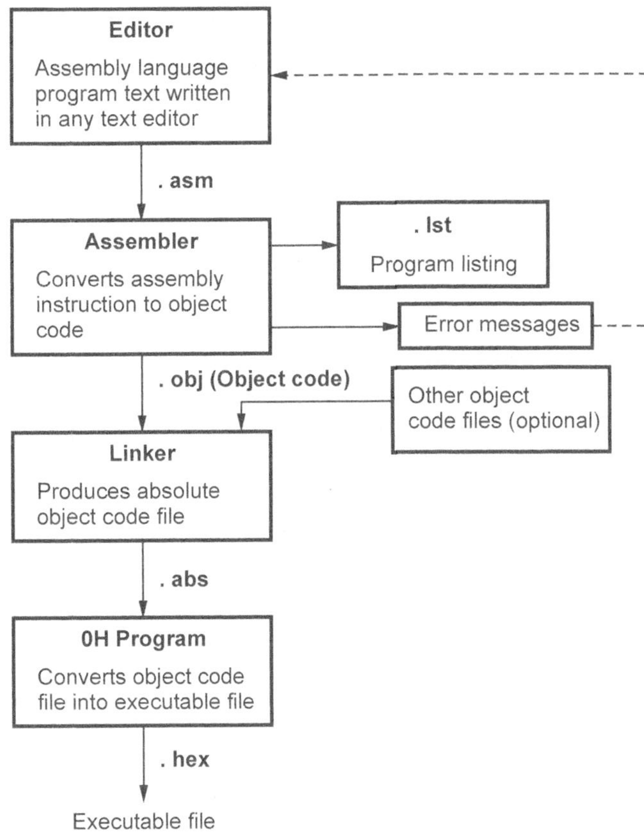

Fig. 18.5 Steps in creating an executable program

18.10.4 Data Types of 8051

The 8051 supports only one data type. It is 8-bits (byte). Each general purpose register is also 8-bits. So to process data larger than 8-bits, the programmer has to break down data in bytes and process them separately.

The data type used by the 8051 can be positive or negative. The most significant bit of 8-bit data indicates the sign of the data.

18.10.5 Assembler Directives

There are some instructions in the assembly language program which are not a part of processor instruction set. These instructions are instructions to the assembler, linker, and loader. These are referred to as **pseudo-operations** or as **assembler directives.** The assembler directives enable us to control the way in which a program assembles and lists. They act during the assembly of a program and do not generate any executable machine code.

Let us study the commonly used assembler directives :

EQU : Equate : It is used to define a constant without occupying a memory location. For example, COUNT EQU 10.

ORG : Origin : It is used to indicate the beginning of the address. The address comes after the ORG can be specified either in hex or decimal. To specify address in hex, the address should be followed by H. For example,
ORG 0100H

DB : Define byte : It is used to define the 8-bit data. The data value comes after the DB can be specified in decimal, binary, hex or ASCII formats. For decimal, the 'D' after the decimal number, for binary 'B' after the binary number and for hex 'H' after the hex number should be specified. For decimal, the 'D' after the decimal number is optional. To indicate ASCII, the characters are placed in quotation marks. For example,

```
NUM 1    DB   32          ;  Num 1 equal to 32 in decimal
NUM 2    DB   32 H        ;  Num 2 equal to 32 in hex, i.e. 50 in decimal
NUM 3    DB   10010001B   ;  Num 3 equal to 10010001 in binary
CHAR     DB   "A"         ;  CHAR equal to ASCII A.
```

END : The END directive is put after the last statement of a 8051 program to tell the assembler that this is the end of the program.

CODE : It assigns a name to the specified memory location in the program memory (Range 0 - 65535). **For example,**

```
LIST CODE 1020H    ;  Memory location 1020H in the program memory is now
                   ;  referred to as LIST
```

DATA : It assigns a name to the specified location in the internal RAM of 8051. (Range 0 - 255). **For example,**

```
TEMP DATA 52 H     ;  Register at address 52H is now
                   ;  named as TEMP
```

IDATA : It assigns a name to the memory location whose address is located in the specified register. **For example,**

```
MARKS DATA 80      ;  Register whose address is in register at
                   ;  address 80 is named as MARKS
```

XDATA : It assigns name to the specified memory location in the external RAM memory (Range 0 - 65535). **For example,**

```
RESULT XDATA 1000H ;  Memory location 1000H in the
                   ;  external RAM memory is now referred
                   ;  to as RESULT
```

USING : This directive is used to define which register bank (Bank0 - Bank3) will be used in the following program. **For example,**

```
USING 1            ;  Bank 1 will be used.
```

18.11 Program Examples

Program 1 : Program to load accumulator A, DPH and DPL with 30H

```
MOV A, #30H     ; Loads 30H in A register
MOV DPH, A      ; (DPH) ← (A)
MOV DPL, A      ; (DPL) ← (A)
```

Program 2 : Copy byte in SCON to register R3.

Method 1 : Using direct address for SCON (98H)

```
MOV R3, 98H      ; copy SCON to R3
```

Method 2 : Using direct address for SCON (98H) and R3 (03H)

```
MOV 03H, 98H     ; copy SCON to R3
```

Method 3 : Using indirect address for R3

```
MOV R1, # 03H       ; initialize pointer to R3
MOV @ R1, 98H       ; copy SCON to R3
```

Method 4 : Using PUSH instruction

```
MOV 81H, #02H       ; set the SP to address 02H in RAM
PUSH 98H            ; Push  SCON (98H) to address (03H)
```

Program 3 : Put the number 90H in R2 and R3

Method 1 : Use immediate addressing mode

```
MOV R2, #90H
MOV R3, #90H
```

Method 2 : Use immediate and register addressing

```
MOV R2, #90H
MOV R3, R2
```

Program 4 : Add two 8-bit numbers.

```
MOV A, #30H      ; (A)← 30
ADD A, #50H      ; (A)← (A) + 50H
```

Program 5 : Add two 16-bit numbers.

```
MOV DPTR, #2040H; (DPTR) ← 2040H (16-bit number)
MOV A, #2BH         ; (A) ← 2BH (lower byte of second
                    ;              16-bit number)
MOV B, #20H         ; (B)← 20H (Higher byte of second
                    ;             16-bit number)
ADD A, DPL          ; Add lower bytes
MOV DPL, A          ; Save result of lower byte addition
MOV A, B            ; Get higher byte of second number
                    ; in A
ADDC A, DPH         ; Add higher bytes with any carry
                    ; from lower byte addition
MOV DPH, A          ; Save result of higher byte addition
```

Program 6 : Find the 2's complement of a number in R0.

```
MOV A, R0           ; (A) ← (R0)
CPL A               ; 1's complement A
ADD A, #01          ; Add 1 to it to get 2's complement
```

Program 7 : Unpack the packed BCD number stored in the accumulator and save the result in R0 and R1 such that (R0)← LSB and (R1) ← MSB.

```
MOV B, A         ; Save the packed BCD number
ANL A, #0FH      ; Mask upper nibble of BCD number
MOV R0, A        ; Save the lower digit
MOV A, B         ; Get the packed BCD number
ANL A, #0F0H     ; Mask lower nibble of BCD number
SWAP A           ; Exchange the lower and upper nibbles
MOV R1,A         ; Save the upper digit.
```

Program 8 : Subtract two 8-bit numbers and exchange digits.

```
MOV A, #9F       ; Get the first number in A
MOV R0, #40      ; Get the second number in R0
CLR C            ; Clear carry
SUBB A, R0       ; A ← A–(R0)
SWAP A           ; Exchange digits
```

Program 9 : Subtract the contents of R1 of Bank0 from the contents of R0 of Bank2.

```
MOV PSW, #10    ; Select Bank2
MOV A, R0       ; (A) ← (R0) from Bank2
MOV PSW, #00    ; Select Bank 0
CLR C           ; Clear carry
SUBB A,R1       ; A ← A–(R1) from Bank0
```

Program 10 : Division two 8-bit numbers.

```
MOV A,#90       ; Get the first number in A
MOV B,#20       ; Get the second number in B
DIV AB          ; A ÷ B, Remainder in B and Quotient
                ; in A
```

Program 11 : Multiply two 8-bit numbers.

```
MOV A, #8F      ; Get the first number in A
MOV B, #79      ; Get the second number in B
MUL AB          ; A × B, Higher byte of result in B
                ; and lower byte of result in A
```

Program 12 : Program to convert 8-bit binary number to its equivalent BCD.

Program Logic :

Step 1 : Divide number with 100 decimal and save quotient i.e. save hundred's digit.

Step 2 : Make remainder as a new number.

Step 3 : Divide number with 10 decimal and save quotient i.e. save tens digit.

Step 4 : Save remainder as ones digit.

Sample Example :

		Quotient	Remainder
76H ÷ 100	=	1	12H
12H ÷ 10	=	1	8
76H	=	$(118)_{10}$	

Flowchart :

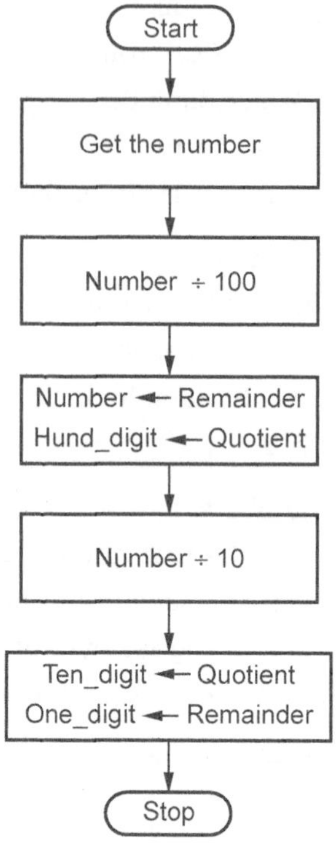

Program :

```
MOV A, #76H      ; Load the binary number in A
MOV B, #100      ; Load B with 100 decimal
DIV AB           ; Divide number with 100
MOV R0 ,A        ; Save the hundreds of the number
                 ; (Quotient of the previous division)
MOV A, B         ; Get the remainder
MOV B, #10       ; Load B with 10 decimal
DIV AB           ; Divide number with 10
MOV R1, A        ; Save the tens of the number
MOV R3, B        ; Save the ones of the number
```

Program 13 : Binary to Gray conversion.

Statement : Write a program to convert a given 8-bit binary number into its Gray code equivalent

Let us see the Binary - Gray conversion process.

- Get the binary number.
- MSB of result ← MSB of the binary number.
- XOR bits from left to right with their adjacent bits.

Example :

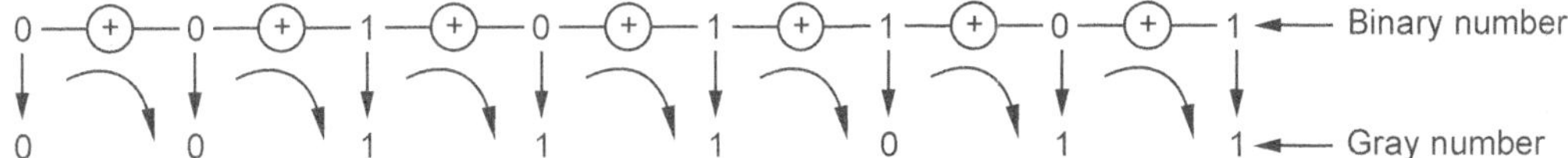

Program Logic :

To XOR each bit with its adjacent bit we right shift the contents of original number and then XOR the result with the original number.

Example :

```
  0 0 1 0 1 1 0 1   <-- Binary number
⊕
  0 0 0 1 0 1 1 0   <-- Right shifted binary number
 -----------------
  0 0 1 1 1 0 1 1   <-- Gray number
```

Flowchart :

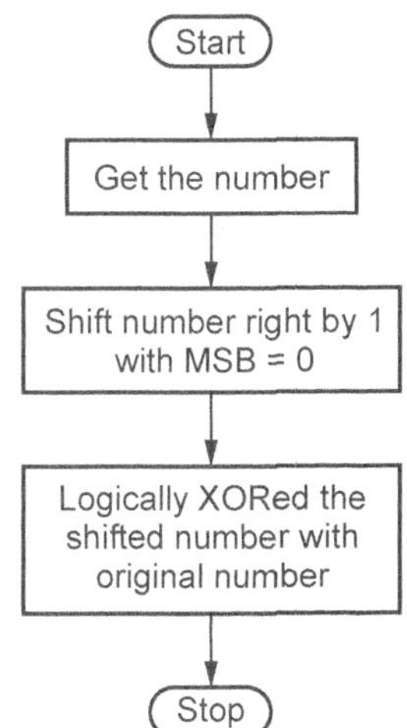

Program :

```
MOV A, #52H     ; Load binary number
MOV R0, A       ; Save binary number
CLR C           ; Clear carry flag so that after shifting
                ; the contents we will get MSB = 0
RRC A           ; right shift
XRL A, R0       ; XOR shifted contents with the original
                ; number
```

Program 14 : To add two 16-bit BCD numbers.

Flowchart :

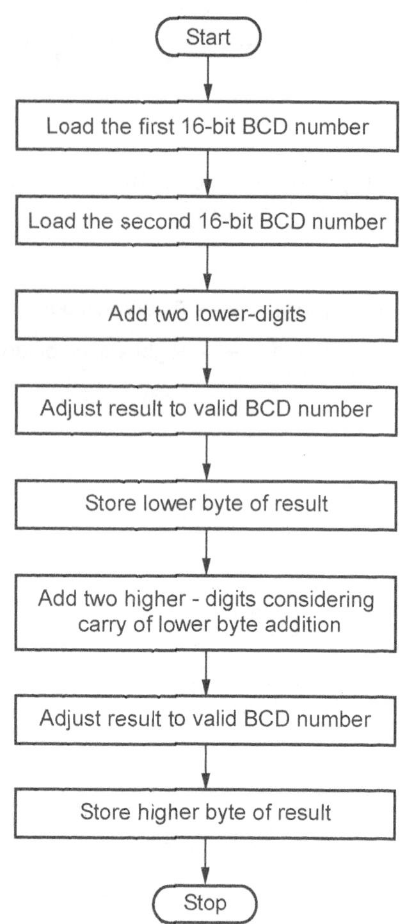

Program :

```
MOV DPTR, #1234H    ; Load first number
MOV R0, #20H        ; Load lower byte of second number
MOV R1, #30H        ; Load higher byte of second number
MOV A, R0           ; Get the lower byte of second number
ADD A, DPL          ; Add two lower bytes
DA A                ; Adjust result to valid BCD
MOV DPL, A          ; Store the sum of lower bytes
MOV A, R1           ; Get the higher byte of second number
ADDC A, DPH         ; Add two higher bytes considering
                    ; carry of lower byte addition
DA A                ; Adjust result to valid BCD
MOV DPH, A          ; Store the sum of higher bytes
```

Program 15 : Implementing a BCD multiply using MUL and DIV

```
MULBCD:   UNPACK TWO BCD DIGITS RECEIVED IN ACC, FIND THEIR
          PRODUCT, AND RETURN PRODUCT IN PACKED BCD FORMAT IN
          ACC
MULBCD :  MOV B, #10H     ; DIVIDE INPUT BY 16
          DIV AB          ; A AND B HOLD SEPARATED DIGITS
                          ; (EACH RIGHT JUSTIFIED IN REGISTER)
          MUL AB          ; A HOLDS PRODUCT IN
                          ; BINARY FORMAT
                          ; (0 - 99(DECIMAL)= 0 - 63H)
          MOV B, #10      ; DIVIDE PRODUCT BY 10
          DIV AB          ; A HOLDS # OF TENS, B
                          ; HOLDS REMAINDER
          SWAP A
          ORL A, B        ; PACK DIGITS
          RET
```

Program 16 : Subtract two 16-bit numbers.

```
MOV DPTR, #9080   ;  (DPTR) ← 9080H (16-bit number)
MOV B, #50H       ;  (B) ← 50H Higher byte of second number
MOV A, #40H       ;  (A) ← 40H Lower byte of second number
CLR C             ;  Clear carry
SUBB A, DPL       ;  Subtract lower bytes
MOV DPL, A        ;  Save result of lower byte subtraction
MOV A,B           ;  Get the higher byte
SUBB A, DPH       ;  Subtract higher byte with borrow
MOV DPH, A        ;  Save result of higher bytes subtraction
```

Program 17 : Generate BCD up counter and send each count to port A.

```
        MOV A, #00    ; Initialize counter
BACK :  MOV P1, A     ; Send count to port A
        ADD A, #01    ; Increment counter
        DA A          ; Decimal adjust the counter
        AJMP BACK     ; Jump BACK
```

Program 18 : Find the maximum number from a given 8-bit ten numbers.

Flowchart :

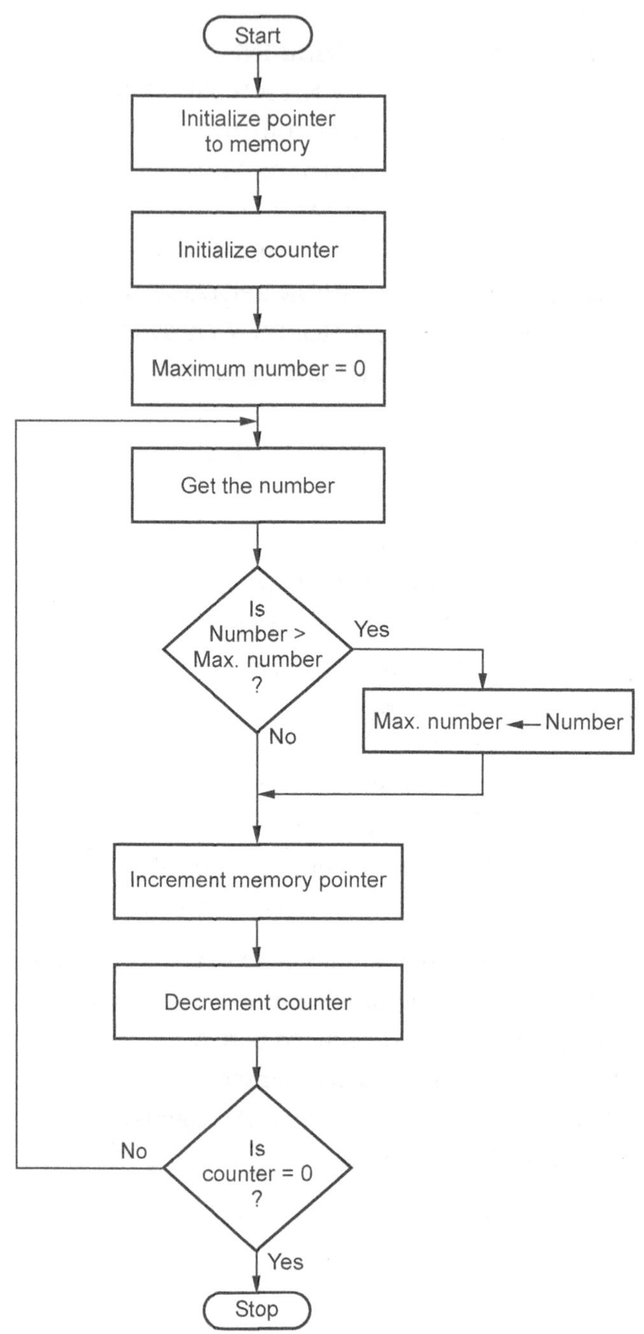

Program :

```
         MOV DPTR, #2000   ; Initialize pointer to memory where
                           ; numbers are stored
         MOV R0, #0A       ; Initialize counter
         MOV R3, #00       ; Maximum  = 0
AGAIN :  MOVX A, @DPTR     ; Get the number from memory
         CJNE A, R3, NE    ; Compare number with maximum number
         AJMP SKIP         ; If equal go to SKIP
NE :     JC SKIP           ; If not equal check for carry, if
                           ; carry go to SKIP
         MOV R3, A         ; Otherwise maximum = number
SKIP :   INC DPTR          ; Increment memory pointer
         DJNZ R0, AGAIN    ; Decrement count, if count = 0 stop
                           ; otherwise go to AGAIN
```

Program 19 : Arrange the given ten 8-bit numbers in the ascending order.

Flowchart : (See on next page)

Program :

```
         MOV R0, #09        ; Initialize counter1
AGAIN :  MOV DPTR, #2000H   ; Initialize memory pointer
         MOV R1, #09        ; Initialize counter2
BACK :   MOV R2, DPL        ; Save lower byte of memory address
         MOVX A, @DPTR      ; Get the number
         MOV B, A           ; Save the number
         INC DPTR           ; Increment memory pointer
         MOVX A, @DPTR      ; Get the next number
         CJNE A,B,NE        ; If not equal check for greater or
                            ; less
         AJMP SKIP          ; Otherwise go to skip
NE :     JNC SKIP           ; If
         MOV DPL, R2        ; [ Exchange
         MOVX @DPTR, A      ;   the contents
         INC DPTR           ;   of two
         MOV A,B            ;   memory
         MOVX @DPTR, A      ;   locations ]
SKIP :   DJNZ R1, BACK      ; If R1 not equal to 0 go to BACK
         DJNZ R0, AGAIN     ; If R0 not equal to 0 go to AGAIN
```

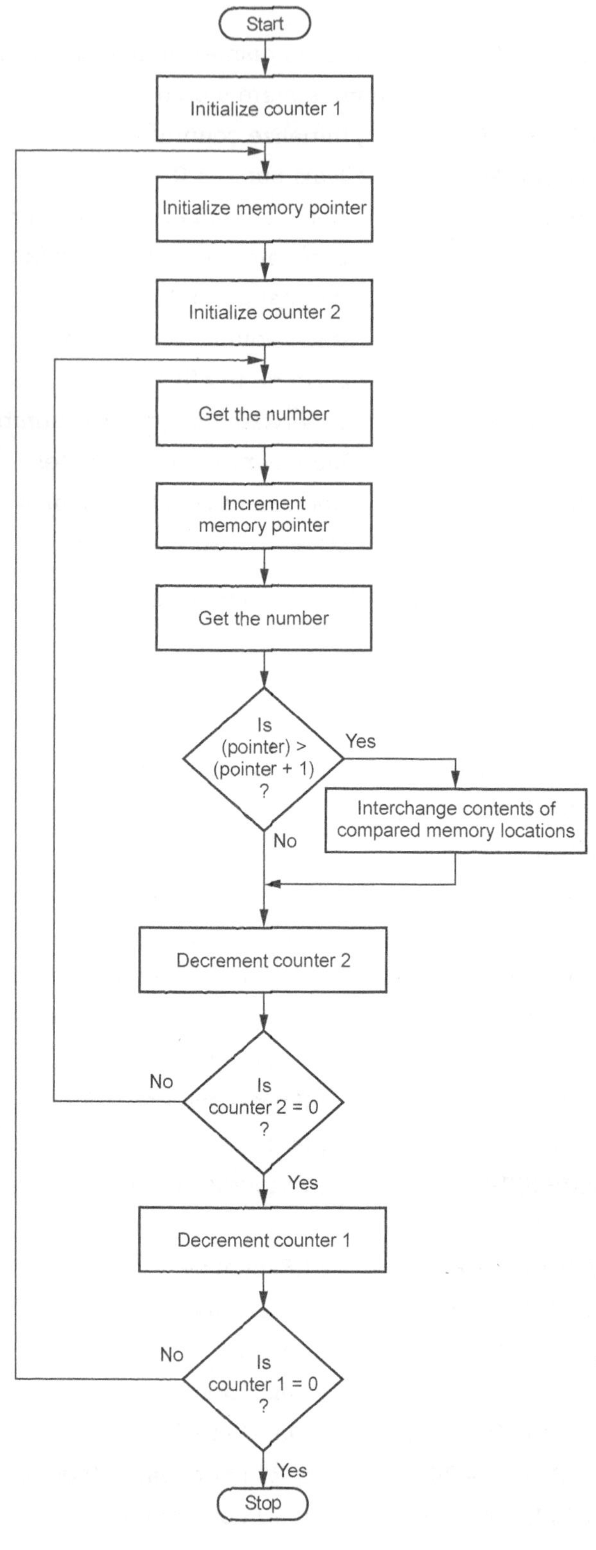
Start
Initialize counter 1
Initialize memory pointer
Initialize counter 2
Get the number
Increment memory pointer
Get the number
Is (pointer) > (pointer + 1) ?
Yes
Interchange contents of compared memory locations
No
Decrement counter 2
No
Is counter 2 = 0 ?
Yes
Decrement counter 1
No
Is counter 1 = 0 ?
Yes
Stop

Program 20 : Find the number of negative and positive numbers in a given array.

Flowchart :

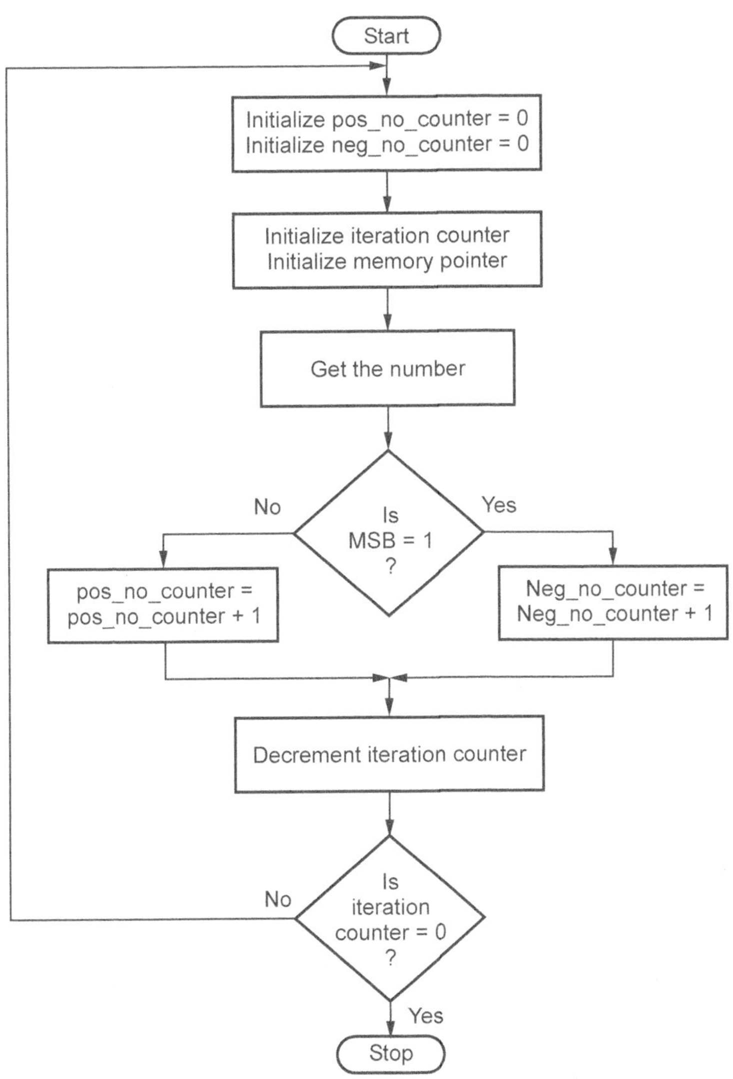

Program :

```
MOV R0, #00         ; Initialize counter = 0 for negative
                    ; numbers
MOV R1, R0          ; Initialize counter = 0 for positive
                    ; numbers
MOV R2, #0AH        ; Initialize counter = 10
MOV DPTR, #2000H    ; Initialize memory pointer
```

```
BACK :  MOVX A, @DPTR     ; Get the number
        ANL A, #80H       ; Mask lower 7 bits
        JZ SKIP           ; If Z = 0 goto SKIP
        INC R0            ; Otherwise increment negative number
                          ; count
        AJMP LAST         ; Go to LAST
SKIP :  INC R1            ; Increment positive number count
LAST:   DJNZ R2, BACK     ; Decrement R2 if not zero goto BACK
```

Program 21 : Count number of one's in a number.

Flowchart :

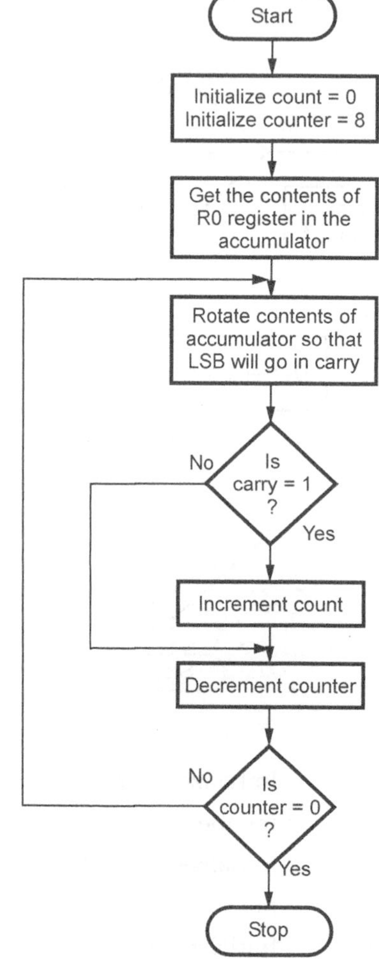

Program :

```
        MOV R2, #0      ; Initialize one's counter = 0
        MOV R1, #08     ; Initialize iteration count
        MOV R0, #56     ; Load number
        MOV A, R0       ; Get the number in accumulator
BACK :  RRC A           ; Rotate A and CY ← LSB
        JNC SKIP        ; If carry is not zero go to skip
        INC R2          ; Otherwise increment one's counter
SKIP :  DJNZ R1, BACK   ; Decrement iteration count and if not
                        ; zero repeat
```

Program 22 : Count number of zero's in a number.

Flowchart :

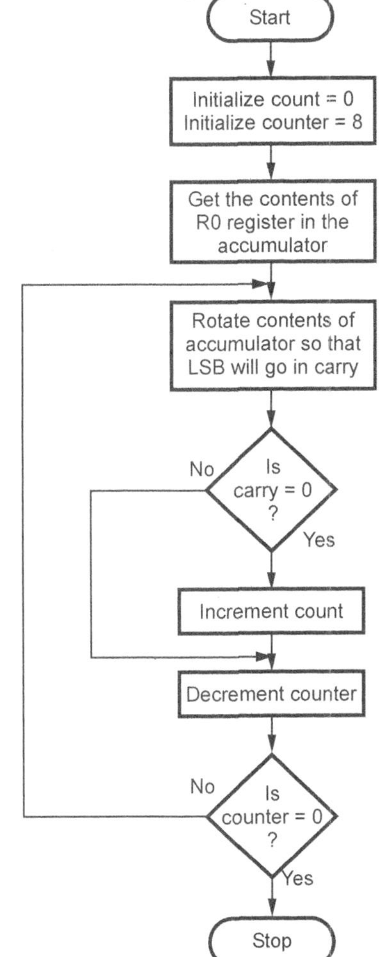

Program :

```
        MOV R2, #0       ; Initialize zero's counter = 0
        MOV R1, #08      ; Initialize iteration count
        MOV R0, #56      ; Load number
        MOV A, R0        ; Get the number in accumulator
BACK :  RRC A            ; Rotate A and CY ← LSB
        JC SKIP          ; If carry is zero go to skip
        INC R2           ; Otherwise increment zero's counter
SKIP :  DJNZ R1, BACK    ; Decrement iteration count and if not
                         ; zero repeat
```

Program 23 : Count number of one's and zero's in a number.

Flowchart :

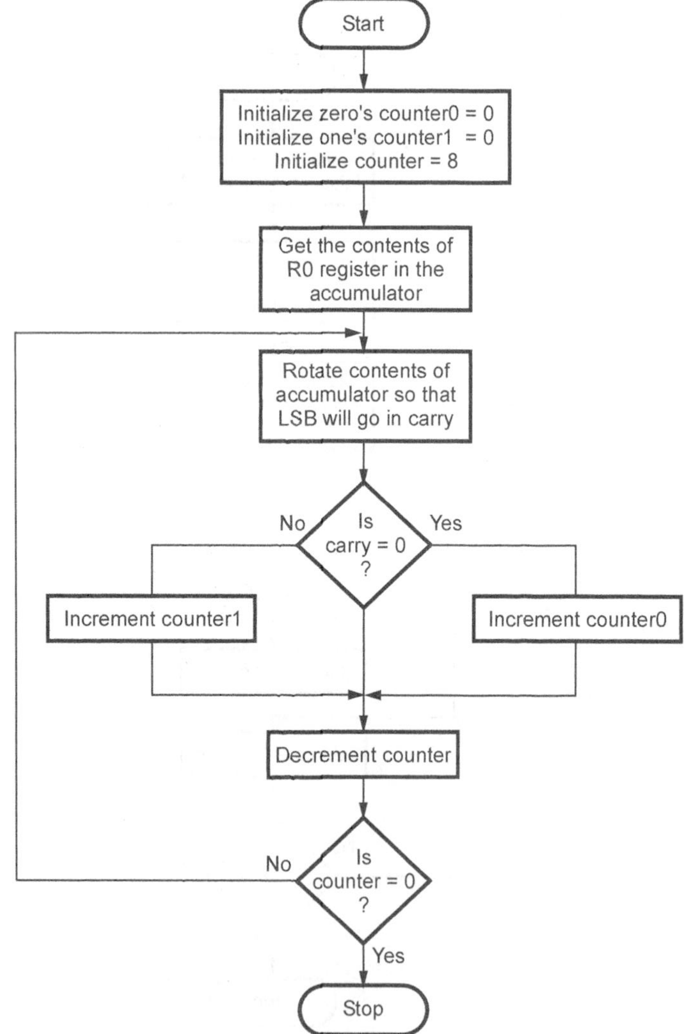

Program :

```
        MOV R2, #0        ; Initialize one's counter = 0
        MOV R3, #0        ; Initialize zero's counter = 0
        MOV R1, #08       ; Initialize iteration count
        MOV R0, #56       ; Load number
        MOV A, R0         ; Get the number in accumulator
BACK :  RRC A             ; Rotate A and CY ← LSB
        JC SKIP           ; If carry is zero go to skip
        INC R3            ; Otherwise increment zero's counter
        AJMP LAST         ; Go to last
SKIP :  INC R2            ; Increment one's counter
LAST :  DJNZ R1, BACK     ; Decrement iteration count and if not
                          ; zero repeat
```

Program 24 : To generate a square wave on the port 1.

```
        MOV SP, #7H           ; Initialize stack pointer since we are
                              ; using subroutine program
BACK :  MOV P1, #00H          ; Send 00H on port 1 to generate low
                              ; level of square wave
        ACALL DELAY           ; Wait for sometime
        MOV P1, #0FFH         ; Send FFH on port 1 to generate high
                              ; level of square wave
        ACALL DELAY           ; Wait for sometime
        SJMP BACK             ; Repeat the sequence
DELAY : MOV R1, #0FFH         ; Load count
AGAIN : DJNZ R1, AGAIN        ; Decrement count and repeat the process
                              ; until count is zero
        RET                   ; Return to main program
```

Program 25 : To generate a square wave on the port pin P1.0.

```
        MOV SP, #7H           ; Initialize stack pointer since we are
                              ; using subroutine program
        CLR P1.0              ; Send 0 on port 1.0 to generate low
                              ; level of square wave
        ACALL DELAY           ; Wait for sometime
        SETB P1.0             ; Send 1 on port 1.0 to generate high
                              ; level of square wave
        ACALL DELAY           ; Wait for sometime
        SJMP BACK             ; Repeat the sequence
DELAY : MOV R1, #0FFH         ; Load count
```

```
AGAIN :    DJNZ R1, AGAIN    ; Decrement count and repeat the process
                             ; until Count is zero
           RET               ; Return to main program
```

Program 26 : To find the sum of 10 numbers stored in the array.

Statement : Calculate the sum of series of numbers. The length of the series is in memory location 2200H and the series itself begins from memory location 2201H.

a. Assume the sum to be 8-bit number so you can ignore carries. Store the sum at memory location 2300H.

b. Assume the sum to be 16-bit number. Store the sum at memory locations 2300H and 2301H.

a. Sample problem

2200H = 04H

2201H = 20H

2202H = 15H

2203H = 13H

2204H = 22H

Result = 20 + 15 + 13 + 22 = 6AH

∴ 2300H = 6AH

Flowchart :

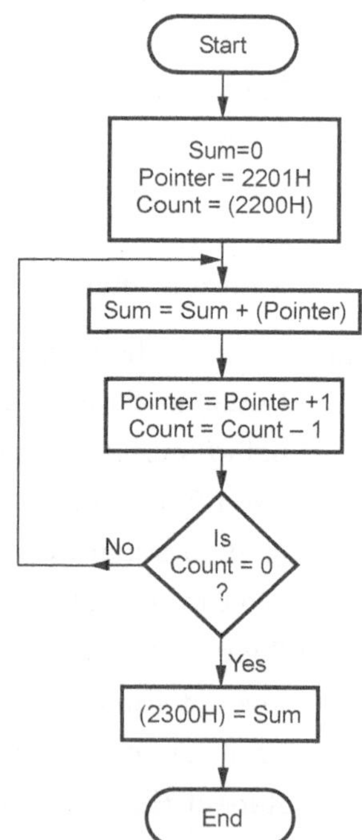

Program :

a)

```
        MOV DPTR, #2200H  ; Initialize memory pointer
        MOVX A, @DPTR     ; Get the count
        MOV R0, #10       ; Initialize the iteration counter
        INC DPTR          ; Initialize pointer to array of numbers
        MOV R1, #00       ; Result = 0
BACK :  MOVX A, @DPTR     ; Get the number
        ADD A, R1         ; A ← Result + A
        MOV R1, A         ; Result ← A
        INC DPTR          ; Increment the array pointer
        DJNZ R0, BACK     ; Decrement iteration count if not zero
                          ; repeat
        MOV DPTR, #2300H  ; Initialize memory pointer
        MOV A, R1         ; Get the result
        MOVX @DPTR, A     ; Store the result
```

b. Sample problem

2200H = 04H 2201H = 9AH

2202H = 52H 2203H = 89H 2204H = 3EH

Result = 9AH + 52H + 89H + 3EH = 1B3H

∴ 2300H = B3H Lower byte 2301H = 01H Higher byte

Flowchart : (See on next page)

Program :

b)

```
        MOV DPTR, #2200H  ; Initialize memory pointer
        MOVX A, @DPTR     ; Get the count
        MOV R0, #10       ; Initialize the iteration counter
        INC DPTR          ; Initialize pointer to array of numbers
        MOV R2, #00       ; [Make
        MOV R1, #00       ; result = 00H]
BACK :  MOVX A, @DPTR     ; Get the number
        ADD A, R1         ; A ← Result + A
        MOV R1, A         ; Result ← A
        ADDC R2, #00      ; If carry exists, add it to MSD
     INC DPTR             ; increment the array pointer
     DJNZ R0, BACK        ; Decrement iteration count if not zero
                          ; repeat
     MOV DPTR, #2300H     ; Initialize memory pointer
     MOV A, R1            ; Get the lower byte of result
```

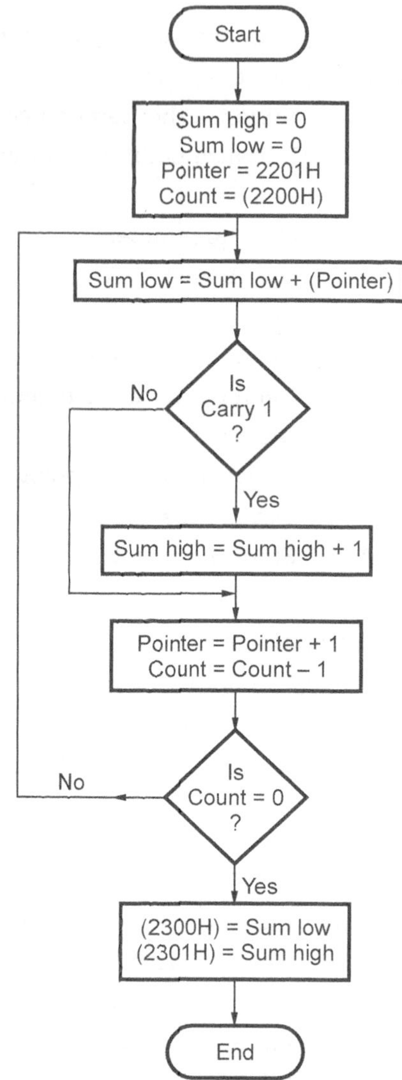


```
MOVX @DPTR, A     ; Store the lower byte of result
INC DPTR          ; Increment memory pointer
MOV A, R2         ; Get the higher byte of result
MOVX @DPTR, A     ; Store the higher byte of result
```

Program 27 : Data transfer from memory block B1 to memory block B2.

Statement : Assume two blocks are non-overlapped.

Flowchart :

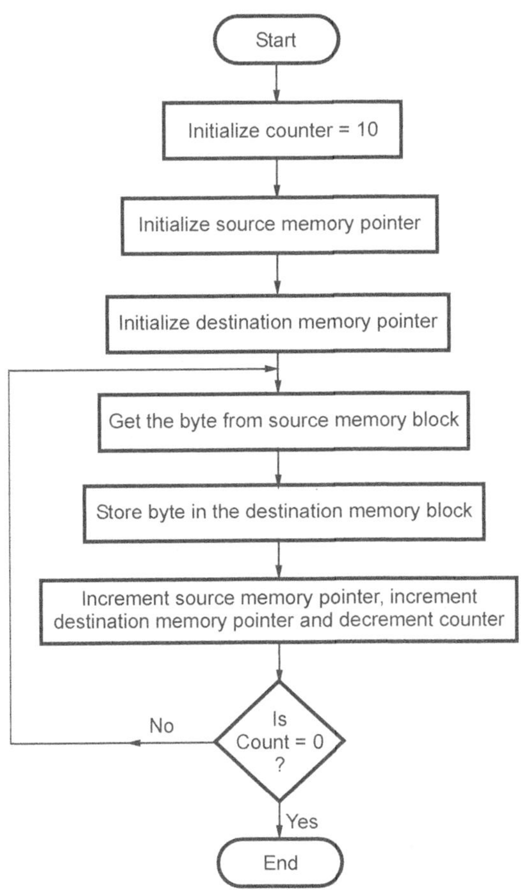

Program :

```
        MOV R2, #1          ; Initialize iteration counter
        MOV R1, #20H        ; Initialize source memory pointer
        MOV R0, #30H        ; Initialize destination memory pointer
BACK :  MOV A, @R1          ; Get data
        MOV @R0, A          ; Store data
        INC R1              ; Increment source memory pointer
        INC R0              ; Increment destination memory pointer
        DJNZ R2, BACK       ; Decrement iteration count and if not
                            ; zero repeat
```

Program 28 : Data transfer from memory block B1 to memory block B2.

Statement : Assume two blocks are overlapped.

Flowchart :

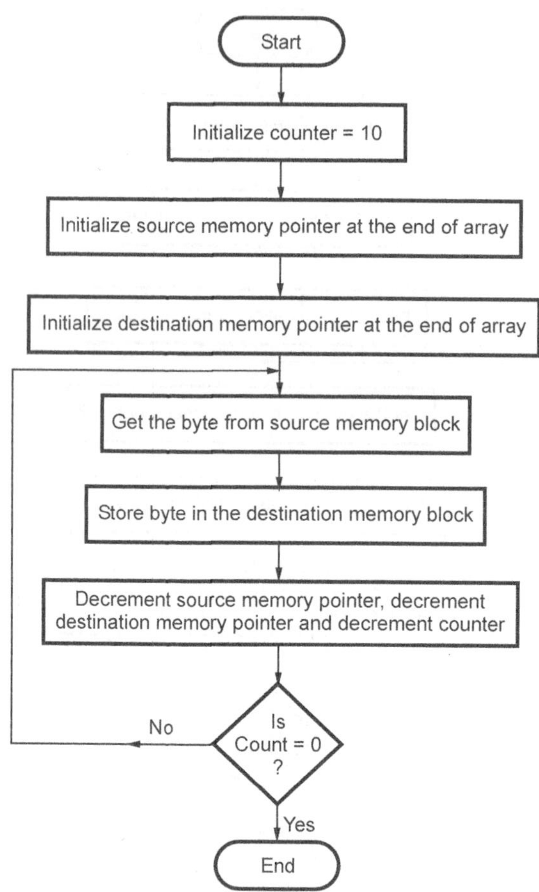

Program :

```
        MOV R2, #10      ; Initialize iteration counter
        MOV R1, #29H     ; Initialize source memory pointer
        MOV R0, #32H     ; Initialize destination memory pointer
BACK :  MOV A, @R1       ; Get data
        MOV @R0, A       ; Store data
        DEC R1           ; Decrement source memory pointer
        DEC R0           ; Decrement destination memory pointer
        DJNZ R2, BACK    ; Decrement iteration count and if not
                         ; zero repeat
```

Program 29 : To search a byte in a given numbers.

Statement : Search the given byte in the list of 50 numbers stored in the consecutive memory locations 2200H and 2201H. Assume that byte is 76H. If byte is not found store 00 at 2200H and 2201H.

Flowchart :

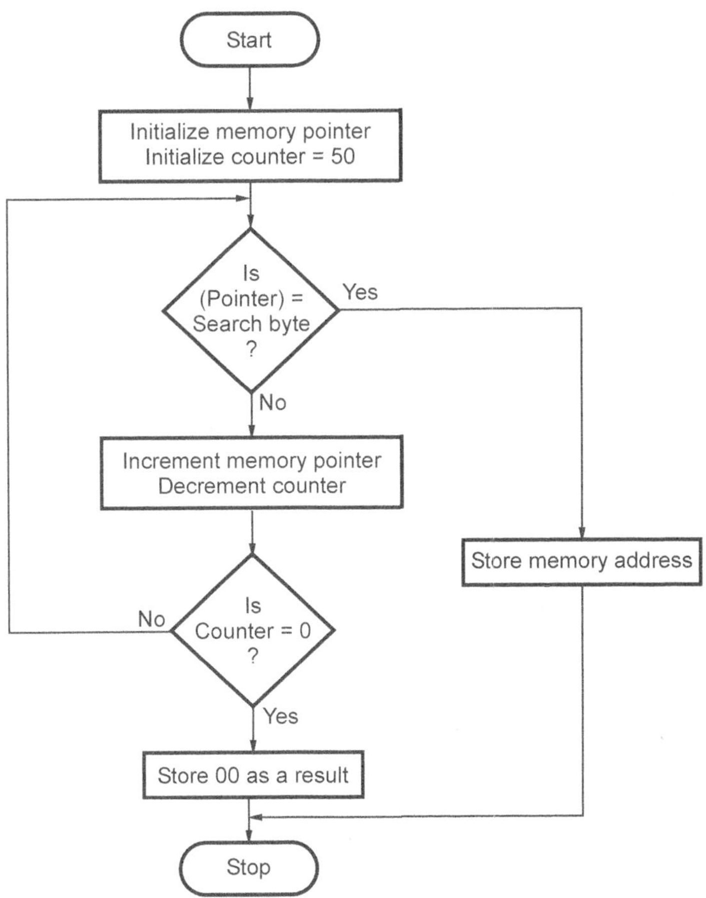

Program :

```
        MOV R1, #00          ; [load R1 and R2 with 00 so that if
        MOV R2, #00          ; byte is not found we can load these
                             ; contents at 2200H and 2201H
                             ; locations]
        MOV R0, #50          ; Initialize iteration counter
        MOV DPTR, #2000H     ; Initialize memory pointer
BACK :  MOVX A, @DPTR        ; Get the number
        CJNE A, #76H, SKIP   ; Search byte 76H if not equal
                             ; go to SKIP
        MOV R1, DPL          ; [otherwise store
        MOV R2, DPH          ; the address of the byte]
        SJMP LAST
SKIP :INC DPTR
```

```
        DJNZ R0, BACK       ; Decrement iteration count and if not
                            ;  zero repeat
LAST :  MOV DPTR, #2200H    ; Initialize memory pointer
        MOV A, R1           ; Get the lower byte of address
        MOVX @DPTR, A       ; store the lower byte of address
        INC DPTR            ; Increment memory pointer
        MOV A, R2           ; Get the higher byte of address
        MOVX @DPTR, A       ; store the higher byte of address
```

Program 30 : Multiply two 8-bit numbers using repetitive addition.

Statement : Multiply two 8-bit numbers stored in memory locations 2200H and 2201H. Store the result in memory locations 2300H and 2301H.

Sample problem

(2200H) = B2H
(2201H) = 03H
Result = B2H + B2H + B2H
= 216H
(2300H) = 16H
(2301H) = 02H

Flowchart :

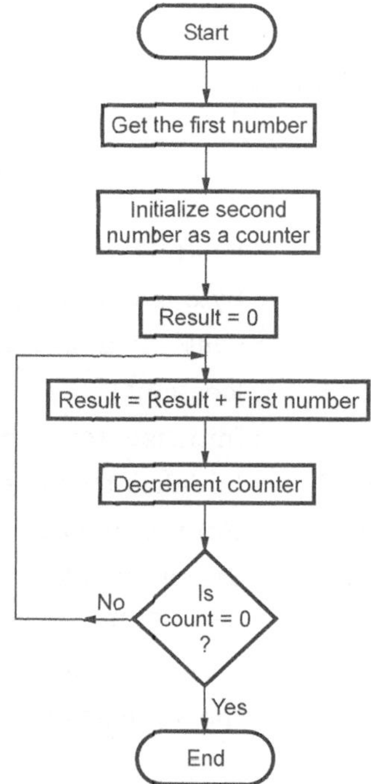

Program :

```
        MOV DPTR, #2200H ; [Get the first
        MOVX A, @DPTR    ; number]
        MOV R0, A        ; store the number
        INC DPTR         ; [Get the second
        MOVX A, @DPTR    ; number]
        MOV R1, A        ; store it as a counter
        MOV R2, #00      ; [Make
        MOV R3, #00      ; result = 0]
BACK :  MOV A, R2        ; Get result (lower byte)
        ADD A, R0        ; Result = Result + number
        MOV R2, A        ; store result (lower byte)
        ADDC R3, #00     ; If carry exists, add 1 to higher byte
        DJNZ R1, BACK    ; Decrement counter, if not zero repeat
        MOV A, R2        ; Get the lower byte of result
        MOV DPTR, #2300H ; [store the
        MOVX @DPTR, A    ; lower byte of result]
        MOV A, R3        ; Get the higher byte of result
        INC DPTR         ; [store the
        MOVX @DPTR, A    ; higher byte of result]
```

Program 31 : To find the average of given N numbers.

Program Logic :

- Calculate the sum of N numbers.
- Divide sum by the N

Flowchart : (See on next page)

Program :

```
        MOV R2, #00     ; [Make
        MOV R3, #00     ; result = 0]
        MOV R0, #10     ; Initialize count
        MOV R1, #20H    ; Initialize memory pointer
BACK :  MOV A, @R1      ; Get the number
        ADD A, R2       ; Add lower byte
        MOV R2 A        ; save result
        ADDC R3, #00    ; If carry exists add Carry to higher byte
        INC R1          ; Increment memory pointer
        DJNZ R0, BACK   ; Decrement counter and if not zero
                        ; repeat
```

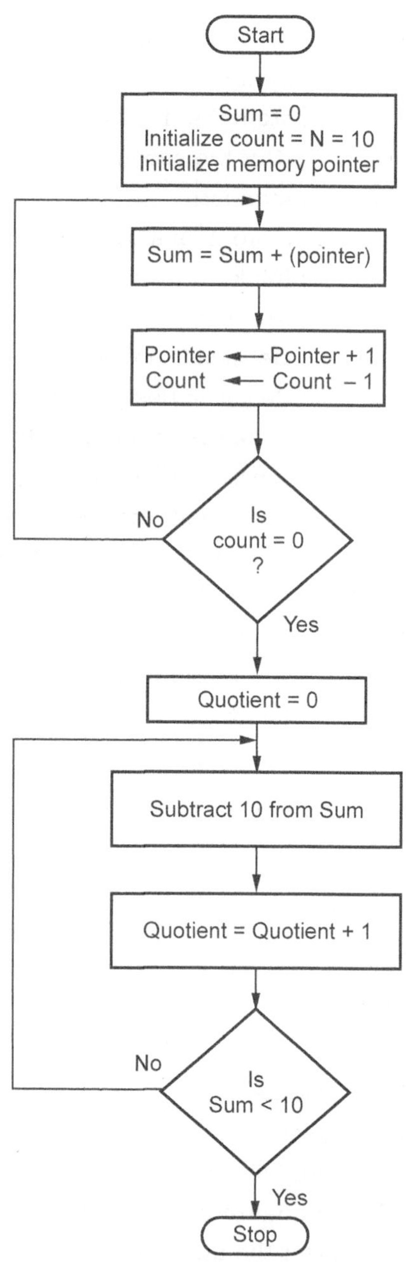


```
        MOV R0, #00      ; Make quotient = 0
AGAIN : CLR C            ; clear carry to perform subtraction
                         ; without borrow
        MOV A, R2        ; Get the lower byte
        SUBB A, #10H     ; Sub 10H from it
        MOV R2, A        ; Store result
```

```
        SUBB R3, #00H           ; If borrow exist subtract 1 from MSD
        INC R0                  ; Increment quotient
        CJNE R3, #00, AGAIN     ; if MSB not equal zero repeat
        MOV A, R2               ; [otherwise check LSB
        CLR C                   ; whether it is
        SUBB A, #10H            ; less than 10H]
        JNC AGAIN               ; If not repeat
```

Note : Quotient in R0 and Remainder in R2.

Program 32 : To find factorial of a number

$$N! = N \times (N-1) \times (N-2) \times (N-3) \times \ldots \times 2 \times 1$$

For example :

$$6! = 6 \times 5 \times 4 \times 3 \times 2 \times 1 = 720$$

Flowchart :

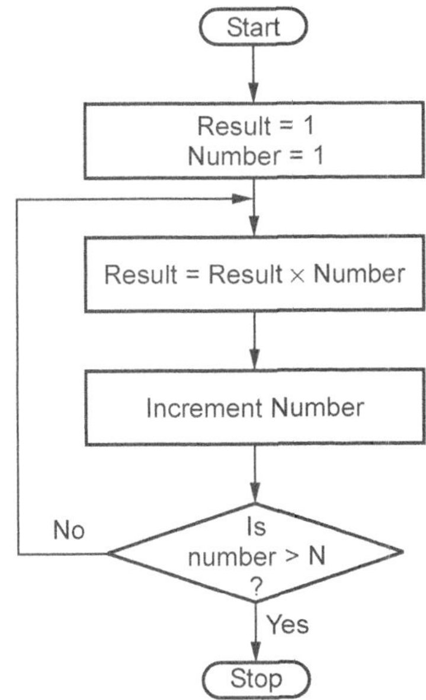

Program

```
        MOV A,#01               ; Store 01 in A register
        MOV B, A                ; Store 01 in B register
CAL :   MUL AB                  ; Multiply two numbers
        INC B                   ; increment number
        CJNE B, #07H, CAL       ; Check whether number is 7. If number
                                ; is 7 we have to stop
```

Note :

- This program can calculate factorial of numbers from 0 through 6.
- Result of factorial is available in A (LSB) and B (MSB) registers.

Program 33 : To find Fibonacci series of N given terms.

The Fibonacci series is given as 0 1 1 2 3 5 8 13 21 ...

Hence we can write :

First term = 0

Second term = 1

Third term = First term + Second term = 0 + 1 = 1

Fourth term = Second term + Third term = 1 + 1 = 2

Fifth term = Third term + Fourth term = 1 + 2 = 3

and so on. In general we can write

N^{th} term = N – 2 term + N – 1 term

Flowchart : (See on next page)

Program :

```
        MOV R0, #10          ; Initialize term count
        MOV R1, #20H         ; Initialize array pointer
        MOV @R1, #0          ; Store 1st term as 0
        INC R1               ; increment memory pointer
        MOV @R1, #1          ; store 2nd term as 1
BACK :  MOV A, @R1           ; Get the current term
        DEC R1               ; Pointer to previous term
        ADD A, @R1           ; Add current term and previous term
        INC R1               ; [Point to
        INC R1               ; next term]
        MOV @R1, A           ; Store next term
        CJNE @R1, 10,BACK    ; Check whether last term calculated
                             ; if not repeat the process
```

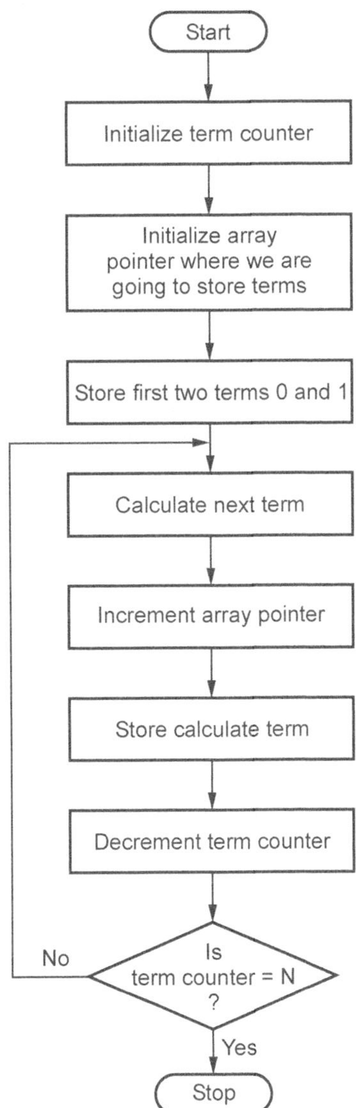

Program 34 : Write an assembly language program to move 5 bytes of data stored at location 8000H onwards to the location C000H onwards and vice-versa.

Solution :

```
        MOV R0, #05       ;  Initialize count = 5
        MOV DPL, #00H     ;  Initialize memory pointer
        MOV DPH, #80H     ;  Adjust the memory pointer to
                          ;  address the first memory
BACK :  MOVX A, @DPTR     ;  Get data 1
```

```
        MOV R1, A           ; Save data 1 temporarily
        MOV DPH, #C0H       ; Adjust the memory pointer to
                            ; address the second memory
        MOVX A, @DPTR       ; Get data 2
        MOV R2, A           ; Save data 2 temporarily
        MOV A, R1           ; Get data 1
        MOVX @DPTR, A       ; Save data 1
        MOV DPH, #80H       ; Adjust memory pointer to
                            ; address the first memory
        MOV A,R2            ; Get data 2
        MOVX @DPTR, A       ; Save data 2
        INC DPTR            ; Increment memory pointer
        DJNZ R0, BACK       ; If count ≠ 0, repeat
```

Program 35 : An array of 10 numbers is stored at location 4000H onwards. Write an assembly language program to sort the numbers and store even numbers from location 5000H onwards and odd numbers from location 6000H onwards.

Program :

```
        MOV R0, # 0A        ; Initialize counter
        MOV R1, #00H        ; Initialize memory pointer
        MOV R2, #40H
        MOV R3, #00H        ; Initialize even memory pointer
        MOV R4, #50H
        MOV R5, #00H        ; Initialize odd memory pointer
        MOV R6, #60H
BACK :  MOV DPL, R1         ; Load memory address
        MOV DPH, R2
        MOVX A, @DPTR       ; Get data
        JB ACC.0, NEXT      ; Check LSB of accumulator
                            ; if 1 goto NEXT (odd)
        MOV DPL, R3         ; Load even memory address
        MOV DPH, R4
        MOVX @DPTR, A       ; Store even data
        INC R3              ; Increment even memory pointer
        SJMP NEXT1
NEXT :  MOV DPL, R5         ; Load odd memory address
        MOV DPH, R6
        MOVX @DPTR, A       ; Store odd data
        INC R5              ; Increment odd memory pointer
```

```
NEXT :  INC R1             ;  Increment memory pointer
        DJNZ R0, BACK      ;  If count #0, repeat
```

Program 36 : Write an assembly language program to realize following logic circuit using Boolean instructions of 8051.

Solution : Let us assume that input a is connected to P1.0, input b is connected by P1.1 and output Y is connected at P2.0.


```
        MOV P1, #0FFH      ;  Configure port1 as input
        MOV A, P1          ;  Read port 1
        JB P1.0 NEXT       ;  If P1.0 is set go to NEXT
        JB P1.1, NEXT1     ;  If P1.1 is set goto NEXT1
        CLR P2.0           ;  If P1.0=P1.1=0 make P2.0=0
        SJMP LAST
NEXT1 : SETB P2.0          ;  If P1.0 = 0, P1.1=1 make P2.0=1
        SJMP LAST
NEXT :  JB P1.1, NEXT2
        SETB P2.0          ;  If P1.0=1, P1.1=0 make P2.0=1
        SJMP LAST
NEXT2 : CLR P2.0           ;  If P1.0 = 1, P1.1 = 1
                           ;  make P2.0 = 0
LAST :  RET
```

Program 37 : Write a program to load accumulator with values 55H and complement 70 times.

```
        MOV R0, #70        ;  Initialize iteration count
        MOV A, # 55H       ;  load 55H in accumulator
HERE :  CPL A              ;  Complement accumulator
        DJNZ R0, HERE      ;  Repeat till R0 = 0
```

Program 38 : Program to count the number of ONE's and ZERO's in two consecutive data memory locations.

Solution :

```
        ORG 100 H          ; Start at location 100 H
        MOV R2, #0         ; Initialize one's counter = 0
        MOV R3, # 0        ; Initialize zero's counter = 0
        MOV R1, # 08       ; Initialize iteration count
        MOV R0, 40H        ; Load number from first memory location
        MOV A, R0          ; Get the number in accumulator
```

```
BACK :   RRC A              ; Rotate A and CY ← LSB
         JC SKIP            ; If carry is zero go to skip
         INC R3             ; Otherwise increment zero's counter
         AJMP LAST          ; Go to last
SKIP :   INC R2             ; Increment one's counter
LAST :   DJNZ R1, BACK      ; Decrement iteration count and if not
                            ; zero repeat
         MOV R1, # 08       ; Initialize iteration count
         MOV R0, 41H        ; Load number from next memory location
         MOV A, R0          ; Get the number in accumulator
BACK1 :  RRC A              ; Rotate A and CY ← LSB
         JC SKIP1           ; If carry is zero go to skip1
         INC R3             ; Otherwise increment zero's counter
         AJMP LAST1         ; Go to last1
SKIP1 :  INC R2             ; Increment one's counter
LAST1 :  DJNZ R1, BACK1     ; Decrement iteration count and if not
                            ; zero repeat
         END                ; end of program
```

Program 39 : Write a program to save the status of bits P1.3 and P1.4 on RAM bit location 5 and 6 respectively.

Solution :

```
         JNB P1.3, NEXT     ;  Check bit P1.3, if 0 then goto NEXT
         SETB 05            ;  P1.3 = 1, therefore, set bit location 5 = 1
         SJMP SKIP          ;  Skip next instruction
NEXT :   CLR 05             ;  Clear bit location 5
SKIP :   JNB P1.4, NEXT 1   ;  Check bit 1.4, if 0 then goto NEXT1
         SETB 06            ;  P1.4 = 1, therefore, set bit location 6 = 1
         SJMP SKIP 1        ;  Skip next instruction
NEXT 1 : CLR 06             ;  Clear bit location 6
Skip 1 : -------
```

Program 40 : What is the content of R5 after execution of the following program ?

```
        MOV A, #0
        MOV R2, #10
AGAIN : ADD A, #03
        DJNZ R2, AGAIN
        MOV R5, A
```

Solution : R5 = $(30)_{10}$ = $(1E)_H$

Review Questions

Section 18.1

Q.1 *What are the addressing modes supported by 8051 ?* **Dec.-09**

Q.2 *Explain the different addressing modes in 8051 in detail.* **June-08, Dec.-07,08,11 Marks 8**

Q.3 *What are the addressing modes of 8051 microcontroller ?* **Dec.-11, Marks 2**

Q.4 *What is register indirect addressing mode of microcontroller 8051 ? Give example.* **June-11, Marks 2**

Section 18.2

Q.1 *List the different types of 8051 instructions.* **May-10**

Q.2 *Give the classification of 8051 instruction set.*

Section 18.3

Q.1 *Write the I/O related instructions in microcontroller 8051.* **Dec.-08**

Q.2 *What is the operation carried out when 8051 executes the instruction MOVC A, @ A + DPTR ?* **Dec.-07**

Q.3 *Mention the I/O instructions of 8051 microcontroller.* **Dec.-11, Marks 2**

Q.4 *Explain the data transfer instructions and program control instructions of 8051 microcontroller.* **May-11, Marks 8**

Q.5 *Explain the operations carried out when the following instructions are executed by 8051.*
i) MOVX @ R0,A ii) MOVC A,@A + PC iii) RLC A iv) CJNE A, 50H, L2
v) XCH A, 30H where L2 and L3 are labels. **Dec.-07, Marks 16**

Section 18.4

Q.1 *What is the operation of the given 8051 microcontroller instructions : XRL A, direct ?* **May-11, Marks 2**

Q.2 *Explain the instruction set of 8051 microcontroller.* **May-10, Marks 10**

Section 18.5

Q.1 *What is the time taken to execute MUL instruction in 8031 ?* **May-05**

Q.2 *How can you perform multiplication using 8051 microcontroller ?* **May-08**

Q.3 *List the arithmetic instructions of microcontroller 8051.* **June-11, Marks 2**

Section 18.6

Q.1 *Name any four bit manipulation instructions in microcontroller 8051.* **May-08**

Q.2 *What are the various operations performed by boolean variable instructions of 8051 ?* **May-10**

Q.3 *What are the different operations performed by boolean variable instructions of 8051 ?* **May-11, Marks 2**

Section 18.8

Q.1 *What are the uses of LCALL and LJUMP instructions of 8051 ?* **Dec-09**

Q.2 *Explain about the instruction DJNZ.* **June-09**

Section 18.10

Q.1 *What is machine language ?*

Q.2 *What is assembly language ?*

Q.3 *Give comparison between assembly language and machine language.*

Q.4 *Write a short note on the following*
a) Assembler b) Compiler c) Linker d) Cross assembler e) Macro assembler.

Q.5 *How assembly language program is created, assembled and made ready to run ?*

Q.6 *List files required during assembly programming.*

Q.7 *Explain the data type of 8051.*

Q.8 *What are assembler directives ? Explain.*

Q.9 *Describe DB, ORG, EQU, END directive of IC 8051 microcontroller.*

Q.10 *Explain the function of following directives.*
i) DB ii) EQU iii) ORG
iv) DATA v) END vi) CODE

Section 18.11

Q.1 *Write an 8051 based assembly language program for performing four basic arithmetic operations on two data.* **May-10, Marks 6**

Two Marks Questions with Answers

Q.1 ***What is the time taken to execute MUL instruction in 8031 ?*** **May-05**

Ans. : Refer section 18.5.4.

Q.2 *Give the PSW setting for making register bank 2 as default register bank in 8051 microcontroller ?* **June-07**

Ans. : Refer program 9.

Q.3 *What is the operation carried out when 8051 executes the instruction MOVC A, @ A + DPTR ?* **Dec.-07**

Ans. : Refer section 18.3.2.

Q.4 *Name any four bit manipulation instructions in microcontroller 8051.* **May-08**

Ans. : Refer section 18.6.

Q.5 *How can you perform multiplication using 8051 microcontroller ?* **May-08**

Ans. : Refer section 18.5.4.

Q.6 *Write the I/O related instructions in microcontroller 8051.* **Dec.-08**

Ans. : Refer section 18.3.

Q.7 *What is output of the program ?*

MOV R0, A

XRL A, #3FH

XRL A, R0 **June-09**

Ans. : The contents of A register will be 3FH and contents of R0 will be the initial contents of A.

Q.8 *Explain about the instruction DJNZ.* **June-09**

Ans. : Refer section 18.8.2.

Q.9 *What are the addressing modes supported by 8051?* **Dec.-09**

Ans. : Refer section 18.1.

Q.10 *Write an 8051 program to divide two 8-bit numbers.* **Dec.-09**

Ans. : Refer program 10.

Q.11 *What are the uses of LCALL and LJUMP instructions of 8051?* **Dec.-09**

Ans. : Refer section 18.8.

Q.12 *List the different types of 8051 instructions.* **May-10**

Ans. : Refer sections 18.2, 18.3, 18.4 and 18.5.

Q.13 *What are the various operations performed by boolean variable instructions of 8051 ?* **May-10**

Ans. : Refer section 18.6.

Q.14 ***Explain DJNZ instructions of Intel 8051 microcontroller ?***

Ans. :

- DJNZ Rn, rel : Decrement the content of the register Rn and jump if not zero.
- DJNZ direct, rel : Decrement the content of direct 8-bit address and jump if not zero.

Q.15 ***Write a program using 8051 assembly language to change the data 55H stored in the lower byte of the data pointer register to AAH using rotate instruction.***

Ans. :

```
MOV DPL, #55H
MOV A, DPL
RL A
```

Q.16 ***Specify the single instruction, which clears the most significant bit of B register of 8051, without affecting the remaining bits.***

Ans. : Single instruction, which clears the most significant bit of B register of 8051, without affecting the remaining bit is CLR B.7.

Q.17 ***Explain the contents of the accumulator after the execution of the following program segments:***

Ans. :

```
MOV A, #3CH
MOV R4, #66H
ANL A, R4
```

ans : A = 3C

R4 = 66

A = 24

Q.18 ***Write a program to load accumulator A, DPH and DPL with 30H.***

Ans. :

```
MOV A, #30
MOV DPH, A
MOV DPL, A
```

Q.19 ***Write a program to subtract the contents of R1 of Bank0 from the contents of R0 of Bank2.***

Ans. :

```
MOV PSW, #10
MOV A, R0
MOV PSW, #00
SUBB A, R1
```

Q.20 ***List the 8051 instructions that affect the overflow flag.***

Ans. : ADD, ADDC, DIV, MUL, SUBB

Q.21 ***List the 8051 instructions that always clear the carry flag.***

Ans. : CLR C, DIV, MUL

Q.22 ***List the 8051 instructions that affect all the flags.***

Ans. : ADD, ADDC and SUBB

Q.23 ***What are the addressing modes supported by 8051 ?***

Ans. : The addressing modes supported by 8051 are :

- Register addressing
- Direct byte addressing
- Register indirect
- Immediate
- Register specific
- index

❑❑❑

Notes

19 8051 I/O Ports, Timer, Serial Port and Interrupts

Contents

19.1 8051 I/O Ports Structure

The 8051 has 32 I/O pins configured as four eight-bit parallel ports (P0, P1, P2 and P3). All four ports are bidirectional i.e. each pin will be configured as input or output (or both). All port-pins are multiplexed except the pins of port 1. Each port consists of a latch, an output driver and an input buffer.

Port 0 (Pins 32 - 39)

Port 0 pins can be used as I/O pins. The output drives and input buffers of port 0 are used to access external memory. Port 0 outputs the low order byte of the external memory address, time multiplexed with the data being written or read. Thus, port 0 can be used as a multiplexed address/data bus.

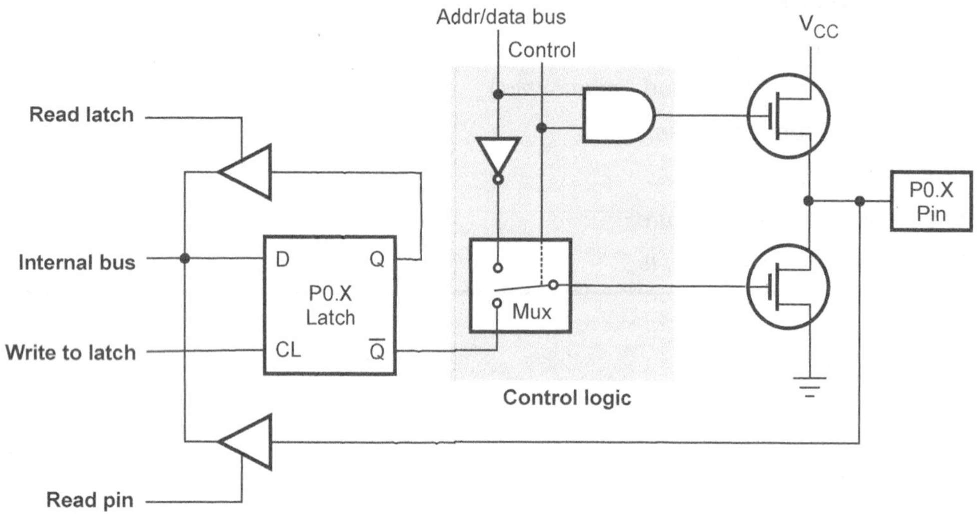

Fig. 19.1 Port 0 bit

Port 1 (Pins 1 - 8)

(See Fig. 19.2 on next page)

Port 1 pins can be used only as I/O pins.

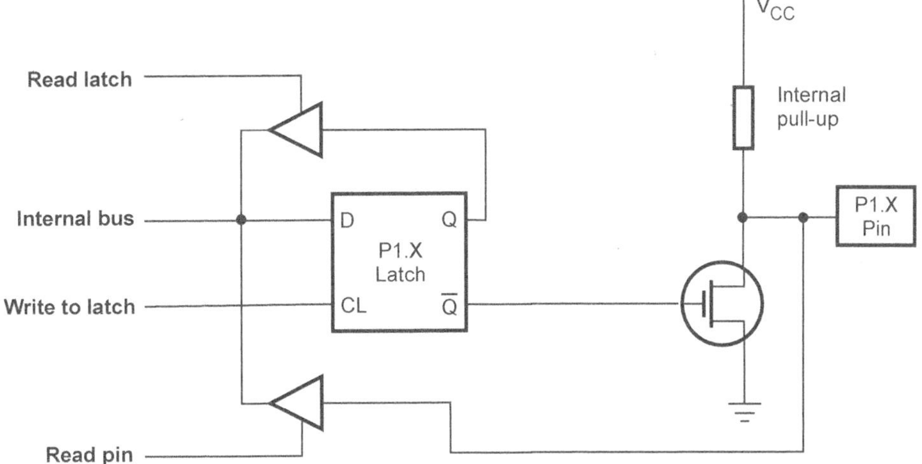

Fig. 19.2 Port 1 bit

Port 2 (Pins 21 - 28)

The output drives of port 2 are used to access external memory. Port 2 outputs the high order byte of the external memory address when the address is 16 bits wide. Otherwise, port 2 is used as an I/O port.

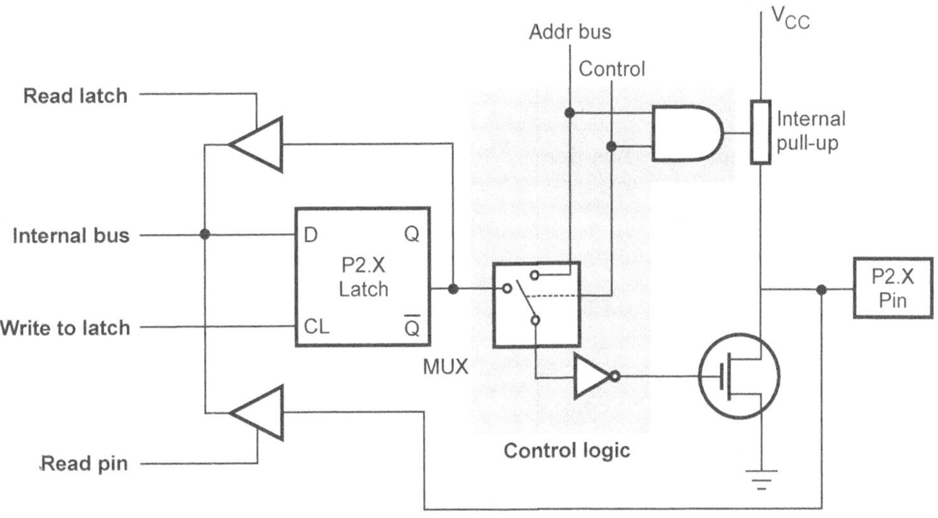

Fig. 19.3 Port 2 bit

Port 3 (Pins 10 - 17)

All port pins of port 3 are multifunctional. Therefore, each pin of port 3 can be programmed to use as I/O or as one of the alternate function. They have special functions as shown below including two external interrupts, two counter inputs, two special data lines and two timing control strobes.

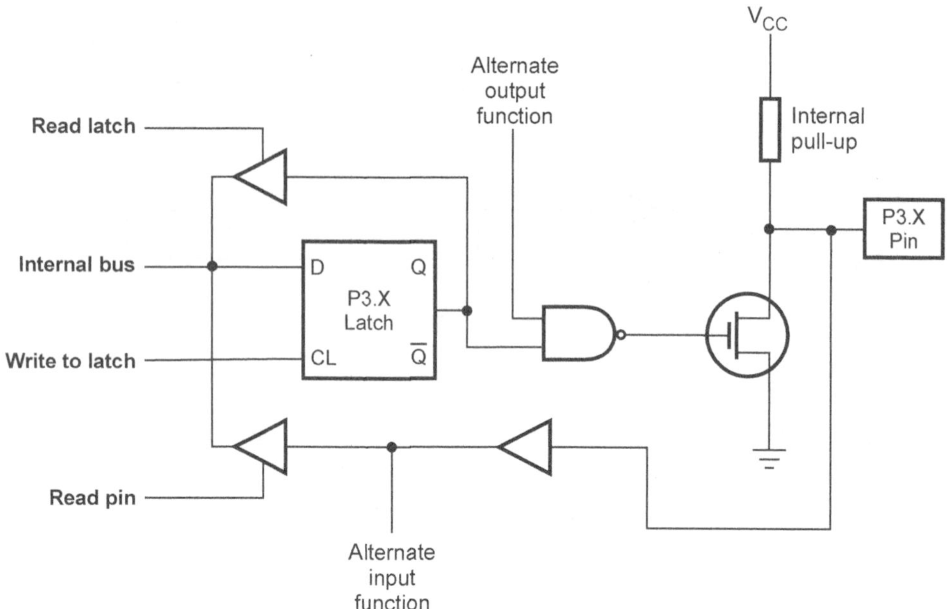

Fig. 19.4 Port 3 bit

Symbol	Position	Alternate use
$\overline{RD}$	P3.7	External memory read signal.
$\overline{WR}$	P3.6	External memory write signal.
T1	P3.5	External timer 1 input.
T0	P3.4	External timer 0 input.
$\overline{INT1}$	P3.3	External interrupt 1 input.
$\overline{INT0}$	P3.2	External interrupt 0 input.
TXD	P3.1	Serial data output.
RXD	P3.0	Serial data input.

Table 19.1

19.2 8051 I/O Port Programming

Minimum system using a microcontroller is a system built with microcontroller having sufficient memory and I/O ports. For a sufficient storage of programs and data, external memory devices are to be interfaced to the microcontroller. According to the application, I/O devices are to be interfaced through I/O ports to the microcontroller so that user can enter data and get the result in either display or print form.

In order to interface memory device or I/O device, supporting circuits such as clock circuit, reset circuit, demultiplexer circuit, and circuit required for generation of control signals are required.

19.2.1 Clock Circuits

Internal clock :

The 8051 microcontroller has on chip clock generator. Fig. 19.5 shows the crystal oscillator circuit. It is the most stable circuit. The 30 pF capacitors in the circuit are connected to assure oscillator start-up at the correct frequency.

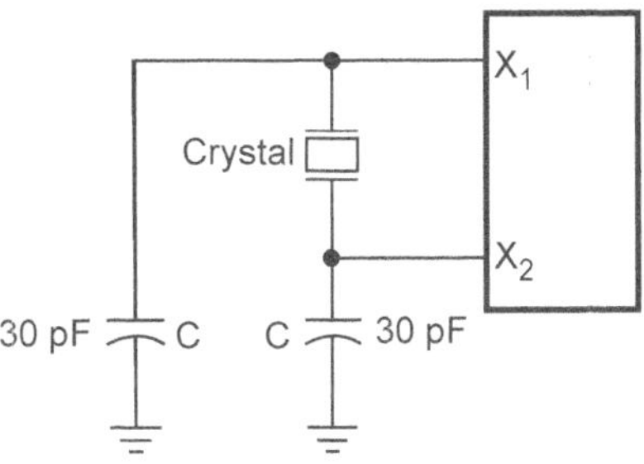

Fig. 19.5 Crystal oscillator circuit

External clock :

Fig. 19.6 shows how to drive clock input of 8051 microcontroller with external frequency source. Here external clock is applied at X_1 input and X_2 input is kept open.

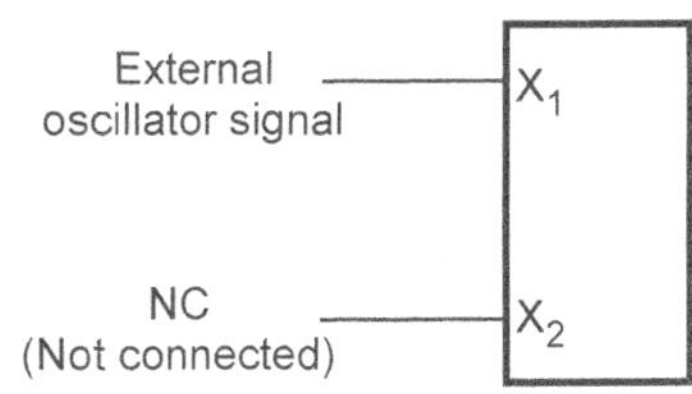

Fig. 19.6

19.2.2 Demultiplexing $P_{0.7}$ - $P_{0.0}$

To keep pin count of 8051 microcontroller minimum, it is provided with multiplexed address and data bus. We have to use external circuitry to demultiplexed these data and address lines with the help of address latch (ALE) signal provided by the microcontroller for external memory interfacing. The Fig. 19.7 shows the hardware connection for latching of an address. The IC 74LS373 is an 8-bit latch, having 8 D flip-flops. The input is transferred to the output only when clock is high. This clock signal is driven by ALE signal from microprocessor or microcontroller. The ALE signal is activated only during T_1, so input is transferred to the output only during T_1 i.e. address (A_0-A_7) on the $P_{0.7}$ to $P_{0.0}$

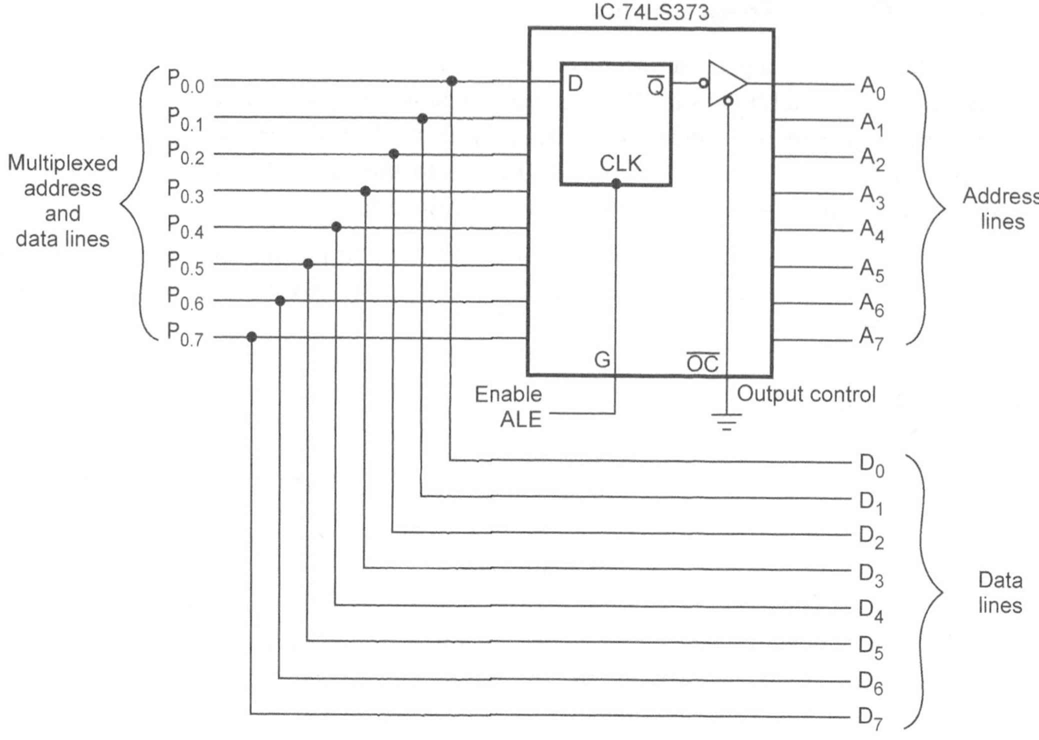

Fig. 19.7 Latching circuit

multiplexed bus. In the remaining part of the machine cycle, ALE signal is disabled so output of the latch (A_0-A_7) remains unchanged. To latch the address, in each machine cycle, the 8051 microcontroller gives ALE signal high during T_1 of every machine cycle.

19.2.3 Reset Circuit

The 8051 microcontroller provides RESETIN pin to itself. For 8051 microcontroller, RESETIN pin is active high. To reset the 8051, the RESETIN pin must be high for at least two-machine period. Then it should be inactive. The Fig. 19.8 shows the reset circuit to generate active high reset.

In Fig. 19.8, upon power up or key press RESET IN immediately goes HIGH and as capacitor charges through R RESET IN signal goes low. This generates active high reset signal for specific time duration decided by the values of components R and C.

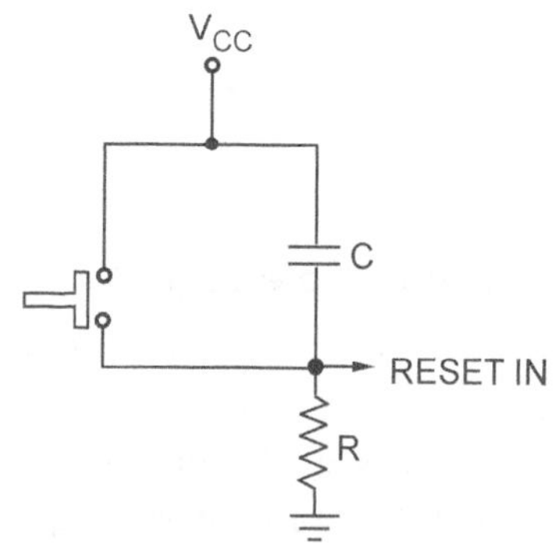

Fig. 19.8 Power on reset to generate active high RESET

19.2.4 Pull-up Resistors for Port 0

Port 0 has open drain outputs and hence to use this port as an input or an output it is necessary to connect external pull-up resistors (value 10 K) as shown in the Fig. 19.9.

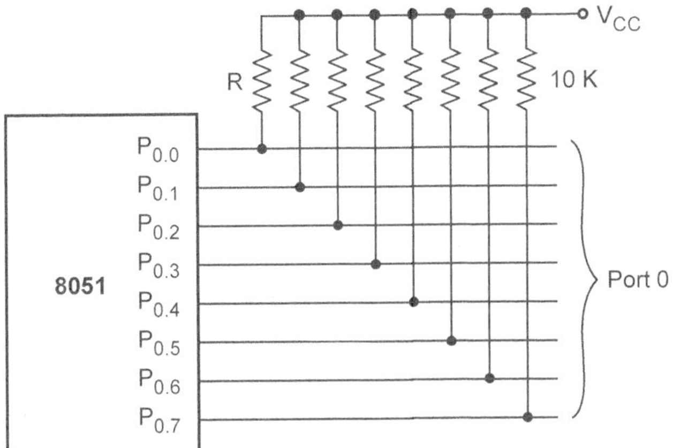

Fig. 19.9 Port 0 with pull-up resistors

Port 1, port 2 and port 3 do not require any pull-up resistors since they have internal pull-up resistors.

The Fig. 19.10 shows the minimum system connectors for 8751/89C51 based systems and for 8051 system without external memory interface.

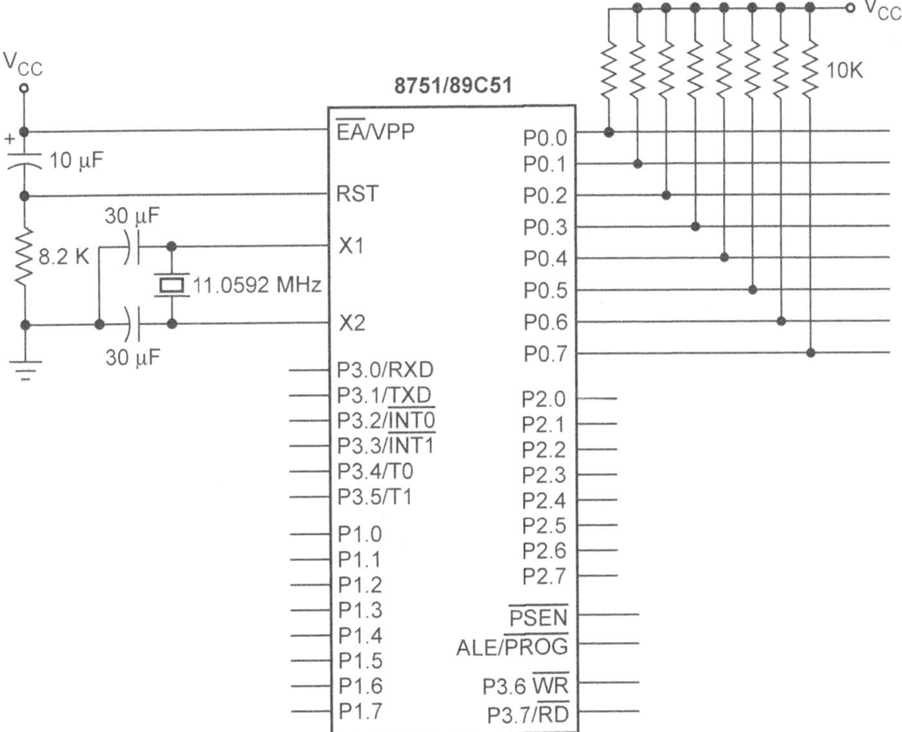

Fig. 19.10 Minimum system connections

19.3 I/O Bit Manipulation Programming

Let us see important points for programming I/O ports :

Port 0 has open drain outputs and hence to use this port as an input or an output it is necessary to connect external pull-up resistors (value 10 K) as shown in the Fig. 19.11.

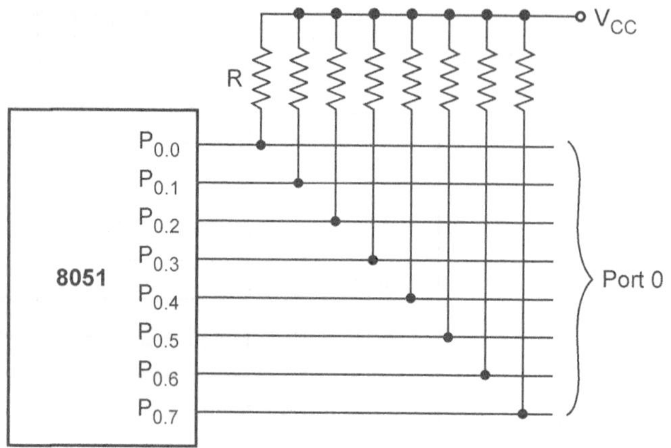

Fig. 19.11 Port 0 with pull-up resistors

Port 1, port 2 and port 3 do not require any pull-up resistors since they have internal pull-up resistors.

On reset, all ports are configured as an input ports.

If the ports are configured as an output ports, to make them input ports again, we have to write FFH (1 to all 8-bits) on these ports.

Now we will see simple programming examples to clearly understand the I/O concepts discussed above.

Example 19.1 : *Write a program to toggle all bits of P0 continuously.*

Solution :

```
BACK :   MOV A, #0AAH     ;   Load AAH in the (A) accumulator
         MOV P0, A        ;   Send contents of A to port 0
         A CALL Delay     ;   Wait for some time
         MOV A, #55H      ;   Load 55H in the accumulator
         MOV P0, A        ;   Send contents of A to port 0
         A CALL Delay     ;   Wait for some time
         SJMP BACK        ;   Repeat
```

The same action can be implemented using following program code.

```
BACK :   MOV P0, A        ;   Send contents of A on port 0
         CPL A            ;   Complement contents of port 0
         A CALL Delay     ;   Wait for some time
         SJMP Back        ;   Repeat
```

Note : Like port 0, we can toggle all bits of P1, P2 or P3 by replacing the corresponding port instead of P0 in the above programs.

Example 19.2 : *Write a program to read the content of P1 and save it in R6 and also send it to P2.*

Solution :

```
MOV A, # 0FFH    ;  A ← FFH
MOV P1, A        ;  Make P1 as an input port by writing all 1's to it
MOV A, P1        ;  Read data from P1
MOV R6, A        ;  Save it in R6
MOV P2, A        ;  Send it to P2
```

19.4 8051 Timers

8051 has two timers, timer 0 and timer 1. Basically both, timer 0 and timer 1 are 16-bit registers. Since 8051 is an 8-bit microcontroller, each 16-bit register can be accessed as low-byte register(TL) and high-byte register(TH). Fig. 19.12 shows the timer 0 and timer 1 registers. These registers can be accessed like other registers (A, B, R0, R1 etc.) in 8051.

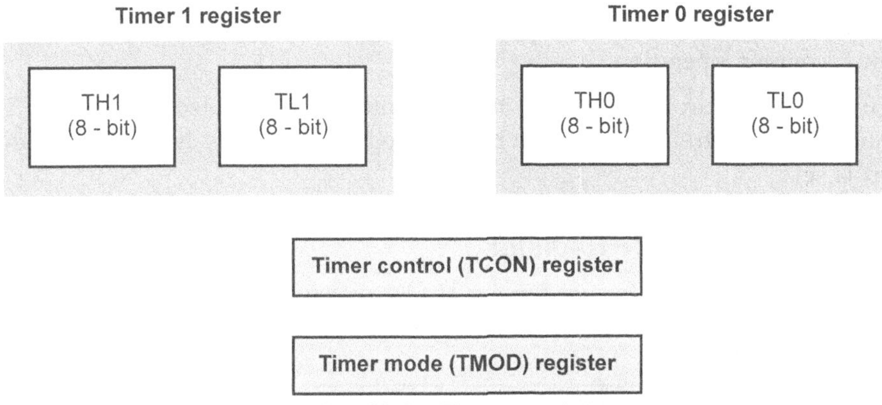

Fig. 19.12 Timer registers

19.4.1 Structure of TMOD Register

Timer/counter mode control (TMOD) is the special function register in 8051 having format as shown in Fig. 19.13.

The TMOD register is responsible for configuring the timers for the following operations :

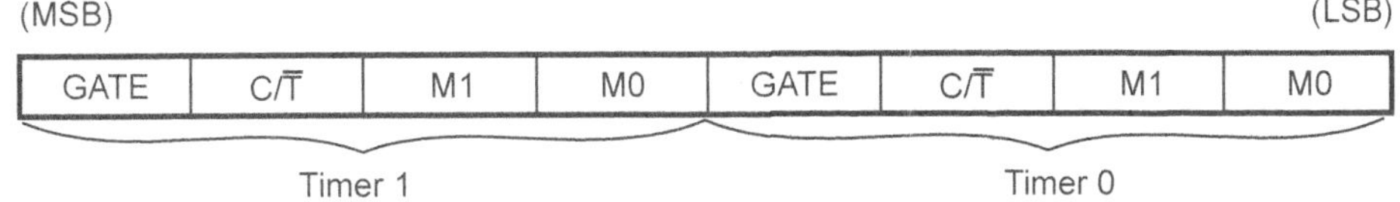

Fig. 19.13 TMOD register

- Select Timer 0 to operate as a counter or timer
- Select Timer 1 to operate as a counter or timer
- Select the mode in which timer should operate.

M1, M0 : These bits select the timer mode. There are four different modes of timer, mode 0, mode 1, mode 2 and mode 3. All these modes are discussed in the further section.

M1	M0	Operating mode
0	0	8-bit Timer/Counter "THx" with "TLx"s 5-bit prescaler.
0	1	16-bit Timer/Counter "THx" with "TLx" are cascaded; there is no prescaler.
1	0	8-bit auto-reload Timer/Counter "THx" holds a value which is to be reloaded into "TLx" each time it overflows.
1	1	(Timer 0) TL0 is an 8-bit Timer/Counter controlled by the standard Timer 0 control bits. TH0 is an 8-bit timer only controlled by Timer 1 control bits.
1	1	(Timer 1) Timer/Counter 1 stopped.

$C/\overline{T}$: This bit is cleared ($C/\overline{T}$ = 0) for selecting 'timer' operation and is set ($C/\overline{T}$ = 1) for selecting 'counter' operation.

GATE : Gating control when set. Timer/Counter "x" is enabled only while "INTx" pin is high and "TRx" control bit is set. When cleared Timer "x" is enabled whenever "TRx" control bit is set.

19.4.2 Structure of TCON Register

The Fig. 19.14 shows the format for the TCON register of 8051.

(MSB) (LSB)

TF1	TR1	TF0	TR0	IE1	IT1	IE0	IT0

Symbol	Position	Name and significance
TF1	TCON.7	Timer 1 Overflow Flag. Set by hardware on timer/counter overflow. Cleared when interrupt processed.
TR1	TCON.6	Timer 1 Run control bit. Set/cleared by software to turn timer/counter on/off.
TF0	TCON.5	Timer 0 Overflow Flag. Set by hardware on timer/counter overflow. Cleared when interrupt processed.
TR0	TCON.4	Timer 0 Run control bit. Set/cleared by software to turn timer/counter on/off.

IE1	TCON.3	Interrupt 1 Edge Flag. Set by hardware when external interrupt edge detected. Cleared when interrupt processed.
IT1	TCON.2	Interrupt 1 Type control bit. Set/cleared by software to specify falling edge/low level triggered external interrupts.
IE0	TCON.1	Interrupt 0 Edge Flag. Set by hardware when external interrupt edge detected. Cleared when interrupt processed.
IT0	TCON.0	Interrupt 0 Type control bit. Set/cleared by software to specify falling edge/low level triggered external interrupts.

Fig. 19.14 TCON-timer/counter control/status register

The TCON register controls the following timer operations :

- Start and stop timer 0 and timer 1
- Provides status of timer/counter overflows
- Provides status of external interrupts
- Configures external interrupts as either low level triggered or falling edge triggered.

Example 19.3 : *Indicate the effect of following 8051 instructions.*

a. MOV TMOD, #00010000B

b. MOV TMOD, #00000001B

c. MOV TMOD, #04

Solution :

a. **MOV TMOD, #00010000B :** The effect of this instruction is to set Timer 1 in mode 1 and Gate = 0 for internal clocking.

b. **MOV TMOD, #00000001B :** The effect of this instruction is to set Timer 0 in mode 1 and Gate = 0 for internal clocking.

c. **MOV TMOD, #04 :** The effect of this instruction is to select timer 0 to run in the counter mode.

Example 19.4 : *Perform the following operations using bit addressable instructions*

a. Start Timer 1

b. Stop Timer 0

Solution : a) SETB TR1 ; starts timer 1 by setting TCON.6 = 1

b) CLR TR0 ; stops timer 0 by clearing TCON.4 = 0

19.5 8051 Timer Modes and Programming

There are four modes of timer, mode 0, mode 1, mode 2 and mode 3. All these modes and their programming are discussed in this section. Mode 1 and mode 2 are widely used, so we will discuss them in detail.

Mode 0

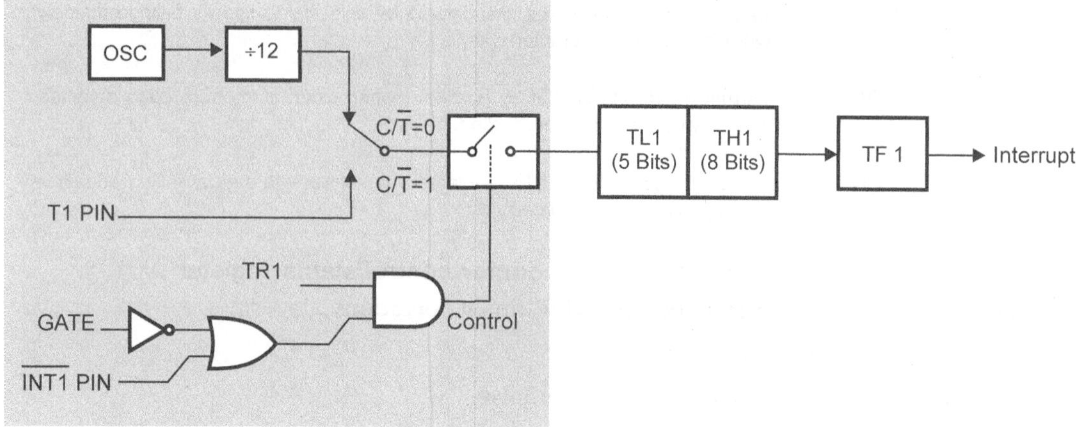

Timer/ counter control logic

Fig. 19.15 Timer/counter 1 mode 0 : 13-bit counter

Both Timers in Mode 0 are 8-bit Counters with a divide-by-32 prescaler. This 13-bit timer is MCS-48 compatible. Fig. 19.15 shows the Mode 0 operation as it applies to Timer 1. In this mode, the Timer register is configured as a 13-bit register. As the count rolls over from all 1s to all 0s, it sets the Timer interrupt flag TF1. The counted input is enabled to the Timer when TR1 = 1 and either GATE = 0 or $\overline{INT1}$ = 1. (Setting GATE = 1 allows the Timer to be controlled by external input $\overline{INT1}$, to facilitate pulse width measurements.) TR1 is a control bit in the Special Function Register TCON GATE is in TMOD.

The 13-bit register consists of all 8 bits of TH1 and the lower 5 bits of TL1. The upper 3 bits of TL1 are indeterminate and should be ignored. Setting the run flag (TR1) does not clear the registers.

Mode 0 operation is the same for Timer 0 as for Timer 1. Substitute TR0, TF0 and $\overline{INT0}$ for the corresponding Timer 1 signals in Fig. 19.15. There are two different GATE bits, one for Timer 1 (TMOD.7) and one for Timer 0 (TMOD.3).

Mode 1

Both Timers in Mode 1 are 16-bit Counters As the count rolls over from all 1s to all 0s, it sets the Timer interrupt flag TF. The counted input is enabled to the Timer when TR = 1 and either GATE = 0 or $\overline{INT1}$ = 1. (Setting GATE = 1 allows the Timer to be controlled by external input $\overline{INT1}$, to facilitate pulse width measurements.)

Timer 0 Mode 1 Programming

The Fig. 19.16 shows the timer control logic for timer 0 in mode 1.

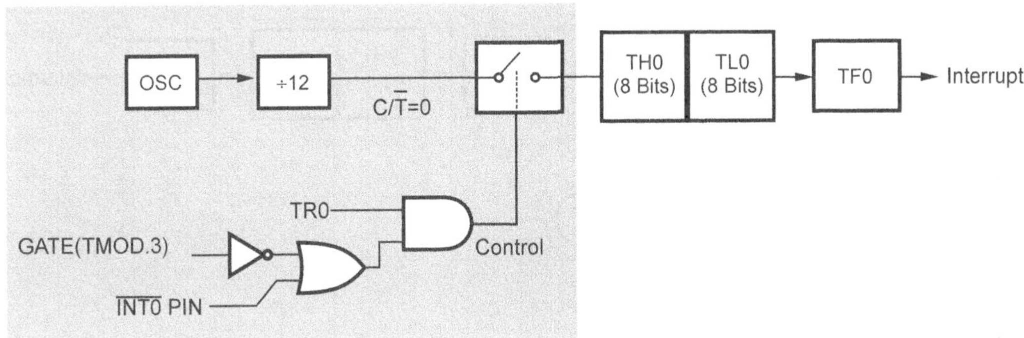

Fig. 19.16 Timer 0 in mode 1

A time delay can be generated using mode 1 of the timer 0 using following steps :

1. Load TMOD register indicating timer 0 is used and mode 1 is selected.

	7	6	5	4	3	2	1	0	
TMOD	**X**	**X**	**X**	**X**	**0**	**0**	**0**	**1**	**= 01**

2. Load TL0 and TH0 registers with count values.
3. Start the timer by setting TR0 bit = 1.
4. Monitor the timer flag (TF0) with the **JNB TF0, target address** instruction. When it is raised, get out of the loop.
5. Stop the timer by clearing TR0 bit = 0 with CLR TR0 instruction.
6. Clear TF0 flag with CLR TF0 instruction.

When start and stop of timer is done using software, no external hardware is needed for the same. This is illustrated in the Fig. 19.17.

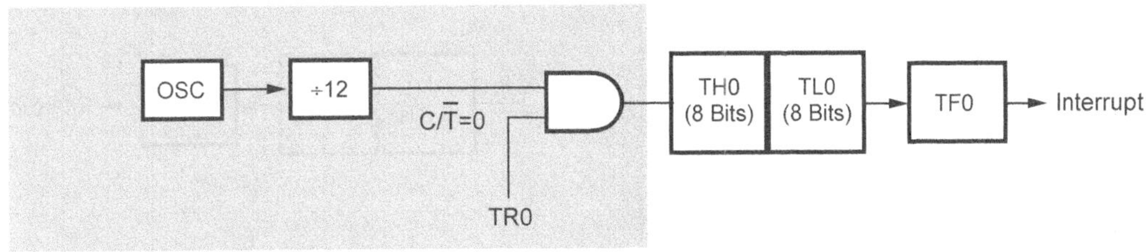

Timer0 control logic when GATE = 0 and $\overline{INT0}$ =1

Fig. 19.17 Timer 0 in mode 1, no external hardware is used to start and stop timer

Timer 1 Mode 1 Programming

The Fig. 19.18 shows the timer control logic for timer 1 in mode 1.

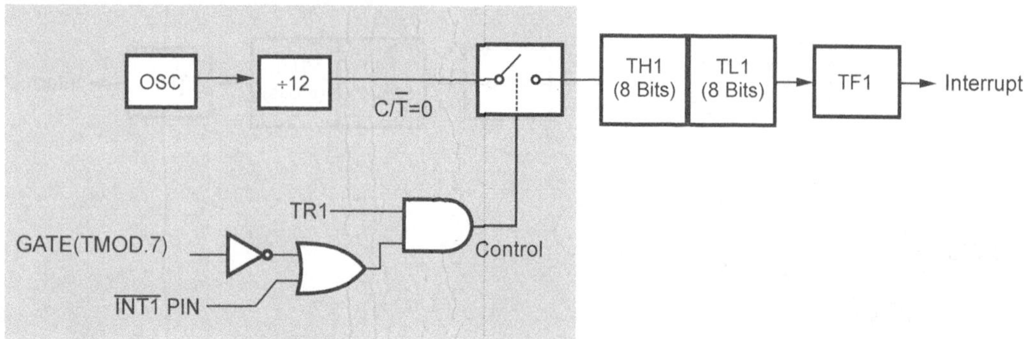

Timer1 control logic

Fig. 19.18 Timer 1 in mode 1

A time delay can be generated using mode 1 of the timer 1 using following steps :

1. Load TMOD register indicating timer 1 is used and mode 1 is selected.

	7	6	5	4	3	2	1	0	
TMOD	0	0	0	1	X	X	X	X	= 10H

2. Load TL1 and TH1 registers with count values.
3. Start the timer by setting TR1 bit = 1.
4. Monitor the timer flag (TF1) with the **JNB TF1, target address** instruction. When it is raised, get out of the loop.
5. Stop the timer by clearing TR1 bit = 0 with CLR TR1 instruction.
6. Clear TF1 flag with CLR TF1 instruction.

When start and stop of timer is done using software, no external hardware is needed for the same. It is illustrated in the Fig. 19.19.

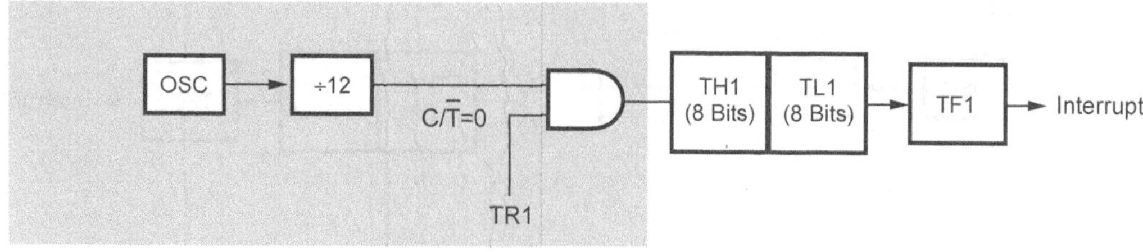

Timer1 control logic when GATE = 0 and $\overline{INT1}$ =1

Fig. 19.19 Timer 1 in mode 1, no external hardware is used to start and stop timer

Mode 2

Mode 2 configures the Timer register as an 8-bit Counter (TL) with automatic reload, as shown in Fig. 19.20. Overflow from TL only sets TF, but also reloads TL with the contents of TH, which is preset by software. The reload leaves TH unchanged.

Timer 0 Mode 2 Programming

The Fig. 19.20 shows the timer control logic for timer 0 in mode 2.

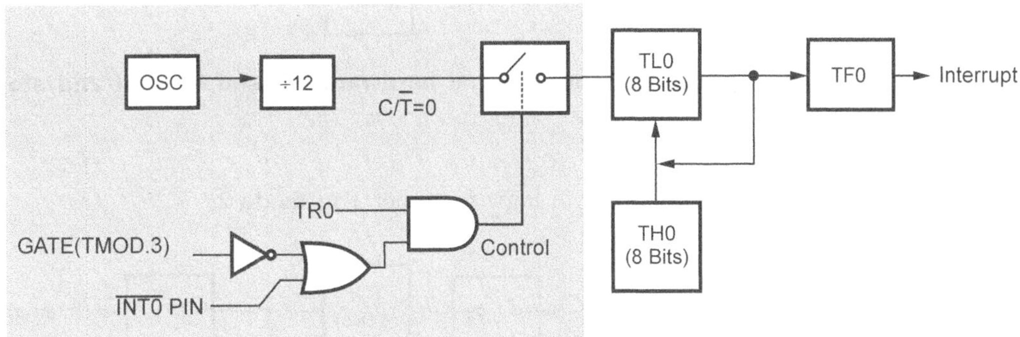

Fig. 19.20 Timer 0 in mode 2

A time delay can be generated using mode 2 of the timer 0 using following steps :

1. Load TMOD register indicating timer 0 is used and mode 2 is selected.

	7	6	5	4	3	2	1	0	
TMOD	**X**	**X**	**X**	**X**	**0**	**0**	**1**	**0**	**= 02H**

2. Load TH0 register with count value.
3. Start the timer by setting TR0 bit = 1.
4. Monitor the timer flag (TF0) with the JNB TF0, target address instruction. When it is raised, get out of the loop.
5. Clear the TF0 flag, with CLR TF0 instruction.
6. Go back to step 4. There is no need to load TH0 register again since Mode 2 is auto-reload.

When start and stop of timer is done using software, no external hardware is needed for the same. It is illustrated in the Fig. 19.21.

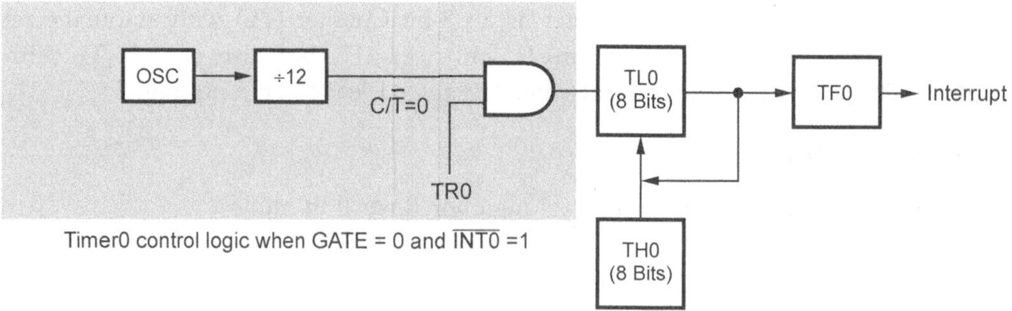

Fig. 19.21 Timer 0 in mode 2, no external hardware is used to start and stop timer

Timer 1 Mode 2 Programming

The Fig. 19.22 shows the timer control logic for timer 1 in mode 2.

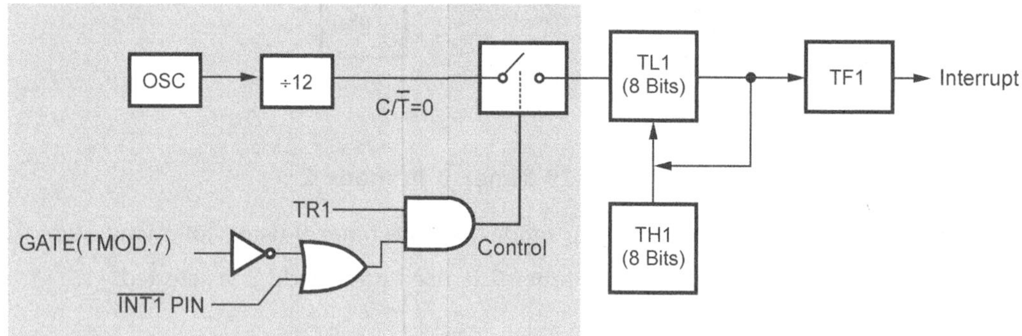

Timer1 control logic

Fig. 19.22 Timer 1 in mode 2

A time delay can be generated using mode 2 of the timer 1 using following steps :

1. Load TMOD register indicating timer 1 is used and mode 2 is selected.

	7	6	5	4	3	2	1	0	
TMOD	0	0	1	0	X	X	X	X	**= 20H**

2. Load TH1 register with count value.
3. Start the timer by setting TR1 bit = 1.
4. Monitor the timer flag (TF1) with the **JNB TF1, target address** instruction. When it is raised, get out of the loop.
5. Clear the TF1 flag, with CLR TF1 instruction.
6. Go back to step 4. There is no need to load TH1 register again since Mode 2 is auto-reload.

When start and stop of timer is done using software, no external hardware is needed for the same. It is illustrated in the Fig. 19.23.

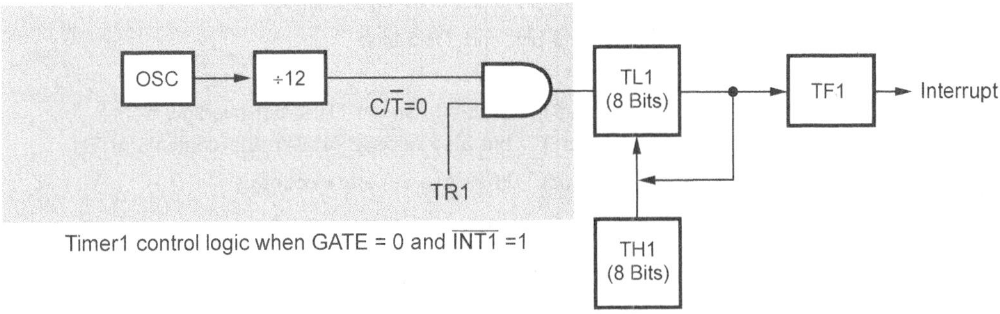

Fig. 19.23 Timer 1 in mode 2, no external hardware is used to start and stop timer

Mode 3

Timer 1 in Mode 3 simply holds its count. The effect is the same as setting TR1 = 0. Timer 0 in Mode 3 establishes TL0 and TH0 as two separate counters. The logic for Mode 3 on Timer 0 is shown in Fig. 19.24. TL0 uses the Timer 0 control bits : $C/\overline{T}$, GATE, TR0, $\overline{\text{INT0}}$, and TF0. TH0 is locked into a timer mode (counting machine cycles) and takes over the use of TR1 and TF1 from Timer 1. Thus, TH0 now controls the : Timer 1 interrupt.

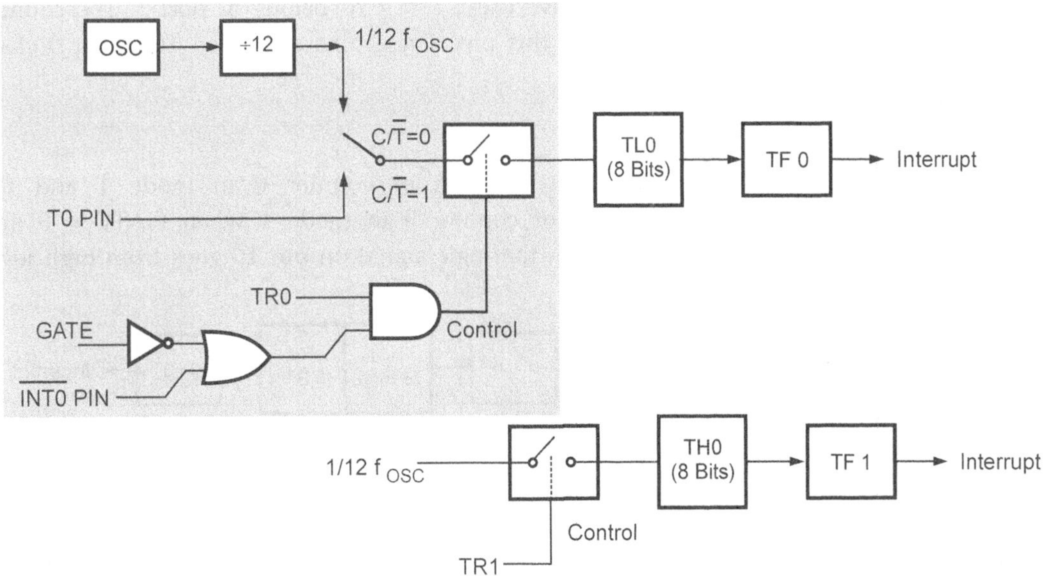

Fig. 19.24 Timer/counter 0 mode 3 : Two 8-bit counters

The Table 19.2 summarizes the modes of timers.

Mode	Brief description
Mode 0	13-bit timer (TL-5-bits and TH-8-bits). Counter overflow is indicated by time interrupt flag.
Mode 1	16-bit timer (TL-8-bits and TH-8-bits) Rest is same as mode 0.
Mode 2	Automatic reload mode. 8-bit counter (TL-8-bit) overflow from TL not only sets TF, but also reloads TL with the contents of TH.
Mode 3	Establishes TL and TH as two seperate counters.

Table 19.2 Summary of timer modes

19.6 8051 Counter Programming

When the timer/counter is used as a counter, the TMOD, TH and TL registers are used, functioning the same as for the timer studied in the last section.

$C/\overline{T}$ Bit in TMOD Register

As seen earlier, the $C/\overline{T}$ bit in the TMOD register decides the timer/counter functioning as a counter or a timer. When $C/\overline{T}$ bit in the TMOD register is 0, the timer mode is selected. When timer/counter is used as a timer, the 8051's crystal is used as a source of the frequency. When $C/\overline{T}$ bit in the TMOD register is 1, the counter mode is selected. When timer/counter is used as a counter, it gets its pulses from outside the 8051. The pin P 3.4 (pin number 14) and pin 3.5 (pin number 15) of 8051 are used for applying pulses counter 0 and counter 1 respectively. These two pins belong to port 3. The counter counts up for each clock pulse applied at this pin. These pins are called T0 (timer 0 clock input) and T1(timer 1 clock input).

Counter 0 in Mode 1

The Fig. 19.25 (a) shows the block diagram of counter 0 in mode 1 and the Fig. 19.25 (b) shows the block diagram of counter 0 in mode 1 when GATE = 0 and $\overline{INT0}$ = 1. Here, counter 0 counts up when the logic signal on pin T0 goes from high level to low level.

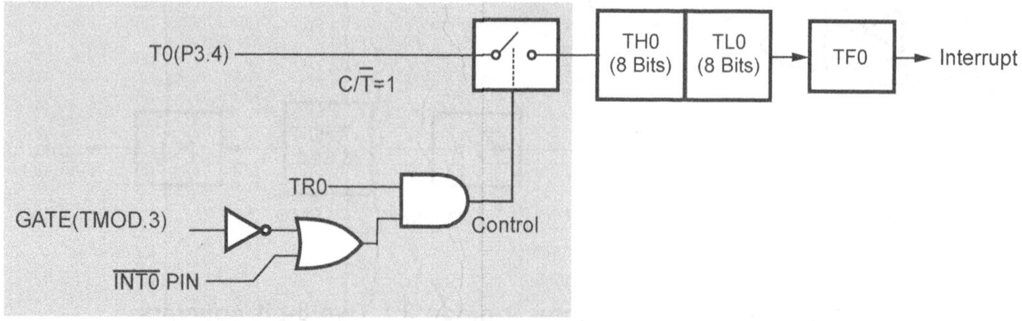

Fig. 19.25 (a)

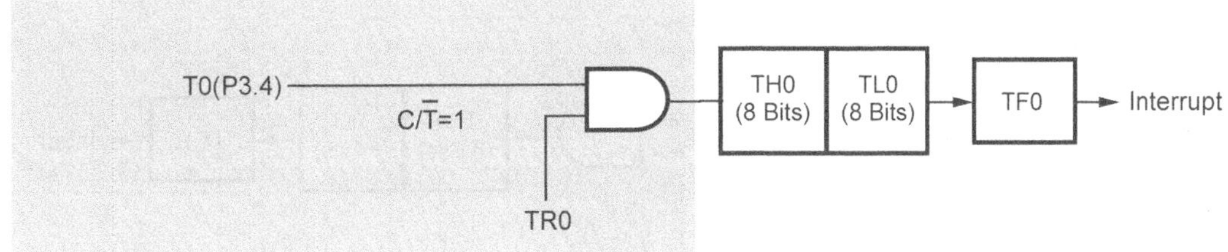

Counter 0 control logic when GATE = 0 and $\overline{INT0}$ =1

Fig. 19.25 (b)

To operate counter 0 in mode 1 we have to perform following steps :

1. $C/\overline{T}$ bit in TMOD register (Bit 2) is set to 1 to allow counter mode operation.
2. M1 : M0 bits (bits 1 : 0) in TMOD register are set to 01 to select mode 1.
3. When Gate bit (Bit 3) in TMOD register is cleared to 0, TR0 bit (bit 4 of TCON) is set to 1 to start the counter.
4. When Gate bit (Bit 3) in TMOD register is set to 1, counter will run only if TR0 is set to 1 and the logic signal on external interrupt pin $\overline{INT0}$ is high.

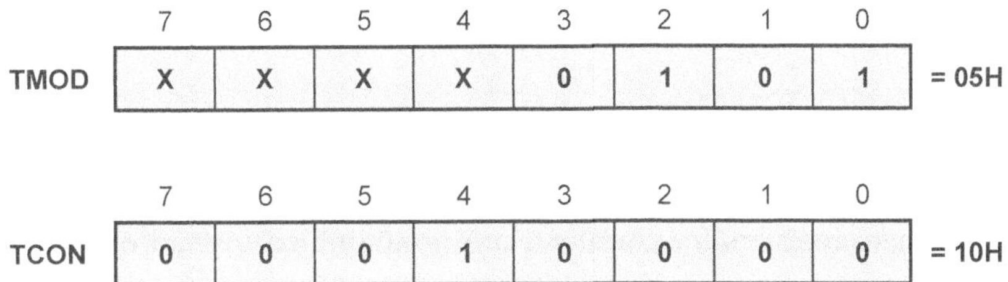

	7	6	5	4	3	2	1	0	
TMOD	X	X	X	X	0	1	0	1	= 05H

	7	6	5	4	3	2	1	0	
TCON	0	0	0	1	0	0	0	0	= 10H

Fig. 19.26 Counter 0 control register settings for mode 1 operation

Counter 1 in Mode 1

The Fig. 19.27 (a) shows the block diagram of counter 1 in mode 1 and the Fig. 19.27 (b) shows the block diagram of counter 1 in mode 1 when GATE = 0 and $\overline{INT0}$ = 1.

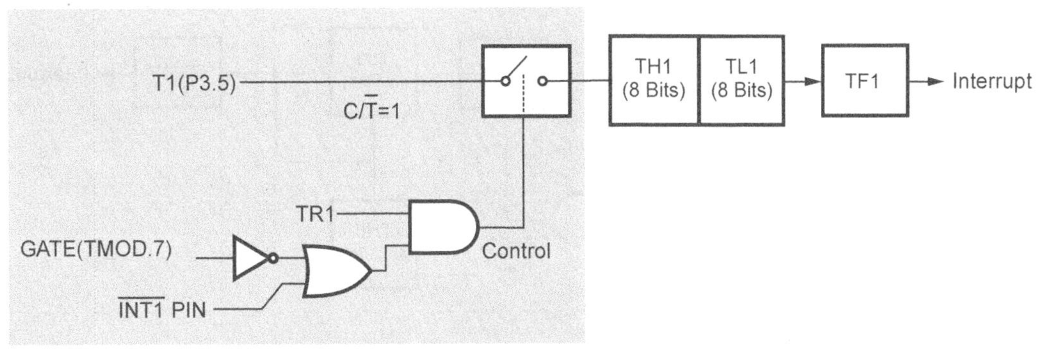

Counter1 control logic

Fig. 19.27 (a)

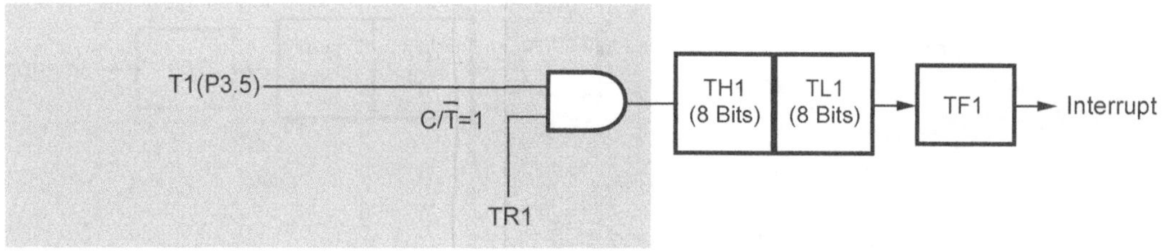

Counter1 control logic when GATE = 0 and $\overline{INT1}$ =1

Fig. 19.27 (b)

	7	6	5	4	3	2	1	0	
TMOD	0	1	0	1	X	X	X	X	= 50H

	7	6	5	4	3	2	1	0	
TCON	0	1	0	0	0	0	0	0	= 40H

Fig. 19.27 (c) Counter 1 control register settings for mode 1 operation

The operation of counter 1 in mode 1 is same as counter 0 operation. The only difference is that here registers for counter 1 are programmed instead of counter 0.

Counter in Mode 2

In this mode, counter is used in auto-reload mode instead of 16-bit counter. Rest of the operation is exactly same as that of Mode 1. The Fig. 19.28 (a) shows the block diagram of counter 0 in Mode 2 and the Fig. 19.28 (b) shows the block diagram of counter 0 in Mode 2 when GATE = 0 and $\overline{INT0}$ = 1

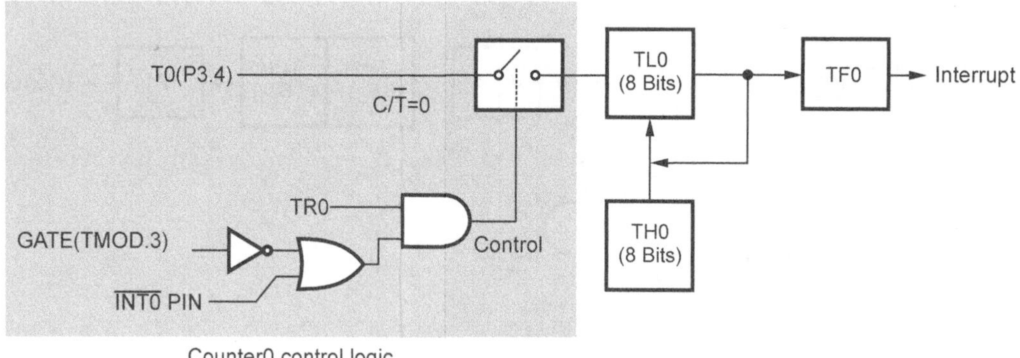

Counter0 control logic

Fig. 19.28 (a)

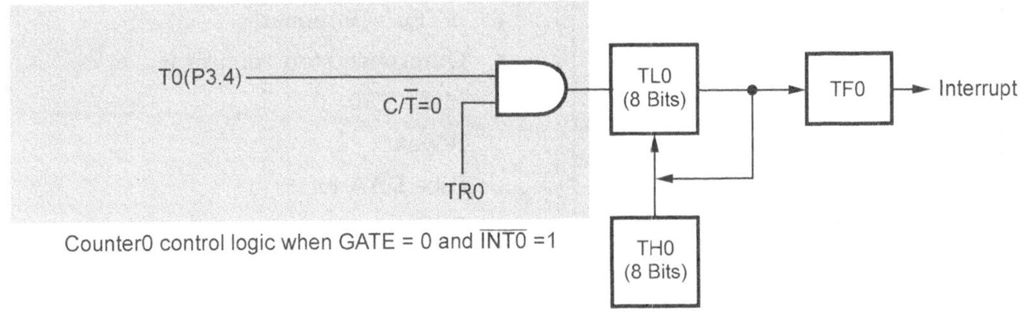

Counter0 control logic when GATE = 0 and $\overline{INT0}$ =1

Fig. 19.28 (b)

Example 19.5 : *Write a program for counter 1 in mode 2 to count the pulses and display the state of TL1 count on port 2. Assume that clock input is connected to T1 pin (P 3.5).*

Solution :

```
        MOV TMOD, #01100000B   ; Initialize counter 1 in
                               ; Mode 2, C/T=1
        MOV TH1, #0            ; Clear TH1
        SETB P3.5              ; Make T1 input
START : SETB TR1               ; Start the counter
BACK :  MOV A, TL1             ; Get the count from TL1
        MOV P2, A              ; Sent it to port 2
        JNB TF1, BACK          ; If TF1 = 0 repeat
        CLR TR1                ; Otherwise stop counter 1
        CLR TF1                ; Make TF1=0
        SJMP START             ; Repeat
```

Note : When 8051 is powered up ports are configured as input ports. To make them work as output port we have to send high output on it. Therefore, to behave T1 as input P 3.5 is set.

Example 19.6 : *Write a program to display counter 0 on 7-segment LEDs. Assume that clock input is connected to pin (P 3.4).*

Solution :

```
        MOV TMOD, #00000110    ; Initialize counter 0 in
                               ; Mode 2, C/T=1
        MOV TH0, #00H          ; Reset counter value
        SETB P3.4              ; Make T0 as input
START : SETB TR0               ; Start counter 0
BACK :  MOV A, TL0             ; Get the count value
        ACALL CONVBCD
```

```
          MOV P2, A          ; Send count value in BCD on port 2
          JNB TF0, BACK      ; If TF0 = 0 repeat
          CLR TR0            ; Otherwise stop counter 0
          CLR TF0            ; Make TF0=0
          SJMP START         ; Repeat
CONVBCD : ADD A, #00H        ; [Use DAA for
          DA  A              ; BCD conversion]
          RET                ; Return to main program
```

Example 19.7 : *Assume that XTAL = 11.0592 MHz. Write a program to generate a square wave of 2 kHz frequency on pin P1.5.*

Solution : T = 1/f = 1/2 kHz = 500 μs is period of square wave. 1/2 of it for high and low portion of the pulse is 250 μs. 250 μs/1.085 μs = 230 and 65536 – 230 = 65306 which in hex is FF1AH.

$\therefore$ TL = 1AH and TH = FFH

Program is as follows

```
        MOV TMOD, #10H     ; timer 1, mode 1
AGAIN : MOV TL1, #1AH      ; low byte of timer
        MOV TH1, #0FFH     ; high byte of timer
        SETB TR1           ; Start timer 1
BACK :  JNB TF1, BACK      ; Stay until timer rolls over
        CLR TR1            ; Stop timer 1
        CPL P1.5           ; Complement P1.5
        CLR TF1            ; Clear timer flag
        SJMP AGAIN         ; reload timer
```

Example 19.8 : *Generate a square wave of frequency 1 kHz using timer 1 in mode 1, on Pin P1.2. Explain the TMOD word used to configure the timer 1 for this application. Show the necessary calculations to find the value of count to be loaded into TH1 and TL1 registers. Assume XTAL frequency = 11.0592 MHz.*

Solution :

T of square wave = 1/f = 1/2 kHz = 500 μs

$$T_{ON} = T_{OFF} = \frac{500\ \mu s}{2} = 250\ \mu s$$

$$\text{T of clock} = \frac{12}{11.0592 \times 10^6} = 1.085\ \mu s$$

$$\text{Count} = \frac{T_{ON}}{\text{T of clock}} = \frac{250\ \mu s}{1.085\ \mu s} = 230$$

∴ Count to be loaded in TH1 and TL1 = 65536 – 230 = 65306 = FF1AH

∴ TH1 = FF and TL1 = 1AH

Program

```
         MOV TMOD, #10H    ; Timer 1, mode 1 (16-bit)
AGAIN :  MOV TL1, #1AH     ; Load lower byte of timer
         MOV TH1, #0FFH    ; Load higher byte of timer
         SETB TR1          ; Start timer 1
BACK :   JNB TF1, BACK     ; Wait for timer rolls over
         CLR TR1           ; Stop timer 1
         CPL P1.2          ; Complement P1.2
         CLR TF1           ; Clear timer flag1
         SJMP AGAIN        ; Reload timer 1 and continue
```

Example 19.9 : *Explain the steps to program timers in model and write an 8051 program to generate a square wave of 50 % duty cycle on the pin P1.5.*

Solution : Square wave

```
         MOV TMOD, #01     ; Timer 0 mode 1
Here :   MOV TL0, #0F2H    ; Load TL0 - 0F2
         MOV TH0, #0FFH    ; Load TH0 - 0FF
         CPL P1.5          ; toggle input  on P1.5
         ACALL Delay
         SJMP Here
Delay :  SETB TR0          ; Start Timer 0
again :  JNB TF0, again    ; Monitor Timer 0 flag until it rolls over
         CLR TR0
         CLR TF0
         RET
```

Example 19.10 : *Write an ALP to generate square wave on pin P1.5 of 500 Hz (approximately) with a subroutine to provide a time delay of 30.38 μs using timer 0. Assume that crystal frequency of 8051 is 11.0592 Hz.*

Solution :

$$T = \frac{12}{\text{Crystal frequency}} = \frac{12}{11.0592 \times 10^6} = 1.085\ \mu s$$

$$\text{Number of counts for roll over} = \frac{30.38\ \mu s}{1.085\ \mu s} = 28$$

$$65536 - 28 = 65508 = \text{FFE4H}$$

∴ To get a delay of 30.38 we have to load TH0 = FFH and TL0 = E4H

$$\text{For square wave T} = \frac{1}{500} = 2 \text{ ms}$$

$$\therefore \quad T_{ON} = T_{OFF} = T/2 = 1 \text{ ms}$$

Thus we have call delay routine (1 ms/30.38 μs) = 33 = 21H times

Program

```
         MOV TMOD, #01      ; Timer0, mode1
HERE:    MOV TL0, #E4H      ; Load TL0 = E4H
         MOV TH0, #FFH      ; Load TH0 = FFH
         CPL P1.5           ; toggle P1.5
         MOV R0, #21H       ; Load count in R0
BACK  :  ACALL Delay        ; wait for 30.38 μs × 33 = 1ms
         DJNZ R0, BACK
         SJMP HERE
DELAY :  SETB TR0           ; start timer 0
AGAIN :  JNB TF0,AGAIN      ; Wait for TF0 to roll over
         CLR TR0            ; stop timer 0
         CLR TF0            ; Clear TF0
         RET                ; Return
```

Example 19.11 : *Find the delay generated by timer 0 in the following code. Calculate the delay generated excluding the instruction overhead. What count has to be loaded in TL0 and TH0 if delay has to be increased to 25 msec ?*

```
         CLR P2.3
HERE :   MOV TMOD, #01
         MOV TL0, #3Eh
         MOV TH0, #0B8h
         SETB TF0,
AGAIN:   JNB TF0, AGAIN
         CLR TF0
         CLR TR0
         CLR P2.3
```

Solution :

$$\text{Timer count} = \text{B83E}$$

$$\therefore \quad (\text{FFFF} - \text{B83E} + 1) = 47\text{C2H} = (18370)_{10}$$

$$\text{Assuming XTAL} = 11.0592 \text{ MHz}$$

$$T = \frac{12}{11.0592 \times 10^{6}} = 1.085 \times 10^{-6}$$

$$\therefore \quad \text{Delay} = 1.085 \times 10^{-6} \times 18370 = \mathbf{19.93\ ms}$$

For 25 msec delay

$$\text{Decimal count} = \frac{25 \text{ ms}}{1.085 \times 10^{-6}} = 23041$$

$$= 5A01\ H$$

$\therefore$ TL0 = 01H and TH0 = 5AH

Example 19.12 : *Find out Hex. number to be loaded in TH0, to produce delay of 4.096 msec in mode '0' operation. Assume clock frequency of 12 MHz.*

Solution :

Timer clock frequency = Crystal frequency ÷ 12 = 12 MHz ÷ 12

= 1 MHz

$\therefore$ Timer clock period = 1 μs

Maximum count in mode 0 is 1FFFH (8191) and we have to count for 4096 counts to get a delay of 4.096 ms

$\therefore$ Count to be loaded in timer is 1FFFH

(8191 in decimal) – 4096 = FFFH (4095 in decimal)

Therefore, we have to load 0FH in TH0 and FFH in TL0.

Example 19.13 : *Using autoreload mode of timer 0 in 8051, generate a frequency of 10 kHz on pin P1.0. Write assembly language program for it.*

Solution : Assume XTAL frequency = 12 MHz. To generate a frequency of 10 kHz, one half of the cycle is of period 0.05 ms. Since XTAL frequency = 12 MHz we have cycle period is 1μs. Therefore, we have to decrement count equal to 50. Thus the initial value to be loaded in TH0 = (256 – 50) = 206.

Program

```
        MOV TMOD,#2H     ; Timer 0, mode 2 (8-bit auto reload)
        MOV TH0,#206     ; TH0 = 206
        SETB TR0         ; Start timer 0
BACK :  JNB TF1, BACK    ; Stay till timer rolls over
        CPL P1.0         ; Complement P1.0
        CLR TF0          ; Clear timer flag 0
        SJMP BACK        ; Continue
```

Example 19.14 : *Write an assembly language program to make LED ON and OFF connected to P 1.0 continuously with ON time 20 msec and off time 40 msec.*

Solution : Assume crystal frequency 12 MHz

Time for one instruction = $(1/12\,\text{MHz}) * 12 = 1$ μsec.

Count to be loaded in TH0:TL0 = >20 μsec/1 μ sec. = 20000 (Decimal)

65536 – 20000 = 45536 = B1E0H

```
            ORG 0000H
START :     MOV TMOD,#01H
            MOV TH0,#0B1H
            MOV TL0,#0E0H
            SETB P1.0
            ACALL DELAY
            CLR P1.0
            ACALL DELAY
            ACALL DELAY
            SJMP START
DELAY20MS : SETB TR0
HERE :      JNB TF0, HERE
            CLR TF0
            CLR TF0
            RET
```

Example 19.15 : *Write an assembly language program to generate a square wave of frequency 5 kHz on pin P3.0 using auto reload mode of timer 0 in 8051.*

Solution : For 5 kHz T = 1/5 kHz = 200μs and T/2 = 100 μs

Assume clock frequency 12 MHz so time for one cycle is 1 μs. So the value of TH0 and TL0 is 255 – 100 = 155

```
       ORG 0000H
       MOV TMOD, #02H      ; Timer 0 in mode 2
       MOV TH0,#155        ; TH0 = 155
       SETB TR0            ; Start timer 0
HERE : JNB TF0, HERE
       CPL P3.0
       ORG 001BH
       CLR TF0
       SJMP HERE
```

19.7 8051 Serial Port

The serial port of 8051 is full duplex, means it can transmit and receive simultaneously. It uses register SBUF to hold data. Register SCON controls data communication, register-PCON controls data rates and pin RxD (P3.0) and TxD (P3.1) do the data transfer.

SBUF is an 8-bit register dedicated for serial communication in 8051. Its address is 99H. It can be addressed like any other register in 8051. Writing to SBUF loads data to be transmitted and reading SBUF accesses received data. There are two separate and distinct registers, the transmit write-only register, and the receive read-only register. This is illustrated in Fig. 19.29.

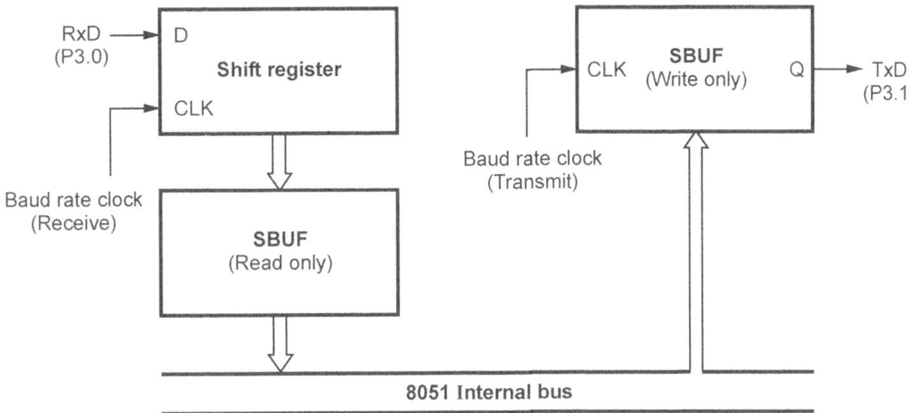

Fig. 19.29

The way in which SBUF is used for the transmission and reception of the data during serial communication is explained below.

- **Transmission :** When a byte of data is to be transmitted via the TxD pin, the SBUF is loaded with this data byte. As soon as a data byte is written into SBUF, it is framed with the start and stop bits and transmitted serially via the TxD pin.
- **Reception :** When 8051 receives data serially via RxD pin of it, the 8051 deframes it. The start and stop bits are separated out from a byte of data. This byte is placed in SBUF register.

Bit pattern of SCON register

The 8051 provides four programmable modes for serial data communication. A particular mode can be selected by setting the SM0 and SM1 bits in SCON. The mode selection also decides the baud rate. The Fig. 19.30 shows the bit patterns for SCON.

7 (MSB)	6	5	4	3	2	1	0 (LSB)
SM0	SM1	SM2	REN	TB8	RB8	TI	RI

Symbol	Position	Name and significance
SM0	SCON.7	Serial port Mode control bit 0. Set/cleared by software (see note).
SM1	SCON.6	Serial port Mode control bit 1. Set/cleared by software (see note).
SM2	SCON.5	Serial port Mode control bit 2. Set by software to disable reception of frames for which bit 8 is zero.
REN	SCON.4	Receiver Enable control bit. Set/cleared by software to enable/disable serial data reception.
TB8	SCON.3	Transmit Bit 8. Set/cleared by hardware to determine state of ninth data bit transmitted in 9-bit UART mode.
RB8	SCON.2	Receive Bit 8. Set/cleared by hardware to indicate state of ninth data bit received.
TI	SCON.1	Transmit Interrupt flag. Set by hardware when byte transmitted. Cleared by software after servicing.
RI	SCON.0	Receive Interrupt flag. Set by hardware when byte received. Cleared by software after servicing.
	Note : **Mode** 0 1 2 3	The state of (SM0, SM1) selects : **SM0 SM1** 0 0 - Shift register ; baud = f/12 0 1 - 8-bit UART, variable data rate. 1 0 - 9-bit UART, fixed data rate ; baud = f/32 or f/64 1 1 - 9-bit UART, variable data rate.

Fig. 19.30 SCON-Serial port control/status register

Bit pattern of PCON register :

(MSB) 7	6	5	4	3	2	1	(LSB) 0
SMOD	-	-	-	GF1	GF0	PD	IDL

Symbol	Position	Name and significance
SMOD	PCON.7	Serial baud rate modify bit. It is 0 at reset. It is set to 1 by program to double the baud rate.
–	PCON.6-4	Not defined
GF1	PCON.3	General purpose user flag bit 1. Set/cleared by program.
GF0	PCON.2	General purpose user flag bit 0. Set/cleared by program.
PD	PCON.1	Power down bit. It is set to 1 by program to enter power down configuration for CHMOS microcontrollers.
IDL	PCON.0	Idle mode bit. It is set to 1 by program to enter idle mode configuration for CHMOS microcontrollers.

Note : PCON is not bit addressable

Fig. 19.31 PCON register

19.7.1 Operating Modes for Serial Port

Mode 0

In this mode, serial data enters and exits through RxD. TxD outputs the shift clock. 8 bits are transmitted/received : 8 data bits (LSB first). The baud rate is fixed at 1/12 the oscillator frequency.

Mode 1

In this mode, 10 bits are transmitted (through TxD) or received (through RxD) : A start bit (0), 8 data bits (LSB first) and a stop bit (1). On receive, the stop bit goes into RB8 in Special Function Register SCON. The baud rate is variable.

Mode 2

In this mode, 11 bits are transmitted (through TxD) or received (through RxD) : A start bit (0), 8 data bits (LSB first), a programmable 9th data bit, and a stop bit (1). On Transmit, the 9th data bit (TB8 in SCON) can be assigned the value of 0 or 1. Or, for example, the parity bit (P, in the PSW) could be moved into TB8. On receive, the 9th data bit goes into RB8 in Special Function Register SCON, while the stop bit is ignored. The baud rate is programmable to either $\frac{1}{32}$ or $\frac{1}{64}$ the oscillator frequency.

Mode 3

In this mode, 11 bits are transmitted (through TxD) or received (through RxD) : A start bit (0), 8 data bits (LSB first), a programmable 9th data bit and a stop bit (1). In fact, Mode 3 is the same as Mode 2 in all respects except the baud rate. The baud rate in Mode 3 is variable.

In all four modes, transmission is initiated by any instruction that uses SBUF as a destination register. Reception is initiated in Mode 0 by the condition RI = 0 and REN = 1. Reception is initiated in the other modes by the incoming start bit if REN = 1.

The Table 19.3 summarizes the four serial port modes provided by 8051.

Mode	Transmission format	Baud rate
0	8-data bits.	$\frac{1}{12}$ oscillator frequency.
1	10-bit (start bit + 8-data bits + stop bit).	Variable.
2	11-bit (start bit + 8-data bits + programmable 9th data bit + stop bit).	Programmable to either $\frac{1}{32}$ or $\frac{1}{64}$ oscillator frequency.
3	11-bit (start bit + 8 data bit + programmable 9th data bit + stop bit).	Variable.

Table 19.3 Summary of serial port modes

19.7.2 Generating Baud Rates

Serial Port in Mode 0 :

Mode 0 has a fixed baud rate which is 1/12 of the oscillator frequency. To run the serial port in this mode none of the Timer/Counters need to be set up. Only the SCON register needs to be defined.

$$\text{Baud rate} = \frac{\text{Oscillator frequency}}{12}$$

Serial Port in Mode 1

Mode 1 has a variable baud rate. The baud rate can be generated by either Timer 1 or Timer 2 (8052 only).

Using Timer/Counter 1 to Generate Baud Rates

For this purpose, Timer 1 is used in mode 2 (Auto-Reload).

$$\text{Baud rate} = \frac{K \times \text{Oscillator frequency}}{32 \times 12 \times [(256 - TH1)]}$$

If SMOD = 0, then K = 1.

If SMOD = 1, then K = 2. (SMOD is the PCON register)

Most of the time the user knows the baud rate and needs to know the reload value for TH1. Therefore, the equation to calculate TH1 can be written as :

$$TH1 = 256 - \frac{K \times \text{Oscillator frequency}}{384 \times \text{Baud rate}}$$

TH1 must be an integer value. Rounding off TH1 to the nearest integer may not produce the desired baud rate. In this case, the user may have to choose another crystal frequency.

Since the PCON register is not bit addressable, one way to set the bit is logical ORing the PCON register. (i.e. ORL PCON, #80H). The address of PCON is 87H.

The Table 19.4 shows the values to be loaded into TH1 to get the corresponding baud rate. It also shows that the baud rates are doubled when SMOD = 1.

TH1 (HEX)	Baud rate (SMOD = 0)	Baud rate (SMOD = 1)
FD	9600	19,200
FA	4800	9600
F4	2400	4800
E8	1200	2400

Note : XTAL = 11.0592 MHz

Table 19.4

Using Timer/Counter 2 to Generate Baud Rates

For this purpose, Timer 2 must be used in the baud rate generating mode. If Timer 2 is being clocked through pin T2 (P1.0) the baud rate is :

$$\text{Baud rate} = \frac{\text{Timer 2 overflow rate}}{16}$$

And if it is being clocked internally the baud rate is :

$$\text{Baud rate} = \frac{\text{Oscillator frequency}}{32 \times [65536 - (\text{RCAP2H, RCAP2L})]}$$

To obtain the reload value for RCAP2H and RCAP2L the above equation can be rewritten as :

$$\text{RCAP2H, RCAP2L} = 65536 - \frac{\text{Oscillator frequency}}{32 \times \text{Baud rate}}$$

Serial Port in Mode 2

The baud rate is fixed in this mode and is $\frac{1}{32}$ or $\frac{1}{64}$ of the oscillator frequency depending on the value of the SMOD bit in the PCON register. In this mode none of the Timers are used and the clock comes from the internal phase 2 clock.

$$\text{SMOD} = 1, \text{ Baud rate} = \frac{1}{32} \text{ Oscillator frequency}$$

$$\text{SMOD} = 0, \text{ Baud rate} = \frac{1}{64} \text{ Oscillator frequency}$$

To set the SMOD bit : ORL PCON, #80H. The address of PCON is 87H.

Note : By changing SMOD bit in PCON from 0 to 1 we can **double the baud rate** in 8051.

Serial Port in Mode 3

The baud rate in mode 3 is variable and sets up exactly the same as in mode 1

19.7.3 Programming 8051 for Serial Data Transfer

To program 8051, to transfer data serially we have to perform following sequence of actions :

1. Load the TMOD register with the value 20H to use timer 1 in mode 2 (8-bit auto-reload) to set the baud rate.
2. Load TH1 to set the desire baud rate for serial data transfer.
3. Load SCON register with the value 50H, to use serial mode 1, where an 8-bit data is framed with start and stop bits.
4. Set TR1 to 1 to start timer 1.
5. Clear TI with **CLR TI** instruction.
6. Write a character to be sent in to the SBUF register.
7. Check the TI flag bit with instruction **JNB TI, XXXX** to see if the character has been transferred completely.
8. Go to step 5 to transfer the next character.

Example 19.16 : *8051 uses 11.0592 MHz crystal. To get 9600 hertz baud rate how will you program it for serial transmission ?*

Solution : When 11.0592 MHz crystal is used and a standard baud rate of 9600 hertz is required then, the setting of TH1 can be found as,

$$TH1 = 256 - \frac{k \times \text{Oscillator frequency}}{384 \times \text{Baud rate}}$$

$$= 256 - \frac{1 \times 11.0592 \times 10^6}{384 \times 9600} = 253 = \text{FDH}$$

Program :

```
MOV TMOD, #020      ; Initialize timer 1 in mode 2
MOV SCON, #4CH      ; Initialize serial mode 1
ORL PCON, #80H      ; Make SMOD = 1
MOV TH1, #FDH       ; Load count
```

Example 19.17 : *Write an 8051 assembly language program to transfer letter "A" serially at 9600 baud rate, continuously.*

Solution :

```
        MOV TMOD, #20H      ; timer 1, mode 2 (auto reload)
        MOV TH1, #FDH       ; 9600 baud rate
        MOV SCON, #50H      ; 8-bit, 1 stop REN enabled
        SETB TR1            ; start timer 1
START:  MOV SBUF, #"A"      ; Letter "A" to be transferred
HERE:   JNB TI, HERE        ; Wait for the last bit to
                            ; transfer
        CLR TI              ; Clear TI for the next character
        SJMP START          ; Go to send the character again
```

Example 19.18 : *Write an 8051 assembly language program to transfer the message "HELLO"serially at 9600 baud, 8-bit data, 1 stop bit.*

Solution :

```
        MOV TMOD,#20H       ; timer 1, mode 2
        MOV TH1, #FDH       ; 9600 baud rate
        MOV SCON,#50H       ; 8-bit, 1 stop bit, REN enabled
        SETB TR1            ; start timer 1
START:  MOV A, #"H"         ; transfer "H"
        ACALL TRANS
        MOV A, #"E"         ; transfer "E"
        ACALL TRANS
        MOV A, #"L"         ; transfer "L"
        ACALL TRANS
        MOV A, #"L"         ; transfer "L"
        ACALL TRANS
        MOV A,#"O"          ; transfer "O"
        ACALL TRANS         ; Serial data transfer subroutine
TRANS:  MOV SBUF, A         ; Load SBUF
HERE:   JNB TI, HERE        ; wait for the last bit to
                            ; transfer
        CLR TI              ; Clear TI for the next
                            ; character
        RET
```

The importance of the TI flag bit :

When a data is to be transmitted via TxD pin, first a data byte is loaded into the SBUF register. A start bit, a data byte and then the stop bit are transmitted sequentially via TxD pin. During the transmission of the stop bit, 8051 sets the TI flag, i.e. TI = 1. This indicates the end of data byte transmission and 8051 is ready for the transmission and 8051 is ready for the transmission of next data. The programmer has to clear the TI flag, i.e. TI = 0, with the 'CLR TI' instruction to transmit next data. The TI flag bit should be monitored to make sure that the SBUF register is not overwritten. If we write the next byte to be transmitted into the SBUF register before setting the TI flag bit, the untransmitted portion of the previous byte will be lost. The programmer can check the TI flag bit by 'JNB TI, XX' instruction or by using an interrupt.

19.7.4 Programming 8051 for Receiving Data Serially

To program 8051, to receive data serially we have to perform following sequence of actions :

1. Load the TMOD register with the value 20H to use timer 1 in mode 2 (8-bit auto-reload) to set the baud rate.
2. Load TH1 to set the desire baud rate for serial data transfer.
3. Load SCON register with the value 50H, to use serial mode 1, where an 8-bit data is framed with start and stop bits.
4. Set TR1 to 1 to start timer 1.
5. Clear RI with **CLR RI** instruction.
6. Check the RI flag bit with instruction **JNB RI, XXXX** to see if an entire character has been received yet.
7. If RI is set, SBUF has the byte. Save this byte.
8. Go to step 5 to receive the next character.

Example 19.19 : *Write an 8051 assembly language program to receive bytes serially with baud rate 9600, 8-bit data and 1 stop bit. Simultaneously send received bytes to port 2.*

Solution :

```
        MOV TMOD, #20H   ; timer 1, mode 2 (auto reload)
        MOV TH1, #FDH    ; 9600 baud rate
        MOV SCON, #50H   ; 8-bit, 1 stop, REN enabled
        SETB TR1         ; start timer 1
HERE:   JNB RI, HERE     ; wait for character receive
                         ; completely
        MOV A, SBUF      ; save the received character
        MOV P2, A        ; send character to port 2
        CLR RI           ; Get ready to receive next byte
        SJMP HERE        ; Go to receive next character
```

The importance of the RI flag bit :

When a data is to be received via RxD pin, first the start bit, and a data byte with one bit at time are received sequentially via RxD pin. When the last bit of a data byte is received, a byte is formed and the SBUF register is loaded with this byte. Then the stop bit is received. During the reception of the stop bit, 8051 sets the RI flag, i.e. RI = 1. This indicates that the entire data byte has been received. This data byte which is loaded in the SBUF register, should be placed to a safe place such as any register or memory before it is lost. The programmer has to clear the RI flag, i.e. RI = 0, with the 'CLR RI' instruction to receive next data and place it in SBUF register. The RI flag bit should be monitored to make sure that the entire byte has been received. This monitoring of the RI flag bit till it becomes one to ensure the reception of complete data place it in SBUF register, copy it to the safe place and then make RI zero with 'CLR RI' instruction are the necessary steps to avoid any loss of received data.

19.7.5 Doubling the Baud Rate in the 8051

We can double the baud rate in 8051 using two way,

- By doubling the crystal frequency.
- By making SMOD bit in the PCON register from 0 to 1.

Example 19.20 : *Write a program to receive message from PC to 8051. Message string is "Hello". After this micro controller sends message to PC "Fine".*

Solution : The Fig. 19.32 shows the connections between 8051 and PC.

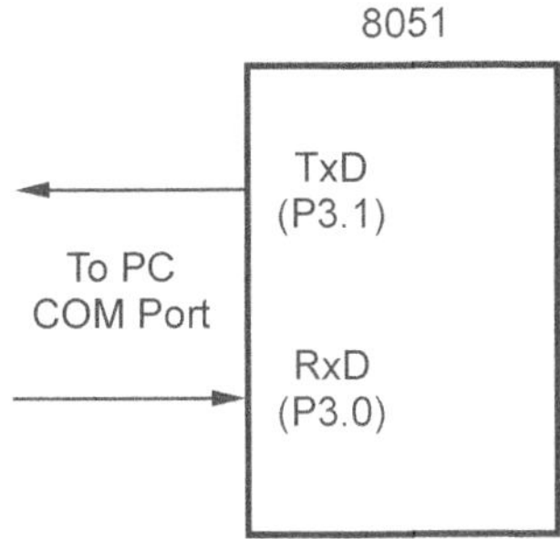

Fig. 19.32

```
MOV TMOD, #20H        ; Initialize timer 1 in mode 2
MOV TH1, #0FDH        ; Load count to get 9600 baud rate
MOV SCON, #50H        ; 8-bit, 1 stop, REN enabled
SETB TR1              ; Start timer 1
MOV DPTR, #2000H      ; Initialize memory pointer to
                      ; save received data
MOV R0,#05H           ; Initialize counter to read
                      ; 5 characters
```

```
RECV:   JNB RI,RECV          ; wait for character
        MOV A,SBUF           ; Read the character
        MOVX @DPTR,A         ; Save it in memory
        INC DPTR             ; increment memory pointer
        CLR RI               ; Get ready for next character
        DJNZ R0, RECV        ; If not last character repeat
        MOV DPTR, #MYDATA    ; Initialize pointer for message
        CLR A
        MOV R0, #4H          ; Initialize counter to send
                             ; 4 characters
        MOVC A, @A+DPTR      ; Get the character
        MOV SBUF, A          ; Load the data
HERE:   JNB TI,HERE          ; Wait for complete byte
                             ; transfer
        CLR TI               ; get ready for next character
```

19.7.6 8051 Connection to RS 232C

In RS 232C the voltage level + 3 V to + 15 V is defined as logic 0; from – 3 V to – 15 V is defined as logic 1. The control and timing signals are compatible with the TTL level. Because of the incompatibility of the data lines with the TTL logic, voltage translators, called line drivers and line receivers, are required to interface TTL logic with the RS 232C signals. The Fig. 19.33 shows the connection between RS 232C and 8051. Here, MAX 232 chip is used as a line driver and line receiver. We know that 8051 assigns two pins RxD (P 3.0) and TxD (P 3.1) for reception and transmission of serial data, respectively.

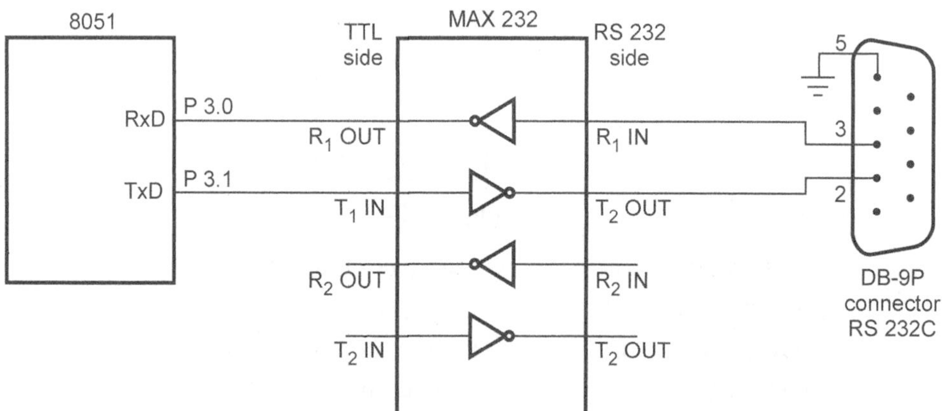

Fig. 19.33 Connection between RS 232C and 8051

These pins are TTL compatible; therefore, they require line driver and line receiver to make them RS 232C compatible. The MAX 232 has two sets of line drivers and line receivers for transmitting and receiving data. Only one set is required for one serial communication.

19.8 8051 Interrupt Structure

The 8051 provides 5 interrupt sources. The 8052 provides 6. These are shown in Fig. 19.34. The external Interrupts $\overline{INT0}$ and $\overline{INT1}$ can each be either level-activated or transition-activated, depending on bits IT0 and IT1 in Register TCON. The flags that actually generate these interrupts are bits IE0 and IE1 in TCON. When an external interrupt is generated, the flag that generated it is cleared by the hardware when the service routine is vectored to only if the interrupt was transition-activated. If the interrupt was level-activated, then the external requesting source is what controls the request flag, rather that the on-chip hardware.

The Timer 0 and Timer 1 interrupts are generated by TF0 and TF1, which are set by a rollover in their respective Timer/Counter registers (except see Timer 0 in Mode 3). The timer flag set upon generation of interrupt is cleared by the on-chip hardware when microcontroller starts execution of particular interrupt service routine.

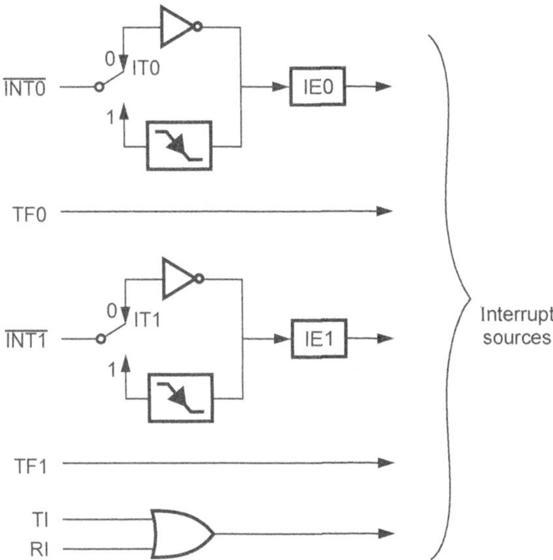

Fig. 19.34 MCS-51 interrupt structure

The serial port interrupt is generated by the logical OR of RI and TI. Neither of these flags is cleared by hardware when the service routine is vectored to service routine. In fact, the service routine will normally have to determine whether it was RI or TI that generated the interrupt and the bit will have to be cleared in software.

19.8.1 Interrupt Control (Enabling and Disabling Interrupts using IE)

When 8051 is reset, all interrupts are disable. These are enabled by software. All of the bits that generate interrupts can be set or cleared by software, with the same result as though it had been set or cleared by hardware. That is, interrupts can be generated or pending interrupts can be canceled in software.

Each of these interrupt sources can be individually enabled or disabled by setting or clearing a bit in Special Function Register IE (Fig. 19.35). IE contains also a global disable bit, EA, which disables all interrupts at once.

Note in Fig. 19.35 that bit position IE.6 is unimplemented. In the 8051s, bit position IE.5 is also unimplemented. User software should not write 1s to these bit positions, since they may be used in future MCS-51 products.

(MSB)							(LSB)
EA	-	ET2	ES	ET1	EX1	ET0	EX0

Symbol	Position	Name and Significance
EA	IE.7	Enable all control bit. Cleared by software to disable all interrupts, independent of the state of IE.4-IE.0.
-	IE.6	(Reserved)
ET2	IE.5	(Reserved)
ES	IE.4	Enable Serial port control bit. Set/cleared by software to enable/disable interrupts from TI or RI flags.
ET1	IE.3	Enable Timer 1 control bit. Set/cleared by software to enable/disable interrupts from timer/counter 1
EX1	IE.2	Enable External interrupt 1 control bit. Set/cleared by software to enable/ disable interrupts from INT1.
ET0	IE.1	Enable Timer 0 control bit. Set/cleared by software to enable/disable interrupts from timer/counter 0.
EX0	IE.0	Enable external interrupt 0 control bit. Set/cleared by software to enable/disable interrupts from INT0.

Fig. 19.35 IE-interrupt enable register

Example 19.21 : *Write a program to enable serial interrupt, Timer 1 interrupt and external hardware interrupt 0 (EX0)*

Solution :

EA	–	–	ES	ET1	EX1	ET0	EX0
1	0	0	1	1	0	0	1

```
MOV IE, #1001 1001B        ;  enable serial, Timer 1, EX0
```

Example 19.22 : *Write an instruction to disable all interrupts*

Solution : By making EA = 0 we can disable all interrupts.

```
CLR  IE.7     ;  Clear EA bit in the IE register
```

Example 19.23 : *Write a program to enable Timer 0 interrupt using bit manipulation instructions.*

Solution :

```
SETB    IE.7   ;   Enable interrupts
SETB    IE.1   ;   Enable timer 0 interrupt
```

19.8.2 Interrupt Priority and Interrupt Destinations (Vector Locations)

Each interrupt source can also be individually programmed to one of two priority levels by setting or clearing a bit in Special Function Register IP (Fig. 19.36). A low-priority interrupt can itself be interrupted by a high-priority interrupt, but not by another low priority interrupt. A high-priority interrupt can't be interrupted by any other interrupt source.

(MSB) (LSB)

-	-	-	PS	PT1	PX1	PT0	PX0

Symbol	Position	Name and Significance
-	IP.7	(Reserved)
-	IP.6	(Reserved)
-	IP.5	(Reserved)
PS	IP.4	Serial port Priority control bit. Set/cleared by software to specify high/low priority interrupts for Serial port.
PT1	IP.3	Timer 1 Priority control bit. Set/cleared by software to specify high/low priority interrupts for timer/counter 1.
PX1	IP.2	External interrupt 1 Priority control bit. Set/cleared by software to specify high/low priority interrupts for INT1.
PT0	IP.1	Timer 0 Priority control bit. Set/cleared by software to specify high/low priority interrupts for timer/counter 0.
PX0	IP.0	External interrupt 0 Priority control bit. Set/cleared by software to specify high/low priority interrupts for INT0.

Fig. 19.36 IP-interrupt priority control register

If two requests of different priority levels are received simultaneously, the request of higher priority level is serviced. If requests of the same priority level are received simultaneously, an internal polling sequence determines which request is serviced.

Thus within each priority level there is a second priority structure determined by the polling sequence, as follows :

Interrupt	Vector location	Priority within level
External hardware interrupt 0 (INT0)	0003H	(highest)
Timer 0 interrupt (TF0)	000BH	
External hardware interrupt 1 (INT1)	0013H	
Timer 1 interrupt (TF1)	001BH	
Serial communication interrupt (RI and TI)	0023H	(lowest)

Table 19.5 Interrupt vector table (IVT) and priority levels

Note that the "priority within level" structure is only used to resolve simultaneous requests of the same priority level.

19.9 Programming Interrupts

19.9.1 Programming Timer Interrupts

The Timer 0 and Timer 1 interrupts are generated by TF0 and TF1, which are set by a rollover in their respective Timer/Counter registers (except see Timer 0 in Mode 3). When a timer interrupt is generated, the flag that generated it is cleared by the on-chip hardware when the service routine is vectored.

We have seen the use of timer 0 and timer 1 with the polling method. Here, we are discussing the use of interrupts to program 8051 timers. We know that the timer flag (TF) is set (=1) when the timer rolls over. In polling method, the TF is monitored with the instruction 'JNB TF, target address'. We have to wait until the TF is raised. The problem with this polling method is that 8051 can not do anything else until TF is set to high. This problem can be solved using interrupt method. If the timer interrupt in the IE register is enabled, TF is set whenever the timer is rolled over and the 8051 is interrupted. Thus the 8051 can perform anything else until it is interrupted. After interruption (timer rolling over) only the 8051 remains busy in executing interrupt service routine.

Example 19.24 : *Write an 8051 ALP that continuously read 8-bit data from port 2 and sends it to port 0. At the same time it should generate square wave of 500 μs period on port 1.0. Assume the crystal frequency = 11.0592 MHz.*

Solution : We will use timer 0 in autoreload mode, i.e. mode 2. To generate square wave of 500 μs we have to toggle port 1.0 pin after every 250 μs.

$$\text{Timer clock frequency} = \frac{11.0592 \times 10^6}{12} = 921.6 \text{ kHz}$$

$$\therefore \quad TH0 = 256 - 250 \ \mu s \times 921.6 \times 10^3$$

$$\approx 26 = 1\text{ AH}$$

Program :

```
        ORG 0000H
        LJMP MAIN          ; Avoid using memory space
                           ; allocated to interrupt vector table

        ORG 000BH          ; ISR for Timer 0 interrupt
        CPL P1.0           ; Complement P1.0 bit
        RETI               ; return from ISR

        ORG 0030H          ; Start main program after
                           ; interrupt vector table
MAIN :  MOV TMOD, #02H     ; Initialize timer 0 in mode 2
        MOV P2, #0FFH      ; Configure Part 2 as input
        MOV TH0, #AH       ; Load timer count
        MOV IE, #82H       ; Enable timer 0 interrupt
        SETB TR0           ; Start timer 0
BACK :  MOV A, P2          ; Read data from P2
        MOV P0, A          ; Send it on P0
        SJMP BACK          ; Repeat
        END
```

19.9.2 Programming External Hardware Interrupts

Pins, P 3.2 (pin number 12) and P 3.3 (pin number 13) in port 3 are used as external hardware interrupts INT0 and INT1, respectively. The external Interrupts $\overline{\text{INT0}}$ and $\overline{\text{INT1}}$ can each be either level-activated or transition-activated, depending on bits IT0 and IT1 in register TCON.

In the level triggered mode, external interrupt pins $\overline{\text{INT0}}$ and $\overline{\text{INT1}}$ are normally high and if a low-level signal is applied to them, if triggers the interrupt. On the other hand, in edge trigger mode, high to low input signal transition its the interrupt.

The flags that actually generate these interrupts are bits IE0 and IE1 in TCON. When an external interrupt is generated, the flag that generated it is cleared by the hardware when the service routine is vectored to only if the interrupt was transition-activated. If the interrupt was level-activated, then the external requesting source is what controls the request flag, rather than the on-chip hardware.

If ITx = 0, external interrupt x is triggered by a detected low at the $\overline{\text{INTx}}$ pin. If ITx = 1, external interrupt x is edge-triggered. In this mode if successive samples of the $\overline{\text{INTx}}$ pin show a high in one cycle and a low in the next cycle, interrupt request flag IEx in TCON is set. Flag bit IEx then requests the interrupt.

Since the external interrupt pins are sampled once each machine cycle, an input high or low should hold for at least 12 oscillator periods to ensure sampling. If the external interrupt is transition-activated, the external source has to hold the request pin high for at least one machine cycle, and then hold it low for at least one machine cycle to ensure that the transition is seen so that interrupt request flag IEx will be set. IEx will be automatically cleared by the CPU when the service routine is called.

If the external interrupt is level-activated, the external source has to hold the request active until the requested interrupt is actually generated. Then it has to deactivate the request before the interrupt service routine is completed, or else another interrupt will be generated.

Example 19.25 : *Write an 8051 ALP to glow LED for a fraction of second when external interrupt INT0 is activated.*

Solution :

```
        ORG 0000H
        LJMP MAIN            ; Avoid using memory space
                             ; allocated to interrupt vector table

        ORG 0003H
        SETB P1.0            ; Turn ON LED
BACK :  MOVE R2, #0FFH       ; Load count
        DJNZ BACK            ; Decrement count and if not zero repeat
        CLR P1.0             ; Turn OFF LED
        RETI                 ; Return to main program

        ORG 0030H            ; Start main program after interrupt
                             ; vector table
MAIN :  MOV IE, #10000001B   ; Enable external interrupt 0
HERE :  SJMP HERE            ; wait for interrupt
        END
```

19.9.3 Programming the Serial Communication Interrupts

The Serial port interrupt is generated by the logical OR of RI and TI. Neither of these flags is cleared by hardware when the service routine is vectored to. In fact, the service routine will normally have to determine whether it was RI or TI that generated the interrupt, and the bit will have to be cleared in software.

Here, we are discussing interrupt based serial communication. In this case, the 8051 can perform other tasks in addition to serial communication, i.e. sending and receiving data from serial communication port.

We know from Chapter 6 that transmit interrupt (TI) flag is set (=1) when the last bit of the framed data (stop bit) is transmitted. This indicates that the SBUF register is ready to transmit the next byte. The receive interrupt (RI) flag is set (=1) when the complete frame of data (with stop bit) is received. RI indicates that the received byte needs to be picked up before it is lost by new incoming serial data.

All the above concepts are applied equally using polling or an interrupt. Only difference is in serving the serial communication needs. In polling method, the flag (TI or RI) is monitored. The 8051 can not do anything else until this flag is set to high. This problem is solved using interrupt method. When 8051 has received a byte or is ready to send the next byte, the RI or TI flag respectively is set. Any other work can be performed while the serial communication needs are served. There is a single interrupt set aside for serial communication. If IE register (IE.4) is enabled, when RI or TI is set (= 1), the 8051 is interrupted. When interrupted, the ISR written at 0023h is executed by 8051. In ISR, the TI and RI flags must be examined to check which one caused the interrupt and according to flag the response is given.

Example 19.26 : *Write an 8051 ALP that continuously read 8-bit data from port 2 and sends it to port 0. At the same time it should read incoming data from serial port at baud rate 9600 and send it to port 1. Assume that crystal frequency = 11.0592 MHz.*

Solution :

```
            ORG 0000H
            LJMP MAIN               ; Avoid using memory space
                                    ; allocated to interrupt vector table
            ORG 0023H
            JNB RI, SKIP            ; If RI is low goto skip
            MOV A , SBUF            ; Otherwise receive serial data
            MOV P1, A               ; Send it to port 1
               CLR RI               ; Clear RI
               RETI                 ; Return to main program
SKIP    :      CLR TI               ; Clear TI
               RETI                 ; Return to main program

               ORG 100H
MAIN :         MOV P2, #0FFH        ; Configure P2 as an input port
```

```
        MOV TMOD, #20H      ; Initialize timer 1 in mode 2
        MOV TH1, #FDH       ; Load count to get 9600 baud rate
        MOV SCON, #50H      ; Select serial mode with receiver
                            ; enabled
        MOV IE, #10010000B  ; Enable serial interrupt
        SETB TR1            ; Start timer 1
BACK :  MOV A, P2           ; Read data from port 2
        MOV P0, A           ; Send it to port 0
        SJMP BACK           ; Repeat
        END
```

Example 19.27 : *Write an 8051 ALP that continuously read 8-bit data from port 2 and sends it to port 0. At the same time it should transmit the same data on serial port. Assume that crystal frequency = 11.0592 MHz.*

Solution :

```
        ORG 0000H
        LJMP MAIN           ; Avoid using memory space
                            ; allocated to interrupt vector table

        ORG 0023H
        JNB TI, SKIP        ; If TI is low goto SKIP
        MOV SBUF, A         ; Transfer data serially
        CLR TI              ; Clear TI
        RETI                ; Return to main program
SKIP :  CLR RI              ; Clear RI
        RETI                ; Return to main program

        ORG 100H
MAIN :  MOV P2, 0FFH        ; Configure P2 as an input port
        MOV TMOD, #20H      ; Initialize timer 1 in mode 2
        MOV TH1, #FDH       ; Load count to get 9600 baud rate
        MOV SCON, #40H      ; Select serial mode
        MOV IE,#10010000B   ; Enable serial interrupt
        SETB TRI            ; Start timer 1
        MOV A, P2           ; Read data from port 2
        MOV SBUF, A         ; Send the first byte serially
BACK :  MOV A, P2           ; Read data from port 2
        MOV P0, A           ; Send it to port 0
        SJMP BACK           ; Repeat
        END
```

Review Questions

Section 19.1

Q.1 *Explain the I/O ports of 8051.* **Dec.-08, Marks 8**

Section 19.4

Q.1 *Explain the timer/counter functional unit of microcontroller 8051 with relevant diagrams.* **May-08, Marks 16**

Q.2 *Discuss in detail the on chip timers supported by 8051, bringing out the various modes of operation of these timers.* **Dec-09, Marks 16**

Q.3 *Draw the TMOD register format and explain.* **Dec.-11, Marks 4**

Section 19.5

Q.1 *Describe the different modes of operation of timers in 8051.* **Dec.-07,11, May-10,11, June-11, Marks 8**

Section 19.6

Q.1 *Write a note on counter programming of 8051.*

Section 19.7

Q.1 *Discuss the serial interface of 8051.* **May-05, Marks 8**

Q.2 *Discuss in detail, the hardware and software support provided by 8051 for serial communication.* **Dec-09, Marks 16**

Q.3 *Describe how the serial communication is performed in 8051.* **May-10, Dec.-08,11, Marks 8**

Q.4 *Draw the flowchart for programming of serial port of 8051.* **Dec.-11, Marks 2**

Q.5 *Explain the different serial communication modes in 8051.* **June-07, Marks 8**

Section 19.8

Q.1 *Explain the register IE format of 8051.*

Q.2 *Explain the interrupt structure of 8051 microcontroller and explain how interrupts are prioritized.* **June-07, Dec.-07, Marks 8**

Q.3 *Explain the interrupt structure with the associated registers in 8051 microcontroller.* **May-11, Marks 8**

Q.4 *Write 8051 ALP to transmit "Hello World" to PC at 9600 baud for external crystal frequency of 11.0592 MHz.* **June-07, Marks 8**

Two Marks Questions with Answers

Q.1 *Write the vector address and priority sequence of 8051 interrupts ?* **June-07**

Ans. : Refer section 19.8.2.

Q.2 *What is the function of SM2 bit in the SCON register of 8051 ?* **Dec.-07**

Ans. : Refer section 19.7.

Q.3 *Name the interrupts available in microcontroller 8051.* **May-08, Dec.-08**

Ans. : Refer section 19.8.

Q.4 *Write a delay routine for 1 millisecond using timer 0 of 8051 for 12 MHz crystal frequency.* **June-07**

Ans. : Crystal frequency = 12 MHz

$$\therefore \quad T = \frac{12}{12 \times 10^6} = 1 \ \mu s$$

i.e. the counter counts up every 1 μs. Out of many 1 μs internals, we have to make a 1 ms delay.

We need 1 ms/1 μs = 1000 clocks

$$N = 65536 - 1000 = 64536 = FC18H$$

We have to load TH with FCH and TL with 18H.

Program :

```
DELAY :   MOV TMOD, # 10H     ; Timer 1, Model
          MOV TL1, # 18H      ; TL1 = 18H, Timer 1 lower byte register
          MOV TH1, # FCH      ; TH1 = FCH, Time 1 higher byte register
          SETB TR1            ; Start timer 1
REPEAT :  JNB TR1, REPEAT     ; Monitor timer flag 1 till it becomes 1.
          CLR TR1             ; stop timer 1
          CLR TF1             ; Clear time 1 flag
          RET                 ; Return to main program
```

Q.5 *Explain the register IE format of 8051.*

Ans. : Refer Fig. 19.35.

Q.6 *Name the five interrupt sources of 8051 ?*

Ans. : The interrupts are :

External interrupt 0	IE0	0003H
Timer interrupt 0	TF0	000BH
External interrupt 1	IE1	0013H

Timer Interrupt 1	TF1	001BH
Receive interrupt	RI	0023H
Transmit interrupt	TI	0023H

Q.7 *How the RS -232C serial bus is interfaced to TTL logic device ?*

Ans. : The RS-232C signal voltage levels are not compatible with TTL logic levels. Hence for interfacing TTL devices to RS-232C serial bus, level converters are used. The popularly used level converters are MC 1488 & MC 1489 or MAX 232.

Q.8 *Define SBUF register in 8051 and mention its use.*

Ans. : SBUF is an 8-bit register dedicated for serial communication in 8051. Its address is 99H. It can be addressed like any other register in 8051. Writing to SBUF loads data to be transmitted and reading SBUF accesses received data.

Q.9 *Explain the use of interrupt enable register in 8051 microcontroller.*

Ans. : The interrupt enable register in 8051 microcontroller allows individually enabling and disabling of all interrupt sources in 8051.

Q.10 *What register keeps track of interrupt priority in the 8051 ? Explain.*

Ans. : Interrupt priority control registers keeps track of interrupt priority in the 8051.

Each interrupt source can also be individually programmed to one of two priority levels by setting or clearing a bit in interrupt priority control register.

A low-priority interrupt can itself be interrupted by a high-priority interrupt, but not by another low priority interrupt. A high-priority interrupt can't be interrupted by any other interrupt source.

Q.11 *What is the function of SM2 bit in the SCON register of 8051 ?* **Dec.-07**

Ans. : Refer section 19.7.

Q.12 *Name the interrupts available in microcontroller 8051.* **May-08, Dec.-08**

Ans. : Refer section 19.8.

Q.13 *Write the vector address and priority sequence of 8051 interrupts ?* **June-07**

Ans. : Refer section 19.8.2

❑❑❑

Notes

20 Microcontroller Applications

Contents

20.1 Keyboard Interface

For interfacing keyboard to the microprocessor/microcontroller based systems, usually push button keys are used. These push button keys when pressed, bounces a few times, closing and opening the contacts before providing a steady reading, as shown in the Fig. 20.1 Reading taken during bouncing period may be faulty. Therefore, microprocessor/microcontroller must wait until the key reach to a steady state; this is known as **key debounce**.

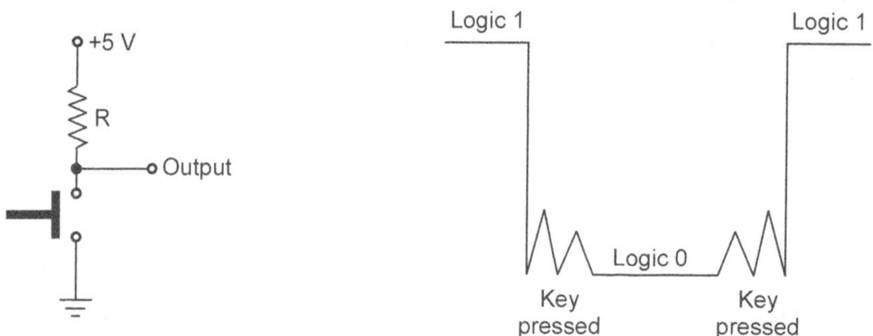

Fig. 20.1 Bouncing of key switch

The problem of key bounce can be eliminated using key debounce technique, either hardware or software.

20.1.1 Key Debounce using Hardware

Key position	a	b	Y	c	d	$\overline{Y}$
A	0	0	1	1	1	0
B	1	1	0	0	0	1
Between A and B	1	$\overline{Y}$	No change	Y	1	No change

Table 20.1

Fig. 20.2 shows the circuit diagram of key debounce. It consists of flip-flop. The output of flip-flop shown in Fig. 20.2 is logic 1 when key is at position A (unpressed) and it is logic 0 when key is at position B, as shown in Table 20.1. It is important to note that, when key is in between A and B, output does not change, preventing bouncing of key output. In other words we can say that output does not change during transition period, eliminating key debouncing.

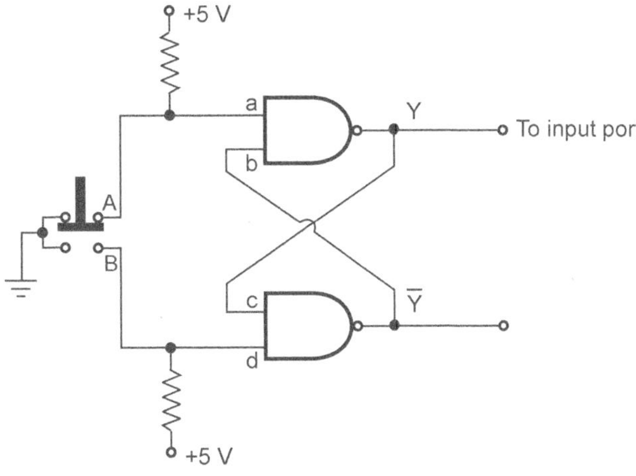

Fig. 20.2

20.1.2 Key Debouncing using Software

In the software technique, when a key press is found, the microprocessor/microcontroller waits for at least 10 ms before it accepts the key as an input. This 10 ms period is sufficient to settle key at steady state. Fig. 20.3 (See on next page) shows the flowchart with key debounce technique.

20.1.3 Simple Keyboard Interface

Fig. 20.4 shows simple keyboard interface.

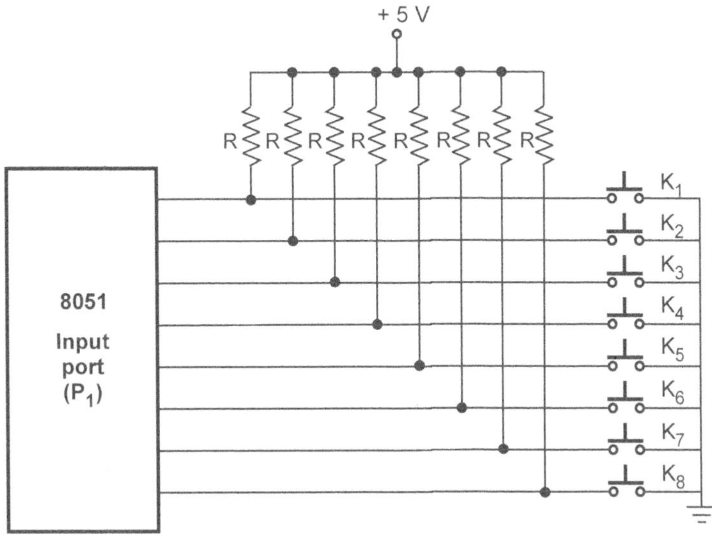

Fig. 20.4 Simple keyboard interface

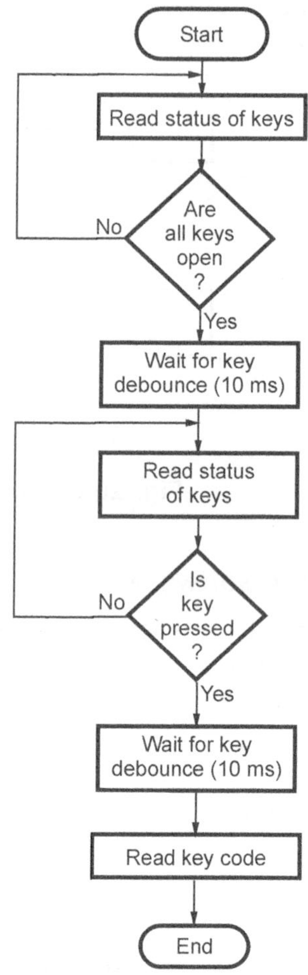

Fig. 20.3 Flowchart of key input with debounce

Here eight keys are individually connected to specific pins of port P1. Each port pin gives the status of key connected to that pin. When port pin is logic 1, key is open, otherwise key is closed.

Software routine to get keycode with key debounce.

```
START :  MOV A, P1                 ; Read key status
                                   ; check if keys are open
         CJNE A,#FFH,START         ; if no, goto start otherwise
                                   ; continue
PRO :    LCALL DEBOUNCE_DELAY      ; call debounce delay
AGAIN :  MOV A, P1                 ; Read key status
         CJNE A, #FFH PRO1         ; check if any key is pressed
         LJMP AGAIN                ; if no, goto AGAIN; otherwise
                                   ; continue
```

```
PRO1 :  LCALL DEBOUNCE_DELAY   ; call debounce delay
        MOV A, P1              ; Get key code
        RET                    ; Return from subroutine
```

This program reads status of all keys by getting data through P1 and compares it with FFH to check whether all keys are open. If all keys are open, instruction compare sets the zero flag, and the program waits for key debounce. After waiting about 10 ms, program checks the P1 for key press. If key press is found, program waits for another 10 ms as a key debounce period. After key debounce period, program reads the keycode from P1.

Key	Keycode							
	D_7	D_6	D_5	D_4	D_3	D_2	D_1	D_0
K_1	1	1	1	1	1	1	1	0
K_2	1	1	1	1	1	1	0	1
K_3	1	1	1	1	1	0	1	1
K_4	1	1	1	1	0	1	1	1
K_5	1	1	1	0	1	1	1	1
K_6	1	1	0	1	1	1	1	1
K_7	1	0	1	1	1	1	1	1
K_8	0	1	1	1	1	1	1	1

Table 20.2

20.1.4 Matrix Keyboard Interface

In simple keyboard interface one input line is required to interface one key and this number will increase with number of keys. Therefore, such technique is not suitable when it is necessary to interface large number of keys. To reduce number of connections keys are arranged in the matrix form as shown in the Fig. 20.5.

Fig. 20.5 shows sixteen keys arranged in four rows and four columns. When keys are open, row and column do not have any connection. When a key is pressed, it shorts corresponding one row and one column. This matrix keyboard requires eight lines to make all the connections instead of the sixteen lines required if the keys are connected individually, as shown in Fig. 20.4. Fig. 20.6 shows the interfacing of matrix keyboard. It requires two ports : an input port and an output port. Rows are connected to the input port referred to as returned lines, and columns are connected to the output port referred to as scan lines. We know that, when all keys are open, row and column do not have any connection. When any key is pressed it shorts corresponding row and column. If the output line of this column is low, it makes corresponding row line low; otherwise the status of row line is high. The key is identified by data sent on the output port and input code received from the input port. The following section explains the steps required to identify pressed key.

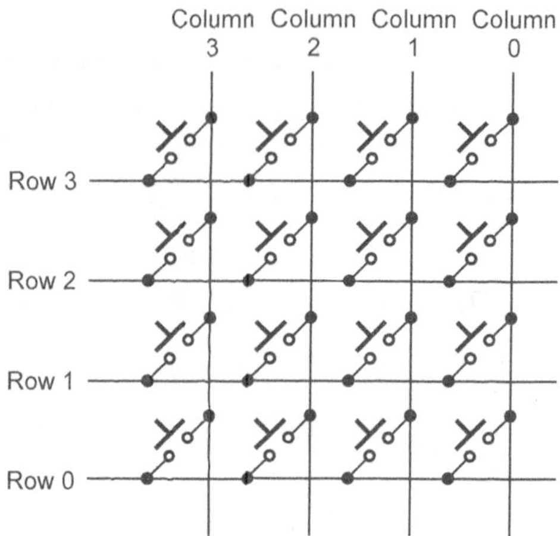

Fig. 20.5 Matrix keyboard

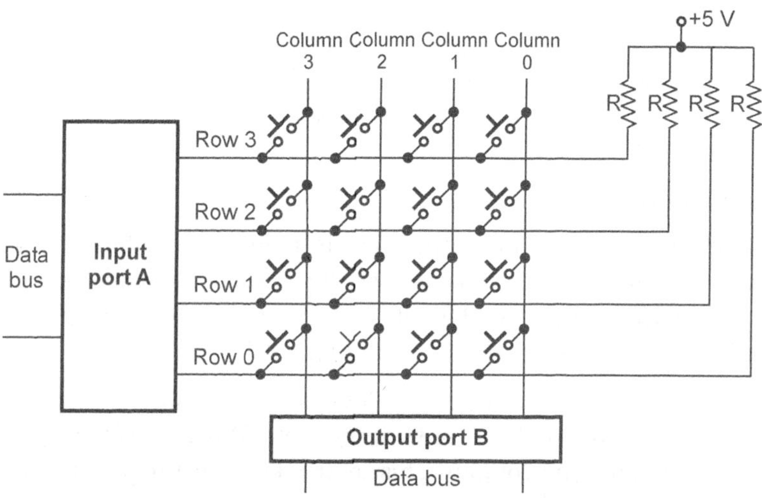

Fig. 20.6 Matrix keyboard connections

Check 1 : Whether any key is pressed or not

1. Make all column lines zero by sending low on all output lines. This activates all keys is in the keyboard matrix. (Note : When scan lines are logic high, the status on the return lines do not change, it will remain logic high.)

2. Read the status of return lines. If the status of all lines is logic high, key is not pressed; otherwise key is pressed.

Check 2 :

1. Activate keys from any one column by making any one column line zero.
2. Read the status of return lines. The zero on any return line indicates key is pressed from the corresponding row and selected column. If the status of all lines is logic high, key is not pressed from that column.
3. Activate the keys from the next column and repeat 2 and 3 for all columns.

We will see how matrix keyboard can be connected to the 8051, a single chip microprocessor/microcontroller. Fig. 20.7 shows the 4 × 4 matrix keyboard connected to the port 1 of 8051. 4 lines of port 1 (P14-P17) are used as a scan lines and remaining 4 lines (P10-P13) are used as return lines.

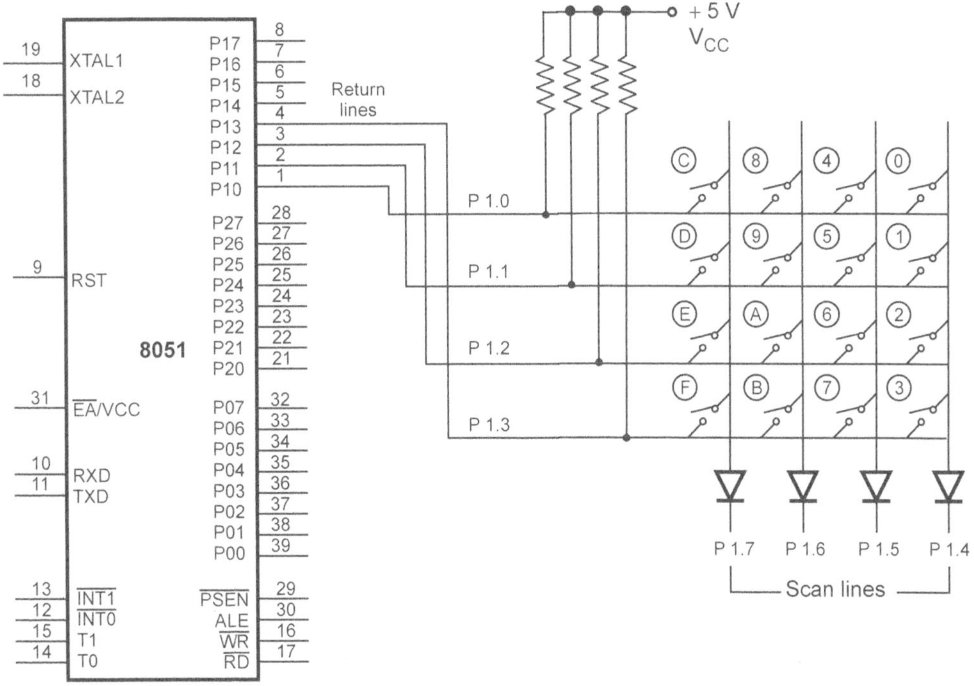

Fig. 20.7 4 × 4 matrix keyboard connected to port 1 of 8051

The steps in algorithm are as follows :

1. Initialise P1.0, P1.1, P1.2, P1.3 as inputs i.e. write '1' to these pins.
2. Check if all the keys are released by writing '0' to P1.4-P1.7 and check if all return lines are in state '1'. If No then wait.

   If Yes then go to step 3.
3. Call debounce.

4. Wait for key closure. Ground all scan lines by writing '0' and then check if at least one of return lines shows '0' level.

   Key pressed ? No step 4

   Yes step 5

5. Call debounce. (allow sufficient time for debounce)

6. Is key really pressed ? (Ground all scan lines by writing '0' and then check if at least one of the return lines shows '0' level.)

   No step 4

   Yes step 7

7. Find key code and display the key pressed on 7-segment display.

   (By grounding one scan line at a time and checking return lines for any one line to go to '0' level.)

8. Go to step 1.

Program :

```
        org lookup_table_address
        db 30h, 31h, 32h, 33h, 34h, 35h, 36h, 37h,
        38h, 39h, 41h, 42h, 43h, 44h, 45h, 46h
        org program_start_address
beg:    mov P1 #0f h        ; configure lower 4 lines of port 1
                            ; as i/p
        mov dptr,#lookup_table_address ; initialise dptr with
                                       ; lookup_table_addr.
aga:    mov a, P1           ;
        anl a, #0fh         ;
        cjne a, #0fh,aga    ; check for key released
        1call delay         ; call delay routine for key debounce
agal:   mov a, P1
        anl a, #0fh
        cjne a,#0fh, go     ; check for key pressed
        ljmp agal
go:     1call delay         ; call delay routine for key debounce
        mov a, P1
        anl a, #0fh
        cjne a,#0fh, go1    ; is  key really pressed ?
        ljmp agal
go1:    mov r1, # 01h       ; initialise counter 1
        mov r0, #0efh       ; store word for column selection
        mov r3, #04h        ; initialise column counter
```

```
aga3: mov P1, r0          ; select only 1 column
      mov a, P1           ; get the status of return lines
      jnb acc.0,display   ; check bit 0 and if it is 0 jump to display
      inc dptr            ; increment lookup_table pointer
      jnb acc.1,display   ; check bit 1 and if it is 1 jump
                          ; to display
      inc dptr            ; increment lookup_table pointer
      inb acc.2,display   ; check bit 2 and if it is 2 jump
                          ; to display
      inc dptr            ; increment lookup_table pointer
      jnb acc.3,display   ; check bit 3 and if it is 3 jump to display
      inc dptr            ; increment lookup_table pointer
      mov a, r0           ; get the word for column selection
      rl a                ; select next column
      mov r0, a           ; store word for column selection
      djnz r3, aga3       ; check for last column
      1jmp beg            ; if any key is not pressed scan again
   end
```

20.2 Display Interface

20.2.1 LED Interfacing

- **Sourcing current :** It refers to the maximum current that the 8051 port pin can supply to drive an externally connected device. The device can be an LED, a buzzer or TTL logic device. For TTL family of 8051 devices the sourcing current is approximately 60 μA.
- **Sinking current :** It refers to the maximum current that the 8051 port pin can absorb through a device which is connected to an external supply. Pins of P1, P2 and P3 can sink a maximum current of 1.6 mA. Port 0 pins can sink current upto 3.2 mA.
- A typical LED consumes 10 to 15 mA. Thus we cannot drive LED directly in current source mode as shown in the Fig. 20.8 (a). However, we can drive LED directly in current sink mode, as shown in the Fig. 20.8 (b). Here, sinking current of 8051 is not enough to drive LED, so the brightness of LED is poor.

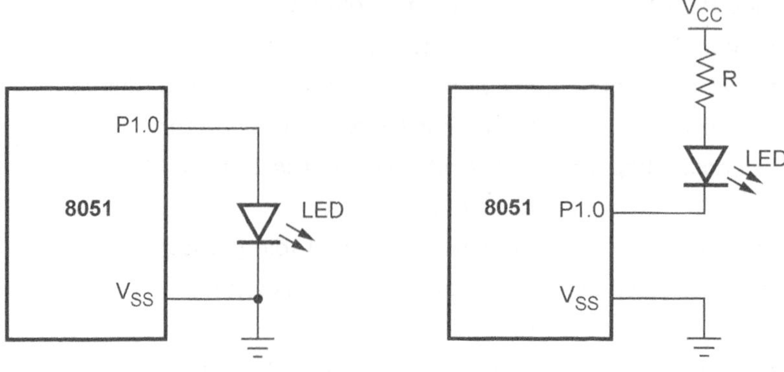

(a) Wrong connection (b) LED connected in current sink mode

Fig. 20.8

- We can use driver transistor to solve the problem of current sinking and sourcing. The Fig. 20.9 shows the LED interface using driver transistor.
- In Fig. 20.9 (a), the source current of 8051 port pin is amplified by the npn transistor to drive the LED. In Fig. 20.9 (b), the pnp transistor is used to amplify the sinking current.

$$R = \frac{V_{CC} - V_{LED}}{I_{LED}} \qquad R_B = \frac{V_{out} - V_{BE}}{(I_{LED} / \beta)}$$

where V_{LED} is the voltage across LED

I_{LED} is the current through LED

V_{out} is the voltage at output pin

β is the current gain (Beta) of the transistor

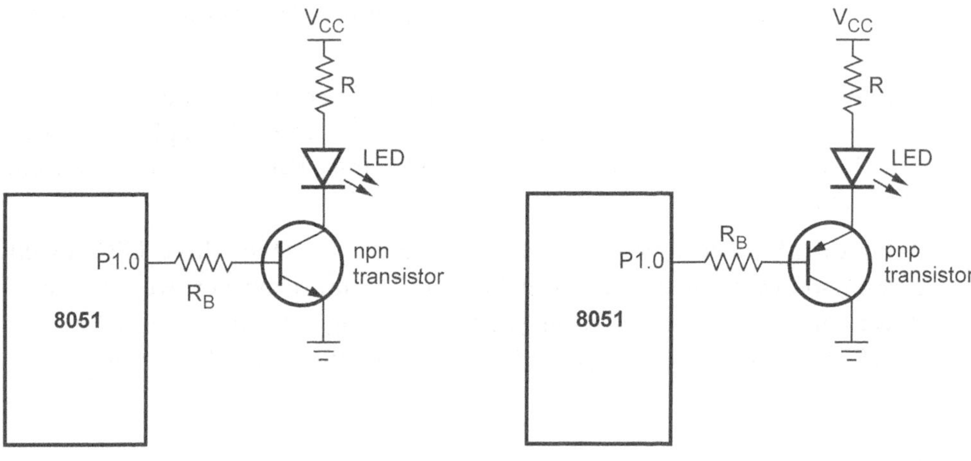

(a) LED interface in current source mode (b) LED interface in current sink mode

Fig. 20.9

Example 20.1 : *Write an ALP to flash the LED connected to port P2.0.*

Solution : Algorithm 1

Step 1 : Make P2.0 High

Step 2 : Wait for some time

Step 3 : Make P2.0 LOW

Step 4 : Wait for some time

Step 5 : Repeat steps 1 through step 4

Algorithm 2

Step 1 : Complement P2.0

Step 2 : Wait for some time

Step 3 : Repeat steps 1 and 2

Program 1 :

```
        ORG 0000H
BACK :  SETB P2.0       ;  Make P2.0 high
        ACALL Delay     ;  Wait for some time
        CLR P2.0        ;  Make P2.0 low
        ACALL Delay     ;  Wait for some time
        SJMP BACK       ;  repeat
```

Program 2 :

```
        ORG 0000H
BACK :  CPL P2.0        ;  Complement P2.0
        ACALL Delay     ;  Wait for some time
        SJMP BACK
```

20.2.2 Multiplexed 7-Segment Display Interfacing

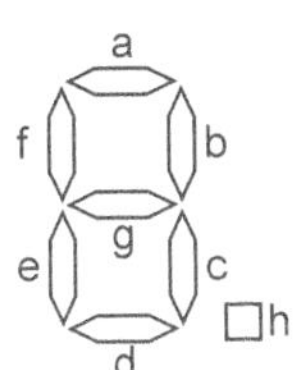

Fig. 20.10 Seven-segment display

Seven-segment display : Seven-segment displays are generally used as numerical indicators and consists of a number of LEDs arranged in seven-segments as shown in the Fig. 20.10.

Any number between 0 and 9 can be indicated by lighting the appropriate segments.

The seven-segments are labelled a to g and dot is labelled as h. By forward biasing different LED segments, we can display the digits 0 through 9. For instance, to display 0, we need to light up a, b, c, d, e, and f. To light up 5, we need segments a, f, g, c and d.

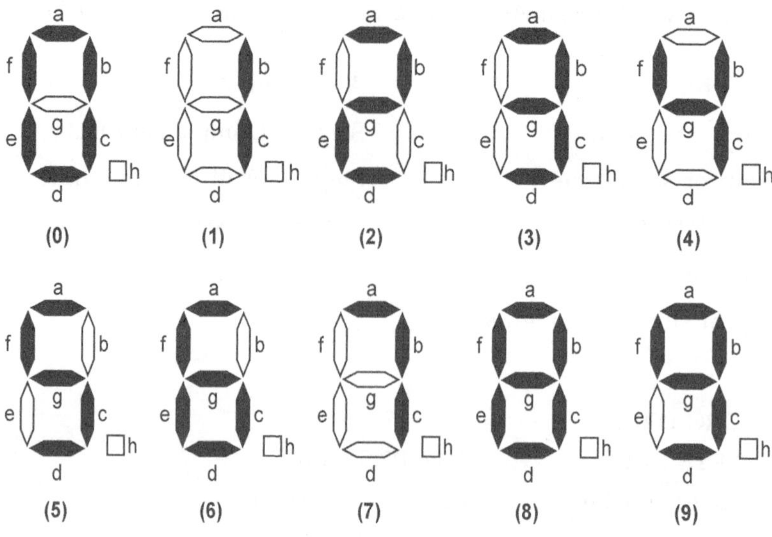

Fig. 20.11

These 7-segment displays are of two types :

- Common anode type
- Common cathode type

In common anode, all anodes of LEDs are connected together as shown in Fig. 20.12 (a) and in common cathode, all cathodes are connected together, as shown in Fig. 20.12 (b).

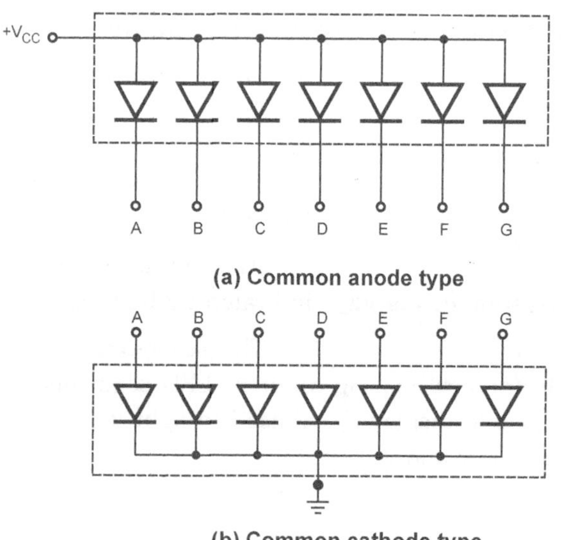

(a) Common anode type

(b) Common cathode type

Fig. 20.12 Internal diagram of 7-segment LED

Static display

Fig. 20.13 shows a circuit to drive a single, seven-segment, common anode LED display. For common anode, when anode is connected to positive supply, a low voltage is applied to a cathode to turn it on. Here, BCD to seven-segment decoder, IC 7447 is used to apply low voltages at cathodes according to BCD input applied to IC 7447. To limit the current through LED segments resistors are connected in series with the segments. This circuit connection is referred to as a static display because current is being passed through the display at all times.

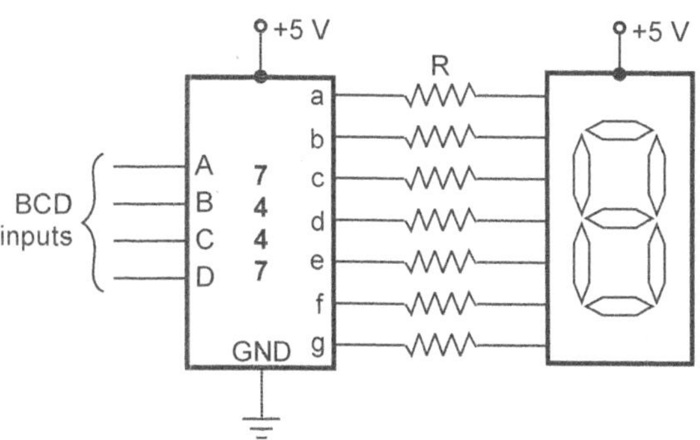

Fig. 20.13 Circuit for driving single seven-segment LED display

The value of the resistor in series with the segment can be calculated as follows :

We know, V_{CC} – drop across LED segment – IR = 0

Drop across LED segment is nearly 1.5 V.

$$\therefore \quad IR = V_{CC} - 1.5\text{ V} = 5 - 1.5\text{ V}$$

$$= 3.5\text{ V}$$

Each LED segment requires a current of between 5 and 30 mA to light. Let's assume that current through LED segment is 15 mA.

$$\therefore \quad R = \frac{3.5\text{V}}{15\text{mA}} = 233\ \Omega$$

In practice, the voltage drop across the LED and the output of IC 7447 are not exactly predictable and the exact current through the LED is not critical as long as we don't exceed its maximum current rating. Therefore, a standard value 220 Ω can be used.

The static display circuits work well for driving just one or two LED digits. However, these circuits are not suitable for driving more LED digits, say 8 digits. When there are more number of digits, the first problem is power consumption. For worst case calculations, assume that all eight digits with all segments are lit. Therefore, worst case current required is

$$I = 8\text{ (digits)} \times 7\text{ (segment)} \times 15\text{ mA (current per segment)}$$

$$= 840\text{ mA}$$

A second problem of the static approach is that each display digit requires a separate BCD to 7-segment decoder.

Multiplexed display

To solve the problems of the static display approach, multiplexed display method is used. Fig. 20.14 shows the 4 seven-segment displays connected using multiplexed method. Here, common anode seven-segment LEDs are used.

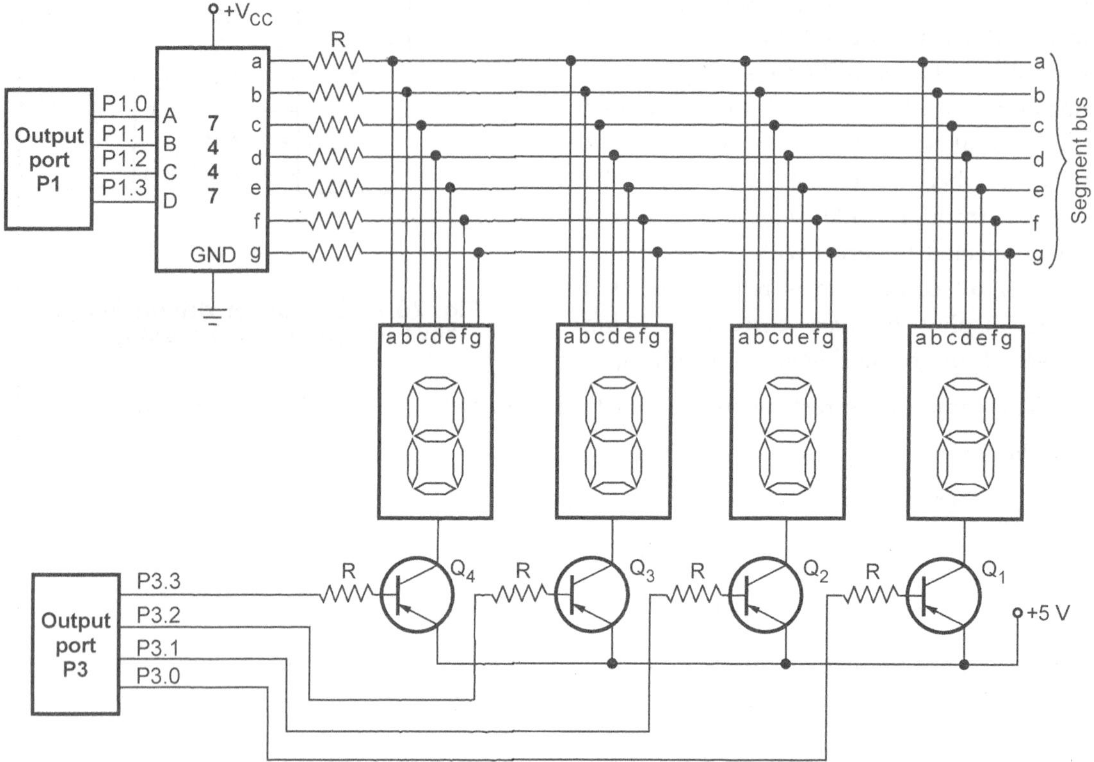

Fig. 20.14 Seven-segment display in multiplexed connection

Anodes are connected to +5 V through transistors. Cathodes of all seven-segments are connected in parallel and then to the output of 7447 IC through resistors. Looking at the Fig. 20.14 the question may occur in our mind that,"Aren't all of the digits going to display the same number?" The answer is that they would show the same number only if all the digits are turned on at the same time. However, in multiplexed display the segment information is sent for all digits on the common lines (output lines of IC 7447), but only one display digit is turned on at a time. The PNP transistors connected in series with the common anode of each digit act as an ON and OFF switch for that digit. Here's how the multiplexing process works.

The BCD code for digit 1 is first output from port 1, to the IC 7447. The IC 7447, BCD to seven-segment decoder outputs the corresponding seven-segment code on the segment bus lines. The transistor Q_1 connected to digit 1 is then turned on by outputting a low to that bit of port 3. All of the rest of the bits of port 3 are made high to ensure no other digits are turned on. After 2 ms, digit 1 is turned OFF outputting all highs to port 3. The

BCD code for digit 2 is then output to the port 1, and bit pattern to turn on digit 2 is output on port 3. After 2 ms, digit 2 is turned off and the process is repeated for digit 3 and digit 4. After completion of turn for each digit, all the digits are lit again in turn.

With 4 digits and 2 ms per digit we get back to digit 1 every 8 ms or about 125 times a second. This refresh rate is fast enough that, to our eye and due to persistence of vision all digits will appear to be lit all the time.

In multiplexed display, the segment current is kept in between 40 mA to 60 mA so that they will appear as bright as they would if not multiplexed. Even with this increased segment current, multiplexing gives a large saving in power and hardware components.

Example 20.2 : *Interface an 8-bit 7-segment LED display to 8051 through port 1 and port 3 and write an 8051 assembly language program to display message on the display.*

Solution : Hardware

The Fig. 20.15 shows the multiplexed 8-digit 7-segment LED display connected in 8051 system using port 1 and port 3. In this circuit port 1 and port 3 are used as a latch, i.e. output port. Port 1 provides the segment data inputs to the display and port 3 provides a means of selecting a display position at a time for multiplexing the displays. Here, instead of BCD to seven-segment decoder (IC 7447) transistors are used to drive the LED segments. Due to this we can also display HEX characters on the display; however in this case we have to send the proper 7-segment code of a particular digit that is to be displayed on the port 1. (See Fig. 20.15 on next page)

Subroutine to Display Message

```
        MOV R0, #8H       ; Initialize counter
        MOV R1, #7FH      ; load select pattern
        MOV DPTR, #6000H  ; Starting address of message to
                          ; be displayed
AGAIN : MOV P3, R1        ; select digit
        MOVX A, @DPTR     ; Get data
        MOV P1, A         ; Send data
        LCALL DELAY       ; Wait for some time
        MOV A, R1         ; [ Adjust
        RR A              ; selection
        MOV R1, A         ; pattern]
        INC DPTR          ; Increment message pointer
        DJNZ R0, AGAIN    ; Decrement R0 and check
        RET               ; if for zero; if not, goto AGAIN
```

Note : This subroutine must be called continuously to display the 7-segment coded message stored in the memory from address 6000H.

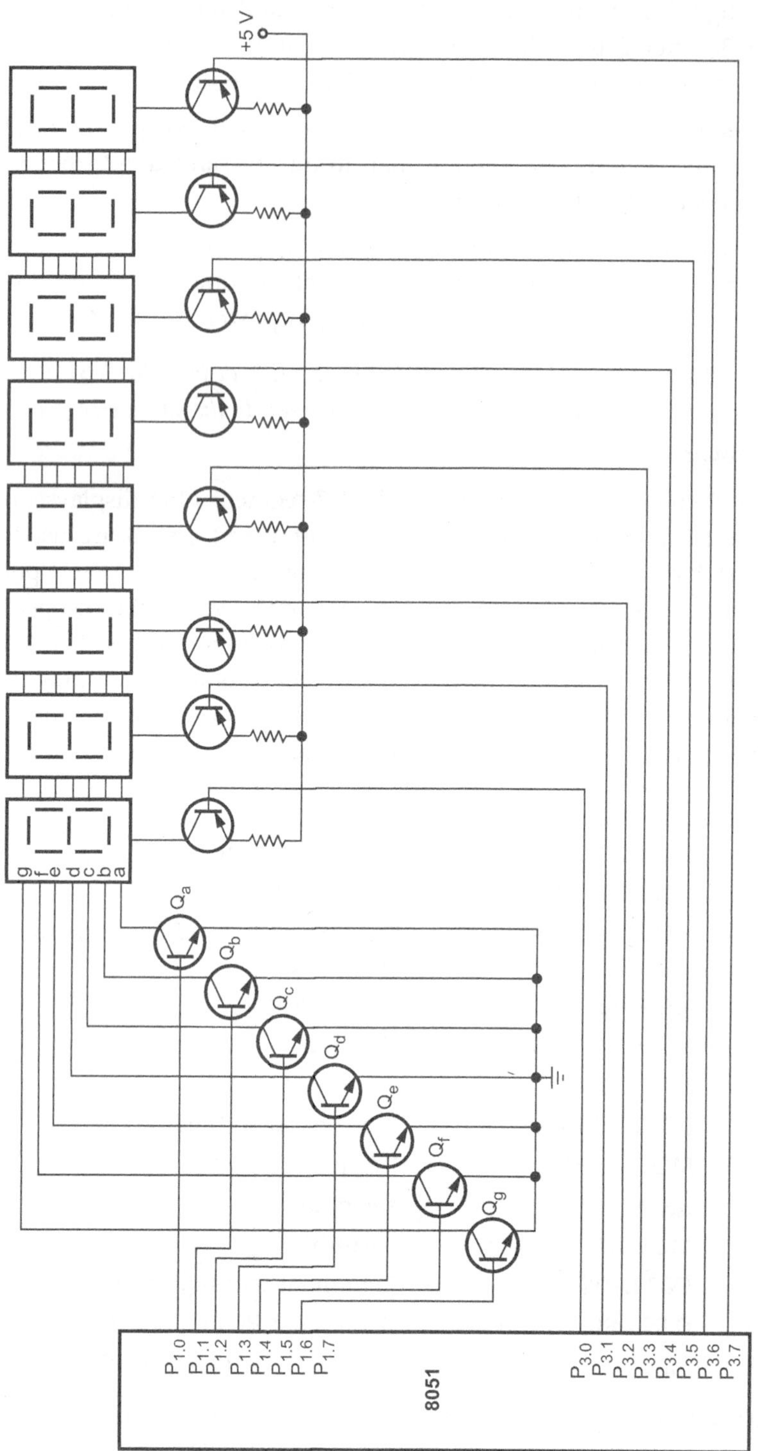
+5 V
a
b
c
d
e
f
g
Qa
Qb
Qc
Qd
Qe
Qf
Qg
P1.0
P1.1
P1.2
P1.3
P1.4
P1.5
P1.6
P1.7
8051
P3.0
P3.1
P3.2
P3.3
P3.4
P3.5
P3.6
P3.7

Fig. 20.15

20.2.3 LCD Interfacing

Now-a-days, many LCD modules are available which have built-in drivers for LCD and interfacing circuitry to interface them to microprocessor/microcontroller systems. These LCD modules allow display of characters as well as numbers. They are available in 16 × 2, 20 × 1, 20 × 2, 20 × 4 and 40 × 2 sizes. The main advantage of using LCD is modules is that they require very less power. The first figure represents number of character in each line and second figure represents number of lines the display has. In this section, we see the interfacing of 20 × 2 LCD display module to microprocessor/microcontroller system through 8255. In this module the display is organized as two lines, each of 20 characters. The module has 14-pins. The function of each pin is given in the Table 20.3.

Pin	Symbol	I/O	Description
1	V_{SS}	-	Ground
2	V_{CC}	-	+ 5 V power supply
3	V_{EE}	-	Used for controlling LCD contrast
4	RS	I	Register select input is used to select either of the two available registers in the module : Data register or command register. When RS = 0 Data register is selected. When RS = 1 Command register is selected.
5	$R/\overline{W}$	I	Allows the user to write information to the LCD or read information from it. For reading $R/\overline{W}$ = 1 and for writing $R/\overline{W}$ = 0
6	E	I	This pin is used by LCD to latch information available at its data pins.
7-14	DB_0-DB_7	I/O	This 8-bit data bus is used to send information to the LCD or read the contents of the internal registers of the LCD.

Table 20.3 Pin description for LCD module

The Fig. 20.16 shows the interfacing of a 20 character × 2 line LCD module with the 8051. As shown in the Fig. 20.16, the data lines are connected to the port 1 of 8051 and control lines RS, $R/\overline{W}$ and E are driven by 3.2, 3.3 and 3.4 lines of port 3, respectively. The voltage at V_{EE} pin is adjusted by a potentiometer to adjust the contrast of the LCD.

The display can be controlled by issuing proper commands to the LCD module. The Table 20.4 lists the command available for LCD module.

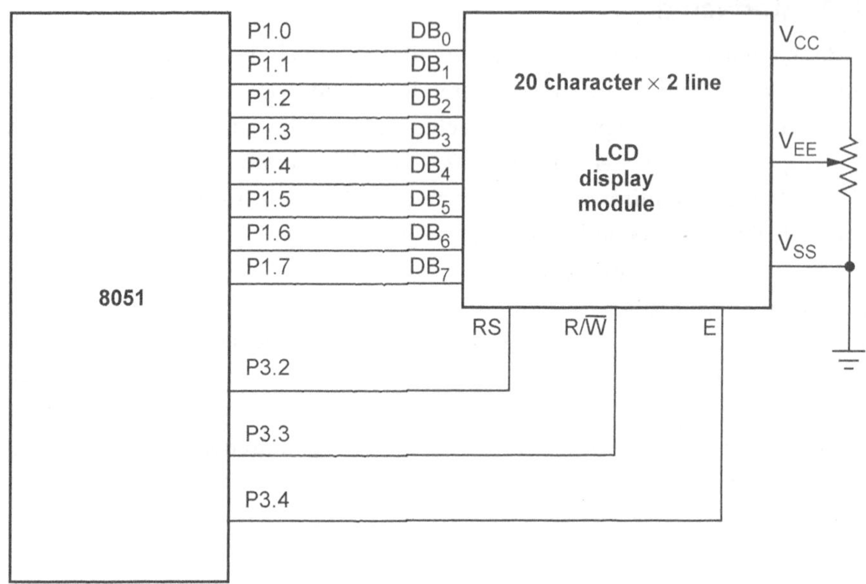

Fig. 20.16 Interfacing LCD module with 8051

Command	Command Code										Description
	RS	$R/\overline{W}$	DB_7	DB_6	DB_5	DB_4	DB_3	DB_2	DB_1	DB_0	
Clear display	0	0	0	0	0	0	0	0	0	1	Sets DD RAM address to 0 and clears entire display.
Return home	0	0	0	0	0	0	0	0	1	-	Sets DD RAM address to 0 and returns the cursor to the home position. DD RAM contents remain unchanged.
Entry mode set	0	0	0	0	0	0	0	1	1/D	S	Sets cursor move direction and specifies or not to shift the display. These operations are performed during data write and read.
Display ON/OFF control	0	0	0	0	0	0	1	D	C	B	Sets ON/OFF of entire display (D), cursor ON/OFF (C), and blink of cursor position character (B).
Cursor and display shift	0	0	0	0	0	1	S/C	R/L	-	-	Moves the cursor and shifts the display without changing DD RAM contents.
Function set	0	0	0	0	1	DL	N	F	-	-	Sets interface data length (DL), number of display lines (N), and character font (F).

Set CG RAM address	0	0	0	1	ACG	Sets CG RAM address. CG RAM is accessed after this setting.
Set DD RAM address	0	0	1	ADD		Sets DD RAM address. DD RAM is accessed after this setting
Read busy flag and address	0	1	BF	AC		Reads busy flag (BF) indicating internal operation is being performed and reads address counter contents
Write data to CG or DD RAM	1	0	Write data			Writes data into DD or CG RAM.
Read data from CG or DD RAM	1	1	Read data			Reads data from DD or CG RAM.

Table 20.4 List of LCD module commands

Abbreviations used in the table

DD RAM	:	Display data RAM			
CG RAM	:	Character generator RAM			
ACG	:	CG RAM address			
ADD	:	DD RAM address			
AC	:	Address counter used for both DD and CG RAM address			
1/D = 1	:	Increment	1/D = 0	:	Decrement
S = 1	:	Accompanies display shift			
S/C = 1	:	Display shift	S/C = 0	:	Cursor move
R/L = 1	:	Shift to right	R/L = 0	:	Shift to left
DL = 1	:	8-bits	DL = 0	:	4-bits
N = 1	:	2 Lines	N = 0	:	1 Line
F = 1	:	5×10 dots	F = 0	:	5×7 dots
BF = 1	:	Busy in internal operation			
BF = 0	:	Can accept command or instruction			

To display a message on LCD module, it is necessary to initialize it by writing series of command codes in the command register in a proper sequence. The initialization includes command codes for clearing the display, returning the cursor home, and shifting cursor automatically after writing a character. After initialisation we can write data to either DD RAM or CG RAM. Both RAMs are read/write RAMs and have unique addresses to access each location. To write data in any RAM we have to set the address for that RAM by issuing proper command. Then we can write data into it by activating write cycle. To activate write cycle we have to make $R/\overline{W}$ signal low, RS signal high, send data on port A and apply high to low pulse of at least 450 ns of duration on E pin of the module. The DD RAM stores the characters in their ASCII code whereas CG RAM stores the character in its internally generated character code. Let us see the 8051 assembly language program to display 'WELCOME' message on the LCD module. Before sending command or data it is necessary to check busy flag, i.e. whether LCD is reading or not.

MAIN Routine :

```
            MOV 81H,#30H        ;  Initialise stack pointer
            MOV A,#3CH          ;  [Send command code to set font
                                ;  = 5×10 dots,
            LCALL COMMAND       ;  DL = 8-bits and N = 2 lines].
            MOV A,#0EH          ;  [Send command code to set display
            LCALL COMMAND       ;  and cursor ON]
            MOV A,#01H          ;  [Send command code to
            LCALL COMMAND       ;  clear LCD]
            MOV A,#86H          ;  [Send command to set DD RAM
            LCALL COMMAND       ;  address to the seventh location]
            MOV A,#'W'
            LCALL DISPLAY       ;  Display letter W
            MOV A,#'E'
            LCALL DISPLAY       ;  Display letter E
            MOV A,#'L'
            LCALL DISPLAY       ;  Display letter L
            MOV A,#'C'
            LCALL DISPLAY       ;  Display letter C
            MOV A,#'O'
            LCALL DISPLAY       ;  Display letter O
            MOV A,#'M'
            LCALL DISPLAY       ;  Display letter M
            MOV A,#'E'
            LCALL DISPLAY       ;  Display letter E
    SJMP HERE:HERE              ;  Loop here after displaying
                                ;  message
```

COMMAND Routine :

```
        LCALL READY             ; Check whether LCD is ready ?
        MOV P1, A               ; Issue command code
        CLR P3.2                ; Make RS = 0 to issue command
        CLR P3.3                ; Make R/W̄ = 0 to enable writing
        SETB P3.4               ; Make E = 1
```

```
        CLR P3.4            ; Make E = 0
        RET                 ; Return
```

READY Routine :

```
        CLR P3.4            ; Disable display
        CLR P3.2            ; Make RS = 0 to access command register
        MOV P1,#0FFH        ; Configure P1 as an input port
        SETB P3.3           ; Make R/W̄ = 1 to enable reading
READ:   SETB P3.4           ; Make E = 1
        JB P1.7,READ        ; Check DB7 bit. If it is 1, LCD is busy
                            ; hence check if until it is 0
        CLR P3.4            ; Make E = 0 to disable display
        RET                 ; Return
```

DISPLAY Routine :

```
        LCALL READY         ; Check whether LCD is ready ?
        MOV P1, A           ; Issue data
        SETB P3.2           ; Make RS = 1 to issue data
        CLR P3.3            ; Make R/W̄ = 0 to enable writing
        SETB P3.4           ; Make E = 1
        CLR P3.4            ; Make E = 0
        RET                 ; Return
```

20.3 Closed Loop Control of Servomotor

A servo motor is a special case of a DC motor to which position or velocity feedback circuitry has been added to implement a closed loop control system. Like the DC motor, the servo motor can rotate in either direction; however, generally the range is less than 360 degrees. Also like the DC motor, the servo motor can be controlled by a pulse width modulated signal; however, the signal used to control position rather than speed.

The function of the servo motor is to receive a control signal that represents a **desired output position of the servo shaft,** and apply power to its DC motor until its shaft turns to that position. It uses the position-sensing device to determine the rotational position of the shaft, so it knows which way the motor must turn to move the shaft to the commanded position.

The servo motor has a 3 wire connection : power, ground, and control. The power source must be constantly applied; the servo has its own power electronics that draw current from the power lead to drive the motor.

The control signal is Pulse Width Modulated (PWM), but here the **duration** of the positive-going pulse determines the **position** of the servo shaft. For instance, a 1.520 millisecond pulse is the center. A longer pulse makes the servo turn to a clockwise-from-center position, and a shorter pulse makes the servo turn to a counter-clockwise-from-center position.

There are two important differences between the control pulse of the servo motor versus the DC motor. First, in the servo motor, duty cycle (on-time vs. off-time) has **no meaning** whatsoever-all that matters is the absolute duration of the positive-going pulse, which corresponds to a commanded output position of the servo shaft. Second, the servo has its own power electronics, so **very little power** flows over the control signal.

Closed-loop servo motor control is usually by 16-bit, high-end microcontrollers and external logic. In an attempt to increase performance many applications are upgrading to DSPs (Digital Signal Processors). However, the very high performance of the microcontrollers makes it possible to implement these servo control applications at a significant reduction in overall system cost.

The Fig. 20.17 shows the microcontroller based close loop, servo motor control circuitry. These systems control a motor with an incremental feedback device known as a sequential encoder. They consist of an encoder counter, a microcontroller, some form of D/A (Digital-to-Analog) converter, and a power amplifier which delivers current or voltage to the motor.

The D/A conversion can be handled by a conventional DAC or by using the microcontroller's pulse-width modulation (PWM). In either case the output signal is fed to a power stage which translates the analog signal(s) into usable voltages and currents to drive the motor.

PWM output can be a duty-cycle signal in combination with a direction signal or a single signal which carries both pieces of information. In the latter case a 50 % duty cycle commands a null output, a 0 % duty cycle commands maximum negative output, and 100 % maximum positive output.

The amplifier can be configured to supply a controlled voltage or current to the motor. Most embedded system use voltage output because its simpler and cheaper.

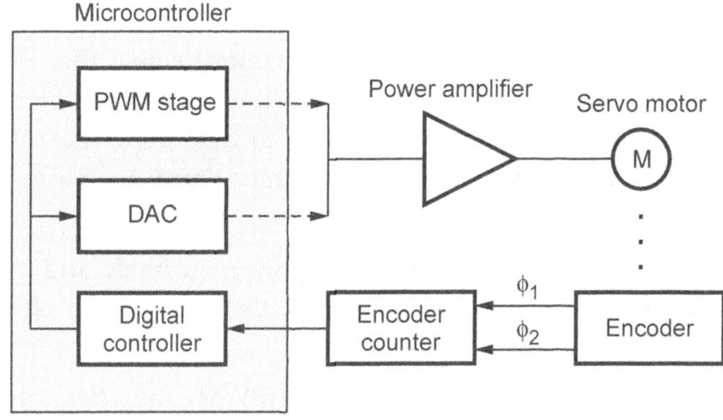

Fig. 20.17 Microcontroller based closed loop servo motor control circuit

Sequential encoders produce quadrature pulse trains, from which position, speed, and direction of the motor rotation can be derived. The frequency is proportional to speed and each transition of $\phi1$ and $\phi2$ represents an increment of position. The phase of the signals is used to determine direction of rotation.

These encoder signals are usually decoded into Count Up and Count Down pulses. These pulses are then routed to an N-bit, up/down counter whose value corresponds to the position of the motor shaft. The decoder/counter may be implemented in hardware, software, or a combination of the two.

20.4 Stepper Motor Control

A stepper motor is a digital motor. It can be driven by digital signal. Fig. 20.18 shows the typical 2 phase motor interfaced using 8051. Motor shown in the circuit has two

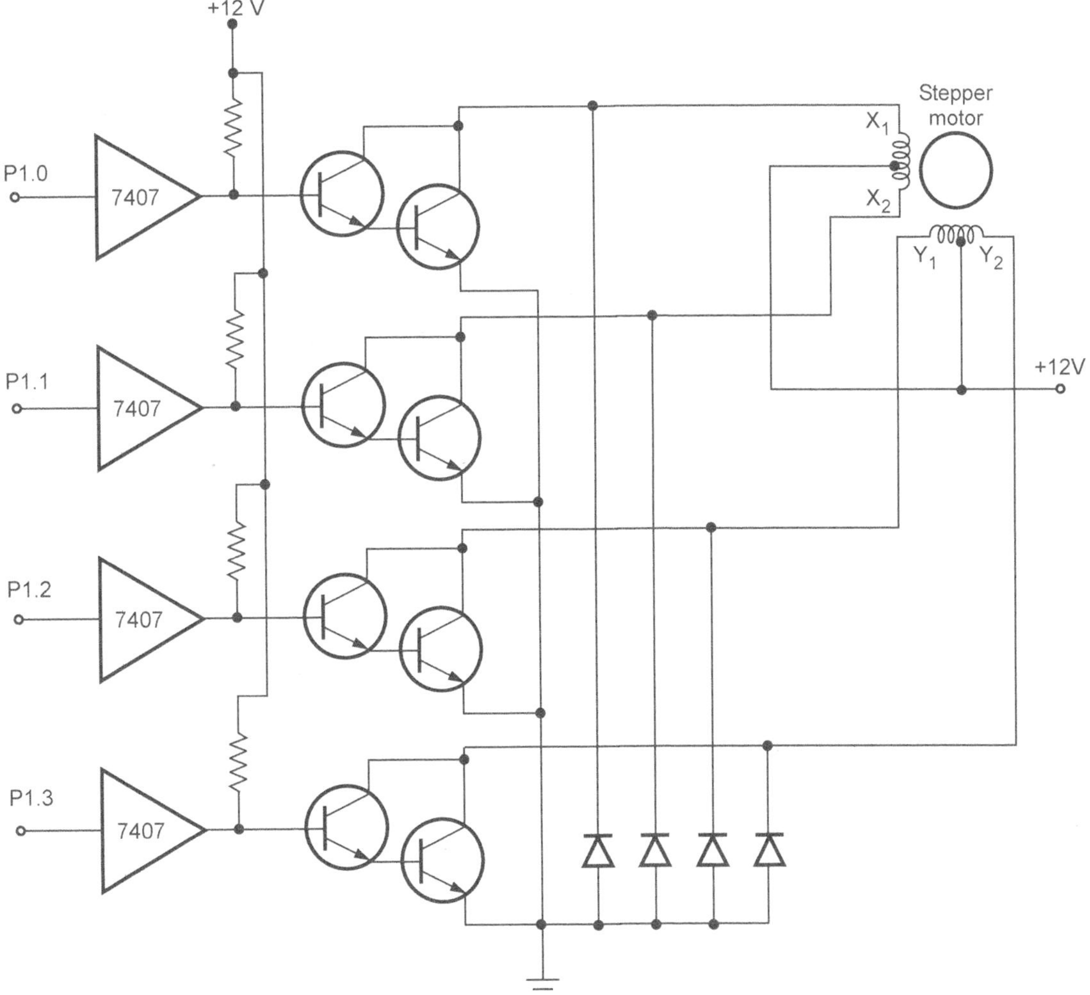

Fig. 20.18 Stepper motor interface

phases, with center-tap winding. The center taps of these windings are connected to the 12 V supply. Due to this, motor can be excited by grounding four terminals of the two windings. Motor can be rotated in steps by giving proper excitation sequence to these windings. The lower nibble of port 1 of the 8051 is used to generate excitation signals in the proper sequence.

The Table 20.5 shows typical excitation sequence. The given excitation sequence rotates the motor in clockwise direction. To rotate motor in anticlockwise direction we have to excite motor in a reverse sequence. The excitation sequence for stepper motor may change due to change in winding connections. However, it is not desirable to excite both the ends of the same winding simultaneously. This cancels the flux and motor winding may damage. To avoid this, digital locking system must be designed. Fig. 20.19 shows a simple digital locking system. Only one output is activated (made low) when properly excited; otherwise output is disabled (made high).

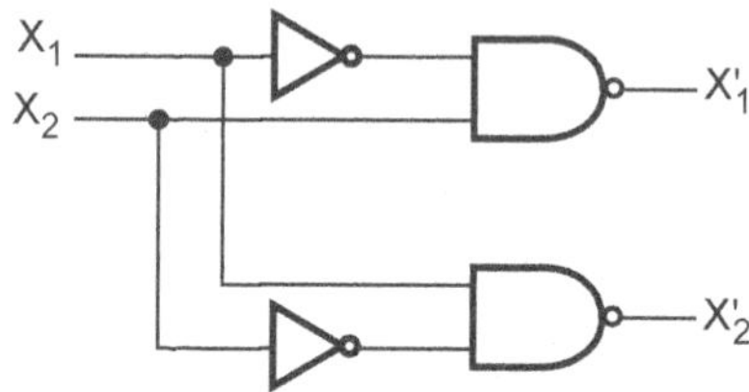

Fig. 20.19 Digital locking system

Step	X_1	X_2	Y_1	Y_2
1	0	1	0	1
2	1	0	0	1
3	1	0	1	0
4	0	1	1	0
1	0	1	0	1

Table 20.5 Full step excitation sequence

The excitation sequence given in Table 20.5 is called **full step sequence**. In which excitation ends of the phase are changed in one step. The excitation sequence given in Table 20.6 takes two steps to change the excitation ends of the phase. Such a sequence is called **half step sequence** and in each step the motor is rotated by 0.9°.

Step	X_1	X_2	Y_1	Y_2
1	0	1	0	1
2	0	0	0	1
3	1	0	0	1
4	1	0	0	0
5	1	0	1	0
6	0	0	1	0
7	0	1	1	0
8	0	1	0	0
1	0	1	0	1

Table 20.6 Half step excitation sequence

We know that stepper motor is stepped from one position to the next by changing the currents through the fields in the motor. The winding inductance opposes the change in current and this puts limit on the stepping rate. For higher stepping rates and more torque, it is necessary to use a higher voltage source and current limiting resistors as shown in Fig. 20.20. By adding series resistance, we decrease L/R time constant, which allows the current to change more rapidly in the windings. There is a power loss across series resistor, but designer has to compromise between power and speed.

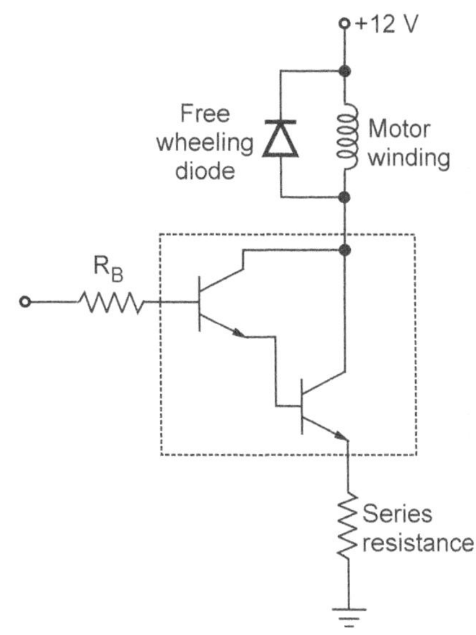

Fig. 20.20 Excitation circuit with series resistance

Example 20.3 : *Write an 8051 assembly language program to control stepper motor using connections given in Fig. 20.18.*

Solution :

```
        MOV R0 # COUNT     ; Initialize rotation count
AGAIN : MOV DPTR, #ETC     ; Initialize pointer to
                           ; excitation code table
        MOV R1, #04        ; Initialize counter to excitation
                           ; code sequence

BACK:   MOVX A, @DPTR      ; Get the excitation code
        MOV P1, A          ; send the excitation code
        LCALL DELAY        ; Wait for some time
        INC DPTR           ; Increment pointer
        DJNZ R1, BACK      ; Decrement R1; if not zero goto BACK
        DJNZ R0, AGAIN     ; Decrement R0; if not zero goto AGAIN
        RET
        ORG 3000H
ETC     DB 03H,06H,09H,0CH; code sequence for clockwise rotation
```

Example 20.4 : *Write assembly language program to control conveyer belt using stepper motor and 8051 controller. Belt moves continuously at rate of 1 step/sec. but stops for 5 sec. when external interrupt occurs and then continues to move.*

Solution :

```
MAIN:   MOV IE, #1000 0001B   ; Enable external interrupt 0
AGAIN:  MOV DPTR,#ETC         ; Initialize pointer to
                              ; excitation code table
        MOV R1, #04           ; Initialize counter to excitation
                              ; code sequence
BACK:   MOVX A, @DPTR         ; Get the excitation code
        MOV P1, A             ; send the excitation code
        MOV A,#14H            ; Initialize count = 20
        LCALL DELAY           ; Wait for 1sec
        INC DPTR              ; Increment pointer
        DJNZ R1, BACK         ; Decrement R1
                              ; if not zero goto BACK
        SJMP AGAIN            ; Repeat
        ORG 3000H
   ETC DB 03H,06H, 09H, 0CH   ; Code sequence for
                              ; Clockwise rotation
```

Assume external interrupt INT0 is used.

```
        ORG 0003H
        MOV A,#64H          ; Initialize count = 100
        ACALL DELAY         ; Called delay routine
        RETI                ; Return to main program
```

Delay Routine

```
DELAY:  MOV TMOD, #01       ; Time 0, mode1 (16-bit mode)
        MOV R0,A            ; Read count and Initialize
BACK:   MOV TL0,#B0H        ; TL0=B0H, the low byte
        MOV TH0,#3CH        ; TH0=3CH, the high byte
        SETB TR0            ; Start the timer 0
RERE:   JNB TF0,REPE        ; Check timer 0 flag until
                            ; it rolls over
        CLR TR0             ; Stop timer 0
        CLR TF0             ; clear timer 0 flag
        DJNZ R0, BACK       ; Decrement counter and
        RET                 ; if not zero repeat
```

Note : Timer 0 gives a delay of 50 ms.

Therefore, to get delay of 1 sec = 50 ms × 20

We load 20 as a count and to get delay of 5 sec. = 50 ms × 100

we load 100 as count.

20.5 Washing Machine Control

Let us assume that the washing machine has following control options :

- Prewash
- Main Wash 1
- Main Wash 2
- Rinse 1
- Rinse 2
- Graduated Spin
- Spin

The user can select option to prewash, or main wash 1 to indicate the initial state for the wash. When the start button is pressed, the cycle begins in the selected initial state. The machine has a program control to indicate the kind of fabrics being washed: cotton or woolen. Cotton program cycles through every state following the initial state. However, woolen program cycles passes through main wash 1, skip main wash 2, enter Rinse 1 but skip the second rinse. Finally, program advances directly to spin skipping the Graduated spin.

The Fig. 20.21 shows the flowchart of washing machine operation.

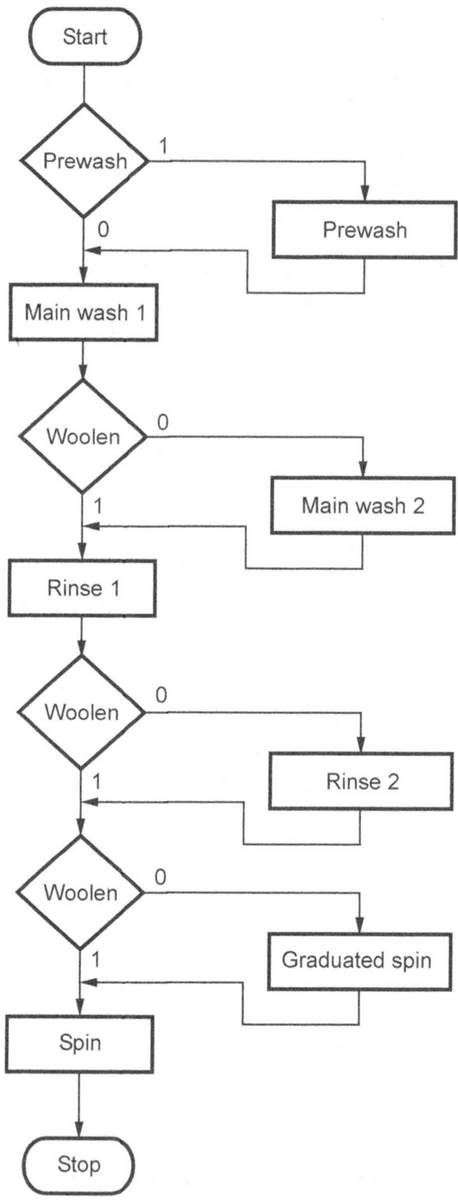

Fig. 20.21 Flowchart for washing machine

Inputs

Pin Name	Pin
Start	P0.0
Prewash Input	P0.1
Cloth Types : 0 : Cotton 1 : Woolen	P0.2

Output

Pin Name	Pin
Prewash Output	P1.0
Main Wash 1	P1.1
Main Wash 2	P1.2
Rinse 1	P1.3
Rinse 2	P1.4
Graduated Spin	P1.5
Spin	P1.6

Hardware Interface

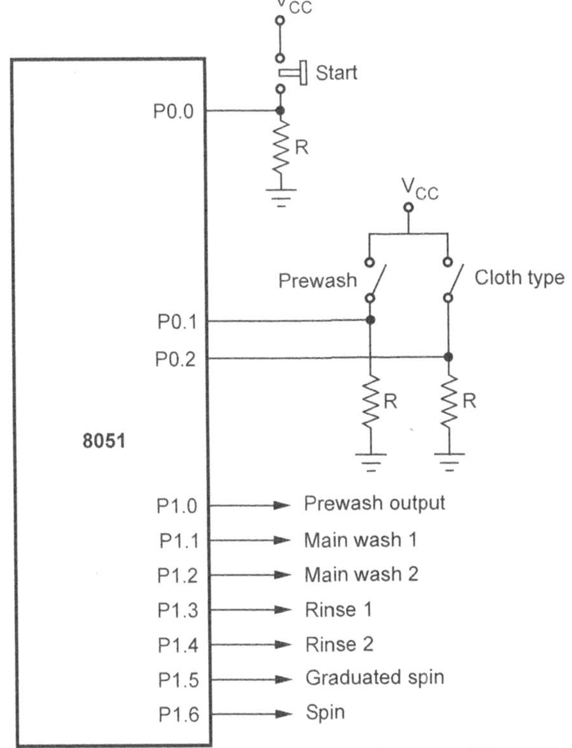

Fig. 20.22 Hardware interface for washing machine

Program :

```
SMRT :        JNB    P 0.0,   START         ; check for star
              JNB    P 0.1,   SKIPPW        ; check if prewash is activated
              SETB   P 1.0,                 ; if yes do prewash
              CALL   D_PREWASH              ; wait for prewash
              CLRB   P 1.0                  ; stop prewash
SKIP PW :     SETB   P 1.1                  ; Do main wash 1
              CALL D_MAINWASH 1             ; Wait for main wash 1
              CLRB   P 1.1                  ; stop main wash 1
              JNB    P 0.2, SKIPMW 2        ; check if cloth type is cotton
              SETB   P 1.2                  ; if yes do main wash 2
              CALL . D_MAINWASH 2           ; wait for main wash 2
              CLRB   P 1.2                  ; stop main wash 2
SKIP MW 2 :SETB P 1.3                       ; Do rinse 1
              CALL D_RINSE 1                ; wait for rinse 1
              CLRB   P 1.3                  ; stop rinse 1
              JNB    P 0.2, SKIPRINSE 2     ; check for cloth type is cotton
              SETB   P 1.4                  ; if yes do rinse 2
              CALL D_RINSE 2                ; wait for rinse 2
              CLRB   P 1.4                  ; stop rinse 2
              JNB    P 0.2, SKIP GS         ; check for cloth type is cotton
              SETB   P 1.5                  ; if yes do gradual spin
              CALL D_GS                     ; wait for gradual spin
              CLRB   P 1.5                  ; stop gradual spin
SKIP GS :     SETB P 1.6                    ; Do spin
              CALL D_SPIN                   ; wait for spin
              CLRB   P 1.6                  ; stop spin
              LJMP START                    ; Go to start
```

Review Questions

Section 20.1

Q.1 *With a neat circuit diagram explain how a 4 × 4 keypad is interfaced with 8051 microcontroller and write 8051 ALP for keypad scanning.* **May-07,08,11, Marks 16**

Q.2 *Interface an 8 × 8 keyboard using 8255 ports and write a program to read the code of a pressed key.* **Dec.-10, Marks 8**

Q.3 *How do you interface a 4 × 4 matrix keyboard using 8051 microcontroller?* **Dec.-11, Marks 8**

Section 20.2

Q.1 *Interface a 20 × 2 LCD with 8051 microcontroller and write assembly language program to display the following message in it at the middle.*
HELLO ! ALL
ARE WELCOME **Dec.-07, Marks 16**

Q.2 *Explain the LCD display interfacing with microcontroller 8051.* **Dec.-08, Marks 16**

Q.3 *Explain the interfacing of keyboard/display with 8051 microcontroller.* **May-11, Marks 8**

Q.4 *How to interface a 7 segment display using 8051 microcontroller.* **Dec.-11, Marks 8**

Section 20.3

Q.1 *Explain the servomotor control using 8051 microcontroller.* **May-11, Marks 8**

Section 20.4

Q.1 *Draw the schematic for interfacing a stepper motor with 8051 microcontroller and write 8051 ALP for changing speed and direction of motor.* **June-07, Marks 16**

Q.2 *Explain the microcontroller 8051 based stepper motor control.* **May-08,10 June-12, Dec.-10, Marks 16**

Q.3 *Write an assembly program in 8051 to rotate the stepper motor in clock wise and anti clockwise direction.* **June-09, Dec.-11, Marks 16**

Q.4 *Write a program to generate pulses to drive and for continuous operation of a stepper motor.* **June-12, Marks 8**

Section 20.5

Q.1 *How 8051 is used in washing machine control ?* **Dec.-11, June-11, Marks 8**

Q.2 *Explain with a neat diagram the application of 8051 microcontroller in Washing Machine control.* **June-12, Marks 16**

Two Marks Question with Answer

Q.1 ***Why do we need opto-isolator circuit between microcontroller and the stepper motor ?*** **Dec.-11**

Ans. : To isolate power circuit of stepper motor and control circuit opto-isolator is needed. It physically separates control circuit ground and power circuit ground connections. Due to such connection, the operation of control circuit is not affected by high current spikes in the power circuit.

Notes